FIFTH EDITION

ETHICAL, LEGAL, AND PROFESSIONAL ISSUES IN COUNSELING

Theodore P. Remley, Jr.

Our Lady of Holy Cross College

Barbara Herlihy

University of New Orleans

Boston   Columbus   Indianapolis   New York   San Francisco   Hoboken   Amsterdam   Cape Town
Dubai   London   Madrid   Milan   Munich   Paris   Montreal   Toronto   Delhi   Mexico City
São Paulo   Sydney   Hong Kong   Seoul   Singapore   Taipei   Tokyo

Vice President and Editorial Director: Jeffery W. Johnston
Vice President and Publisher: Kevin M. Davis
Editorial Assistant: Marisia Styles
Executive Field Marketing Manager: Krista Clark
Senior Product Marketing Manager: Christopher Barry
Project Manager: Lauren Carlson
Procurement Specialist: Deidra Skahill
Senior Art Director: Diane Ernsberger
Cover Designer: Studio Montage
Cover Art: Charles Bonham Photography/Getty Images
Full-Service Project Management: Parul Trivedi, iEnergizer Aptara®, Inc.
Printer/Binder: Courier/Westford
Cover Printer: Courier/Westford
Text Font: Times LT Std

Credits and acknowledgments for material borrowed from other sources and reproduced, with permission, in this textbook appear on the appropriate page within the text.

Every effort has been made to provide accurate and current Internet information in this book. However, the Internet and information posted on it are constantly changing, so it is inevitable that some of the Internet addresses listed in this textbook will change.

Library of Congress Cataloging-in-Publication Data

Remley, Theodore Phant,
    Ethical, legal, and professional issues in counseling / Theodore P. Remley, Jr., Barbara Herlihy.—Fifth edition.
        pages cm
    ISBN-13: 978-0-13-406164-1
    ISBN-10: 0-13-406164-0
    1. Counseling—Moral and ethical aspects—United States.   2. Counselors—Professional ethics—United States.
3. Counseling—Law and legislation—United States.   4. Counselors—Legal status, laws, etc.—United States.
I. Herlihy, Barbara. II. Title.
    BF636.67.R46 2015
    174'.91583—dc23

                                                                                    2015000981

10 9 8 7 6 5 4 3 2 1

ISBN 13: 978-0-13-406164-1
ISBN 10:   0-13-406164-0

*To Dr. Patrick M. Flanagan, this counselor's counselor
and a true role model*

—Ted Remley

*To my colleagues—far too numerous to mention—who have questioned my
assumptions, challenged my thinking, asked me the tough questions, and in
many other ways helped me learn and grow*

—Barbara Herlihy

PREFACE

We think you will find it useful to know something about us, the co-authors, and how we came to write this text. From 1997 to 2006, we were both professors in the counseling graduate program at the University of New Orleans. Ted Remley is an attorney with several years of legal experience and also has been a school and community college counselor. Barbara Herlihy has worked as a school counselor and a Licensed Professional Counselor in private practice and agency settings. She currently is a counselor educator with special interests in counselor ethics and social justice.

Before we became colleagues at the same institution, we worked together over many years, co-authoring articles and presenting numerous workshops on law and ethics in counseling. It was through these workshops that the idea for this text was born. The counselors who attended our workshops had much in common, although they practiced in a variety of settings with diverse clientele. They shared a deep and abiding commitment to the welfare of their clients, a desire to stay current with the ethical standards of their profession, and a need to feel competent in dealing with legal issues that arose in their work. At the same time, they sometimes felt overwhelmed by the complex and conflicting demands of situations they encountered. They frequently had difficulty distinguishing between legal and ethical issues. As we worked together in our presentations to these counselors, we found that we very rarely disagreed with each other, but we did bring differing perspectives. Barbara's ethics orientation led her to focus on client welfare and to emphasize protecting the client. Ted, with his legal orientation, helped us to consider another dimension—that of protecting the counselor. We believe both perspectives are important.

Because both of us regularly teach graduate courses in professional orientation and ethics, we found ourselves discussing the need for a text written specifically for counselors that would address ethical, legal, and professional issues. Thus, out of our backgrounds and shared interests was conceived a text that is unique in that it approaches each professional issue in counseling from both an ethical perspective and a legal viewpoint. We believe you will find this integrated approach particularly helpful as you grapple with the complexities inherent in the work of the counselor.

We also believe that the best learning is active rather than passive, and personalized rather than abstract. We hope that you will actively discuss and even argue the issues that are raised throughout the text and that you will work to develop your own personal stance on these issues. Typical situations and dilemmas that counseling practitioners encounter are presented in each chapter. We ask you to imagine that you are the counselor in each case study and to attend to what you would think, how you would feel, and what you might do in the situation. In these case studies, as in real life, there is rarely a single right answer to the counselor's dilemma, so we hope that the situations will spark lively discussion.

NEW TO THIS EDITION

- This edition is fully updated to include the 2014 American Counseling Association (ACA) *Code of Ethics*. Readers will be brought up to date on the 2014 ACA *Code of Ethics*, which includes new guidelines in the areas of professional and personal values, technology, counselor competence, social justice, and numerous additional changes.
- A new chapter focuses on the use of technology in counseling, teaching, and supervision and on the use of social media by clients. Technology and social media are being utilized more

frequently by counselors and clients, and counselors are given additional guidelines on how to deal with technology and social media in an ethical, legal, and professional manner.

- A thorough discussion is provided around the contemporary issue of ensuring that counseling students and practitioners do not allow their personal or religious values to interfere with their ability and willingness to counsel all clients, including those who are lesbian, gay, bisexual, or transgender. This issue in counseling has been at the heart of more than one lawsuit, has resulted in changes in the 2014 ACA *Code of Ethics*, and has caused counseling graduate programs and licensure boards to enact new policies and procedures.

- Additional guidelines are provided on how to manage boundary issues with clients. The counseling profession has moved in the last few decades from a position of prohibiting multiple relationships with clients to a more nuanced understanding of the issue and an acceptance that multiple relationships are inevitable. The focus now is on helping counselors understand how to manage these relationships in a manner that is not harmful to clients.

- A discussion is provided of new developments in the credentialing of counselors that have been initiated because of policies adopted by the U.S. Veterans Administration and state counseling boards, requiring that counselors hold master's degrees that are accredited by the Council on Accreditation of Counseling and Related Educational Programs (CACREP). This is a new development that counseling students and practicing counselors need to understand because it affects their employment possibilities.

- The role of counselors as advocates for clients and the profession is addressed. Advocacy is a relatively new concept in the field of counseling, and counselors, counseling students, and counselor educators and supervisors need to understand appropriate and inappropriate advocacy positions.

- The globalization of counseling as a profession is addressed. Counseling, like most other professions, is expanding globally. Understanding the vast differences in cultures and stages of development of the counseling profession in other cultures and countries is essential as the world becomes technologically interconnected.

ACKNOWLEDGMENTS

The comments of the following reviewers were invaluable: Robin Lee, Middle Tennessee State University; Claudia Lingertat-Putnam, The College of Saint Rose; Keith Mobley, University of North Carolina–Greensboro; Elizabeth A. Prosek, University of North Texas; and Edward A. Wierzalis, University of North Carolina–Charlotte.

BRIEF CONTENTS

CONTENTS

Introduction

PROFESSIONAL ORIENTATION

This text is intended primarily for prospective counselors; thus, most readers are likely to be graduate students in counselor education programs. However, many counselors who are already practicing use this text as a resource to help them address legal and ethical issues. As you, the reader, digest and discuss the material, we hope you will develop a thoughtful understanding of ethical, legal, and professional issues in counseling. These issues, collectively, make up the *professional orientation* content area of your graduate studies. The Council for Accreditation of Counseling and Related Educational Programs (CACREP), an organization that sets standards for counselor preparation and accredits training programs that meet these standards, requires the curriculum for counselors in training to include studies that provide an understanding of professional functioning. These required studies include, but are not limited to, the history and philosophy of the profession, counselor roles and functions, professional organizations, professional credentialing, advocacy, ethical standards, and applications of ethical and legal considerations (CACREP, 2009).

The National Board for Certified Counselors (NBCC), a voluntary organization that credentials counselors, also requires the counselors it certifies to complete course work in the area of professional orientation to counseling (NBCC, 2011). If you plan to become licensed as a professional counselor, you should be aware that state counselor licensure boards mandate that licensees demonstrate knowledge of professional orientation issues, which include ethical and legal issues.

Beyond external requirements, an important part of your professional development as a counselor is to acquire a firm grounding in the area of professional orientation. This content area includes three main components:

- *Developing a professional identity as a counselor.* This includes understanding the history and development of counseling and related professions, knowing the professional roles and functions of counselors and how these are similar to and different from other professions, learning about and becoming involved in professional organizations, gaining awareness of counselor preparation standards and credentialing, knowing how to advocate for your clients and your profession, and developing pride in your profession. Professional identity is discussed in detail in Chapter 2.
- *Learning about ethics.* This involves becoming familiar with ethical standards for counselors, understanding the ethical issues that counselors encounter, developing ethical reasoning and decision-making skills, and being able to use an ethical decision-making model to apply your knowledge and skills in your day-to-day professional activities.
- *Learning about the law as it applies to counseling.* This includes being able to distinguish among legal, ethical, and clinical issues; acquiring a basic knowledge of legal issues in counseling and laws that affect the practice of counseling; and knowing what to do when you are faced with a legal problem.

It is essential that you develop a strong professional identity as a counselor during this time in our history when we are still a relatively new profession. Counselors today are constantly being asked questions such as "What kind of counselor are you?" or "Is being a counselor like being a psychologist?" or "How are counselors different from social workers?" These are legitimate questions, and you must be prepared to clearly explain who you are as a member of a professional group, what you believe, how you are similar to other mental health professionals, and, more important, how you are different. You must also be prepared to practice in ways that are ethically and legally sound and that promote the welfare of your clients. Information throughout this text will provide you with an understanding of your chosen profession of counseling and will prepare you to practice in an ethical and legal manner.

We hope that seasoned practitioners, as well as counselors in training, will read this text and find it useful. Professional, ethical, and legal standards are constantly changing, and it is important to keep up to date. Also, as Corey, Corey, Corey, and Callanan (2015) have pointed out, issues that students and beginning practitioners encounter resurface and take on new meanings at different stages of one's professional development.

Morals, Values, and Ethics

The terms *morals*, *values*, and *ethics* are sometimes used interchangeably, and they do have overlapping meanings. All three terms involve judgments about what is good and bad, or right and wrong, and all pertain to the study of human conduct and relationships. Nonetheless, distinctions must be drawn when these terms are applied to the behaviors of professional counselors.

The term *moral* is derived from the Latin word *mores*, which means customs or norms. Moral actions are determined within a broad context of a culture or society. Although some moral principles, such as "Do no harm to others," are shared by most civilized groups of people, how these moral principles are interpreted and acted on will vary from culture to culture and from individual to individual within a culture. Thus, conduct that you evaluate as moral might be judged as immoral by another person or by people in another society. It is important to remember that what you view as moral behavior is based on the values you espouse. In this text, when we refer to moral conduct, we ask you to think in terms of your *personal* belief system and how this affects your interactions with others in all aspects of your life.

Although *values* are very similar to morals in that they serve as a guide to determining what is good or right behavior, we use the term *values* to apply more broadly to both the personal and professional functioning of counselors. Our *personal* values guide our choices and behaviors, and each of us holds some values more strongly than other values (Strom-Gottfried, 2007). Although your value system is unique to you, it has been influenced by your upbringing, the culture in which you live, and quite possibly your religious beliefs. What is important about your personal values as they relate to professional practice is that you have a high level of self-awareness of your values, and that you learn to *bracket* (Kocet & Herlihy, 2014), or set aside, your personal values within the counseling relationship. One of the hardest lessons counselors must learn is to respect values that are different from their own and to avoid imposing their own personal values on their clients. This can be a particularly challenging task when a client holds values that are very different from those of the counselor. For example, if you believe deeply that a fetus is a human being and that abortion is morally wrong, then it will be challenging for you to keep your values in check as you counsel a woman who is considering having an abortion (Millner & Hanks, 2002). Similarly, it may be difficult for counselors who believe strongly in the sanctity of marriage to counsel clients who are seeking divorce. A series of court cases have involved counselors with strong religious beliefs who declined to counsel lesbian, gay, bisexual, and transsexual (LGBT) clients. Partly as a result of the controversy generated by these court cases, the recently revised *Code of Ethics* of the American Counseling Association (ACA, 2014) states quite clearly that counselors must avoid imposing their own personal values on their clients.

Members of the counseling profession share certain *professional* values. These include enhancing human development across the life span, honoring diversity and embracing a multicultural approach, promoting social justice, safeguarding the integrity of the counselor–client relationship, and practicing competently and ethically (ACA, 2014, *Code of Ethics* Preamble). These core values are articulated in the code of ethics to help acculturate students to the expectations of the profession (Francis, 2015). If a counseling student's personal values were so strong that he or she could not learn to counsel clients who held differing beliefs, or if a student could not embrace the professional values of the profession as articulated in the ethics code, we would be concerned that the student is not well suited for the counseling profession.

Ethics is a discipline within philosophy that is concerned with human conduct and moral decision making. Certainly, you have developed your own individual ethical stance that guides you in the ways you treat others, expect them to treat you, and make decisions about what behaviors are good or right for you. In this text, however, we think of ethics as it relates to the profession of counseling; that is, ethics refers to conduct judged as good or right for counselors as a professional group. When your fellow professionals have come to sufficient consensus about right behaviors, these behaviors have been codified and have become the ethical standards to which you are expected to adhere in your professional life (ACA, 2014). Therefore, think about ethics as referring to your *professional* behavior and interactions. Keep in mind that ethics must prevail over your personal values when value conflicts arise within a counseling relationship. Because the counseling relationship exists to benefit the client, you must avoid imposing your own values on your clients.

Legal, Ethical, and Professional Behavior

Law is different from morality or ethics, even though law, like morality, is created by a society and, like ethics, it is codified. Laws are the agreed-upon rules of a society that set forth the basic principles for, living together as a group. Laws can be general or specific regarding both what is required and what is allowed of individuals who form a governmental entity. Criminal laws hold individuals accountable for violating principles of coexistence and are enforced by the government. Civil laws allow members of society to enforce rules of living with each other.

Our view is that there are few conflicts between law and ethics in professional counseling. Keep in mind, though, that there are important differences. Laws are created by elected officials, enforced by police, and interpreted by judges. Ethics are created by members of the counseling profession and are interpreted and enforced by ethics committees and licensure and certification boards. Laws dictate the *minimum* standards of behavior that society will tolerate, whereas ethics pertains to a wider range of professional functioning. Some ethical standards prescribe the minimum that other counselors will tolerate from fellow professionals (for example, sexual or romantic relationships with clients are prohibited), and some standards describe ideal practices to which counselors should aspire (for example, counselors aspire to foster meaningful and respectful professional relationships).

Rowley and MacDonald (2001) discussed the differences between law and ethics using concepts of culture and cross-culture. They argued that "law and ethics are based on different understandings of how the world operates" (p. 422). These authors advise you to learn the different culture of law, seek to understand how law operates, and develop collaborative partnerships with attorneys. We agree with the perspective that the cultures of counseling and law are different and that seeking legal advice is often an important step in the practice of counseling.

Where does the notion of *professionalism* fit into the picture? Many factors, including the newness of the counseling profession, the interpersonal nature and complexity of the counseling process, and the wide variety of types of counselors and their work settings, make it essential for counselors to conduct themselves in a professional manner. It is not easy to define what it means to be *professional*, and we discuss this in more detail in Chapter 2. We note here that professionalism is closely related to the concept in a profession of *best practice*, and perhaps the concepts of law, ethics, and best practice in the field of counseling are on a continuum. Legal standards are the minimum that society will tolerate from a professional. Ethical standards occupy a middle ground, describing both the minimal behaviors expected of counselors and the ideal standards to which counselors aspire. Best practice is the very best a counselor could be expected to do. Best practice guidelines are intended to provide counselors with goals to which they can aspire, and they are motivational, as distinguished from ethical standards, which are enforceable (Marotta & Watts, 2007).

Although there is no consensus among counseling professionals about what constitutes best practice (Marotta, 2000; Marotta & Watts, 2007), you will want to strive to practice in the best possible manner and provide the most competent services to your clients throughout your career. Meeting minimum legal standards or minimum ethical standards is not enough for the truly professional counselor. Professionalism demands that you be the best counselor for your clients that you are capable of being.

1-1 The Case of Alicia

Alicia will be seeing a 16-year-old minor for his first counseling session. Alicia knows that legally and ethically she must have one of his parents sign an agreement for her to disclose information regarding his sessions to his parent's health insurance company so that the parent will be reimbursed partially for the cost of her counseling services. Alicia also is aware that, according to the ACA *Code of Ethics* (2014), she may include parents in the counseling process, as appropriate (§A.2.d.; §B.5.b). However, she realizes how important confidentiality is to adolescents, and she wants to provide services to this minor in a way that would meet best practice standards.

- What are some of the things Alicia might do in this situation to go beyond what is minimally required by law or the code of ethics?
- How will Alicia know if what she finally decides to do is best practice?

Discussion: You will have the information you need to answer these questions after you have read material on ethical decision making, informed consent, confidentiality, and counseling minor clients, all presented later in the text. For now, a brief answer is that Alicia would be well advised to hold a conversation with both the client and his parent(s) present, in which she discusses confidentiality and its limits (including the information she would share with the insurance company). Including the client in the decision-making process is good practice, and Alicia can ask the client to sign the agreement to signify his assent, in addition to having the parents sign to give legal consent. Best practice for Alicia will mean keeping a careful balance, honoring both her minor client's right to privacy and his parents' rights to information about their son, and working to establish and maintain a cooperative relationship with all parties.

A Model for Professional Practice

One source of very real frustration for prospective and beginning counselors is that there are so few absolute, right answers to ethical, legal, or best practice questions. Throughout your career, you will encounter dilemmas for which there are no *cookbook* solutions or universally agreed-upon answers. We visualize professional practice as entailing a rather precarious balance that requires constant vigilance. We also see counseling practice as being built from within the self but balanced by outside forces, as shown in Figure 1-1.

In this model of professional practice, the internal building blocks are inside the triangle. The most fundamental element, at the base, is *intentionality*. Being an effective practitioner must start with good intentions, or wanting to do the right thing. The overwhelming majority of counselors have the best intentions; they want to be helpful to those they serve.

The second building block contains *principles and virtues*. Principles and virtues represent two philosophies that provide the underpinnings for ethical reasoning. Moral principles are a set of shared beliefs or agreed-upon assumptions that guide the ethical thinking of helping professionals (including physicians, nurses and other medical specialists, teachers, and mental health professionals). Basic moral principles include respect for autonomy (honoring freedom of choice), nonmaleficence (doing no harm), beneficence (being helpful), justice (fairness), fidelity (being faithful), and veracity (being honest). Virtue ethics focuses on the traits of character or dispositions that promote the human good. We discuss these in more detail later in this chapter.

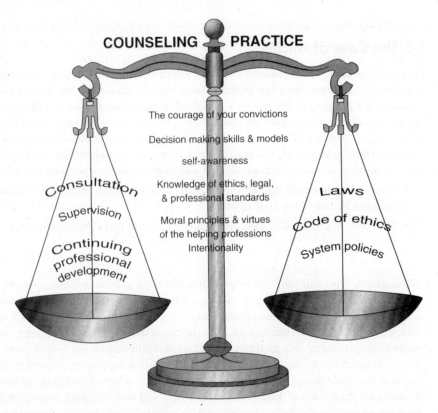

FIGURE 1-1   Professional practice—built from within and balanced from outside the self

Source: Pearson Education, Inc., Hoboken, NJ.

The third element is *knowledge* of ethical, legal, and professional standards. You will find that there is a wealth of resources available to you as you work to gain, maintain, and expand your knowledge base. Texts such as this one, casebooks, professional journals, codes of ethics, workshops and seminars, professional conferences, and your supervisors and colleagues are all excellent resources that can help to increase your knowledge.

The fourth element is *self-awareness*. As discussed earlier in this chapter, counselors must maintain a high level of self-awareness so that they do not inadvertently impose their own values, beliefs, and needs onto their clients. Knowledge of ethical, legal, and professional standards is not sufficient; best practice is achieved through constant self-reflection and personal dedication, rather than through mandatory requirements of external organizations (Francis, 2015).

Even after you have developed a solid knowledge base and the habit of self-reflection, you must have *skills* for applying your knowledge and reasoning through the questions and dilemmas that will arise in your practice. It also helps to have a *model* that will serve as a road map to guide your ethical decision making and bring some consistency to the process.

The final internal element is *the courage of your convictions*. This element can challenge even the most conscientious counselors who have the best intentions. As a counselor, you will face ethical quandaries. It can take courage to do what you believe is right, especially when there is a high cost to yourself, when your personal needs are involved, when you know that others may not agree with or approve of your actions, or when (as is the case in ethical dilemmas) there is no single, clear, right answer to the problem.

The following are some examples of ethical quandaries that take courage and that involve the behavior of other counseling professionals: What if you know that one of your professors has published, under her or his own name only, an article based largely on a paper you wrote? What if your supervisor at your internship site is engaging in a behavior that you strongly believe is unethical? What if you know that one of your fellow interns, who is also your friend, is engaging in inappropriate relationships with clients? In such instances, it can be easier to *turn a blind eye* than to confront the individual involved and run the risk of retaliatory action by the professor, a poor evaluation from your supervisor, or the loss of a friend. Chapter 8 discusses important points you must consider if you suspect another professional is behaving in an unethical manner and actions you might take.

Examples of ethical dilemmas that involve your own behavior include the following: What if you know that you are supposed to maintain personal boundaries between you and your clients, but just once you agree to allow a client to buy you a cup of coffee and have a social conversation immediately after a session has ended? What if you know you are supposed to render diagnoses of mental and emotional disorders for your clients based on criteria in the *Diagnostic and Statistical Manual of Mental Disorders*, Fifth Edition (American Psychiatric Association, 2013), yet you generally render the same diagnosis of *adjustment disorder* for most clients because you think this diagnosis is the least stigmatizing? What if you report to a counselor certification board that you attended a continuing education workshop you paid for, even though you did not actually attend it? In these situations, it might be tempting to make some minor compromises to your usual ethical behavior, especially when you feel no harm comes to a client or to anyone else as a result.

Nonetheless, if you do nothing when you know the behavior of other professionals is unethical, or if you compromise your own ethical behavior, you have set foot on an ethical slippery slope. The *slippery slope phenomenon* is a term used by moral philosophers to describe what happens when one begins to compromise one's principles—it becomes easier and easier to slide down the slope, diminishing one's sense of moral selfhood along the way.

The diagram of the model also includes external forces that can support counselors in their efforts to maintain sound, professional practice. External sources of guidance and support include consulting with colleagues, seeking supervision, and increasing your knowledge and skills through continuing education activities. Your code of ethics is certainly a major source of guidance. Some laws support counselors in fulfilling ethical obligations; for example, privileged communication statutes can help you to uphold your clients' confidentiality when called to testify in court or produce records. The system (school, agency, or institution) in which you are employed may also have policies on which you can rely when confronted with a challenge or a request to compromise your ethics.

PROFESSIONAL ETHICS

Concern about ethics acknowledges the awesome responsibilities inherent in the practice of counseling. A counselor's work can make a difference in whether an abused child's life situation is recognized and addressed, whether a battered spouse finds the self-affirming courage to move to a safe environment, or whether a suicidal client finds the hope needed to choose life. Other clients come with less dramatic, more mundane problems, yet counseling can play a vital role in their struggle to lead more meaningful and effective lives (Pope & Vasquez, 2010). Ethical counselors take these responsibilities seriously.

Foundations of Ethics

For many centuries, philosophers have debated what characterizes a moral and ethical person and how to behave in a moral and ethical manner, and these issues have been addressed within the helping professions since ancient times. The Hippocratic Oath was written about 2,500 years ago in ancient Greece, and in fact Greek philosophers such as Plato and Aristotle created most of the ethical principles that helping professionals use today.

Ethical Theories

Ethical theories provide a framework that counselors can use to decide whether an action or contemplated action is ethical. It is important for you to have an ethical theory because it will enable you to resolve the ethical dilemmas you encounter in your work and help you defend the solutions you reach. A number of ethical theories take opposing positions on what it means to be and act as an ethical person. Having some familiarity with a few of these positions may help you become aware of the approach you take in your ethical decision making as a counselor and perhaps challenge the assumptions you make. Remember that ethical reasoning is an acquired skill, not an inherent gift, and it can be sharpened through practice.

One set of opposing viewpoints on ethics is *ethical absolutism* versus *ethical relativism*. Ethical absolutists believe that there are some absolute moral standards that are universally applicable; that is, they must prevail in all circumstances and are not dependent on a person's beliefs or cultural values. These standards exist a priori (they exist before a situation arises) and independently of whether or not one believes in them. Ethical relativists, on the other hand, do not believe that any absolute moral standards exist that can be universally applied. Rather, they take the position that if the members of a culture believe an action is morally right, then it is morally right to perform that act in that culture (Freeman, 2000). As you begin to study the codes of ethics for counselors, these codes may seem to you to be written in absolutist terms. They are written in terms such as "counselors do not . . ." and "counselors ensure that . . . ," which appear to suggest that there are absolute *do's* and *don'ts* of ethical behavior. We believe, however, that ethical standards must be interpreted in a relativistic manner, taking into account the uniqueness of the client, the situation, and any cultural variables that are involved. These distinctions should become clearer to you as you progress through the chapters of the text and begin to grapple with the ethical issues and dilemmas that are presented.

A related issue that is raised by philosophers of ethics is that of *utilitarianism* versus *deontology*, or consequential versus nonconsequential ethics. Utilitarian thought, represented by thinkers such as John Stuart Mill, argues that people should choose the act that will do the greatest good for the greatest number. In other words, an act is evaluated by its consequences. By contrast, deontologists, represented by the thinking of Emmanuel Kant, believe that an action is justified by its being inherently right, not by its consequences. Another way to state this idea is that what makes an action right is the principle that guides it. This philosophical question underlies much of the reasoning that counselors use in attempting to determine what is ethical professional behavior.

A third set of opposing philosophical viewpoints has to do with what motivates people to act morally or ethically. *Egoism* is the term used to describe actions taken out of self-interest, whereas *altruism* is the word that describes actions taken to benefit others (Freeman, 2000). Most people who choose counseling as their life's work tend to see themselves as altruists, and indeed one of the most fundamental ethical values of counselors is that "client welfare comes first." Although this ethical value is well established in the counseling profession, this does not mean that there is no place for egoism or self-interest in our work. When we consider the possible consequences of a decision or action we might take, we would be prudent to reflect on the effects that action could have on us as well as on our clients. This dual consideration of altruism and self-interest, in fact, is reflected in the differences between the ethical and legal perspectives that are presented throughout this text. The ethical perspective is focused more on the welfare and protection of the client, whereas the legal perspective is focused more on protecting the counselor.

1-2 The Case of Edward

Edward is a high school counselor. His administrative supervisor is the school principal, Ms. Wilcox. Although Ms. Wilcox has no training as a counselor, she generally has been supportive of the counselors on her staff. She asks Edward to provide, for her eyes only, a list of his clients and presenting concerns. Edward trusts the supervisor to be responsible and refrain from sharing the list with others. Nonetheless, Edward believes it would be wrong to produce the list because it would violate his clients' right to confidentiality. At the same time, he realizes he could be at risk for disciplinary action for refusing to produce the list. He thinks that no real harm would be likely to result from giving it to Ms. Wilcox. He is also concerned that a refusal could negatively affect Ms. Wilcox's supportive attitude toward the counselors.

- What should Edward do? Do you believe the *principle* of confidentiality is the overriding consideration?
- Or, do you believe that it is more important for Edward to consider the *consequences* of the decision?

Discussion: If Edward reasons that the ethical principle is most important, he would be committing himself to uphold the moral principle of fidelity. *Fidelity* refers to fulfilling a responsibility of trust in the counseling relationship: Counselors strive to be faithful to the promises they make, such as keeping clients' disclosures confidential. If Edward adheres to this line of reasoning, he could be said to be thinking as an ethical absolutist—that the principle always applies, regardless of the situation. He would also be thinking as a deontologist, by deciding that keeping the students' confidentiality is the right thing to do, regardless of the consequences. In addition, he might be relying on altruism, in that he believes that his actions must uphold client welfare rather than serve his own interests.

If Edward decides to produce the list for Ms. Wilcox, he might be motivated by egoism, or a focus on protecting himself and his fellow counselors from negative repercussions. He could be using utilitarian reasoning as suggested by Mill, that because no harm is likely to come to the students, his decision will do the greatest good for the greatest number of people—not only himself and his fellow counselors but also the students who would be better served by having a supportive school administration.

We believe the best course of action in this situation would be for Edward to have an open discussion with his principal and explain his concerns about providing her with the list of students he has seen in counseling. Hopefully, his principal will either understand his concern and withdraw her request or convince Edward of the need for the list that would override his ethical concerns about the privacy of his students.

All of the theories discussed up to this point have focused on the question of what constitutes ethical action. Other theories focus on what constitutes ethical character. Virtue ethics, which originated with Aristotle, explores the question of what character traits or dispositions form the basis for right action. Aristotle believed that positive personal character is developed when individuals consistently take actions that are based on their society's values. Virtue ethics focuses on individuals rather than actions and evaluates the whole individual instead of isolated decisions the individual makes. Virtue ethicists believe that moral choices cannot be made by rule; what is needed instead is good judgment.

The ethic of care, or relational ethics, is based on the recognition that human beings exist in relationship and connection with one another. Psychologist Carol Gilligan (1982), who represents this perspective, believes that ethics exist in a world of relationships in which the awareness of connection among people gives rise to a recognition that we are responsible for each other. Thus, the solution to an ethical dilemma is not found in a contest between opposing philosophies but, rather, in a strengthening of the relationship on which the actors in the dilemma depend. Feminist ethicists have further articulated the ethic of care. Manning (1992) has stated, "An ethic of care involves a morality grounded in relationship and response. . . . In responding, we do not appeal to abstract principles . . . rather we pay attention to the concrete other in his or her real situation [and to] the effect of our response on the networks that sustain us both" (p. xiv). Relational or feminist ethicists do not disagree with principle ethicists, but their focus is different—they view moral actions as those that empower individuals, promote social justice, and ensure that all people are cared for and nurtured to develop their potentials (Vasquez, 2008).

With these general ethical theories in mind, we now turn to a consideration of ethical reasoning as it has been applied in the field of counseling.

Linking Theory to Practice: Principles and Virtues

Thoughtful mental health professionals have struggled with questions of ethical ideals, concepts, principles, and values, and how to link these to ethical decisions in professional practice (Beauchamp & Childress, 1994; Jordan & Meara, 1990; Kitchener, 1984; Meara, Schmidt, & Day, 1996). Two helpful perspectives are *principle ethics* and *virtue ethics*. Even though these two approaches are quite different from one another, they are complementary. When integrated into a holistic framework for ethical decision making, they can serve as a bridge from philosophy to practice.

Principle ethics have their foundation in moral principles, which are agreed-upon assumptions or beliefs about ideals that are shared by members of the helping professions. They are prima facie obligations that are always considered in ethical decision making (Meara et al., 1996). Although moral philosophers do not agree about the nature or number of moral principles, the following six are included in the Preamble to the ACA *Code of Ethics* (ACA, 2014):[†]

- *Respect for autonomy* means to foster self-determination. According to this principle, counselors respect the rights of clients to choose their own directions, act in accordance with their beliefs, and control their own lives. Counselors work to decrease client dependency and foster independent decision making.
- *Nonmaleficence* means to avoid actions that cause harm. This principle, long established in the medical profession, obligates counselors to avoid actions that risk hurting clients, even inadvertently.
- *Beneficence* is the counterpoint to nonmaleficence. It could be argued that the obligation of ordinary citizens in our society ends with doing no harm to others, whereas professionals have a higher obligation to provide a service that benefits society. Thus, counselors actively work for the good of individuals and society by promoting the mental health and well-being of their clients.
- *Justice* refers to the counselor's commitment to fairness in professional relationships and treating people equitably. Counselors' actions and decisions must be fair to all concerned. Justice demands equality, which has implications for nondiscrimination and equitable treatment of all clients.

[†]*Source:* Based on Preamble to the ACA Code of Ethics (2014), American Counseling Association.

- *Fidelity* refers to fulfilling a responsibility of trust in the counseling relationship by honoring commitments and keeping promises. Counselors strive to be faithful to the promises they make, such as keeping clients' disclosures confidential.
- *Veracity* means truthfulness and addresses the counselor's obligation to deal honestly with clients and others with whom they relate professionally.

Some writers have suggested additional principles such as *respect for persons*, which refers to a duty to honor others and their rights and responsibilities (Kenyon, 1999), and self-care, which reminds counselors that we must take good care of ourselves as a prerequisite to being able to be fully present for others (Barnett, 2008). Another principle that may have increasing salience in the future is *reparation*, which is the duty to make up for a wrong. This principle seems foundational to our profession's commitment to social justice and advocacy (which we discuss in more detail in Chapter 3).

In theory, all of these principles have equal value and should be considered along with all the others when weighing an ethical decision. In reality, however, these principles can compete with one another, and counselors may need to sacrifice one in order to uphold another. For example, a counselor who is counseling a suicidal client may decide to intervene by notifying family members against the client's wishes (thus breaching confidentiality and sacrificing fidelity) or by seeking involuntary hospitalization (thus sacrificing client autonomy) in order to uphold the obligations to prevent harm and do good (nonmaleficence and beneficence).

Virtue ethics start from a premise very different from principle ethics. The basic assumption of virtue ethics is that professional ethics involve more than moral actions; they also involve traits of character or virtue. Virtue ethics focus on the actor rather than on the action. Principle ethics ask the question "What should I do?"; virtue ethics asks "Who should I be?" Patterns of virtuous behavior are evident throughout the career of a professional, rather than being found in any particular action or decision. Thus, this perspective asks you to look at who you are, rather than at what you do. Certain characteristics of virtuous agents have been suggested as appropriate for mental health professionals (Meara et al., 1996). We hope that you will read about these characteristics with an eye to whether you see them as representing the ideals you hold for yourself, and that you will assess their relevance for you as an aspiring counselor.

- *Integrity.* Virtuous agents are motivated to do what is right because they believe it is right, not because they feel obligated or fear the consequences. They have stable moral values and are faithful to these values in their actions.
- *Discernment.* Discerning counselors are able to perceive the ethically relevant aspects of a situation, know what principles apply, and take decisive action. Discernment involves a tolerance for ambiguity, the ability to maintain perspective, and an understanding of the links between current behaviors and future consequences.
- *Acceptance of emotion.* Without discounting the value of logic and systematic deliberation about ethical issues, virtuous agents also recognize the role of emotion in ethical decisions. Rather than assume that emotion hinders reason, they believe that emotion informs reason. Virtuous counselors are compassionate and sensitive to the suffering of others.
- *Self-awareness.* Virtuous agents know their own assumptions, convictions, and biases and how these may affect their relationships and interactions with others.
- *Interdependence with the community.* Virtuous agents realize that values cannot be espoused without awareness of context. They are connected with and understand the expectations and values of their communities.

Both perspectives—a focus on principles and a focus on virtues—can contribute to your understanding of the basis for professional ethics. Principle ethics help you to systematically evaluate what you should do when trying to resolve an ethical dilemma. Virtue ethics can help you examine your ideals and define the kind of person you aspire to be as a helping professional. Thinking about principles and virtues requires you to look inward in order to identify internal resources that can assist you in ethical decision making. There are external resources as well, and primary among these is your professional code of ethics.

Codes of Ethics

Promulgating a code of ethics is one way that a group of practitioners can establish its professional status. Codes of ethics serve a number of other important purposes as well. They educate members of the profession as well as consumers about what constitutes ethical practice, help to ensure accountability through enforcement of the standards, protect the profession from government by allowing the profession to regulate itself and function more autonomously, promote stability within the profession by helping to control internal disagreement, and serve as a catalyst for improving practice (Herlihy & Corey, 2015; Mappes, Robb, & Engels, 1985; Van Hoose & Kottler, 1985). An established code of ethics also can protect practitioners—if professionals behave according to established guidelines, their behavior is more likely to be judged in compliance with accepted standards in a malpractice suit or licensing board complaint. Most fundamentally, codes of ethics exist to protect and promote the welfare of clients.

Some counselors practice *mandatory ethics*; that is, they function at a level of ethical reasoning that merely keeps them in compliance with minimal standards. By complying with these basic *musts* and *must nots*, they meet the letter but not the spirit of the ethical standards. Corey et al. (2015) use the term *fear-based ethics* to describe a level of ethical functioning that is motivated by a desire to avoid lawsuits, complaints to ethics committees or licensing boards, or getting into trouble in some other way. According to Pope and Vasquez (2010), counselors who set their sights at this level are vulnerable to denial and to other means of distorting, discounting, or dismissing ethical questions they encounter. Some of the self-statements that these counselors use to justify their actions include the following:

"It can't be unethical if I don't see it as an ethical issue."

"It isn't unethical if there is no ethical standard that specifically prohibits it."

"It can't be unethical if I know other practitioners who do it."

"It isn't an ethical problem as long as no client has ever complained about it."

"It's not unethical as long as no one finds out about it."

Other counselors practice *aspirational ethics*, a term that describes the highest standards of conduct to which counselors can aspire. They understand the spirit behind the code and the moral principles on which it rests. They not only look outward to established standards, but also look inward and ask themselves whether what they are doing is best for their clients. Aspirational ethics, or *concern-based ethics* (Corey et al., 2015), means striving for the highest level of care for clients and is closely related to the concept of best practice. Corey et al. (2015) have emphasized that clients' needs are best met when counselors monitor their own ethics and challenge their own thinking and behavior.

A code of ethics that would address every possible situation that a counselor might encounter would probably fill an entire library. You cannot expect your code of ethics to provide an answer to every question you might have. Codes are a crucial resource, but they are not a substitute for an active, deliberative, and creative approach to fulfilling your ethical responsibilities (Pope & Vasquez, 2010). You must attend to both the letter and the spirit of the code and work to understand the intentions that underlie each standard. As Herlihy and Corey (2015) have noted, "there is a very real difference between merely following the ethics code and living out a commitment to practice with the highest ideals" (p. 13).

Your primary professional association, the ACA, has established a code of ethics to guide you in your practice. We encourage you to review it when you complete this chapter to become familiar with how the code relates to issues discussed throughout the text. The ACA *Code* can be found in Appendix A and at counseling.org.

Figure 1-2 presents a brief overview of the nine sections of the code and their general provisions.

Preamble describes the American Counseling Association and its members, defines counseling, and enumerates core professional values and ethical principles.

Purpose sets forth six purposes for the Code of Ethics and describes the ethical decision-making process.

Section A: The Counseling Relationship addresses important issues in forming, maintaining, and ending the counseling relationship. This section includes guidelines to help counselors keep client welfare foremost. It contains standards that emphasize the importance of informed consent and of avoiding the harm that can be caused by imposing one's own personal values. It provides guidance on how to maintain appropriate professional boundaries, advocate for clients, manage fees and business practices, and terminate the counseling relationship. Standards are also provided for working with multiple clients, groups, and clients served by other professionals.

Section B: Confidentiality and Privacy addresses the client's right to privacy of information shared during counseling sessions and of records. Exceptions and limitations to confidentiality are specified, and special considerations in working with families, groups, and clients who lack capacity to give informed consent are addressed. Guidelines are offered for maintaining confidentiality when consulting.

Section C: Professional Responsibility contains standards related to competence. It emphasizes the importance of advertising services and qualifications in an accurate manner. It also addresses the counselor's responsibilities to the public and other professionals and offers cautions regarding treatment modalities.

Section D: Relationships with Other Professionals offers guidelines for relationships with colleagues, employers, employees, and consultees. This section highlights the importance of respecting and establishing good working relationships with professionals in related mental health professions.

Section E: Evaluation, Assessment, and Interpretation includes standards on competence to select, use, and interpret assessment instruments. Client rights in testing, test security, and proper testing conditions are addressed. This section also includes standards related to diagnosis of mental disorders and forensic evaluations.

Section F: Supervision, Training, and Teaching presents guidelines for counselor supervisors, trainers, and educators. Responsibilities of supervisors and counselor educators are elucidated, and standards address relationship boundaries, evaluation and remediation, endorsement of students to enter the profession, and student welfare.

Section G: Research and Publication describes research responsibilities, rights of research participants, and the reporting of research results. A range of issues is covered from protection of human subjects to ethical procedures in seeking publication.

Section H: Distance Counseling, Technology, and Social Media presents guidelines to assist counselors to best serve clients using distance counseling, technology, and social media. This section addresses ethical issues that are specific to these new and emerging resources.

Section I: Resolving Ethical Issues addresses the responsibility of counselors to know ethical and legal standards and explains procedures for resolving and reporting suspected ethical violations.

Glossary of Terms provides definitions of terms used in the code.

FIGURE 1-2 ACA *Code of Ethics*: A synopsis

Source: Pearson Education, Inc., Hoboken, NJ.

The current ACA *Code of Ethics*, adopted in 2014, is the seventh version of the ethics code established by ACA and its predecessor organizations. Development of the first code was initiated in 1953 by Donald Super, then president of the newly formed American Personnel and Guidance Association (APGA). The code was adopted in 1961. It was revised in 1974 and has been revised approximately every 7 to 10 years since that time. The current code is the result of a lengthy revision process that began in 2011, when a code revision task force was appointed to revise the 2005 code that was then in effect (Francis, 2015).

As you learn about ethical standards that you will be expected to uphold, keep in mind that codes of ethics are living documents that change over time. They are periodically revised as the profession's knowledge base grows and as consensus emerges about new and controversial ethical issues. Although the fundamental ethical principles do not change, new questions are constantly arising as to how to apply them in a changing world of counseling practice. For instance, when computer technologies first became widely available, ethical concerns centered around the security of client information stored on computers. Later, as Internet usage burgeoned, many questions arose around the ethics of Internet counseling. Today, the popularity of social media has raised new issues, such as whether counselors should "friend" clients, former clients, or supervisees. These developments led to the creation of a separate section on distance counseling, technology, and social media (ACA, 2014, §H) that reflects current issues when counselors use electronic means to provide services, store records, advertise their services, and communicate with clients (Francis, 2015).

It is also important to keep in mind that historically, counseling has not been a unified profession. Codes of ethics have proliferated as various specialty groups within counseling (Jordan, 2001a; Kelly, 2001), certification bodies, and state licensure boards have developed their own ethical standards. When you are established in your own professional practice, it is likely that you will hold multiple affiliations and will be bound to know and adhere to multiple codes. For instance, you might be a member of ACA and several of its divisions that have published specialty guidelines, be a National Certified Counselor (NCC), and be licensed as a counselor in your state. Holding each of these credentials will require you to abide by its particular code of ethics. The existence of multiple codes of ethics has created difficulties in enforcement, confusion for consumers of counseling services, and confusion for counseling professionals themselves (Herlihy & Remley, 1995). Efforts are being made by various organizations to bring standards into alignment, but until a single, universally accepted code of ethics for the counseling profession is established, you will need to be knowledgeable about all the codes of ethics that pertain to your practice.

Ethical Decision Making

Ethical decisions are rarely easy to arrive at, and dilemmas can be very complex. When counselors encounter ethical dilemmas, "they are expected to engage in a carefully considered ethical decision-making process" and use a "credible model of decision making that can bear public scrutiny of its application" (ACA, 2014, Purpose). Although no particular decision-making model has been shown to be universally effective or applicable, a number of models do exist, and we briefly review them here for your consideration.

One of the earliest models was *A Practitioner's Guide to Ethical Decision Making* (Forester-Miller & Davis, 1996). This guide presented a practical, sequential, seven-step model (Herlihy & Corey, 1996) that was based on the moral principles already discussed in this chapter. Over a decade later, Koocher and Keith-Spiegel (2008) presented a nine-step model that took a similar, logical, and primarily cognitive approach to ethical decision making. The assumption inherent in these models, that the goal of ethical decision making is to minimize subjectivity (Woody, 2013), has been challenged by some writers, particularly those with a feminist orientation (Hill, Glaser, & Harden, 1995; Meara et al., 1996; Rave & Larsen, 1995). Feminists have cautioned that traditional ethical decision-making models represent the information processing style of White males, in that they are linear, logical, rational, dispassionate, abstract, and paternalistic. Feminists have suggested that ethical decision making that is also holistic, intuitive, emotional, compassionate, personal and contextual, and mutual may be more inclusive of other processing styles and more culturally appropriate. Feminist theorists have emphasized the importance of remembering that ethical decision making does not occur solely within the mind of the professional. Walden (2015) urged including the client in the process, noting that clients are empowered when counselors make ethical decisions *with* them rather than *for* them.

Early models were also criticized for neglecting to consider multicultural issues. Garcia, Cartwright, Winston, and Borzuchowska (2003) offered a transcultural integrative model as being more appropriate when working with clients from diverse cultural backgrounds. They incorporated virtue ethics (already described in this chapter), along with the feminist concepts of reflecting on one's own feelings and balancing the perspectives of all involved. They suggested that a vital component, to be included early in the decision-making process, is for counselors to reflect on their own world views and how these affect their interpretation of the ethical dilemma. Frame and Williams (2005) presented a culturally sensitive ethical decision-making model that, like the feminist models, was based in an ethic of care and a consideration of power dynamics. To increase multicultural sensitivity, they added the element of assessing acculturation and racial identity development of the counselor and client. Finally, Herlihy and Watson (2006) offered a model based in a social justice perspective that puts multicultural competence at the core of the ethical reasoning process. The model is grounded in virtue ethics, cultural identity development, and collaborative decision making.

Cottone (2001) proposed a social constructivist model. Social constructivism is a relatively recent movement in the mental health field and purports that a person cannot know reality through individual contemplation because reality does not exist as objective fact. Rather, reality is socially constructed through interactions with others. Social constructivists see ethical decision making not as a process that occurs in the mind of the decision maker but as a process that is always made in interaction with at least one other person and that involves negotiating and consensualizing (Cottone, 2001).

A recent trend in ethical decision-making models seems to be the development of specialized models that are focused on counseling specific populations or on particular ethical issues (Deroche, Eckart, Lott, Park, & Raddler, 2015). Models have been offered for managing boundary issues (Herlihy & Corey, 2015b), resolving value conflicts (Kocet & Herlihy, 2014), integrating spirituality and religion into counseling (Barnett & Johnson, 2011), treating eating disorders (Matusek & O'Dougherty, 2010), school counseling (Luke, Goodrich, & Gilbride, 2013), and practicing play therapy (Seymour & Rubin, 2006).

There is much to be learned from each of these models, and we do not endorse any one particular model as being the *right* one for everyone. Instead, what follows is a description of steps that many of the models seem to have in common. We have tried to incorporate lessons that can be learned from principle and virtue ethics, feminist and multicultural ethics, social constructivism, and specialty models. We caution you to keep in mind that a listing of steps portrays ethical decision making as a linear progression, when in reality counselors rarely follow a set sequence of steps to resolve an ethical dilemma. In practice, numerous aspects of ethical decision making occur simultaneously in a dynamic process (Woody, 2013).

Identify and define the problem. Before deciding what action to take when faced with a dilemma, "determine whether the matter truly involves ethics" (Koocher & Keith-Spiegel, 2008, p. 21) or is actually a legal or clinical issue. If a legal issue is involved, consult with an attorney. If you have a clinical issue, consult with your supervisor or a trusted colleague. If, indeed, you have an ethical dilemma, it is prudent to take time to reflect and gather information. Although you may feel some sense of urgency, rarely will decisions that have ethical dimensions have to be made immediately. Take time to consider what you know (or what you can find out) about the situation, applicable ethical guidelines, and any laws that might be relevant. Try to examine the problem from several perspectives and avoid searching for simplistic solutions.

Involve your client in the decision-making process. This is not a separate step in ethical decision making; rather, it should occur throughout the process. Walden (2015) reminded counselors that the client is an integral part of the ethical community of the counseling relationship. Including clients in the process both empowers them and is culturally appropriate practice. We can think of very few situations that would preclude making the client an active partner in decisions affecting that client.

Review relevant codes of ethics and the professional literature. Examine the codes of ethics of the professional organizations to which you belong (as well as the ethical standards of your state licensing board if you are licensed as a counselor), to see if your issue is addressed in them. Be sure to read the codes carefully, as there may be several standards that pertain to different aspects of the dilemma. Also, read the recent literature on the issue at hand. This will help to ensure that you are using the most up-to-date professional knowledge on the issue (Herlihy & Corey, 2015a).

Consider the principles and virtues. Reflect on how the moral principles apply to the problem. Identify ways that they compete with each other, and rank them in order of their priority in this situation. Consider how virtue ethics might apply in the situation as well. Rather than focus exclusively on what you need to *do* in the situation, also consider who you want to *be* and how any possible action might affect your sense of moral selfhood.

Tune in to your feelings. Virtue ethicists believe that emotion informs judgment. Your feelings will influence how you interpret the dilemma, so it is important to consider what emotions you are experiencing as you contemplate the situation and your possible actions. To what extent are you being influenced, for instance, by emotions such as fear, self-doubt, or an overwhelming sense of responsibility? Being aware of your emotions, beliefs, values, and motivations can help guide you in your decision making.

Consult with colleagues or experts. Decisions made in isolation are rarely as sound as decisions made in consultation. Corey et al. (2015) have pointed out that poor ethical decision making often stems from our inability to view a situation objectively because we are emotionally invested in it or because our prejudices, values, or emotional needs are clouding our judgment. In addition, consultation would serve as an important element of your defense in court if your decision were challenged legally (Wheeler & Bertram, 2012).

Consider the context. Keep in mind that your worldview will affect how you interpret the dilemma, and that the client's worldview and culture may differ from your own. The resolution that is chosen for the dilemma must feel right not only to you but must also be appropriate for the client. It is also important to remember that decisions occur in a context. Therefore, it is useful to reflect on the potential ramifications of a decision for the client's family members, the community, and other professionals.

Identify desired outcomes and consider possible actions to achieve the outcomes. Even after thoughtful consideration, a single desired outcome rarely emerges in an ethical dilemma. There may be a number of outcomes you would hope to see achieved in a situation. Consider possible actions that you could take to achieve the desired outcomes. It may even be useful to list desired outcomes on one side of a page, and on the other side to generate possible actions that would facilitate the achievement of each of those outcomes. It is possible that implementing a particular action may achieve one desired outcome while eliminating another, forcing you to prioritize and choose one outcome at the expense of the other. Ponder the implications and consequences of each option for the client, for others who will be affected, and for yourself.

Choose and act on your choice. Once you have selected an action or series of actions, check to see whether your selected options are congruent with your ranking of the moral principles. Pay attention to how you feel about your choice. This final step involves strengthening your ego or gathering the moral courage to allow you to carry out your decision.

Even after the most careful deliberation, conscientious counselors cannot help but ask the question "How can I know whether I've done the right thing?" Van Hoose and Paradise (1979) suggested that decisions are probably ethically responsible if the counselors (a) maintained personal and professional honesty, coupled with (b) promoting the client's best interests (c) without malice or personal gain; and (d) can justify their actions as the best judgment regarding what should be done based on the current state of the profession.

You can also apply several self-tests after you have resolved an ethical dilemma. The first three tests were suggested by Stadler (1986). First is the test of *justice*, in which you ask whether you would treat others the same in this situation. Second is the test of *universality*, which considers if you would be willing to recommend the course of action you followed to other counselors who find themselves in a similar situation. Third is the test of *publicity*: Are you willing to have your actions come to light and be known by others? Another test is the *reversibility* test, which is a version of the Golden Rule; in this test you ask yourself if you would have made the same choice if you were in the client's shoes or if your child or life partner were subject to that choice. The *mentor* test asks you to consider an individual whose integrity and judgment you trust and admire, and ask how that person might solve the dilemma (Strom-Gottfried, 2007). Finally, you can check for *moral traces*, which are lingering feelings of doubt, discomfort, or uncertainty that counselors may experience after they have resolved an ethical dilemma, particularly when expediency, politics, or self-interest have influenced the decision. Moral traces are unpleasant but perform an important function. They act as a warning sign that you may have set foot on an ethical slippery slope, as defined earlier in this chapter.

We hope you will return to this material on the ethical decision-making process as you ponder the case studies that are presented throughout this text. As you reflect on what you might do if you were the counselor in the case study, you can gain practice in applying a systematic model, as required by your code of ethics. Being an ethical professional involves a combination of knowledge, problem-solving skills and strategies, understanding of philosophical principles, and a virtuous character that leads one to respond with maturity, judgment, and wisdom (Bersoff, 1996). It is a task that requires a lifelong commitment and is never really finished. Even the most experienced counselors who are intimately aware of the ethical standards wrestle with difficult ethical issues and dilemmas (Walden, Herlihy, & Ashton, 2003).

1-3 The Case of Carla

Carla has been counseling a 15-year-old girl, Danielle, for several weeks. Carla has had to work hard to gain Danielle's trust. Danielle was raised by abusive parents until she was 13, when she went to live with her grandparents. Today she tells Carla that she is having some problems with her boyfriend. As Danielle describes these problems, Carla realizes that the boyfriend is treating her in an abusive manner. When Carla expresses her concern about this, Danielle replies that she loves him and can get him to change, that her grandparents don't know about his behavior, and that she absolutely does not want Carla to tell them or anyone else.

- How might you apply each of the six moral principles to this situation? In this case, which moral principle do you think must take precedence? How might you apply the ethic of care or relational ethics to this dilemma?
- Try to apply to this scenario the steps of the ethical decision-making process described in this chapter. To what course of action does this process lead you? How well did it work for you?

Discussion: The moral principles could be applied in several ways. The principle of respect for autonomy would support deferring to Danielle's wishes and not telling anyone about her abusive boyfriend. The principle of nonmaleficence would require Carla to weigh the risk for harm. Telling someone who could prevent further abuse would support nonmaleficence. However, if Danielle becomes upset by this action and refuses to continue in counseling, telling someone also could violate the principle of do no harm. Likewise, beneficence could be interpreted in more than one way. Beneficence means that professionals have an obligation to provide a service that benefits society, so taking action that would stop the abuse would best serve society's interests. Yet, beneficence also means to promote clients' mental health, and Carla could respect Danielle's wishes and continue to work to increase her awareness and self-esteem, which, for now, could be the most beneficent thing to do. How Carla adheres to the principles of justice, fidelity, and veracity will depend largely on whether she has informed Danielle that she would have to breach confidentiality to prevent harm to Danielle. If so, then telling her grandparents would be just and truthful, and would not be breaking her promise to keep Danielle's disclosures confidential.

If Carla reasons through her dilemmas from the perspective of the ethic of care, she will put primary importance on preserving and nurturing her relationship with Danielle. She would also be concerned about Danielle's other supportive networks, such as her relationship with her grandparents and what she considers to be a loving relationship with her boyfriend despite his problem behaviors.

Obviously, there is no one correct way to reason through this dilemma and no single, clear, right answer. We believe it would be a good learning experience for you to work your way through the decision-making process and then discuss your decisions with your classmates.

LEGAL ISSUES

The discussion of professional ethics that precedes this section emphasized the serious responsibility you have to clients, the difference you can make in their lives, and the duty you have to practice in an ethical manner. Understanding the legal system and your role in it, the legal rights of your clients, and your legal responsibilities to clients is also essential to practicing counseling in a professional manner. Legal issues within counseling are somewhat frightening because the law is an area that is complex, often vague, threatening, antithetical to the nature of counselors, and difficult to fully grasp. The process of decision making around legal issues is presented in this chapter. In addition, throughout this text, you are given information about the legal dimensions that surround your functions as a professional counselor.

Origins of Law

There are a number of sources of law in the United States. The basic source is the U.S. Constitution. The 50 states, the District of Columbia, and the U.S. possessions also have constitutions. Laws created by the federal, state, district, and possession governments cannot violate either federal or state constitutional principles. The United States has adopted English common law, which includes a set of societal principles that were not written into documents but have been accepted over time as obvious within U.S. society. An example of common law that is very important to counselors is the law of torts. Tort law relates to the principle that individuals will be held responsible for any harm they cause to other members of society. Malpractice is an area of tort law that holds professionals accountable for any harm they might cause to the public. The public relies on professionals to provide services in a manner that benefits and does not harm them.

A primary source of law is statutes passed by federal and state legislatures. These statutes may modify the common law but may not violate constitutional principles. Governmental regulations, both federal and state, are procedures adopted by agencies to carry out laws created by statutes. Regulations, which are created by governmental agencies, may implement statutes but may not exceed the authority of the statute. Finally, federal and state courts interpret the law. Whereas some accuse judges of creating law, courts are limited to interpreting constitutions, common law principles, statutes, and regulations.

Almost all areas of counselor practice are affected by law. Most seasoned counselors are keenly aware of the law of malpractice and the fact that they might be sued by a client. As a counselor, you will probably come to share this awareness. You also must be aware of laws related to confidentiality, records, parental rights, and licensing statutes, among others. In addition, you must be able to identify legal problems as they arise, and you must adhere to legal requirements when you are involved in any way with a legal proceeding. Legal issues are an important part of the day-to-day professional practice of counselors in all settings.

Recognizing Legal Issues

Many of the ethical and professional judgment questions you will encounter as a counseling practitioner will have legal implications as well. Sometimes counselors find it difficult to determine when they have a legal problem or to know what to do once a legal problem has been identified. This section of the chapter discusses how to recognize legal issues, how to get legal advice, and what steps to take to ensure proper and professional practice.

The following are examples of legal issues that counselors face in their practices:

- The secretary tells you that there is a deputy sheriff in the reception area asking for you. When you introduce yourself, the deputy hands you a subpoena that orders you to produce your case notes and any other documents related to one of your current clients.
- One of your clients asks you to come to a child custody hearing that will determine whether she will get permanent custody of her children.
- One of your clients has been arrested for drug possession. You receive a subpoena in the mail that orders you to appear at her criminal trial.

- A new client tells you that his lawyer sent him to see you. He is suing his employer for having fired him and wants you to verify that he has emotional stress that is job related.
- A client tells you that her former husband's lawyer called and told her she had to let her former husband have their children for the summer. She wants to know if the lawyer is right.
- A former client has sent you a letter demanding her money back. She thinks the 10 sessions she had with you were a waste of money because you did not help her. She has sent a copy of the letter to her lawyer.
- A client you are seeing appears suicidal and refuses to go voluntarily to the local hospital for a psychiatric evaluation.
- You receive a notice from your state licensure board that a formal complaint has been filed against you and that a hearing will be held on the matter.
- In your office mail, you receive a formal legal complaint against you that has been filed with the local court, accusing you of professional malpractice. One of your clients murdered his girlfriend 9 months ago. The complaint alleges that you were responsible for the girl's death and asks for $1 million in damages.

A simple test to determine whether there is a legal issue involved in a situation you are facing is to review the situation to see if any of the following apply: (a) legal proceedings of some type have been initiated, (b) lawyers are on the scene in some capacity, or (c) you are vulnerable to having a complaint filed against you for misconduct. If you are providing professional counseling services and one or more of these three components exist, then you definitely are dealing with a legal issue. Sometimes, all you need to do with a legal situation is clarify the nature of a counselor's role with your client and refer the client to attorneys for legal advice. When you are dealing with a legal issue and you are unsure which course of action you should take, often you will need to consult a lawyer.

Obtaining Legal Advice

Most counselors are employed by organizations or entities that provide counseling services, such as community mental health agencies, schools, businesses, hospitals, outpatient treatment programs, or colleges. These entities all have administrators and organizational structures that require the regular services of attorneys. It is the employees' responsibility to request legal advice when dealing with an issue that has legal implications beyond their ability to resolve. It is the obligation of employers to provide employees with the legal advice they need to perform their jobs appropriately.

Counselors seldom have direct access to lawyers, primarily because the cost is prohibitive. Also, administrators seek the advice of lawyers, but they must maintain their authority in making administrative decisions. When a counselor identifies a legal issue in the work setting and defines the legal questions to ask, the counselor should pose the questions to the immediate supervisor and ask for assistance. If the counselor thinks an attorney needs to have special information regarding the situation in order to render sound advice, the counselor should request a personal consultation with the attorney, although such consultations are not normally allowed. The supervisor will then either answer the counselor's questions based on previous experience with similar issues or seek legal advice through proper administrative channels within the organization.

In some circumstances, it is possible for counselors to give their legal problems to administrators within their agency. Many legal issues that arise are administrative in nature and should be handled by administrators rather than by counselors. Examples of legal issues that counselors might easily turn over to administrators include the following:

- A noncustodial parent demands from a school counselor that he be allowed to see his child's academic records.

- The police arrive at a counselor's door and want to see the counseling file for a current client.
- A health insurance company representative calls a counselor and wants to know why the counselor's agency has so many claims signed by the same psychiatrist.
- A client becomes irate because a counselor terminates the counseling relationship after five sessions because that is the agency's policy.
- A lawyer for a former client calls a counselor and threatens to sue if the counselor does not immediately give the lawyer the information being sought.
- A secretary who reports to an administrator appears to be revealing confidential information about clients to friends.
- A client tells a counselor that the counselor's colleague in the agency has made sexual advances during a counseling session.

If legal problems cannot be handed over to an administrator, then counselors themselves must take responsibility for resolving situations in an appropriate manner. Once counselors have disclosed their legal questions to their immediate supervisors and have received a response either from the supervisor or an attorney advising them as to the proper course of action, counselors must follow that advice. It is essential for counselors to follow legal advice given to them, even if they do not agree with it. Only then will counselors be indemnified by their employers and supported if problems arise later. By seeking and following legal advice when legal questions arise, counselors are taking steps that may protect them from being held individually responsible in the event their actions are challenged.

Counselors in independent private practice do not have the luxury of seeking legal advice without charge within their work environment, and they are not protected from responsibility because they do not have employers. Private practitioners must establish relationships with attorneys for legal advice just as they must retain accountants to handle their financial and business affairs. The cost of legal advice for a counselor in private practice is a necessary expense related to establishing and maintaining a business. However, finding a lawyer who understands the nature of mental health practices and is prepared to represent counselors effectively is not always an easy task (Remley, 1991). Counselors who are planning to open private practices are advised to identify an attorney while they are establishing their business so they will have a working relationship in place when problems arise. The best attorney probably would be a local one who is already representing one or more successful mental health practitioners—counselors, social workers, or psychologists. Such an attorney would already have been educated regarding the special issues surrounding mental health practices. If an attorney who is experienced in representing mental health professionals is not available, then a lawyer who represents other types of professionals—such as accountants, other lawyers, or physicians—would be a good alternative.

Some counselors have jobs in which they testify in court on a routine basis or provide services to clients who frequently are involved in litigation. These counselors learn their roles over time and do not need to consult attorneys for advice each time they encounter a legal situation. For most counselors, however, it is infrequent that they deal with legal proceedings, have clients who are represented by lawyers, or think they are in danger of being sued. When such situations arise for the majority of counselors, it is essential for them to obtain legal advice.

Exercising Professional Judgment

Throughout the workday, counselors often have to exercise their professional judgment in areas that are difficult. They are held accountable for making professional decisions that are sound and reasonable, given the information they have available when they make such judgments. If a client believes that he or she was harmed because of a professional decision made by a counselor, then the client might sue a counselor for malpractice. As a result, when a counselor exercises professional judgment, there is always a risk afterward of being accused of wrongdoing.

A few of the areas particularly vulnerable to later legal challenges in which counselors make judgments include the following:

- Determining whether a client is suicidal or a danger to others
- Deciding what to do to prevent harm after determining that a client is a danger to self or others
- Rendering a clinical diagnosis that could have negative implications for a client at a later time
- Terminating a counseling relationship over the client's objections
- Deciding whether to enter into a counseling relationship with a client who has a problem that you have not treated before or have not been specifically trained to treat
- Reacting appropriately to a client who has expressed an interest in having a sexual relationship with you
- Using a paradoxical intervention with a client

Just as counselors must obtain legal advice when legal questions arise in their practice, they must obtain professional consultation to the extent possible when making difficult professional judgments. It is inappropriate to ask counselor colleagues about how to handle legal problems, and at the same time it is inappropriate to consult with an attorney when making difficult clinical decisions. A counselor colleague might give you advice about a legal situation, but you cannot rely on the accuracy of that advice because your counselor colleagues are not lawyers. Likewise, a lawyer might give you advice about how to handle a difficult clinical issue, but lawyers are not educated as mental health professionals. If you ask attorneys about what to do in difficult clinical situations, they will focus on protecting you rather than on knowing what might be best for your client.

1-4 The Case of Fatima

Fatima is a counselor in a university counseling center who is in the process of planning for a month-long vacation. She will be leaving in 2 months. She has been having a series of conversations with her supervisor and several of her colleagues at the center about the proper way to handle her existing clients: when to tell them she is leaving; whether to refer them permanently to other counselors; whether to refer them temporarily to other counselors and take them back when she returns; whether to terminate with those who are nearing readiness; and what to do about those clients who have been at risk for suicide in the recent past. At the staff meeting today, the counseling center director announced that he had talked to the university attorney about the situation and her advice was to just tell all of Fatima's clients that she will be gone for a month and to let them decide what to do in the interim. The director said that the attorney said that Fatima had no other legal obligations to the clients.

- To what degree should the university attorney's advice on this issue affect Fatima's decision making?
- Because the director told Fatima and the staff about the advice of the university attorney, how should Fatima interact with the director if she decides to do something different from what the attorney advised?

Discussion: It is good for counselors to get advice from attorneys regarding their legal obligations. However, a counselor's ethical obligations may go beyond what is required legally. Fatima will want to be careful not to offend the director, so perhaps she could thank the director for obtaining legal advice. Later and in private, she might share the ACA *Code of Ethics* with the director and point out some of the ethical obligations she wants to meet. She could continue by suggesting that a good goal for the center would be to follow ethical and best practice guidelines, in addition to legal obligations, in order to provide the best possible service to clients.

When counselors face issues that require them to exercise their clinical judgment, particularly where there are no clear right or wrong responses, it is essential to consult with colleagues to the extent possible. In some situations consultation might be impossible, such as when emergencies arise. When time does allow, however, consulting about clients provides a substantial protection to counselors whose clinical decisions are later challenged. The legal standard of care for counselors is that counselors must practice in a manner consistent with the way in which a reasonable, similarly educated counselor would practice under the same set of circumstances. By consulting with others, counselors can prove later that they indeed met the standard of care by doing what other, presumably reasonable, counselors advised or agreed on. If experts are available for consultation, it is wise to talk with them as well. Experts might include former university professors, counselors who are known for their expertise in a particular area, or counselors with extensive clinical experience.

It is impossible for counselors to know for certain whether they are making decisions that will protect their clients or others from harm. Because of this uncertainty, it is essential that counselors maintain a current personal professional liability insurance policy at all times. Professional liability insurance policies are discussed in detail in Chapter 8.

Summary and Key Points

This introductory chapter has familiarized you with some key concepts that form the foundation for studying ethical, legal, and professional issues in counseling. The professional orientation content area of graduate training involves the study of professional identity, ethics, and law. *Morals, values,* and *ethics* are all interrelated terms, but they have different meanings. As used in this text, the term *morality* refers to personal beliefs and how these beliefs affect your conduct, whereas *ethics* refers to professional behaviors. Counselors share certain professional *values,* and they hold their own unique personal values, which they must take care not to impose on clients. *Laws* are agreed-on rules which set forth principles that allow people to live together in a society. Laws dictate minimal standards of behavior, and ethics prescribe both minimal professional behaviors and ideal or aspirational behaviors. *Best practice* goes beyond what is minimally required by laws or codes of ethics and is the very best a counselor could be expected to do.

A model of professional practice was presented as one way to conceptualize how all these terms might fit together in your actual practice as a counselor. In this model, both internal and external building blocks contribute to the development and maintenance of sound, professional practice.

Following are some of the key points made in this chapter about ethics and law in counseling:

- Ethical theories have existed for centuries and provide a foundation for the ethical reasoning of contemporary professional counselors.

- Principle ethics, based on the moral principles of the helping professions, and virtue ethics, focused on traits of character, are two complementary ways of looking at the foundations of counselor ethics.
- Codes of ethics are vital resources in ethical decision making, but they cannot answer every question that might arise in actual practice. The ACA *Code of Ethics* (ACA, 2014) is the primary code on which counselors rely.
- Of critical importance to counselors is the development of ethical decision-making skills. Counselors are required to use an ethi-

cal decision-making model to reason through the ethical dilemmas confronting them.
- Most areas of counselor practice are affected by law.
- Counselors must know how to recognize legal issues and how to obtain legal advice.
- Counselors should seek advice from fellow mental health professionals when they have clinical or ethical questions, and seek advice from lawyers when they have legal questions.
- There is no substitute for professional judgment on difficult ethical or legal questions encountered by counselors, although many helpful resources exist.

Professional Identity of Counselors

Counselors are a relatively new professional group compared to such other mental health professionals as psychologists, social workers, and psychiatrists. Potential consumers of mental health services often are unaware that counseling is a distinct profession that can be clearly distinguished from similar mental health professions. Even counselors themselves sometimes find it difficult to describe the distinctions. Thus, a vital professional task for counselors is to adopt a strong professional identity and to be able to articulate that unique identity to others (Gale & Austin, 2003; Healey & Hays, 2012; Smith, 2001).

Professional identity is a nebulous concept, but it is vital to the long-term success of a profession. In discussing the professional identity development of school counselors, Brott and Myers (1999) argued that professional identity is a process rather than an outcome, and that seasoned counselors must constantly reexamine their identities to meet new challenges. Individuals who have a strong professional identity can easily explain the philosophy that underlies the activities of their professional group, describe the services that their profession renders to the public, describe the training programs that prepare them to practice their profession, explain their qualifications and the credentials they possess, and articulate the similarities and differences between members of their own profession and other similar groups. In addition, those with a strong professional identity feel a significant pride in being a member of their profession and can communicate this special sense of belonging to those with whom they interact.

A number of articles have appeared regarding counselor identity over the last few years. Counselor professional identity development has been discussed and studied from various perspectives (Dollarhide, Gibson, & Moss, 2013; Healey & Hays, 2012; Moss, Gibson, & Dollarhide, 2014; Reiner, Dobmeier, & Hernandez, 2013). Scholars have recognized the importance of understanding counselor professional identity development for the success of the counseling profession.

Although it may seem strange to some, it wasn't until 2010 that a definition of *counseling* was agreed upon by the various organizations that represent the profession (Kaplan, Tarvydas, & Gladding, 2014). This agreed-upon definition can be found on the ACA website at counseling.org.

2-1 The Case of Rebekah

Rebekah is a third-grade teacher who recently completed her master's degree in counseling. Because her school district employs counselors only at the high school level, she has assumed that she will have to move to another district to fulfill her goal of being an elementary school counselor. She is very excited when her principal calls to tell her that the school board is going to consider hiring either counselors or school social workers for the elementary schools. The principal asks her to attend the next school board meeting and speak about what an elementary school counselor does and how counselors differ from social workers. Rebekah wants to give a very persuasive talk so that the board will decide to hire counselors and, she hopes, offer her one of the new positions. She asks you for advice on what to say and how to say it.

- What advice would you give Rebekah, in terms of the information she should present?
- What arguments do you think would be most persuasive in influencing the board members to hire counselors?

Discussion: Rebekah might gather all the information available from the American School Counselor Association (ASCA; schoolcounselor.org) regarding the unique role of school counselors in elementary schools. She should summarize this information for the school board members. She should also be prepared to explain the differences between the roles of school social workers and school counselors at the elementary school level.

The most influential information Rebekah could present would be data showing that elementary school counselors make a difference in schools in terms of students' academic achievement; satisfaction of parents with the school; and satisfaction of parents, teachers, and administrators with elementary school counseling programs. Providing testimonials from students, parents, teachers, and principals in schools that have effective elementary school counseling programs might also be very effective.

We hope this chapter helps you clarify your professional identity as a counselor and also helps you tell others about the profession of counseling. It is also intended to help you understand and appreciate the history of the counseling profession, the professional associations that serve counselors, graduate program accreditation, and the credentials available to counselors.

PHILOSOPHY UNDERLYING THE COUNSELING PROFESSION

Counselors have a distinct belief system regarding the best way to help people resolve their emotional and personal issues and problems. This belief system provides the foundation for the professional identity of counselors. Basically, counselors share the following four beliefs regarding helping others with their mental health concerns:

1. The best perspective for assisting individuals in resolving their emotional and personal issues and problems is the wellness model of mental health.
2. Most of the issues and problems that individuals face in life are developmental in nature, and understanding the dynamics of human growth and development is essential to success as a helper.
3. Prevention and early intervention are far superior to remediation in dealing with personal and emotional problems.
4. The goal of counseling is to empower individual clients and client systems to resolve their own problems independently of mental health professionals and to teach them to identify and resolve problems autonomously in the future.

The Wellness Model

The first belief that counselors share is that the wellness model of mental health is the best perspective for helping people resolve their personal and emotional issues and problems (Hermon & Hazler, 1999; McAuliffe & Eriksen, 1999). Myers, Sweeney, and Witmer (2000) have developed a comprehensive model of wellness specific to counseling. Historically, the primary model used by other mental health professionals in the United States to address emotional problems was the medical or illness model, an approach created by physicians in caring for persons with physical illnesses.

In the medical model, the helper identifies the illness presented by the person asking for assistance. The diagnosis of the illness is always the first step in helping. This perspective assumes that the client is diminished in some significant way. The goal of the professional helper is to return the help seeker to the level of functioning enjoyed before the illness occurred. Once the illness has been isolated, the helper applies scientific principles in curing the illness. If the helper is successful and the illness is cured, the client then goes on about life. If another illness negatively affects the client's well-being, the client returns to the helper to be cured again.

Psychiatrists, who are physicians, are educated to approach mental health issues utilizing the medical model. Other mental health professions, including clinical psychology, psychiatric nursing, and clinical social work, came into existence when the medical model was prevalent, and these mental health professionals have their roots in this tradition as well.

Counselors, on the other hand, belong to a newer profession with a different tradition. Counselors have adopted the wellness model of mental health as their perspective for helping people, and there is evidence that counseling from a wellness perspective is an effective method of helping clients (Myers & Sweeney, 2004b; Prochaska, DiClemente, & Norcross, 1992; Tanigoshi, Kontos, & Remley, 2008; Westgate, 1996). In the wellness model, the goal is for each person to achieve

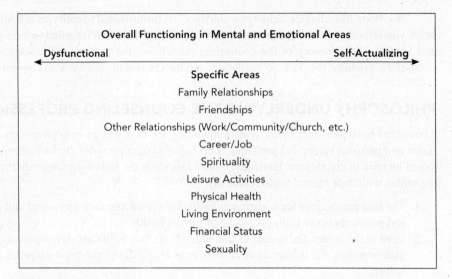

Overall Functioning in Mental and Emotional Areas

Dysfunctional ←————————————————————————→ Self-Actualizing

Specific Areas

Family Relationships

Friendships

Other Relationships (Work/Community/Church, etc.)

Career/Job

Spirituality

Leisure Activities

Physical Health

Living Environment

Financial Status

Sexuality

FIGURE 2-1   The wellness orientation to mental health

Source: Pearson Education, Inc., Hoboken, NJ.

positive mental health to the degree possible. From a wellness perspective, mental health is seen as occurring on a continuum (Smith, 2001). At one end of the scale are individuals who are very mentally healthy. Maslow (1968) described people who are fully functioning mentally and emotionally as *self-actualizing*. At the other extreme are persons who are dysfunctional because of mental problems. Such people might include persons with schizophrenia who do not respond to any kind of treatment or intervention.

In addition to this general continuum of mental health, the wellness orientation also views mental health as including a number of scales of mental and emotional functioning (see Figure 2-1). These scales represent an individual's mental and emotional wellness in important areas of living. Counselors assess a client's functioning in each of these areas to determine where attention within counseling might best be focused to increase wellness. These areas include family relationships, friendships, other relationships (work/community/church, etc.), career/job, spirituality, leisure activities, physical health, living environment, financial status, and sexuality.

Counselors assess clients' current life situations and help determine which factors are interfering with the goal of reaching their maximum potential. Many persons are limited by physical disabilities or environmental conditions that cannot be changed. Keeping such limitations in mind, counselors assist their clients in becoming as autonomous and successful in their lives as possible.

Although the distinctions between the medical model and the wellness model can be clearly articulated, there is considerable overlap when they are put into practice. Many individual practitioners within the other mental health professions deviate from the illness model. In fact, evidence that the medical profession has adopted many elements of the wellness model can be seen in current trends toward preventive medicine, consumer education, and patient rights. Increasingly, medical practitioners are coming to view patients as partners in their own health care, and this trend is also evident in the approaches of many psychiatrists, psychologists, and other mental health professionals. At the same time, today's counselors are educated to use the medical model of diagnosing mental disorders (the *DSM* system) and often render such diagnoses as a component of the services they provide.

Within the counseling profession there is an increasing recognition of the importance of advocating for clients who face societal and institutional barriers that inhibit their access or growth and development (Hunt, Matthews, Milsom, & Lammel, 2006; Ingersoll, Bauer, & Burns, 2004; Myers & Sweeney, 2004a). Client advocacy has long been a tradition in social work practice, but until recently it has not been emphasized in the training of counselors, other than rehabilitation counselors. Mental health professionals who operate from the illness model might treat patients or clients in ways that appear similar to the way they would be treated by mental health professionals who embrace the wellness model. For example, mental health professionals who espouse either model would most likely provide individual or group counseling services, spend time talking with clients, take clinical notes, and render a diagnosis of any mental disorders the person may have. Perhaps the primary differences between the two are in the attitude of the professional toward the client and the focus of the professional's clinical attention. Counselors see the client as having both the potential and the desire for autonomy and success in living rather than having an illness that needs to be remediated. In addition, the goal of counseling is to help the person accomplish wellness rather than cure an illness. Hansen (2003; 2005; 2006; 2007; 2012) and Hansen, Speciale, and Lemberger (2014) have written a series of articles that question many of the current practices and language used by counselors, suggesting that the counseling profession may be moving away from its foundational beliefs by classifying itself as a health care profession.

A Developmental Perspective

A second belief that counselors share is that many personal and emotional issues can be understood within a developmental perspective. As people progress through the life span, they meet and must successfully address a number of personal challenges. Counselors believe that most of the problems people encounter are developmental in nature and therefore are natural and normal. Problems that some other mental health professionals might view as pathological, and that counselors would see as developmental, include the following:

- A 5-year-old crying as if in terror when his mother drops him off for the first time at his kindergarten class
- An 11-year-old girl who seems to become obsessed with boys
- A teenager vigorously defying his parents' directives
- A 19-year-old boy becoming seriously depressed after breaking up with his girlfriend
- A young mother becoming despondent soon after the birth of a child
- A 35-year-old man beginning to drink so much he is getting into trouble after 15 years of social drinking
- A 40-year-old woman feeling worthless after her youngest child leaves home for college
- A 46-year-old man having an affair with a younger woman after 23 years of a committed marriage
- A 65-year-old woman feeling very depressed as her retirement approaches
- An 80-year-old man concerned that he is losing his mind because he is forgetting so much

By studying the developmental stages in life and understanding tasks that all individuals face during their lives, counselors are able to put many problems that clients experience into a perspective that views these problems as natural and normal. Even problems viewed as psychopathological by other mental health professionals, such as severe depression, substance addiction, or debilitating anxiety, could be seen as transitory issues that often plague people and that must be dealt with effectively if individuals are to continue living in a successful fashion.

Prevention and Early Intervention

A third philosophical assumption of counselors is our preference for prevention rather than remediation of mental and emotional problems (Conyne & Horne, 2001; Kulic, Dagley, & Horne, 2001; McCarthy & Mejía, 2001; McCormac, 2014; Owens & Kulic, 2001; Sapia, 2001; Wilson & Owens, 2001). When prevention is impossible, counselors strive toward early intervention instead of waiting until a problem has reached serious proportions.

A primary tool that counselors use to prevent emotional and mental problems is education. Counselors often practice their profession in the role of teacher, using psychoeducation as a tool. By alerting clients to potential future areas that might cause personal and emotional distress and preparing them to meet such challenges successfully, counselors prevent problems before they arise. Just a few examples of prevention activities are parenting education programs, assertiveness training seminars, career exploration groups, and premarriage counseling.

When the time for prevention has already passed and a client is experiencing personal or emotional problems, counselors prefer seeing clients early in the process. Counselors believe that counseling is for everyone, not just for individuals who have mental illnesses or emotional disorders. By providing services to individuals when they begin to experience potentially distressing events in their lives, counselors hope to intervene early and thereby prevent problems from escalating. For instance, counselors would prefer to see a client who is beginning to have feelings of depression rather than someone who could be diagnosed as having an episode of severe depression, and counselors would encourage couples who are beginning to experience problems in their relationship to seek counseling rather than wait for their problems to escalate into serious marital discord.

Empowerment of Clients

The fourth belief that counselors share regarding the helping process is that the goal of counseling is to empower clients to problem-solve independently (Chronister & McWhirter, 2003; Dailey, Gill, Karl, & Barrio Minton, 2014a; Lynch & Gussel, 1996; Savage, Harley, & Nowak, 2005). Through teaching clients appropriate problem-solving strategies and increasing their self-understanding, counselors hope that clients will not need assistance in living their lives in the future. Realizing that individuals often need only transitory help, counselors also try to communicate to clients that asking for and receiving help is not a sign of mental or emotional weakness but, instead, is often a healthy response to life's problems.

It is quite easy for individuals to become dependent on those who provide help to them. Some systems of mental health care seem to encourage a pattern of lifelong dependence. Counselors recognize this problem and encourage clients to assume responsibility for their lives and learn to live in a manner that allows them autonomy and independence as those concepts are understood within the clients' cultures. Although some people may need assistance throughout their lives because of a physical or mental disability, all clients are helped to become as independent as their circumstances will allow. Counselors do not present themselves as experts in mental health who must be consulted when problems arise. Rather, counselors communicate the belief that clients are capable of developing the skills they need for independent living and wellness.

COUNSELING SERVICES

To achieve a strong professional identity as a counselor, it is essential that you understand the philosophy of helping we have just described. In addition, you need to be knowledgeable about the kinds of services that counselors provide to the public, even though the services that counselors provide do not define the profession. Actually, counselors engage in a number of the same activities as do other professionals. The key to a strong professional identity is the philosophy underlying the services, not the services being rendered.

The basic service that counselors provide is counseling—for individuals, couples, families, and groups. All other mental health professionals counsel patients and clients, too. A major difference between counselors and other mental health professionals who counsel is that counseling is the *primary* professional service that counselors provide. By contrast, the primary service that psychiatrists provide is the diagnosis and medical treatment of mental disorders as a physician; psychologists primarily provide assessment and research; psychiatric nurses provide management of mental health care within a hospital setting; and social workers primarily link clients to community resources. For mental health professionals other than counselors, counseling may be a secondary or ancillary service.

In addition, a number of other professionals outside the mental health field call the service that they provide to clients *counseling*. For example, attorneys provide legal counseling, accountants offer financial counseling, and physicians offer counseling to their patients regarding their physical health. Counselors, in contrast to these non–mental-health professionals, provide mental health counseling services to clients.

In conjunction with counseling, counselors also perform a number of other professional services. These services include assessment, teaching, diagnosis, case management, and advocacy. Despite performing these other duties, the primary service provided by counselors is mental health counseling.

Counselors have a number of job titles, roles, and duties in their professional positions. To develop a strong professional identity, you must know when you are functioning as a counselor and when you are performing other roles in your professional position. You must also be able to identify the types of professional services that counselors render to the public.

COUNSELOR PREPARATION PROGRAMS

Ask lawyers what they were taught in law school, physicians what they were taught in medical school, and engineers what they were taught in engineering school, and they can easily and clearly describe the courses they were taught, the practical components of their educational experience, and the topics covered in their preparation programs. To develop a strong professional identity, it is vital that you are also able to describe your training program components. By describing the educational programs that prepare counselors, you summarize the essential nature of counseling as a profession and emphasize the basic knowledge required for becoming a counselor.

An important aspect of counselor training is that the profession considers individuals to be professionals after they have completed a master's degree. Although a master's degree is the required professional degree in both psychiatric nursing and clinical social work, psychiatry requires a medical degree and a residency in psychiatry, and psychology requires a doctoral degree for the achievement of professional status. One of the primary differences between counseling psychology and the profession of counseling is that counseling psychologists must hold doctorates to be considered professionals, whereas counselors are considered professionals at the master's-degree level.

In addition, counseling skills are the primary focus of the counseling master's-degree training programs. Although other subjects are taught, all of the training emphasizes competency in the areas of individual and group counseling. The other courses required in master's-degree programs, such as research, assessment, multicultural counseling, and career counseling, are meant to strengthen the counseling skills of graduate students.

Counseling graduate programs generally are located in colleges of education within universities. The profession of counseling has its foundations in pedagogy and psychology, particularly in counseling psychology and human growth and development. All these fields have their roots in colleges of education, which is why counseling graduate programs are usually located there. Some counselor educators and counselors are concerned that this implies that counselors are being prepared to function only in educational settings, such as schools or colleges. They believe that the general public's perception is negatively affected when they think of all counselors as being prepared and practicing in the same way that school guidance counselors were prepared and practiced at the beginning of the school counseling movement in the 1950s. The reality is that the counseling process is educational in nature, and although counselors do not educate in formal classrooms like traditional teachers do, counselors do educate their clients. Being located in colleges of education strengthens counseling graduate programs because the colleges emphasize pedagogy, human growth and development, applied research, and field placements as essential components of learning skills.

The counseling profession created the Council for Accreditation of Counseling and Related Educational Programs (CACREP) to set national standards for the preparation of master's- and doctoral-level counselors (CACREP, 2014; Urofsky, 2013). CACREP was begun during the 1960s under the leadership of Robert O. Stripling, a counselor educator at the University of Florida. CACREP began as a project of the Association of Counselor Education and Supervision (ACES), a division of the ACA, and now functions as a separate corporation.

CACREP has established standards for the preparation of counselors (CACREP, 2014). These standards require a minimum of 2 years or 48 to 60 semester hours in master's-degree programs that prepare counselors. In addition, the programs must include instruction in the following content areas: (a) human growth and development, (b) social and cultural foundations, (c) helping relationships, (d) group work, (e) career and lifestyle development, (f) appraisal, (g) research and program evaluation, and (h) professional orientation (which includes professional identity and ethics). CACREP requires that students complete a 100-hour practicum and a 600-hour internship. The CACREP standards also require that program faculty also be counselors, that programs have a laboratory for training, and that a number of other requirements for quality instruction be met (Bobby, 2013; Even & Robinson, 2013; Lee, 2013).

Currently, of the more than 1,600 master's- and doctoral-degree programs in counseling in the United States (Schweiger, Henderson, McCaskill, Clawson, & Collins, 2011), about one-third are CACREP accredited (CACREP, 2014). Many programs that are not yet accredited have patterned their master's-degree programs after the standards developed by CACREP. Although not all of the counseling graduate degree programs in the United States are accredited by CACREP, it is accurate to say that CACREP standards have been accepted by the profession as the model curriculum for preparing master's- and doctoral-level counselors. The doctoral standards have recently been strengthened (Adkison-Bradley, 2013). Because graduation from a CACREP-accredited program is one type of credential that a counselor might possess, CACREP accreditation will be discussed further in the next section.

In 2018, Ohio will be the first state to require that those licensed as counselors hold CACREP-accredited master's degrees (Bray, 2013). This is a major change and verifies that CACREP has become the educational standard for the counseling profession.

CREDENTIALING

One of the greatest challenges faced by those entering the counseling profession is to understand counselor credentialing. Credentialed individuals possess some type of indicator that they are legitimate professionals. Credentialing comes in many forms, which is the basic reason people are so confused by it. In addition, some credentials are essential to the practice of the profession, others are desirable but not necessary, and still others are of questionable value or even worthless.

This section contains a discussion of credentials and should assist you in conceptualizing and understanding counselor credentials.

A major problem that causes confusion among counselors and the public is that terminology is not consistent within the area of credentialing. The major types of counselor credentials are degree, state license, state agency certification, national voluntary certification, and program accreditation.

Degree

The most obvious credential that counselors hold is the master's degree. Other degrees, such as specialist or doctoral degrees, are credentials as well.

Counselors hold a variety of master's-degree titles. A legitimate counselor might hold a Master of Education (MEd), Master of Arts (MA), Master of Science (MS), Master of Divinity (MDiv), or another, more unusual, master's-degree title such as Master of Counseling (MCoun). Most of the titles of master's degrees given in various universities were decided long ago and generally have little to do with any differences in the actual program content. The degree title in no way indicates whether a degree program requires a specified number of credits, includes a thesis, or has other specific requirements. In many universities, degree titles are decided politically among the various faculties. For example, a number of counseling master's-degree programs award MEd degrees because the degree programs are offered within university colleges of education.

Although the basic credential for a professional counselor is a master's degree in counseling, many counselors hold higher degrees, including specialist's degrees, certificates of advanced study, and doctoral degrees. Doctoral degrees in counseling usually are either the Doctor of Philosophy (PhD) or the Doctor of Education (EdD), although some counseling doctoral programs might have titles such as Doctor of Arts (DA) or Doctor of Divinity (DDiv).

State License

In most states, a license issued by the state is required before a person is allowed to practice counseling in that state (Bergman, 2013). This licensure affects private practice counseling most directly because most licensure statutes state that counselors who practice in many other settings are exempt from the licensure requirement. For example, in most states, counselors who practice in local, state, or federal agencies; in nonprofit corporations; or in schools or other educational institutions are exempt from the licensure requirement. Often when professions are first licensed, many exemptions are granted to the licensure requirement. This occurs because of a concern that, if licensure were required for all members of that profession, agencies that traditionally pay less for the professionals' services would not be able to attract employees. For example, when physicians were first licensed by states, physicians employed in a number of settings were exempt from licensure. Over the years, these licensure exemptions have been removed for physicians, and now almost all physicians, no matter where they practice, must have a state license. The same removal of exemptions will most likely occur over time in the counseling field.

Unfortunately, counseling licensure statutes have various titles. In some states, counselors credentialed by the state are called *licensed*, and in other states they are referred to as *certified*. In some states, they have even been called *registered*.

In the more general arena of state regulation of professions, the terms *licensed, certified,* and *registered* have separate and specific meanings. A licensure law is referred to as a *practice law*, which means that the professional must be licensed to practice that profession in that state. A certification law is what is known as a *title law*, which means that a person must be certified to use the title of *certified professional* but that the practice of that profession is not regulated by the state. Finally, a registration law was intended to mean that a professional had to *register* with the state but that no credentials would be required for registration. These terms, however, have been used interchangeably from state to state and from profession to profession. For example, registered nurses in almost all states in reality are *licensed* even though their title indicates they are *registered*. In addition, most current state registration laws do require that registered persons have some type of credentials before they will be added to the state registry.

Currently, in some states licensed counselors actually function under title laws, and some certified counselors, in reality, are operating under practice laws. As an individual counselor who wants to practice in a particular state, you should ascertain exactly what the state credential (whether a license, a certificate, or a registry) entitles the credentialed person to do. You do not have to fully understand the complexity of all state regulatory laws to understand what the particular law means in your state. The American Association of State Counseling Boards (AASCB; aascb.org) provides a listing of contact information for state licensure boards (AASCB, 2014). In addition, the National Board for Certified Counselors (NBCC; nbcc.org provides contact and testing information for state counselor licensure boards (NBCC, 2014). All 50 states, the District of Columbia, Puerto Rico, and Guam now have laws that regulate the profession of counseling.

To add to the confusion regarding state counselor licensure laws, states have given a number of titles to counselors who are licensed. The most common title is that of professional counselor. However, other states use titles such as mental health counselor or clinical counselor. The individuals who proposed the counselor licensing laws in each state decided which title to use. In some cases, titles were chosen to satisfy political compromises that had to be made to obtain legislative support for the bills.

State Agency Certification

As the term is used here, *state agency certification* is different from state licensure. It was explained previously that counselors in some states are certified rather than licensed. However, in this section, the term *certification* is used to refer to the process whereby official agencies of the state certify individuals as qualified to hold certain state jobs. In most states, this agency process is referred to as *certification*, although some call it *licensure*.

The most obvious state agency certification process is for school counselors. In each state the department of education determines which counselors may be certified as school counselors. To maintain their school accreditation, schools in that state must hire certified school counselors, just as they must hire only certified school teachers. The requirements for being certified as a school counselor vary widely from state to state. In some states, school counselors must first be certified and experienced school teachers before they can become certified as school counselors, although this teacher certification requirement is being eliminated in most states. The requirements for state school counselor certification should be obtained from the state department of education in the state in which you wish to practice.

Another area in which counselors are certified by the state is in substance abuse counseling. Most states have various levels of certified substance abuse counselors, sometimes including counselors who hold less than a bachelor's degree. State agencies that provide substance abuse treatment services are required to hire only certified counselors who meet state requirements for certification. Information regarding state requirements for substance abuse counselors can be obtained from NAADAC: The Association for Addiction Professionals (NAADAC, 2014; naadac.org).

Rehabilitation counseling is another specialty area that involves varying state requirements. Although state rehabilitation agencies do not certify vocational rehabilitation counselors, they have established minimum requirements for rehabilitation counselors that vary from state to state. Information regarding the requirements for being hired as a vocational rehabilitation counselor can be obtained from each state's rehabilitation agency.

National Voluntary Certification

The two national certification agencies of the counseling profession are the National Board for Certified Counselors (NBCC; nbcc.org) and the Commission on Rehabilitation Counselor Certification (CRCC; crccertification.com). In 2014, NBCC certified more than 55,000 counselors in more than 40 countries (NBCC, 2014). In 2014 CRCC had over 17,000 certified rehabilitation counselors (CRCC, 2014). National certification is voluntary in that there is no governmental requirement that a counselor be certified for private practice. Even though a counselor may be required to be licensed in a state to practice counseling, there is no legal need for that same counselor to be certified by NBCC or CRCC. Counselors choose to become nationally certified to demonstrate they have met the highest national standards developed by their profession. National certification is sometimes used as a job prerequisite as well, especially in the field of rehabilitation counseling.

The counseling profession created NBCC in 1982 as the national agency to certify counselors who had met the minimum requirements of the profession (Stone, 1985). A National Certified Counselor (NCC) is an individual who has met the requirements set forth by NBCC. NBCC now functions as an independent corporation with its own board of directors. It was important for the profession to create NBCC so that the profession, rather than each individual state legislature, could determine the minimum requirements for being a professional counselor. In the same vein, it is important for counselors to support NBCC by becoming NCCs as soon as they are qualified to do so. In addition, counselors who hire other counselors should indicate that NCCs are preferred.

To become an NCC, a counselor must complete a master's degree in counseling, have 2 years of post-master's experience, and pass the National Counselor Examination. The 2 years of post-master's experience is waived for graduates of CACREP-accredited programs.

Every profession has national voluntary certification of specialists within that profession. NBCC has created specialty certification for the counseling profession. Although some believe that states should license counselors as specialists (Cottone, 1985; Emener & Cottone, 1989), Remley (1995) has argued that states should license counselors generally and NBCC should certify specialists. His position is that the role NBCC plays in certifying counselors as specialists within their chosen areas is vital to the success of the counseling profession. He believes that specialty designations should be voluntary and should be offered by a national body such as NBCC.

To become certified as a specialist by NBCC, a counselor first must be an NCC. Currently, NBCC offers specialty certification in mental health, school, and addictions counseling. The specific requirements for becoming specialty certified in one or more of these fields can be obtained by contacting NBCC (nbcc.org). In addition, an affiliate of NBCC, the Center for Credentialing & Education (CCE, 2014; cce-global.org) offers additional specialty certifications, including Approved Clinical Supervisor (APS), Distance Credentialed Counselor (DCC), Global Career Development Facilitator (GCDF), Thinking for a Change Certified Facilitator (T4C-CF), Board Certified Coach (BCC), Educational and Vocational Guidance Practitioner (EVGP), and Human Services-Board Certified Practitioner (HS-BCP).

Rehabilitation counseling specialists began certifying rehabilitation counselors before NBCC was formed. As a result, that specialty certification is offered by a separate certifying agency, the Commission on Rehabilitation Counselor Certification (CRCC; crccertification.com).

In addition to NBCC and CRCC, many other national voluntary counselor certifications are available to counselors. Some of these certifications have high standards and are multidisciplinary in nature. Others are simply designed to make money for the individuals who created them. If you are interested in a national certification for counselors offered by a group other than NBCC or CRCC, you should investigate the group's reputation among members of the counseling profession, the organizational structure of the group, and the general legitimacy of the credential.

NBCC is providing leadership in helping other countries establish the profession of counseling. The international affiliate of NBCC, known as NBCC International, has established relationships with counselors in a number of countries and is helping them become recognized as professionals (NBCC International, 2014; nbccinternational.org).

Program Accreditation

The training of counselors was summarized previously in this chapter. The standards for preparing counselors that have been agreed upon by the counseling profession are included in the accreditation standards of CACREP, also detailed in the previous section. The Council on Rehabilitation Education (CORE, 2014; core-rehab.org) accredits master's-degree programs in the specialty area of rehabilitation counseling.

A counselor's graduation from a CACREP-accredited or CORE-accredited counseling graduate program is a credential. Although many highly competent counselors are graduates of non-CACREP-accredited programs, the CACREP credential does distinguish counselors as having completed a preparation program that meets the standards of excellence for the profession. Counselors can indicate on their résumés that they are graduates of CACREP-accredited or CORE-accredited programs. Many job announcements now indicate that CACREP-accredited or CORE-accredited program graduates are required or preferred.

The most comprehensive listing of graduate programs in counseling is found in a directory produced by Schweiger et al. (2011). In the most recent edition of that directory, more than a thousand master's-level programs and more than two hundred doctoral programs were listed. The master's-degree programs focus on the following specialty areas: community counseling, marriage and family counseling or therapy, mental health counseling, pastoral counseling, rehabilitation counseling, school counseling, college counseling, and miscellaneous specialty areas. The doctoral programs listed are divided into the following areas: counselor education and supervision, counseling psychology, marriage and family counseling/therapy, rehabilitation counseling, college counseling, pastoral counseling, and miscellaneous specialty areas.

Only master's- and doctoral-degree programs offered by regionally accredited universities are listed in the directory. Nonaccredited universities also offer graduate degrees in counseling. However, individuals who graduate from these nonaccredited university-degree programs often are unable to have their degrees recognized for the purposes of licensure, certification, or employment.

Accreditation of the university that offers degree programs in counseling, therefore, is essential for recognition. In addition to university accreditation, separate accreditation of counseling programs is important. Many state licensure statutes for counselors require the same preparation courses and field experiences as CACREP requires. In addition, NBCC has essentially the same preparation standards as CACREP.

Because the rehabilitation counseling specialty established a mechanism for accrediting master's-degree programs before counseling in general began accrediting master's- and doctoral-degree programs, the counseling profession has two recognized program accreditation groups—CORE and CACREP. CORE (2014) accredits only master's-degree programs in rehabilitation counseling. CACREP (2014) accredits master's-degree programs in career counseling; student affairs and college counseling; clinical mental health counseling; marriage, couple, and family counseling; school counseling; and addiction counseling; and doctoral programs in counselor education and supervision.

In 2008, CACREP adopted program accreditation changes that went into effect in 2009 (CACREP, 2009). One major change was that the community counseling and mental health counseling specializations were combined into one program that includes 60 semester credits and requires 600 hours of internship rather than 900. Another major change was that newly hired full-time faculty members now must hold a doctoral degree in counselor education if they do not have previous experience teaching in a counselor education program.

CORE and CACREP reflect the minimum preparation program standards that have been agreed upon by the profession for master's- and doctoral-degree programs in counseling. If you want to determine whether programs that are not accredited by CORE or CACREP reflect these minimum standards, you could compare the degree requirements of those programs to the CORE or CACREP standards.

In established professions such as medicine, law, and even psychology, all preparation programs are either accredited by their professional accreditation bodies or are actively pursuing accreditation. Graduates of nonaccredited programs in those professions are unable to obtain state licenses to practice or are unable to secure desirable jobs (LaFountain & Baer, 2001). It is likely that, eventually, all master's- and doctoral-degree programs in counseling will be either CORE accredited or CACREP accredited as well. Ohio has recently passed a law that requires all future counselors who are licensed in that state to have degrees from CACREP-accredited programs (Bray, 2013).

Ethical Standards Related to Credentialing

Professional counselors are ethically required to present their credentials accurately. According to the ACA *Code of Ethics* (2014), counselors must claim or imply only professional qualifications actually completed and correct any known misrepresentations of their qualifications by others. They must clearly distinguish between paid and volunteer work experience and accurately describe their continuing education and specialized training (§C.4.a.). With respect to degrees held, counselors may advertise only the highest degree earned that is in counseling or a closely related field (§C.4.d.). Some counselors hold a master's degree in counseling and a doctoral degree in another field.

As you acquire various professional credentials, you certainly will want to advertise them. Your professional association's code of ethics imposes few restrictions on advertising (ACA, 2014, §C.3.), and those are limited to restrictions that can be clearly justified to protect the public. Nonetheless, you must know precisely what limits are contained in the code. In some circumstances, however, it is difficult to determine what the ACA *Code of Ethics* allows.

2-2 The Case of Kevin

Kevin earned his master's degree in counseling 8 years ago and has been working as a staff counselor in a psychiatric hospital since he graduated. In addition to this employment, he opened a part-time private practice when he became licensed as a professional counselor. Kevin recently completed his doctorate in health care administration from a nontraditional distance learning university in California. He is now focused on his goals of moving into an administrative position within the hospital as well as building up his private practice in case an administrative job opportunity does not occur. He has decided to update the business cards and brochures he uses in his private practice, and he has changed the wording to present himself as "Kevin Smith, PhD, MS, LPC, Professional Member of the American Counseling Association."

- Do you see anything wrong with the wording on Kevin's cards?
- Do you believe a doctorate in health care administration could be considered a doctorate in counseling or a closely related field?

Discussion: All of Kevin's credentials on his card are directly related to counseling except perhaps his PhD, which is in health care administration. If his doctorate was earned from a university that was not accredited by one of the regional accrediting bodies, then the legitimacy of his degree would be questionable. He must be careful not to mislead the public into believing that he has a legitimate counseling doctoral degree. Whether the university from which he earned his degree is accredited by a regional accrediting body is not known. Many nontraditional distance learning universities do hold regional body accreditation.

According to the ACA *Code of Ethics* (2014), "Counselors do not imply doctoral-level competence when possessing a master's degree in counseling or a related field by referring to themselves as *Dr.* in a counseling context when their doctorate is not in counseling or a related field" (§C.4.d.). There are arguments for and against recognizing a PhD in health care administration as a doctorate in a field closely related to counseling. On one hand, counseling is a form of health care, and a specialty within health care could easily be mental health care administration. On the other hand, general health care administration is not a mental health field. Perhaps the best way for Kevin to ensure that he is acting ethically, even though it might be a bit awkward, would be for him to specify on his business cards that his PhD degree is in health care administration and his MS degree is in counseling.

Basically, advertising must be accurate and must not be false, misleading, deceptive, or fraudulent (ACA, 2014, §C.3.a.). When you become aware of any misrepresentation of your credentials that might be made by others, you are responsible for making reasonable efforts to correct the misinformation (§C.3.c.). Because many counselors hold multiple credentials, their business cards and advertising brochures can sometimes resemble a kind of alphabet soup. A counselor's degrees, licenses, certifications, and professional memberships might include, for instance, MS (Master of Science) from a CACREP-accredited counseling program, LPC (Licensed Professional Counselor), NCC (National Certified Counselor), CCMHC (Certified Clinical Mental Health Counselor), CADAC (Certified Alcohol and Drug Abuse Counselor), and ACA Professional Member. It is important for counselors to make reasonable efforts to ensure that the *meaning* of these credentials is clear to potential consumers of their services.

In addition, as a credentialed counselor, you must be careful not to attribute more to your credentials than the credentials actually represent (ACA, 2014, §C.4.a.), and you should not imply that other counselors are not qualified because they do not possess the same credentials as you do or because they lack certain credentials (§§C.4.a. and D.1.a.). For example, it would be inappropriate for a Certified Alcohol and Drug Abuse Counselor to say or infer that a mental health professional had to have that credential in order to be competent to counsel clients regarding substance abuse or dependency problems. Also, it would not be professional to denigrate the preparation of licensed psychologists by inferring that their degree programs have prepared them less adequately for mental health practice than have the degree programs of licensed professional counselors. The ACA *Code of Ethics* (ACA, 2014) states, "Counselors acknowledge the expertise of other professional groups and are respectful of their practices" (§D.1.a.).

EVOLUTION OF THE COUNSELING PROFESSION

History is in the eye of the beholder. In other words, people view history from their own personal perspectives. A number of authors have attempted to summarize the history of the counseling profession, and each summary is different (Bradley & Cox, 2001; Gibson & Mitchell, 2008; Hershenson, Power, & Waldo, 1996; Sweeney, 2001). Various authors emphasize different events and give their own interpretations to facts that have led them to various conclusions. The following summary represents a brief view of the history of the counseling profession that recognizes the input of others and adds our perspectives based on our observations as leaders and members of the profession.

Origins of the Profession

At the same time that the psychology profession was establishing the doctoral level as the requirement for professional status and counseling psychology was developing as a specialty area within it, historical events were leading to the rapid development of school counseling programs and vocational rehabilitation counseling. Eventually, changes within counseling psychology, the school counseling movement, and federal funding of vocational rehabilitation counseling led to the emergence of the new profession of counseling.

Counseling Psychology

The counseling profession basically shares its history with the emergence of counseling psychology as a specialty within the psychology profession (Goodyear, 2000). Early leaders in the specialty of counseling psychology distinguished themselves from other psychologists by declaring that they were interested in the normal, healthy development of human beings rather than in illness and psychopathology. In counseling psychology, the focus was on developmental stages in people's lives and career concerns. World War I and the work of Frank Parsons on career classifications provided the impetus for the development of counseling psychology as a separate specialty within psychology. Parsons created a concept in the United States that citizens should be assisted in selecting careers that would be rewarding and matched to their abilities and interests (Gibson & Mitchell, 2008).

Although the field of psychology has offered doctoral degrees for quite some time, at the beginning of its political movement to become a profession, psychology recognized individuals with master's degrees as professional psychologists. Several decades ago, the American Psychological Association (APA) declared that, in the future, only psychologists who held doctoral degrees would be recognized as professionals. The profession decided to continue to recognize all existing psychologists who held master's degrees and allow them to practice, but in the future to allow only individuals who held doctoral degrees in psychology into the profession. Licensure laws in psychology throughout the United States were changed to reflect this new political position.

Despite APA's declaration that only psychologists at the doctoral level would be recognized as professionals, universities throughout the United States continue even today to offer master's degrees in clinical and counseling psychology. Essentially, these master's-degree programs in psychology have produced and are continuing to produce graduates who have limited or no professional recognition in psychology. Graduates of these master's-degree programs most often seek and obtain licensure as counselors in states that have counselor licensure laws. When graduates of master's-degree programs in clinical or counseling psychology become counselors through the process of state counselor licensure, the professional identities of both psychologists and counselors become blurred, and the public becomes more confused about the differences between the two professions. In addition, a number of licensure boards have adopted rules in the last few years that do not recognize master's degrees in psychology as acceptable for licensure as professional counselors.

School Counseling

When the Russians launched the first spacecraft, *Sputnik*, in 1957, politicians in the United States feared that, because the Russians had exceeded U.S. technology and beat the United States in the *race to space*, they might overpower the country politically as well. In response to this fear, the U.S. Congress created and funded substantial programs to encourage young people to seek careers in technical and scientific fields. Part of this effort included placing counselors in high schools to channel students into math and science courses. Throughout the United States, universities created summer institutes in which high school teachers were given basic courses that led to their placement in high schools as guidance counselors. In most instances, high school teachers were given two or three courses in *guidance* or *counseling*, which then allowed them to be certified as school counselors and assume guidance counselor positions within schools. Because the primary purpose of this effort was to encourage students to take math and science courses, it did not seem necessary for counselors to be prepared beyond the training provided in these summer institutes.

In a very short time, school accreditation groups required that high schools have guidance counselors in order to receive or continue their accreditation. Today, almost all middle and high school accreditation agencies require that these schools have counselors, and in some areas of the country elementary schools are required to have counselors as well. Almost all states now require that certified school counselors have received the master's degree and have completed specified courses and an internship. For a school counseling program to achieve CACREP-accredited status, the master's degree must include a minimum of 48 semester hours.

Vocational Rehabilitation Counseling

In the 1950s, it was recognized in the United States that citizens with physical and mental disabilities were not being given the help they needed to become productive members of society. As a result, legislation was passed that provided counseling and educational resources that were meant to rehabilitate persons with disabilities so that they could function as autonomously as possible.

A major component of this rehabilitation legislation was funding to prepare counselors to help disabled persons evaluate their disabilities, make plans to work, and find satisfactory employment. As a result of this funding, master's-degree programs in rehabilitation counseling were developed and existing programs were expanded. State rehabilitation agencies created positions in rehabilitation case management and counseling for the graduates of these programs.

In summary, the dynamics around the creation of the specialty of counseling psychology, the decision within the psychology profession that professionals would be recognized only at the doctoral level, the emergence of school counseling, and the funding of vocational rehabilitation counseling programs led to the creation of counseling as a separate profession. Clearly, the origins of the profession lie in the convergence of several disparate forces rather than in a single event.

Counseling as a New Profession

An entire area of scholarly inquiry in the field of sociology studies the emergence of new professions. Scholars within this field have identified the essential factors that define what a profession is and what steps a group must go through to establish itself as a legitimate, separate, and unique profession. In relation to other professional groups in general and to mental health professional groups in particular, counseling is a relatively new professional entity. To understand some of the difficult problems facing the counseling profession today, it is important for counselors to compare counseling to other, older mental health professions, to ascertain where we are in the process of becoming a fully recognized profession.

Toren (1969) defined a fully developed profession as one that has the following traits: a body of theoretical knowledge, members who possess competence in the application of this knowledge, and a code of ethics focused on the client's well-being.

A different concept of a profession has been offered by Hughes (1965). He has said that, compared to nonprofessions, emerging professions demand more independence, more recognition, a higher place, a clearer distinction between those inside and those outside the profession, and more autonomy in choosing colleagues.

Six criteria for determining professional maturity have been described by Nugent (1981). According to Nugent, a mature profession and its members have the following characteristics:

- They can clearly define their role and have a defined scope of practice.
- They offer unique services (do something that members of no other profession can do).
- They have special knowledge and skills (are specifically trained for the profession).
- They have an explicit code of ethics.
- They have the legal right to offer the service (have obtained a monopoly, through licensure or certification, over the right to provide the services).
- They have the ability to monitor the practice of the profession (the profession can police itself).

By considering these traits, conceptualizations, and definitions of a mature profession, it is possible to see that the field of counseling fully meets the criteria in some areas and is still struggling in others. Certainly counselors have a well-established code of ethics and have achieved societal recognition through state licensure. Areas that are still weak include identifying services that are uniquely offered by counselors, developing a body of knowledge that belongs specifically to counseling and does not borrow so heavily from psychology, and achieving a higher status within society.

Steps in Becoming a Profession

According to sociologists who have studied emerging professions within society (Abbott, 1988; Caplow, 1966; Dugan, 1965; Etzioni, 1969; Friedson, 1983; Hughes, 1965; Scott, 1969; Toren, 1969), professions must go through a developmental process if they are to be successful in establishing themselves as fully recognized professions.

Caplow (1966) maintained that the steps whereby a group achieves professional status are quite definite, and that the sequence of steps is explicit. The first three steps toward professionalization are (a) forming associations, (b) changing names to reduce identification with the previous occupational status, and (c) developing a code of ethics. Certainly the counseling profession has accomplished these three steps. First, ACA was chartered in 1952 from three long-standing subgroups. Second, the association's name was changed from the American Personnel and Guidance Association (APGA) to the American Association for Counseling and Development (AACD), and then to the ACA. Each change reduced the identification with words such as *guidance*, *student personnel*, and *student development* and embraced more fully the word *counseling*. In addition, ACA has had a code of ethics since 1961.

According to Caplow (1966), the fourth step in accomplishing the goal of becoming a profession is prolonged political agitation. Members of the occupational group obtain public sanction to maintain established occupational barriers. Counselors have been involved in substantial political agitation since the first counselor licensure law was passed in Virginia in 1976. That political activity has been continued as similar licensure laws have been passed in state after state. In addition, counselors have lobbied state legislators to mandate school counseling programs, to include counselors as providers in health care programs, and to ensure that the professional services of counselors are reimbursed by health care insurance companies. Clearly, counselors have engaged in Caplow's prolonged political agitation, and this process is continuing today.

Counselors have been fighting hard and making a number of changes to overcome the deficiencies that have hindered the development of the profession. Some of the changes that have taken place in the last 20 to 30 years in the field of counseling include the following: The length of most training programs has increased from 30 to 48 or 60 semester hours; efforts have been made to improve the professional status of counselors through credentialing and legislation; laws are continually passed in states granting privileged communication to interactions between counselors and their clients; the body of knowledge is being increased through scholarly publications specifically in counseling, as distinguished from psychology; and counselor licensure laws have brought autonomy from being supervised by others to practice counseling. Evidence suggests that counseling is now close to being a fully recognized profession in the United States.

Progress Toward Professionalization

It is discouraging for graduate students preparing to enter the field to realize that counseling, despite its progress, still has some way to go before achieving recognition on a par with other mental health professions within our society. On the other hand, it is encouraging to note that counseling is making progress toward recognition as a profession at a relatively fast rate when compared to professionalization efforts in other fields. For example, scholars within psychology wrote as late as 1982 in one of their own profession's journals that they doubted that psychology could validly claim to be a profession (Phillips, 1982). The first law establishing psychologists as independent health practitioners was passed in 1968 in New Jersey (Dorken & Webb, 1980), and some states still do not require a license to practice psychology. In comparison, the first counselor licensure bill was passed in Virginia in 1976, and already all states and the District of Columbia have passed licensure bills for counselors.

Although counselors are continuing to work toward full professional status, we will continue to refer to ourselves as professionals and to our field as a profession.

PROFESSIONAL ASSOCIATIONS OF COUNSELORS

Professional associations are formed by professional groups for a number of reasons. First, associations provide a forum for professionals to gather to discuss issues and problems that exist within the profession. An association allows the members of a profession to address issues as a group rather than work independently on behalf of the profession. Second, professional associations provide leadership by speaking for the profession on critical legislative issues that affect the profession at all levels of government. Professional associations also provide continuing education for their members. Earning a master's degree in counseling is only the beginning of the learning process for counselors. As new information becomes available, counselors must attend conferences and workshops to update their skills and expertise. Professional associations provide such learning opportunities and also publish scholarly journals, texts, monographs, and other media resources for the continuing education of their members. In addition, professional associations publish and enforce a code of ethics for their members. Important hallmarks for professionals are having a code of ethics and policing themselves.

American Counseling Association

The American Counseling Association (ACA, 2014; counseling.org) has a number of divisions and state branches that represent the counseling profession and serve counselors in various ways.

You should join ACA when you begin your graduate degree program in counseling and maintain active membership throughout your career as a counselor. Students receive discounted membership. All members, including students, receive a subscription to the counseling professional journal, the *Journal of Counseling & Development*. In addition, members receive a monthly magazine and bulletins, which include current political and professional news related to counseling as well as announcements of professional development opportunities, job openings, and advertisements for professional products. Other benefits of membership include the ability to purchase professional liability insurance policies, reduced registration fees for the national convention and national workshops, and discounted prices for texts and media products published by ACA. Professional liability insurance is free to student members of ACA.

2-3 The Case of Juanita

Juanita recently received her master's degree in counseling and has taken her first full-time job as a counselor at an outpatient substance abuse treatment facility. Although her beginning salary was lower than she anticipated, Juanita is confident that with hard work and determination, she will get promotions and pay raises in the next few years. Immediately after beginning her job, Juanita paid a $200 fee to register with her state counselor licensure board so that she could complete her 2 years of supervised experience required to become licensed. She also made arrangements with a local licensed counselor to meet weekly at $90 per meeting for supervision. During her 2 years in graduate school, Juanita had been a student member of ACA and two ACA divisions, the American Mental Health Counselors Association (AMHCA), and the International Association of Addiction and Offender Counselors (IAAOC). In addition, she had been a student member of her state counseling association and the state branch divisions of AMHCA and IAAOC. Juanita is also a member of the national counseling scholarship honorary, Chi Sigma Iota, and is a National Certified Counselor (NCC). Both the organization and the certification board require annual dues or renewal payments. Juanita is on a tight budget and is thinking that she might not rejoin ACA and the two national divisions or her state counseling association and its two divisions.

- What will Juanita miss if she drops her ACA and national division memberships?
- What will Juanita miss if she drops her state counseling association and two state division memberships?
- How would you advise Juanita?

Discussion: Most important, if Juanita drops her ACA and national division memberships, she will miss the opportunity to stay informed of new developments in the counseling profession from a national perspective. She will no longer get ACA and division newsletters, announcements of national conferences, discounts for texts and conference registration fees, and bulletins on important matters of interest to counselors. Juanita will also miss opportunities for continued development of her professional identity as a counselor by not knowing what is going on in the counseling profession at the national level. She will no longer be able to purchase the high-quality professional liability insurance policy ACA makes available to its members.

If she drops her state association memberships, Juanita will miss the opportunity to stay informed of new developments in the counseling profession at the state level, where state licensure issues are addressed, and where funding for counseling positions and state laws affecting counselors are monitored. She will no longer get state counseling association and division newsletters, announcements of state conferences, discounts for conference registration fees, and bulletins on important matters of interest to counselors in her state. Juanita will also miss opportunities for continued development of her professional identity as a counselor by not knowing what is going on in the counseling profession at the state level and not being connected professionally to her state colleagues.

You might remind Juanita that she has spent considerable amounts of money to earn her master's degree in counseling. Not only has she paid for tuition and texts, but she has also lost income she would have earned by working while she was taking her graduate classes. Although all of these expenses may seem overwhelming to a new professional, if Juanita is to be successful in her career as a counselor, she will need to continue her professional association affiliations and maintain her counseling credentials. Counselors who isolate themselves from their professional peers seldom have successful careers. Professionals in all fields have similar expenses. These membership dues, certification renewal fees, and licensure board fees are part of the costs of being a professional.

ACA Divisions

Currently, ACA has 20 divisions. ACA members, if they choose, may join one or more divisions in addition to their basic ACA membership. Division members receive scholarly journals from divisions that publish them, periodic newsletters, and from time to time information related to the divisions' special purposes.

There are two types of divisions within ACA, and all divisions are subgroups of ACA. One type of division has as members counselors who practice in various employment settings, such as schools, colleges, or mental health centers. The other type of division has as members counselors who have special interests within counseling such as group counseling, multicultural counseling, or marriage and family counseling. Figure 2-2 provides a listing of the 20 ACA divisions with a description of their members.

ACA State Branches

Most states plus the District of Columbia, the Virgin Islands, Puerto Rico, the Philippines, and Europe have ACA branches. Although these branches are chartered by ACA, they are separate, independent organizations. To join a state branch, you must contact that organization. Most branches offer discounted membership rates for graduate students. Telephone and address information for state branch associations can be obtained by contacting the ACA (counseling.org). State branches

NAME OF ACA DIVISION	MEMBERSHIP INCLUDES
Association for Adult Development and Aging (AADA)	Counselors who have a special interest in counseling issues of adults and those who specialize in gerontology
Association for Assessment and Research in Counseling (AARC)	Counselors who are interested in testing and research
Association for Child and Adolescent Counseling (ACAC)	Counselors who have a special interest in counseling children and adolescents in all settings
Association for Creativity in Counseling (ACC)	Counselors who have an interest in understanding creative approaches to counseling (such as art, music, or dance therapy)
American College Counseling Association (ACCA)	Counselors who work in college and university settings, including technical and community colleges
Association for Counselors and Educators in Government (ACEG)	Counselors employed by federal and state governments
Association for Counselor Education and Supervision (ACES)	University professors who teach in counseling graduate programs, supervisors of counselors, and individuals who specialize in counseling supervision
The Association for Humanistic Counseling (AHC)	Counselors who are oriented toward humanistic principles
Association for Lesbian, Gay, Bisexual, and Transgender Issues in Counseling (ALGBTIC)	Counselors who have a special interest in providing counseling services to lesbian, gay, bisexual, and transgender clients
Association of Multicultural Counseling and Development (AMCD)	Counselors who have a special interest in multicultural issues in counseling
American Mental Health Counselors Association (AMHCA)	Counselors who practice in community mental health settings and who are in private practice
American Rehabilitation Counseling Association (ARCA)	Counselors who work in government and private vocational rehabilitation settings
American School Counselor Association (ASCA)	Counselors who practice at all levels of school counseling: elementary, middle, and secondary
Association for Spiritual, Ethical, and Religious Values in Counseling (ASERVIC)	Counselors who have special interests in spiritual, ethical, or religious values issues in counseling
Association for Specialists in Group Work (ASGW)	Counselors who have a special interest in group counseling
Counselors for Social Justice (CSJ)	Counselors who are interested in the eradication of oppressive systems of power and privilege
International Association of Addictions and Offender Counselors (IAAOC)	Counselors who work in substance abuse or prison settings
International Association of Marriage and Family Counselors (IAMFC)	Counselors who specialize in marriage and family counseling
National Career Development Association (NCDA)	Counselors who have a special interest in career counseling
National Employment Counseling Association (NECA)	Counselors who work in employment agency settings

FIGURE 2-2   The 20 divisions of the American Counseling Association

Source: Pearson Education, Inc., Hoboken, NJ.

hold annual conventions, represent counselors from their states in legislative matters, publish periodic newsletters, and sometimes provide publications and workshops for members.

Most state ACA branches have state branch divisions that parallel the national ACA divisions. So, in addition to a state ACA association, often there will exist, for example, state divisions for school counselors, mental health counselors, and counselors interested in multicultural counseling issues. When you join your state ACA branch, you will also have the opportunity to join any divisions that exist in your state that interest you.

Many important professional issues, such as licensure and school counselor certification, can be addressed only at the state level. In addition, it is very important for counselors to know and interact with their colleagues throughout the state in which they are practicing. Therefore, throughout their professional careers counselors should belong to their ACA state branch in addition to belonging to ACA and should provide leadership for the counseling profession (Meany-Walen, Carnes-Holt, Minton, Purswell, & Pronchenko-Jain, 2013).

Other Associations

In addition to ACA and its national divisions and state branches, counselors belong to a number of other national and international associations. These associations represent a variety of interests. Associations consist of multidisciplinary groups of mental health professionals, professionals interested in specializations within the mental health field, special political-purpose groups, and even associations that are in opposition to the professional and political interests of the ACA and counselors. It might be beneficial for counselors to join multidisciplinary professional associations to gain from cross-disciplinary interactions and fresh perspectives on mental health issues. Counselors may also want to purchase materials developed by other associations or attend workshops these associations sponsor.

One association that was created as a result of ACA's success in the area of state licensure for counselors is the American Association of State Counseling Boards (AASCB, 2014; aascb.org). This group has as its members state boards that license counselors and individuals who have been appointed to those boards or who administer them. The group meets annually to update members regarding developments in the area of counseling licensure.

Not all other mental health professional associations are supportive of counseling as a profession. The APA opposed counselors as they achieved recognition in state legislatures as an independent profession and currently opposes licensed counselors' efforts to pass legislation making it clear that counselors can diagnose and treat mental disorders, can test, and can be reimbursed by health insurance companies for their services. A number of associations focus on the certification of counselors and the accreditation of facilities that offer counseling services. Groups that have not already been mentioned in this chapter include the Commission on Accreditation of Rehabilitation Facilities (CACRF International; carf.org); the International Association of Counseling Services (IACS; iacsinc.org), which accredits university counseling centers; and the Joint Commission (jointcommission.org), which accredits hospitals, home care organizations, laboratory services, and nursing care centers, among others.

CURRENT ISSUES RELATED TO PROFESSIONAL IDENTITY

One of your tasks as a graduate student preparing to enter the counseling profession is to develop a strong identity as a counselor. Yet, as we have seen, the profession itself seems confused about its identity. Highlighting and discussing some of the current professional identity problems in the profession may help you acknowledge and put these problems in perspective as you develop your own professional identity as a counselor.

Specialties Versus One United Profession

Probably the most significant problem that the counseling profession faces today is determining whether the profession will develop a strong identity as one united profession with a common philosophical foundation and knowledge base, or whether the specialties will emerge as the dominant force within counseling (Myers & Sweeney, 2001). If the specialties prevail, counseling has little chance of becoming a unified and societally recognized profession.

The problems associated with the specialties within the counseling profession were discussed two decades ago in the November/December 1995 issue of the *Journal of Counseling & Development* (Myers, 1995). In that issue of the primary professional journal of the counseling profession, authors discussed the following established and emerging counseling specialties: career counseling (Engels, Minor, Sampson, & Splete, 1995), college counseling (Dean & Meadows, 1995), school counseling (Paisley & Borders, 1995), marriage and family counseling (Smith, Carlson, Stevens-Smith, & Dennison, 1995), mental health counseling (Smith & Robinson, 1995), rehabilitation counseling (Leahy & Szymanski, 1995), addictions counseling (Page & Bailey, 1995), and sports counseling (Miller & Wooten, 1995).

A complex profession must include specialties because no one practitioner can be proficient in all areas of the profession (Abraham, 1978; Kett, 1968; Napoli, 1981). Specialties are necessary to ensure that research, training, and improved practice occur in specialized areas of counseling with unique needs and issues. If members of subgroups within a profession believe that their specialties are significantly different from the general profession, however, then those specialty groups will attempt to establish themselves as separate professions (Etzioni, 1969). This phenomenon seems to continue to occur in counseling, particularly within the specialties of mental health counseling (Messina, 1999), marriage and family counseling, school counseling (Johnson, 2000), and career counseling. It would be wise for new counseling professionals to recognize that the specialty group members with whom they wish to affiliate may be working against the overall goal of establishing counseling as a strong, viable, and societally recognized mental health profession (Fox, 1994).

Our position on this issue is that counseling is our primary profession, and that counselors who are members of specialty groups should support the overall profession while paying attention to their special interests and needs within the counseling profession. When you enter the profession, you will have opportunities to voice your own position, and you will want to consider carefully the issues involved.

Organizational Structure of ACA

Historically, some specialty groups in counseling (school counselors, college counselors, career counselors, and counselor educators) came together to form the first professional association, which they named the American Personnel and Guidance Association (APGA) in 1952. The name was later changed to the American Association for Counseling and Development (AACD) and is now ACA.

An unfortunate event occurred during the history of the association when, at some point, the divisions within ACA were incorporated as separate legal structures. This makes ACA appear to be a federation, or a group of groups, rather than one unified organization with subgroups of specialties. The separate incorporation of the divisions within ACA has led to many disagreements among association leaders as to whether ACA is a manager meant to serve the interests of the divisions, or whether the divisions are subgroups of individuals whose primary interest is in being members of a unified professional association.

These disagreements led the American College Personnel Association (ACPA) to disaffiliate from ACA in 1992 and become a separate, autonomous professional association. Three additional ACA divisions have seriously discussed, and taken some actions that could lead to, disaffiliation. They are the American School Counselor Association (ASCA), the American Mental Health Counselors Association (AMHCA), and the National Career Development Association (NCDA). Leaders and members of the association have spent energy on the conflict rather than on the tasks of strengthening the counseling profession and ensuring that members' continuing professional development needs are met.

When ACPA left ACA, ACA immediately created a new division, the American College Counseling Association (ACCA), for members who worked in higher education settings. Some ACA leaders have stated their intent to do the same thing if the mental health counseling, school counseling, or career counseling associations disaffiliate from ACA. In the future, AMHCA (Beck, 1999), ASCA, NCDA, and perhaps others might disaffiliate from ACA and establish themselves as separate autonomous associations. If major divisions within ACA leave, ACA could create entities within ACA to replace them. In any eventuality, ACA members will be able to continue their affiliation with ACA and will have opportunities within ACA to affiliate with members who have their same specialty interests.

A basic aspect of human nature is that people tend to identify with the group they know best and with which they are most familiar. Members and leaders within the specialty subgroups in counseling have naturally tended to create well-organized entities that represent their specialized interests. It also is clear that counseling is at a critical stage of development (Collison, 2001). Either the profession of counseling will find a way through its conflict and will emerge as a unified profession, or it will fragment and its various specialties will attempt to establish themselves as separate independent professions. Bradley and Cox (2001) have suggested that perhaps a new organizational structure is needed that will allow the larger ACA to accommodate the differences within its divisions. Only time will reveal the outcome of the current struggles.

CACREP Accreditation of Specialties

Sweeney (1995) has pointed out that CACREP actually accredits master's-degree programs leading to specialty degrees in counseling, rather than accrediting general master's-degree programs in counseling. If a university that offers a master's-degree program in counseling wants to obtain CACREP accreditation, the program must declare that it prepares master's-level counselors for one or more of the following specialty areas: addictions counseling; student affairs and college counseling; career counseling; marriage, couple, and family counseling; clinical mental health counseling; or school counseling (CACREP, 2014). Even though CACREP accredits master's-degree programs leading to specialty degrees in counseling, a core curriculum that includes basic instruction for all counselors is required for accreditation in any of the specialty areas. Bobby (2013) has explained how the CACREP standards have helped to unify the counseling profession.

This requirement that students specialize at the master's-degree level does cause some professional identity problems for graduate students. Although professors encourage graduate students to develop identities as counselors in general, these same graduate students are being told that they must choose and prepare for one specialty area within counseling. There are questions as well about what constitutes a particular specialty, such as clinical mental health counseling, and what makes it different from other specialties (Hershenson & Berger, 2001).

Varying State Licensure and Certification Requirements

As explained previously in this chapter, the states that license counselors vary significantly in requirements. Licensure statutes require from 30 to 60 hours of graduate course work and from 1 to 3 years of post–master's-degree supervision, and they include a variety of requirements that are unique to the state (ACA, 2014). State requirements for certification as a school counselor also vary considerably from jurisdiction to jurisdiction.

These differences in licensure and certification standards reflect a profession that has not been able to establish an agreed-upon set of standards and then to get those standards accepted by political entities throughout the United States. Because of this lack of uniformity, individual counselors who move from state to state often find that they must take additional course work or even earn another master's degree to meet the new state's standards. Established professions, such as law, medicine, and even psychology, have been able to establish licensing laws across the United States that are uniform and allow members of their professions to be licensed and to practice no matter where they live. Eventually, the licensing and certification laws for counselors will become more uniform, but currently the lack of uniformity causes problems for counselors who relocate. Ohio's recent new law that will require those seeking licensure as counselors to have graduated from a CACREP-accredited program beginning in 2018 (Bray, 2013) may be the foundation for other states passing similar laws. Leaders in ACA and AASCB are working to resolve problems associated with licensure *portability* from state to state (Mascari & Webber, 2013).

LEGAL AND POLITICAL ISSUES

In addition to the professional identity problems that currently exist for counselors, you must be familiar with a number of legal and political issues. The successful resolution of these issues is critical to the continued movement of counseling to establish itself as a legitimate societally recognized profession.

Challenges to the Scope of Practice of Counselors

Counselors believe that they are qualified to perform a number of professional services for clients, based on their training and expertise. Two areas in which counselors have been challenged by psychologists and other mental health professionals are testing and the diagnosis and treatment of mental and emotional disorders. Some psychologists and social workers claim that they are adequately prepared to perform these professional services and that counselors are not.

There is an economic component to these issues. Counselors who test and diagnose and treat mental and emotional disorders in their practices often compete in the marketplace with psychologists and social workers. Many health insurance companies and health maintenance organizations require that mental health professionals be qualified to perform these two tasks before they will reimburse their insured for the services of these professionals. Therefore, there is a significant economic advantage for psychologists and social workers to claim that counselors are not qualified in these professional practice areas.

This debate has taken place in state legislatures in the form of arguments over the language in state statutes that license counselors for practice. In most states, counselors have been successful in inserting language into their licensing statutes that says they are competent and therefore qualified to test and to diagnose and treat mental and emotional disorders. There are some states, however, where these issues are still unresolved.

TESTING   One of the core curriculum requirements for preparation of counselors is in the area of testing, or assessment. All counselor master's-degree programs require at least one graduate course in testing principles that includes evaluating the validity and reliability of tests, selecting appropriate tests for clients, administering tests, and interpreting test results. Counselors have used tests in their practices since the profession was first established.

Of course, testing is a very broad area, and counselors might not be prepared at the master's-degree level to administer and interpret a number of psychological tests, such as individual intelligence tests or projective tests. Psychologists have claimed that counselors should not be allowed to test at all within their practices, or should be allowed to use tests only in a very limited fashion. Counselors, on the other hand, believe that they have the basic education needed to test and that each counselor should determine the particular tests he or she is qualified by education or experience to administer and interpret.

Some state licensure statutes give counselors broad testing privileges, whereas others either are silent on whether testing is part of a counselor's practice or are very restrictive in enumerating which tests a counselor may administer and interpret. In some states (Butler, 1998), counselors have been accused of practicing psychology without a license because of their testing activities. In states in which the testing practices of counselors are restricted, political activities are taking place to change the statutes to broaden the authority of counselors to test.

DIAGNOSIS AND TREATMENT OF MENTAL AND EMOTIONAL DISORDERS   Counselors are taught to diagnose and treat mental disorders as part of their specialized training (Seligman, 1999). Ivey and Ivey (1999) have explained how counselors, with their wellness orientation, can utilize a developmental approach when using the *DSM* system. In most states, course work is required in this area for counseling licensure. In addition, counselors are tested before they are licensed to determine whether they are proficient in the diagnosis and treatment of mental and emotional disorders. Despite the preparation of counselors in this area, it appears that the general public may need to be better educated regarding the skills of counselors in the area of diagnosis and treatment of mental disorders (Fall, Levitov, Jennings, & Eberts, 2000).

The *Diagnostic and Statistical Manual of Mental Disorders* (*DSM*-5), published by the American Psychiatric Association (2013), clearly states that many mental health professionals are engaged in the diagnosis and treatment of mental disorders and that the manual is meant to be a reference for all of those professionals. The use of this standard manual is taught to counselors who wish to be licensed.

As with the testing issue, in many states the scope of practice of licensed counselors includes the diagnosis and treatment of mental disorders. In states in which the authority of counselors to diagnose and treat mental disorders is being challenged, efforts are being made to change the language of the licensure statutes to state clearly that counselors are qualified to perform this professional activity.

Job Classifications for Counselors

Positions for counseling professionals exist in many state and federal agencies. In some of these agencies, however, no job classification categories have been established for counselors. As a result, when counselors are hired, their job titles might be *psychologist I*, *social worker I*, or *mental health technician I*. Although being hired into these positions gives counselors jobs and entry into agencies, counselors may be discriminated against later because promotions might require a license in psychology or social work or a graduate degree in one of those fields.

As a result of this problem, efforts are being made to have job titles established specifically for counselors. Convincing a state or federal agency that job titles or classifications should be changed is not an easy task. Bureaucracies are very slow to change. Nonetheless, professional associations and leaders within the counseling profession must address this problem if counselors are to be fully accepted as professionals within these agencies.

In Louisiana, a series of job categories for counselors who work in the state civil service system was created in 2003 (C. Gagnon, personal communication, September 10, 2003). Until that time, counselors were hired in job categories that limited their ability to receive promotions. Creation of these new counselor job categories (which are equivalent to those that existed already for social workers) was completed in a unique manner because of the political and legal environment in that state. The success in this endeavor will have a significant positive impact on all counselors currently working in that state and future counselors who will be hired there. NBCC reported that in July 2014, a U.S. Senate subcommittee went on record urging the creation of an occupation series for mental health counselors (NBCC, 2014).

Third-Party Reimbursement

It is essential for counselors in private practice that their clients be able to access counselors' mental health services as part of clients' health care plan (Palmo, 1999). If clients are participating in health maintenance organizations (HMOs) or preferred provider organizations (PPOs), then counselors must be on the list of eligible providers for the clients. If clients are part of an indemnity health care plan, then counselors must be acknowledged as qualified mental health care providers so that clients can be reimbursed for counselor services.

HMOs, PPOs, and health insurance companies can voluntarily acknowledge counselors as qualified mental health care providers, and most do. However, these health care organizations have a legal right to refuse to give their clients access to counselors unless there is legislation to the contrary. This type of legislation, called *freedom of choice legislation*, requires health care providers to give access to licensed counselors for mental health care if they give access to other mental health care providers such as psychologists or social workers. Many states have passed freedom-of-choice legislation. In states that have not, counselors are active in trying to get freedom-of-choice legislation passed.

ACA and NBCC are active in seeking national legislative and regulatory changes that would allow Medicaid recipients, military personnel, and federal employees to receive mental health services from counselors as part of their health benefits. An important goal is for all Americans to have access to mental health services from counselors, not just from psychiatrists, psychologists, or social workers.

Counselors have been successful in being recognized as providers for individuals who are on active duty in the military and their dependents through TRICARE and for individuals who are war veterans (ACA, 2014; NBCC, 2014).

IDENTITY AND PROFESSIONALISM

Counseling and Other Mental Health Professions

As we noted at the beginning of this chapter, counselors are a relatively new professional group, and counselors are often asked what they do. A weak answer would be that counselors do things similar to what psychologists do. A strong answer would be to describe the process of counseling, including its philosophical foundations, the services that counselors provide, and the components of training programs that prepare master's-level counselors. A counselor or prospective counselor with a strong professional identity will be able to describe the process of counseling without reference to other mental health professions.

The material provided in this chapter should allow you to state clearly what a counselor does. However, a further challenge for counselors is to be able to describe objectively, accurately, and dispassionately the similarities and differences between counselors and other mental health professionals. Listeners should take away from a conversation with a counselor the conclusion that counselors have a clear and unique identity within the field of mental health and that the counselor with whom they have been talking takes pride in her or his chosen profession.

How are counselors similar to other mental health professionals, including psychiatrists, psychologists, and social workers? We are all prepared at the master's-degree level or higher, and we all provide mental health services for clients. All mental health professionals follow a similar process of assessing a person's mental health needs, developing a plan for assisting the person, and then providing mental health services consistent with the assessment and plan for treatment. All mental health professionals counsel clients in some fashion. Mental health professionals of all types can be found in agencies and institutions where mental health treatment is offered to individuals.

How are counselors different from other mental health professionals? The primary difference between counselors and other mental health professionals is that counselors espouse the wellness model of mental health instead of the illness or medical model. The wellness model of mental health emphasizes helping people maximize their potential rather than curing their illness. Counselors believe that human growth and development stages and processes make life's problems normal and natural rather than pathological. Counselors emphasize prevention and early intervention rather than remediation. Empowerment of clients is a goal of counselors. The training of counselors focuses on teaching counseling skills rather than skills in physical health care, psychopathology, assessment, or social service linkages.

Definitions of the mental health professions, including counseling, have been published by professional associations. The definition for *counselor* is from the American Counseling Association (2014; counseling.org); the definition for *social worker* is from the Council on Social Work Education (2014; cswe.org); the definition for *psychologist* is from the American Psychological Association (2014; apa.org); and the definition for *psychiatrist* is from the American Psychiatric Association, as provided by MedicineNet (2014; medterms.com). These definitions provide insight into how professional organizations view themselves. The *counselor* definition focuses on the counseling process that was derived from mental health, psychological, and human development principles. The *social worker* definition emphasizes the goals of promoting social justice, human rights, and quality of life as well as eliminating poverty. The *psychologist* definition states the requirement that psychologists must hold doctoral degrees and that psychologists focus on the understanding of human behavior. The *psychiatrist* definition begins by saying that psychiatry is a specialty for physicians who focus on mental illnesses. Figure 2-3 summarizes the differences in preparation program requirements for the major mental health professions of counseling, social work, psychology, and psychiatry. This figure was developed using information provided by the organizations that accredit these four mental health professions: for counseling, the Council on Accreditation of Counseling and Related Educational Programs (CACREP, 2014); for social work, the Council on Social Work Education (CSWE, 2014); for psychology, the American Psychological Association Commission on Accreditation (American Psychological Association Commission on Accreditation, 2014); and for psychiatry, the Liaison Committee on Medical Education (LCME, 2014) and the American Board of Psychiatry and Neurology (ABPN, 2014). This figure illustrates the differences in the amount of post–bachelor's-degree study required (ranging from 2 years of graduate study for counseling and social work, and 3 years of

COMPARISON OF PREPARATION PROGRAM REQUIREMENTS
FOR THE MENTAL HEALTH PROFESSIONS

Profession and Graduate Education Required	Summary of Required Courses and Required Supervised Field Experience
Counseling 48–60 graduate credits required for master's degree	Graduate coursework required in professional identity; social and cultural diversity; human growth and development; career development; helping relationships; group work; assessment; research and program evaluation; and specialty area (mental health counseling, community counseling, school counseling, career counseling, marriage and family counseling/therapy, college counseling, gerontological counseling, and student affairs).
Social Work 60 graduate credits required for master's degree	A 100-hour practicum and 600-hour internship are required. Coursework required in professional social worker identity; ethical principles; critical thinking; diversity and difference; advancing human rights and social and economic justice; research-informed practice and practice-informed research; human behavior and the social environment; policy practice; contexts that shape practice; and engaging, assessing, intervening, and evaluating individuals, families, groups, organizations, and communities.
Psychology 3 full-time years of graduate study required for doctoral degree	A total of 900 hours of field experience is required. Coursework required in biological aspects of behavior; cognitive and affective aspects of behavior; social aspects of behavior; history and systems of psychology; psychological measurement; research methodology; techniques of data analysis; individual differences in behavior; human development; dysfunctional behavior or psychopathology; professional standards and ethics; theories and methods of assessment and diagnosis; effective intervention; consultation and supervision; evaluating the efficacy of interventions; cultural and individual diversity; attitudes essential for life-long learning, scholarly inquiry, and professional problem solving.
Psychiatry 130 weeks required for medical degree (usually 4 years) plus 36-month residency in psychiatry required	One full-time year of residency required. MD requires coursework in anatomy; biochemistry; genetics; physiology; microbiology and immunology; pathology; pharmacology and therapeutics; preventive medicine; the scientific method; accurate observation of biomedical phenomena; critical analysis of data; organ systems; preventive, acute, chronic, continuing, rehabilitative, and end-of-life care; clinical experiences in primary care, family medicine, internal medicine, obstetrics and gynecology, pediatrics, psychiatry, and surgery in outpatient and inpatient settings; multidisciplinary content areas, such as emergency medicine and geriatrics; disciplines that support general medical practice, such as diagnostic imaging and clinical pathology; clinical and translational research, including how such research is conducted, evaluated, explained to patients, and applied to patient care; communication skills as they relate to physician responsibilities, including communication with patients, families, colleagues, and other health professionals; addressing the medical consequences of common societal problems—for example, providing instruction in the diagnosis, prevention, appropriate reporting, and treatment of violence and abuse; the manner in which people of diverse cultures and belief systems perceive health and illness and respond to various symptoms, diseases, and treatments; gender and cultural biases; medical ethics and human values.

FIGURE 2-3   Comparison of preparation program requirements for the mental health professions

Source: Pearson Education, Inc., Hoboken, NJ.

> The psychiatry residency must prepare physicians in the psychiatric areas of development through the life cycle; behavioral and social sciences; epidemiology and public policy; diagnostic procedures; clinical aspects of psychiatric disorders; treatment of psychiatric disorders; special topics (suicide; dangerousness; seclusion/restraint; risk management; child abuse, sexual abuse, and domestic violence; psychiatric consultation; professionalism/ethics; other). In addition, the psychiatry residency must prepare physicians in the neurologic areas of development through the life cycle; basic neurosciences; diagnostic procedures; clinical aspect of neuropsychiatric disorders; treatment of neuropsychiatric disorders; diagnostic and clinical evaluation of neurologic disorders/syndromes; and management and treatment of neurologic disorders.

FIGURE 2-3   (continued)

graduate study for psychology, to 7 years of graduate study for medicine). The content of the course work requirements demonstrates that the counseling curriculum has a primary focus on counseling, the social work curriculum emphasizes social issues, the psychology curriculum has a heavy emphasis on evaluation and research, and the curriculum for psychiatry prepares physicians who specialize in behavior disorders and neuroscience. An examination of the actual required courses within accredited counseling, social work, psychology, and psychiatry programs would further demonstrate these different emphases among the preparation programs of these mental health professions.

The similarities to and differences from other mental health professionals, as previously summarized, are easy to articulate. It is vital that counselors learn to state both the traits we share in common with our other mental health colleagues and the differences that make us unique as mental health care providers (Sweeney, 2001).

In addition to understanding differences and similarities, it is important to keep in mind that you will also have working relationships with other mental health professionals when you enter practice as a counselor. Psychologists often contribute articles to counseling professional journals (Weinrach, Lustig, Chan, & Thomas, 1998; Weinrach, Thomas, & Chan, 2001). In addition, many counselors work closely with other mental health professionals on a day-to-day basis—for example, as members of multidisciplinary treatment teams in hospitals or as members of school teams that provide services to students with special needs. Increasingly, collaboration with other mental health professionals is regarded as best practice, so it is vital for counselors to understand the scope of practice of these other professionals. There is some evidence that counselors hold stereotyped views of psychologists as primarily focused on testing and of social workers as primarily experts in case management (Mellin, Hunt, & Nichols, 2011).

In the previous section we discussed some conflicts that currently exist between counselors and certain other mental health professional groups. Despite the likelihood that you and your colleagues will disagree about professional issues, in the practice environment these differences are always set aside in the interest of providing clients with the best possible mental health services (ACA, 2014, *Code of Ethics*, §D.1.c.). You have an ethical obligation to respect approaches to mental health treatment that are different from your own, and to acknowledge the expertise of other professional groups and be respectful of their practices §D.1.a.).

Pride in the Counseling Profession

In Chapter 1, we defined *professionalism* as an internal motivation to perform at the level of *best practices* that represent the ideals of the profession, enhance its image, and promote its development. A crucial component of professionalism is having a sense of pride in one's chosen profession. Counselors who have strong professional identities are proud to be members of their profession. By understanding and appreciating the counseling profession's history, philosophical foundations, services that are offered to the public, training program contents, and similarities to and differences from other similar mental health professions, counselors with strong professional identities are satisfied with their chosen profession and communicate this pride to those with whom they come into contact.

It is important for members of a profession to be self-critical and to seek advancements in knowledge and improvements within the profession. At the same time, members of a profession must be comfortable with the career choice they have made in order to develop a professional identity that serves them and the profession well.

Counselors with strong professional identities express pride in their profession by defending the profession when inaccurate statements are made concerning the profession itself or members of the profession. To represent the profession vigorously to the public, counselors must be thoroughly familiar with the information presented in this chapter. Individual counselors who provide quality counseling services are responsible for the positive reputation that the counseling profession enjoys. Similarly, individual counselors who can articulate the strengths of the counseling profession are responsible for informing the public about the unique contributions to society that members of the counseling profession are making.

Counseling Around the World

Although counseling is a profession that was established and developed in the United States, there is evidence that the counseling profession, in a form similar to that which exists in the United States, is being established throughout the world. In other words, today's counseling profession is trending toward globalization.

Despite cultural differences in other countries, there appears to be an interest worldwide in having counseling services available to citizens. It appears that counseling imported from the United States is being adapted to the cultures of the countries where counseling is being established.

Countries have a variety of political environments that are affecting the way in which counseling is developing. For example, in European countries, counseling is not accepted as a field of study in universities, so counselors are being prepared in private schools. In some African countries, counseling is being established to assist citizens cope with the AIDS epidemic. In many Asian countries, counseling is closely following the model of the profession in the United States, despite the vast cultural differences between Asians and Americans.

A book published by the American Counseling Association, *Counseling Around the World: An International Handbook*, edited by Hohenshil, Amundson, and Niles (2013), summarized how the profession of counseling is developing in 40 countries located on six continents. In addition, the leading journal in the counseling profession, the *Journal of Counseling and Development*, has published a series of articles summarizing the beginnings of the counseling profession in a multitude of countries including, but not limited to, Australia (Schofield, 2013); Ecuador (Smith & Valarezo, 2013); Hong Kong (Yuen, Leung, & Chan, 2014); Italy (Remley, Bacchini, & Krieg, 2010); Russia (Currie, Kuzmina, & Nadyuk, 2012); South Korea (Lee, Suh, Yang, & Jang, 2012); Switzerland (Thomas & Henning, 2012); Taiwan (Guo, Wang, Combs, Lin, & Johnson (2013); and Uganda (Senyonyi & Ochieng, 2012).

CACREP has established a registry that includes counselor preparation programs that are different from those in the United States but meet CACREP standards (CACREP, 2014). The registry is known as the International Registry of Counsellor Education Programs (IRCEP; ircep.org).

Summary and Key Points

The aim of this chapter is to help you clarify and strengthen your professional identity as a counselor. We hope that after reading the material in this chapter, you will have a clear sense of your professional identity and be able to do the following:

- Explain the philosophy that underlies the activities of your professional group
- Describe the services your profession renders to the public
- Describe the components of your profession's preparation programs
- Articulate the similarities and differences between members of your profession and other, similar professional groups
- Communicate your pride in being a member of the counseling profession

We begin the chapter with a discussion of the philosophy underlying the counseling profession. This philosophy, which makes the counseling profession unique and distinguishes us from other mental health professions, includes the following four components: the wellness model of mental health, a developmental perspective, a strong preference for prevention and early intervention into problems, and a goal of empowerment for clients.

Other aspects of professional identity presented in this chapter include counselor preparation programs; credentialing; professional associations for counselors; and current professional, political, and legal issues. A brief history of the counseling profession provided a foundation for a careful look at its present status as an emerging profession. Following are some of the key points of this chapter:

- A vital professional task for counselor trainees is to develop a strong professional identity and to be able to articulate that identity to others.
- Counselors espouse the wellness model of mental health as their perspective for helping people. Other mental health professions have their roots in the tradition of the medical model. Although the differences between the two traditions are clear, in actual practice many other mental health practitioners use the wellness model and counselors are educated to use the medical model of diagnosing mental disorders.
- Counselors take a developmental perspective to understanding people's personal and emotional issues and problems. From this perspective, problems that other mental health professionals might view as pathological are seen by counselors as natural and normal.
- Counselors believe that prevention of and early intervention into mental health problems is far superior to remediation.
- The goal of counseling is to empower clients so that they will be able, in the future, to resolve their problems independently of counselor assistance.
- For counselors, mental health counseling is the primary service they provide. By contrast, other mental health professionals provide counseling as a secondary or ancillary service.
- Counselors are considered to be professionals after they have completed the master's degree. Preparation programs emphasize the development of counseling skills and are generally located in colleges of education within universities.
- Credentialing in counseling is complicated and can be confusing. It is important that you are able to distinguish among state licensure, state certification, national voluntary certification, and program accreditation. It is also important that you plan your program of studies carefully so that you will qualify for the credentials you will need to practice effectively.
- Professional codes of ethics impose only a few restrictions, designed to protect the public, on advertising one's credentials in counseling. You must attend carefully to these restrictions as you prepare to practice and as you develop your business cards, brochures, or other advertising materials.
- The counseling profession emerged out of a convergence of several disparate forces,

including counseling psychology, school counseling, and vocational rehabilitation counseling.

- The field of counseling meets the criteria generally accepted as constituting a mature profession and is making rapid progress toward becoming a societally recognized profession.
- The primary professional association for counselors is the ACA. This organization has various divisions and state branches that serve the particular needs and interests of its members. You should join ACA now, if you have not already done so.
- Currently, the counseling profession is struggling with several professional identity problems. One issue presently being debated is whether counseling will develop as a united profession or as separate specialties. Another issue that is being decided is the organizational structure of ACA. A third problem is that requirements for becoming licensed as a counselor vary from state to state.

- Contemporary legal and professional issues include challenges to the scope and practice of counselors, particularly in the areas of testing, diagnosis, and treatment of mental disorders; job classifications for counselors; and third-party reimbursement for counseling services.
- Counselors have an ethical obligation to maintain positive working relationships with other mental health professionals and to respect and understand their differing approaches.
- Having a sense of pride in being a member of the counseling profession is essential both for your own internal satisfaction with your chosen career and for the continued progress of counseling toward being a societally recognized profession.
- The profession of counseling is developing in countries around the world. Each country is adapting the profession to fit its own political climate and cultural heritage.

CHAPTER 3

Multicultural Competence and Social Justice

1. What do you see as the characteristics of a *culturally competent counselor?*

2. In what ways is cultural competence an ethical issue?

3. How would you define *social justice?*

4. How can you ensure that you are competent to provide counseling services to the culturally diverse clients who may seek your assistance?

Over the past 65 years, the counseling profession has evolved significantly in its stance toward multiculturalism and social justice. We have moved from a position of *cultural encapsulation*, to an awareness of our ethical responsibility to serve diverse clients effectively by practicing in a multiculturally competent manner, to an emphasis on social justice and advocacy aimed at improving the lives of all people in our society and across the world.

In the early years of the development of the counseling profession, the impact of cultural diversity was virtually ignored. Wrenn (1962) was one of the first counseling professionals to draw attention to this issue when he introduced the term *culturally encapsulated counselor*. As Wrenn explained, culturally encapsulated counselors define reality according to one set of cultural assumptions and fail to evaluate other viewpoints. Because they assume that their view is the only legitimate one and tend to ignore evidence that challenges or disconfirms their own assumptions, they become locked into stereotypical thinking.

In addition to Wrenn's (1962) call for counselors to develop cultural awareness, a number of societal factors worked to draw the attention of counseling professionals to diversity issues during the 1960s. The civil rights and women's movements increased societal awareness of equity issues. One effect of these movements was that counselors began to recognize that cultural issues that had been ignored in society had also been ignored in counseling.

In 1973, the growing concern about mental health practitioners' lack of preparedness to counsel diverse clients provided the impetus for the Follow-up Commission to the American Psychological Association's (APA) Vail Conference to publish a declaration that forged the link between ethical practice and competence to serve culturally diverse clients (Korman, 1974). At about the same time, the American Counseling Association (ACA) and its divisions were providing leadership in the effort to make mental health services responsive to the needs of diverse clientele. Throughout the 1980s, multicultural counseling was increasingly recognized as a major discipline within the profession. The need became apparent for counselors to be multiculturally competent practitioners who are able to establish a working alliance that takes into consideration both the personal and cultural dynamics of the client and counselor (Lee, 2013). As the twentieth century entered its last decade, the Association for Counselor Education and Supervision (ACES) and the Association for Multicultural Counseling and Development (AMCD), in a joint effort, developed and operationalized the *Multicultural Counseling Competencies and Standards* (Arredondo et al., 1996). Later, Arredondo and Aricniega (2001) added grounding principles that placed these competencies in an ecological frame.

The twenty-first century has been marked so far by a shift beyond awareness of societal inequities to an emphasis on social justice, advocacy, and global literacy. Multiculturalism, social justice, and advocacy are closely related (Ratts, 2011). Social justice has been defined as a commitment to promote access and equity with the aim of empowering and ensuring full participation of all people in a society, especially those who have been marginalized and systematically excluded on the basis of race, ethnicity, gender, age, ability status, sexual orientation, socioeconomic status, or other characteristic of group membership. Advocacy translates that commitment into action. When issues of power, privilege, and discrimination arise, counselors are called on to address client issues at successively broader levels (Durodoye, 2013). Counselors as advocates are able to intervene to improve the social context that affects clients' lives as well as the lives of individual clients.

In recent years, the counseling profession has given increased attention to global literacy, which is "the information a person needs to know in order to navigate life in the technologically sophisticated, globally interconnected world of the 21st century" (Lee, 2013, p. 310). With the burgeoning globalization of counseling (which we discuss in Chapter 2), multicultural competence—or the ability to work effectively with clients from diverse cultures within the United States—is no longer assumed to be sufficient. Transcultural counseling competence is also needed if counselors are to be effective advocates for marginalized client populations around the world.

MULTICULTURALISM, ADVOCACY, AND ETHICAL STANDARDS

Because the counseling profession was slow, historically, to recognize the connection between multicultural competence and ethical behavior, multicultural considerations have been infused only gradually into our profession's code of ethics. Watson, Herlihy, and Pierce (2006) traced this gradual infusion into successive revisions of the ACA *Code of Ethics* over the years. When the organization (then APGA) adopted its first code of ethics in 1961, counselors were essentially a monocultural group, and no mention was made in the first version of the code of cultural awareness as a component of ethical practice. Revised codes of ethics that appeared in the 1970s and 1980s gave only slight attention to cultural diversity.

As the 1980s drew to a close, writers expressed concern that the ACA *Code of Ethics* was continuing to overlook the needs of disenfranchised groups (e.g., Ibrahim & Arredondo, 1990). In 1995, the code was revised extensively, and multicultural considerations were given a position of prominence (Sue, 1996).

In 2002, the leadership of ACA began the process of revising the 1995 *Code of Ethics*. David Kaplan, then president of ACA, charged the Ethics Revision Task Force with proposing revisions to the ethics code with special focus on multiculturalism, diversity, and social justice. The 2005 version of the ACA *Code of Ethics* (ACA, 2005) gave centrality to multiculturalism by addressing diversity in the Preamble and in every major section of the code. This emphasis on diversity issues and the infusion of diversity throughout the *Code* continue in the current (ACA, 2014) version.

The strong commitment to diversity and multicultural competence is evident throughout the 2014 ACA *Code of Ethics* (ACA, 2014). The Preamble articulates the core professional values of counselors, which include "honoring diversity and embracing a multicultural approach in support of the worth, dignity, potential, and uniqueness of people within their social and cultural contexts" and "promoting social justice." In the Introduction to Section A, which focuses on the counseling relationship, counselors are urged to "actively attempt to understand the diverse cultural backgrounds of the clients they serve. Counselors also explore their own cultural identities and how these affect their values and beliefs about the counseling process." The code clarifies that "multicultural counseling competency is required across all specialties" and that counselors must "gain knowledge, personal awareness, sensitivity, dispositions, and skills pertinent to being a culturally competent counselor in working with a diverse client population" (Standard C.2.a.). The code provides additional guidance regarding nondiscrimination in several standards, including Standard C.5., which states that counselors do not condone or engage in discrimination "based on age, culture, disability, ethnicity, race, religion/spirituality, gender, gender identity, sexual orientation, marital status/partnership, language preference, socioeconomic status or any basis proscribed by law." Lee (2015) identified 26 standards in the 2014 Code that address diversity issues, including specific standards related to confidentiality, assessment, diagnosis, relationship boundaries, technology, supervision, counselor training, and research.

The 2014 *Code of Ethics* also addresses the commitment of counselors to advocate on behalf of their clients. Advocacy involves confronting the social issues that negatively affect clients and working to eradicate systems that perpetuate discrimination. Standard A.7.a. addresses this obligation in the statement that "When appropriate, counselors advocate at individual, group, institutional, and societal levels to address potential barriers and obstacles that inhibit access and/or the growth and development of clients." To assist counselors in carrying out advocacy activities ethically and effectively, a set of *Advocacy Competencies* were developed and were approved by ACA in 2003. We encourage you to familiarize yourself with these competencies by visiting the ACA website (counseling.org). Competencies for advocacy at all levels have been explained by Lewis, Ratts, Paladino, and Toporek (2011).

COMPONENTS OF MULTICULTURAL COMPETENCE

Multiculturally competent counselors need to be aware of their own values, biases, and assumptions about human behavior. They also need to be knowledgeable about the cultural values, biases, and assumptions of the diverse groups of clients with whom they work. Third, they must develop culturally appropriate intervention strategies for assisting these diverse clients (Sue & Sue, 2013). In the following sections, we suggest some strategies that you might implement to strengthen your own multicultural competence.

Self-Awareness

A starting place for you to develop cultural self-awareness is to learn how your own cultural and racial identities have an impact on your values and beliefs about the counseling process. Although it may be uncomfortable, you must engage in self-reflection and acknowledge your own biases and assumptions.

For members of the dominant race in the United States, developing multicultural self-awareness takes conscious effort because Whites have not had to experience themselves as racial or ethnic beings (Kiselica, 1999). McIntosh (1998) argued that White privilege in our society allows and even encourages a lack of awareness. She described *White privilege* as an invisible package of unearned assets on which White people can rely and about which they are intended to remain oblivious. Her contention is that Whites have been taught not to see this inherited systemic overadvantage because remaining blind to its existence maintains the status quo. McIntosh cited numerous examples of White privilege that were grounded in her own experience, such as being able to watch television and see people of her race widely and positively represented; knowing that if she needs legal or medical help, her race will not work against her; and not needing to teach her children about systemic racism for their own daily protection.

You can assess your self-awareness by checking your ability to judge a situation accurately, both from your own viewpoint and from the points of view of members of other cultures (Pedersen, Draguns, Lonner, & Trimble, 2002). How would you evaluate the counselor's multicultural self-awareness in the following example?

3-1 The Case of Marlene

Marlene, a White high school counselor, is conducting a group for non–college-bound senior girls. The topic of this session is "preparing for life after graduation." The nine-member group is composed of equal numbers of African American and Euro-American girls, and one Hispanic American girl. The discussion has turned to a consideration of the advantages and disadvantages of continuing to live at home with parents for a while versus moving into an apartment with friends as soon as one finds a job. Marlene notices that the Hispanic American group member has remained silent for the past several minutes. In an effort to draw her in, Marlene asks her, "Consuela, isn't it more of an expectation among Hispanic families that girls will continue to live at home until they marry?"

- What do you think of the question that Marlene posed to Consuela?
- What are some other ways Marlene might have used to draw Consuela into the conversation?

Discussion: The case of Marlene illustrates how lack of awareness of one's own assumptions can be manifested in a counseling situation. Marlene had good intentions when she asked Consuela the question to draw her into the group. However, she failed to consider how Consuela may have felt about being asked to speak for all Hispanic families. It hardly seems likely that Marlene would have asked a similar question of one of the White students. In fact, being able to count on not being asked to speak for all members of one's racial or ethnic group is an element of White privilege. Had Marlene examined her unconscious assumptions that may have originated in her own status of White privilege, she would not have used this particular strategy to draw Consuela into the discussion.

Knowledge

In addition to developing cultural self-awareness, you must also seek out knowledge that will enhance your understanding of clients who are culturally different from you (Lee, 2013; Milsome, 2002; Yeh, 2001). When counselors do not have this knowledge base, therapeutic error is likely to occur. Of course, it would be impossible for any counselor to be completely knowledgeable about the cultural beliefs, values, communication styles, and behaviors of every potential client in our highly diverse society. What is important is that you acquire basic competencies with respect to knowledge of different cultures and that you are open to continuing to learn.

How does the counselor's lack of knowledge affect the counseling relationship in the following scenario?

3-2 The Case of Jack

Jack, a counselor intern, is working in a college counseling center. Mai-Ling, a freshman who came to the United States from mainland China with her parents 8 years ago, has come for her first session with Jack and has agreed to let him audiotape the session for his supervisor. Mai-Ling states that she has come for help in deciding whether to continue in her 2-year associate degree program in computer operations or switch to a baccalaureate program in computer science. Jack, very much aware that his supervisor will be listening for reflections of feelings and other attending skills, asks Mai-Ling how she feels about being confronted with this decision. She responds by simply restating her problem. The session continues in this fashion, with Jack probing for the client's feelings and the client responding in a cognitive, content-oriented manner. After the session ends, Jack determines to ask his supervisor how to build rapport with this difficult client.

- What does Jack need to know about the culture of persons from mainland China that could have been helpful to him in this counseling session with Mai-Ling?
- What do you think about Jack labeling Mai-Ling as a *difficult client*?

Discussion: If Jack had known that many Asian clients are very uncomfortable with the idea of discussing their feelings with a stranger, he might not have perceived his client as *difficult*. His lack of understanding led him to make an error that is common among counselors who lack knowledge of different cultures—he blamed the client for his failure to establish a therapeutic alliance.

A variety of avenues are available for gaining and increasing knowledge of different cultures. A number of excellent texts are available that address multicultural counseling in general or that focus on specific groups such as lesbian, gay, bisexual, and transgender (LGBT) clients, African American youth, and older individuals, to cite just a few examples. Specialized training is readily available through workshops and seminars, on-line courses, and other resources. In seeking out knowledge about diversity, however, there is a limit to what can be learned through reading and taking courses and seminars. Experiential learning can be powerful. Serving one's practicum or internship at a culturally pluralistic site can provide invaluable learning experiences. Before beginning to work with culturally diverse clients, though, you can become better prepared by pushing yourself to actively engage, outside the counselor education program, with people from cultures different from your own. For example, Wehrly (1991) suggested that a White student can experience the discomfort and isolation often felt by members of minority groups by going alone to a function where the student is clearly in the minority, such as an NAACP or La Raza meeting or an African American church service.

Keep in mind, too, as you begin to practice, that the most important resource for your continued learning will be your clients. They are the most expert source of knowledge about their own cultural values, beliefs, customs, and behaviors, and they are often willing to teach their counselors.

Skills

The third component of ethical multicultural practice is culturally appropriate skills and intervention strategies for counseling diverse clients. To develop these skills, you must recognize that the conventional counselor role often has been misapplied when working with ethnic clients (Atkinson, Thompson, & Grant, 1993). It is also crucial to realize that many of the traditional approaches to counseling that focus on the internal dynamics of the individual client may not be as useful to clients whose problems originate in societal oppression, discrimination, and marginalization. To serve these clients effectively, you will need to develop a repertoire of helping strategies that consider not only the individual client but also the larger social systems in which the client functions. It will be equally vital for you to develop skills in performing alternate roles such as client advocate, consultant, social change agent, and liaison with existing support systems in the client's community (Lee, 2001; Lee & Kurilla, 1997).

How would you assess the multiculturally appropriate helping skills repertoire of Theo, the counselor in the following case example?

3-3 The Case of Theo

Tameika, a 28-year-old African American woman, comes to the community mental health center seeking counseling. During her initial session with Theo, a novice counselor who is White, Tameika reports several symptoms suggestive of depression, including disturbance in her sleep patterns, loss of appetite, general fatigue, and unexplained weeping spells. Theo inquires as to whether she has experienced any losses or significant life changes recently. She replies, "Not really. I just keep trying to keep it all together. And it's hard when I earn a minimum wage and so much of it goes for child care for my two little ones. Some months I can't afford both to feed my kids and pay the utility bills. I can't see how it's going to get any better." Theo suggests that she might get some short-term relief by taking an antidepressant medication and offers to refer her to the mental health center's consulting psychiatrist. Tameika agrees to make an appointment, but she never returns to the center.

- What do you think of Theo's suggestions for assisting Tameika with her problems?
- What kind of help does Tameika need?

Discussion: In this case, the counselor would have been more effective had he taken more of a systemic approach to helping Tameika. Rather than focus on her intrapsychic dynamics and her depression, he might have explored with her whether there were any social support systems available in her community. He might have discovered, for instance, that her religious faith was an important source of strength for her and helped her connect with a church in her neighborhood that offers free or reduced-fee child care for its members. He might have helped her contact social services agencies such as Aid to Families with Dependent Children or a community organization that could help her manage her financial problems. His failure to implement any such culturally appropriate strategies could have been a major factor in Tameika's failure to return to the center.

ETHICAL CONSIDERATIONS IN MULTICULTURAL COUNSELING AND ADVOCACY

The primary ethical issue that relates to multicultural counseling and advocacy is competence. Although there are certainly some counselors practicing today who remain culturally encapsulated, counseling professionals now generally recognize that they must learn to practice in a diversity-sensitive manner and must develop advocacy skills for intervening in unjust systems. Nonetheless, prejudicial attitudes and biases are deeply ingrained in Western society, and counselors, as members of that society, have internalized these biases. Thus, counselors can practice discrimination without being aware that they are doing so.

Our own understanding of multiculturalism is based on the premise that *all counseling is cross-cultural*. We define *culture* broadly to include numerous cultural variables, including characteristics into which people are born or which are visible, such as race or ethnicity, social class, gender, age, and disability status. Culture also encompasses characteristics that may not be visible, such as educational attainment, geographic origin, marital status, language, religion, and citizenship status. Ethical issues related to prevalent forms of bias based on these cultural characteristics are discussed in the following subsections, along with strategies to advocate for clients who are members of disenfranchised groups in our society. As advocates, counselors have an ethical responsibility to confront the *isms* of prejudice and discrimination at the individual, group, and societal levels.

Racism

Racism refers to prejudice and discrimination against people of color and people of certain ethnic origins. Because the multicultural counseling movement historically has focused on race, a substantial body of professional literature addresses the effects of race and ethnicity on the counseling relationship, process, and outcomes (D'Andrea & Foster Heckman, 2008). When a client and counselor are racially or ethnically different from each other, counselor insensitivity to the differences can lead to client reluctance to self-disclose, mistrust of the counselor by the client, and premature termination of counseling. Very rarely do counselors behave toward clients in a manner that is deliberately racist. However, even counselors who are strongly committed to multiculturalism are not exempt from deeply embedded racial/ethnic biases and prejudices (Utsey, Ponterotto, & Porter, 2008). Just a few examples of unintentional racism as it is manifested among counselors are avoiding the issue of cultural differences by claiming to be *color blind* and treating all people as if they were alike; being too *color conscious*, thus attributing all problems to a client's cultural background; *misunderstanding* a client's defensive reactions to the counselor's stereotypical thinking; and *misinterpreting* a client's culturally learned patterns of communicating or behaving (Ridley, 1989). Unintended racism can lead to violations of the counselor's fundamental ethical obligation to do no harm (Pack-Brown, Thomas, & Seymour, 2008).

Recent literature has focused on racial microaggressions, which are "brief and commonplace daily verbal or behavioral indignities, whether intentional or unintentional, that communicate hostile, derogatory, or negative racial slights and insults" (Sue & Sue, 2013, p. 154) and have a potentially harmful or unpleasant impact on the target person or group. Sue and Sue (2013) have identified three forms of microaggressions: Microassaults are blatant verbal or nonverbal attacks that are intentional and convey discriminatory and biased sentiments; microinsults are unintentional comments or behaviors that convey rudeness or insensitivity or demean a person's cultural identity in some way; and microinvalidations are verbal comments or behaviors that exclude, negate, or dismiss a person's thoughts, feelings, or experiences. Some examples are telling an individual who is visibly of Asian heritage that he or she "speaks good English," mistaking a female doctor for a nurse, staring at two men who are holding hands in public, or saying "Merry Christmas" as a universal holiday season greeting. Ample research evidence exists that microaggressions have a negative impact on the mental health of people of color (Nadal, Griffin, Wong, Hamit, & Rasmus, 2014; Rivera, Forquer, & Rangel, 2010; Sue, Bucceri, Lin, Nadal, & Torino, 2007; Sue, Capodilupo, & Holder, 2008). It is important to remember that no one, even the most well-intentioned counselor, is free from these biases. Therefore, the biases that exist in society are often recreated and reenacted in the dynamics between counselor and client within counseling sessions.

As advocates, counselors recognize that racial and ethnic discrimination are rooted in the social organization of our society and that mental health is profoundly affected by experiences of marginalization and oppression. Advocacy involves extending the work of counseling beyond the individual client to address the external forces that create barriers to clients' full participation in society. This includes engaging in community empowerment strategies, political action, and other activities aimed at systemic change. Counselors can take the lead in mobilizing the provision of mental health services to communities in need. Holcomb-McCoy and Mitchell (2007) have reminded counselors that it is also imperative to challenge racism and oppression in their own communities.

Sexism

Gender issues may be overlooked in counseling for at least two reasons. First, there is a widely held assumption that women have achieved equality in contemporary U.S. society and that we have entered a *post-feminist era* (Atkinson & Hackett, 2004) in which marginalization and oppression are less likely to be relevant to the issues women bring to counseling. Second, the vast majority of master's-level counseling practitioners are female, and it might be assumed that these practitioners have the awareness and skills to counsel other women effectively. In reality, women and men are equally influenced by gender-role socialization experiences that, if left unexamined, can lead to gender discrimination and incompetent counseling practices.

Counselor self-awareness is an essential starting point to avoid bringing gender bias into the counseling relationship. Self-awareness begins with reflection on the impact of one's own gender-role socialization experiences. From birth, stereotyped beliefs about what it means to be male and female are reinforced by virtually every significant force in a child's life, including parents, schools, religious institutions, books, toys, language, television, movies, and other mass media. Unless counselors bring these stereotyped messages to explicit awareness, they are likely to contribute to this status quo.

In addition to self-awareness, counselors need to acquire knowledge that is foundational for counseling women, which includes understanding the specific life experiences and world views of diverse groups of women. This includes becoming familiar with theories of development that are specific to females, such as the pioneering work of Gilligan (1982). The developmental model offered by Conarton and Kreger-Silverman (1988) not only describes developmental stages, but it also suggests areas of counseling focus for each stage. Knowledge of women's identity development models, such as the feminist identity development model (Downing & Roush, 1985) and the womanist model (Ossana, Helms, & Leonard, 1992) preferred by some women of color, can help counselors meet clients where the clients are and collaboratively determine goals for change. These models help counselors to understand that women tend to be relationally oriented and to view this orientation as a strength. Relational cultural theory (RCT) arose from the recognition that traditional models of human development do not accurately address the relational experiences of women (Comstock et al., 2008). Comstock et al. wrote that RCT complements multicultural counseling competencies by providing another framework from which counselors can explore the effects of gender-role socialization, power, dominance, marginalization, and subordination on the mental health and development of all clients.

Counselors who work with female clients also should have an understanding of the high-prevalence problems and issues experienced by women, including domestic violence, sexual assault and harassment, body image and objectification, and conflicts between work and family responsibilities. They must also develop skills that are specific to counseling women clients. They must know how to build collaborative relationships and have a repertoire of strategies for empowering women (Enns, 2004). They should be cautious in assigning diagnoses and selecting treatments so that they do not inadvertently perpetuate sexist bias in the counseling relationship and process. Counselors can increase their competence by learning feminist therapy strategies, such as gender analysis and intervention and power analysis and intervention, that are designed to meet the unique needs of women (Enns, 2004; Worell & Remer, 2003).

As advocates, counselors are aware that discrimination and violence against women are societal issues. A first step in advocacy is to help women become aware of the gender-biased messages they have received and internalized, so that they may choose to move beyond unquestioning acceptance of gender stereotyping and oppression (Lewis, 2007). Beyond the individual client level, counselors can facilitate change by engaging in social and political advocacy. They can lobby legislators and policy makers and create, join, and support existing alliances. Discrimination against women is also a global issue that needs to be confronted abroad as well as in the United States (Lewis, 2007). According to Amnesty International (2012), a global culture of discrimination against women exists that allows violence to occur daily and with impunity, and no country is exempt. A challenge for counselors in the United States as they move into the global arena will be to find ways to navigate their ethical obligation to advocate for women without imposing their own Westernized values.

Classism

The counseling literature has not given much attention to socioeconomic status (SES) or class as a cultural variable (Smith, Foley, & Chaney, 2008). Yet, SES affects all dimensions of a person's life, including sense of self-worth, access to mental health care, exposure to violence, and sense of personal power or agency (Robinson-Wood, 2009). Socioeconomic status transcends other cultural dimensions such as race, gender, religion, and ability status. The link between mental health and poverty is clear: people suffering from mental illness are more likely to be poor, and poverty is linked to problems with inadequate housing, unemployment, and involvement in substance abuse and the criminal justice system (Draine, 2013). Research has demonstrated bias against low-SES clients in mental health services: clients from low-SES backgrounds are more frequently and more severely diagnosed, are prescribed different treatments based solely on class, and have fewer services available to them and less experienced clinicians to serve them (Aponte & Wohl, 2000).

Most counselors come from or have achieved middle-class status (Bienvenu & Ramsey, 2006), and a middle-class bias prevails in the training of counselors (Robinson-Wood, 2009). Both of these factors may make it difficult for counselors to relate to the phenomenon of poverty and to become aware of their class biases. For instance, middle-class bias is present in the expectation that clients will self-disclose and will be able to articulate their feelings and affective responses.

Culturally competent counseling includes the ability to hear class conditioning when listening to clients' stories. For example, a client might be reluctant to take certain occupational risks because of socialization experiences that emphasized security and practicality. Rather than focusing exclusively on personal relationships and insight with a client, counselors should remain aware of and address the social and economic issues that affect the client's life. Bienvenu and Ramsey (2006) have suggested that counselors need the following advocacy competencies for culturally sensitive counseling across the socioeconomic divide:

- Individual and group counseling skills that are grounded in empowerment
- A systemic approach that includes an understanding of the educational, family, political, criminal justice, and social welfare systems that affect clients' lives
- Skills in advocating for low-income clients
- The ability to collaborate with families and community resources

As advocates, counselors can work to change the entrenched political and social systems that allow poverty to continue. Counselors need to be able not only to work effectively within systems but also to work toward change when programs are ineffective, inaccessible to some clients, uncoordinated, or disempowering to the people they serve (Armstrong, 2007). Poverty is a worldwide problem, and counselors working transnationally must have expertise in interventions that focus on change in the environment as well as in the individual if they are to fulfill their commitments to social justice and advocacy.

Homoprejudice

Lesbian, gay, bisexual, transgender, queer, intersex, and questioning (LGBTQIQ) individuals have experienced a long history of oppression and stigmatization in the United States. Homosexuality was once considered to be criminal and was a diagnosable mental disorder until 1973. Today, LGBTQIQ persons continue to experience societal stigmatization and seek assistance with associated life challenges. LGBTQIQ clients use counseling at a higher rate and participate longer in counseling relationships than do heterosexual clients (Bieschke, McClanahan, Tozer, Grzegorek, & Park, 2000; Rudolph, 1990). These factors attest to a clear need for counselors who can provide culturally competent services to these clients (Israel, 2004).

As is true for working with clients who are members of any marginalized group, counselors need to explore their own biases as a starting place for developing their cultural competence. Internalized attitudes of homophobia, homonegativity, and heterosexism among mental health professionals have led to harmful practices, such as assuming that a client is heterosexual, referring a client who discloses his or her sexual orientation, acquiescing in the dissolution of a relationship because it is with a person of the same sex, and failing to support the desire for child custody of gay parents (Garnets, Hancock, Cochran, Goodchilds, & Peplau, 1991).

One practice that has been highly controversial is reparative/conversion therapy, the goal of which is to change an individual's sexual orientation from homosexual to heterosexual. In 1999, the ACA Governing Council adopted a statement opposing the promotion of reparative therapy as a cure. In 2006 the ACA Ethics Committee issued an interpretation of the ACA *Code of Ethics* concerning conversion therapy and the ethics of referring clients for this practice. The committee concluded that research indicates that conversion therapies may harm clients. The committee strongly advised counselors not to refer clients to someone who engages in this type of therapy, or to discuss the potential harm if clients indicate they are still interested in a referral (Whitman, Glosoff, Kocet, & Tarvydas, 2006). The 2014 ACA *Code of Ethics* clarifies that counselors "do not use techniques/ procedures/modalities when substantial evidence suggests harm, even if such services are requested" (ACA, 2014, §C.7.c.).

Cultural competencies for working with LGBTQIQ clients have been identified by several writers (e.g., Appleby, 2001; Hutchins, 2006; Logan, 2006; Robinson-Wood, 2009). These competencies include being able to talk about sex and sexuality and become familiar and comfortable with gay and lesbian sexuality and its expression; not assuming that sexual orientation will be the focus of counseling for an LGBTQIQ client, being prepared to assist clients in the coming-out process, understanding that sexuality is not dichotomous, and understanding the stages of identity development for LGBTQIQ clients.

Lassiter and Barret (2007) have offered a number of strategies for advocating for LGBTQIQ clients. These include joining the Association for Lesbian, Gay, Bisexual and Transgender Issues in Counseling (ALGBTIC), PFLAG National (community.pflag.org), or other organizations that work to eradicate discrimination based on sexual orientation; working to establish domestic partner benefits at one's place of work; confronting prejudice among co-workers, friends, and family; and contacting elected officials when relevant issues arise. ALGBTIC has developed comprehensive statements of Competencies for Counseling LGBQQIA [Lesbian, Gay, Bisexual, Queer, Questioning, Intersex, and Ally] Individuals (2012) and for Counseling with Transgender Individuals (2009). These documents can be found on the organization's website (algbtic.org).

Throughout the world, LGBT individuals continue to face the fear of discovery, actual and potential economic disenfranchisement, ridicule and shame, and penalties for alleged criminal behavior (Dworkin & Yi, 2003), and working for their human rights can place them in imminent peril for their lives (Amnesty International, 2001). Counselors working in these countries as advocates for social justice can play a significant role in working toward achieving human rights for members of sexual minority groups.

Ableism

People with disabilities constitute the largest minority group in the United States (Hanjorgiris & O'Neill, 2006). According to the Americans with Disabilities Act of 1990 (ADA, 42 U.S. Code §12101), a person is considered to have a disability if she or he has an impairment that creates a functional limitation in a major life activity.

Ableism is a form of discrimination or prejudice against individuals with physical, developmental, or mental disabilities that is characterized by the belief that these individuals cannot function as full members of society. Counselors are subject to the same negative images and stereotypes of people with disabilities (PWD) as the rest of society (Reeve, 2000). This problem may persist because disability has not been widely recognized as a multicultural concern by counselors (Smith et al., 2008), and most counselor education programs (other than rehabilitation counseling programs) have not given much attention to disability issues (Hanjorgiris & O'Neill, 2006; Smart & Smart, 2006).

Developing the competencies that are necessary for providing effective counseling services to PWDs begins with counselors' awareness of their own assumptions, values, and biases about disability. Counselors must first confront their own ableism, which can cause them to hold limited expectations of a client and hinder the client's progress toward reaching his or her full potential. Counselors need to remain aware that not all disabilities are visible; a counselor who is unaware of a hidden disability might erroneously assume that the client's slow progress in counseling is due to client resistance. It is also important to remember that a client's presenting problem may or may not be related to disability. As Caron (1996) has stated, counselors need first to see the person, not the disability, and to listen as clients identify their own needs.

Counselors need to understand the world views of their clients with disabilities. PWDs experience barriers related to architecture as well as economic, social, educational, and occupational opportunity. Experiences with discrimination, alienation, and barriers to independence and opportunity can affect the coping skills and self-concept that clients bring to the counseling endeavor. Counselors can gain an understanding of how disability is interpreted by the client by exploring the client's world view and cultural context (Hanjorgiris & O'Neill, 2006).

In addition, counselors need to have a repertoire of appropriate intervention strategies for assisting people with disabilities. To establish the therapeutic alliance, Hanjorgiris and O'Neill (2006) advise counselors to be willing to listen and provide the client with opportunities to have a voice and exercise power and control during sessions. The counseling process might include countering deficit thinking by focusing on a client's abilities rather than limitations, helping the client gain personal control and self-efficacy, and working to overcome social isolation.

Disability issues generally have not been included in social justice agendas (Fabian, 2007), and marginalization is perpetuated when counseling PWDs is assumed to be exclusively the province of rehabilitation counselors. Problems that are related to disability are often related to systemic barriers, so counselors should be skilled in advocacy approaches that focus on systems change (Smith et al., 2008), both in the United States and worldwide.

Ageism

Older adults are the fastest-growing population group in the United States (Robinson-Wood, 2009). The number of older adults with mental illnesses was 35 million in 2000 and is expected to grow to 70 million by 2030 (Lum, 2007). Clearly, there will be a burgeoning need for culturally competent counselors to serve this population in coming years.

In some respects, ageism is a problem unique to the United States. Unlike many other cultures in which the elderly are respected and valued, the U.S. mainstream culture prizes youthfulness, and age discrimination tends to be against the elderly. If you expect to work with older adults, you will need to be alert to your own biases. It is important to guard against stereotyping and monolithic thinking or assuming that all older people share the same life issues and counseling concerns. There is a great deal of difference between a *young-old*, healthy and active 65-year-old and an *old-old*, frail, 95-year-old whose health is in decline. You can check yourself for unconscious biases by paying attention to the terminology you use in everyday language, such as describing someone as *crotchety* or referring to ordinary instances of forgetfulness as *senior moments*. Even the terms *elderly* and *aged* suggest that older persons share common, negative characteristics (Myers, 2007).

Older adults tend to underutilize mental health services, perhaps partly because of the stigma they attach to seeking psychological services. Kunkel and Williams (1991) found that very few of the 100 older adults they surveyed thought that counselors were appropriate sources of help for retirement issues, fear of death, or sexual problems. Counselors need to be prepared to address the reluctance of some older clients to enter into counseling relationships. Counselors can best promote client welfare and respect for autonomy by assessing the client's social supports (both family and community) and level of involvement in meaningful work and social activities, and by assisting some older clients with issues of loss around death of a spouse or family members, mental acuity, physical abilities and mobility, income, and the sense of purpose they once derived from work or their roles in their families. Counselors should be alert to signs of possible elder abuse or neglect (see Chapter 11 for a further discussion of this topic). Counselors also can play a vital role in assisting family members and caregivers to reduce stress and manage their multiple roles as members of the *sandwich generation*.

As advocates, counselors are uniquely positioned to assist older individuals because our developmental perspective recognizes and supports the possibility of positive growth across the life span (Myers, 2007). Working both with and on behalf of older individuals, counselors can work to effect changes in laws, policies, and organizations.

Spiritual and Religious Bias

Spirituality and religion play an important part in the lives of many clients (Ivey, D'Andrea, Ivey, & Simek-Morgan, 2007; Robinson-Wood, 2009; Steen, Engels, & Thweatt, 2006). According to the results of one survey, 79% of clients believed that religious and spiritual values and experiences are important to address in counseling (Myers & Truluck, 1998). *Spirituality* can be defined as a personal relationship with a higher power and faith that may be used to find meaning in life. Religion is a shared set of practices and beliefs that is associated with denominational affiliations (Halbert et al., 2007; Robinson-Wood, 2009).

Some counselors are uncomfortable with the idea of addressing spiritual or religious issues within the therapeutic relationship. This discomfort may be due to lack of clarity about their own views on spirituality and religion, a fear of imposing values, concerns about maintaining separation of church and state in school and some other secular settings, or lack of training and questions about competence (Genia, 2000; Hall, Dixon, & Mauzey, 2004; Steen et al., 2006).

Because many clients believe spirituality is integrally connected to their personal growth and mental health (Ivey, Ivey, Myers, & Sweeney, 2005), counselors must be open to discussing client spirituality. Although it would not be ethical for counselors to impose their own spiritual or religious beliefs and values on a client, counselors should be able to explore spiritual themes when the client opens a spiritual discussion (Corey, Corey, Corey, & Callanan, 2015). Results of one study suggested that client welfare can be positively affected, by decreasing symptoms of depression and anxiety, when the counselor creates an environment that accommodates spiritual exploration (Young, Cashwell, & Shcherbakova, 2000).

The counseling profession has recognized spirituality as an integral component of wellness (see Chapter 2), but the question of integrating religious beliefs into the counseling process poses difficult dilemmas for some counselors. For instance, if the counselor's religious belief is that abortion is always a sin, can the counselor work effectively with a client who wants to explore whether or not to terminate her pregnancy? If the counselor's religious beliefs hold homosexuality to be a sin, can the counselor work effectively with LGBT clients? Several court cases have addressed this issue. These cases are discussed in detail in Chapter 4 and Chapter 14.

As a counselor, you will have to develop the competencies needed to explore spiritual and religious issues with clients. To practice competently and ethically, counselors must be aware of and sensitive to the importance and role of spirituality and religion in the lives of their clients (Barnett & Johnson, 2011). Some self-assessment questions you might ask yourself include the following:

- Have I examined my own prejudices and biases (both positive and negative) about spirituality and religion?
- Am I familiar with how spirituality is viewed by the major world religions, and do I understand the various models of religious and spiritual development?
- Do I have the skills to assess the relevance of spirituality and religion in my clients' therapeutic issues?
- Do I have the skills for using a client's spiritual beliefs to help advance the client's therapeutic goals?
- Do I know the limitations of my understanding of spiritual/religious beliefs and have appropriate referral resources available for my clients?

MULTIPLE CULTURAL IDENTITIES

It is important to recognize that individuals have multiple, interrelated cultural characteristics. Recent literature in multicultural counseling has addressed the intersection among multiple group memberships and identities (Ivey et al., 2007; Robinson & Watt, 2001; Robinson-Wood, 2009). Race, ethnicity, gender, and social class are salient cultural variables for all people, and considering

Draw two columns on a piece of paper and label the two columns *Dominant-Group Characteristics* and *Subordinate-Group Characteristics*. In the left-hand column, list your cultural characteristics that give you membership in a dominant group. Some examples might be Caucasian, middle class, Protestant, male, able bodied, heterosexual. Then, in the right-hand column, make a list of your cultural characteristics that give you membership in a subordinate or marginalized group. Some examples might be person of color, lower-class/working-poor family of origin, female, Jewish, from a rural community in the South.

What are some ways in which you enjoy *privilege* in your daily life due to your membership in each group you listed on the left? What are some ways that your membership in the groups you listed on the right affects what you are able to do, or are presumed by others to be able to do, in your everyday life?

FIGURE 3-1 Cultural characteristics exercise

Source: Pearson Education, Inc., Hoboken, NJ.

any of these variables in isolation fails to reflect the complexities of a person's life experiences and world view (Constantine, 2001, 2002). Constantine suggested that counselors should examine how race, class, gender, and other cultural factors interact in their own lives. If you engage in this process, you will recognize that you simultaneously experience both privilege and oppression (as, say, a middle-class White heterosexual woman, or a Christian African American man). Realizing that you occupy both positions on the power spectrum and reflecting on your own experiences of privilege and oppression may increase your understanding and sense of empathy for your clients (Croteau, Talbot, Lance, & Evans, 2002).

The exercise presented in Figure 3-1 may help you begin to identify your own life experiences as a member of both dominant and nondominant cultures.

If you give some thought to the many ways that your multiple memberships in cultural groups have an impact on your day-to-day living, you may be more aware of the complexities of the cultural identities of your clients. Perhaps because much of the literature has focused on racial and ethnic differences, other cultural variables sometimes are overlooked. Notice the number of cultural considerations that Horst, the counselor in the following case example, must consider.

3-4 The Case of Horst

Arthur is a 32-year-old African American man who is employed as a nursing instructor at a community college and is married with two children. He seeks counseling from Horst after he becomes involved in an intimate relationship with Mark, an openly gay man. Mark also works at the community college, and their co-workers have gossiped among themselves about the relationship although no one has said anything directly to either Arthur or Mark. Arthur believes he has come to the point in his life when heterosexual marriage is no longer viable for him. He presents with several issues, including coming out to his wife and children and redefining himself as a gay man. He believes that his wife suspects the truth and will come to accept who he is, but he fears losing the close relationship he has enjoyed with his children.

- What are the issues Horst must address in providing counseling to Arthur?
- What information will Horst need in order to be a culturally competent counselor in this situation?
- What skills will Horst need to be a culturally competent counselor in this situation?

Discussion: Horst, as Arthur's counselor, must have awareness, knowledge, and skills across several dimensions if he is to be effective in helping Arthur. First, Horst must be aware of the impact of Arthur's multiple cultural identities. Until recently, Arthur has enjoyed heterosexual privilege, and he may not be prepared to deal with the realities of being an openly gay man. He may find that some of his friends will not be able to accept his gay identity. On the other hand, Arthur has had experience in coping with a marginalized status—he is African American and works in a predominantly female occupation. Horst must be knowledgeable about sexuality so that he does not make erroneous assumptions, such as believing that Arthur must be bisexual because he has engaged in heterosexual intercourse for many years (Janson & Steigerwald, 2002). If Arthur's wife and children want to join in the counseling process and Horst decides to accept them as counseling clients, Horst must have family counseling skills so that he can help Arthur and his family create new family rules and boundaries. He must have a range of competencies—in multicultural counseling, family counseling, and LGBT counseling—to be effective in helping Arthur.

Harley, Jolivette, McCormick, and Tice (2002) recommended several conceptualizations and strategies for incorporating the interplay of race, class, and gender in the counseling process:

- Take an integrative approach to considering race, class, and gender, as most people of color, women, and the poor do not separate these issues.
- Ask culturally relevant questions.
- Postpone assessment and diagnosis until trust and rapport have been established, recognizing that it may take longer for people of color, women, and lower SES clients to become active participants in the counseling process.
- Recognize the complexities of *positionalities* on the power spectrum to avoid stereotyped assumptions.

It is essential that you realize that culture influences a person's view of reality and thus every aspect of life. A multicultural perspective in counseling recognizes that the client may hold values and beliefs that are different from those of the counselor. It seeks to provide a conceptual framework that recognizes the complex diversity of a pluralistic society while building bridges of shared concern that allow culturally different individuals to connect with one another (Pedersen, 1991).

Mental health professionals have become increasingly aware that when counselors and clients are from different cultural groups, differences may exist between them related to values, perceptions of events, and communication styles. In fact, counselors must understand that even the counseling process may be uncomfortable or unacceptable to clients from some cultural backgrounds. At the same time, to avoid stereotypical and erroneous assumptions about clients based on their race, ethnicity, social class, or gender, it is crucial to keep in mind that there are within-group differences for all cultural groups as well as overlap across groups. You must ascertain the extent to which each of your clients is actually representative of the patterns of the cultural groups to which he or she belongs (Sciarra, 1999).

A danger to studying specific cultural differences is the natural tendency to stereotype once information about a culture is known. For example, counselors who know that many Asians are deferential to elders might assume that a particular Asian client is in conflict because of that cultural norm when, in fact, that Asian client may not be particularly deferential to his or her elders. Lee (2001) has stated this conflict best as follows:

> If counselors are to be effective with clients from a variety of ethnic backgrounds, then they must approach the helping process from a perspective that simultaneously acknowledges human difference and celebrates human similarity. They must adopt a philosophy that promotes the ability to view each client as a unique individual while, at the same time, taking into consideration the client's common experience as a human (i.e., the universal developmental challenges that face all people regardless of ethnic background) and the specific experiences that come from his or her ethnic background. (p. 583)

Every client, and every counselor, belongs to multiple cultures, and the salience of membership in any of these cultural groups changes according to the situation. At the same time, each individual is unique. You will need to keep your attention balanced in your work with clients. If you pay too much attention to cultural group membership, you may inadvertently stereotype your client. If you focus too narrowly on the individual client, you might overlook the impact of the cultural environment on that client (Corey, Haynes, Moulton, & Muratori, 2010).

ETHICAL PRINCIPLES AND DIVERSITY

With respect to cultural diversity, perhaps more than any other ethical issue, it is crucial that counselors attend to the *spirit* of the *Code of Ethics* (ACA, 2014). Standards regarding nondiscrimination and honoring diversity are included throughout the code, but we believe it would be a mistake to think that only these specific standards are pertinent to multiculturally competent practice. Rather, we believe that *all* of the ethical standards are best seen as multicultural standards. Sensitivity to cultural diversity should be inherent in our interpretation of all our ethical obligations. Diversity-sensitive interpretation requires us to keep in mind that the ethical reasoning of every counselor is embedded within the counselor's world view, which is shaped by sociocultural conditioning of which we are often unaware (Helms & Cook, 1999). The moral principles (discussed in Chapter 1) that provide the foundation for much of our ethical reasoning are not universally endorsed by all cultures. Herlihy and Watson (2003) suggested some ways to interpret these principles through a multicultural lens, which might help to avoid culturally encapsulated ethical reasoning.

Multicultural scholars have suggested that the principle of *respect for autonomy* is often misapplied when Euro-American counselors work with clients whose cultural identity differs from their own. As has been noted, many clients make choices and decisions in the context of family, tribe, group, or community. Counselors who reframe the principle to consider the client's *cultural autonomy* (Burn, 1992) will be better prepared to allow the client's cultural self-definition and beliefs to direct the course of the counseling process.

Although all counselors intend to uphold the principle of *nonmaleficence* by doing no harm, it is possible for harm to occur when counselors who work with culturally diverse clients are not multiculturally competent. If counselors lack cross-cultural awareness, knowledge, and skills, they will not be capable of protecting the welfare of these diverse clients. Multicultural competence is essential to upholding the principle of do no harm.

There are numerous ways in which a counselor who fails to practice with an understanding of, and respect for, a client's cultural identity and belief system can violate the principle of *beneficence*. For example, counselors who are not sensitive to their dominant power position in the counseling relationship may function from an assumption that they know what is good for the client. As was discussed in Chapter 1, feminist and multicultural theorists have reminded us that ethical decisions are best made *with* the client rather than *for* the client. They also have recommended that counselors strive to avoid replicating in the counseling relationship the power dynamics that exist in society for women and clients who are members of marginalized societal groups.

The principle of *justice* has particular significance when counseling clients whose problems arise from discrimination, oppression, and marginalization. Social justice and advocacy competence require that counselors be able to implement empowering intervention strategies that assist clients in coping with, and making changes in, the larger systems in which these clients live.

As the counseling profession continues to expand into the international arena, more questions are emerging with respect to the universal applicability of these basic principles (Herlihy, James, & Taheri, in press). Across different nations, the principles will need to be interpreted differently depending on the cultural context in which they are being applied. For example, working to increase a client's autonomy might actually be harmful in non-Western nations that do not share Euro-American values of individualism, independence, and self-determination. If the principle of justice is to be applied transnationally, it will need to be defined more broadly than treating each individual fairly. It must be rooted in the awareness that "the ethical implications of inequalities in mental health for people and nations are profound and must be addressed" (Ngui, Khasakhals, Ndetei, & Roberts, 2010, p. 235). Counselors working across the globe can advocate for oppressed and underserved groups of people and help them overcome systemic barriers to health and equity.

Some ethics scholars have suggested that integrating virtue ethics with principle ethics can enhance the ethical conduct of counselors in multicultural interactions (Herlihy & Watson, 2006; Meara, Schmidt, & Day, 1996; Vasquez, 1996). The virtue ethics perspective, with its focus on counselor self-awareness of assumptions and values, on recognizing the importance of cultural context, and on mutual respect in the counseling relationship, may help counselors maintain sensitivity to issues of diversity.

Garcia, Cartwright, Winston, & Borzuchowska, (2003) have suggested a transcultural integrative model for resolving ethical dilemmas that is founded in both principle and virtue ethics. They offered a four-step model based primarily on the work of Tarvydas (1998), with elements of social constructionism and collaborative models (see Chapter 1 to review these models). They identified transcultural issues to be considered in each step. Some of these issues include the following:

- Awareness of the counselor's own and the client's cultural identity, acculturation, and role socialization
- Determining whether resolutions being considered reflect the world view of the counselor, the client, or both
- Gathering relevant cultural information, such as immigration history, family values, and community relationships
- Examining potentially discriminatory laws and institutional policies
- Considering the consequences of potential actions within the cultural world view of each of the parties involved
- Anticipating cultural barriers such as biases, discrimination, stereotypes, and prejudices, and developing culture-specific countermeasures

If cultural diversity is a theme that runs throughout the *Code of Ethics* (ACA, 2014), it is also a theme that runs throughout this text. This chapter only introduces the multitude of considerations that are involved in ethically sensitive multicultural counseling practice. Each of the ensuing chapters focuses on a specific ethical/legal/professional issue, and there is a section devoted to diversity issues that relate to that topic. For instance, some diversity issues that arise in informed consent are discussed in the next chapter. Diversity is far too important an issue in the professional practice of counselors to be limited to one section of this text.

CLIENTS WHO MAY BE VICTIMS OF ILLEGAL DISCRIMINATION

Section C.5. of the *Code of Ethics* (ACA, 2005) states that counselors do not condone or engage in discrimination based on age, culture, disability, ethnicity, race, religion/spirituality, gender, gender identity, sexual orientation, marital status/partnership, language preference, socioeconomic status, or any basis proscribed by law. Counselors have a duty to ensure that individuals who are under their care are not harmed (see Chapters 5, 7, and 11). There may be circumstances in which you must take action to ensure that individuals from minority groups are not harmed physically or emotionally by others. For example, McFarland and Dupuis (2001) have argued that professionals have a legal duty to protect gay and lesbian clients from violence in schools. Legal duties of counselors related to discrimination are found in the U.S. Constitution as well as laws and statutes.

The U.S. Constitution provided a foundation for making discrimination illegal through the Due Process Clause of the Fifth Amendment (*Adarand Constructors, Inc. v. Pena,* 1995), the Due Process and Equal Protection Clauses of the Fourteenth Amendment (*Truax v. Raich,* 1915), and the First Amendment. In addition, Title VII of the Civil Rights Act of 1964 prohibits public and private employers, labor organizations, and employment agencies from discriminating on the basis of race, color, sex, religion, and national origin. After Title VII was enacted, federal laws were passed that prohibit discrimination on the basis of age (Age Discrimination in Employment Act of 1967) and disability (Title I of the Americans with Disabilities Act of 1990).

The *Code of Ethics* (ACA, 2014) lists the groups that counselors are admonished not to discriminate against and includes groups that are not protected from discrimination by the federal constitution or by federal statutes. The groups that are not legally protected include subgroups based on culture, ethnicity, race, spirituality, gender identity, sexual orientation, marital status/partnership, language preference, and socioeconomic status. Some states and local government entities, however, have passed nondiscrimination laws for some specific purposes related to these groups (Belton & Avery, 1999). In our view, counselors do not have a professional responsibility to expose those who they think may be illegally discriminating against protected groups or to encourage clients to assert their legal rights or to assert those rights for the clients, which could be disempowering. On the other hand, counselors do have an obligation to assist clients in making decisions about whether to take action, and what action to take, if they are struggling with value conflicts or if they believe their legal rights have been violated, just as counselors would help clients make other types of important decisions in their lives.

Many clients who believe they have been victims of illegal discrimination also have other concerns arising from their membership in stigmatized cultural groups. To illustrate, let us return to the case of Arthur, Horst's client in the scenario previously presented. Assume that Arthur discloses to Horst that he had several one-time sexual encounters with men before he met Mark. He recently has been tested and has been diagnosed HIV positive. In addition, he is outraged that he has been passed over at work for promotion to department chair, a position he believes he deserves but was denied because of the rumors about his relationship with Mark.

When clients express concern that they may have been illegally discriminated against, counselors should first help the clients decide whether they want to take any kind of action. In Arthur's case, if he decides he wants to try to assert his legal rights, Horst can refer him to an advocacy group for advocacy guidance or to an attorney for legal advice. Advocacy groups or attorneys can determine whether clients like Arthur may have been a victim of illegal discrimination and, if so, can tell them what options exist to address the wrong. Arthur may want to discuss these options with his counselor after speaking with an advocacy group representative or an attorney. Counselors can be very helpful in assisting clients to consider their options and the possible consequences, both positive and negative, regarding these options. It is important that counselors stay within their bounds in these situations and that they not render legal advice or promote their own political or moral agendas through the client.

In addition to helping Arthur think through his options for dealing with what he sees as discrimination at work, Horst can assist him with issues of disclosure, health care, sexual behavior, and family decisions. He may be faced with several ethical dilemmas in the process. What if Arthur refuses to disclose his HIV status to his wife? What if he wants to postpone disclosing his status to Mark until they have formed a more stable relationship? What if he decides he is so upset by being denied a promotion that he wants to quit his job? What would be the consequences if he were to lose health care coverage? What if he refuses to seek medical care? What if he decides to end his relationship with Mark rather than risk exposing Mark to HIV? With disclosure comes the risk that he could become estranged from his family and from Mark. Feeling isolated and alone, and facing the prospect of medical treatment that carries many side effects and of possibly developing AIDS, Arthur might become suicidal. Horst needs to be prepared to deal with all these potential challenges in his work with Arthur.

GAY AND LESBIAN CLIENTS AND FAMILY LAW ISSUES

Counselors should be aware of a number of family law issues in contemporary society that may be affecting their gay and lesbian clients. Counselors clearly should not provide legal advice to their clients; rather, counselors should refer their clients to attorneys or legal advocacy groups if clients need assistance.

The law regarding same-sex marriages in the United States is rapidly changing (National Conference of State Legislatures, 2015). The U.S. Supreme Court will hear four same-sex marriage cases in 2015. A total of 36 states currently allow same-sex marriages either through state legislatures passing laws recognizing same-sex marriage or through courts striking down laws disallowing same-sex marriage. It is likely that by the end of 2015, the U.S. Supreme Court will decide whether it is constitutional for states to prohibit same-sex marriage and whether states may refuse to recognize same-sex marriages that were performed out of state. On the federal level, the Defense of Marriage Act (DOMA, 1996, 1 U.S.C. § 7), a statute passed in 1996 that explicitly defined marriage in federal law as a union of one man and one woman, has been held to be unconstitutional in two federal district courts (Gerstein, 2012; Lat, 2010). In the United States today, same-sex couples can be legally married in some states, but their marriage may not be recognized as legal in other states. In the past, gay or lesbian parents of children were automatically denied custody of their children during divorce proceedings (Wilcoxon, Remley, & Gladding, 2013). In contemporary courts, however, judges seem more inclined to require evidence that a parent's gay or lesbian status is likely to harm a child before denying the parent custody or visitation rights.

CULTURAL ISSUES IN CRISIS COUNSELING

Managing a crisis is important to counselors from a legal perspective. Because they may be liable for harm that comes to their clients if a crisis situation is not managed properly, counselors must understand and react well in crises.

Counselors who assess and manage crisis situations must be sensitive to cultural differences in their work. In discussing models of assessing crisis situations, Irish (1993) and Myer (2001) have cautioned that individuals from various cultures react differently to crisis events. According to Sue and Sue (2013), nonverbal behavior such as hand gestures and eye contact probably are influenced by culture. As a result, Myer has suggested that crisis counselors distinguish physiological responses from gestures. Myer also has recommended that counselors avoid stereotypical conclusions regarding nonverbal behaviors such as sitting on one's hands (which could mean the person is cold rather than wants to hide his or her feelings) or lack of eye contact (which could mean the individual is showing respect for the other person rather than showing a sign of sadness).

Crisis counselors often assess an individual's time orientation to determine whether a client is focused on the past and a loss, the present and a transgression, or the future and a threat (Myer, 2001). According to Sue and Sue (2013), Asian Americans are primarily oriented to the past or present, with little attention paid to the future, and crisis events are likely to be interpreted from a past or present perspective. Native Americans tend to be present oriented and experience crises in that way.

Myer (2001) has recommended that crisis counselors avoid imposing their values on individuals they counsel in crisis situations. For example, Southeast Asian immigrants may be reluctant to seek assistance from the police when they are victims of crimes because of police oppression in their countries, and gay or lesbian victims of domestic violence may refuse to seek help because of fear of ridicule. What may seem to crisis counselors like self-defeating reactions could have foundations that are culturally appropriate.

Goldman and Beardslee (1999) maintained that some cultural factors increase the risk of suicidal behaviors of children and adolescents. For example, high rates of suicide have been reported in Micronesians and in Native Americans, and both groups have experienced dramatic shifts in their cultures. On the other hand, Berlin (1987) found that Native American tribes with traditional structures have very low adolescent suicide rates. Jilek-Aall (1988) concluded that countries that have highly competitive and goal-directed populations (such as the United States, Japan, and Sweden) have high rates of suicide among children, whereas countries that have less competitive citizens (such as Norway) have lower suicide rates.

Cultural differences were discovered by Nock and Marzuk (1999) when they investigated murder–suicides. Rage associated with suicide (which sometimes results in murder before suicide) has been given names in various cultures. In Malaysia, it is known as *amok*; in Cree Indian tribes, *wihtiko psychosis*; in Canada, *jumping Frenchman*; and in Japan, *imu*. Counselors, when assessing crisis situations as serious as suicide or murder, must understand that cultural differences can influence behaviors.

Summary and Key Points

This chapter addresses vitally important ethical and legal issues in counseling related to multicultural counseling, social justice, and advocacy. The following are key points:

- The counseling profession has evolved over the years, from a lack of awareness of cultural differences, to a commitment to multiculturally competent practice, to an emphasis on social justice and advocacy aimed at improving the lives of all people in our society and across the globe.

- Goals of ethical multicultural practice include counselors becoming culturally aware of their own biases, values, and assumptions; gaining knowledge about other cultural groups; and developing culturally appropriate advocacy skills and intervention strategies for assisting diverse clientele.

- Counselors are ethically obligated to understand and advocate to eliminate racism, sexism, classism, homoprejudice, ableism, ageism, and religious bias.

- All people have multiple cultural identities and belong to cultural groups that are dominant and cultural groups that are peripheralized in U.S. society.
- The basic ethical principles of respect for autonomy, nonmaleficence, beneficence, and justice must be interpreted differently, depending on the context in which they are being applied, both in the United States and abroad.
- Although the ACA *Code of Ethics* contains a number of standards that specifically address cultural diversity, counselors are advised to view all of the standards as being multicultural in spirit and intent.
- The U.S. Constitution and various statutes prohibit discrimination. When counselors work with clients who believe they have suffered illegal discrimination, counselors can assist these clients to consider their options and the possible consequences of those options.
- Counselors need to be aware of family law issues that affect LGBT clients.
- Crisis counselors must be sensitive to cultural differences in the ways that clients respond to crises.

CHAPTER 4

Client Rights and Counselor Responsibilities

FOCUS QUESTIONS

1. What are some steps that counselors should take to safeguard the welfare of their clients?

2. Do you believe a counselor should be allowed to refuse to provide counseling services to a client when the client's beliefs or behaviors conflict with the personal value system of the counselor?

3. What kinds of information do you think clients need in order to be able to give their fully informed consent to enter into a counseling relationship?

4. Under what circumstances do you think it would be acceptable to terminate counseling services to a client?

Trust is the cornerstone on which the counseling relationship is built (American Counseling Association, 2014, *Code of Ethics*, Introduction). If clients are to make progress in achieving their goals in counseling, they need to feel safe in the relationship and to trust that the counselor is committed to safeguarding their welfare and respecting their rights. In your work as a counselor, it is fundamental that you put client welfare first and foremost. The counseling profession attaches such importance to this principle that it is the very first ethical standard in the *Code of Ethics* of the American Counseling Association (ACA, 2014). Standard A.1.a. states that the "primary responsibility of counselors is to respect the dignity and to promote the welfare of clients." There are very few exceptions to this principle, and exceptions occur only in rare circumstances when the good of others in society outweighs what might appear to be best for a particular client.

Counselors have what is known in law as *fiduciary relationships* with their clients. An individual who is a fiduciary has a position of trust and confidence (Ludes & Gilbert, 1998). Clients rely on their counselor fiduciaries to act only in their best interests. The duties of fiduciaries are so strong that any transaction between a fiduciary and the recipient of services is presumed to be fraudulent and void if the fiduciary benefits from it. Transactions that benefit a fiduciary (or counselor) will be upheld in court only when the counselor can present clear and convincing proof that the transaction was legitimate (Ludes & Gilbert, 1998). Because of the law related to fiduciaries, counselors have a significant legal burden to protect the best interests of their clients and to avoid any interactions or transactions with clients that benefit the counselors themselves at the client's expense.

COUNSELOR RESPONSIBILITIES

Counselors have a number of responsibilities related to safeguarding client welfare. These responsibilities begin when a counseling relationship is entered and extend through termination of the relationship. Counselors must remain aware of their own needs and motivations when they are working with clients. They also must be aware of and able to *bracket* or set aside their personal values. In addition, ethical practice entails being able to avoid fostering dependent relationships, use appropriate counseling techniques, and manage any interruptions that might occur in the counseling process. Services must be terminated in an appropriate manner, without abandoning clients who need continued services. Mandated or involuntary clients have certain rights that counselors need to safeguard as well.

Counselor Needs and Motivations

It is vitally important for counselors to be aware of their own needs and motivations in order to maintain a fiduciary relationship that keeps client welfare foremost. Without this self-awareness, counselors run the risk of meeting their own needs at the expense of the client. See if you can discern how this may be occurring in the following case.

4-1 The Case of Lynn

Lynn has been counseling Elaine, a 30-year-old client. During this session, Elaine states that she wishes she could just walk away from her marriage, but she can't do it because it would traumatize the children. Lynn, herself a child of divorce whose father abandoned the family, further explores Elaine's fears for the children. At one point Lynn says to her client, "Well, yes, the statistics do show that a lot of kids lose touch with their fathers after a divorce. It would be really hard for them if that happened. It could even have repercussions well into their adult years."

- What do you think motivated Lynn to respond the way she did?
- Do you see any problem with Lynn's response?

Discussion: It appears that the counselor, Lynn, is interjecting her own feelings about paternal abandonment into the session. Lynn is focusing on her own feelings rather than trying to help Elaine clarify her own feelings about the issue. By focusing on the client's children rather than the client herself, Lynn is discounting the client's feelings and imposing her own values about the effects of divorce on children onto the client.

This case example illustrates that, if counselors lack self-awareness of their *unfinished business*, areas of vulnerability, and defenses, there is a risk that they will inadvertently be working on their own issues in the counseling relationship rather than the client's issues. As Corey, Corey, Corey, and Callanan (2015) have noted, counselors who are unaware of their own issues are in a poor position to recognize the ways in which their personal lives are influencing their interactions with clients. This is particularly true when the client's problems or issues are similar to the unresolved issues of the counselor.

We are not suggesting that counselors do not have their own needs or that it is unethical to get some of these needs met by choosing counseling as a profession. In fact, most counselors would probably say that they get a real sense of satisfaction or fulfillment from their work and from knowing that they have made a difference in the lives of others. Still, it is important for you to explore your own answers to the questions "What motivates me to choose the counseling profession?" and "What do I get out of being a counselor?" and "What needs of mine am I getting met?" Knowing your own needs will help you identify potential areas of vulnerability and sources of therapeutic error.

For example, if you have a strong need to nurture others, you may be tempted to encourage client dependency. If you have a strong need to be liked and appreciated, you may avoid confronting your clients. If you have a strong need to feel useful or prove your competence, you may want to rush in and give answers or advice. If you can recognize your potential areas of vulnerability, you will be better able to keep the best interests of your clients foremost and less likely to allow your needs to intrude into your work with clients. You will be better able to avoid actions that meet your personal needs at the expense of your clients.

When counselors project their emotions onto a client and the counselors' own needs become entangled in the therapeutic relationship, this phenomenon is sometimes referred to as *countertransference* (Safran & Kriss, 2014). Countertransference can benefit a counseling relationship if counselors are aware of and can monitor their internal reactions to a client and how those reactions are influencing the counseling process (Corey et al., 2015), but countertransference becomes problematic when counselors lack self-awareness and lose their objectivity. What is important to remember is that sound ethical practice requires counselors to pay attention to their emotional reactions to clients and seek consultation or supervision when these emotional reactions are interfering with the work that is occurring in the counseling relationship.

It is important for you to keep in mind that professionals, by the nature of the relationship, have power over their clients (Haug, 1999). Because professionals possess knowledge and skills beyond those of the ordinary citizen, our society extends privileges to professionals. Individuals who seek services from professionals must trust those professionals to practice in a manner that is helpful, and not harmful, to them. Thus, clients may not know whether counselors are treating them in a way that benefits them or are taking advantage of them or their lack of knowledge of how the counseling process is supposed to proceed. Counselors could use the power they have in professional counseling relationships to meet their own personal needs rather than the needs of the client. As a member of the counseling profession, you have an ethical obligation to avoid misusing your power and to keep the needs of your clients foremost in the therapeutic relationship.

Counselors' Personal and Professional Values

Because ethical issues related to counselors' personal and professional values have generated a great deal of discussion in recent years, we discuss these issues in some detail here. The primary ethical standard related to counselor values is §A.4.b. of the ACA *Code of Ethics* (ACA, 2014), which requires that counselors be aware of—and avoid imposing—their own values, attitudes, beliefs, and behaviors on clients. Although this ethical obligation is easy to state, it can be extremely difficult to uphold in practice. A counselor's values will influence the counseling process in many ways (Levitt & Moorhead, 2013), including which goals are considered appropriate or desirable in counseling, whether and how the client will be diagnosed, and which client issues will become the focus of therapy. Even the theory from which the counselor operates can influence the counseling process in value-laden ways. Certain theories promote specific values. For instance, the Adlerian approach emphasizes the development of social interest as a benchmark of mental health, whereas the existential approach emphasizes individual freedom and responsibility. The influence of counselor values on the counseling process can be very subtle, and counselors can communicate their values in many indirect ways: through nonverbal responses, by focusing on some elements of a client's story while not responding to others, and through the interventions they select (Francis & Dugger, 2014). Counselor values can significantly affect counseling outcomes. Research has shown that the degree of congruence between the values of the counselor and those of the client can influence therapeutic outcomes and that clients tend to change in ways that are consistent with the values of their counselors.

Both the client and the counselor enter counseling relationships with their own sets of values that they have acquired through years of experience and exposure. Value conflicts may never become a problem in counseling when the value systems of the client and counselor are similar or compatible. When the value systems of the counselor and clients differ, however, particularly around emotionally charged issues, these differences can become problematic (Barrett & McWhirter, 2002; Kiselica & Robinson, 2001; Millner & Hanks, 2002). Value-laden issues can create problems if counselors have not clarified how their own beliefs might affect their therapeutic work with clients who present with these issues. Just some of the issues that might cause problems include abortion, end-of-life decision making, beliefs and behaviors of members of cults or gangs, child or elder abuse, genetic engineering, extramarital sex, and sexual orientation. Values conflicts between the beliefs and behaviors of certain clients and the personal values of their counselors have been at the heart of a series of recent court cases that have generated a great deal of controversy.

COUNSELORS AND COURT CASES   At issue in at least four lawsuits has been the question of whether counselors can use their religious beliefs as the basis for refusing to counsel LGBT clients. In two court cases, counseling practitioners were terminated from their employment, and in two other cases counseling students were dismissed from their training programs after they refused to counsel LGBT clients regarding same-sex relationships.

In *Bruff v. North Mississippi Health Services, Inc.* (2001), a client asked her employee assistance program (EAP) counselor (Bruff) for help with improving her relationship with her same-sex partner. Bruff explained that *homosexual behavior* was against her religious beliefs and offered to refer the client to another counselor. Although the client accepted the referral, she did not return for counseling and eventually filed a complaint with Bruff's employer. The employer tried to accommodate Bruff's religious beliefs but determined that it would place too great a burden on Bruff's fellow counselors if Bruff were allowed to refer all clients whose issues presented a conflict with her religious values. Bruff was placed on leave without pay and was terminated from employment after she refused opportunities to transfer to other positions within the company. Bruff filed suit against her former employer. One of her claims was that her employer had violated her right to freedom from religious discrimination under Title VII of the Civil Rights Act of 1964. Eventually, the Fifth Circuit Court of Appeals ruled against Bruff. The court determined that, although employers do have a legal obligation to make reasonable accommodations for religious beliefs, Bruff's *inflexible* position caused undue hardship to her fellow EAP counselors.

A second legal case, *Walden v. Centers for Disease Control and Prevention* (2010), presented issues very similar to those in *Bruff*. In this second case, an employee of the Centers for Disease Control and Prevention (CDC) sought same-sex relationship counseling from Walden, an EAP counselor. Walden told the client that same-sex relationships conflicted with her religious values and referred the client to another counselor. The client later brought suit, stating that she had felt judged and condemned even though the referral had been satisfactory. Walden's employer tried to accommodate her religious beliefs by asking her to refer future clients without telling them about her religious objections or personal values. When Walden refused, she was laid off and was later terminated after she did not avail herself of opportunities to apply for other positions within the CDC. Like Bruff, Walden filed suit, and the court ruled against Walden due to her rigid position regarding referrals.

Both the Bruff and Walden rulings were based primarily on issues of employment law rather than on the ethical issues related to refusing to counsel LGBT clients regarding their same-sex relationships. Ethical issues related to values conflicts have played a more prominent role in the cases of two counseling students who were dismissed from counselor education programs at Eastern Michigan University and Augusta State University (now Georgia Regents University) in Georgia after they refused to counsel LGBT clients because same-sex affectional relationships were not acceptable to their religious beliefs. Both students sued their universities. The students claimed that the counseling graduate programs violated their constitutional right to express their religious beliefs.

In *Ward v. Wilbanks* (2010), Julea Ward, a master's degree student in the counseling program at Eastern Michigan University (EMU), was dismissed from the program in 2009 after she refused to counsel an LGBT client. Ward was enrolled in her practicum course when she learned that a clinic client she had been assigned to counsel had previously sought counseling for same-sex relationship issues. Ward told her faculty supervisor that she would not be able to counsel this client effectively due to conflicts with her religious beliefs. The supervisor reassigned the client. Later, the faculty held an informal review meeting with Ward to express their concern that Ward was not complying with the counseling program's policies or the ACA *Code of Ethics*, which prohibits discrimination based on sexual orientation (ACA, 2014). The faculty offered Ward the choices of completing a remediation plan, leaving the program, or requesting a formal hearing. After a formal review, Ward was dismissed from the graduate program.

Ward then brought suit against EMU, with the backing of the Alliance Defending Freedom (formerly the Alliance Defense Fund). The U.S. District Court for the Eastern District of Michigan granted a motion made by the university for summary judgment (*Ward v. Wilbanks*, 2010), which means that the judges on the court found that the student did not have a foundation for her lawsuit based on the pleadings that had been filed by both sides (the claim of discrimination by the student plaintiff and the response by the university). A higher court (U.S. 6th District Court of Appeals) overturned the lower court's summary judgment decision (*Ward v. Wilbanks*, 2012) and remanded the case back to the district court for a jury trial. The suit was settled out of court. According to Rudow (2013), the resolution upheld EMU's program policies and confirmed the right of the program to use the ACA (2014) *Code of Ethics* as the guide for defining ethical behavior.

According to *Keeton v. Augusta State University* (2011), Jennifer Keeton was asked by faculty at Augusta State University (ASU) in Georgia to complete a remediation plan after completing her first year of the master's-degree program in counseling. In classes, Keeton had often expressed her condemnation of homosexuality based on her religious beliefs, and the faculty was concerned that she "might not be able to separate her religious views on sexual morality from her professional counseling responsibilities" (*Keeton v. Augusta State University,* 2011, p. 4). When Keeton failed to complete the remediation plan, she was dismissed from the master's-degree program. She brought suit against the faculty and the university, claiming that her rights to freedom from religious discrimination had been violated. The student also asked for a preliminary injunction to prevent ASU officials from dismissing her from the program if she did not complete the remediation plan. The federal district court denied the student's motion for a preliminary injunction, and the student appealed the decision. The U.S. Court of Appeals upheld the lower court's denial of the preliminary injunction.

The particular circumstances surrounding this case are included in the court's written decision.

The Court of Appeals concluded that "the evidence in this record does not support Keeton's claim that ASU's officials imposed the remediation plan because of her views on homosexuality. Rather, as the district court found, the evidence shows that the remediation plan was imposed because she expressed an intent to impose her personal religious views on her clients, in violation of the ACA *Code of Ethics*, and that the objective of the remediation plan was to teach her how to effectively counsel LGBTQIQ clients in accordance with the ACA Code of Ethics" (*Keeton v. Anderson-Wiley, et al.,* 2011, p. 17). The court found that ASU officials did not tell the student that she had to change her religious beliefs, as she had claimed, but instead had required her to separate those beliefs from her work in counseling clients. Keeton's motion for a preliminary injunction to keep the university from dismissing was denied, and her lawsuit against the university claiming that her rights were violated was dismissed by a federal judge in a U.S. District Court in June 2012.

The issues raised by the students in these two lawsuits have not been confined to the courts; they have been introduced into the legislative arena as well. A law has been enacted in Arizona that prohibits a state university from discriminating against or disciplining a student in a counseling or related mental health program because the student "refuses to counsel a client about goals that conflict with the student's sincerely held religious beliefs" (AZ Rev Stat §15-1862, 2011). Similar bills have been introduced in other states, including Michigan, but none have been enacted into law as of December 2014.

END-OF-LIFE DECISION MAKING   Another value-laden issue that merits discussion is end-of-life decision making. A controversial issue in today's society is whether people who are terminally ill, have an incurable condition, or are in intolerable pain have the right to choose the time and means of their own deaths (Herlihy & Watson, 2004). As more members of U.S. society live to an advanced age and as life-sustaining medical technologies continue to advance, it is likely that counselors will be called on more frequently to counsel clients who are considering hastening their own deaths (Manis & Bodenhorn, 2006). In recognition of this growing need, ACA signed on to an amicus brief submitted to the U.S. Supreme Court in 1997 in support of the role of mental health professionals in assisting individuals with their end-of-life decision making.

In the previous ACA *Code of Ethics* (ACA, 2005), §A.9, acknowledged that not every counselor will feel comfortable or competent to work with terminally ill clients who wish to explore their end-of-life options. This standard, which allowed counselors to refer a terminally ill client who wished to explore end-of-life options, based on the counselor's personal values and beliefs around the issue (Martz & Kaplan, 2014), does not appear in the current *Code* (ACA, 2014). Counselors are expected to be competent to work with clients across the entire developmental spectrum, which includes clients who are nearing the end of their lives (Bevacqua & Kurpius, 2013).

Before you work with terminally ill clients, you will need to answer a number of questions for yourself. Under what circumstances do you think hastening one's own death is an acceptable option to explore? When a person is terminally ill and death is imminent? When the illness is fatal but the person could live for several more years if he or she undergoes multiple, painful surgeries or must take potent medications with severe side effects? When a condition is not terminal but has left a person in constant, intolerable pain? When a terminally ill person wants to hasten his death to avoid being a burden to his family? When the person already has lived well into her 90s? What if the individual is only 30 years old? When you work with clients who want to consider end-of-life options, it is essential that you do not impose your own values, even inadvertently, about such issues as living and dying, quality of life, or religion or spirituality. An excellent resource for learning more about issues surrounding end-of-life decisions is a book entitled *Counseling Clients Near the End of Life: A Practical Guide for Mental Health Professionals* (Werth, 2013).

RESOLVING VALUE CONFLICTS   As noted, the most basic standard related to values is §A.4.b. of the ACA *Code of Ethics*, which states that "counselors are aware—and avoid imposing—their own values, attitudes, beliefs, and behaviors" (ACA, 2014). To strengthen the foundation for this standard and others that deal with values, referrals, competence, and discrimination, the Preamble was revised in the 2014 *Code* to spell out the professional values of enhancing human development, honoring diversity, promoting social justice, safeguarding the integrity of the counseling relationship, and practicing with competence and ethical diligence (Francis, 2015). In previous versions of the code, it was not clear that referrals must be based on lack of competence rather than value conflicts (Herlihy & Corey, 2105a). A new standard (§A.11.b.) prohibits making referrals "based solely on the counselor's personally held values, attitudes, beliefs, and behaviors" and requires counselors to "seek training in areas in which they are at risk of imposing their values onto clients, especially when the counselor's values are inconsistent with the client's goals or are discriminatory in nature." The definition of competence has been strengthened to clarify that "counselors must develop multicultural competency in working with a diverse client population" (§C.2.a.).

If you are a student in a counseling program, you may be wondering what these new standards, as well as the outcomes of the court cases that involved counseling students, portend for you as you progress through your program of studies. We believe that it is crucial that you reflect on how you will manage the value conflicts that inevitably will arise between you and your future clients. For example, if you are a strong feminist you might find it difficult to counsel a client whose religious beliefs dictate subservience to her husband. You will need to keep in mind that it is not your job to convert the client to feminism but, rather, to assist this client in finding her own way. It is essential that you learn to *bracket* or set aside your values while engaged in a counseling relationship, so that you promote the welfare of the client and avoid imposing your own values. If, during your training experiences you find it difficult to work with certain clients whose behavior conflicts with your personal or religious values, you will need to be open to acquiring the knowledge and learning the skills necessary to assist these clients as well as future clients who may present with the same or similar issues. A special section in the April 2014 issue of the *Journal of Counseling & Development* was devoted to professionalism, ethics, and values-based conflicts in counseling and is an excellent resource for learning more about these issues.

DIVERSITY CONSIDERATIONS   Values and value conflicts in the counseling relationship often can be understood within the context of differing world views, or ways that people see the world. An individual's world view is influenced by culture and is the source of that person's values, beliefs, opinions, and assumptions (Pedersen et al., 2002). World views affect how people think, make decisions, act, and interpret events (Sue & Sue, 2013). Values of cultures vary in how they relate to nature, time, social relations, activity, and collectivism versus individualism, among other dimensions (Hopkins, 1997). When a counselor and a client are from different cultural backgrounds, they may hold differing world views, which can lead to misinterpretations, misunderstandings, and conflicts (Chung & Bemak, 2002). This mismatching can, in turn, lead to clients dropping out of counseling or terminating prematurely (Sue, Fujino, Takeuchi, Hu, & Zane, 1991).

4-2 The Case of Brian

Brian is a counselor who works in an urban community agency. The agency provides reduced-fee services to some clients who cannot pay the standard fee. Three months ago, Brian began counseling with Kimberly, a 28-year-old single mother. Kimberly works as a maid in a local hotel and receives Aid to Families with Dependent Children (AFDC). During the weekly staffing conducted by the agency counselors, Brian presents the case of Kimberly and states that she often calls to cancel her appointments at the last minute and sometimes simply fails to show up, and when she does keep her appointments, she usually arrives late. When Kimberly attends sessions, she talks at length about the problems she encounters in daily living but self-discloses very little. Brian questions whether she has a sincere commitment to counseling.

- What might be some possible explanations for Kimberly's behavior?
- What do you think of Brian's questioning the sincerity of Kimberly's commitment to counseling?

Discussion: If Brian had considered Kimberly's life circumstances in attempting to understand his client, he might have given a different explanation of her behavior. Had Brian explored with Kimberly the context of her daily life, he might have learned that she gets to the counseling agency by bus, transferring twice. Brian might have discovered that she relies on various family members to babysit for her when she comes for counseling. When the buses don't run on time or when family members fail to keep their promise to babysit, Kimberly is late for appointments or is unable to come at all.

Kimberly may be focusing on her problems in daily living because she expects the counselor to help her solve these problems rather than disclose her feelings. Brian may be blaming the client for his inability to establish a therapeutic alliance with her.

A growing body of literature suggests that counselors must develop *cultural empathy* in order to be effective in counseling clients who hold world views and come from cultures different from their own (Chung & Bemak, 2002; Pedersen et al., 2002; Ridley, 1995; Ridley & Lingle, 1996). Acquiring cultural empathy requires counselors not only to have fundamental empathy skills but also to learn advanced skills that will enable them to decode cultural messages (Chung & Bemak, 2002). Some of these skills or strategies include the following:

- Expressing lack of knowledge or awareness of some aspects of the client's cultural experience
- Communicating an interest in learning more about the client's culture
- Conveying a genuine appreciation for cultural differences
- Acquiring knowledge about the historical and sociopolitical background of the client's culture

- Being sensitive to the oppression, marginalization, and discrimination that clients may encounter on a daily basis
- Clarifying language and other modes of communication
- Incorporating culturally appropriate strategies and treatment goals into the counseling process

Avoiding Dependent Relationships

Counselors must avoid fostering dependent counseling relationships with clients. Clients have a right to expect that the counseling process will help them move toward increased independence. In counseling, clients learn new skills for living, including an increased ability to make decisions without the counselor's help.

We have mentioned the possibility that some counselors might encourage client dependency on them. This could happen to you in a number of ways if you are not alert to the potential problem. During your internship, you must complete a certain number of contact hours with clients, and you might be tempted to keep some clients in counseling longer than necessary in order to fulfill your requirement. You also might do so in hopes of demonstrating to your supervisors that your clients keep coming because you are so helpful to them. After you graduate and are in practice, temptations to foster dependency might arise out of a need to feel needed, a need to nurture others, a need to feel that you are important or indispensable to your clients, or even a need for income from client fees if you are in private practice.

Sometimes it is not the counselor's needs but rather the client's needs that work to foster a dependent relationship. Some clients may attempt to maintain or even increase their dependency on the counselor. They may request more frequent sessions, have a new crisis every time the counselor suggests that they may be nearing the end of their work together, or engage in other strategies to avoid progress toward independent functioning. For these clients, remaining dependent on the counselor is less risky than learning to live autonomously. Counselors must find ways to balance ongoing support for them while encouraging independence and risk taking.

The dramatic increase in the number of clients who participate in managed care health plans has had an impact on this issue. Managed care plans limit clients to a certain number of sessions and require counselors to justify any requests for additional sessions. Thus, it is much more difficult for counselors to unnecessarily prolong a counseling relationship. Nonetheless, counselors are obligated to work toward helping clients reach a place where they no longer need counseling and should be motivated by an internalized sense of responsibility to promote client welfare.

DIVERSITY CONSIDERATIONS   As we noted in the previous chapter, when counselors work to uphold their ethical obligations to avoid fostering dependency and to promote client independence and autonomy, they sometimes misapply the principle of autonomy. Counselors need to keep in mind that autonomy is a highly individualistic concept (Meara, Schmidt, & Day, 1996) and that the counseling goal of achieving individual independence or autonomy may not be appropriate for clients whose choices are made in the context of family, group, or community (Herlihy & Watson, 2003). For example, Yamamoto and Chang (1987) suggested that, in counseling Asian Americans, counselors could incorporate knowledge of the family-oriented Asian culture by acknowledging and communicating cultural empathy toward the client's family and by including the family in treatment. At the same time, counselors must not lose sight of the fact that there are within-group differences and that each client is unique. Cultural misunderstandings often occur because counselors indiscriminately apply textbook norms regarding racial and ethnic groups and fail to maintain their stance as learners (Ridley, 1995). Counselors working globally need to remember that many cultures in the world are collectivistic rather than individualistic in nature. In these contexts, a counseling goal of promoting a client's individual autonomy would be culturally inappropriate and would likely even be harmful.

Involuntary or Mandated Clients

Special ethical considerations exist when counselors are assigned to work with reluctant clients (Borsari & Tevyaw, 2005; Kiracofe & Wells, 2007). In some situations, clients may attend counseling sessions because someone else has pushed them in that direction, even though they are not convinced that counseling is a good idea for them. In other, more serious circumstances, clients may have been ordered to attend counseling or suffer negative consequences. Sometimes judges require individuals to attend counseling or go to jail. School principals may require students to attend counseling or face expulsion from school or other disciplinary action. There is nothing unethical about accepting clients in such circumstances.

The term *involuntary client* probably is not the best pairing of words. A client who chooses to enter into counseling rather than accept an alternative or an unwanted consequence is, in fact, making a choice. Mandated counseling situations might appear to conflict with the ACA *Code of Ethics*, which states that mandated clients may refuse services (ACA, 2014, §A.2.a.). However, mandated clients do choose counseling over other options (such as jail or school expulsion), even though the choice may be made reluctantly. When clients refuse counseling services, counselors are ethically obligated to explain, to the best of their ability, the potential consequences of such refusal (§A.2.a.).

Involuntary clients usually are required to sign a waiver of their privacy rights when they begin a counseling relationship. Because they are being required to participate in counseling and would suffer some type of negative consequences if they refuse, the person or entity requiring the counseling also requires some type of report regarding their participation in the counseling process.

The legal issue involved in these situations is to ensure that involuntary clients know that reports must be made and understand the types of information that will be included in the reports. The privacy waiver form that involuntary clients sign should contain as much specific information as possible. Because different individuals and entities require that various types of information be reported, the form should allow for detailed information to be added. A model agreement form for involuntary clients that includes a waiver of privacy is included in Appendix B.

An ACA *Code of Ethics* provision (ACA, 2014, §C.6.b.) that applies to counseling involuntary or mandated clients states that counselors are accurate, honest, and objective in reporting their professional activities and judgments to third parties, including courts or those who receive evaluation reports. We believe that counseling and evaluation are two separate processes and that counselors who counsel individuals should refuse to evaluate those same clients. Reporting on counseling attendance and progress toward reaching counseling goals set by clients is different from evaluating clients for issues such as fitness for parenting, ability to work after an injury, or a mental condition.

Sometimes counselors do perform such evaluations, but counselors who evaluate individuals must be unbiased. If they have counseled a client in the past, they are biased and should not agree to evaluate that same person. If a counselor is evaluating a client, the counselor must make clear to the client that the purpose of their meetings is to gather information for an evaluation, not to provide counseling services. Further, clients must understand that there is no confidentiality in such situations and that their counselors will report their findings to a third party. See Chapter 7 regarding the requirements of counselors who serve as evaluators.

The ACA *Code of Ethics* addresses role changes in the professional relationship. When counselors change from an evaluative role to a therapeutic role, or vice versa, they must obtain the client's informed consent for the change and explain the client's right to refuse services related to the change (ACA, 2014, §A.6.d.). Counselors must be particularly sensitive to the rights of reluctant, involuntary, or mandated clients. It is essential that counselors fully disclose to such clients any privacy rights that clients are waiving as they enter into such arrangements. For example, if a judge who orders an individual to counseling requires periodic reports to a court official (such as a probation officer) on the person's attendance and progress toward counseling goals, counselors must obtain written permission from the client for such reports and must ensure that the client has a full understanding of the types of reports that will be made. Granello and Hanna (2003) have suggested that counselors who provide services to individuals involved with the criminal legal system must develop a good understanding of the system in order to serve their clients well.

Because mandated clients may feel coerced into counseling, they may lack motivation to change. Counselors must self-monitor to ensure that they do not develop a cynicism in their work with these clients. If both the client and the counselor are just *going through the motions* in their counseling sessions, little (if any) meaningful work will be accomplished. It is the counselor's responsibility to engage the client in the counseling process, and if that cannot be accomplished, to terminate the counseling relationship.

Counseling Techniques

Another consideration in promoting client welfare is the counselor's obligation to select appropriate counseling strategies or techniques. In recent years, the mental health professions have worked to develop guides for treatment planning that match client concerns with the strategies that research has demonstrated to be the most effective in treating those concerns. Lambert and Cattani-Thompson (1996) reviewed studies on counseling effectiveness and found that some specific techniques seemed to be more efficacious with certain symptoms and disorders. They cautioned, however, that successful client outcome is determined in large part by client characteristics such as motivation, locus of control, and severity and duration of symptoms. Hansen (2005, 2006) has expressed a concern that the movement in the counseling field in which a particular approach is required to treat a particular presenting problem takes away the essence of counseling in which human beings connect in a creative, meaningful, and therapeutic manner. Despite such cautions, the ACA *Code of Ethics* requires counselors to use techniques, procedures, and modalities that are grounded in theory and/or have an empirical or scientific foundation (ACA, 2014, §C.7.a.). Therefore, if you use any techniques that could be considered experimental or unusual, you should do so very cautiously (Ho, D'Agostine, Yadegar, Burke, & Bylund, 2012). The client should be informed of any potential risks and benefits and should consent to your use of such techniques. Before attempting them, you should be sure that you are adequately trained and have a sound clinical rationale for their use. Before employing an experimental or unusual counseling technique, think about how you would justify your procedures if a complaint were filed against you with a licensing board or in a court of law.

As a counselor, your selection of techniques will depend on a number of factors, including your theoretical orientation and your training. Corey et al. (2015) put it best when they advised that your strategies should fit your counseling style and be tailored to the specific needs of your client. Of course, counselors should not use techniques when research has indicated that those techniques may cause harm to a client. One example of such a technique is conversion/reparative therapy, which has been used with some LGBT clients (see Chapter 3 for a fuller discussion).

Counselors have an ethical responsibility to work jointly with clients to devise counseling plans that offer reasonable promise of success (ACA, 2014, §A.1.c.). As we have mentioned, managed care organizations typically limit the number of sessions for which a client will be reimbursed and require counselors to justify any requests for additional sessions. Counselors will be more successful in making such requests when they can present empirical support for their clinical judgments. Managed care organizations demand accountability from their providers, and counselors must be able to present data that demonstrate their efficacy (Glosoff, Garcia, Herlihy, & Remley, 1999).

DIVERSITY CONSIDERATIONS   Counselors who espouse traditional counseling theories and their associated techniques must be aware that these approaches have limited applicability in working with culturally diverse clients (Jencius & West, 2003).

Psychodynamically oriented counselors and ego psychologists who focus on their clients' early childhood relationships with their parents and on intrapsychic conflicts may overlook a client's historic experiences with discrimination and oppression. A psychodynamic therapist's strategy of remaining relatively anonymous in order to serve as a projection screen for the client's transferences could be a poor fit for clients from cultures that value cooperative relationships or for clients who expect the helper to take an active role.

Cognitive behavior therapists are more active in implementing strategies such as direct teaching of skills and assigning homework. However, some techniques, such as identifying cognitive distortions or irrational self-talk, fail to consider the language-bound nature of cognitions. Cognitive behavioral approaches, like psychodynamic approaches, may not incorporate variables such as race, ethnicity, class, gender, and culture that may be salient to the client's core identity.

Humanistic counselors, particularly those with a Rogerian orientation, offer clients acceptance, unconditional positive regard, and empathy, all of which may help to transcend cultural differences and establish a therapeutic alliance. However, these approaches may fail to consider that barriers to self-actualization may exist in the client's environment rather than within the self. In addition, the nondirective stance may not meet the needs of clients who might benefit from advocacy and assistance in navigating an oppressive culture.

Today's counselors must have repertoires of helping strategies that extend beyond those offered by traditional counseling theories (nearly all of which were created by and reflect the world views of Euro-American White males). It is particularly important for counselors, as they step into the international arena, to have training in a wide variety of counseling techniques, including those that originated in non-Western cultures, and to be competent in working in nontraditional roles.

Interruptions and Termination

Termination is an important stage in the therapeutic relationship that sometimes is given inadequate consideration. Termination is an intentional process that occurs over time when a client has achieved most of the treatment goals, and it provides opportunities for consolidating, making plans for maintaining, and generalizing client gains made in counseling. Effective terminations model how healthy relationships should end and provide clients with opportunities to work through their feelings about ending their therapeutic journeys.

In an ideal world, once a counselor has accepted a client and begins providing services, those services will continue on a regular basis until the client is able to function effectively without the ongoing assistance of the counselor. In reality, however, counselors must sometimes interrupt counseling services for a period of time, and counselors occasionally terminate counseling relationships before clients are prepared to discontinue counseling services. Sometimes, clients will terminate counseling prematurely, for various reasons. From both an ethical and a legal perspective, counselors must be careful to protect the best interests of clients when services have to be interrupted or are prematurely terminated.

INTERRUPTIONS IN SERVICES   There is truth in the wry observation of Pope and Vasquez (2010) that both counselors and clients tend to find comfort in the fantasy that the counselor is invulnerable. The reality is, however, that counselors fall seriously ill, have accidents, or are called away by family emergencies. Counselors must plan ahead for emergency absences by developing procedures to safeguard their clients' welfare. Anticipating that unexpected events might occur, counselors should have plans in place regarding who will notify the clients, who has access to client records, and how the transfer of clients to another counselor will be handled.

Counselors are no different from other workers in that they take vacations, go out of town to attend conferences, and do other things that cause interruptions in the weekly rhythm of the therapeutic relationship. Clients sometimes have strong and even puzzling reactions to their counselor's absence, so it is important that counselors give clients adequate notice and ensure that clients know whom to contact in a crisis or emergency. The ACA *Code of Ethics* requires counselors to make appropriate arrangements for the continuation of treatment during interruptions caused by vacations or illnesses and, when necessary, following termination (ACA, 2014, §A.12).

Counselors who counsel clients at risk for harm to self or others are well advised to arrange for those clients to also be under the care of other professionals who have accepted responsibility for the well-being of the clients. Counselors should work to ensure that all clients are able to tolerate counselor absences for reasonable periods of time.

TERMINATION   Proper termination of the counseling relationship conveys caring and helps to prevent harm, which are important ethical considerations (Vasquez, Bingham, & Barnett, 2008). Clients should be able to expect that their counseling sessions will end when they have received what they were seeking from counseling, or when they have realized the maximum benefit from the services. Counselors always anticipate termination as a phase or stage in the counseling relationship, and they provide pre-termination counseling or recommend other service providers when necessary (ACA, 2014, §A.11.c.). Counselors should raise and discuss the issue of termination with the client well in advance of the final session. This allows ample time to plan for the client's transition to functioning without the counselor and to deal with the natural and appropriate issues of separation and loss. It is best if the timing of the termination is mutually agreed on by the counselor and client. However, depending on the circumstances, the ultimate decision might be made independently by either the counselor or the client.

PREMATURE TERMINATION   Not all counseling relationships end smoothly by mutual agreement. In reality, circumstances can arise that allow the counselor to terminate the counseling relationship even against a client's wishes (Welfel, 2013). According to the ACA *Code of Ethics* (ACA, 2014, §A.11.c.), it is ethically permissible for counselors to terminate counseling relationships in the following circumstances:

- It is apparent that the client no longer needs assistance, is not likely to benefit, or is being harmed by continued counseling.
- Clients do not pay the fees as agreed upon.
- The counselor is in jeopardy of being harmed by the client or someone with whom the client has a relationship.

When counselors are unable to be of continued assistance to clients or decide to end the relationship over the client's objection, counselors must give adequate notice and give the client time to secure another mental health care provider (Hilliard, 1998). In addition, counselors should suggest an appropriate referral and do all they can to facilitate a smooth transition to the new mental health professional. If the client is unable to continue to pay the counselor's fee, an appropriate referral can be made to free services or to an agency that uses a sliding fee scale, if such alternatives are available. If a client refuses to accept the suggested referral, the counselor is not obligated to provide free services.

Many clients are able to afford counseling services only because they have managed health care plans that will reimburse for a significant portion of the cost. Under managed care plans, people are given only the services that the managed care company deems to be necessary and appropriate through a process known as *utilization review* (see Chapter 13 for a detailed discussion of health care plans). Counselors face difficult ethical challenges when further treatment is denied by utilization review panels. Counselors maintain clinical responsibility for the clients' welfare, and when clients need further counseling, counselors cannot allow financially motivated decisions to supersede their clinical judgment. Vasquez et al. (2008) have advised that counselors always appeal, or have their clients appeal, adverse utilization review decisions.

Sometimes it is the client who terminates the counseling relationship prematurely. In fact, research has indicated that 30% to 57% of all psychotherapy clients drop out prematurely (Garfield, 1994). Even when the counselor believes that a client is making progress and that treatment goals are being met, clients may call and cancel with or without giving an explanation, fail to keep appointments, or fail to reschedule. The counselor's ethical obligation in these situations is to attempt to communicate a willingness to continue to meet with the client, either to continue counseling or to summarize and end treatment, or to refer the client to another mental health professional. Vasquez et al. (2008) have offered sample letters that counselors can use when clients in need of continued counseling drop out, when clients making progress initiate termination, when counseling is being terminated due to lack of benefit to the client, and when counseling is being terminated due to a decision made by a managed care company.

Avoiding Abandonment

Abandonment can be considered a form of inappropriate termination and can occur when the client's counseling needs are not adequately addressed by the counselor, either when treatment ends or during the course of treatment due to counselor unavailability (Vasquez et al., 2008). Ethical guidelines in the ACA *Code of Ethics* (ACA, 2014, §A.12) and legal decisions related to physicians (*Allison v. Patel*, 1993; *Manno v. McIntosh*, 1994) prohibit counselors from abandoning their clients. Once a counseling relationship has been established, the counselor cannot arbitrarily end it if the client will be put at risk as a result.

As noted, advance planning can help avoid the risk that clients will feel abandoned by their counselors. Counselors should take care to give clients ample advance notice when planned interruptions are anticipated, such as the counselor taking maternity or paternity leave, undergoing a surgical procedure, or taking a vacation.

The key to ending a professional relationship with a client properly, and thus not being exposed to charges of abandonment, is to give the client adequate notice that you are ending the professional relationship and ample opportunity to locate a new counselor. It might be important, too, to discuss with the client how to locate agencies and individuals who offer counseling services. Giving notice of termination and time for the client to find a new counselor may not lead to the client taking the initiative to find a new counselor. If a client refuses to see another counselor after you have given notice that you are withdrawing your services, it will be essential for you to document carefully and fully the notice you gave, your assistance with the referral process, and the time you gave the client to locate a new professional.

Hilliard (1998), an attorney who represents mental health professionals who are sued by their clients, has observed the events that lead individuals to sue their mental health providers. As a practical consideration, Hilliard has recommended that mental health care providers never terminate a professional relationship over a client's objection when the client is angry or when the client is in a serious crisis situation. Taking the time to address a client's distress is very important to avoid unresolved angry feelings that could lead to a lawsuit. Also, a judge or jury probably would not support a mental health professional's decision to end a relationship in the midst of a crisis (*Allison v. Patel*, 1993; *Manno v. McIntosh*, 1994). Ending a counseling relationship because insurance benefits have run out, when the client is still at risk for suicide, is very risky (Packman & Harris, 1998) for both the client and the counselor.

Of course, counselors may always refer an at-risk client to a psychiatrist or health care facility that evaluates individuals for suicide or danger to themselves or others. This referral does not always lead to a transfer of that client to another professional or termination. In many circumstances, counselors continue to provide services to a referred client in collaboration with another mental health professional. When a referral of an at-risk client is made, however, it is very important that the counselor informs all parties whether the referral is a transfer of the client to another professional, or the counselor will be providing services in conjunction with another professional.

To protect mental health professionals from being held accountable for abandonment of their clients, Hilliard (1998) and Macbeth, Wheeler, Sither, and Onek (1994) developed the following guidelines for mental health professionals to use when they are terminating clients in adverse circumstances:

- Honestly discuss with the client your intention to terminate and the specific reason for your decision.
- Give the client an opportunity to make changes that would be necessary to continue the relationship.
- Give written notice to the client that the relationship will be terminated.
- Offer the client one to three termination sessions.
- Give your client up to three good referrals.
- Give your client places to contact in the event of emergencies.
- Place a summary of your interactions with the client related to the termination issue in the client's file. Do not transfer that document to another individual or entity without an express written request from the client.
- Give the client plenty of time to find another mental health professional. If more time is requested, allow it.
- Transfer records to the new mental health professional promptly.

DIVERSITY CONSIDERATIONS   As we have noted, clients sometimes drop out of counseling without discussing their intentions with the counselor. This can happen for many reasons—sometimes clients just need to *take a break* from the intense personal explorations involved in counseling, or they may drop out or discontinue the counseling relationship because they do not believe they are benefitting from counseling. Client self-termination will occur in any counselor's practice, and it may be helpful to remember that no counselor is skilled enough to be able to assist every client. There is some evidence to suggest that when counselors are ethically or linguistically different from their clients, clients are more likely to terminate prematurely (Maramba & Nagayama Hall, 2002). Thus, it is important that you self-monitor to discern whether the clients who are discontinuing counseling with you are those who are culturally different from you. If you see such a pattern, this is a signal that you must work to increase your cross-cultural counseling skills.

INFORMED CONSENT

As an ethical obligation, the rationale for informed consent is simple: clients have a right to know what they are getting into when they come for counseling. Most clients are not experts in counseling, so they must trust their counselors to provide them with the information they need to make a good decision (Handelsman, 2001). Providing clients with the opportunity to make an informed decision about entering into a counseling relationship demonstrates respect for a client's autonomy and self-determination and is integral to the formation of an effective therapeutic alliance. By communicating the client's role in making treatment decisions, informed consent can increase the client's sense of ownership over the process, establish that the counselor and client are partners working toward common goals, and reduce the client's anxiety by demystifying the counseling process (Fisher & Oransky, 2008; Margolin, Chien, & Duman, 2005).

Counselors believe that obtaining consent from clients before counseling begins constitutes best practice and is the proper and ethical way to proceed. In addition, certain concepts in law require that informed consent be obtained from clients before counseling relationships are initiated. Some state counseling licensing laws or regulations require that licensed counselors provide written documents to clients (e.g., La. Rev. Stat. Ann. 5 37:1101–1115). These written documents constitute informed consent (Madden, 1998). Counselors must provide prospective clients with information that will enable them to make wise choices. This includes deciding whether to enter into a counseling relationship and, if so, choosing the mental health professional who seems best suited to their needs and the type of counseling they will receive.

Marczyk and Wertheimer (2001) have noted that, in the past, it was difficult for mental health professionals to provide clients with adequate information regarding treatment choices because the field of counseling and psychology was "still very much a philosophy and not a science" (p. 33). They have suggested that mental health professionals should be required to provide clients with the success rates of various forms of mental health treatment based on empirical, research-based evidence, as do physicians who treat patients with conditions such as cancer. In the future, such a duty could be imposed on counselors, but at this point it certainly is not an ethical or legal requirement.

Contract Law

Contract law is complex. Counselors do not need to understand the technical principles of contract law such as offer, acceptance, and consideration (Calamari, Perillo, & Bender, 1989) in order to appreciate their contractual obligations to clients, but a basic understanding of those principles can be helpful.

Generally, relationships with professionals who provide services are contractual in nature (Murphy, Speidel, & Ayres, 1997). In terms of contract law, a professional in a private practice offers services to a recipient for a fee. The professional says to the client that services will be provided that will benefit and not harm the recipient if the recipient will pay the professional the amount of money required. Once the client accepts the professional's offer of services, a legal contract is formed, and all the laws of the contract govern the relationship. The process that leads up to professional services being rendered to a recipient does not look at all like a contractual process to non-lawyers. Because of the fiduciary duty owed to clients of professionals, and because clients must trust professionals to treat them appropriately, the idea of signing a contract before accepting services from a professional seems almost contradictory. If you trust someone, why would you need a contract?

Some contracts, such as real estate deals, must be in writing (Murphy et al., 1997). Contract law does not generally require, however, that contracts be in writing to be valid and enforceable. As a result, most contracts for professional services are not in writing. Although written contracts are generally not necessary under the law, many parties choose to execute them. One practical reason for reducing to writing the terms of a contract is to ensure that both parties understand exactly what they are agreeing to (i.e., the terms of the contract).

If two parties enter into a contractual arrangement, nothing goes wrong, and both are satisfied with the result, then a written contract was not needed. However, written contracts allow the parties to ensure they both understand the specifics in the agreement that they have reached. In addition, written contracts often anticipate changes or problems that might occur and set forth the agreement in the event such things happen. Agreements that are complex or must anticipate changes, therefore, should be in writing to protect both parties.

Informed Consent in Medicine

The process of informing recipients of professional services and obtaining their consent to receive such services is a relatively new legal concept. The requirement that health professionals obtain informed consent from their clients before rendering services began in medicine (Appelbaum, Lidz, & Meisel, 1987).

Twenty-five years ago, it probably rarely occurred to physicians that they should explain to patients what they knew about their medical conditions, tell their patients about various treatment options, or allow their patients to decide which option to choose. Perhaps consumers of medical services were once less educated or less aware of their right to receive information. It has only been in the last half-century that courts have created the requirement that patients must be educated or informed regarding their medical treatment options and consequences before they are able to give valid consent to treatment that is legally binding. The first case in the United States that took this position was *Salgo v. Leland Stanford Jr. Univ. Bd. of Trustees* (1957).

The *Salgo* case provided the essential elements that physicians must give to patients. According to Appelbaum et al. (1987), these elements are "disclosure of the nature of the ailment, the nature of the proposed treatment, the probability of success, and possible alternative treatments" (p. 41). *Canterbury v. Spence* (1972), a later case, took a different position on informed consent. It found that physicians were required to disclose information about a proposed treatment that a reasonable person, such as the patient receiving treatment, would find necessary to make a decision to either accept or refuse treatment.

After considering the case law on informed consent, Berner (1998) has argued that there are two elements to the informed consent legal standard. These elements are professional and materiality. The *professional element* is defined as information that a reasonable physician would have provided to a patient in similar circumstances. *Materiality*, on the other hand, is defined as the amount of information that the average patient would consider adequate in deciding whether to accept treatment. If Berner is correct, then courts will most likely require that physicians provide basic information to all patients *and* require that physicians ensure that the particular patient with whom they are dealing understands the information.

The Health Insurance Portability and Accountability Act (HIPAA), which went into effect April 15, 2003, has had a powerful impact on informed consent practices in medicine and mental health. This federal law and its regulations are explored in detail in Chapter 6. Essentially, HIPAA

To comply with the HIPAA law, here are some areas you must include on the form that your clients sign stating that they have been informed about your proposed treatment and agreeing to the treatment and the arrangement with you:

✓ State that your client's personal information may be used and disclosed to complete treatment. Also state that information may be provided to health care companies related to payment for your services.

✓ Develop a complete written description of the procedures you will follow in your office regarding keeping or disclosing personal information of clients.

✓ Tell your client that you have a more complete description of the way in which you will keep or disclose their personal information, and that the complete description is available for them to see. State that the client has a right to review the complete description before signing this consent form. Explain that your practices may change in the future, and that if the client wants to see any revisions the client must make that request in writing and that you will then make them available.

✓ Tell your client that he or she may request that you restrict how the client's personal information is used or disclosed. Explain that you will consider any such requests and will notify the client whether you have agreed to them.

✓ Explain that the client has the right to revoke his or her consent in writing, except to the extent actions have already been taken by you based on prior consent.

✓ Get the client's signature and have him or her indicate the date on the form.

✓ Keep the form for at least 6 years.

FIGURE 4-1 HIPAA requirements for informed consent disclosure statements

Source: Pearson Education, Inc., Hoboken, NJ.

requires all health care providers who transmit records electronically (which most likely includes all providers) to comply with procedures to ensure consumer privacy. The requirements include explaining to health care recipients in detail their rights related to privacy and records (which essentially is the informed consent process discussed earlier). This federal law has transformed the concept of informed consent, which once was rather vague, into a concrete framework that includes disclosure of steps taken to ensure client privacy, and it also requires clients to sign a document stating that they have been informed of their rights. Figure 4-1 includes a listing of essential elements for informed consent documents to ensure that counselors and agencies meet the legal HIPAA requirements.

Informed Consent in Mental Health

At present, there have been no appellate legal cases involving the responsibility of mental health professionals to obtain informed consent from their clients. But like other legal areas in mental health, most of the precedents and rules are created first with physicians and later become verified for mental health professionals through cases involving psychologists, counselors, and social workers. Beyond legal requirements, however, we believe it is best practice to provide clients with written information about the counseling relationship before the relationship begins (Herlihy & Remley, 2001).

It is probably safe to conclude that counselors do have a legal obligation to obtain informed consent from their clients before they begin treatment with them. Further, the informed consent should include information that would be given to the client by other reasonable professionals and should be delivered in a way that the client understands. HIPAA requires that the informed consent of clients be verified with their signatures.

Written Disclosure Statements

In mental health, written contracts for informed consent are commonly referred to as *disclosure statements*. These documents disclose to clients the nature of the counseling relationship they are entering into. Disclosure statements are also legal contracts. Often, they are signed by both the client and the counselor. Appendix B includes model disclosure statements for counselors who are providing counseling services to clients in a private practice and for employed counselors who are providing counseling services to clients in an agency or mental health center, respectively. The model counseling disclosure statements for private practice and agencies or mental health centers are similar in many ways. However, fee issues and some other aspects of the disclosure statements are quite different. Additional disclosure statements in Appendix B are for counselors who evaluate individuals, who counsel mandated or involuntary clients, and who counsel in schools.

The ACA *Code of Ethics* spells out in considerable detail the elements that need to be included in securing informed consent ethically (ACA, 2014, §A.2.b.). Therefore, these elements should be included in counseling disclosure statements:

- The purposes, goals, techniques, procedures, limitations, potential risks, and benefits of services
- The counselor's qualifications, including relevant degrees held, licenses and certifications, areas of specialization, experience, and approach to counseling
- Arrangements for continuation of services if the counselor dies or becomes incapacitated
- The role of technology
- The implications of diagnosis and the intended use of tests and reports
- Fees and billing information, including procedures for nonpayment of fees
- Confidentiality and its limitations
- Clients' rights to obtain information about their records and to participate in ongoing counseling plans
- Clients' rights to refuse any recommended services or modality change and be advised of the consequences of refusal

In addition to the elements addressed by the code, various writers have recommended that the following additional topics be included:

- A description of the counselor's *theoretical orientation*, in lay language, that the client can understand (Corey et al., 2015), or a brief statement of the counselor's *philosophy* (how the counselor sees the counseling process)
- Information about *logistics* of the counseling process, such as length and frequency of sessions, procedures for making and canceling appointments, policies regarding telephone contact between sessions, and how to reach the counselor or an alternative service in an emergency (Haas & Malouf, 1995)
- Information about *insurance reimbursement*, including the fact that any diagnosis assigned will become part of the client's permanent health record; what information will be provided to insurance carriers and how this limits confidentiality (Welfel, 2013; and, if applicable, a description of how the *managed care* system will affect the counseling process (Glosoff et al., 1999)
- Information about *alternatives to counseling*, such as 12-step groups or other self-help groups, books, medications, nutritional or exercise therapy, or other services (Bray, Shepherd, & Hays, 1985)

- If applicable, a statement that sessions will be *videotaped or audiotaped*, along with the information that the client's case may be discussed with a supervisor or consultant (Corey et al., 2015)
- The client's *recourse if dissatisfied with services*, including names and contact information for supervisors, and addresses and telephone numbers of licensing boards and professional organizations (Welfel, 2013)

Beyond the informed consent areas required by the ACA *Code of Ethics* (ACA, 2014) and areas suggested by others, some legal concerns need to be addressed in disclosure statements. The following informed consent areas are particularly sensitive and could lead to legal problems if not handled properly. Examples of problems that could arise are included. A client might have the basis for a lawsuit against a counselor if the client believed, for some reason, that the counselor had done any of the following:

1. *Failed to include required HIPAA elements (see Chapter 6).* Example: A client was not notified when she began counseling that she had the right to review her counseling records. She complained to the federal government, and the counselor subsequently was asked to verify that he had informed her of these rights.

2. *Guaranteed an outcome as a result of counseling.* Example: A wife reluctantly agreed to enter marriage counseling with her husband. She believed that, by agreeing to engage in counseling, she was guaranteed that her marriage would not end. She says the counselor told her that counseling was "the only thing that would save her marriage." She felt betrayed by the counselor when, after five sessions, her husband moved out of their home and filed for divorce. She sued the counselor for breach of contract, conspiracy, and alienation of affection.

3. *Guaranteed privacy with no exceptions.* Example: A new client expresses concern to his counselor that others might find out what he tells the counselor in their sessions. To reduce the client's anxiety, the counselor explains her ethical and legal responsibilities to protect his privacy. The client believes that his counselor told him that she would never, under any circumstances, reveal to anyone else information given to her in counseling sessions. Later the counselor informs the client's wife, over his objection, that he has expressed suicidal ideas and that she believes he should be evaluated to determine whether he is at risk. He sues the counselor for breach of contract, malpractice, and intentional infliction of emotional distress.

4. *Agreed to fee arrangements different from what was intended.* Example: A counselor begins a counseling relationship with his client, charging the client his standard rate of $75 per hour. After 3 months of sessions once a week, the counselor tells his client that his fees will be increased in 1 month to $90 per hour. The client objects, saying that he believes the new hourly rate is too high. The counselor replies that he is not willing to provide further counseling services to the client unless the client agrees to pay the new rate. The client sues the counselor for breach of contract and abandonment.

5. *Touched without implied or actual permission.* Example: In the course of a group counseling experience, a counselor asks group members who are blindfolded to allow themselves to fall backward into the arms of another group member to demonstrate the difficulty of trusting another person. A female group member reluctantly participates and is caught by a male group member. The female group member is very upset after the exercise and leaves the session visibly shaken. The female client sues the counselor for breach of contract, breach of fiduciary duty, assault, battery, and sexual assault.

6. *Misrepresented credentials.* Example: A client begins counseling sessions with a master's-level licensed counselor. The client tells his family members and friends that he is seeing a psychologist for therapy. The client makes out his checks to *Dr.*, notes on the checks that he is paying for *psychological services*, and gives the checks each week to the office receptionist, who deposits them. At the ninth session, the client calls the counselor "Doctor," and she corrects him. He then says, "You are a psychologist, aren't you?" He is very upset when he realizes that she is a master's-level licensed counselor. The client sues the counselor for breach of contract and fraudulent misrepresentation.

   7. *Failed to communicate the nature of counseling.* Example: A client has taken a new job in which she is required periodically to give presentations to small groups of potential clients. She is very anxious about speaking before groups and has sought counseling to overcome her anxiety. The counselor believes that her anxiety is the result of low self-esteem and focuses on positive reinforcement of the client's positive attributes. After five sessions, the client complains that she is still as anxious as she was when she began counseling. She tells the counselor that she had expected to be taught how to give presentations without being anxious and she does not understand why the counselor has not given her books to read, given her advice on how to be less anxious, or practiced making presentations with her. The client sues the counselor for breach of contract and malpractice.

   8. *Neglected to warn client about possible stigma.* Example: After the first session with a new client, the counselor completes an insurance form at the client's request. The counselor indicates on the form that the client has had a single episode of depression and assigns the appropriate *DSM* diagnosis. The counselor counsels the client for 10 sessions, terminating when the client moves to a new city hundreds of miles away. Two years later the client contacts the counselor and complains that he has been denied a security clearance for a job he has applied for because she diagnosed him, without his knowledge or agreement, with a mental disorder. He sues the counselor for breach of contract, malpractice, and defamation.

These eight hypothetical situations illustrate the importance of ensuring that counselors and their clients have the same understanding regarding their relationship before counseling begins. All of these problems could have been avoided if the counselors had fully informed the clients regarding the counseling relationship. Since HIPAA has been implemented, all counselors must give their clients written informed consent documents to sign. To be effective, however, these documents must include essential information beyond the HIPAA requirements.

4-3 The Case of Mark

Mark, a new Licensed Professional Counselor (LPC), works in a very efficient community mental health agency that utilizes the latest technology. Before he begins his first counseling session with each client, Mark types in the client's name and prints out a personalized disclosure statement that includes all of the HIPAA, ethical, and legal requirements for such documents. Mark is counseling Maureen, a young mother, who discloses that her husband, Jake, gets angry with their infant daughter when she cries and shakes the child severely to stop her crying. Mark informs Maureen that he must report Jake's actions to the authorities as possible child abuse. Mark, being sensitive to Maureen's concerns, explains in detail what may happen as a result of the report and assures her that he will continue counseling her. Maureen complains that she never would have told Mark about Jake's actions if she had known he would make a report to authorities. Mark responds that Maureen signed the informed consent form when they began their counseling relationship, and that the form clearly stated that counselors are legally obligated to report incidents of suspected child abuse. Maureen responds that she didn't read the document. She says she just signed it along with all those other papers for insurance. Maureen says she will not continue her counseling relationship with Mark because she no longer trusts him.

- What could Mark have done at the outset of his counseling relationship with Maureen that might have prevented this unfortunate situation? What would have constituted *best practice* in this situation?
- How can counselors balance the need to inform new clients of the limits of confidentiality in the relationship and to establish rapport at the same time?

Discussion: Mark might have considered the following actions to prevent this unfortunate situation:

- Mark might have spent some time with Maureen in their first session pointing out some of the major exceptions to confidentiality. One such major exception is a counselor's legal duty to report suspected child abuse.
- Mark might have asked the intake person in his agency, if such help had been available, to go over some of the major details in the documents with Maureen before he began his first session with her.

In order to discuss confidentiality limits and establish rapport, counselors should consider taking the following actions:

- Focus on establishing rapport in a first session and, at the end of the session, go over important details regarding the counseling relationship.
- Highlight certain parts of the many papers that clients sign in bold type or large type to draw clients' attention.
- Create a written brochure that explains the counseling relationship, including confidentiality limits, and send the brochure to prospective clients for them to read before their first appointment.

In the process of having clients sign counseling disclosure statements, counselors should attempt to ensure that clients know what they have read and what was in the document being signed. If questions arise later about what counselors may have said, a signed written document demonstrates the intent of the parties much more clearly than does a statement of what someone says he or she intended. In addition, counseling disclosure statements can be used to correct misunderstandings on the part of clients before counseling begins.

You may be thinking that a lot of information must be included in a disclosure statement, and, indeed, this is true. In order for clients to give truly informed consent, they must have considerable information before deciding whether to enter into a counseling relationship. This may raise your concern that inundating prospective clients with information will overwhelm them and give the impression that the counseling relationship is nothing more than a complex, contractual business arrangement. It is difficult for counselors to achieve the delicate balance between giving clients too little information and giving them so much information that they feel overwhelmed or intimidated (Barnett, Wise, Johnson-Greene, & Bucky, 2007). Written disclosure statements allow counselors to provide detailed information. Oral exchanges between counselors and potential clients can then focus on areas that the counselor wishes to emphasize or that cause particular concern for clients.

As noted, every counselor should have a professional disclosure statement that can be given to clients. A complete and signed disclosure statement will fulfill a counselor's legal obligation to obtain informed consent from a client. Keep in mind, though, that disclosure statements are necessary but not sufficient strategies for securing genuine informed consent. They cannot serve as a substitute for dialog with the client. We cannot rely on standard forms, no matter how well they are written, to do our work for us (Pope & Vasquez, 2010). Prospective clients are likely to have many questions, and some of these are best addressed in face-to-face conversation. Such a dialog gives clients an opportunity to clarify any information that seems confusing to them and gives counselors the opportunity to gauge the extent to which the clients comprehend the information. At the outset of the relationship, informed consent discussions present a mutual opportunity for the client and the counselor to ensure that they understand their shared journey.

Pope and Vasquez (2010) also have noted that informed consent procedures must fit the situation and setting and be sensitive to the client's ability to understand. The ACA *Code of Ethics* (ACA, 2014) affirms the obligation of counselors to communicate information in ways that are both developmentally and culturally appropriate (§A.2.c.). To ensure client comprehension, it may be necessary in some cases to arrange for a qualified interpreter or translator. Counselors are cautioned, though, that having a translator present may not be sufficient to ensure the client's informed consent if the translator lacks understanding of the counselor's role and the purpose of the informed consent information. Paone and Malott (2008) have advised counselors to have a presession briefing with a translator to review informed consent concepts and how these concepts should be communicated to the client.

Some clients may be presumed to lack the capacity to give informed consent. Such clients might include minors or adults who are developmentally disabled or who suffer from cognitive impairments or a severe thought disorder. In these cases, counselors seek the consent of legal guardians. Counselors should also seek clients' assent to services and include clients in the decision-making process to the extent possible (ACA, 2014, §A.2.d.). Bennett et al. (2006) have advised counselors to view informed consent capacity as being on a continuum rather than as an all-or-none ability. The informed consent process should be designed to fit each client's cognitive strengths, vulnerabilities, and decision-making capabilities (Fisher, Cea, Davidson, & Fried, 2006).

Managed care arrangements present some specific considerations in informed consent. Clients often do not understand how their health plans affect the duration of their treatment, the implications of diagnosis, or the extent to which their insurance providers require counselors to provide them with information about treatment plans and counseling progress (Glosoff, 1998). Because it would be impossible for counselors to know the details of each of the health care plans of their clients, it is preferable for counselors to stress to clients that they should investigate the terms and limits of their coverage, rather than for counselors to undertake that entire burden. Once the provisions of the plan are known, counselors should discuss with clients the limitations of their coverage; perhaps they will need to agree on treatment goals that are more limited than if cost were no object (Vasquez et al., 2008). See Chapter 13 for further discussions regarding managed care.

From an ethical perspective, ensuring informed consent is not a one-time event. Rather, it is a recurring process that begins with the initial contact between client and counselor and continues throughout the counseling relationship. It is not always possible for counselors to provide complete informed consent information during the first session. For example, insurance policies often dictate the number of sessions that will be reimbursed, and counselors may not be able to accurately inform clients about the duration of reimbursed counseling until they receive the necessary information from the client's managed care company. Specific goals of counseling and the techniques that may be used to accomplish those goals are not always clearly formed during the initial meeting. Some elements of informed consent are best left until a trusting therapeutic relationship has been established; for instance, a client who suffers from a phobia might become anxious when told about exposure therapy, a technique that has proven effectiveness for treating phobias but includes elements (such as getting on an elevator) that might seem frightening at first (Fisher & Oransky, 2008). The ACA *Code of Ethics* (ACA, 2014) describes informed consent as an ongoing part of the counseling process and advises counselors to document discussions of informed consent throughout the counseling relationship (§A.2.a.). As counseling progresses, the goals, issues, risks, and benefits often change, and clients need to have updated information so that they can continue to make sound decisions (Handelsman, 2001).

It is impossible to predict which clients will need what information and when they will need it, so it is best to be as thorough as possible in a written disclosure statement. Later, in a face-to-face discussion, issues that arise frequently in one's practice can be emphasized, and rare events can be given less attention. For example, Weinrach (1989) has suggested that the two most common problems for private practitioners concern (a) fees and billing and (b) late cancellations or no-shows. Thus, it behooves counselors in private practice to be clear with their clients about methods of payment and policies regarding missed appointments.

Research supports the wisdom of securing informed consent. Studies have suggested that clients want information about their prospective counselors (Braaten, Otto, & Handelsman, 1993; Hendrick, 1988); that they perceive counselors who provide informed consent information as being more expert and trustworthy (Sullivan, Martin, & Handelsman, 1993); and that clients who have received appropriate information are more likely to follow their treatment plans, to recover more quickly, to be less anxious, and to be more alert to possible negative consequences (Handler, 1990). In addition, some legal problems can be avoided by the use of disclosure statements. If allegations do arise that a counselor did not fully explain the counseling relationship to a client, a disclosure statement signed by a client often can go a long way toward vindicating an accused counselor who has done no wrong.

DIVERSITY CONSIDERATIONS   It is important for us to question whether the individualism inherent in our concept of informed consent is truly respectful of people of all cultures. We need to be aware that the full and truthful disclosure that counselors value may be at variance with some clients' cultural beliefs about hope and wellness, that autonomous decision making may run counter to family-centered or group-centered values, and that uncoerced choices may contradict cultural norms about obedience to the wishes of elders or spouses (Gostin, 1995). The following two case examples illustrate this point.

4-4 The Case of Henry

Joseph, a Navajo Indian who espouses the traditions of his culture, is Henry's new client. During the initial interview, Henry wants to secure Joseph's informed consent, which would include giving him information about the implications of diagnosis and the potential risks associated with counseling. Henry says, "Sometimes clients in counseling seem to feel worse before they feel better." He adds that, based on the symptoms Joseph has described, Joseph seems to be experiencing mild depression.

- What would Henry need to know about Joseph's culture that would help him conduct informed consent procedures in a culturally sensitive way?
- Can you identify any problems with what Henry told Joseph?

Discussion: Henry should have made an effort to gain some basic understanding of the Navajo culture before meeting with Joseph. In traditional Navajo culture, it is believed that language has the power to shape reality and control events. Therefore Henry, in following his standard informed consent procedures, could be *creating* a reality for Joseph that he is depressed and thus will feel worse before he feels better.

4-5 The Case of Loretta

Soo Jung is a 22-year-old immigrant from Korea who is brought to the counseling center by her husband. During the intake interview, she tells her counselor, Loretta, that she has been having crying spells, has lost her appetite, and is not sleeping well. She gave birth to her first child 2 months earlier. When Loretta suggests to Soo Jung that she may be experiencing postpartum depression, Soo Jung becomes upset and says, "Why are you telling me this? You need to talk to my husband."

- Why do you think Soo Jung became upset?
- How might Loretta have handled the intake interview differently to avoid upsetting this client?

Discussion: Soo Jung appears to share a family-oriented world view that is common among people from some Asian cultures. Because the counselor did not include this client's husband in this discussion, Soo Jung may have interpreted the counselor's actions as attempting to undermine her marital relationship. An awareness of the Korean culture and its views on marriage might have led Loretta to interview Soo Jung and her husband together as the counseling relationship was being established.

Joseph and Soo Jung illustrate the point that there are communities of clients in our pluralistic society who do not claim Euro-American values as their own. Counselors must remember to put the client's needs first. Weinrach and Thomas (1996) suggested that counselors identify, and then focus on, the frame of reference or belief and value systems that are central to the client as one way to remain sensitive to differences. Expanding our frame of reference regarding informed consent does not mean that we must abandon our commitment to client autonomy, but it does encompass respect for the cultural values that our clients bring with them to counseling.

Counselors must also be sensitive to clients' rights to informed consent when clients have been legally adjudicated as incompetent. Clients with developmental disabilities, older adults who have cognitive impairments, and persons who have been diagnosed with a psychotic or thought disorder often are judged to have diminished capacity to consent. Keep in mind that *diminished* capacity is not the same as an absence of capacity. Counselors have an ethical obligation to discuss consent with these clients in a manner that they can understand and to obtain their assent to services even though their agreement may not be legally recognized (Fisher & Oransky, 2008; Handelsman, 2001).

The importance of using language that clients can understand is equally important with clients who are children, adults who are not well educated, and clients whose first language is not English. If you work with such clients, it would be wise to carefully check the readability level of your written disclosure statement. When English is a second language for clients, it would be helpful to have a copy that has been translated into the client's primary language. The overarching principle is that consent procedures, both oral and written, must be developmentally and culturally appropriate.

Summary and Key Points

This chapter addresses two vitally important and interrelated ethical and legal issues in counseling: client rights and counselor responsibilities. Following are key points regarding these rights and responsibilities:

- Counselors are ethically responsible for putting client welfare first and foremost in their work.
- Counselors have a fiduciary relationship with their clients, which means that they have a legal obligation to protect their clients' best interests and to avoid interactions that benefit themselves.
- Respecting diversity is fundamental to protecting client welfare and promoting client dignity in our pluralistic society.
- It is vital for counselors to be aware of their own needs and motivations, unfinished business, areas of vulnerability, and defenses so that they will not inadvertently be working on their own issues in the counseling relationship rather than on the client's issues.
- Counselors must be aware of their personal values and must not impose their values on clients. Recent court cases have highlighted issues related to value conflicts between counselors and clients.
- Counselors must avoid fostering client dependency. They have an obligation to promote client autonomy and independence.
- When counseling involuntary or mandated clients, counselors must inform these clients of the limits of confidentiality and the nature of any reports that may be made to courts or other entities that are requiring the clients to attend counseling. Counselors must be sensitive to these clients' rights and ensure that

clients understand any privacy rights they may be waiving.
- Counselors have an obligation to select appropriate counseling strategies or techniques and to make clients active partners in treatment decisions.
- Counselors must protect the best interests and welfare of clients when counseling services have to be interrupted or terminated prematurely.
- It is unethical, as well as illegal, for counselors to abandon their clients. Although there are valid reasons for a counselor to end a counseling relationship, care must be taken not to put the client at risk when doing so. Several guidelines were offered for counselors to use when they are terminating counseling relationships in adverse circumstances.

The following are key points regarding informed consent in counseling:

- As an ethical obligation, informed consent is based on the rationale that clients have a right to know what they are getting into when they come for counseling.
- Counselors should understand that counseling services are contractual in nature. Agreements should be put in writing in an informed consent document.
- The requirement that health professionals inform prospective recipients of services and obtain their consent to treatment originated in the field of medicine. More recently, it has been applied to the mental health field. A number of model disclosure statements are available to assist counselors who work in various settings with a variety of clientele.

- The requirements of HIPAA have transformed informed consent into a legal requirement, and counselors must ensure that their procedures are in compliance with this law.
- Informed consent in counseling involves a number of elements that are required by the ACA *Code of Ethics*, recommended by various writers, and suggested as a means to address legal concerns.
- Counselors need to be aware of at least eight areas of informed consent that, if not handled properly, could lead to legal problems.

- It can be difficult to achieve a balance between providing prospective clients with too little information and giving them so much information that they feel overwhelmed or intimidated. Informed consent is an ongoing process that should be conducted both orally and in written form.
- It is important for counselors to be sensitive to the fact that informed consent as traditionally conceptualized may not be respectful of people of all cultures and to educate themselves as appropriate for their clients.

CHAPTER 5

Confidentiality and Privileged Communication

FOCUS QUESTIONS

1. What do you think are the distinctions among the terms *privacy, confidentiality,* and *privileged communication*?

2. Some studies have shown that clients are not very concerned about privacy or confidentiality when they seek counseling services. What do you think about such findings?

3. How would you respond if a client asked to see the notes you have taken related to his or her counseling sessions?

4. What do you think should happen to clients' records after they die?

Confidentiality is one of the most fundamental of all professional obligations in counseling. It is also one of the most complex and problematic duties to manage in day-to-day practice. Consider, for instance, what you would do if you were the counselor in each of the following situations.

5-1 The Case of Elena

Elena has been working with Pete, age 28, who came for counseling to resolve some family-of-origin issues that he believes are creating problems in his relationship with his partner, Jacob. During their last counseling session together, Pete tearfully revealed that before he met Jacob, he had a series of casual sexual encounters and that he was terrified that he might have contracted the AIDS virus through these encounters. He comes to today's session with the news that he has been fully tested and is confirmed to be HIV positive. He says he cannot tell Jacob because he is sure Jacob will leave him if he knows.

- As Pete's counselor, is Elena obligated to keep his secret? Or do you believe she has a duty to inform Jacob of Pete's condition, even though this would involve breaching Pete's confidentiality?
- Suppose Pete tells Elena, after further discussion, that he realizes he must tell Jacob but needs some time to gather his courage. Should Elena keep his secret in this circumstance? If yes, for how long?

Discussion: Counselors have both an ethical and a legal (except in Texas) duty to take action to prevent harm if they believe their client is intentionally harming someone else. The ethical duty exists because the obligation to prevent harm outweighs the rights of a client to privacy. The legal duty exists (except in Texas) because of the *Tarasoff* case (*Tarasoff v. Regents of University of California*, 1976), which is discussed in detail in Chapter 8.

Therefore, Elena cannot keep Pete's secret. It might be best if Elena were to contact Pete's physician (because only the physician knows for sure that Pete is HIV positive), inform the physician of the situation, and ask the physician to take action to protect Jacob.

If Pete asks for some time before he tells Jacob, it would be risky for Elena to agree to the request. If Jacob is later found to be HIV positive, there would be no way to tell whether he was infected before or after Pete told Elena about his condition. Therefore, Jacob might argue that Elena is responsible for his becoming HIV positive because she did not warn him. Perhaps, however, Elena might have Pete promise not to have unprotected sex with Jacob before telling him. Elena might then decide to agree to give Pete some time if she has been counseling him for quite some time and feels confident that he will honor his promise.

5-2 The Case of Nancy

Nancy, a high school counselor, has been conducting a group for freshman and sophomore girls. The focus of the group is on building self-esteem and making wise choices. During the fourth session today, the group members begin discussing boyfriends and whether to *just say no* to sex. Marlee, a 15-year-old freshman, shares that she and her boyfriend are having sexual relations and that she thinks it's okay because they are really in love. She mentions, almost in passing, that her boyfriend is 20 years old and that her parents would *kill her* if they found out about him.

- Can Marlee's counselor keep her disclosure in confidence, or must she notify Marlee's parents?
- If Nancy breaches confidentiality, what are the risks to her relationship with Marlee?
- If Nancy breaches confidentiality, what are the risks to the group process, to the trust that other group members may have come to feel toward her, and to her reputation for trustworthiness among the student population in general?
- Are these risks greater than the risks posed by keeping Marlee's relationship with her boyfriend a secret from her parents?

Discussion: Nancy cannot keep Marlee's disclosure a secret; she must notify Marlee's parents, although she should first inform Marlee of her obligation and explain why she cannot keep the secret. If Nancy does not tell the parents and Marlee becomes pregnant or is harmed by the relationship with an adult male, the parents might attempt to hold Nancy responsible. Nancy should check her state law, as she may also be required to report suspected child abuse to authorities.

It certainly is possible that Marlee will be very upset after Nancy tells her parents, and Marlee may not want to continue the counseling relationship. Nancy should do her best to maintain the relationship, however. This may be possible if she is able to convince Marlee that it is in her best interest for her parents to know, or if she can obtain Marlee's agreement that Marlee will tell her parents, perhaps in Nancy's office with Nancy present.

This group might not continue, although Nancy should try to keep it functioning and work through the issue with the other students. Hopefully, Nancy has already discussed the limits of confidentiality with the group members so they will understand why she cannot keep Marlee's secret. It is likely, however, that Nancy's reputation among the students for trustworthiness will be compromised, and other students probably will be reluctant to share confidential information with her in the future.

After pondering these scenarios, you may not be surprised to learn that counselors encounter dilemmas of confidentiality more frequently than other types of ethical challenges and find them the most difficult to resolve (Fisher, 2008). Questions surrounding confidentiality can be very complex and often involve legal as well as ethical considerations.

A useful starting place may be to clarify the distinctions among three terms—*privacy, confidentiality*, and *privileged communication*. These terms are sometimes used interchangeably by counselors, but the concepts have important differences. Both confidentiality and privileged communication arise from our societal belief that individuals have a right to privacy. *Privacy* is the broadest of the three concepts and refers to the right of persons to decide what information about themselves will be shared with or withheld from others. Confidentiality and privileged communication both apply more specifically to the professional relationship between counselors and clients. *Confidentiality* is primarily an ethical concept that refers to the counselor's obligation to respect the client's privacy and the promise to clients that the information they reveal during counseling will be protected from disclosure without their consent. *Privileged communication* is the narrowest of the three terms and is a legal concept. Privileged communication laws protect clients from having confidential communications with their counselors disclosed in a court of law without their permission (Garner, 2014). For a communication to be privileged, a statute must have been enacted that grants privilege to a category of professionals and to those whom they serve.

In this chapter, we first explore confidentiality as an ethical issue and then discuss privileged communication. Later, we look at the numerous exceptions that exist, both to confidentiality and to privilege.

CONFIDENTIALITY

Origins of Confidentiality

Helping professionals assume that an assurance of confidentiality is an indispensable requirement for effective therapy and that, without this assurance, many clients would not feel safe to discuss openly the intimate and personal aspects of their lives or would not seek counseling. Actual studies, however, show only mixed support for this assumption. Some studies have supported the belief that privacy assurances are essential (McGuire, Toal, & Blau, 1985; Merluzzi & Brischetto, 1983; Miller & Thelan, 1986), whereas other studies have indicated that such assurances have little effect on encouraging disclosures (Muehleman, Pickens, & Robinson, 1985; Schmid, Appelbaum, Roth, & Lidz, 1983; Shuman & Weiner, 1987), or that limits to confidentiality matter only to some clients in some circumstances (Taube & Elwork, 1990; VandeCreek, Miars, & Herzog, 1987). Despite this lack of unequivocal evidence, confidentiality has become such an internalized norm in the counseling profession that it is rarely questioned. A brief look at some of the historical origins of the profession may be helpful in understanding how this norm developed.

Counseling represents the fusion of many diverse influences. One of these influences was the emergence of the field of psychiatry in the treatment of mental illness. Almost until the beginning of the nineteenth century, mental illness was viewed as mystical and demonic. These early times are associated with images of "lunatics" in chains in asylums. It was not until the 1800s that significant strides were made in the understanding of mental illness, and not until the 1960s that the deinstitutionalization of the mentally ill brought these individuals back into contact with society. Another force that bears mentioning is the emergence of psychoanalysis in the early to middle twentieth century. Patients of Freudian analysts were expected to work through their socially unacceptable urges, sexual fantasies, and repressed feelings and thoughts, and to do so in a society that held Victorian social mores. Early notions about mental illness and negative impressions about the nature of personal material discussed in analysis helped to create a social stigma. In this climate, it is understandable that the patient's need for absolute privacy was assumed and that people would want to hide any information related to their having sought and received treatment.

It was not until the middle of the twentieth century that other, countervailing influences emerged in the mental health field. Carl Rogers's humanistic views, other theorists who emphasized the natural developmental life stages that all individuals pass through, and the career guidance movement all helped to shift thinking away from counseling as a service only for the mentally ill or the sexually repressed. Concurrently, as scientists began to discover the biological bases for some mental disorders and to find medications that could alleviate conditions formerly thought to be untreatable, the stigmatization associated with mental illness and psychotherapy began to decrease. Nonetheless, even in current society, a notion stubbornly persists that there is something shameful about seeking the services of a mental health professional. Note, for instance, the language used by the U.S. Supreme Court in its 1996 decision in *Jaffee v. Redmond et al.* (1996, p. 8), a case we describe later in this chapter:

> Because of the sensitive nature of the problems for which individuals consult psychotherapists, disclosure of confidential communications made during counseling sessions may cause *embarrassment or disgrace.*

The Rationale for Confidentiality

Whatever its origin, confidentiality is universally viewed today as being essential to the counseling process, which depends on an atmosphere of confidence and trust in which clients are able to tell their stories freely and honestly disclose their feelings, fears, thoughts, memories, and desires. Clients need to know that they can trust their counselors to respect their privacy, and the counselor's confidentiality pledge is the cornerstone on which this trust is built (ACA Code of Ethics, 2014, §A: Introduction).

Confidentiality is a strong moral force that helps shape the manner in which counselors relate to their clients. Bok (1983) has suggested that confidentiality is based on four premises. The first two premises relate to respect for client rights in counseling. The principle of *respect for autonomy* (which is described in Chapter 1) means that counselors honor their clients' ability to be self-determining and to make their own choices. Applied to confidentiality, it also means that counselors honor the rights of clients to decide who knows what information about them and in what circumstances. The second premise is *respect* for human relationships and for the secrets that certain types of relationships entail. In the professional relationship, the intimate context in which these secrets are shared is seen as essential to counseling. The third premise has to do with the counselor's obligation that arises from autonomy and respect. Bok contends that an additional duty is created by a *pledge of silence*, which is the offer of confidentiality extended by the counselor to the client. Counselors are bound to this pledge both in word and in deed; when they have given their word, they are obligated to actively work to protect clients' secrets from disclosure. The final basis for confidentiality is its *utility*. The rationale here is that confidentiality in counseling relationships is useful to society, because clients would be reluctant to seek help without an assurance of privacy. Society gives up its right to certain information and accepts the risks of not knowing about some problems and dangers in society in exchange for the benefit that is gained when its members improve their mental health.

Respect for autonomy is only one of the moral principles on which confidentiality rests. Another is *fidelity*, which means being faithful and keeping promises, as we describe in Chapter 1. Certainly one of the most important promises that counselors make to clients is that they will keep the secrets shared in counseling. Today, confidentiality is an issue not only of counselor belief systems but also of consumer rights. U.S. culture has placed increasing emphasis on the rights of service recipients, and clients are more likely to hold an expectation that their privacy will be maintained by the professionals whose help they seek. This expectation of privacy has important legal as well as ethical implications, as you will discover later in this chapter.

Counselor Practices and Confidentiality

How well do practicing counselors deal with confidentiality issues? There is some evidence to suggest that counselors feel confident of their ability to make sound ethical judgments about confidentiality issues. Gibson and Pope (1993) surveyed a large national sample of counselors regarding their beliefs about whether a wide range of behaviors were ethical or unethical and how confident they were in making these judgments. Twenty-nine percent of the items for which the confidence rating was very high (at least 9.0 on a 10-point scale) concerned confidentiality. In a more recent survey, Neukrug and Milliken (2011) asked American Counseling Association (ACA) members to rate 77 behaviors as ethical or unethical. In their study, two confidentiality-related behaviors about which the respondents were in overwhelming agreement (over 95%) were that it is ethical to break confidentiality if a client is threatening harm to self and that it is unethical to fail to reveal the limits of confidentiality to a client.

Counselors' confidence in their ethical judgments may be well founded. Complaints made against helping professionals for violations of confidentiality are not as common as one might expect. Various studies have shown that only 1% to 5% of complaints made to the ethics committees and state licensing boards of counselors involve violations of confidentiality (Anderson & Freeman, 2006; Garcia, Glosoff, & Smith, 1994; Garcia, Salo, & Hamilton, 1995; Neukrug, Healy, & Herlihy, 1992). It appears that mental health professionals take seriously their pledge to maintain their clients' confidentiality and are diligent in honoring it. Grabois (1997/1998) reported that there had been only a few cases in which mental health professionals had been sued for breaching confidentiality. Counselors should not become complacent about their confidentiality practices, however. Statistics regarding formal complaints may not accurately reflect the actual frequency of breaches of confidentiality. According to one study, 61.9% of psychologists reported that they had *unintentionally* violated their clients' confidentiality (Pope, Tabachnick, & Keith-Spiegel, 1987b). Clients may not have been aware of these unintentional breaches. Although it may be startling to think that the majority of practitioners may have violated their clients' confidentiality, it is somewhat understandable when we pause to consider the myriad ways that an inadvertent or careless breach could occur. The following examples illustrate this point.

Counselors do not always have the luxury of having a separate entrance and exit for their clients to use. When clients who are leaving their sessions must pass through a waiting area, counselors need to take special precautions to guard their clients' privacy. We know one very conscientious counselor in private practice who routinely left 15-minute intervals between the end of one scheduled appointment and the beginning of the next, and who avoided scheduling consecutively any clients from the same part of town. Nevertheless, one day she ran late with a client, who exited into the waiting room and ran into a friend from church. Both clients appeared uncomfortable to have encountered each other in this way.

Counselors are encouraged to consult with each other regarding clients who present challenges to them, and most consultations can be managed without revealing a client's identity. However, it is important not to obtain a colleague's advice while walking through the halls of an agency or institution, at a restaurant, or in another public place. Pope and Vasquez (2010) related the story of a counselor who was consulting a colleague about a particularly *difficult* client while they were on a crowded elevator. The counselor did not mention the client's name but gave enough detail that the client, who happened to be standing only a few feet behind them in the elevator, was able to ascertain that he was the subject of the discussion and to listen with intense interest and dismay.

Clearly, it is easy for even seasoned practitioners to violate a client's privacy unintentionally. Students in counselor training programs must also take special care to maintain client confidentiality. Although it may be tempting to share with family, friends, or fellow students your excitement about what you are learning in a practicum, a practice session with a peer client, or an experiential group, it is important to keep in mind that the ethical obligations of students are the same as those of practicing counselors (ACA, 2014, §F.5.a.). Your conversations must not reveal any information that could conceivably allow listeners to ascertain the identity of a client. Case notes, test protocols and interpretations, audiotapes, and videotapes of work with clients must not be left in places where they might be seen by anyone other than authorized supervisors or professors. It is a good idea to get into the habit of zealously safeguarding client confidentiality from the very beginning of your graduate studies.

A question that surfaces quite often for beginning counselors is whether they have an obligation to maintain the confidentiality of private information that is disclosed to them when they are not in the role of counselor—for example, when a neighbor tells a counselor about an event that occurred a few houses away. The answer is that confidentiality and privileged communication exist only when counselors are functioning in the role of professional counselor. As explained by Sydow (2006), courts have held that—even when a counselor is at work—privilege exists only when a counselor–client relationship exists and when the counselor is providing professional counseling services.

Ethical Standards and Confidentiality

Confidentiality is the only specific ethical issue to which an entire section of the *Code of Ethics* (ACA, 2014) is devoted. Section B: Confidentiality and Privacy emphasizes the client's right to privacy in the counseling relationship. Exceptions and limitations to confidentiality are addressed and, because exceptions to confidentiality may be mandated by legal as well as ethical considerations, the standards are carefully written to minimize conflicts between law and ethics. This section addresses special circumstances in counseling minors, families, and groups and offers guidelines for maintaining confidentiality when consulting or conducting research.

The Introduction to Section B is general and states, "Counselors recognize that trust is a cornerstone of the counseling relationship." An early standard in this section states, "Counselors respect the privacy of prospective and current clients" (ACA, 2014, §B.1.b.). Sometimes counselors, in their zeal to protect a client's privacy, mistakenly believe that they should maintain a client's confidentiality even when the client asks them to share information with others (Herlihy & Corey, 2015a). When clients request that information be disclosed, counselors should honor these requests. If the counselor believes that releasing the information might be detrimental to the client's best interests, these concerns should be discussed with the client, but the ultimate decision belongs to the client. In many instances, client requests for disclosure are not particularly problematic for counselors, such as when clients move and later request that their records be sent to their new counselor. Other situations may cause counselors some discomfort, such as when clients ask to see their own records. It is important to realize that records are kept for the benefit of clients and that counselors are obligated to provide clients with access to their records, unless the records contain information that may be misleading or harmful to the client (ACA, 2014, §B.6.e.). The Health Insurance Portability and Accountability Act (HIPAA), a federal statute that is discussed at length in Chapter 6, requires that clients be given access to their counseling records except in exceptional circumstances in which clients may be harmed by seeing their records.

One of the reasons that confidentiality is such a difficult ethical issue is that *confidentiality is not absolute*. Although counselors should make every effort to avoid inadvertent breaches, sometimes confidentiality *must* be breached. Counselors must inform clients at the outset that there are limitations to their confidentiality. It is important to discuss thoroughly these limitations and to identify foreseeable situations in which confidentiality must be breached (ACA, 2014, §B.1.d.). Prospective clients may not be aware at the time they seek your services that confidentiality is not absolute. In one survey of the general public, 69% of respondents believed that everything discussed with a professional therapist would be held strictly confidential, and 74% thought that there should be no exceptions to maintaining confidential disclosures (Miller & Thelan, 1986). Counselors may be hesitant to explain the exceptions to confidentiality to new or prospective clients for fear that clients will feel constrained in discussing their problems. However, some researchers have found very little evidence that explaining in detail the limits of confidentiality actually inhibits client disclosures. Others have concluded that the advantages of informing clients about limits outweigh any disadvantages in terms of inhibited disclosure (Baird & Rupert, 1987; Muehleman et al., 1985).

There are numerous exceptions to confidentiality. We have identified at least 15 types of situations in which compromising a client's confidentiality might be permissible or required. Because most of these exceptions to confidentiality have both a legal and an ethical basis, we will explore them in more detail after we have discussed the legal counterpart to confidentiality: privileged communication.

PRIVILEGED COMMUNICATION

At the beginning of this chapter, we noted that privacy is a broad concept that provides the underpinnings for both confidentiality and privileged communication. The right to privacy is guaranteed to all citizens by the Fourth Amendment to the U.S. Constitution, which prohibits government searches without warrants. This privacy right is not absolute, however. When the interests of society outweigh the individual's right to privacy, the privacy right is compromised in the interest of preserving a stable societal structure. The U.S. Supreme Court has never addressed the question of whether the Fourth Amendment supports the concept that some relationships are privileged because of this constitutional right to privacy. State and lower federal courts have been mixed in their results on the issue (Knapp & VandeCreek, 1987).

Basically, privileged communication means that a judge cannot order information that has been recognized by law as privileged to be revealed in court. The concept of withholding any relevant evidence is antagonistic to the entire system of justice in the United States because legal procedures demand that all evidence relevant to a case be presented to a judge or jury. The legal system also demands that the opposing side in a court case have access to the evidence before the trial takes place through a process called *discovery*. As a counselor, you will surely want to guarantee that the information that clients give you will be kept confidential. The idea that information and secrets revealed in a counseling session might someday be disclosed in court is very unsettling for counselors. However, the idea that a judge or jury might have to decide the outcome of a court case without the benefit of essential privileged information is very unsettling to judges.

A good question to ask, then, is "Why did the idea of privileged communication emerge in the U.S. legal system in the first place?" According to Slovenko (1966), the evidence presented in a court determines the quality of a trial in a court of law. Despite the strong belief that all evidence should be available to the judge or jury who will decide the outcome of a case, federal and state legislators have realized that the requirement to make available all evidence compromises many important interactions. Legislators have been convinced that, without a guarantee of absolute privacy for conversations between citizens and certain professionals, it would be impossible for professionals to provide necessary assistance to those who seek their help. As a result, statutes have been enacted that specifically exempt certain conversations between citizens and professionals from the general rule in law that all relevant evidence will be presented in a court case. These laws are called *privileged communication statutes*.

Origins of Privileged Communication

According to Shuman and Weiner (1987), the first reference to courts recognizing a legal privilege between professionals and the citizens they served was in early Roman law. This privilege was based on the duty of servants (attorneys) to their masters (clients) rather than on the modern principle of a right to privacy.

Under English common law, the foundation on which the legal system in the United States is based, there was no need for privileged communication. In early England, truth during trials was determined by various modes, including witnesses swearing to tell the truth, defendants being put to a physical endurance test, or individuals who were disagreeing engaging in a battle (Shuman & Weiner, 1987). Even when witnesses were used in trials, they also served as the jurors and relied on information they had gathered as members of the community. Individuals who were not jurors but volunteered information were viewed as meddlers and could be sued for interfering with the legal process.

About 1450, English equity courts began recognizing subpoenas for nonparty witnesses and started using them in law courts in 1562 (Wigmore, 1961). Yet few communications were privileged under English common law. Other than government secrets, the common law recognized as privileged only attorney–client and husband–wife relationships (Knapp & VandeCreek, 1987).

Once the English legal system allowed judges to compel witnesses to testify at trials, a question arose as to whether certain information obtained by professionals should be excluded from testimony for one reason or another. Wigmore (1961), the leading authority on evidence, described four requirements for a relationship to be privileged under the law:

1. The communications must originate in a *confidence* that they will not be disclosed.
2. This element of *confidentiality must be essential* to the full and satisfactory maintenance of the relation between the parties.
3. The *relationship* must be one that, in the opinion of the community, ought to be sedulously *fostered*.
4. The *injury* to the relationship that disclosure of the communications would cause must be *greater than the benefit* gained for the correct disposal of the litigation.

State and federal legislatures have used these requirements as criteria in considering whether to grant privilege to relationships between citizens and various categories of professionals. The question of which professional relationships meet these criteria and, therefore, should be accorded privilege has been a source of controversy that continues to this day. Some legal scholars have criticized all statutes that have been passed by legislatures granting privilege to relationships with professionals (Chafee, 1943; Cleary, 1984; Curd, 1938; Morgan, 1943; Wigmore, 1961). The attorney–client relationship was the first professional relationship to be recognized under English common law, during the reign of Queen Elizabeth I. Currently in the United States, the attorney–client privilege is universally recognized (Rice, 1993).

Physicians, on the other hand, have been less successful at obtaining legal privilege with their patients. According to Shuman and Weiner (1987), most legal scholars agree that the concept of a physician–patient privilege fails Wigmore's test. Almost every jurisdiction in the United States now has privileged communication statutes for physician–patient interactions. However, many of the statutes include a multitude of exceptions, including criminal cases, workers' compensation proceedings, will contests, cases where the condition for which treatment or diagnosis was sought is raised by the patient to support a claim or defense, or cases in which the parent–child relationship is at issue.

According to Knapp and VandeCreek (1987), the clergy–communicant privilege is unique because it has its roots in common law, but it is now protected by statute. Every state except West Virginia now has a clergy–communicant privilege statute (Gumper, 1984). These statutes were passed to ensure that confessions by penitents to priests would be absolutely confidential. The clergy, in persuading legislators to pass such statutes, stressed that there was a substantial societal benefit in ensuring citizens that their confessions would never be repeated by priests or by members of the clergy outside the confessional. The clergy argued that unless citizens were absolutely convinced that their confessions would remain confidential, they would not confess their sins, which could cause serious disruption to the framework of society. They asserted that the need for privacy in the confessional far outweighed the need for all evidence to be presented in a trial. The notion of extending the clergy–communicant privilege to include counseling has been criticized by Knapp and VandeCreek (1987). They argue that the privilege for recipients of mental health services should apply only when citizens have relationships with professionals with specialized training in counseling or psychotherapy, and that only a few specially trained pastoral counselors have such qualifications.

McCreary (2011) has explored the unusual situation in which a clergy member was also a licensed professional counselor (LPC) and was providing mental health services. In a Texas case (*Westbook v. Penley,* 2007), a minister disclosed to his congregation private information about a female client's extramarital affair that was revealed in a counseling relationship with the minister (it is standard practice in this church to discuss personal issues brought to the minister with the entire congregation). The Texas court determined that the minister's action was church related and a civil court should not interfere, despite the fact that the minister was also an LPC and would not have been allowed to reveal the private information of his client if he had not also been her minister. In this particular case, the court decided that the role of minister outweighed the role of LPC when the two roles were in conflict.

It is very important for counselors who have other roles to avoid trying to assume both roles at the same time. Counselors with dual roles should be clear in their own minds which role they are performing at a given point and communicate effectively their role with the persons they are helping.

Once citizens had been granted privileged communication with attorneys, physicians, and clergy, a variety of other professionals, including mental health professionals, began arguing successfully for privileged communication statutes for the benefit of their clients. Remember, though, that any exception to the general rule that all evidence will be presented in court is compromised by privileged communications statutes. Each time such a statute is passed, the legislators have to be convinced that making an exception to the rule is vital to the well-being of society, and that an individual citizen's need for privacy outweighs the need for evidence in court cases.

The earlier scholars who argued for a mental health professional–client privilege (Cottle, 1956; Fisher, 1964; Guttmacher & Weihofen, 1952; Heller, 1957; Slovenko, 1960; Slovenko & Usdin, 1961) did not base their arguments on the physician–patient privilege. Instead, they contended that citizens who sought the services of mental health professionals required more privacy than patients needed with physicians (Knapp & VandeCreek, 1987). Because of physicians' status in U.S. society, you might think that physician–patient privilege could be considered more important than mental health professional–client privilege. However, some legal scholars (Guttmacher & Weihofen, 1952; Louisell & Sinclair, 1971; Slovenko, 1960; Wigmore, 1961) have concluded that it is more important to protect the privacy of clients of mental health professionals than it is to protect the privacy of physicians' patients because of the unique nature of the psychotherapeutic relationship.

Before World War II, no state had a privileged communication statute for mental health professionals, although some psychiatrists were covered under physician–patient privilege statutes (Knapp & VandeCreek, 1987). State legislative bodies meet annually, changing statutes each time they meet, and sections affecting privileged communication statutes might be found in obscure places in state statute volumes. Therefore, it is impossible to give a completely accurate picture of privileged communication statutes for counselors and other mental health professionals. However, it is true that all 50 states and the District of Columbia have enacted some type of privileged communication statute for mental health professionals and their clients (*Jaffee v. Redmond*, 1996).

Statutes making relationships between mental health professionals and their clients privileged vary substantially from state to state in their language and construction. States have taken four approaches in formulating privilege laws for relationships between clients and their mental health providers (Knapp & VandeCreek, 1987). Some privilege statutes are modeled on attorney–client privilege laws. Others take the approach of the proposed, but rejected, Rule 504 of the Federal Rules of Evidence (28 U.S. Code §504). This rule has advantages over the attorney–client privilege laws because the proposed rules specify the extent and limitations of the privilege with great precision. A third approach provides for a privilege but allows judicial discretion in its waiver. The last group of statutes is idiosyncratic and does not follow any special pattern.

The Rationale for Privileged Communication in Counseling Relationships

Over the past few decades, counselors have been working to convince state legislators to enact privileged communication laws that protect their relationships with clients. Many of the arguments used to justify passage of these statutes were accepted and repeated by the U.S. Supreme Court

(Remley, Herlihy, & Herlihy, 1997) when *Jaffee v. Redmond et al.* (1996) was decided in favor of the existence of such a privilege under the Federal Rules of Evidence.

Counselors have argued that society benefits when individuals seek counseling to help them lead more productive lives as citizens. Mental health professionals have argued that because clients must reveal personal secrets that could be embarrassing, sensitive, or against their best interests, clients must be assured that the content of their counseling sessions will not be revealed without their permission. Society benefits when clients receive counseling that allows them to be more independent and productive, and these benefits outweigh the negative consequences of some evidence being privileged and therefore unavailable in court cases.

However, after an extensive review and analysis of empirical research studies related to confidentiality and privileged communication in the mental health professions, Shuman and Weiner (1987) concluded that although confidentiality is important in therapeutic relationships, privilege is not. Among their more interesting findings were (a) few laypersons know whether privilege exists in their states, (b) many mental health professionals indicate that clients are reassured by their disclosure or threat of disclosure of potential harm to self or others, and (c) judges do not find privilege a great impediment to finding the truth at trials. The first two findings argue against privileged communication statutes that protect relationships with mental health professionals, whereas the last one would seem to support the existence of such statutes.

Another argument used to get counselor privileged communication statutes passed is that the evidence lost to courts because of privilege statutes would never have been produced in the first place if the statutes did not exist. Clients would not go to counselors and reveal their secrets if they did not have the protection of legal privilege. As a result, society does not lose important evidence in lawsuits by granting privilege to counselor–client relationships because the evidence would never have come into existence if there were no privilege.

Psychiatrists, psychologists, and social workers have been successful in their efforts to have statutes enacted that grant privileged communication to their relationships with clients. Counselors have argued that their services are similar to those of other mental health professionals and that they are as deserving of the protection.

Counselor–client privilege of some type existed in 44 of the 45 states that licensed counselors in 2000 (Glosoff, Herlihy, & Spence, 2000), whereas psychologist–client privilege statutes existed in all 50 states (Glosoff, Herlihy, Herlihy, & Spence, 1997). Privileged communication statutes vary, ranging from some that protect counselor–client relationships to the fullest extent allowed by law to others that are quite weak. Professional counselors in jurisdictions where there are no counselor–client privileged communication statutes, or where existing ones are weak, are continuing in their efforts to get such laws passed or strengthened. Auerbach (2006) has pointed out that clients who seek mental health services in a particular state have varying degrees of privacy, depending on the exact language found in multiple statutes that grant privilege of clients with psychiatrists, licensed counselors, licensed psychologists, licensed social workers, and other licensed mental health professionals. Auerbach has argued that states need to reform their privileged communication statutes, and clients should have the same privacy protection, no matter which category of mental health professional provides services.

Privileged communication statutes are not always limited to interactions between clients and licensed professional counselors. In some states, school counselors, substance abuse counselors, or other designated categories of counselors have privilege. On the other hand, if a category of mental health professional is not listed in a privileged communication statute, courts deny privilege to the relationships of clients with those professionals (Moberly, 2007). You must investigate the statutes of the state in which you practice to determine whether your interactions with clients enjoy privilege and to determine exactly what *privilege* means in your state.

If you practice in a state that does not offer statutory privilege, you should inform your clients that you will keep confidential the content of your counseling sessions with them, but that one of the exceptions would be if a judge orders you to disclose information. You must include the same exception even if you practice in a state that does include a counselor–client privileged communication statute, but it is much less likely that a judge will order disclosure in a state with such a statute.

Occasionally, counselors will be involved in court cases heard in federal rather than state courts. The U.S. Supreme Court ruling in *Jaffee v. Redmond et al.* (1996) has interpreted the Federal Rules of Evidence to mean that there is a licensed psychotherapist–patient privilege in some cases heard in federal courts (Remley et al., 1997). In the *Jaffee* case, the psychotherapist was a social worker. It seems probable, but not guaranteed, that a similar privilege would be acknowledged for licensed counselor–client relationships in future cases. In a review of psychotherapist–patient privilege decisions in federal courts, Boumil, Freitas, and Freitas (2012) concluded, "The law that has evolved around the exercise of this privilege is complex and far from uniform around the country. In most cases, the goal is to balance the imperative of confidentiality with the need to disclose useful information" (p. 31). The same lack of uniformity in applying the law could be said to describe privileged communication statutes and case law in all states.

Counselors struggle with deciding the exact language to use when writing disclosure statements for clients or when informing clients orally regarding the confidentiality and privilege that might exist in the relationship. On one hand, counselors want to fully inform clients of the exceptions that exist to confidentiality and privilege, so that clients will be able to give truly informed consent to entering the counseling relationship (see Chapter 4 under Informed Consent). On the other hand, counselors do not want to be so technical and detailed in describing exceptions to confidentiality and privilege that clients become confused or lose confidence in the privacy of the counseling relationship. Suggested disclosure statements regarding confidentiality and privilege are included in Appendix B.

Asserting the Privilege

A statutory privilege belongs to clients rather than to counselors. If you or your records are subpoenaed or if you are asked during a legal proceeding to disclose privileged information, it is up to your client to assert the privilege so that you will not have to disclose the information (Boumil et al., 2012). However, sometimes the client cannot be located or is not present when counselors are asked to disclose privileged information. In these circumstances, the counselor has an obligation to assert the privilege on behalf of the client. In our opinion, counselors should secure the advice of an attorney if they are put in the position of asserting a client's privilege because legal procedures and questions regarding privilege are quite technical.

Responding to Subpoenas

Subpoenas are legal documents that might require counselors to give a written response to a written list of questions; produce copies of records; appear for a deposition, court hearing, or trial; or appear and bring their records with them. Subpoenas are official court documents and cannot be ignored. Counselors who do not respond appropriately to subpoenas can be held in contempt of court and could be fined or jailed until they comply. Unless you deal with subpoenas on a regular basis in your work, you should obtain legal advice before responding to a subpoena. Methods of obtaining legal advice are discussed in Chapter 1.

An attorney will review a subpoena for you and will advise you how to respond. If you must appear at a deposition, hearing, or trial as a result of a subpoena, you should ask your attorney to prepare you for what to expect, to advise you about how you should conduct yourself, and if possible to go with you so you can be given advice throughout the proceeding. More information on responding to subpoenas is contained in Chapter 6.

Suits for Disclosure

When counseling relationships are privileged under state or federal laws, clients have a right to expect counselors to keep information from their sessions private. With or without the privilege, counselors have a legal duty to maintain the privacy of their clients. Clients enter the counseling relationship with assurances of privacy and with very high expectations that information they disclose will not be revealed.

If a counselor discloses confidential information and the disclosure does not qualify as one of the exceptions to confidentiality and privilege, a client could sue the counselor for malpractice. The client would be required to prove the elements of a malpractice suit, as explained in Chapter 8. Clients who could show that they were harmed by the counselor's disclosure might prevail in such lawsuits and collect damages from the counselor. Thus, it is crucial that you understand the exceptions to confidentiality and privileged communication and know how to apply these exceptions in your practice.

Exceptions to Confidentiality and Privileged Communication

The general rule that counselors must keep their clients' disclosures confidential is easy to understand and follow. Exceptions to this general rule, however, occur frequently in the course of counseling, and counselors must understand these exceptions and be able to apply them to real situations (ACA, 2014, §B.2.). After reviewing counselor privileged communication statutes in all states, Glosoff et al. (2000) concluded that exceptions are numerous and extremely varied. As a result, it is very important for counselors to know the content of the privileged communication statute that exists in their state (if there is one) and the specific exceptions that are included. Glosoff et al. categorized exceptions into nine areas and listed those areas from the most to the least frequently cited in state statutes:

> (a) in cases of a dispute between counselor and client; (b) when a client raises the issue of mental condition in legal proceedings; (c) when a client's condition poses a danger to self or others; (d) in cases of child abuse or neglect (in addition to mandated reporting laws); (e) when the counselor has knowledge that the client is contemplating commission of a crime; (f) during court ordered psychological evaluations; (g) for purposes of involuntary hospitalization; (h) when the counselor has knowledge that a client has been a victim of a crime; and (i) in cases of harm to vulnerable adults. (p. 455)

To facilitate understanding, we have organized the exceptions into clusters according to the purposes they serve. First, we discuss client waiver of the privilege or right to privacy and exceptions that deal with sharing information with subordinates or other professionals in order to improve the quality of services. Next, we turn to exceptions that involve protecting clients or others who may be in danger. Then we look at ways that confidentiality and privileged communication are different when working with multiple clients as opposed to individuals, and with minor clients as opposed to adults. Finally, we note some exceptions that are legally mandated.

Client Waiver of the Privilege

Confidentiality and privilege belong to clients, not to counselors. As a result, clients can waive their privacy. This occurs most often when clients explicitly ask counselors to give information regarding the counseling relationship to third parties. Usually, clients who waive the privilege have an understanding that their secrets will be revealed. In some circumstances, however, clients may unknowingly waive the privilege by their actions (Knapp & VandeCreek, 1987). For example, clients might implicitly waive the privilege by filing a lawsuit seeking damages for emotional distress caused by an accident or by filing a malpractice lawsuit against a mental health professional, as discussed later in the section on exceptions. In *Cynthia B. v. New Rochelle Hospital* (1982), the court found that the client (rather than the mental health professional) had responsibility for any embarrassment or inconvenience that resulted from the disclosure of privileged mental health information in a lawsuit she had filed.

Death of the Client

According to Cleary (1984), the common law doctrine is that privilege does not end with a person's death. In some states, statutes specify how privilege is controlled after an individual dies. When there is no statutory language dealing with privilege and the death of the holder, then the common law practice of allowing a legal representative of the deceased person to assert the privilege generally is followed (Knapp & VandeCreek, 1987). An executor of an estate is not always recognized by a court as a deceased person's legal representative for the purposes of privilege (*Boling v. Superior Court*, 1980). If you believe that a deceased client's privilege must be asserted or waived, you should contact his or her family members, probate attorney, or executor to determine whether a legal representative is available to deal with the matter. The ACA *Code of Ethics* states simply that counselors must protect the confidentiality of deceased clients according to legal requirements and documented preferences of the client (ACA, 2014, §B.3.f.).

Sharing Information with Subordinates or Fellow Professionals

In some situations, the *umbrella* of confidentiality can be extended to cover others who assist or work with the counselor in providing services to clients. Although these situations do not involve a breach of the client's confidentiality, they do constitute exceptions to the general rule that only the counselor and client are privy to information shared in sessions. Sharing information with others in order to provide the best possible services to clients is permissible when (a) clerical or other assistants handle confidential information, (b) counselors consult with colleagues or experts, (c) counselors are working under supervision, and (d) other professionals are involved in coordinating client care.

CLERICAL OR OTHER ASSISTANTS MAY HANDLE CONFIDENTIAL INFORMATION It is routine business practice for many types of professionals, including physicians and attorneys as well as counselors, to employ clerical assistants and other subordinates who handle confidential client information. Some state statutes that grant privilege to counselor–client relationships may also specifically extend the privilege to communications when assistants are present or when assistants see privileged information, but such specific language is rare. Knapp and VandeCreek (1987) have concluded that common law principles most likely would extend privilege to unprivileged assistants who are involved in activities that further the treatment of the client.

Counselors should be aware, however, that they are ethically responsible for any breach of confidentiality by someone who assists them. The *Code of Ethics* alerts counselors to "make every effort to ensure that privacy and confidentiality of clients are maintained by subordinates, including employees, supervisees, students, clerical assistants, and volunteers" (ACA, 2014, §B.3.a.). Counselors may also be held legally responsible for breaches of confidentiality by their subordinates.

Under the general legal principle of *respondeat superior*, employers are held responsible for the acts of their employees. Counselors, then, can be held accountable for assistants who breach confidentiality through the doctrine of vicarious liability. It is important for counselors to impress on their employees the importance of keeping information confidential and to supervise them in such a way as to ensure that they are complying with this requirement.

Counselors can take certain precautions to help ensure that their subordinates understand both the importance of confidentiality and the procedures for maintaining it. Counselors are obligated to determine whether individuals they may hire are trustworthy. Counselors could be held accountable for hiring persons notorious for disregarding the privacy of others if these persons later disclose confidential client information. We suggest that counselors take an inventory periodically of everyone who may handle confidential information about their clients. This might include answering service personnel, an office receptionist, clerical assistants, billing service staff, counselor interns or supervisees, and paraprofessionals. The counselor can conduct training sessions for these employee groups to ensure that they understand the importance of confidentiality and know how the counselor wants them to handle confidential material. The federal HIPAA law (see Chapter 6) requires that employees be trained to protect the privacy of clients. Therefore, training sessions that are held should be documented.

COUNSELORS MAY CONSULT WITH COLLEAGUES OR EXPERTS   Counselors are encouraged to consult with peers or experts whenever they have questions about their ethical obligations or professional practice (ACA, 2014, §C.2.e.). If the questions have to do with clinical practice, counselors should seek consultation from a practitioner who has experience or expertise in the particular area of concern. If an ethical question is involved, it is a good idea to consult a fellow mental health professional who has expertise in ethics. In a particularly perplexing ethical dilemma that involves a difficult judgment call, it is wise to seek more than one opinion.

Consultation usually does not need to involve a breach of confidentiality because most consultations can be managed without revealing the identity of the client. The *Code of Ethics* (ACA, 2014) gives some guidance in this respect. Standard B.7.a. states that "Written and oral reports present only data germane to the purposes of the consultation, and every effort is made to protect client identity and to avoid undue invasion of privacy." Standard B.7.b cautions that, during consultations, counselors should not disclose confidential information that could lead to the identification of a client. Nonetheless, nearly 30% of the counselors in Neukrug and Milliken's (2011) study believed it was ethical to share confidential client information with a colleague. Although every effort should be made to protect confidentiality, it is sometimes impossible to avoid revealing the identity of the client because of the nature of a particular situation or because the identity of the client might be obvious. In these instances, best practice would be for the counselor to obtain client consent, if possible, and the identity of the consultant should be revealed to the client. Of course, in some situations neither step might be possible.

Finally, counselors should choose consultants who have the appropriate expertise for the question at hand. If you have an ethical or clinical question, consult with a professional colleague. If you have a legal question, ask an attorney.

CONFIDENTIAL INFORMATION MAY BE SHARED WHEN THE COUNSELOR IS WORKING UNDER SUPERVISION   While you are a counselor in training or when you are gaining post-master's degree experience as a counselor in preparation for licensure, your work with actual clients will be supervised by experienced professionals. During your practicum, internship, and other field experiences, university supervisors and on-site supervisors will review your counseling sessions with you and provide you with feedback about your performance. After graduation, if you are planning to obtain a credential such as a license, your initial post-master's counseling work will also be under supervision. Experienced counselors may want to provide supervision to beginning professionals or may need to work under supervision while acquiring skills in a new specialty area of practice. Supervision is likely to be a part of your experience throughout your professional career.

Supervision is similar to consultation in that information about clients is shared with other professionals who subscribe to the ethic of confidentiality. However, in supervision, unlike consultation, the client's identity cannot be concealed. Supervisors may observe actual counseling sessions from behind a one-way mirror, review videotapes or audiotapes of sessions, and review case notes and counseling records. Supervisors have the same obligations as you do: they must keep confidential any information revealed in counseling sessions that they are supervising. Nonetheless, your clients have the right to know that you are working under supervision. According to *Informed Consent and Client Rights* (ACA, 2014, §F.1.c.), you have an ethical obligation to inform your clients that their confidentiality is limited because your supervisor will have access to information about them. When you are involved in group supervision, clients have the right to know that a group of your fellow practicum students or interns may also be discussing their cases. The *Code of Ethics* also requires counselors to obtain permission from clients before they observe counseling sessions or review transcripts or videotaped recordings of sessions with their supervisors, faculty, or peers (ACA, 2014, §B.6.d.).

You may feel some reluctance to divulge to your clients that you are working under supervision, or to explain to them all the circumstances in which information about them might be shared. You may be concerned that clients will have less confidence in your professional abilities, or that they will feel constrained about revealing personal information. These concerns must be set aside in the interest of your clients' right to informed consent. It is best to inform your clients about the limits to confidentiality in a straightforward manner and to do so at the very outset of the counseling relationship. Clients can be told that the purpose of supervision is to help you do a better job and that the focus of the supervision will be on you and your performance rather than on them and their problems. Sometimes clients will be unnerved by the idea of a supervisor, who is a faceless stranger to them, sitting behind the mirror. In these cases, it is a good idea to arrange for the client to meet the supervisor and have the opportunity to express concerns and ask questions directly. In our experience as supervisors, we have seen that clients typically forget their initial concerns once they become engaged in the counseling process. You may be pleasantly surprised to find that this will happen for you, too.

The relationships between counseling students who are in supervision and their clients may not be privileged. As a result, students may be forced to reveal the contents of counseling sessions if ordered to do so by a judge in a legal proceeding. If the relationship between a client and the student's supervisor would be privileged if the supervisor were providing the counseling services, then it is likely that privilege will exist between the client and the counselor–supervisee as well. Usually, under the law of privilege, a privilege is extended to assistants or supervisees of professionals who have statutory privilege with their clients.

OTHER PROFESSIONALS MAY BE INVOLVED IN COORDINATING CLIENT CARE In some settings, such as inpatient units in hospitals, treatment teams routinely work together in caring for patients. Although the benefits of coordinating the efforts of various professionals are obvious, as an ethical matter clients need to be told what information about them is being shared, with whom, and for what purposes (Herlihy & Corey, 20014a). According to §B.3.b. (ACA, 2014,), when client care

involves a continuing review by a treatment team, the client must be informed of the team's existence and composition, the information being shared, and the purposes of sharing the information.

In numerous other situations, you might want to share confidential client information with
fellow professionals in order to ensure coordination or continuity of care. A client might be receiving psychotropic medications from a physician while seeing you for counseling. A client might be
seeing you for individual counseling while participating in group counseling with another counselor. Clients might move and later request that you send their records or communicate by telephone
with their new counselor. In all these situations, it is ethically appropriate for you to communicate
with the other professionals *when the client has given permission for you to do so.* Several standards
in the *Code of Ethics* (ACA, 2014) address these kinds of circumstances. Standards A.3. and B.3.
both speak to the need for mental health professionals to work cooperatively. When clients are
receiving services from another mental health professional, the code directs counselors to obtain
client consent and then to inform the other professional and develop clear agreements to avoid confusion and conflict for the client. Standard B.6.g. (ACA, 2014) requires counselors to obtain written
permission from clients to disclose or transfer records to legitimate third parties and reminds counselors that they are required to work to ensure that receivers of their records are sensitive to the
client's confidentiality. HIPAA requires that client permission to give information to third parties
be obtained in writing, and that counselors who transfer records notify the receiving third parties
that the information being transferred is confidential and should be protected. Fisher (2008) suggested that counselors mark any records that contain identifiable client information as confidential
and not to be released.

From a legal perspective, situations in which counselors function in treatment teams or coordinate client care are similar to situations in which counselors' assistants or supervisors learn confidential information about clients. If the relationship between a counselor and a client is privileged,
then it is likely that the privilege will continue to exist when confidential information is discussed in
treatment teams or with other professionals when coordinating client care.

Protecting Someone Who Is in Danger

Situations sometimes arise that require counselors to breach confidentiality in order to warn or protect someone who is in danger. Some of these situations also involve a duty to report the dangerous
situation to responsible authorities. These three types of duties—to warn, to protect, and to report—
constitute some of the most stressful situations you will encounter as a practicing counselor.

Because these exceptions require that you make a deliberate decision to breach a client's confidentiality, there must be a compelling justification for doing so. Winston (1991) suggested that
breaching a confidence can be justified by the concept of vulnerability. A duty to protect from harm
arises when someone is especially dependent on others or is in some way vulnerable to the choices
and actions of others. Persons in a vulnerable position are unable to avoid risk of harm on their own
and are dependent on others to intervene on their behalf. When counselors, through their confidential relations with clients, learn that a vulnerable person is at risk of harm, they have a duty to act to
prevent the harm. This is a higher duty than the duty to maintain confidentiality.

**COUNSELORS MUST TAKE ACTION WHEN THEY SUSPECT ABUSE OR NEGLECT OF CHILDREN
OR OTHER PERSONS PRESUMED TO HAVE LIMITED ABILITY TO CARE FOR THEMSELVES** Counselors have both an ethical and a legal duty to disclose confidential information when such disclosure is required to protect clients or identified others from serious and foreseeable harm (ACA,
2014, §B.2.a.). Duties to protect children and vulnerable adults from abuse are discussed at length
in Chapter 11.

COUNSELORS MUST TAKE ACTION TO PROTECT CLIENTS WHO POSE A DANGER TO THEM-SELVES   When counselors determine that clients are suicidal, they must do something to prevent the clients from harming themselves (ACA, 2014, §B.2.a.). A leading cause of malpractice lawsuits against counselors is a charge by surviving family members that counselors were negligent and there-fore committed malpractice if their clients commit suicide or harm themselves while attempting sui-cide. This duty to protect your clients from suicide attempts is explained and discussed in Chapter 7.

COUNSELORS MUST TAKE ACTION WHEN A CLIENT POSES A DANGER TO OTHERS   When counselors believe their clients may harm someone else, even when such information is commu-nicated by someone other than the client (Edwards, 2006), counselors must take steps to prevent harm to the person who is in danger (ACA, 2014, §B.2.a.). This duty, like the duty to prevent clients from harming themselves, could lead to a charge of negligence or malpractice. The duty to protect others who may be harmed is explained and discussed in Chapter 7.

COUNSELORS MUST DETERMINE WHETHER TO BREACH CONFIDENTIALITY WHEN A CLIENT HAS A COMMUNICABLE AND LIFE-THREATENING DISEASE AND THE CLIENT'S BEHAVIOR IS PUTTING OTHERS AT RISK   This exception to confidentiality is the same as the exception to pro-tect others if you believe your client may harm other people (ACA, 2014, §B.2.c.). This excep-tion also is reviewed in Chapter 7.

Counseling Multiple Clients

Unique confidentiality problems arise when working with multiple clients. Generally, when your client and one or more additional persons are in the room, confidentiality is compromised and privi-lege usually is waived. Although you can make your own pledge not to disclose certain information, you cannot guarantee the behavior of others such as group participants or family members. Despite the fact that others in the room might not keep a client's secrets, a counselor's responsibility is not diminished by the presence of additional persons in a counseling session.

CONFIDENTIALITY CANNOT BE GUARANTEED IN GROUP COUNSELING   Confidentiality is a particularly difficult ethical issue in group counseling. Although confidentiality certainly is as important in group counseling as it is in individual counseling, it is difficult to enforce, and counse-lors should not offer guarantees. It appears that this caution may not be well understood—37% of the ACA members surveyed by Neukrug and Milliken (2011) believed it was ethical to guarantee confidentiality for group members. Group counselors frequently encounter problems with maintain-ing confidentiality among group members who are not bound by the same professional standards. They may inadvertently breach confidentiality or yield to the temptation to discuss group experi-ences with family or friends. The *Code of Ethics* (ACA, 2014) gives some guidance for dealing with confidentiality in groups in §B.4.a., which states that "counselors clearly explain the importance and parameters of confidentiality for the specific group." A significant portion of the best practice guidelines of the Association for Specialists in Group Work (Thomas & Pender, 2008) is devoted to confidentiality among group members. This is an especially helpful resource with which you will want to familiarize yourself.

A few states specifically provide for privilege to extend to group counseling situations, but most privileged communication statutes are silent on this issue (Knapp & VandeCreek, 1987). It is impor-tant, then, that you read the privileged communication statute in your state (if one exists for counseling relationships) to determine whether group counseling sessions are privileged. In states where group counseling situations are not mentioned, at least one court has found privilege to exist (*State v. Andring*,

1984). As a result of the Andring case, it is possible that group counseling sessions would be found by courts to be privileged even if statutes do not specify that privilege exists for group counseling clients. Confidentiality dilemmas related to group counseling are discussed further in Chapter 12.

CONFIDENTIALITY CANNOT BE GUARANTEED IN COUPLES OR FAMILY COUNSELING   When the focus of counseling shifts from the individual to the family system, new ethical issues arise and existing ones become more complicated. Counselors who provide services for couples and families encounter some unique confidentiality concerns, such as how to deal with family secrets. For example, consider the situation in the following case example.

5-3 The Case of Alexis

Bob and Carla, a husband and wife, are seeing Alexis for marriage counseling. Generally, when Alexis provides counseling to couples, she sees each partner alone for one or more sessions because she believes counseling progresses better that way. Bob shared during one of his individual sessions with Alexis that he is having an affair with another woman and that Carla doesn't know it. Bob doesn't plan to tell Carla, and he insists that Alexis not tell Carla either.

- How should Alexis respond to Bob's insistence?
- How might this situation have been avoided?

Discussion: According to the *Code of Ethics*, in couples and family counseling "Counselors seek agreement and document in writing such agreement among all involved parties regarding the confidentiality of information. In the absence of an agreement to the contrary, the couple or family is considered to be the client" (ACA, 2014, §B.4.b.). From the wording of the standard, it appears the agreement could be oral or written, but if it is oral, the agreement should be documented in the counselor's notes. Therefore, Alexis should have obtained an agreement from Bob and Carla before their counseling sessions began, and documented their agreement in writing, regarding the confidentiality of information, especially since Alexis generally sees each partner in individual sessions. Since Alexis takes that approach to couples counseling, it is very important to establish with the couple how information that is shared individually will be handled. Each partner should know whether or not information shared with the counselor without the other partner being present will be told to the partner who is not present. In this situation, because the *Code of Ethics* states that in the absence of a written agreement the couple "is considered to be the client," Alexis will have to insist that Bob disclose the affair to Carla if Alexis is to continue counseling the couple. Alexis could refer the couple to another counselor.

Alexis might have avoided the problem in several ways. She could have counseled the couple together only, and not individually. She could have told Bob and Carla at the outset that she would not keep any secret that would interfere with the goals or process of counseling, and if either of them objected to disclosing the secret, she would not be able to continue the counseling relationship. Alexis could have included an explanation of her policy on family secrets in her written disclosure statement. In addition, to comply with the ACA *Code of Ethics*, she should have gotten a written signed agreement from the couple regarding how confidential information would be handled during their couple's counseling.

This case example points out the importance of informed consent procedures. You must make clear at the outset to both of a couple's partners the limitations of confidentiality and how you will handle confidentiality issues, obtain an agreement with the couple, and document the agreement in writing (ACA, 2014, §B.4.b.). In an analysis of the problem of *family secrets*, Brendel and Nelson (1999) pointed out that the ethical code of the International Association of Marriage and Family Counselors (IAMFC) specifically states that information learned by counselors in individual counseling sessions may not be repeated to other family members without the client's permission. They provided guidelines for counselors on how to deal with situations similar to the previously cited case example. This frequently occurring problem is discussed further in Chapter 12.

Counseling couples or families can also lead to very difficult legal questions regarding confidentiality and privilege. Under general legal principles, any statutory privilege that exists between a counselor and client is waived if there is a third party present when information is being disclosed. However, privilege laws in some states specifically cover relationships between counselors and married couples or between counselors and family members (Knapp & VandeCreek, 1987). In these states, it is clear that a counseling relationship will be privileged despite specific additional persons being present during the counseling session. In states without such statutes, it is unclear whether an individual who is being counseled with a spouse or other family members present could assert the privilege. Appellate court decisions are split as to whether a privilege that otherwise would exist by statute would be extended to sessions that include a married couple (*Clausen v. Clausen*, 1983; *Ellis v. Ellis*, 1971; *Sims v. State*, 1984; *Hospital and Community Psychiatry*, 1979; *Wichansky v. Wichansky*, 1973; *Yaron v. Yaron*, 1975).

A very difficult dilemma for counselors is posed when one spouse demands that the counselor not reveal information related in a marital counseling session, and the other spouse demands that the counselor reveal it. Situations like this often arise when a married couple enters counseling because of marital problems and then later engages in divorce proceedings.

The spouse who does not want the contents of the counseling sessions revealed should assert the privilege through his or her attorney. Of course, a counselor never wants to reveal in court private information that was related in a counseling session (ACA, 2014, §B.1.c.). Counselors generally will cooperate with the spouse and attorney as arguments are made to maintain the privilege of the client who does not want the private information revealed. Counselors are quite vulnerable legally in these situations because revealing privileged information inappropriately could lead to a malpractice lawsuit. On the other hand, refusing to disclose information that is not privileged could lead to being held in contempt of court by a judge. If you find yourself in a situation like this and are unsure of your legal responsibilities, you should consult your own attorney, who will advise you regarding your legal obligations and rights.

Counseling Minor or Legally Incompetent Clients

WHEN CLIENTS ARE MINOR CHILDREN OR LEGALLY INCOMPETENT, COUNSELORS CANNOT GIVE THE SAME ASSURANCES OF CONFIDENTIALITY AS THEY GIVE OTHER CLIENTS Minors and adults who have been adjudicated incompetent in a court of law do not have a legal right to enter into contracts. Thus, their parents or guardians control their legal rights. As a result, counselors owe legal duties to the parents or guardians of minors or incompetent adults. At the same time, counselors have ethical obligations to the clients themselves (ACA, 2014, §B.5.). This conflict between law and ethics regarding the privacy rights of minors and incompetent adults is discussed in detail in Chapter 11.

Court-Ordered Disclosures

COUNSELORS MUST DISCLOSE CONFIDENTIAL INFORMATION WHEN ORDERED TO DO SO BY A COURT   There will be instances when counselors are called to testify in court and their clients ask them not to reveal information shared in counseling sessions. If the relationship is privileged, either the client or the counselor will assert the privilege. In cases where no privilege exists, counselors should ask the court not to require the disclosure and should explain the potential harm that could be done to the counseling relationship (ACA, 2014, §B.2.c.). If the judge still requires the disclosure, only essential information should be revealed (§B.2.e.). Counselors who are ordered by a judge to reveal confidential information should not worry that clients may sue them for violating their privacy. Complying with a judge's order is a defense to any charge of wrongdoing (Prosser, 1971). Remember, though, that a subpoena that a counselor receives may not be valid. Confidential or privileged information should not be revealed in response to a subpoena until an attorney representing the counselor has advised that course of action. See Chapter 6 for a complete discussion of subpoenas.

Legal Protections for Counselors in Disputes

COUNSELORS MAY REVEAL CONFIDENTIAL INFORMATION WHEN IT IS NECESSARY TO DEFEND THEMSELVES AGAINST CHARGES BROUGHT BY CLIENTS   When ethical or legal complaints are filed against counselors by their clients, the concepts of confidentiality or privilege could become problematic for counselors who must defend themselves. It would be odd if a client could claim that a counselor had done something wrong in a counseling relationship, and then the same client could claim that confidentiality or privilege prevented the counselor from explaining the details of the counseling relationship in presenting his or her defense. As a result, the law of privileged communication requires that clients waive their privilege when they bring complaints or malpractice lawsuits against their counselors (Knapp & VandeCreek, 1987).

Other Legal Exceptions

CLIENTS WAIVE THEIR PRIVILEGE WHEN THEY BRING LAWSUITS CLAIMING EMOTIONAL DAMAGE   If clients claim emotional damage in a lawsuit, then the law automatically waives their privilege associated with counseling relationships (Knapp & VandeCreek, 1987). It would be unfair to allow individuals to claim in court that they had been emotionally damaged and then to prohibit the counselor who had treated the person for the damage from testifying. The person accused of damaging the client must be given an opportunity in a court proceeding to cross-examine the counselor regarding the nature and extent of the damage.

Nonetheless, most courts have held that suits for normal distress or physical injuries arising out of a physical trauma do not automatically waive a plaintiff's right to privilege in counseling relationships (*Ideal Publishing Corp. v. Creative Features*, 1977; *Roberts v. Superior Court*, 1973; *Tylitzki v. Triple X Service, Inc.*, 1970; *Webb v. Quincy City Lines, Inc.*, 1966). Only when individuals bringing lawsuits claim that they were emotionally damaged and that damage required them to seek mental health treatment will their therapeutic privilege be waived.

PRIVILEGE IS GENERALLY WAIVED IN CIVIL COMMITMENT PROCEEDINGS   Privilege is usually waived by law for individuals who are being evaluated by a court to determine whether they should be involuntarily committed to a psychiatric hospital. Obviously, the contents of an evaluation conducted for the purpose of rendering an opinion to a court concerning the advisability of a commitment will not be privileged. Evaluators should carefully explain the nature of the interview to individuals who are being evaluated to ensure that the individual does not misconstrue the relationship as involving mental health treatment (ACA, 2014, §E.13.b.; Knapp & VandeCreek, 1987).

> **Sharing information with subordinates or fellow professionals is permissible under the following circumstances:**
>
> - Clerical or other assistants handle confidential information.
> - A counselor consults with colleagues or experts.
> - The counselor is working under supervision.
> - Other professionals are involved in coordinating client care.
>
> **Protecting someone who is in danger may require disclosure of confidential information when the following conditions exist:**
>
> - The counselor suspects abuse or neglect of children or other persons presumed to have limited ability to care for themselves.
> - A client poses a danger to others.
> - A client poses a danger to self (is suicidal).
> - A client has a fatal, communicable disease and the client's behavior is putting others at risk.
>
> **Confidentiality is compromised when counseling multiple clients, including the following:**
>
> - Group counseling.
> - Counseling couples or families.
>
> **There are unique confidentiality and privileged communication considerations when working with minor clients:**
>
> - Minor clients do not have privilege under the law.
> - Privilege belongs to parents or guardians.
>
> **Certain exceptions are mandated by law, including the following:**
>
> - Disclosure is court ordered.
> - Clients file complaints against their counselors.
> - Clients claim emotional damage in a lawsuit.
> - Civil commitment proceedings are initiated.

FIGURE 5-1   Exceptions to confidentiality and privileged communication

Source: Pearson Education, Inc., Hoboken, NJ.

When a mental health professional seeks a commitment of a client who initiated treatment voluntarily, privilege may also be waived by the client by law (*Commonwealth ex rel. Platt v. Platt*, 1979), although in *People v. Taylor* (1980) a Colorado court refused to waive the privilege. Individuals who are involuntarily committed do not have privileged relationships with their treating mental health professionals at a judicial review of that commitment (*State v. Hungerford*, 1978; *State v. Kupchun*, 1977). The important distinction to remember is that evaluation interviews are different from counseling interviews in terms of privilege. Evaluation interviews conducted to help determine whether a client should be committed to a residential facility are not privileged. Appendix B includes an informed consent form that may be used by counselors who conduct evaluations.

See Figure 5-1 for a listing of the exceptions to confidentiality and privileged communication that are summarized in this chapter.

DIVERSITY CONSIDERATIONS IN CONFIDENTIALITY AND PRIVILEGED COMMUNICATION

Counselors must be sensitive to the cultural meanings of privacy and confidentiality (ACA, 2014, §B.1.a.). Because U.S. society is becoming more diverse and the international movement in counseling is burgeoning, it is more important than ever before to be aware that some clients may not want their confidentiality upheld in the traditional manner. Confidentiality requirements in counseling have been a reflection of cultural values that emphasize autonomy and respect for individualism (Casas, Park, & Cho, 2010). In collectivist cultures the individual is seen as less important than the family or group, and clients might not place much importance on their individual privacy, although the privacy of their families or groups might be highly valued (Hoop, DiPasquale, Hernandez, & Weiss Roberts, 2008). In such cases, counselors might need to share confidential information with family members or members of the client's community, if the client so desires.

Maintaining client confidentiality becomes more complicated when the counselor and client do not speak the same language and an interpreter is required. If a family member is used as the interpreter, the counselor should carefully explain the purpose and importance of confidentiality and ask the interpreter to keep all disclosures completely confidential. It is preferable to use a professional interpreter, if one is available who understands the context of the client's life. The counselor might consider holding a presession meeting with the interpreter to review confidentiality, its limits, and how the concept can be communicated to the client (Paone & Malott, 2008). During the initial session, the client should be informed of the limits to confidentiality and privilege that are created by the presence of the interpreter.

Summary and Key Points

After reading this chapter, we expect that you have developed a healthy appreciation for the complexities of the ethic of confidentiality and its legal counterpart, privileged communication. We also expect that you have a clearer understanding of why counselors encounter dilemmas of confidentiality more frequently than they encounter other types of dilemmas and find them the most difficult to resolve. The considerable amount of information contained in this chapter should be helpful. These dilemmas, nevertheless, will challenge you to use your clinical judgment and your skills in ethical reasoning and in researching the current status of professional knowledge and the law. We hope we have emphasized how important it is that you do not try to go it alone when you encounter questions about confidentiality and privileged communication, but rather that you seek consultation from colleagues or an attorney. Following are some of the key points made in the chapter:

- Both confidentiality and privileged communication are based on the client's right to privacy. *Confidentiality* is an ethical concept, and *privileged communication* is a legal term.
- Although research does not clearly support the notion that assurances of privacy are essential

to clients' willingness to disclose, counselors view confidentiality as a strong moral force and a fundamental ethical obligation.

- In general, counselors seem to do a very good job of protecting their clients' confidentiality. It is easy for an inadvertent breach to occur, however, and counselors need to be zealous in safeguarding client privacy.
- Privileged communication means that a judge cannot order a counselor to reveal information in court that has been recognized by law as privileged. Because privileged communication is antagonistic to the entire U.S. system of justice, courts and legislatures have been reluctant to extend privilege to relationships between mental health professionals and their clients.
- Except for cases heard in federal courts, privileged communication in counseling is determined by state statutes. It is essential that you learn your state laws regarding privileged communication in counseling relationships.
- Confidentiality and privilege both belong to the client, not to the counselor, and clients can waive their privacy.

- Confidentiality and privilege are not absolute. There are at least 15 exceptions to confidentiality and privileged communication. You must understand each exception and be able to apply exceptions to real situations you encounter in your practice.
- It is permissible to share information with subordinates and fellow professionals in order to provide the best possible services to clients.
- Stressful situations for counselors often involve decisions regarding the duties to warn, protect, or report when a client's condition poses a danger to self or others.
- Confidentiality cannot be guaranteed when counseling couples, families, groups, minors, or adults who have been adjudicated as legally incompetent.
- Certain exceptions to confidentiality and privileged communication are legally mandated.
- When in doubt about your obligations regarding confidentiality or privileged communication, consult!

Records and Subpoenas

Although records were mentioned in Chapter 5 in relation to counselors' responsibilities regarding confidentiality and privileged communication, records are such an important (and somewhat complex) area of a counselor's practice that we discuss them in detail in this chapter. Counselors typically receive little training in proper record keeping, and they tend to dislike and neglect paperwork (Fulero & Wilbert, 1988; Luepker, 2012; MacCluskie, 2001). Nonetheless, maintaining adequate records is necessary for ethical, legal, and professional reasons. Records are often subject to being subpoenaed, and counselors must be prepared to respond to legal demands for their records.

RECORDS

Records are any physical *recording* made of information related to a counselor's professional practice. When you consider the kinds of records counselors create and maintain, you probably think of the notes that counselors take concerning sessions with clients. These types of records are referred to as *clinical case notes* in this chapter. Other types that might come easily to mind are administrative records related to clients, such as appointment books, billing and payment accounts, copies of correspondence, intake forms, or other routine papers. Additional records that are often generated are audiorecordings or videorecordings of sessions with clients. These recordings usually are used for supervision purposes, but they might also be created for clients to review or by counselors for the purpose of training other counselors. Unusual records generated in counseling practices might include records of clients logging on to computerized information systems, telephone bills indicating clients' numbers called, computerized records that clients had used for parking or building passes, or videorecordings of clients entering or leaving a counseling office. All of these items are records, and the privacy of clients could be compromised if these records were not kept confidential.

Although records are a necessary part of a counselor's practice, it is important that counselors balance their need to keep documents with their obligation to provide quality counseling services to clients. Counselors who find themselves devoting inordinate or excessive amounts of time creating and maintaining records probably need to reevaluate how they are spending their professional time and energy.

In today's litigious environment, many administrators and lawyers who represent counseling agencies are requiring counselors to keep voluminous records to protect the agencies in the event a lawsuit is filed. Although counselors are wise to document actions they take when they are fulfilling an ethical or legal obligation (such as protecting an intended victim against a client's threat of harm), it is not appropriate for counselors to neglect the counseling services they provide to clients in order to produce excessive amounts of records that are self-protective (Kennedy, 2003). Counselors, their administrators, and the lawyers who advise them must balance the need to protect themselves in the event of legal claims against their duty to provide quality counseling services. It is possible to keep adequate records *and* provide quality counseling services.

Purposes of Records

Counseling records are created for a number of reasons (Corey, Corey, Corey, & Callanan, 2015). Some of these reasons benefit clients, whereas others benefit counselors or their employers.

One of the first standards in the *Code of Ethics* (American Counseling Association, 2014, §A.1.b.) states that counselors maintain documentation necessary for rendering professional services to their clients. From an ethical perspective, this is the primary purpose of keeping records—to assist you in providing clients with the best possible counseling services. Unless you have perfect recall, you will find that the clinical case notes you have recorded will help to refresh your memory prior to sessions. These notes will allow you to review progress toward goals that you and the client have jointly determined, to know when and in what circumstances important decisions and actions were taken, and to maintain an overall perspective on the content and process of the entire counseling relationship.

Clinical case notes benefit the client because they allow the counselor to summarize each interaction with the client and record plans for future sessions. The work of counselors can be more consistent, precise, and systematic when accurate and thorough notes are kept.

Keeping good records allows counselors to stay on track by documenting which kinds of treatment were undertaken and why. It is helpful to us, our clients, and the therapeutic process when we work to maintain a clear conceptualization of counseling goals and our progress toward those goals. Good records can assist us in helping clients measure their change and growth. We can use our notes to reference and affirm significant turning points and successes in our clients' work.

Clinical case notes can be particularly important when a client decides to resume counseling with you after an extended break. It would be a daunting task to try to remember details of a client's life and concerns after months or even years have passed, during which so many other clients' lives and concerns have consumed your attention. If you can use your notes to refresh your recollections about former issues and events that occurred during the counseling process, you will take a significant step toward reconnecting with your returning client.

Continuity of care is a consideration when a client is referred from one mental health professional to another as well. Records are used to transfer the information that one health care provider has about a client's condition to another health care provider. Health care records create a history of a client's diagnosis, treatment, and recovery. Health care providers can render better services when they have access to information regarding a client's past that is more thorough and accurate than a client's oral recall.

Notes should be written with enough clarity so that another helping professional, by learning what did and did not help the client, can provide continuation of counseling. The receiving counselor can get attuned to the meaningful aspects of a client's work if records clearly describe goals, treatment strategies, and progress that was made. If you are the receiving counselor, you will particularly appreciate these records.

Counselors also keep clinical case notes for their own benefit (Schaffer, 1997). Counselors document any steps they have taken in an emergency or critical situation. Later, if counselors are accused of not having provided competent services, the records serve as evidence of their thinking, and the notes document any actions taken. Without adequate documentation, there is no clear record of the course and progress of counseling (Wiger, 1999).

In our opinion, before you write any type of note or create a record, you should carefully consider why you are taking that action. In many counseling offices or agencies, records are routinely created without giving any thought to the simple question of *why* they are being kept. It makes no sense for a counselor who is keeping clinical case notes for the sole purpose of refreshing her memory to write her notes the same way the counselor in the local hospital writes notes on a patient's chart. In a hospital, a patient's chart is read by physicians, nurses, physical therapists, counselors, and others. Each person who makes an entry on a patient's chart is writing so that other professionals will know what types of services were rendered, for the benefit of the patient. If counselors ask themselves why they are writing a note for a client record, who will read the record, and what those who read it will be looking for, there will be a better chance that the record will be appropriate for its purpose.

Counselors keep a number of business records associated with their counseling practice for their own purposes. Counselors who work within agencies or other facilities that provide counseling services often need to document the number of persons who have been served, the categories of services rendered, and other types of information. Counselors in private practice have to keep business records to justify tax deductions they take in relation to their counseling business. Regardless of whose purpose is being served in creating records, it is the privacy of clients that dictates how records must be handled.

6-1 The Case of Paolo

Paolo has recently taken his first counseling job in the local community mental health center, after receiving his master's degree in counseling. During his first week at work, he meets with his section supervisor, who goes over the records the agency keeps for each client. His supervisor shows him an intake form that is 12 pages long. The form requires the counselor to collect all types of personal information on the client, including a thorough medical, health, and social history, and detailed information regarding the client's education, work background, and current job. A diagnosis and treatment plan form requires the counselor to enter a diagnosis from the *Diagnostic and Statistical Manual*, 5th Edition (*DSM-5*; American Psychiatric Association, 2013) and at least five measurable and behavioral goals for counseling. Paolo's supervisor explains that after each counseling session, Paolo must note in the client's folder a summary of issues discussed in the session, the client's progress toward each of the counseling goals listed, and what Paolo plans to do in the next counseling session. The supervisor suggests that Paolo write about three pages of notes for each client after each session. His supervisor says there are more forms to be completed after clients have their last session, but they will go over those forms later. When Paolo asks his supervisor why so much information is collected for each client, his supervisor replies in a patronizing tone, "This is the way all professional counseling agencies keep records. Weren't you taught record keeping in your master's degree program?"

- How should Paolo respond to his supervisor's training session?
- What kinds of records do you think would be reasonable for a community mental health agency to keep on each client?

Discussion: Because Paolo has accepted employment at the agency, he should do his best to understand exactly what types of records he is expected to keep and to create those kinds of records. After he has been at the agency for a period of time, he might suggest to his supervisor and other staff members that record-keeping procedures be reviewed to determine if records are being kept appropriately, given the goals and objectives of the agency's counseling program.

Regarding the types of information that would be reasonable for a community mental health agency to keep, intake information might be limited to basics, such as contact information and current medications or health problems. A diagnosis should be rendered only if required by third-party payers. In addition, treatment plans and goals for counseling should be flexible, and the number of goals should be determined individually for each client. In clinical case notes, only information needed to refresh the counselor's memory should be written down. There is no need to summarize the content of sessions.

Ethical Standards Related to Records

Standard A.1.b. of the ACA *Code of Ethics* (ACA, 2014) states that counselors include in their records "sufficient and timely documentation to facilitate the delivery and continuity of services." This standard acknowledges that *continuity of services* is an important reason for keeping records. Standard A.1.b. also requires that counseling records document client progress and services provided, and that errors in client records be corrected according to agency or institutional policies.

Section B.6. of the *Code of Ethics* (ACA, 2014) includes nine standards that specifically address counseling records. Standard B.6.b. addresses the importance of keeping records in a secure location. Counselors must strive to keep records in a place that is not accessible to unauthorized persons. Counselors are responsible for securing the safety and confidentiality of any counseling records they create, maintain, transfer, or destroy. This caveat includes records that are written, taped, computerized, or stored in any other medium. In Chapter 5, we discussed at some length how easy it can be for a counselor to inadvertently breach a client's confidentiality. That discussion is as pertinent to counseling records as it is to other aspects of the counseling relationship, as is evident in the case of Vanessa, presented here.

6-2 The Case of Vanessa

Vanessa is a Licensed Professional Counselor (LPC) in private practice with a group that includes three other counselors. One afternoon at 1:00 p.m., she has had a client cancellation and is using the time to work at her computer writing clinical case notes from her morning sessions. Margie, the counselor whose office is next door, pokes her head in the door and asks Vanessa for a case consultation. Vanessa and Margie go into Margie's office and close the door for privacy. Unbeknownst to Vanessa, her 2:00 p.m. client arrives early, sees that her office door is open, and goes in. The client reads the clinical case notes that Vanessa had left on her computer screen.

- What actions can counselors take to ensure that a client's records are not seen by anyone not authorized to see them?
- What steps must counselors take to preserve client privacy when they keep case notes on a computer?

Discussion: Counselors should use the following guidelines to avoid unfortunate situations like the one just described:

- In your office, be extra careful not to leave records out in the open, so that other clients do not see them. Always put them away, even if you leave your desk for only a few minutes.
- Use a secure password for accessing client records on your computer. Always close a secure file when you leave the room.
- If your computer is networked, be sure your client records are not accessible to others. Position your computer so that others in your office cannot see what you have on your screen.

Standards B.6.c. and B.6.d. (ACA, 2014) address the issue of informed consent and require counselors to obtain client permission before they electronically record or observe sessions. Recording and observing sessions, common practices in supervision, are discussed in more detail later in this chapter.

Standard B.6.e. (ACA, 2014) alerts us to the fact that we have an ethical obligation to provide competent clients with access to their records, unless the records contain information that might be misleading or detrimental to the clients. There is a presumption that clients have a right to see records that counselors keep related to the counseling services that the clients have received. Standard B.6.e. states, "Counselors limit the access of clients to their records, or portions of their records, only when there is compelling evidence that such access would cause harm to the client." This standard also provides guidance on a trickier situation that occurs when clients have been seen in the context of group or family counseling. In situations involving multiple clients, counselors limit access to those parts of the records that do not include confidential information related to another client. When clients are given access to their counseling records, counselors provide them with assistance and consultation in interpreting the records (§B.6.f.).

Standard B.6.g. (ACA, 2014) requires counselors to obtain written permission from clients to disclose or transfer records to legitimate third parties unless exceptions to confidentiality exist.

Interestingly, this standard also makes counselors responsible for taking steps to ensure that receivers of counseling records are sensitive to the confidential nature of those records. It is not possible for a counselor to guarantee anyone else's behavior, including that of a fellow mental health professional who receives records. However, steps that can be taken to promote professionally appropriate transfer of records are to include a cover letter that explains the confidential nature of any transferred records, mark each page *confidential*, and include a statement on the records that the copy of the records is not to be transferred to any third party.

Standard B.6.h. (ACA, 2014) provides guidelines to counselors regarding storage and disposal of counseling records after a counseling relationship has ended. Although this standard could be interpreted to infer that counselors must keep counseling records indefinitely, our suggestion is that some records be kept and others destroyed when it is clear that a client will no longer receive services from a counselor. The issue of whether to keep or destroy counseling records is discussed at length in later sections of this chapter.

Standard B.6.i. (ACA, 2014) imposes on counselors the duty to take *reasonable precautions* to protect their clients' privacy if counselors terminate their practice, become incapacitated, or die.

One important client privacy issue is how much information third-party payers (health insurance companies) should be allowed to demand from counselors and how much information counselors should be willing to provide them (MacCluskie, 2001). Welfel (2013) has suggested that before counselors sign a contract with a health insurance organization, they should learn the type, frequency, and extent of patient information the organization requires in order to authorize and review treatment. As an informed consent procedure, of course, this information should be thoroughly discussed with the client. Standard B.3.d. (ACA, 2014) requires counselors to obtain authorization from their clients before disclosing information to third-party payers.

Legal Requirements

Overall, clinical health care records are seen as being created to benefit the person who is receiving the services. In fact, legal principles indicate that the contents of the records about a particular client belong to that client, even though the paper or recording instrument belongs to someone else (*Claim of Gerkin*, 1980; *People v. Cohen*, 1979). Records can benefit clients in a number of ways.

The *Code of Ethics* (ACA, 2014) provisions regarding records do not conflict with any legal requirements regarding counseling records. In fact, one ethical standard (§B.6.g.) goes beyond legal requirements and indicates that written permission should be obtained from clients before records are transferred, unless specific exceptions exist. The common law in the United States does not require that counselors obtain written permission from clients to give copies of their records to third parties. However, many federal laws—such as the Health Insurance Portability and Accountability Act (HIPAA) and the Family Educational Rights and Privacy Act (FERPA), state statutes, and agency policies—have such written permission requirements. In addition, it is generally advisable for counselors, in order to protect themselves, to obtain written authority from clients before transferring records to third parties. If a client later denies that such permission was given or a client is not available to say whether oral permission was granted, the counselor will have a document as evidence that permission was obtained. Counselors should use the client request for records forms created by the agency in which they work. If the agency does not have a standard form, or if a counselor in private practice does not have such a form, the sample form provided in Appendix C can be used.

There is no common law principle, nor are there any general federal or state statutes, requiring counselors to keep clinical case notes. On the other hand, the *Code of Ethics* (ACA, 2014), in §A.1.b., infers that ethical counselors must keep clinical case notes that document services rendered to clients and client progress. Counselors do keep various types of records for a number of legally related reasons. For example, counselors in private practice must keep administrative records regarding their expenses and income for federal and state income tax purposes. As is discussed later in this chapter, some specific federal statutes require counselors to handle records in particular ways if counselors work in settings in which these statutes apply. In addition, lawyers always advise counselors to document carefully everything they do so that they can protect themselves if their actions or judgments are later questioned in a lawsuit.

Confidentiality and Privileged Communication Requirements

All the points made in Chapter 5 regarding the confidentiality and privileged communication responsibilities of counselors apply to records to the same degree they apply to oral comments related to the privacy of clients. However, because records have physical properties, whereas *information* may not, it is important to consider carefully the responsibility of counselors to handle records appropriately.

Types of Records Kept by Counselors

The *Code of Ethics* (ACA, 2014) provides only limited information about the types of records that must be kept; rather, the code allows each counselor to determine which types of clinical case notes are needed to render professional services. Many record-keeping requirements are imposed on counselors by laws, regulations, and procedures, rather than being required by the ACA *Code of Ethics*.

Standards A.1.b. and B.6.a., A.1.c., A.2.a., and B.6.g. (ACA, 2014) provide guidance to counselors regarding the types of records they must keep.

Standards A.1.b. and B.6.a. both state that counselors maintain documentation "necessary for rendering professional services." This section also indicates that records must "include sufficient and timely documentation to facilitate the delivery and continuity of services." Records must accurately reflect client progress and the services that they have provided to clients. Any amendments to records must be made according to agency or institutional policies. From these standards, it is clear that counselors are expected to keep some type of records for all clients and that records should be kept in such a way that another counselor could take over the care of the client, if necessary.

Standard A.1.c. requires that counselors develop counseling plans with their clients and revise the plans as necessary. Although the code does not specifically require that such plans be in writing, there could be that expectation.

Standard A.2.a. states that "Counselors have an obligation to review in writing and verbally with clients the rights and responsibilities of both counselors and clients." This standard suggests that there is an ethical obligation to have a written record of informed consent for counseling relationships.

Standard B.6.g. requires a written record of permission to transfer records.

It may be helpful for counselors to receive more instructions about the record-keeping responsibilities that will be a part of most of the jobs they will hold. However, it would not be wise for the profession or the ACA *Code of Ethics* to tell counselors the types of records they must keep, the contents of such records, and the ways in which those records should be created. It is best for counselors to determine the kinds of records they need based on their position and the kinds of clinical notes they need to create in order to be effective practitioners. Keeping in mind that there will be variations depending on a counselor's style and the requirements imposed by employment settings, we offer some general guidelines regarding three types of records: administrative records, recordings, and clinical case notes.

ADMINISTRATIVE RECORDS   All settings that provide counseling services keep some type of administrative records. The type of agency and external pressures determine how many and what types of records are kept. When counselors accept employment in an agency, school, hospital, or other setting, they agree to conform to agency rules and procedures, which include record-keeping requirements.

Administrative records are any types of records that would not be considered recordings or clinical case notes. Administrative records include appointment books, billing and payment accounts, copies of correspondence, signed informed consent documents, client permission to release information, intake forms, or other routine papers that are created as a result of providing counseling services to clients. In most businesses, records of these types are not considered confidential. Yet the very fact that someone has applied for or received counseling services is a private matter. Therefore, business records that reveal the identity of individuals who have had contact with the agency must be treated as confidential and must be protected in the same way that clinical case notes are protected.

RECORDINGS   Clinical supervision of counseling services takes place in some form in most settings. Agencies often accept practicum or internship students who must record their sessions with clients for the purposes of clinical supervision. Mental health professionals, after they have received their graduate degrees, usually have to practice under clinical supervision for 2 to 3 years before they can become licensed. In addition, many practicing counselors continue supervision throughout their careers and might record sessions for supervision purposes.

Counseling sessions could be recorded when counselors want clients to listen to or view their own behavior or interpersonal interactions during sessions. Although this therapeutic use of client session recordings is not unusual, a few cautions should be mentioned. Counselors should emphasize to their clients that these recordings would compromise their privacy if the clients did not keep them secure or erase them after using them. Counselors also should make sure clients know that until these recordings are erased or destroyed, they would be available for subpoena in some lawsuits that could arise. We suggest that counselors who give recordings of sessions to their clients for any purpose have their clients sign a form to ensure that they understand the problems that might arise and their responsibility for their own privacy protection.

A number of procedures must be followed when recordings of client sessions are created. Clients must know that recordings are being made and must agree to the process. The *Code of Ethics* (ACA, 2014, §B.6.c.) requires that consent of clients be obtained prior to recording sessions. The consent of clients must be *informed* in that clients must understand the reason the recordings are being made and who will have access to them. It would be a violation of privacy if sessions were recorded without a client's knowledge, or if consent were given and then the recordings were used for purposes not agreed to or accessed by persons unknown to the client. The tapes, once they are created, must be kept as secure as any confidential record is kept. Once the recordings have been used, they must be erased or destroyed.

Although there is no ethical or legal requirement that the client's permission be obtained in writing, counselors often obtain written permission from clients to record counseling sessions in order to protect themselves. This self-protection would be necessary if a client later claimed that permission had never been given for the recording or that the client did not fully understand how the recording would be used. In addition, many agencies require written permission before client counseling sessions may be recorded. If such policies exist, counselors must comply. Any signed form of this type obtained from a client should be placed in the client's folder and kept until the record is destroyed. If you wish to obtain a client's permission to record a session for supervision and your agency does not have a standard form to use, a form is provided in Appendix D.

6-3 The Case of Téa

Téa counsels children in the counseling lab at the university where she is working on her master's degree in counseling. Before she begins her first session with Ana, an 8-year-old, Téa explains to Ana that there is a camera in the corner of the room and that their sessions will be recorded so that Téa's instructor can review their counseling sessions. Ana says she understands and doesn't mind that their sessions will be recorded. After their session is over, on the drive back home, Ana tells her mother that the counseling session was recorded. Ana's mother calls the director of the counseling lab and tells the director that Téa recorded the counseling session with Ana without Ana's knowledge and without the mother's knowledge or permission.

- What should Téa have done to avoid this problem?
- Why is it important to obtain written permission to record counseling sessions, even though verbal permission is adequate?

Discussion: Since Ana is a minor, it was necessary for Téa to obtain at least verbal permission from Ana's mother to record the counseling session. It would have been best practice for Téa to obtain written permission to record from both Ana and her mother. Even though written permission to record is not ethically or legally required, it is best to get permission in writing so you have proof that permission was obtained in case a question arises later as to whether permission was obtained.

Clinical Case Notes

Clinical case notes that counselors keep regarding their sessions with clients are the records that concern counselors and clients most. These notes sometimes contain specific details clients have told counselors, counselors' clinical impressions of clients, and generally very sensitive and personal information about clients.

A problem with clinical case notes is that counselors often think of them as being personal notes to themselves that will be seen only by them in the future. However, the reality of clinical case notes is much different, and we have found that even seasoned counselors are sometimes surprised to learn how many people have a right to access their clinical case notes. Counselors must be aware of how these notes are viewed by clients, agencies, and the law.

We often have heard the suggestion that counselors simply should not take clinical case notes, so that they will not have to worry about the notes being subpoenaed or being seen at a later time by the client or any other person. This is not sound advice. In the first place, the *Code of Ethics* (ACA, 2014, §A.1.b.) specifically states that ethical counselors do keep records. In addition, it seems to be general practice today for mental health professionals, no matter what their credentials or orientation, to routinely create and use clinical case notes in their practices. If counselors were to fail to create these notes, it is likely that they would be accused of unprofessional practice and probably would be called on to explain how they could render quality counseling services without taking clinical case notes (Anderson & Bertram, 2012). Second, not having clinical case notes would not keep a counselor from having to reveal confidential information orally from memory if someone had a legal right to that information. In addition, counselors should take the clinical notes they need in order to function effectively as professionals. Counselors should not feel inhibited about creating clinical case notes just because the notes may later be seen by clients themselves or by third parties.

ASSUME NOTES WILL BE READ   Counselors never know whether others will read the clinical case notes they create. Thus, counselors should assume that notes they write will become public information at some later date. Counselors who make this assumption will be very cautious in deciding what to include in their notes. At the same time, counselors should write whatever they need to render quality counseling services to their clients.

Situations in which the clinical case notes of counselors appropriately and legally are read by others are discussed in the following sections. It is important for you to remember the following sobering information when you are writing clinical case notes:

- Your clients have a legal right to review the notes and to obtain copies of them.
- Your clients have a legal right to demand that you transfer copies of those clinical case notes to other professionals, including other mental health professionals, attorneys, physicians, and even accountants.
- Your clients can subpoena the clinical case notes when they are involved in litigation.
- Other parties can legally subpoena the clinical case notes when involved in litigation situations involving the client, sometimes over the client's objection and even when the records are privileged if legal exceptions to privilege exist.
- The legal representatives of deceased clients, in most states, have the same rights to clinical case notes as the clients had when they were alive.
- Clinical case notes sometimes do become public information and get published in the media.

APPROPRIATE CONTENT OF CLINICAL CASE NOTES   Unfortunately, very little instruction occurs in counseling graduate programs regarding the purposes and the actual creation of clinical case notes (Cottone & Tarvydas, 2007). In other professions, such as medicine, nursing, and social work, a heavy emphasis is placed on how to write health records, what information should and should not be included, and proper ways of creating such clinical notes. Most health records are passed from one professional to another, and professionals rely on each other to record information so it can be used in the care and treatment of a patient. Counseling clinical case notes, on the other hand, generally are written by a counselor for the counselor's own use. Sometimes, however, these records are read by others and counselors even offer such records to prove they acted professionally. Luepker (2012), Mitchell (2007), Merlone (2005), Piazza and Baruth (1990), and Snider (1987) have provided suggestions for keeping records. Some guidelines, based largely on those developed by the American Psychological Association (2007), are included in Appendix E. We offer some recommendations here regarding the creation of clinical case notes to assist counselors in their practices.

You should never lose sight of the purposes of clinical case notes. There are two basic reasons to keep notes: (a) to provide quality counseling services to clients and (b) to document decisions you have made and actions you have taken as a counselor. Both of these purposes are legitimate and reasonable.

It is critical that you take your notes either during sessions or immediately after. It does no good to write clinical case notes long after the counseling session occurs. The whole purpose of the notes is to record on paper what your memory will not hold. If you wait too long, you will be relying on your memory, which is what you are trying to avoid.

Your own personal style should dictate whether you take notes during a counseling session or after it is over. Both approaches have advantages and disadvantages. Taking notes during sessions allows you to record accurate information immediately without having to rely on your memory. Some counselors can take notes unobtrusively during sessions. Other counselors may have trouble taking notes and listening to clients at the same time. Clients could be distracted or inhibited by your note taking during sessions, if it is not done easily. Some counselors find that waiting until after the session is over is the best way for them to take clinical case notes. We suggest that you try both methods and adopt the approach that works best for you.

As we have emphasized, the first purpose for creating clinical case notes is to render quality counseling services. A very important part of writing clinical case notes is to separate objective information (what was said by anyone or observed by you during the session) from your clinical impressions (hypotheses or conclusions you developed as a result of what was said or observed). Quite often, you will review notes to determine what a client actually said during a session. You must be able to separate what was actually said from what you thought about as a result of what was said. In addition, your notes may be used someday as evidence in a legal proceeding, and being able to determine what was actually said by a client could be critical. A common format for clinical case notes is the use of *SOAP* notes, which include four separate sections:

Subjective:	information reported by the client
Objective:	results of the counselor's tests and other assessments administered
Assessment:	the counselor's impressions generated by the data
Plan:	diagnosis and treatment plan, along with any modifications to them

Another format that is similar and is also used frequently is the *DAP*, which is comprised of three sections:

• Data:	objective description of what occurred during the session
Assessment:	counselor's interpretations based on the data, in the context of the presenting problem and treatment plan
Plan:	what the counselor intends to accomplish in the next session or sessions

The second purpose for keeping clinical case notes is to document decisions you have made or actions you have taken (Woody, 1988b). Such documentation would be important when you determine that a client is a danger to self or others and you take some actions to prevent harm. Documentation is also important when you consult with others regarding a client's situation. When you make decisions that clients may not like, you should also document your actions in your clinical case notes. If you decide to terminate counseling over a client's objection, instruct a client to take some action the client is reluctant to take, or impose limits to a client's interactions with you outside of sessions, it is wise to document how and why you did these things and the client's reactions.

When you document decisions or actions in your case notes, you are doing that to protect yourself in the event such decisions or actions are questioned later by anyone else (Mitchell, 2007). As a result, it is important to provide as much detailed information as possible. For example, listing the exact time a conversation took place could be vital. When you are talking to people other than your client, it is important to include the person's name, title, and contact information; date and time the conversation took place; and any other information that might be needed later. Recording exact words used by you and others often can be important as well. When documenting to protect yourself, it is essential that you do so immediately after conversations take place. If you write notes hours, days, or weeks after conversations have occurred, such notes will be much less helpful to you if you are trying to prove that you made the decisions or took the actions you are claiming to have taken in your notes.

It would be impossible to write a summary of every action you take as a counselor or to make an audio recording or video of every counseling session. Excessive documentation can take away

Generally, counselors must provide access to client records to clients upon request (ACA, 2014, §B.6.e.). However, if there is *compelling evidence that such access would cause harm to the client*, then counselors can limit clients' access to their records. If counselors do decide to deny client access to their counseling records, then "Counselors document the request of clients and the rationale for withholding some or all of the record in the files of clients" (§B.6.e.).

1. Documentation should be undertaken in circumstances in which a counselor's actions or inaction may be later reviewed by an ethics panel, licensure board, or administrator, or within the context of a legal proceeding.

2. Some of the situations in which some level of documentation is called for include the following:
   • Someone accuses a counselor of unethical or illegal behavior.
   • A counselor reports a case of suspected child abuse.
   • A counselor determines that a client is a danger to self.
   • A counselor determines that a client is a danger to others.
   • A client who is being counseled is involved in a legal controversy that could lead to the counselor's being forced to testify in court. Such controversies include counseling a child whose parents are arguing about custody in a divorce case, a husband or wife involved in a contentious divorce case, a couple contemplating a divorce, or a person involved in a personal injury lawsuit.

3. Documentation efforts should begin as soon as counselors determine they are in a situation in which documentation is important.

4. When documenting for self-protection, as much detail as possible should be included. Dates, exact times events occurred, and exact words spoken should be included to the degree that details are remembered. Only factual information should be included. Thoughts, diagnoses, and conclusions of counselors should be avoided when documenting. If these must be written down, they should be included in clinical case notes rather than in records kept for documentation.

5. The best documentation is created very soon after a conversation or event has occurred. Indicate the date and time anything is written. Never backdate anything that is written. In other words, do not imply or state that something was written on an earlier date than it was actually written.

6. In the event counselors realize that they should have begun documentation sooner, they should write a summary of what happened up to that point in time. Include as much detail as can be remembered, as well as the date and time the summary was written.

7. Maintain a documentation file that includes the originals of notes written to counselors, copies of notes written by counselors to others, copies of relevant papers that counselors cannot keep for themselves, and other papers that might be relevant to the situation.

8. Records kept for documentation should be kept secure in a locked file drawer or cabinet or in a secure computer file. If counselors agree to provide their files, they should never release their originals, only copies.

FIGURE 6-1   Documentation through records for self-protection

Source: Pearson Education, Inc., Hoboken, NJ.

valuable time that might be spent providing counseling services. On the other hand, in some circumstances counselors should document their actions to create a record showing that they have done what they should have done.

Guidelines for documenting for self-protection are included in Figure 6-1.

Another important part of note taking is to write notes that are legible, at least to you. For notes to be useful in the future, you must be able to read and understand them. If your notes are transferred to clients or third parties at a later date and they cannot read them, you will be called on to explain what you wrote. This can be very inconvenient for you, because it could occur in a court after you have been subpoenaed and put under oath to tell the truth. It is much better to write your notes so that others can read them than to have to interpret them later. It is definitely not a good idea to purposefully write notes so that they cannot be read by others or to use symbols that only you can understand. When clients or third parties try to read such notes, they often become irritated. You can be put in a difficult position because it may appear that you are not cooperating with people who have a legal right to review the notes.

Client Access to Records

It would never occur to most health care providers to have concerns about patients having access to copies of their records. However, mental health care is different from physical health care in many respects. Some mental health care professionals believe it is not appropriate and could even be harmful for patients or clients to have information about the diagnoses of mental disorders, treatment approaches being taken, or clinical impressions that have been formulated by the professional.

The legal perspective on health care records is that they are kept for the benefit of the patient, and therefore, the patient should have access to them and must receive copies if requested (*Claim of Gerkin*, 1980; *People v. Cohen*, 1979). Further, the patient has the right to demand that one health care provider transfer the records to another health care provider. Mental health care is not seen as different from physical health care concerning patient or client records. It is important, then, for counselors to assume that clients will have access to clinical case notes created, a right to copies of those notes, and a right to request that copies of the notes be transferred to other professionals.

In the event that a client requests a copy of your clinical case notes and you have any reason to think that it would be best if the client did not see them, you can take practical steps that could resolve the matter. You could explain to your client why you believe it would not be best to see your notes, and your client might accept your explanation and withdraw the request. You also could suggest that it might be more helpful for the client or for the person to whom the client wants the records transferred if you were to create a summary of your notes rather than copy the notes themselves. You might explain that the notes were written for your own clinical purposes, and that others probably would be more interested in summaries than in day-to-day notes.

If you were to refuse to show a client your clinical case notes regarding treatment or refuse to provide copies for the client or for a third party that the client has designated, the client probably could take legal steps to compel you to comply with the demand. It would appear that the law supports the client's rights to the records (*Application of Striegel*, 1977). In the following section, you will find that HIPAA requires counselors to give clients access to their records. However, there is an exception in which counselors can refuse to provide client access when counselors believe a client would be harmed by the contents of the record, but the exception is narrow, and the assumption is typically that a client should have access.

In some circumstances, your clinical case notes may contain information about other parties involved in sessions in which the client was counseled. Such situations could arise in couples, family, or group counseling. If your clinical case notes contain information that would compromise another person's privacy if they were given to a client or to someone designated by the client, you might try to convince your client to withdraw the request or you might suggest that you provide a summary for your client. If your client insists, however, on having copies of your original records, then you should copy what you have written, eliminate references to others, and provide your client with the portions of the records that deal only with that client. When counselors provide clients with copies of their counseling records, counselors do not include confidential information related to any other clients (ACA, 2014,§B.6.e.).

Federal Laws Affecting Counseling Records

It would be impossible to describe every federal law or regulation that contains requirements for counseling records. The most far-reaching federal law related to mental health records is HIPAA.

Most other federal statutes related to mental health records apply only to programs that are funded by federal tax money. Counselors who work in settings that are administered by the federal government or in agencies that receive federal funding should ask their employers whether there are any federal laws or regulations that affect the counseling records they keep as part of their jobs. Many private agencies as well as state and local government programs receive federal funding. Three federal laws affect a number of counselors: the Health Insurance Portability and Accounting Act (HIPAA), the Family Educational Rights and Privacy Act of 1974 (FERPA), and the Comprehensive Alcohol Abuse and Alcoholism Prevention, Treatment and Rehabilitation Act of 1972.

Health Insurance Portability and Accountability Act

Public Law 104-191, commonly known as HIPAA, caused a huge stir in the health care industry in the United States when it was first enacted. According to the U.S. Department of Health and Human Services (HHS, 2014a), the HIPAA rules protect the privacy of individually identifiable health information.

HIPAA was enacted on August 21, 1996. The HIPAA statute required HHS to issue privacy regulations governing individually identifiable health information if Congress did not enact privacy legislation within 3 years of the passage of HIPAA. After Congress failed to act on time, HHS issued HIPAA rules, known as the *Privacy Rule*, on December 28, 2000. Final modifications to the rule were published on August 14, 2002. A full text of the rule and modifications are located at 45 CFR Part 160 and Part 164, Subparts A and E, on the agency Web site: www.hhs.gov.

HIPAA applies only to organizations and individuals who transmit health care information in electronic form in connection with a health care transaction. As it would be very difficult to have a *paper only* mental health care practice (Blakely, Smith, & Swenson, 2004), we recommend that all mental health organizations and professionals in private practice comply with the HIPAA requirements.

The Privacy Rule requirements went into effect on April 14, 2003. All records and other individually identifiable health information held or disclosed by a covered entity in any form—whether communicated electronically, on paper, or orally—are covered by the HIPAA Privacy Rule.

Counselors must give clients a clear written explanation of how counselors use, keep, and disclose their health care information. Clients must have access to their records. A process must exist and must be in writing for clients to request amendments to their records. A written history of most disclosures must be available to clients. In addition, counselors must have available for clients to see, if they request it, a set of written privacy procedures that include who has access to protected information, how it will be used within the counseling office, and when the information would or would not be disclosed to others. Under HIPAA, clients must be given a means to make inquiries regarding their counseling records or to make complaints regarding the privacy of their records.

Counselors must obtain uncoerced client consent to release information for treatment, payment, and health care operations purposes, and for nonroutine uses and most non–health care purposes, such as releasing information to financial institutions determining mortgages and other loans or selling mailing lists to interested parties, such as life insurers.

Disclosures of treatment information without specific consumer authorization are allowed in certain circumstances, including but not limited to quality assurance oversight activities, research, judicial and administrative hearings, limited law enforcement activities, emergency circumstances, and facility patient directories.

One provision is quite unique and could be very helpful to counselors when they provide services to clients who need a great deal of family support. If clients are first informed and given an opportunity to orally object, counselors may give health care information to family members or others assisting in the client's care. Standard B.1.a. of the *Code of Ethics* (ACA, 2014) cautions counselors to maintain sensitivity to cultural meanings of confidentiality and "respect differing views toward disclosure of information." We recommend that counselors who wish to utilize the HIPAA provision allowing private information to be given to family members indicate in their initial client agreement form the intention to communicate with family members when needed and to specifically ask clients orally whether that is acceptable to them. Under this same section in the rules, counselors may provide information to the public in the form of facility directories and to disaster relief organizations, such as the Red Cross.

·   When clients do give permission to transfer their personal information regarding their counseling, only the minimum amount of information to accomplish the purpose may be transferred. As a result, it is important for counselors to have on their record release form a place for clients to specify the purpose of their request that their records be transferred. Standard B.2.e. of the *Code of Ethics* (ACA, 2014) states that when disclosure of confidential information is required, counselors reveal only essential information. When clients request that their records be transferred to another health care professional in conjunction with anticipated treatment from that individual, then, according to HIPAA, the full record must be transferred so that the receiving professional can provide the best quality care.

Under HIPAA, each counseling office must designate a privacy officer. In a private practice, the counselors would also serve as the privacy officers. The privacy officer of an agency must train employees to handle confidential information appropriately, ensure that procedures to protect client privacy are in place and are followed, and ensure that proper forms are used by counselors and other health care personnel.

When counselors transfer records based on client written permission, they must take steps to ensure that recipients of the records protect the privacy of the information they have received. We recommend that counselors record and insert statements that the contents are confidential and should not be transferred to any other individuals.

What we have called *clinical case notes* are known as *psychotherapy notes* under HIPAA. Psychotherapy notes that are used only by the psychotherapist, to which no one else has access, are held to a much higher standard of protection. The rationale is that such notes are not a part of the health care record and were never intended to be shared with anyone else. When a client wants to have psychotherapy notes transferred to a third party, the client must specifically request that these notes be transferred. A general request for transfer of records is insufficient. Clients must give their specific permission and authorization for the sensitive information contained in psychotherapy notes to be released. Health care plans cannot refuse to provide reimbursement if a client does not agree to release information covered under the psychotherapy notes provision.

Civil penalties for violations of the HIPAA rules are $100 per incident, up to $25,000 per person, per year, per standard. Criminal penalties for providers who knowingly and improperly disclose or obtain health care information include substantial fines and terms of imprisonment.

The U.S. Department of Health and Human Services (2014b) reported that in 2003 a total of 3,744 complaints were received alleging HIPAA violations (by all health care providers, not just mental health care providers). The number of complaints has steadily increased since 2003, and in 2013, a total of 12,915 complaints were received (U.S. Department of Health and Human Services, n.d.).

The extent to which HIPAA protects the privacy of clients is still unclear. One state court has ruled that, under HIPAA rules, a patient who was undergoing review for mandated court-ordered outpatient treatment would have to be given notice and the opportunity to object before the patient's records could be provided to a court through a subpoena (Gomez & Knight, 2013; *In the Matter of Miguel M. v. Barron*, 2011).

HIPAA is a federal law, so it applies throughout the United States and overrides state laws that are more lax. However, state laws that are stricter than HIPAA about protecting consumer health care privacy must be adhered to, if they exist.

Family Educational Rights and Privacy Act

The Family Educational Rights and Privacy Act of 1974 (FERPA), which is sometimes referred to as the *Buckley Amendment*, affects all public educational institutions and any private or parochial educational institution that receives federal funding in one form or another (Doll, Strein, Jacob, & Prasse, 2011). Almost all private and church-sponsored educational institutions receive some type of federal funding. The penalty for violating provisions of FERPA is the loss of all federal funding, which could be devastating for many educational institutions. Individuals cannot bring lawsuits under FERPA (*Tarka v. Franklin*, 1989).

Since the HIPAA rules were enacted, school personnel have wanted to know whether HIPAA requirements for health care records must be followed in educational institutions. In some cases, HIPAA applies in schools, and in other situations it does not. Under 24 CFT 164.501, health information contained within student educational records that are subject to FERPA is exempt from the requirements of HIPAA. On the other hand, school-based health centers may be subject to HIPAA requirements if such centers are operated by HIPAA-compliant health organizations. Also, school nurses may be subject to HIPAA requirements if they engage in electronic billing. Communications between schools and health care providers may be subject to HIPAA rules as well.

FERPA legislation basically says that parents of minor students (and students who are 18 or older or who are in college) have two rights: (a) to inspect and review their education records and to challenge the contents to ensure the records are not inaccurate or misleading and (b) to have their written authorization obtained before copies of their education records can be transferred to any third party (U.S. Department of Education, 2014).

After students are 18 years old or are attending a postsecondary institution, the legal rights under this legislation are vested in them. However, parents or guardians of dependent students may be given copies of the records of such students without the student's consent. *Dependent students* are defined as children or stepchildren, over half of whose support was received from the taxpayer the previous tax year (Family Educational Rights and Privacy Act of 1974, 26 U.S.C.A. §152). As a result of this definition, most educational institutions give access to student records to parents who can show they claimed their child as a tax dependent the previous year.

Education records are defined in the federal legislation as records kept by educational institutions regarding students. The law specifically exempts from the right to inspect and review, any records that "are in the sole possession of the maker" [FERPA, 1997, 20 U.S.C.A. §1232g(a)(B)(i)]. To qualify under this exemption, counselors in schools and other educational institutions should keep their case notes separate from other records and should not let anyone else have access to those records. Treatment records "made or maintained by a physician, psychiatrist, psychologist, or other recognized professional or paraprofessional" are also exempt [20 U.S.C.A. §1232g(a)(B)(iv)]. As a result of these exemptions, clinical case notes kept by counselors in educational institutions do not have to be shown to students, parents, or guardians under FERPA requirements.

Schools are not required by FERPA to obtain written permission from parents or students to release a student's records to "other schools or school systems in which the student intends to enroll" [FERPA, 1997, 20 U.S.C.A. §1232g(b)(1)(b)]. Nonetheless, when copies of records of transfer students are forwarded to other schools, parents must be notified of the transfer and must be given copies of the transferred records if they desire copies.

These access exemptions to inspect and review one's records under FERPA do not in any way diminish a person's rights to counselors' records under a subpoena in relation to a lawsuit. A valid subpoena for records must be complied with in all circumstances. When an educational institution intends to release records pursuant to a subpoena, the institution must notify parents and students in advance of the release [FERPA, 1997, 20 U.S.C.A. §1232g(b)(2)(B); *Mattie T. v. Johnston*, 1976; *Rios v. Read*, 1977], although notification is not required if the subpoena orders that the existence of the subpoena not be disclosed [FERPA, 1997, 20 U.S.C.A. §1232g(b)(J)(i–ii)].

In an emergency situation, an amendment to FERPA (1997) has given permission to release private information without parent or student written permission. The information must be "necessary to protect the health or safety of the student or other persons" [20 U.S.C.A. §1232g(a)(1)(I)]. This provision would allow counselors to release their records on students to medical personnel or law enforcement authorities without violating FERPA, if they determined that a student was a danger to self or others.

Educational institutions may release to an alleged victim of any violence the results of any disciplinary proceeding conducted against the alleged perpetrator with respect to that specific crime [FERPA, 1997, 20 U.S.C.A. §1232g(b)(6)]. FERPA also allows institutions to include in educational records any disciplinary action taken against students and to disclose such action to school officials in other schools [20 U.S.C.A. §1232g(h)]. However, institutions may not release to newspapers the names of students who have been found guilty of disciplinary proceedings (*United States v. Miami University*, 2002).

No general common law principle requires counselors to obtain *written* authorization from clients to transfer records to third parties. Oral permission is legally adequate, but obtaining written authorization is always recommended. Under FERPA, however, written authorization is required to transfer records.

Federally Funded Substance Abuse Programs

The federal government funds a multitude of substance abuse prevention and treatment programs. Private and public agencies apply for federal funds to operate many of these programs. Programs that receive federal funds must comply with federal laws related to substance abuse treatment.

A federal statute (Comprehensive Alcohol Abuse and Alcoholism Prevention, Treatment and Rehabilitation Act of 1972, 1997, 42 U.S.C.A. §290dd-2) declares that records kept by any facility that is "conducted, regulated, or directly or indirectly assisted" by the federal government are confidential. Disclosure of records of individuals receiving substance abuse services (including education, prevention, training, treatment, rehabilitation, or research) is permitted only in a few circumstances. Exceptions to the nondisclosure of records requirement include the following: (a) when the person gives prior written consent, (b) medical emergencies, (c) audits or evaluations, and (d) to avert substantial risk of death or serious bodily harm if a court order is secured. Records cannot be used for criminal charges or investigations [42 U.S.C.A. §290dd-2(c)]. However, a counselor's direct observations are not a record and can be used in criminal proceedings against clients or patients (*State v. Brown*, 1985; *State v. Magnuson*, 1984).

The statute related to federal substance abuse programs does not prohibit exchange of information between the military and the Department of Veterans Affairs. The statute also permits the reporting of suspected child abuse and neglect under state laws.

Unlike FERPA, the violation of this statute or the regulations that implement it can result in criminal charges and a fine. As a result, clients may file criminal complaints against counselors in federally supported substance abuse treatment programs who violate their rights to privacy, although individuals whose confidentiality rights are violated cannot file civil lawsuits for damages (*Logan v. District of Columbia*, 1978).

Other Federal Statutes

Additional federal statutes prohibit or limit the disclosure of counseling records for the following clients who are served by federally assisted programs: (a) runaway and homeless youth [42 U.S.C.A. §5731], (b) individuals with sexually transmitted diseases [42 U.S.C.A. §247c(d)(5)], (c) voluntary clients in federal drug abuse or dependence programs [42 U.S.C.A. §260(d)], (d) older persons [42 U.S.C.A. §3026(d); 42 U.S.C. §3027(f)(1)], and (e) victims of violence against women [42 U.S.C.A. §14011(b)(5)]. On the other hand, privacy is sometimes expressly limited by statutes. A federal statute specifically denies confidentiality to individuals who are examined by a physician in civil commitment proceedings due to drug abuse [42 U.S.C.A. §3420].

Handling, Storing, and Destroying Records

Creating counseling records is an important process, but maintaining and ultimately disposing of them are crucial matters for counselors as well. According to the *Code of Ethics* (ACA, 2014), counselors must ensure that records are kept in a secure location and that access to counseling records is limited to authorized persons (§B.6.b.). The privacy of clients and the self-protection of counselors both have an impact on the manner in which records are handled, stored, and destroyed.

Because counseling records are so sensitive, agencies should develop written policies regarding how these records will be handled day to day. Agencies or practices regulated under HIPAA must have written policies regarding records and must make those policies available for client review. Typically, counselors create and keep their own clinical case notes. These notes should be kept in locked drawers or cabinets, or on a secure site if the records are computerized. In offices with more than one person, an individual should be designated as the records manager. Generally, this person would be a clerical or administrative employee. The records manager should have the responsibility of ensuring that counseling records are kept secure, checked out and back in properly, stored safely, and, eventually, eliminated according to a set schedule and policy.

Everyone who handles counseling records should make sure that the records are not left unattended in such a manner that unauthorized persons can read them. Care should be taken to promptly return counseling records to their proper place after they have been used.

No general laws dictate how long a particular counseling record must be kept (Woody, 1988b). However, some federal or state statutes require that certain types of records created for certain purposes be kept for a certain period of time. For instance, some state counselor licensure laws dictate that counselors' records be kept for a certain number of years. Attorneys who advise counseling agencies should be asked to review statutes and regulations to identify any requirements regarding records, including the length of time they must be maintained.

Many agencies have determined that they want to keep their counseling records for a set period of time. Generally, agencies also have rules and guidelines regarding how records should be handled, stored, and eliminated. Counselors should always inquire as to whether the agency in which they work has such requirements. All agency rules and regulations should be followed by counselors.

Counseling records often also are affected by agency accreditation rules. Many counseling centers, hospitals, and treatment facilities are accredited by private agencies such as the Joint Commission, the International Association of Counseling Services (IACS), and the Commission on Accreditation of Rehabilitation Facilities (CARF International). Appendix B contains contact information for these organizations. These accreditation agencies have specific requirements regarding counseling records, and many require that records be kept for a set period of time. Counselors who work in agencies that are accredited should ask about record-keeping requirements.

If there are no laws, agency rules, or accreditation standards that require records to be kept for a specific length of time, then counselors should encourage their agency to establish a written policy and to destroy counseling records on a periodic basis. There are a number of reasons for not keeping counseling records indefinitely. Practically speaking, it is expensive to keep records locked away and to keep up with logging them in and out. In addition, confidential records that exist could be compromised in some way, whereas confidential records that are destroyed cannot be seen by unauthorized persons.

It is wise to establish a record-destroying policy stipulating that certain categories of records will be destroyed on a specific date each year unless one of the following applies: (a) there is reason to believe the records may be subpoenaed in a current or future lawsuit or (b) the records contain documentation of actions taken by counselors that must be kept longer than the usual period of time. There are no guidelines about how to determine whether individuals *believe records may be subpoenaed*. Common sense should dictate this determination. If records are purposefully destroyed when someone knows or should have reasonably known that those records would be subpoenaed later, the person destroying them can be charged with a serious crime (Woody, 1988a). Records documenting actions that counselors have taken to protect themselves probably should be kept longer than counseling records normally would be kept.

Voluntarily Transferring Records

Clients often request that their counseling records be provided to another professional who is rendering services to them. In addition, professionals often request your clients' counseling records when they begin treating your current or former clients. The *Code of Ethics* (ACA, 2014), §B.6.g.) requires that counselors obtain written permission from clients to disclose or transfer copies of records. After clients have requested or given permission in writing that their counseling records be transferred to a third party, counselors have an obligation to comply. A form is provided in Appendix C for clients to sign when they wish to have their records transferred.

Counselors should make sure the written request of the client is followed precisely and that only copies of records the client authorizes for transfer are actually sent. In addition, counselors should never send originals of records, only copies. Also, records located in client files from other professionals or agencies should never be transferred to a third party. If clients want those records sent, they must contact the agency that created the records and authorize that agency to forward them.

The written and signed authorization from the client should be filed in the client's folder. In addition, a notation should be entered in the client's file that indicates which records were sent and when, the method of transfer (e.g., U.S. mail, courier service, personal delivery), to whom they were sent, and to what address.

SUBPOENAS

Receiving a subpoena can be an intimidating, and even frightening, experience for a counselor (Gutheil & Drogin, 2013). Unless counselors deal with subpoenas on a routine basis in their work, this reaction is somewhat justified. Dealing with a subpoena places a counselor in the legal arena—a system that is adversarial in nature and operates by a different set of rules than those to which counselors are accustomed. If you should receive a subpoena, the information that follows will help guide you through the process of responding to it.

6-4 The Case of Paulette

Paulette, an elementary school counselor, has been counseling Billy Rosen, a third-grader whose parents are going through a contentious divorce. One afternoon after school, Paulette is working in her office when a gentleman appears at her door. He announces that he has a subpoena for her records that has been issued by Mr. Rosen's attorney. He offers to wait while she makes a copy of the records of her counseling sessions with Billy.

- How should Paulette respond to the gentleman's offer?
- What should Paulette do about the subpoena?

Discussion: Paulette should first inform the gentleman that she will confer with her supervisor to determine how to respond to the subpoena. She should tell him she will not produce the records until some later time, if the subpoena is valid. Paulette should notify her immediate supervisor that she has received a subpoena and request legal advice regarding her response to it. If her supervisor does not provide her with access to a lawyer, then Paulette should follow the supervisor's directives regarding how to respond to the subpoena.

Subpoenas are legal documents that might require counselors to produce copies of records; appear for a deposition, court hearing, or trial; or appear and bring their records with them (Barsky & Goud, 2002; Childress-Beatty & Koocher, 2013; Cottone & Tarvydas, 2007; Levy, Galambos, & Skarbek, 2014). Subpoenas are official court documents and cannot be ignored. Even though subpoenas might result in health care professionals having to turn over records or appear in court for various reasons (Palusci, Hicks, & Vandervort, 2001), counselors must know whether they have a legal obligation to do what a subpoena says.

In Chapter 5, one of the exceptions to confidentiality and privileged communication that was noted is a court order. Court orders might be issued in hearings or trials at which judges are present and give verbal orders, or they might be issued when judges sign written orders in their official capacity. All citizens must obey court orders. The sanctions for not obeying orders issued by judges are imprisonment, fines, or both. The only alternative to obeying a court order is to appeal to a higher court. Such appeals must be filed immediately by a lawyer. Although a subpoena is a type of court order, counselors should always consult with their own attorneys before turning over records or appearing at a deposition, hearing, or trial in response to a subpoena.

Discovery in Litigation

Lawyers who are representing parties in lawsuits are members of the bar in the jurisdiction in which they are practicing. Therefore, they are considered official officers of the court. One of the privileges extended to officers of a court is to issue valid subpoenas for information related to cases they are litigating.

One of the concepts in lawsuits of any kind is that attorneys representing the parties are entitled to *discovery*. Discovery is the process whereby attorneys have the right to ask for and receive information relevant to their case before the case is tried (Swenson, 1997). The idea is that there should be no surprises during trials. Instead, before the actual trial begins each side in a lawsuit should know all the information that will be entered into evidence during the trial.

Subpoenas are used extensively during the discovery or pretrial phase of lawsuits. Attorneys from both sides ask potential witnesses to respond in writing to written questions (interrogatories), to provide copies of records they are entitled to see, and to come to their offices for depositions. In addition, witnesses can be subpoenaed to testify at hearings before the judge presiding over the case, as well as at the trial.

Validity of Subpoenas

If a subpoena is issued to you by an attorney, your first step is to consult your own lawyer to determine whether the subpoena is valid and whether you must respond to it (Woody, 1988a). Guidelines for obtaining your own legal advice, whether you are an employee or are in private practice, are provided in Chapter 1.

The records of counselors may be subpoenaed, as may counselors themselves for their oral testimony at depositions, hearings, or trials. Also, written questions may be submitted with a demand for written answers. Counselors might also be subpoenaed to appear at a legal proceeding and instructed to bring records with them (Bowerbank, 2006). In the event you receive a subpoena to appear at a legal proceeding, but no mention is made of records, do not take records with you unless you are instructed to do so by your own attorney.

An attorney will review a subpoena for you and will advise you regarding the proper manner in which to respond. Attorneys might assist you in a number of ways. For example, they could ask the attorney who issued the subpoena to withdraw it, file a motion to quash the subpoena, or advise you to comply with the subpoena.

Attorneys who are litigating cases may not issue subpoenas for records or for witnesses to testify if the attorneys know they do not have a right to the information. However, because attorneys may not realize that material may be privileged, you could receive a subpoena that is not enforceable because of privilege (American Psychological Association, 2006; Woody, 2007). Subpoenas could be unenforceable or invalid for other reasons as well. You must obtain legal advice regarding your response to any subpoena you receive. If you refuse to respond to a valid subpoena, you could be held in contempt of court and either imprisoned or fined. On the other hand, if you provide information in response to an invalid or unenforceable subpoena, you could be held legally accountable to a client or former client for any damages suffered.

When you receive a subpoena, you should take action immediately because most subpoenas must be complied with within a fixed number of hours. Many counselors mistakenly believe that subpoenas must be personally handed to them to be valid and enforceable. In fact, in most cases, if you have knowledge through any means that a subpoena has been issued to you, you should immediately take the steps listed in the following sections.

Your first step, if you are employed, should be to notify your immediate supervisor that you have received a subpoena and to request legal advice regarding your response to it. If your employer does not provide you with access to a lawyer, then follow the directives of your supervisor. If you are in an independent private practice, then your first step should be to call your own practice attorney.

Your lawyer or supervisor should be informed if you think the information being requested might be privileged. You should also inform your attorney or supervisor if you believe testifying or producing records regarding the matter would compromise the privacy of a former or current client, even if the relationship was not privileged by law. You should feel free to openly discuss the situation with a lawyer because your relationship with the lawyer is privileged. Often, it is necessary to explain to your lawyer the general concepts of counseling, the nature of your relationship to the parties involved in the lawsuit, and the details regarding clients who are involved or affected by the litigation. You should give complete information to your lawyer and answer any questions regarding the situation.

Once your attorney or supervisor understands the situation and has given you advice, follow the instructions precisely. If you have doubts or questions, discuss them with your attorney or supervisor, but ultimately you must follow the advice given to you.

Generally, a subpoena received from the attorney of your client or former client will not be problematic because the individual in most cases has waived his or her privilege, if it exists, by calling you as a witness. Nonetheless, legal advice in such situations still is needed to ensure that you are proceeding properly.

Interrogatories

One of the easiest types of subpoenas to deal with involves interrogatories. Included with the subpoena will be a set of written questions with a requirement that you respond to each question in writing. You must sign an oath that your answers are truthful.

If you receive a set of interrogatories and your attorney informs you that you must respond to them, you should discuss each question and your proposed answer with your attorney before you begin writing. After composing your answers and before you submit them, you should ask your attorney to review your answers. Take your attorney's advice about changes or rewording of your answers. Again, if you are an employed counselor and do not have access to an attorney, follow the directives of your immediate supervisor.

Appearances at Proceedings

In the event you are directed by your attorney or supervisor to appear at a legal proceeding, ask that you be told what to expect. Ask your attorney or supervisor to explain in detail how such events take place. Also, ask the attorney to tell you what questions you might be asked and request advice on responses you think you should make to the anticipated questions. Ask the attorney to accompany you to the proceeding if possible.

Depositions usually take place in the office of the lawyer who has issued the subpoena. Although the judge will be present at hearings and trials, the judge does not attend depositions. Generally, depositions are attended by the attorney who issued the subpoena, the attorney representing the other party involved in the lawsuit, a court reporter, and the witness being deposed.

It is important to have your own attorney present at your deposition if possible. During a hearing or trial, the judge will rule on controversies and will instruct witnesses whether to answer questions. With no judge present at depositions, you need your own attorney there to tell you how to proceed and to protect you from being pressured by the other attorneys. In some circumstances, one attorney could tell you that if you do not answer a question, she or he will issue a rule to show cause and require you to appear before a judge to explain your refusal to answer, and that the judge could then hold you in contempt of court and fine or imprison you. The other attorney could then threaten that if you do answer the question, that attorney will sue you for violating his or her client's privacy. When situations like this arise, you need the presence of an attorney who will advise you how to proceed.

Testimony Under Oath

Testimony that you give at any legal proceeding will be *under oath*, which means that you will be required to swear to tell the truth. Once an oath has been administered, false statements usually are considered perjury, which is a serious crime. You might be instructed by your attorney not to answer questions at a deposition, but you should always, in all circumstances, answer questions truthfully when you do respond.

Turning Over Records

In the event that your attorney or supervisor directs you to turn over your records in response to a subpoena, you should follow the advice you have been given. Sometimes attorneys who issue subpoenas will accept summaries of notes rather than case notes themselves, or other similar compromises may be needed. Your attorney will negotiate appropriately on your behalf.

You should never forward the originals of your records. Instead, make copies and deliver the copies. Sometimes records of other individuals are mixed in with records that must be turned over. In that situation, sometimes it is permissible to obliterate private information related to other parties. Again, follow the advice of your attorney in this situation.

If your records include records that you have received from other professionals, such as physicians, other mental health professionals, or hospitals, do not copy and forward those records. If the attorney issuing the subpoena wants copies of those records, the individual or entity that created them will have to be subpoenaed.

The *Code of Ethics* (ACA, 2014) states that when counselors receive subpoenas for counseling records of their clients, counselors must obtain written informed consent from their clients to release the records, or, if that is impossible, must "take steps to prohibit the disclosure or have it limited as narrowly as possible due to potential harm to the client or counseling relationship" (§B.2.d.). In our experience, clients who do not wish to have their counseling records exposed rarely agree to sign a written consent document. Usually, clients whose records have been subpoenaed, after being informed by their counselors that a subpoena exists, take appropriate legal steps through their attorneys to have the subpoena quashed. It is the duty of clients to assert their legal privilege, if one exists. In the event a client is not available to be informed that his or her counseling records have been subpoenaed and it is believed the relationship with the client was privileged, the counselor or the counselor's attorney should assert the client's privilege on behalf of the client and should take other steps that are legally available to avoid complying with the subpoena. If the subpoena is determined to be valid, then counselors and their attorneys should do what they can to limit the disclosure of private client information.

Summary and Key Points

This chapter familiarizes you with the complexities of counseling records and record keeping. Subpoenas were also addressed because records are often subject to being subpoenaed.

With respect to *records*, some key points made in this chapter include the following:

- Counselors keep records for two legitimate reasons: to provide the best possible quality of services to clients and for their own self-protection.
- Keeping good records can benefit clients in several significant ways. Some benefits to clients include continuity of care when client information is transferred from one mental health professional to another, or when a former client returns to counseling after an extended absence; helping clients measure and affirm their growth and change; and the creation of an accurate history of a client's diagnosis, treatment, and recovery.
- Records can also serve to protect counselors. In the event that your decisions are ever challenged, it is essential that you have documented decisions that you have made and actions you have taken.

- Counselors keep three major types of records: administrative records, recordings, and clinical case notes. It is important for you to understand what is involved in keeping each of these kinds of records and that you follow sound procedures for keeping them secure and protecting the privacy of your clients.
- Many counselors are surprised to learn how many people can have access to their records. You should always make records with the assumption that they will be seen by others, including clients who have the right to access their records.
- Three important federal laws that affect counseling records are the Health Insurance Portability and Accountability Act (HIPAA); the Family Educational Rights and Privacy Act (FERPA); and the Comprehensive Alcohol Abuse and Alcoholism Prevention, Treatment and Rehabilitation Act of 1972, a statute related to federally funded substance abuse programs. If you work in an educational institution or in an agency that receives federal funds to provide substance abuse treatment, you will need to understand the major provisions of these laws.
- HIPAA is a recently enacted federal law that contains numerous, detailed provisions regarding client privacy, informed consent, and transfer of records. Counselors in all settings must understand how this law affects their practices.
- When you begin working with clients, you will need to have clear and consistent policies and procedures for creating, maintaining, transferring, and destroying your records. Although your personal style and preferences may play some role, many of these policies and procedures will be dictated by your employer, laws, and accreditation standards.

The thought of receiving a subpoena might make you quite anxious. *Subpoenas* are official court documents that you cannot ignore. Unless you deal with subpoenas on a routine basis in your work, you should consult your supervisor (if you are employed) or your practice attorney (if you are in private practice) whenever you receive a subpoena. Your attorney will be an invaluable resource in helping you respond appropriately to subpoenas and deal with legal proceedings such as interrogatories, depositions, and trials. Always seek the counsel of your supervisor or attorney and follow the advice you are given.

CHAPTER **7**

Competence, Assessment, and Diagnosis

FOCUS QUESTIONS

1. If you were a prospective client seeking counseling, how would you go about finding a counselor who is competent to help you?

2. How do counselors determine whether they are competent to counsel a particular client?

3. Do you think it is appropriate for a counselor to refer a client whose beliefs and behaviors conflict with the personal values of the counselor?

4. What do you think should be done if a counselor becomes addicted to alcohol and is not counseling effectively?

5. Evaluation as an end in itself is a very different process from counseling. Why would a counselor want to be an evaluator?

6. To what degree do you believe counselors are competent to administer and interpret psychological tests?

7. The *DSM-5* system for diagnosis is based on pathology and the medical model of mental illness, whereas counseling is grounded in the wellness model. Why must counselors learn to diagnose clinical disorders?

COMPETENCE AS AN ETHICAL AND LEGAL CONCEPT

When clients come for counseling, they invest a great deal of trust and reliance in their counselors. The client's role in the therapeutic relationship, which involves dependency, self-disclosure, vulnerability, and expectations of finding relief and solutions to problems in a safe environment, underscores the counselor's obligation to provide competent services. When clients put their trust in counselors as professionals, one of their most fundamental expectations is that their counselors will be competent (Pope & Vasquez, 2011). Herlihy and Corey (2015a) noted that the trust that clients bestow on us is "a source of power that must not be abused; clients need to be able to rely on their counselor's competence as a helper" (p. 183).

Competence in counseling is not easy to define. According to Welfel (2013), competence involves a combination of *knowledge*, *skill*, and *diligence*. Knowledgeable counselors have a thorough grounding in the core areas of study required to practice the profession. As we noted in Chapter 2, the Council for Accreditation of Counseling and Related Educational Programs (CACREP, 2009) has identified core areas of instruction, including professional orientation and ethical practice, social and cultural diversity, human growth and development, career development, helping relationships, group work, assessment, and research and program evaluation. Most counselor training programs, whether or not they are CACREP accredited, offer instruction in these basic areas. Knowledge is acquired through attaining a graduate degree in counseling and is maintained through continuing education activities.

Skill building is a complex process that begins in graduate school with applied courses such as counseling techniques, group work, and practicum and internship. Skills are then honed and expanded through postdegree supervised counseling experience. Skilled counselors are able to select and use appropriately a range of basic interviewing techniques and therapeutic interventions.

Diligence has been defined by Welfel (2013) as a consistent attentiveness to the client's needs that means putting client welfare first and foremost, above all other concerns. The first standard of the *Code of Ethics* (ACA, 2014) is "The primary responsibility of counselors is to respect the dignity and to promote the welfare of clients" (§A.1.a.). Evidence of diligent practice includes being willing to do extra reading, research, training, consultation, and follow-up to ensure that clients are served effectively.

Counselors are neither totally competent nor totally incompetent, although legal arguments during malpractice lawsuits might imply otherwise. In discussing the competency of lawyers, Cramton (1981) distinguished between "the ability to perform a task at an acceptable level" and "the reality of actually doing so in a particular situation" (p. 161). From Cramton's perspective, competency is not an abstract concept; instead, it is based on performance. Neither is competency a dichotomous concept; there is a continuum of professional expertise with gross negligence at one end and maximum effectiveness at the other extreme. As discussed in Chapter 1, the difference between law and ethics is that law demands a minimum level of practice from counselors, and ethics encourages counselors to approach the ideal in their level of practice. Competency is a parallel concept in that external forces require counselors to demonstrate minimum competency for professionals, whereas an internal force demands that counselors strive for ideal practice. For example, state licensure boards set the *minimum* requirements that counselors must meet to practice in that state, and counseling graduate programs require *minimum* levels of performance in order for students to be granted a degree. On the other hand, counselors are constantly striving to attain *maximum* knowledge and skills, and national voluntary credentialing organizations such as the National Board for Certified Counselors (NBCC) certify counselors who have distinguished themselves beyond the minimum in the field.

So, as we discuss competence in this chapter, keep in mind that competency is not an either/or concept. Rather, competence is a complex construct with many possible levels along a continuum.

Competency in counseling involves both ethical and legal considerations. From an ethical perspective, the most salient moral principle is *nonmaleficence:* Do no harm. Incompetence is often a major factor in causing harm to clients. Counselors rarely intend to harm their clients, but harm *can* occur if counselors are not knowledgeable, skillful, and capable.

The most basic ethical standard related to competence in the *Code of Ethics* (ACA, 2014) is that counselors "practice only within the boundaries of their competence" (§C.2.a.). How can a counselor determine just where these boundaries lie? It is difficult to answer this question because counseling is an exceptionally broad profession. Just as attorneys and physicians could never be competent to practice in every area within law and medicine, counselors could never be competent to offer counseling services in all areas of practice or to everyone who seeks their services

(Barnett & Johnson, 2015). A counselor who is qualified and experienced in counseling children might not be competent to provide counseling services to a geriatric population. Expertise in counseling basically healthy clients who are having difficulty coping with life transitions does not qualify a counselor to counsel clients who suffer from chronic psychotic disorders. Competence in individual counseling does not necessarily translate into competence to lead a particular type of counseling group or to counsel families. In fact, Hughes (2014) has suggested that competence is comprised of the knowledge, skills, attitudes, and values needed to provide effective counseling services to a specific client in a specific context.

Competence is also a legal issue, because society expects professionals to be competent and holds them to this standard through licensing boards and the courts. Legal issues relating to competence include state licensure and the law of malpractice. Counselor incompetence is the second most frequently reported area of ethical complaints (after dual relationships with clients), according to one survey of state counselor licensure boards (Neukrug, Milliken, & Walden, 2001). When a client is harmed, the counselor could be sued for malpractice and held legally responsible in a court of law. Many lawsuits brought by plaintiffs alleging that they were harmed as clients focus on competence.

In this chapter, we first explore methods of developing and assessing competence to *enter* the counseling profession. Next, we focus on ways to *maintain* competence during one's professional career. Competence is a fluid concept, and achieving competence at one time does not ensure that one will remain competent over time (Barnett & Johnson, 2015). In addition, we address issues that arise when a counselor's competence is *questionable*. These issues include counselor burnout and impairment.

Counselor Preparation

Competence is based on "education, training, supervised experience, state and national professional credentials, and appropriate professional experience" (ACA, 2014, *Code of Ethics*, §C.2.a.). To be competent, counselors are also expected to "gain knowledge, personal awareness, sensitivity, dispositions, and skills pertinent to being a culturally competent counselor in working with a diverse client population" (§C.2.a.). Counselor preparation is obviously a basic component in developing competence to counsel. The process of becoming competent to enter professional practice begins with university counselor preparation programs. Measuring a student's competency as a counselor has proven to be a difficult process (Erikson & McAuliffe, 2003).

The initial responsibility for producing competent practitioners lies with those who do the preparation: counselor educators and supervisors. During the period of time when prospective counselors are working toward their master's degrees and are working under supervision toward licensure, the responsibility for ensuring an acceptable level of competence rests with counselor educators and supervisors. These professionals have an ethical obligation to protect the public by acting as *gatekeepers* for the profession (Dufrene & Henderson, 2009; Henderson, 2010; McCaughan & Hill, 2014; Swank & Smith-Adcock, 2014).

Counselor educators must select and admit to graduate programs individuals who are likely to succeed at developing the skills, knowledge, and characteristics needed to become effective counselors (Erikson & McAuliffe, 2006). Academic ability is one important factor. Selection criteria typically include grade-point averages and scores on standardized tests such as the Graduate Record Examination (GRE) or Miller Analogies Test (MAT). It is entirely possible, however, for a student to have strong intellectual abilities and still not possess the personal characteristics needed to be a *therapeutic person*. Personal characteristics such as openness to new ideas, flexibility, cooperativeness, being open to feedback, awareness of one's impact on others, ability to deal with conflict, ability to express feelings, and acceptance of personal responsibility have been identified as necessary for effective performance as a counselor (Baldo, Softas-Nall, & Shaw, 1997; Frame & Stevens-Smith, 1995; McAdams, Foster, & Ward 2007). In addition, a tolerance for ambiguity and a willingness to explore one's own biases, values, and personal issues have been shown to be related to the ability to develop effective therapeutic relationships. Although these characteristics are difficult to measure, most counselor preparation programs rely on a personal interview, written essay, or other subjective criteria in selecting candidates for admission. The admissions criteria most commonly used for master's program admission among CACREP-accredited programs surveyed by Swank and Smith-Adcock (2014) were letters of recommendation (96%), GPA (95%), personal statement (89%), and interviews (82%).

Once candidates have been selected and admitted into a graduate program, the next question that arises is "What does a master's degree program need to include in order to produce competent counselors?" As we described in Chapter 2, CACREP has developed standards for preparing counselors, and the Council on Rehabilitation Education (CORE) has set forth similar standards for rehabilitation counselors. CACREP and CORE accredit preparation programs that have undergone a rigorous review, so it can be reasonably assumed that graduates of approved programs possess certain competencies (Herlihy & Corey, 2015a). It should be noted, however, that the majority of counselor preparation programs are not CACREP or CORE accredited (Schweiger, Henderson, McCaskill, Clawson, & Collins, 2011), and many competent counselors are educated in programs of sound quality that have not sought this accreditation. Another approach to ensuring adequacy of preparation programs is regional accreditation of universities. Regional accrediting agencies have set the minimal standard for universities in the United States. If a university is accredited by a regional accrediting agency, its legitimacy is assumed. The *Code of Ethics* (ACA, 2014) requires that "Counselors accurately represent the accreditation status of their degree program and college/university" (§C.4.e.). Counselors should not explicitly state or imply that the university that granted their degree was regionally accredited if it was not at the time that the degree was granted.

Although these approaches to ensuring quality of counselor preparation are both necessary and helpful, the reality remains that successful graduation from an accredited program does not guarantee competence (Kitzrow, 2002). Much depends on the individual student's motivation and ability to learn, the quality of instruction, the competencies of the faculty members, the breadth and extent of supervised counseling experience provided by the program, and the quality of supervision received. In our own experience as counselor educators, we have found that most students who are about to graduate are keenly aware that they have only just begun to develop competence as practitioners. As a novice counselor, you need not be hobbled by a concern over your limitations and lack of experience. In most states, you will continue to be supervised closely and supported in your work as a counselor until you have been licensed for independent private practice. Nonetheless, a healthy awareness of your limitations can help you avoid exceeding your boundaries of competence in your eagerness to begin practicing your new profession (Gaubatz & Vera, 2006).

Credentialing

Credentialing is a "method of identifying individuals by occupational group" (Sweeney, 1995, p. 120). As was discussed in Chapter 2, two important types of credentialing found in counseling are certification, which takes various forms, and licensure. These credentials provide a tangible indicator of certain accomplishments and, as such, they have implications for assessing the competence of the credential holder. Counselor credentials were discussed in Chapter 2 and are revisited in this chapter with a focus on how credentials are related to determining counselor competence.

The terms *licensure, certification,* and *registration* have many different meanings but are sometimes used interchangeably, which causes a great deal of confusion. As was explained in depth in Chapter 2, the strict uses of the terms in governmental regulation of a profession are as follows: (a) *Licensure* refers to the most rigorous form of regulation in that only those who are licensed may practice the profession in a state; (b) *certification* is the term used when a title, such as *professional counselor*, can be used only by those who are certified, but anyone can practice the profession without being certified; and (c) *registration* is the form of governmental regulation in which members of a profession must *sign up* with the government if they practice the profession in the state, but anyone may sign the registry without a review of their credentials (Anderson & Swanson, 1994). National private organizations, such as the NBCC, offer national certification, which is a credential that is voluntary (not required by a government for practice). In addition, state departments of education require certification of school counselors employed in public school districts. In this chapter, we use the term *licensure* to refer to state regulation of a profession generally, and the term *certification* to refer to national voluntary credentials and state department certification of school counselors.

Licensure

In Chapter 2, we explained that all 50 states, the District of Columbia, and Puerto Rico now license counselors (ACA, 2014), but many exemptions to the licensure requirement exist. The differences in state laws that license, certify, or register counselors were explained in Chapter 2 as well.

Licensure is related to counselor competency in that it is the most powerful type of credentialing and is established by state law. When state legislators determine that the public's best interests are best served by creating a license to practice a particular profession, the minimum standards for practice of that profession in that state are established through a political process. State governments would rather not be involved in regulating the practice of professions. Legislators agree to license a professional group only when it can be shown that members of the public (a) do not have the ability to determine who is competent to practice within a particular profession, and (b) could be harmed by incompetent practitioners.

When a state legislature passes a statute that establishes counselor licensure or passes amendments to an existing licensure statute, part of that statute specifies the minimum standards for becoming licensed to practice in that state. When these bills or amendments are introduced, political pressures are put on politicians. Economists oppose counselor licensure, arguing that licensing of professions is self-serving, restricts entry into professions, and causes fees for services to rise unreasonably (Rottenberg, 1980). Organizations whose purpose it is to limit the role of government in citizens' lives also oppose licensure statutes. They often are joined in their opposition by other mental health professionals (including psychologists, psychiatrists, and social workers) who do not want to see counselors licensed to provide mental health services because marketplace competition will increase. When these groups of related mental health professionals realize that a bill or amendment is going to be passed over their objection, they often demand very high standards for licensure to keep as few individuals as possible from being licensed. All these groups put political pressure on legislators to set the minimum standards for licensure very high.

On the other side are pressures to set the minimum standards very low. For instance, individuals who are already practicing counseling in a state when counselor licensure statutes are being considered or amended often lobby for statutes that include very low standards so that they will not lose their status and will be entitled to licenses. The U.S. Constitution requires that individuals who were practicing counseling in a state when a licensure statute is passed be automatically licensed. This process has been referred to as *grandparenting*.

As a result of these various political pressures, states now have differing standards. According to Harris (1997) and ACA (2014), licensing statutes for counselors range from a low of 30 required graduate credits to a high of 60 credits. In addition, the number of required post-master's-degree supervised hours range from 2,250 to 4,000. Some statutes specify a significant number of required courses; others require fewer specific courses. Most state statutes require the same courses as those required by CACREP and NBCC, although some differences exist. For instance, some states require a course in marriage and family counseling or a course in substance abuse counseling.

Although there is variation from state to state, all licensed counselors (except those who were grandparented) have completed at least a master's degree, have had post-master's supervised experience, and have successfully completed an examination or other form of screening. Thus, when clients select licensed professionals as their counselors, they can be assured that their counselors have demonstrated certain knowledge, skills, and abilities to the satisfaction of those professionals who evaluated them. Nonetheless, as is true of other approaches, there are limitations to what licensing can accomplish in terms of ensuring competence. Some writers have questioned whether there is evidence that licensure actually ensures general competence, protects consumers, or promotes higher standards of practice (Keith-Spiegel & Koocher, 1985; Pope & Vasquez, 2011). Others have pointed out that the licenses of mental health professionals are sometimes revoked for incompetent practice (e.g., Morris, 1984).

A limitation to licensure is that the possession of a license does not ensure that practitioners will competently *do* what their license permits them to do. The counselor license is a generic one. This leaves it up to licensed counselors, as individuals, to discriminate among professional titles and the professional *functions* they are competent to perform. In addition, whereas licensure boards can restrict or terminate the practice of incompetent practitioners against whom they have received complaints, they are not in the business of monitoring the practices of counselors about whom they have received no complaints.

Clearly, licensing of counselors is an attempt to ensure competent practice. Government regulation may have a positive influence on competency within the counseling profession, but it falls short of accomplishing its objective of ensuring competence. In reality, the standards set for licensure are often the result of political compromises rather than of standards set by the profession for minimum competency.

Certification

In addition to becoming licensed, counselors can offer evidence that supports their competence by becoming certified. The various types of counselor certification, the history of state agency counselor certification and national voluntary counselor certification, and the requirements for certification were summarized in Chapter 2. Some types of certification are mandatory for practicing in certain settings and occur at the state level. For instance, public school counselors must be certified by the states in which they practice. There are also national, voluntary certifications, such as those offered by the NBCC. National Certified Counselors (NCC), like licensed counselors, have received preparation in specific content areas and clinical instruction, have had supervised counseling experience, and have passed an examination.

Specialties

In addition to generic certification as an NCC, NBCC offers three specialty certifications: Certified Clinical Mental Health Counselor (CCMHC), Master Addictions Counselor (MAC), and National Certified School Counselor (NCSC; NBCC, 2014). An affiliate of NBCC, the Center for Credentialing and Education (CCE), offers a specialty credential in supervision (CCE, 2014).

Specialty certifications are another means of establishing a counselor's competence to work with certain types of clients, in certain settings, or in specialized areas of counseling. A host of other, narrower specialty certifications are offered by various groups in such areas as hypnotherapy, biofeedback, or sex therapy.

Specialty preparation is a controversial issue in counseling. Some have argued that only practitioners who have specialized preparation should be allowed to practice that specialty. Some have called for specialty *licensing* (Cottone, 1985), whereas others (Remley, 1995) strongly oppose specialty licensing. Remley has pointed out that the other major professions of medicine and law license professionals to practice their profession generally. Physicians and lawyers may practice any type of medicine or law. The only force that restrains them in limiting themselves to specialties is their own understanding that they must be competent in the professional services they render, and that no one can be competent in all areas. Specialty *accreditation* of counselor education programs is another approach that suggests that only certain counselors are qualified to practice in specified areas. This is the approach that is currently being taken by CACREP (Sweeney, 1995).

There appears to be tension between proponents of two schools of thought regarding specialty preparation. Some counselors believe that establishing competence boundaries should be left up to individual professionals, who then would be accountable to licensure or certification boards if they exceeded those boundaries to the detriment of a client. Others believe that counselors should be prevented by licensure boards from practicing within specialty areas unless they have received specific preparation in the form of graduate courses or supervision. The issues of specialty preparation and specialty licensing and certification will likely be debated within the counseling profession for some time. Currently, however, the prevailing school of thought is that counselors who have proven their minimal preparation and are licensed can decide for themselves the boundaries of their competence and may practice in areas considered specialties without holding any specialty certifications. Nonetheless, counselors have an ethical responsibility to practice in specialty areas new to them only after they have obtained appropriate education, training, and supervised experience, and they must take steps to ensure the competence of their work while developing skills in new specialty areas (ACA, 2014, *Code of Ethics*, §C.2.b.).

Maintaining Competence

Once counselors have completed their formal education and are licensed or certified to practice, the burden of determining competence shifts away from counselor educators and supervisors and onto the counselors themselves. Counselors are autonomous professionals, responsible for monitoring their own effectiveness. The *Code of Ethics* underscores this responsibility, stating that "Counselors continually monitor their effectiveness as professionals and take steps to improve when necessary" (ACA, 2014, §C.2.d.). Even when counselors are employed in agencies or institutions, they are held individually accountable for practicing in an ethical and professional manner. One of the indicators of a profession, which distinguishes it from a semiprofession or a nonprofession, is that the members of the profession practice autonomously. In return for this privilege of independence, professionals must limit themselves to practicing within the areas in which they are competent. Professionals individually determine the limits of their competence and practice accordingly.

Continuing Education

Although competence can certainly be enhanced by the skillful application on a day-to-day basis of the knowledge gained in a formal preparation program, experience alone is no guarantee against errors. Considering the constant contributions that new research makes to knowledge in the field, as well as significant, ongoing changes in the environment in which counseling is practiced, we doubt that a counselor could retain even a modicum of professional competence over a 30- or 40-year career without further education. Counselors must keep up with new knowledge related to emerging issues; for instance, there is a growing body of literature on counseling clients who are involved in self-injurious behaviors (Choate, 2012; Kinch & Kress, 2012; Kress, 2003; Whisenhunt & Kress, 2013). The *Code of Ethics* (ACA, 2014) states that counselors recognize the need for continuing education to acquire and maintain awareness of current scientific and professional information (§C.2.f.), and most counselor licensure and certification boards have established continuing education requirements for maintaining one's license. As Herlihy and Corey (2015a) have noted, however, there are limits to what continuing education requirements can accomplish. "It is difficult to monitor the quality of continuing education offerings or their relevance to a particular counselor's needs. The number of clock hours obtained may have little relation to how much the counselor has actually learned and integrated into practice" (p. 185). The focus should be on maintaining competence, rather than on simply accumulating the continuing education credits required to maintain a license or certification (Corey, Corey, Corey, & Callanan, 2015; Johnson, Barnett, Elman, Forrest, & Kaslow, 2012).

Many other questions could be raised regarding what constitutes a legitimate effort to maintain competence. For instance, is attending a seminar commensurate with teaching one? Is writing an article for a professional journal an indicator of continuing competence? What is the relative value of reading books and scholarly articles about new techniques and theories? Can counselors who regularly but informally consult with colleagues about their cases be considered to be as diligent in working to maintain competence as counselors who attend formal seminars? There may be no way to objectively assess whether a counselor has maintained competence over time. External criteria such as continuing education credits earned are not sufficient to ensure continuing competence. Perhaps more important are counselors' own efforts, as autonomous professionals operating at the aspirational level of ethics, to remain aware of their own limitations, to recognize that these limitations can increase over time, and to seek to keep skills current by both formal and informal means (Keith-Spiegel & Koocher, 1985).

Peer Review

Peer review is a convenient and cost-effective approach to monitoring competence that can be very effective (Truneckova, Viney, Maitland, & Seaborn, 2010). Peer review is a system by which mental health professionals assess one another's services. Granello, Kindsvatter, Granello, Underfer-Babalis, and Moorhead (2008) have argued that peer consultation or peer supervision should continue as a lifelong learning process, and we agree that peer review is useful for counselors at all levels of experience and offers many benefits to counselors. These benefits include enhanced self-awareness and a deeper understanding of the complexities of counseling (Granello et al., 2008); opportunities to discuss a wide variety of answers to clinical and professional questions (Barnett & Johnson, 2015); mutual support; objective feedback in dealing with countertransference issues; information on therapeutic techniques, new research, and referral sources; and help in dealing with difficult cases, stress, and the isolation often experienced by private practitioners. Ideally, peer consultation or supervision groups would meet on a regular, scheduled basis to discuss practice challenges and ethical issues, with a structured but flexible agenda determined by the needs of the members (Borders, 1991; Greenburg, Lewis, & Johnson, 1985). If a peer consultation group is not available, Johnson et al. (2013) recommended that counselors maintain close collegial relationships with several fellow professionals who can provide consistent and honest feedback.

Independent private practitioners are expected to seek peer supervision (ACA, 2014, *Code of Ethics*, §C.2.d.), and this is a strategy we recommend for counselors in all work settings. Several models have been developed for peer supervision that can be used by counseling practitioners (e.g., Benshoff & Paisley, 1996; Gottlieb, 2006; Johnson, Barnett, Elman, Forrest, & Kaslow, 2012; Remley, Benshoff, & Mowbray, 1987; Stoltenberg, McNeill, & Delworth, 1998; Truneckova et al., 2010).

Technology

The Internet presents counselors with myriad opportunities for keeping current and improving their competence as practitioners. New information technologies are developing at such a rapid pace that any attempt we might make to describe them would be obsolete almost immediately. We can, however, highlight a few key resources.

The counseling profession has established a solid presence on the Internet. This offers opportunities to access virtual libraries for researching the latest information on client problems and effective counseling techniques, as well as to collaborate and consult with other professionals around the world. Many of ACA's divisions, NBCC, and CACREP have home pages on the World Wide Web, so you can communicate quickly and directly with professional groups that are working to strengthen counseling as a profession. Videoconferencing on the Internet enables you and counselors everywhere to obtain further preparation and even supervision without having to travel great distances. You can subscribe to mailing lists that allow you to share experiences, ask questions, and exchange information and ideas.

Making Referrals

Standard A.11.a. of the *Code of Ethics* (ACA, 2014) requires that counselors make appropriate referrals when they lack the competence to be of professional assistance to clients. Ethical counselors recognize that they will need to refer a client when accepting or continuing to work with that client would exceed their boundaries of competence. Sometimes it can be difficult for counselors to acknowledge that they are not competent to provide professional services to every client who might request their help. There are many sources of temptation to accept clients who might be better served by a referral. These might include a reluctance to disappoint a valued source of referrals, financial pressures to increase your client load when business has been slow, or the ego-enhancing nature of requests from clients who hold exaggerated beliefs about your talents and abilities to help them. To succumb to these kinds of temptations would not be ethical and would not be in your clients' best interest.

An issue that has become the focus of much controversy is whether or not value conflicts between a counselor and client are an appropriate basis for referring a client. In Chapter 4, we discussed four lawsuits that involved counseling practitioners and counseling students or practicing counselors who refused, based on their religious beliefs, to counsel LGBT clients regarding their same-sex relationships. These cases have brought the issue of values-based referrals into bold relief. A standard was added to the *Code of Ethics* that clarifies that counselors do not refer prospective or current clients "based solely on the counselor's personally held values, attitudes, beliefs, and behaviors" (ACA, 2014, §A.11.b.). In an interview (Martz & Kaplan, 2014), members of the Ethics Revision Taskforce explained counselors' responsibilities when making referrals, stating that the foundation for referrals should be skill-based competence, and that lack of competence cannot be used as an excuse to discriminate against an entire class of people (such as LGBT clients).

In the interview with Martz and Kaplan (2014), members of the Ethics Revision Taskforce, acknowledged that it can sometimes be difficult to distinguish referrals based on competence from those that are discriminatory. They offered the example of a client who seeks counseling to discuss possible gender reassignment. Because the developmental process involved in gender reassignment is complex and specific, a counselor who has no experience with this issue would be justified in suggesting a referral to another provider with experience and expertise. However, that referral would need to be based on lack of experience and lack of competence, not on the counselor's values and beliefs regarding gender reassignment.

A particular type of challenge is posed when counselors need to refer a client with whom they are already engaged in a counseling relationship. Despite the best efforts of counselors to accept only those clients whom they believe they can provide with competent services, the course of counseling is unpredictable. A client's presenting problem may be well within the counselor's scope of competence, and the counselor might in good faith begin working with that client, only to discover as therapy progresses that the client has unanticipated counseling needs. The following case is an example.

7-1 The Case of Marianne

Marianne, a Licensed Professional Counselor (LPC) in private practice, began working with Ellen, a young woman who came for counseling to deal with what at first appeared to be moderate anxiety. Ellen described herself as a perfectionist and sought counseling to learn to "stop being so hard on myself." It was only after several counseling sessions that Ellen felt safe enough in the counseling relationship to reveal to Marianne that she was so fearful of becoming *fat* that she regularly engaged in self-induced vomiting after meals, abused laxatives, and exercised excessively. Marianne recognized these behaviors as symptoms of anorexia nervosa or bulimia nervosa (American Psychiatric Association, 2013), a problem area with which she had no experience.

- How should Marianne approach this situation with Ellen?
- If Marianne decides to take workshops and do independent reading on treatment of individuals who have eating disorders, how will she know when she is competent to provide counseling services to clients like Ellen?
- What if Marianne is able to find a suitable referral source but Ellen refuses, stating that she has complete faith in Marianne's ability to help her?
- What if Marianne practices in an isolated, rural community and a local referral resource or expert consultants or supervisors are not available?

Discussion: Marianne has an ethical obligation to either refer Ellen to a specialist or to another therapist who is competent to work with clients who suffer from eating disorders, or to ensure that she provides quality counseling services to Ellen by obtaining educational experiences and consultation, or supervision from experts. Also, because both anorexia nervosa and bulimia nervosa can be life-threatening conditions, Marianne will need to develop a relationship with a local physician who will treat Ellen's physical issues at the same time.

If Marianne decides to refer, it might be difficult for her, after establishing rapport with Ellen, to tell Ellen she now needs to see a different counselor. Marianne will have to be clear in explaining her reasons for making the referral, and at the same time be sensitive to Ellen's concerns.

If Marianne decides to take workshops and do independent reading on the treatment of individuals who have eating disorders, she will need to consider a number of issues in determining whether she is competent to provide counseling services to clients like Ellen. There are no rules about how a counselor adds a new area of expertise—Marianne will have to decide for herself when she is competent in a new area. Should someone later challenge her regarding this competence, she should be ready to defend her new competence by providing evidence of how she developed it.

If Marianne is able to find a suitable referral source, but Ellen refuses, Marianne will need to be firm in refusing to continue to work with Ellen. If Marianne has trouble being firm in a situation like this, she should seek clinical supervision for support in doing what has to be done.

If Marianne practices in an isolated, rural community and no local referral resource, expert consultant, or supervisor is available, then there really is no absolutely correct way to proceed in a situation like this.

Marianne might consider her options—for example, she could (a) enter into an Internet supervisory arrangement with a specialist in eating disorders and continue to counsel Ellen under that person's clinical supervision and in collaboration with a physician who is monitoring Ellen's physical health or (b) investigate and find the closest and best treatment option available for Ellen, and inform Ellen that this is really her best option, despite travel hardships.

Other situations that might raise the question of referring a client are less clear-cut. Even the most experienced counselors will at times seriously wonder whether they have the personal and professional abilities to work with some of their clients. Difficulty in working with some clients does not, in itself, imply incompetence. In fact, counselors who refer all clients with whom they encounter difficulties will probably have few clients. Instead, counselors can extend their boundaries of competence through reading, participating in workshops and other professional development opportunities, consulting, co-counseling with colleagues who have expertise in a needed area, and working under supervision. The key is to keep a careful balance, referring when necessary and in other situations extending your areas of competency while keeping clients. Counselors can avoid stagnation and can continue to learn and grow as professionals by taking on clients who present new concerns and issues, thus extending their scope of competence. In fact, it would be impossible to develop expertise in a new counseling specialty area without eventually accepting a client with an issue in that area. At the same time, counselors must take care to ensure that clients are not harmed while the counselor is in the process of learning new skills and developing new competencies. You must make careful judgments regarding when to refer and when to keep new clients when you are preparing to provide services in a new area.

Diversity Considerations

As we emphasized in Chapter 3, recognizing diversity in U.S. society and developing intercultural counseling competence are essential to ethical practice. When you think of your own future practice, keep in mind that if you are not trained and competent to work with culturally diverse clients, you are at risk of practicing unethically if you attempt to provide services to such clients. Counselors have an ethical obligation to actively attempt to understand the diverse cultural backgrounds of their clients and to learn how their own cultural, racial, and ethnic identities have an impact on their values and beliefs about the counseling process. The *Code of Ethics* has incorporated, throughout the document, provisions requiring counselors to be culturally competent. The introduction to Section A (ACA, 2014) states, "Counselors actively attempt to understand the diverse cultural backgrounds of the clients they serve. Counselors also explore their own cultural identities and how these affect their values and beliefs about the counseling process." Every section of the code reminds counselors of their duty to be aware of cultural differences in their counseling practices. Fortunately, the counseling profession's attention to cultural diversity has increased dramatically in recent decades. Research on multicultural competence continues to appear at a rapid pace (e.g., Hall, Barden, & Conley, 2014; Katz & Hoyt, 2014; Magaldi-Dopman, 2014). There is an abundance of professional literature that can enhance counselor awareness and knowledge. The *Journal of Multicultural Counseling and Development*, the publication of the Association for Multicultural Counseling and Development (AMCD, an ACA division), contains excellent cutting-edge articles and has published the *Multicultural Competencies and Standards* (Arredondo et al., 1996). *Advocacy Competencies* have been developed as well (see Chapter 3). Diversity issues are addressed frequently in ACA publications that have a more general focus. The *Journal of Counseling and Development* regularly includes articles related to counseling clients from cultures that are different from a counselor's own background and contains articles in each issue devoted to counseling in other countries. Numerous books on multicultural counseling and social justice and advocacy are now available, including several that can be purchased from the ACA bookstore at a discounted price for members. If you want to learn more about counseling across the world, we recommend a book published by the ACA entitled *Counseling Around the World: An International Handbook* (Hohenshil, Amundson, & Niles, 2013).

At the same time, work remains to be done to improve counselor multicultural competence (Delphin & Rowe, 2008), although research has indicated that counselors as a group perceive themselves to be multiculturally competent (Holcomb-McCoy & Myers, 1999; Patureau-Hatchett, 2008). Holcomb-McCoy and Myers found that counselors perceive their multicultural preparation to have been less than adequate and that differences in self-perceived multicultural competence could be explained by whether a counselor is a member of an ethnic minority group. They suggested that the experience of being a member of an ethnic minority group and interacting daily with members of the majority group provides in vivo multicultural education. These findings underscore the need for White counselors to seek out experiences that will allow them to interact with those who are culturally different from themselves.

Counselors who work in urban and suburban settings are able to limit their scope of practice because they typically have numerous referral resources available to them. Counselors who practice in rural areas, however, do not enjoy this luxury and often practice as generalists out of sheer necessity (Welfel, 2013). The geographic location of their practice places extra demands on them to increase their knowledge and skills in order to respond to the varied needs of their clientele. At the same time, they must practice diligence. They must weigh the risk of causing harm if they provide services to a client who presents problems or issues in which they are not adequately trained. Fortunately, maintaining competence is no longer as difficult as it was in the past now that opportunities to increase knowledge and skills are readily available through distance consultation and supervision, interactive webinars, and online continuing education courses.

Erosion of Competence: Burnout and Impairment

The work of the counselor can be stressful and emotionally demanding. Counselors, as partners in the therapeutic journey, can be deeply affected by the pain of their clients (Corey et al., 2015). This stress occasionally takes its toll on practitioners (Barnett, 2008). Ironically, the counseling relationship itself can be a source of stress. In other interpersonal relationships, such as friendships, there is give and take and a reciprocal meeting of needs. This balance does not exist in a counseling relationship. Counselors are experts in one-way caring (Skovholt, 2001) who make a *loan of the self* to the therapeutic relationship (Squyres, 1986), receive little in return, and sometimes doubt the effectiveness of counseling. Of counselors surveyed by Farber and Heifetz (1982), 74% saw lack of therapeutic success as the most stressful aspect of their work, and 55% felt depleted by the unreciprocated attentiveness, giving, and responsibility that the therapeutic relationship demands. Stress can lead to distress which can, over time, lead to burnout and impairment. The terms *distressed*, *burned out*, and *impaired* have been used somewhat interchangeably in the counseling literature. However, these terms might be better viewed as ranging along a continuum from the least to the most serious in relation to their impact on competent professional performance.

Most counselors probably could be described as *distressed* at some time during their professional lives. In fact, results of one survey indicated that 82% of psychotherapists had experienced at least one episode of psychic distress (Prochaska & Norcross, 1983). Distressed counselors may experience irritability, anxious and depressed moods, somatic complaints, lowered self-esteem, and feelings of helplessness, but they are not necessarily impaired in their professional functioning. They know at some subjective level that something is wrong and that distress is usually a transitory and temporary condition.

When distress remains unalleviated, however, it can lead to *burnout*, which has been described as "physical, emotional, and mental exhaustion brought on by involvement over prolonged periods with emotionally demanding situations and people" (Pine & Aronson, 1988). Burned-out counselors, exhausted and depleted, have little energy left for their clients. According to Zur (2011a), signs of burnout include emotional depletion, an unrelieved sense of worry, loss of perspective, helplessness, inefficiency, and an inability to leave clients' concerns at the office. Some writers have suggested that few counselors can expect to stay immune from burnout, and even that burnout may be nearly inevitable after 10 years in the field (Grosch & Olsen, 1994; Kottler, 1993). Burnout is not so much a state or condition as it is a process that, if not corrected, can lead to impairment.

It would be rare for a counselor to never experience a frustrating week, a difficult client, an emotional overload, or occasional symptoms of burnout, yet counselors who are functioning well can put these experiences into perspective. *Impaired counselors*, by contrast, are unable to transcend periods of stress (Stadler, 2001). Their therapeutic skills have diminished or deteriorated to the point that they are unable to perform their responsibilities appropriately (Emerson & Markos, 1996). The medical profession has described *impairment* as "the inability to deliver competent patient care" (Stadler, Willing, Eberhage, & Ward, 1988, p. 258). Substituting *client* for *patient*, this definition can be applied to counseling, and incompetence raises the risk that clients might be harmed. Impairment is often associated with alcohol and other drug abuse and with the blurring of therapeutic boundaries that can lead to sexual exploitation of clients.

Why do some counselors become impaired, whereas others manage to bounce back from periods of distress or burnout? Sometimes *environmental factors* can play a key role. A counselor may experience the death of a loved one, divorce or desertion, physical or sexual assault, the severe physical illness of a family member, or other personal loss or trauma. These events can unbalance anyone's emotional equilibrium. If the counselor takes time off from work, goes for counseling, or in some other overt way takes control and works toward a return to full functioning, this type of impairment is usually transitory and need not be a cause for ongoing concern about the counselor's competence (Emerson & Markos, 1996).

Sommer (2008) has pointed out that traumatic events occur more frequently than is generally recognized, and that there is a high likelihood that most counselors will work with traumatized clients. Human-created tragedies such as the 9/11 terrorist attacks and natural disasters such as Hurricane Katrina are examples of events that can put counselors at risk of experiencing *vicarious traumatization*, also known as compassion fatigue or secondary traumatic stress disorder. Counselors who fail to recognize the warning signs of vicarious traumatization in themselves may become less skilled and less able to be emotionally present with clients who have been traumatized. Thus, counselors have an ethical obligation to know about these hazards in advance and be prepared to deal with them (Sommer, 2008).

In other instances, *preexisting conditions* may put the counselor at risk. Some individuals enter the helping professions in order to work through their own unresolved problems. Personal difficulties that have led some counselors to enter the profession may be exacerbated by the practice of the profession. The practice of counseling can reactivate early experiences, open old wounds, and reawaken unresolved issues. Counselors with a history of addictions or a vulnerability to substance abuse seem to be predisposed to problems after entering the profession. Studies indicate that a significant number of impaired counselors experience alcoholism or other substance abuse problems (Deutsch, 1985; Thoreson, Nathan, Skorina, & Kilberg, 1983). Glickhauf-Hughes and Mehlman (1996) contended that certain personality characteristics make counselors more vulnerable to impairment. These characteristics include parentification (a willingness to take responsibility for others), perfectionism, imposter feelings and self-doubt, and audience sensitivity (strong awareness of others' feelings and responsiveness to them).

Stressful or traumatic events in a counselor's personal or social life and preexisting conditions are not the only factors that can contribute to counselor impairment. Certain kinds of *clients* and *client problems* can promote counselor distress (Stadler, 2001). Working with suicidal clients has been shown to take an emotional toll. For counselors who work with clients with substance abuse problems, the high relapse rate among these clients can lead to counselor discouragement and cynicism about the sincerity of clients' desires to change. Certain client characteristics such as lack of empathy for others, manipulativeness, and refusal to accept responsibility for one's behavior are often present in clients diagnosed with some personality disorders, sex offenders, and clients who abuse women or children. These characteristics also can exacerbate the stress felt by counselors. As has been noted, counselors who work with victims of trauma and abuse are at increased risk for developing secondary posttraumatic stress symptomology. Having a practice that includes a large number of clients in managed care plans, with the accompanying demands for demonstrable, short-term results and often-burdensome paperwork, can put counselors at greater risk for emotional exhaustion (Thompson, 1999). Factors that can contribute to burnout and impairment among addictions counselors include heavy caseloads of mandated clients, staff turnover, funding cuts, low salaries, and limited career opportunities (Vilardaga et al., 2011).

The counseling profession has been slow to recognize the problem of impairment among its members; however, research and attention to the problem have increased in recent years. In 2003, ACA created a Taskforce on Counselor Wellness and Impairment. The Taskforce has organized and presented information on risk factors, assessment, wellness strategies, and resources, all of which can be accessed through the ACA's website (www.counseling.org). In a national survey of counselor wellness and impairment, Lawson (2007) found that counselors generally rated themselves high in wellness, but rated the wellness of their colleagues significantly lower. A substantial number of counselors who participated in the study (5% to 10%) had scores on an instrument that indicated they were at risk for burnout and compassion fatigue or vicarious traumatization. More recently, Lawson and Myers (2011) surveyed over 500 ACA members and found that counselors scored higher on the measure of wellness (Professional Quality of Life; ProQOL) than did populations previously studied, and they had lower scores on compassion fatigue and burnout.

The *Code of Ethics* (ACA, 2014) provides clear guidance regarding counselors who may be impaired (§C.2.g.). This standard states that counselors monitor themselves for signs of impairment from their own physical, mental, or emotional problems. If they determine they are impaired, counselors must limit, suspend, or terminate their professional responsibilities until they can safely resume their work and seek assistance to address their problems.

1. Deterioration in personal relationships, including marital problems and family dysfunction

2. Becoming isolated and withdrawn from others

3. Feelings of disillusionment with the profession

4. Emotional distancing during counseling sessions

5. Poor health habits with respect to nutrition, exercise, and adequate sleep

6. Alcohol and drug abuse

7. Changes in work habits such as increased tardiness and absenteeism

8. Moodiness, depression, and symptoms of anxiety

9. Blurring of professional boundaries with clients

10. Procedural errors and sloppy record keeping

FIGURE 7-1 Warning signs of professional impairment

Source: Pearson Education, Inc., Hoboken, NJ.

The Code of Ethics (ACA, 2014) also requires counselors to assist their colleagues or supervisors in recognizing their own impairment (§C.2.g.). If counselors believe that their colleagues or supervisors may be harming their clients, counselors must intervene as appropriate. It might be difficult for counselors to assist their colleagues and supervisors in recognizing their own impairment. At what point would you decide that a colleague or supervisor was impaired? For example, how much social drinking is too much? Or, how many absences from work indicate impairment? Once you have formulated in your mind that a colleague or supervisor is impaired, how do you go about addressing the issue with him or her? Most individuals who are impaired go through an extended period of denial and probably would reject your input. In our opinion, this requirement in the *Code of Ethics* (ACA, 2014) may be very difficult to comply with, especially if the counselor you believe is impaired is your supervisor, who has control and authority over you. Of course, you would need to intervene in some way to prevent harm to clients, but you should be very concerned that imminent harm will occur if you do not intervene and, if you do intervene, you must be prepared for a negative reaction. If you ever believe you need to confront a colleague or supervisor about your belief that he or she is impaired, this would be a good time to consult with other counselors or related professionals regarding your ethical obligations.

Ethical practice requires, first, that counselors be aware of warning signs of impairment. Some of the most common symptoms are presented in Figure 7-1.

Suzanne, the counselor in the following case example, is experiencing some of these symptoms.

7-2 The Case of Suzanne

Suzanne is an LPC who went to work at a community agency when she earned her master's degree. After 5 years at the agency, Suzanne resigned and opened a private practice on her own. Now, 8 months into this venture, she finds that she isn't sleeping well at night. She tosses and turns, worrying about whether she will be able to pay the monthly bills, and trying to think of new ways to market her practice. She misses the camaraderie she enjoyed with her colleagues at the agency and feels increasingly isolated. She has lost weight recently and is starting to have episodes of gastric distress. She realizes that she needs a break from the stresses of her work. However, because she feels trapped by her financial situation, she is taking on more clients during evening hours and on the weekends rather than taking time for self-care activities.

- What are some indicators that Suzanne is experiencing problems that might lead to impairment?
- If Suzanne does not change her behavior, what kinds of problems might you expect her to experience?
- If you were Suzanne's friend, what options might you suggest to her to relieve her distress?

Discussion: There are numerous indicators that Suzanne is experiencing problems that might lead to impairment: she isn't sleeping well at night, is worrying about whether she can pay her monthly bills and about finding ways to market her practice, misses her friends at her former work site, feels isolated, has lost weight recently, is having gastric distress, and has taken on more clients than she really wants to serve.

If Suzanne does not change her behavior, she is at risk for impairment. The quality of her counseling services to clients may decline. She may develop additional psychological problems or physical health problems, and she may end up in a financial crisis.

If you were Suzanne's friend you might suggest that she try to find another job and close her practice after she does. Other suggestions might be that she could find one or more other counselors in private practice to share her expenses and provide her with professional stimulation, join a peer support or supervision group, or seek counseling for burnout management.

Burnout and impairment can be prevented when individual counselors monitor their own vulnerabilities and are aware of the ethical ramifications of practicing when they are unable to function effectively (Witmer & Young, 1996). Many resources and strategies are available to counselors when they recognize that they need to make changes in their lives if they are to remain competent practitioners (Kottler & Schofield, 2001). Some of these are (a) seeking counseling for themselves; (b) seeking supervision, especially of their work with clients who are difficult and tend to drain their personal resources; (c) taking a break or vacation from practice; (d) joining a peer support group; (e) getting regular exercise, meditating, and taking time to enjoy hobbies; and (f) seeking support from family and friends. Attending to self-care is an ethical obligation that must be taken seriously; counselors cannot provide nourishment to clients if they do not nourish themselves (Corey et al., 2015; Culver, 2011; Patsiopoulos & Buchanan, 2011; Skovholt, 2012; Warren, Morgan, Morris, & Morris, 2010).

It is crucial that you develop self-monitoring skills so that you can stay psychologically and emotionally healthy as a counselor. Because graduate school is often stressful, now is a good time to learn and practice these skills (Roach & Young, 2007). Newsome, Waldo, and Gruszka (2012) suggested that counselor training programs provide insufficient education about self-care and that counselor trainees should view self-care as an essential element of their professional development. If you are a student, we recommend that you learn the symptoms of burnout, familiarize yourself with various wellness models, and periodically take the time to assess how you are managing the stressors in your life. Corey et al. (2015) have suggested that you ask yourself some questions if you think you might be experiencing burnout. Your questions might include whether you ask supervisors or peers for help when you need it, whether you are willing to seek personal counseling if you think you need it, whether you engage in self-care practices, whether you are engaged in life outside of work, and whether you are staying connected to family members and friends.

Diversity Considerations in Burnout Prevention

The results of a study conducted by Myers, Mobley, and Booth (2003) on the wellness levels of counseling graduate students bode well for the future of the profession. These investigators found that counseling students scored higher than an adult norm group on the Wellness Evaluation of Lifestyle (WEL), and that doctoral students scored even higher than entry-level students.

Cause for concern in differences was found along cultural variables, however. Female students scored higher than male students on the measure of Gender Identity, and non-Caucasian students scored higher than Caucasian students on the measure of Cultural Identity. The researchers suggested that these findings may reflect greater awareness of gender and cultural issues on the part of persons who belong to historically oppressed groups in U.S. society. Still, the fact that doctoral students scored higher than entry-level students on gender and cultural identity subscales may indicate that counselor preparation programs are succeeding at developing awareness of diversity issues among their students.

ASSESSMENT AND DIAGNOSIS

In Chapter 2, we noted that psychologists and other mental health professionals have challenged the boundaries of competence, or scope of practice, of counselors in two major areas: testing and diagnosis. Testing and diagnosis are both components of the more general professional activity of assessment, or evaluation. The ethical and legal pitfalls in the areas of evaluation, assessment, testing, and diagnosis are numerous (Welfel, 2013), and an entire section (Section E) of the *Code of Ethics* (ACA, 2014) is devoted to this topic. We begin this section with a discussion of ethical requirements and related legal issues in evaluation and assessment generally. Then we focus on two types of assessment—testing and diagnosis.

Evaluation and Assessment

COMPETENCE IN EVALUATION   Despite arguments to the contrary made by psychologists and some other mental health providers, counselors have the education and skills necessary to conduct certain types of evaluations. Some counselors have jobs in which they conduct evaluations on a regular basis, and some have private practices in which they conduct evaluations occasionally or exclusively. In order to conduct an evaluation, a counselor should have expertise in the area that is being evaluated and must be prepared to serve as an expert witness in court. According to the *Code of Ethics* (ACA, 2014), counselors utilize only those testing and assessment services for which they have been trained and are competent (§E.2.a.).

Counselors commonly conduct evaluations for a number of purposes. To give some examples, counselors evaluate:

- What type of custody arrangement would be in the best interests of a child
- The extent of an individual's disability and the potential for future employment
- Whether an individual has a substance abuse problem and, if so, the type of treatment that is needed
- Whether a person is at risk for abusing children in the future
- Whether a person is at risk for harming others
- Whether a person is at risk for suicide or other self-injurious behavior
- Whether a person has a diagnosable mental disorder
- Whether a person would perform well in a particular job

FORMAL EVALUATIONS   Counseling most often involves face-to-face interviews between a counselor and client that are focused on the client's well-being and on assisting the client in personal decision making and problem solving. Evaluations completed by a counselor might include a personal interview, but interviews in which persons are being evaluated have a different purpose than counseling interviews. When a counselor who is also going to treat the client completes an evaluation, the sole purpose should be to gain information to allow the counselor and client to understand the problems and establish appropriate counseling goals. Dual roles should be avoided (ACA, 2014, §E.13.c.).

Because counselors may sometimes be evaluators, and because evaluators usually conduct personal interviews as part of the evaluation process, it is understandable that individuals may become confused about their interactions with evaluators. For example, a woman who goes to a counselor's office for an interview related to a child custody dispute may not understand that she is not entering into a counseling relationship, although the counselor may be asking questions about life events that are very upsetting. The purpose of a child custody evaluation is to report findings to a judge or jury about which parent may be best to have custody of a child, not to assist the person being evaluated in dealing with the stressors of the situation. Child custody evaluations require that unbiased and objective recommendations be made to a judge (J. W. Gould, 1998). An evaluator must be objective and dispassionate. Counselors always have the best interests of their clients in mind and, therefore, could not be objective evaluators if the findings might negatively affect their clients.

Before counselors begin an evaluation interview, it is essential that they fully describe the difference between being counseled and being evaluated. Counselors must ensure that the individual understands this is not a counseling relationship and that the counselor may use any information gathered in the interview as the basis of a report and opinion that will be given to a third party. These obligations are described in the *Code of Ethics* (ACA, 2014). Standard E.13.a. clarifies that when counselors provide forensic evaluations, their primary obligation "is to produce objective findings" to be used in reports or testimony.

When an assessment or evaluation is completed, the assessment itself is the end product. A counselor or any number of other individuals might then use the assessment report for purposes other than for counseling. As noted, a personal interview of the person being evaluated is quite often a part of the process. Clients who are being assessed need to understand that the process is different from counseling, what the process entails, what the final product will be, and how and by whom the assessment is intended to be used. Counselors have a responsibility to secure their clients' informed consent to evaluation procedures. According to the *Code of Ethics* (ACA, 2014), the client's *written* informed consent should be secured before beginning a forensic evaluation (§E.13.b.). Before counselors conduct any type of assessment, they must explain its nature and purposes in language that the client can understand (§E.3.a.).

THE COUNSELOR AS EXPERT WITNESS   Counselors should avoid conducting evaluations that cast them in the role of expert witness unless they have agreed to do so. If your job requires that you conduct evaluations or if you complete evaluations in your private practice, you must be prepared to testify in court as an expert witness. There is a good chance that eventually you will be subpoenaed and ordered to explain and defend your conclusions and recommendations.

Counselors also should be certain that they understand the circumstances when an attorney appears to be referring a client for counseling. Such referrals may be attempted for legal purposes as well as for clinical reasons, in that attorneys may be seeking a counselor who would later be subpoenaed to repeat in court what the attorney's client has said in counseling sessions, or the attorney may simply want to demonstrate that the client has gone through the motions of seeking counseling. Counselors should ascertain whether a referral from an attorney is related to an existing or potential legal case and take this information into consideration when deciding whether to accept the client (Reid, 2010).

7-3 The Case of April

April has recently completed her master's degree in counseling and has taken a job in the probation and parole office at the local county courthouse. April's new supervisor has told April that her master's degree in counseling will be very helpful to her in her new position. April's job is to interview people after they have been convicted of a crime to determine whether they are good candidates for probation or whether they should be put in jail or prison. April is told that good candidates for probation are those who have never committed crimes in the past or have had only minor violations, have a stable place to live, have jobs they have held for a while, and are truthful. April will look over the records of each convicted person, conduct an interview with that person, and then make a report to the judge, giving her opinion regarding whether the person is a good candidate for probation. In her first interview with Tom, who has been convicted of a crime, Tom tells April he is really glad to be able to talk to a counselor. Tom and April develop an easy rapport. In the course of the interview, Tom tells April about a number of crimes he has committed that did not show up on his criminal record and explains that he is about to lose his job because of absenteeism, has recently been evicted from his apartment, and doesn't know where he is going to live. In court 2 weeks later, April reports to the judge that, based on information she has gathered from Tom, she does not believe he is a good candidate for probation. Tom angrily tells the judge that April misled him into thinking she was his counselor and was trying to help him and now she has betrayed him by telling the judge private information. Tom's lawyer makes a motion to have April's recommendation stricken from the record because she has no experience conducting probation evaluations and misled his client.

- When April began her meeting with Tom, what should she have said or done to avoid this unfortunate situation?
- How should counselors react if a person they are evaluating indicates during an interview that he or she believes this is a counseling session, even though the counselors have explained that it is an evaluation interview?

Discussion: April should have carefully explained to Tom the purpose of the interview and ensured that he understood before beginning. She also should have given him a written document to sign that reiterated these explanations. When Tom stated that he was glad to be able to talk to a counselor, April should have interrupted the interview and again explained her role as an evaluator. She should call herself an *evaluator*, *probation consultant*, or some other title, rather than *counselor*. She also should have explained to Tom that whatever he said could become a part of the report she is required to make and may be used in determining his probation decision.

An expert's testimony in court usually supports one side in a legal controversy and damages the other side. As a result, the attorney for the side that is damaged has a professional obligation to minimize the impact of the expert's testimony. The attorney will do this in one or more of the following ways: (a) object to the expert's credentials, arguing that the counselor is not expert enough to give an opinion in court; (b) attack the process the counselor used in completing the evaluation, claiming that it was not adequate; (c) attempt to get the counselor to contradict statements, hoping that the judge or jury will give less credibility to a witness who is not consistent; and (d) offer another expert witness's testimony that contradicts the counselor's conclusions and recommendations, hoping the judge or jury will give more credibility to the other expert's testimony. Aggressive cross-examinations can be challenging and uncomfortable for counselors who testify in court as expert witnesses (Brodsky & Terrell, 2011).

Counselors who agree to provide expert testimony in the belief that judges, attorneys, and juries will listen respectfully to the counselor's opinions and be appreciative of their input are in for a big surprise. Hagan (1997) has argued that all mental health expert testimony is a fraud. She has taken the point of view that mental health, as a science, is too inexact to allow its opinions as evidence. Ziskin (1995) has produced a three-volume set of texts designed to assist lawyers in discrediting the testimony of mental health expert witnesses.

Counselors who plan to serve as expert witnesses should take courses to prepare themselves, observe other experts testifying over a period of time, and read written materials (e.g., Becker, 1997; D. Gould, 1998; Stokes & Remley, 2001; Strasburger, 1998).

ASSESSMENT WITHIN THE COUNSELING RELATIONSHIP   As described, counselor involvement in child custody determinations consists of a formal evaluation that is separate from the counseling process. Formal evaluations are different from the types of assessment that occur throughout a counseling relationship. In its broadest sense, assessment is the process of gathering information about a client (Leppma & Jones, 2013). Counselors use assessment to ascertain information about clients such as the nature of their problem; the severity and impact of the problem; the interplay between family, relationships, and past experiences with respect to the problem; the impact of environmental conditions on the problem; the client's challenges, strengths, and readiness for counseling; and whether counseling can be beneficial to the client (Drummond & Jones, 2010). Assessment is a collaborative process to which both the counselor and the client contribute with the aim of gaining a better understanding of the client's problems. An accurate assessment of the problems, in turn, increases the likelihood that the problems will be resolved successfully in counseling. The most commonly used method for gathering this initial information is the unstructured clinical interview (Leppma & Jones, 2013). Other forms of assessment often are used within the counseling relationship to provide the counselor and client with more specific information than was gained during the initial interview. The most commonly used forms of assessment are tests of various types and diagnosis. In the following sections, we first explore the ethical issues associated with testing and then turn our attention to diagnosis.

Testing

Counselors use tests in various ways. Occasionally they may be involved in developing new tests, but more often they select existing tests, administer them, and interpret them for their clients. Selecting and administering a test may not seem like a complicated process that has ethical implications, but formal testing is vulnerable to abuse (Welfel, 2013). For example, consider the case of Aaron.

7-4 The Case of Aaron

Kathleen has sought counseling from Aaron, LPC. Her job situation is tentative because the company where she has worked for the past 12 years is downsizing. She is experiencing a number of somatic complaints related to anxiety along with a general feeling of apprehension. By the end of their second session together, Aaron believes that Kathleen may be experiencing depression as well as anxiety. Because her company's managed health care plan allows them only six sessions, Aaron doesn't want to use precious time for assessment activities. He gives Kathleen a standardized depression scale and tells her to complete it at home.

- What do you think of Aaron's decision to let Kathleen complete the test at home?
- Can you identify any problems with this procedure?

Discussion: Aaron should not have allowed Kathleen to take the test home unless it was specifically designed to be self-administered (ACA, 2014, *Code of Ethics*, §E.7.d.). Counselors have a responsibility to appropriately supervise the test-taking process. Any number of things could happen that would produce invalid results if Kathleen takes the test at home. She might misread or misunderstand the directions, exceed the time limits for completing the test, try to complete the test while watching TV or being otherwise distracted, or become alarmed by feelings evoked by the wording of some of the test items.

COMPETENCE TO TEST   Counselors generally do not use testing as much as psychologists do in their practices. The preparation that master's-level counselors receive in testing usually includes the following: (a) a 3-credit assessment course, (b) some testing principles in a research class, (c) testing information in courses such as career counseling and diagnosis of mental disorders, and (d) supervised practice of the use of tests in practicum and internship. Because of the limited use that counselors generally make of tests and the educational level of counselors in the area of testing, it is important both ethically and legally for counselors to administer and interpret only tests for which they have been trained and are competent (ACA, 2014, *Code of Ethics*, §E.2.a.).

At first glance, testing procedures might seem to be fairly simple and straightforward. Test manuals give detailed step-by-step instructions for administration, and many tests can be scored and interpreted by a testing service. In reality, however, considerable knowledge and professional judgment are needed to select the right test for the intended purpose and clientele, administer the test properly, and interpret the findings to the client. In order to select wisely, counselors must have a solid knowledge of the various tests that are available, what they measure, and their limitations. Leppma and Jones (2013) have reminded counselors of their ethical responsibility to use *multiple* methods of assessment. This means that counselors should never use a test as the sole criterion for making clinical or educational decisions. To illustrate this point, even if Aaron (the counselor in the previous case example) had asked his client to complete the depression scale in his presence, Aaron should not use only the client's score on the scale to determine whether a diagnosis of depression is warranted. Aaron should also consider his clinical impressions and the client's behavioral indicators, consult the diagnostic criteria for depression in the *Diagnostic and Statistical Manual* (*DSM-5*), and perhaps (with the client's permission) interview individuals who know the client well and have observed her general daily behaviors.

There is no absolute standard for adequate preparation to use particular tests. Formal educational experiences such as for-credit courses and internships are not the only methods of training. Counselors could become proficient in testing through workshops, supervised practice, and independent study as well. The amount of training needed to develop proficiency varies greatly depending on the test. Developing competence to use complex personality tests such as the Minnesota Multiphasic Personality Inventory–2 requires extensive training (Pope, Butcher, & Sheelen, 1993). There are many tests, however, that counselors can learn to use through the instruction and supervised practice provided in a typical master's degree program. Competence to use a test always depends on the individual counselor's training and experience with the particular test.

Although assessment, including the use of various tests, has always been an integral component of the counseling process, the question of who is qualified to use assessment instruments remains a contentious battleground (Watson & Sheperis, 2010). For this reason an advocacy group, the National Fair Access Coalition on Testing (FACT), has been formed to protect counselors' rights to conduct assessment and testing (National Fair Access Coalition on Testing, 2014).

As we noted in Chapter 2, counselor licensure laws now exist in all 50 states; however, some state laws either restrict counselors to certain testing activities or are ambiguous about whether counselors are qualified to make assessments. For example, some states prohibit counselors from using projective tests, and at least one state statute requires licensed counselors to be further *privileged* to test (*Louisiana Licensed Mental Health Counselor Act*, 1999). Counselors should review their licensing statutes and regulations to determine whether there are any tests they cannot legally administer and interpret. If licensed counselors exceed their statutory authority to test, they could be accused and found guilty of practicing psychology without a license. This happened to an LPC in Louisiana (*State of Louisiana v. Atterberry*, 1995).

Counselors should regulate themselves in the practice of testing. This is the position taken by the ACA as is explained in the *Standards for Qualifications of Test Users* (ACA, 2014). Although counselors typically do not have extensive training in testing, many resources are available to assist counselors in maintaining and increasing their competence to test. The website of the Association for Assessment in Counseling and Education (AACE; www.theaaceonline.com), an ACA division, offers links to a variety of resources and testing documents. Two particularly useful documents are the *Code of Fair Testing Practices in Education* and the *Responsibilities of Users of Standardized Tests*. As the international counseling movement continues to grow, counselors who use tests in their work should familiarize themselves with the international guidelines for test use (International Test Commission, 2001).

DEVELOPING AND PUBLISHING TESTS   Most counselors are not involved in developing testing instruments. Designing, developing, validating, and marketing a new test requires specific knowledge and skills and is a complex and lengthy process. These factors undoubtedly deter many counseling practitioners from undertaking the task.

Even if you are never involved in constructing a test, however, you should understand the ethical responsibilities of test producers. Test producers must produce and market tests that have demonstrated validity and reliability and appropriate norms, as well as a manual that clearly explains how to use the test, the clientele for whom it is and is not suitable, and its strengths and limitations. They must provide information that will help users interpret the results accurately.

Test publishers should make their tests available only to professionals who are qualified to use them. Typically, test publishers require those who wish to purchase their tests to state their degrees, licenses, graduate courses in testing, and training in the use of the specific test.

Test Security

Counselors have both ethical and legal obligations to protect the security of tests from improper usage, copying, or dissemination (ACA, 2014, *Code of Ethics*, §E.10.). Almost all tests depend on the user being unfamiliar with the test items. Therefore, counselors must keep testing materials safely locked away when not in use to prevent unauthorized users from gaining access to them. Of course, test security measures must also be carefully maintained when the test materials are accessed and stored on a computer. A problem related to test security occurs when counselors and other professionals break the law by violating copyrights of tests held by test authors and publishers. The general principles of copyright law are explained in Chapter 16. Once a test has been created, the author (or publisher, if the author transfers the rights) owns the test for 75 years from the date of first publication or 100 years from its date of creation, whichever date expires first (Henn, 1991).

Tests that are published by commercial testing companies must be purchased. Materials include answer sheets, question booklets, report forms, manuals, and other items related to the test. Computer software of all types related to testing is copyrighted and may not be duplicated or used without permission of the publisher. Some commercial testing companies are aggressive in protecting their copyrights because their business profits are negatively affected by violations.

Some tests have never been published by the author or may have been published in a journal. Such tests are not available from a commercial testing company. However, permission must be obtained from the copyright holder before counselors can use the tests either to administer to clients or for research. In most situations, authors transfer their rights to the owners of journals when materials are published.

Release of Testing Records

Records of test results are the same as other counseling records. Counselors should not release test data to anyone who is not qualified to receive the information. The *Code of Ethics* (ACA, 2014), states that counselors should release test data only to persons recognized by counselors as competent to interpret the data (§E.4.). You may feel uncomfortable asking someone who requests test records to verify his or her qualifications, but releasing test data to unqualified individuals carries such a high risk to client welfare that counselors must stand firm on this point (Welfel, 2013).

Counselors also have an ethical obligation to ensure that testing records are transferred in a secure manner. Counselors who receive test results for clients they have been counseling should never transfer those records to another person. In the event that testing records received from another professional are requested or subpoenaed, counselors should refer the individual asking for the records to the professional who originally created them. Reviewing the section in Chapter 6 that deals with transfer of records in general will alert you to possible pitfalls and recommended procedures to ensure safe transfer of test data.

Providing Explanations to Clients

Clients have the right to make an informed choice about whether they want to participate or refuse to engage in testing procedures. They can also expect to receive an explanation of the results of any test they take.

Standard E.3.a. of the *Code of Ethics* (ACA, 2014) clearly indicates that informed consent applies to testing. Before counselors test, they must explain the nature and purposes of assessment and the specific use of the results in language that the client can understand. It is particularly important that clients understand what uses will be made of their test results. They have a right to know in advance if tests will be used as a factor in employment decisions, as a criterion for placement in a special educational program, as a device for screening potential members of a psychotherapy group, or as a means of making other decisions that will affect their lives.

After clients have participated in testing procedures, they have a right to receive feedback about the results (ACA, 2014, §E.1.b.). Many standardized inventories are now computer scored, and counselors can receive results along with printouts that present a fairly extensive explanation of those results. What do you think of the way Louis, the counselor in the following case example, utilized the computer-generated score report and interpretation of his client's test?

7-5 The Case of Louis

Louis is a counselor in a university career counseling and placement center. Last week he began counseling Alicia, a freshman who sought his assistance in deciding which major to pursue. In their first session, he explored with Alicia her sense of being overwhelmed with so many interesting options. After the session ended, Alicia sat at a computer in the next room and completed a career interest inventory. Before his second session with Alicia, Louis obtains her computer-generated score report and interpretation. He reads it over, is impressed with its thoroughness, and decides to give it to her to read at home. He decides he would rather use their time together to explore some other issues she has mentioned, which seem to him to be related to her career indecisiveness.

- What are the problems with giving a client computer-generated test results without also providing an interpretation of the results?
- In what types of situations might you ethically use computer-based testing with clients?

Discussion: Although it is easy to understand Louis's reasoning, it would not be wise for him to follow his plan. Alicia might think *the computer has given her the answer* and may attribute too much power to the test results. Using computer-based testing with clients is not problematic so long as the counselor interprets the results to the client in person and puts the results in the context of other information about the client.

It is essential that counselors communicate test results and interpretations directly to their clients. Counselors appreciate commercial services that score and interpret psychological tests because the services save time and relieve them of the task of scoring the tests, but they should avoid overreliance on them. Interpretations generated by commercial services cannot, by themselves, provide sufficient feedback to clients. They do not take into account the individual characteristics of the test taker and may not generate sufficient alternative explanations of results (Matarazzo, 1986). Counselors must exercise their professional judgment and personal knowledge of the client in using reports provided by test interpretation services.

A face-to-face conversation with the client regarding test results can serve additional purposes. Clients sometimes view test results—particularly elaborate, computer-generated score reports—as being infallible. Counselors need to educate clients about the limitations of tests and to keep these limitations prominent in their own thinking. This will help them avoid any tendency to present results in absolute language. In addition, a dialog with the client can shed light on any unclear or unexpected test results.

For some clients, taking a test is an anxiety-producing event, and they may worry until they see their results. Counselors should keep in mind that some clients have had negative experiences with test taking. In addition, feedback can have therapeutic value. Finn and Tonsager (1992) found that clients who received feedback on their Minnesota Multiphasic Personality Inventories (MMPI) found the feedback to be a positive experience and actually showed a reduction in symptoms.

In practice, counselors often struggle with the question of how much feedback or explanation of test results they should give their clients. They want to be thorough, without overwhelming the client with detail. For many counselors, the pressures of time-limited counseling relationships imposed by managed care are also a factor. Welfel (2013) has suggested that the criteria for deciding how much time to devote to test interpretation should include the following: (a) clients' satisfaction that they understand the meaning and implications of the results, (b) the counselor's assessment that feedback has clarified any confusion or unclear results, (c) a mutual agreement about ways the test results should influence the counseling process, and (d) implications of releasing the findings to others if the client has agreed to such a release.

Diversity Issues in Testing

Counselors must be cautious in using tests with culturally diverse clients. They must select tests carefully to avoid inappropriate testing that may lack appropriate psychometric properties for a particular client population (ACA, 2014, §E.8). It is important to be aware that many traditional assessment instruments have been developed by theorists and practitioners who are themselves lacking in diversity and multicultural training (Helms & Cook, 1999). Because many tests have been validated on mostly middle-class people of European extraction, special populations may not be represented in the norm group on which a test was standardized. Therefore, the test results may be less valid for them. When you use tests, you need to be knowledgeable about the characteristics of the norm group and recognize the limitations of the test with other populations.

Ethical standards (American Counseling Association [ACA], 2014) require counselors to recognize the effects of age, color, culture, disability, ethnic group, gender, race, language preference, religion, spirituality, sexual orientation, and socioeconomic status on test administration and interpretation. Especially when working with culturally diverse clients, test results must be placed in perspective with other relevant factors (§E.8.).

No test is completely culture free. A considerable body of literature provides examples of how assessment instruments have been misused with ethnic and racial minority clients, women, clients with limited English proficiency, the physically challenged, and other special populations (Herlihy & Watson, 2003). The use of educational and psychological tests, in the school setting in particular, has been challenged. There is evidence that these tests tend to discriminate against African American and Hispanic children (Walsh & Betz, 1995). Academic placement or advancement decisions should never be made on the basis of test data alone.

In addition to knowing about the norm groups on which tests are standardized, counselors should examine tests for content bias. When some items in a test refer to experiences that are not familiar to certain populations, the test is content biased. For example, an item on a test that refers to milking cows may make no sense to an urban child who lives in an impoverished socioeconomic environment. There is evidence that content bias of tests of cognitive abilities, in particular, is partly responsible for lower scores among cultural minorities (Lonner & Ibrahim, 1996). Disparities between the average scores of African American and White individuals on tests of intellectual ability are at least partly attributable to culture-specific variables associated with racial and ethnic minority group members' experiences (Axelson, 1993; Perry, Satiani, Henze, Mascher, & Helms, 2008).

Counselors must be alert to the passage of laws that affect testing practices. Two examples are the Education for All Handicapped Children Act (1975) and the Americans with Disabilities Act

(1990). The Education for All Handicapped Children Act requires that tests be in a child's language and be appropriate for the intended use. It also requires that parents give their consent to testing and that they be given access to test protocols after testing has been completed. The Americans with Disabilities Act mandates that testing be appropriate for the individual being tested, that reasonable accommodations be made in testing, and that results may not be used to discriminate in employment choices for people with disabilities.

In summary, counselors must be alert to cultural bias in tests and in test interpretation, and must use caution in interpreting results with minority clients. Ethical practice requires counselors both to understand how clients' cultures and world views can influence their performance on standardized tests and to place test results in perspective with other factors in evaluating these clients. A good resource for developing competence in assessment with culturally diverse clients is *The Handbook of Multicultural Assessment* (Suzuki & Ponterotto, 2007).

Diagnosis

Counselors are sometimes uncomfortable with participating in the diagnosis of mental disorders. Diagnoses usually are made using the *DSM-5* (American Psychiatric Association, 2013), which is the world's most widely used system for identifying and describing mental disorders (Gray, 2011). This system of diagnosis is based on the medical model of mental illness. In contrast to the medical model, counselors espouse a wellness model that focuses on client strengths rather than on simply ameliorating symptoms (see Chapter 2 to review the wellness model). Thus, there is an inherent philosophical conflict between the *DSM* system and the wellness orientation of counselors (Kress, Hoffman, & Eriksen, 2010).

A lively conversation has taken place in the professional literature regarding whether counselors, with their wellness perspective, should diagnose clients with clinical disorders using the *DSM* system (Ginter, 1999, 2001; Hohenshil, 1996; Ivey & Ivey, 1998; Smart & Smart, 1997). Hohenshil has suggested that the antidiagnostic position of some counselors arises from mistaken assumptions, including the following: Counselors counsel clients with less severe problems than clients who are counseled by other mental health professionals; because counselors focus on wellness, the pathology in the *DSM* is not helpful; and the client-centered relationships utilized by most counselors do not need *DSM* diagnoses for treatment planning. Ginter (2001) concluded that "ignorance of the *DSM* system is not congruent with current expectations concerning counseling practice" (p. 70). We agree that counselors in today's world, no matter where they work, must be knowledgeable of the *DSM-5* and be able to converse with other mental health professionals regarding its contents.

When clients want to use their health insurance to help pay for mental health care, counselors usually must assign a diagnosis in order for their services to be reimbursable. As we discuss more fully in Chapter 12, health insurance companies generally will not reimburse for counseling services unless a *DSM* diagnosis accompanies the insurance claim (Comer, 2007). Counselors want to serve their clients by helping them receive reimbursement for counseling services, yet their philosophical objections make them reluctant participants in diagnosis. Braun and Cox (2005) have warned that discomfort with diagnostic labeling can lead to problems. Some counselors may try to diagnose most or even all of their clients as having an adjustment disorder, which is the mildest and least stigmatizing type of disorder. Some might assign a more serious diagnosis than is clinically warranted so that a client can qualify for health insurance reimbursement. These practices of under-diagnosing, or *downcoding,* and over-diagnosing, or *upcoding,* are dishonest and inaccurate (Herlihy, Watson, & Patureau-Hatchett, 2008). Even more serious is the practice of deliberately changing a diagnosis for insurance reimbursement purposes. Some research has indicated that approximately 35% to 44% of mental health practitioners may be engaging in this behavior (Danzinger & Welfel, 2001; Tubbs & Pomerantz, 2001). Clients can be harmed by inappropriate diagnostic procedures, and counselors are on shaky ground both ethically and legally. Standard E.5.a. of the *Code of Ethics* (ACA, 2014) states that "Counselors take special care to provide proper diagnosis of mental disorders."

If you use the *DSM*-5 in your work as a counselor, it is vital that you use it appropriately. A first step is to clarify your own stance toward diagnosis. Diagnosis involves much more than assigning labels to clients. It is best conceptualized in context, as a part of the overall process of assessment that helps counselors understand their clients. Sleek (1996) has likened the diagnostic process to working a jigsaw puzzle in that it involves putting together pieces of information about the client to build an overall picture of the person. The primary purpose of diagnosis is to facilitate effective treatment. The relationship between diagnosis and treatment is like a driving trip and a road map. The diagnosis is a map that helps travelers develop a plan for reaching their destination. Diagnosis should point the way to treatment planning and to the selection of effective treatment strategies for identified disorders.

Diagnosis serves other important functions (Fong & Silien, 1999). First, an accurate diagnosis can help counselors make a prognosis or predict the course of a disorder. Second, the diagnostic system in mental health care was developed to facilitate communication among professionals (Kutchins & Kirk, 1987) and provides a common language and shared frame of reference for mental health professionals. Third, it helps counselors identify conditions that may require the attention of a physician, such as organic disorders or medical conditions that are contributing to psychological problems, so that a referral can be made. Finally, the diagnostic system provides a framework for research. Clinical outcome studies build our knowledge base regarding the effectiveness of various treatment approaches.

While keeping in mind all the useful functions of diagnosis, you should be aware of the risks involved, even when it is done honestly and accurately. For clients, learning their diagnosis can be a double-edged sword. It can be comforting for clients to learn that their condition has a name, that they are not alone in what they are experiencing, and that they are not *going crazy*. On the other hand, clients may feel embarrassed or ashamed of their diagnosis, or feel stigmatized by a diagnostic label and refuse treatment rather than have the diagnosis become part of their record. It is also possible that a diagnosis can lead to a self-fulfilling prophecy; for instance, a client who is diagnosed with depression may become even more deeply depressed. Counselors must be sensitive to the powerful effect that diagnosis can have on clients. Although the *Code of Ethics* (ACA, 2014) allows counselors to "refrain from making and/or reporting a diagnosis if they believe it would cause harm to the client or others" (§E.5.d.), in most circumstances clients have access to their counseling records, including any diagnoses that counselors have rendered.

Diagnoses can affect in significant ways not only clients' feelings and self-concepts but also their lives. Severe diagnoses can have harmful effects far into a client's future, including difficulty obtaining certain kinds of employment or having their diagnosis used negatively in child custody proceedings (Overton & Medina, 2008). Under managed care, some diagnoses can "shadow a client's life like hounds from hell" (Wylie, 1995, p. 32).

The process of diagnosing a client's condition can have effects on the counselor as well as on the client. Studies have shown that the very availability of diagnostic labels can bias counselors in favor of using them, even when a client's condition does not warrant a *DSM* diagnosis (Langer & Abelson, 1974; Rosenhan, 1973). Particularly when a client's eligibility for health insurance coverage depends on a diagnosis, counselors may be tempted to *pathologize* behaviors that are developmentally normal. A rebellious adolescent might be diagnosed as having *oppositional defiant disorder* or *conduct disorder*. A very shy young adult might be diagnosed as having an *avoidant personality disorder.* Welfel (2013) has cautioned counselors against jumping ahead to naming a problem before they have verified that one exists. Counselors who use diagnosis must take care to avoid losing sight of the uniqueness of each client. Even while using a system that is focused on mental disorders and pathology, counselors must maintain the wellness perspective that is unique to their profession. This can be a challenging task.

The most recent edition of the diagnostic manual, the *DSM-5*, was published in 2013 after a lengthy revision process. ACA offered input regarding proposed changes throughout that process, and the leadership has applauded some changes, such as reversing the pathologizing of normal bereavement, that have the effect of reducing the dissonance between the *DSM* and the wellness orientation of counselors. We believe it has been important for ACA to offer input into the revisions as a means to work to establish the parity of professional counselors with other mental health professionals in the realm of diagnosis. Nonetheless, many of the changes are controversial, both among counselors and within the psychiatric profession, and the *DSM* system remains firmly grounded in the medical model. Practicing counselors who have used the previous edition have an ethical responsibility to acquire the continuing education they need to become proficient in using the *DSM-5*. Fortunately, abundant resources exist to assist counselors: journal articles appear regularly that explain new diagnoses and changes in diagnostic categories, and ACA has provided podcasts and webinars that can be found on the website, www.counseling.org, under *continuing education.*

Some ethical issues that arise for counselors when they use diagnosis are securing the client's fully informed consent, working with physicians, and having the qualifications to diagnose. Multicultural considerations are also important in diagnosis. Following is a discussion of these issues as well as legal issues related to accurate diagnosis.

Informed Consent

Some clients do not understand the stigma that might be associated with being diagnosed with an emotional or mental disorder, whereas others may be very concerned about the implications of diagnosis for their future employment. Although it would be inappropriate to overemphasize the possibility that a client may be discriminated against in the future as a result of receiving a diagnosis, counselors do have a responsibility to raise the issue with clients. The challenge is to present a fully adequate explanation of the diagnostic process without deterring the client from seeking counseling services (Kress et al., 2010).

When clients are participants in managed care plans, there is an increase in the information that must be discussed (Applebaum, 1993; Glosoff, 1998; Haas & Cummings, 1991). Clients must understand the impact that their insurance policy may have on the types and length of treatment that will be reimbursed. They must be aware that third-party payment might end before they believe they have met their counseling goals. They must also know what and how much information will be released to managed care companies, and they must give the counselor permission to release the information. The *Code of Ethics* (ACA, 2014) specifies that "Counselors disclose information to third-party payers only when clients have authorized such disclosure" (§B.3.d.).

So that clients cannot later claim that they did not even realize they might receive a diagnosis of an emotional or mental disorder, counselors' disclosure statements should include a phrase regarding diagnosis. We also recommend that, whenever possible, counselors should disclose to clients (or their parents or guardians) their diagnosis when the diagnosis is recorded. If an initial diagnosis is changed after the counseling process has begun as a result of a counselor's reassessment of the client's condition, of course this change should also be discussed with the client. As we note in Chapter 4, informed consent should be viewed as an ongoing process, not a one-time event. This may be particularly important to remember with respect to diagnosis, as noted by Grover (2005), who has cautioned that some clients may not adequately understand, at the time of their initial consent, the full implications of being assigned a diagnosis and having it communicated to others.

Consulting with Physicians

Counselors have a responsibility to understand that some client behaviors or reported thoughts and feelings could have a physiological basis. Counselors are wise to determine the physical condition of their clients when they begin the counseling process. Intake forms or interview protocols must ask clients whether they have any negative health conditions and, if so, the details regarding their treatment. Counselors must also know whether their clients are taking any medications and, if so, the purpose of the medications and the effects and side effects that the medications produce (King & Anderson, 2004). When clients have not had a physical exam in a long time, or if a possibility exists that a problem may be physical in nature, counselors should recommend that clients have a physical exam. They should ask the clients to report the results to them or to sign a release of information so that the counselor and physician can communicate with each other.

When clients have physical complaints that obviously might be related to medical problems (such as headaches, dizziness, or chest pains), counselors must insist that these clients have physical examinations as a condition to their continued mental health treatment. Mental health professionals who overlook or ignore the obvious need for a referral to a physician could be held negligent if a client's supposed mental condition later turned out to be caused by a physical problem.

The symptoms of some mental disorders can be alleviated by psychotropic medications. For example, several medications have been demonstrated to be effective in reducing symptoms of bipolar disorder (formerly called *manic depression*) in many sufferers. When counselors diagnose conditions that can be helped by taking medication, they must make clients aware of this option. Counselors can then refer to a psychiatrist those clients who are willing to consider taking medication. With the client's permission, the counselor and psychiatrist can work cooperatively in assisting the client.

Qualifications to Diagnose

An issue that has been controversial is whether counselors are qualified to diagnose mental disorders. Of course, counselors should not assign a diagnosis of an emotional or mental disorder unless they have had adequate training to do so (ACA, 2014, §C.2.a.), but there is no absolute standard for determining adequate training. In terms of academic preparation, most contemporary programs that prepare counselors for clinical mental health or community agency practices require counselors to complete a course in diagnosis of emotional and mental disorders. Counselors should also have had supervised experiences in diagnosing as part of their practicum or internship in their master's degree programs, should continue to gain supervised experience in diagnosis while they are working toward their licenses, and should seek ongoing consultation and supervision of their diagnostic practices (Kress et al., 2010). New research about effective treatments is appearing constantly, so counselors must continue to learn in order to stay current (ACA, 2014, §C.2.f.).

In some states, licensed counselors have been challenged and accused of practicing outside their scope of authority when they have diagnosed emotional and mental disorders. The following quotation from the *DSM-5* clearly states that it is applicable in a wide diversity of contexts and:

> is of value to all professionals associated with various aspects of mental health care, including psychiatrists, other physicians, psychologists, social workers, nurses, counselors, forensic and legal specialists, occupational and rehabilitation therapists, counselors, and other health professionals. (American Psychiatric Association, 2013, DSM-5, preface, p. xii)

Accusing counselors of practicing outside their scope of authority when diagnosing emotional and mental disorders is an example of a *turf issue* that can pit counselors against other mental health professionals such as psychiatrists, psychologists, and social workers, who have traditionally endorsed the medical model. The issue is very important because if mental health professionals are unable to render diagnoses of emotional and mental disorders, some agencies may refuse to employ them, and health insurance companies may not reimburse their clients for mental health services that counselors provide.

Counselors have responded to this problem by introducing legislation that amends the scope of practice in their state licensure statutes. The amendments specifically indicate that licensed counselors may diagnose and treat emotional and mental disorders. In states that do not have such specific language in their counselor licensure statutes, counselors still diagnose emotional and mental disorders. However, they must argue that doing so is part of the counseling process in general that is covered in other language in their counselor licensure statutes.

Diversity Considerations in Diagnosis

It is important to keep in mind when dealing with diagnosis that *mental disorders* are defined in a cultural context. Standard E.5.b. of the *Code of Ethics* (ACA, 2014) states, "Counselors recognize that culture affects the manner in which clients' problems are defined and experienced. Clients' socio-economic and cultural experiences are considered when diagnosing mental disorders." Behaviors that may seem bizarre in one culture may be considered perfectly normal in another.

The *DSM* system has long been criticized for pathologizing normal behaviors and for bias against women, members of ethnic and racial minority groups, geriatric populations, children, people living in poverty, and LGBT individuals (Rapp & Goscha, 2012; Zur & Nordmarken, 2010). In the *DSM-5* (American Psychiatric Association, 2013), an attempt was made to give more attention to the diverse ways people from different cultural groups can experience and describe their distress (Dailey, Gill, Karl, & Barrio Minton, 2014a). A section on *cultural formation* has been expanded to include cultural syndromes, idioms, and explanations.

Despite attempts to increase cultural sensitivity, it is important to remember that the *DSM* only *describes* mental disorders. It does not consider the etiology, or possible origin, of mental disorders. The manual does not ask clinicians to consider, for instance, why twice as many women as men are diagnosed with Major Depressive Disorder. Is it because women are more prone to depression than are men, because it is generally more acceptable in our society for women to express sadness and to ask for help for symptoms of depression, because women are more likely as an oppressed group to experience feelings of hopelessness and depression, or due to other reasons? Several studies have demonstrated gender bias against women among mental health professionals, including mental health counselors (Schwartz, Lent, & Geihsler, 2011). These studies have been an outgrowth of a well-known study by a group of researchers (Broverman, Broverman, Clarkson, Rosencrantz, & Vogel, 1970), who found that mental health professionals used nearly identical adjectives to describe a *healthy male* and a *healthy adult* but a different set of adjectives to describe a *healthy female*.

Herlihy and Watson (2003) identified three ethical problems in the use of the *DSM* system with diverse clients. First, the *DSM* is based on the medical model of mental illness that defines problems as residing within the individual. Failure to consider social, political, economic, and cultural factors in clients' lives does a disservice to clients whose problems originate in or are exacerbated by oppression, marginalization, and discrimination.

Second, the *DSM* system tends to pathologize the problems of racial and ethnic minority clients, as well as women. A number of studies have demonstrated that members of minority groups tend to receive more severe diagnoses than members of the majority culture for the same symptoms.

Studies have shown that African Americans are more likely to be diagnosed as suffering from schizophrenia (Neighbors, Ford, Trierweiler, & Stillman, 2002; Neighbors, Trierweiler, Ford, & Muroff, 2003; Pavkov, Lewis, & Lyons, 1989) and childhood disorders (Feisthamel & Schwartz, 2009) than are Euro-Americans. Latinos/Latinas also are more likely to be diagnosed with psychotic illnesses (Manderscheid & Barrett, 1991).

Third, the *DSM* system tends to perpetuate a paternalistic approach to mental health care and thus to reinforce the societal oppression of women and minority clients. The medical, pharmaceutical, and psychotherapy industries profit tremendously from the treatment of mental disorders (Herlihy & Watson, 2003; Rave & Larsen, 1995). Women receive more prescriptions than do men in all classes of drugs, particularly psychotropic medications. The medical model mirrors the dominant/subordinate relationships between the authority who diagnoses and prescribes and women and minority culture clients who are the recipients of these services (Feisthamel & Schwartz, 2009; Rapp & Goscha, 2012). Counselors who strive to avoid replicating in the counseling relationship the inequities experienced by women and minority clients will reframe many symptoms as coping mechanisms and evidence of survival skills in an oppressive culture rather than as evidence of pathology.

The *Code of Ethics* (ACA, 2014) reflects the concern of counselors regarding historical and social prejudices in the diagnosis of pathology. Standard E.5.c. states that counselors recognize these prejudices that have led to the misdiagnosing and pathologizing of certain individuals and groups and strive to become aware of and address such biases in themselves or others.

Despite the problems inherent in the *DSM* system and despite the discomfort of many counselors in using this system, it would be impractical for counselors to refuse to participate in the *DSM* diagnostic process. Rather, counselors have an ethical responsibility to reframe their thinking about the *DSM* system in more culturally competent ways (Herlihy et al., 2008; Zalaquett, Fuerth, Stein, Ivey, & Ivey, 2008). Counselors must be careful to maintain their wellness and holistic orientation and to avoid equating clients with their disorders through diagnostic labeling. For example, a client is never referred to as *a schizophrenic* but, rather, is described as an individual who suffers from schizophrenia (Dorre & Kinnier, 2006).

Legal Issues in Diagnosis

Earlier in this section, we made the point diagnoses rendered by counselors must be accurate and honest despite any philosophical uneasiness or cognitive dissonance they may be experiencing. We noted that some mental health professionals record what they consider to be less serious disorders than what they believe the client has in an effort to avoid stigma for the client. At the other end of the spectrum, they sometimes assign diagnoses that are more serious than warranted so that their clients will receive third-party reimbursement for counseling services. These practices are not uncommon. Inappropriate use of a diagnostic category to obtain insurance reimbursement is the type of financial misconduct that is most frequently brought before ethics committees, licensing boards, and courts (Peterson, 1996).

7-6 The Case of Charlotte

Charlotte has been a counselor in a group private practice for 6 years. She shares office space with other counselors but maintains her own separate private practice business. Most of the managed health care companies for which Charlotte is an approved provider require her to identify an emotional or mental disorder before they will agree to pay for her counseling services. Most companies require that Charlotte diagnose each client using the *DSM–5*. *Other Conditions That May Be a Focus of Clinical Attention*, sometimes called *V-Codes*, are not acceptable. Charlotte, having been educated from a wellness perspective of mental health, worries about labeling her clients negatively by diagnosing them with mental disorders. In reviewing the *DSM–5*, Charlotte has decided that Adjustment Disorder is the least objectionable diagnosis and is least likely to distress her clients if she diagnoses them with it. Even though many of her clients do not meet the technical criteria for receiving a diagnosis of Adjustment Disorder, Charlotte uses that diagnosis anyway. About 80% of Charlotte's clients are diagnosed with Adjustment Disorder.

- Do you agree with Charlotte's diagnostic practices? Why or why not?
- How can a counselor with a wellness perspective justify diagnosing clients with *DSM–5* mental disorders?

Discussion: Charlotte's motives in diagnosing most of her clients with Adjustment Disorder are understandable, but her actions are not ethical and also constitute insurance fraud because she is lying to managed care companies in order to collect payments from them. She can be sued by the companies and charged with a crime by a prosecutor. Charlotte must make the effort to reconcile her wellness perspective with using the *DSM* system so that she diagnoses honestly and accurately. She should remember that rendering a diagnosis means that a counselor has identified the criteria for the diagnosis in the client at a given time.

In Chapter 13, we identify practices such as those Charlotte is using as insurance fraud, which can expose counselors to both civil and criminal liability. A client could bring a civil malpractice suit against the counselor, and a prosecutor could bring criminal charges against the counselor based on the fraud. A client who was assigned a false diagnosis would have an excellent foundation for a successful malpractice suit against the counselor if the client later lost a job, was denied a license, or was denied a security clearance because of the false diagnosis. If it could be shown that a mental health professional knew or should have known that a client had a serious disorder but recorded a less serious disorder, and that the client received inadequate treatment that led to harm, or was denied health insurance reimbursement because of the false diagnosis, the mental health professional could be found to have committed malpractice. Obviously, you want to avoid ever having to face such a situation. It is crucial that you do not engage in the practice of assigning a diagnosis to fit insurance companies' criteria for reimbursement, even if you observe others doing it or hear justifications for such fraudulent practices.

Summary and Key Points

Counselor competence is an important concept, even though it is difficult to define from an ethical viewpoint and difficult to demonstrate in a court of law. It is best viewed as being based on performance and as existing along a continuum from gross negligence to maximum effectiveness. Some of the key points regarding competence that are made in this chapter include the following:

- The law demands a minimum level of practice from counselors, whereas ethics encourages counselors to aspire to an ideal level of practice.

- Counselors must practice within their boundaries of competence. It can be difficult to determine just where these boundaries lie.
- The development of competence begins with preparation and education, and the initial responsibility for producing competent practitioners rests with counselor educators and supervisors.
- Preparation standards established by accrediting bodies help to ensure that graduates of accredited programs possess certain competencies. Nonetheless, graduation from an accredited counselor education program does not guarantee competence.
- Licensure is a legal process that establishes minimum standards for a counselor to practice in a given state. Because licensure is a political process, counselor licensure requirements are not uniform across the states.
- Certification is another approach to attempting to ensure competence.
- Once counselors begin to practice, they are responsible for determining their own competence.
- Counselors are required to seek continuing education in order to maintain their competence. Peer review is an effective approach to monitoring competence.
- Counselors must know when and how to refer clients when they are not able to provide competent services to these clients. Referrals must not be made on the basis of value conflicts; referrals must be based on a lack of competence to work with a client.
- Counselors must exercise care while stretching their boundaries of competence to include client populations and concerns with which they have little or no experience.
- It is essential in today's society that counselors possess intercultural counseling competence.
- When counselors are experiencing distress, burnout, or impairment, they must take steps to protect clients from harm and to restore themselves to their full level of functioning.

Assessment is a collaborative process between counselor and client during which they work to gain a better understanding of the client's problems. An accurate assessment then guides the treatment planning. Testing and diagnosis are two specific types of assessment that are particularly vulnerable to ethical and legal problems. Multicultural considerations are vital in both testing and diagnosis. Key points made in this chapter regarding evaluation and assessment include the following:

- Counselors are competent to conduct many types of evaluation.
- Evaluations must be objective, and for this reason counselors should avoid taking on dual roles, such as counselor and child custody evaluator.
- Clients have a right to understand what an assessment process will involve, what its purposes are, and the uses to which it will be put.
- When counselors conduct evaluations, they must be prepared to serve as expert witnesses in court.
- Counselors are responsible for maintaining the security of tests that they use and for appropriately supervising the test-taking process.
- Counselors are competent to administer and interpret many tests, but they should keep in mind that some tests require specific training in their use.
- In order to be competent in using a test, a counselor should have completed formal coursework and have had supervised experience in using the test.
- Other mental health professionals in some states have attempted to prohibit counselors from using certain kinds of tests.
- Counselors must use caution in releasing test records to third parties and should release the records only to those individuals who are qualified to receive them.
- Clients have the right to receive a full explanation of their test results.
- Counselors must be cautious in using tests with culturally diverse clients. Many tests have been shown to be culturally biased, and minority groups often are not represented in the norm groups on which the tests were standardized.

- Counselors must be knowledgeable about laws that affect testing practices.
- Counselors are often uncomfortable with diagnosing mental disorders because the prevalent diagnostic system is based on the medical model.
- Clients must understand the implications of any diagnosis that might be assigned to them.
- Counselors must be prepared to work cooperatively with physicians when clients may have a physical condition that is contributing to their mental or emotional problems or when they could benefit from taking medications for their condition.

- A controversial issue has been whether counselors are qualified to diagnose.
- Multicultural considerations are of paramount importance in diagnosis because all mental disorders occur in and are defined by a cultural context.
- Counselors must be alert to sources of bias against women and minority group members in the diagnostic process and must take care not to perpetuate historical and social prejudices in diagnosing pathology.
- Counselors are guilty of insurance fraud when they do not diagnose honestly and accurately, and they can be subject to both civil and criminal liability.

CHAPTER 8

Malpractice and Resolving Legal and Ethical Challenges

FOCUS QUESTIONS

1. What do you think are the most common reasons that clients bring malpractice lawsuits against counselors and other mental health professionals?

2. How does a counselor determine whether a client is suicidal?

3. How do you think you would react if you were a licensed counselor and received a registered letter from your licensure board informing you that you had been accused of professional incompetence by a former client?

4. Do you think it is wise to avoid telling anyone if you receive notification of a complaint against you? Why or why not?

5. In what circumstances do you think you would report another counselor for unethical behavior?

MALPRACTICE

Malpractice involves professional misconduct or unreasonable lack of skill and has been defined as the failure to render professional services to the level expected in a particular community by a prudent member of the profession with the result that a recipient of services is harmed (Garner, 2014).

Malpractice includes intentional wrongdoing, incompetency, or unintentional wrongdoing of the professional involved. The concept of competency might be extended so that a counselor guilty of *professional misconduct*, *evil practice*, or *illegal* or *immoral conduct* also could be defined as incompetent.

Malpractice is also a type of civil lawsuit that can be filed against professionals for practicing in a manner that leads to injury to a recipient of their services. Professionals have a legal obligation not to harm individuals who come to them for professional services. Although the law cannot restore people who have been injured to their former state of existence, it can require the person who harmed them to compensate them financially for their damages. If clients believe they have been harmed by their counselors, they can file a malpractice lawsuit against the counselors. Counselors who are sued must then defend themselves against the lawsuit before a judge or jury. Although there is widespread belief that juries favor plaintiffs in professional malpractice suits against health professionals, evidence from a study of physicians has demonstrated that juries' findings follow what physicians themselves consider to be negligence, and probably even favor the professionals (Vidmar, 1995).

In order for a client plaintiff to prevail in a malpractice lawsuit against a counselor, the plaintiff must prove the following elements (Schwartz, Kelly, & Partlett, 2010):

- The counselor had a duty to the client to use reasonable care in providing counseling services.
- The counselor failed to conform to the required duty of care.
- The client was injured.
- There was a reasonably close causal connection between the conduct of the counselor and the resulting injury (known as *proximate cause*).
- The client suffered an actual loss or was damaged.

Proximate cause is a difficult legal concept to understand. *Actual cause* means that a person actually caused the injury of another person. *Proximate cause* has to do with whether the individual would have been injured had it not been for the action or inaction of the other person. Cohen and Mariano (1982) explained that "an intervening cause which is independent of the negligence absolves the defending negligent actor of liability" (p. 121). In other words, just because professionals are negligent does not make them responsible for an injury. It must be proven that some other intervening event did not, in fact, cause the injury. Foreseeability is important in determinations of proximate cause (Cohen & Mariano, 1982). *Foreseeability* has to do with whether the professional knew or should have known that the professional's actions would result in a specific outcome.

Counselors have become increasingly concerned about being sued for malpractice. Many counselors are hesitant to even touch clients in today's litigious environment (Calmes, Piazza, & Laux, 2013). Although malpractice lawsuits against mental health professionals have increased dramatically over the past decade, the total number of these lawsuits is relatively small. Hogan (1979) concluded that few malpractice lawsuits are filed against counselors because it is difficult for plaintiffs to establish an adequate case. It is not easy to prove that a counselor deviated from accepted practices and that the counselor's act or negligence caused the harm that a client suffered.

It appears that mental health professionals continue to be sued most often because of sexual relationships with their clients. However, it is likely that the next leading cause of malpractice lawsuits against counselors revolves around situations in which clients attempt or complete suicide (McAdams & Foster, 2000; Roberts, Monferrari, & Yeager, 2008). Whether to have sex with clients is certainly under the control of a mental health professional. Predicting whether a client will attempt suicide, however, is scientifically impossible. Yet, counselors will be held accountable in courts if they fail to follow procedures endorsed by the profession when a client is at risk. Suicidal clients, potentially violent clients, and the duty to warn intended victims of client violence are discussed in the following sections, and guidelines for practice in these areas are offered.

Suicidal Clients

When a client threatens to commit suicide, an ethical duty arises to protect the client from harm to self. The ethical standard that applies to clients who pose a danger to others applies to suicidal clients as well: confidentiality requirements are waived when disclosure is necessary to protect clients or others from *serious and foreseeable harm* (American Counseling Association [ACA], 2014, *Code of Ethics,* §B.2.a.). Evaluating and managing suicide risk is one of the most stressful situations that you will encounter in your work (Corey, Corey, Corey, & Callanan, 2015; Miller, McGlothlin, & West, 2013). You must be prepared to take measures to prevent suicide attempts (Slaby, 1999), and a study by Ting, Sullivan, Boudreaux, Miller, and Camargo (2012) has shown that hospital emergency department admissions of suicidal patients is increasing, particularly among those who are ages 15 to 19. Suicide prevention measures begin with a thorough risk assessment and then, depending on the level of danger, might include involving the client's family or significant others, working with the client to arrange for voluntary hospitalization, or even initiating the process that leads to an involuntary commitment of the client. All of these interventions are disruptive and compromise the client's confidentiality. Ethically (ACA, 2014, §B.2.e.), and legally under the Health Insurance Portability and Accounting Act (HIPAA), it is important to disclose only information you consider essential in order for someone else to help prevent a suicide attempt.

Similar to situations in which clients threaten harm to others, the counselor's first responsibility is to determine that a particular client is in danger of attempting suicide. There is no sure way to determine this, but experts agree that individuals who commit suicide generally give cues to those around them (Capuzzi, 2002; Capuzzi & Golden, 1988; Curran, 1987; Davis, 1983; Hafen & Frandsen, 1986; Hussain & Vandiver, 1984; Jacobs, Brewer, & Klein-Benheim, 1999; Johnson & Maile, 1987; Laux, 2002; Myer, 2001; Rogers, 2001; Rogers, Lewis, & Subich, 2002; Schwartz, 2000; Schwartz & Cohen, 2001; Stanard, 2000). Day-Vines (2007) has alerted counselors to the soaring rates of suicide among African Americans in the United States, and information such as this must guide the day-to-day work of counselors when they assess clients for suicide potential. In most circumstances, a counselor's determination of a client's level of risk must be based on clinical observations, not on test results. If counselors were not prepared in their graduate programs to handle crises (Allen et al., 2002), they must overcome this deficit through independent reading, workshop attendance, post-master's-degree course completion, and supervised practice (McGlothlin, Rainey, & Kindsvatter, 2005; Morris & Minton, 2012).

As noted, determining that a client is at risk of committing suicide leads to actions that can be exceptionally disruptive to the client's life. Just as counselors can be accused of malpractice for neglecting to take action to prevent harm when a client is determined to be suicidal, counselors also can be accused of wrongdoing if they overreact and precipitously take actions that violate a client's privacy or freedom when there is no basis for doing so (Hermann, Remley, & Huey, 2011). As a result, counselors have a legal duty to evaluate accurately a client's potential for suicide. Counselors can be held liable for overreacting and for underreacting. So, how should a determination be made as to whether a client is suicidal?

First, no matter where you work as a counselor, you are likely to provide services to individuals who might express suicidal thoughts (Hermann, 2001; O'Dwyer, 2012). Therefore, it is necessary for all counselors to know the warning signs that indicate that a particular person is at risk for committing suicide. A legal case from the 1960s (*Bogust v. Iverson,* 1960) held that a college counselor was not a mental health professional and therefore had no duty to assess a client's risk of suicide. Since then, however, counselors have established themselves as mental health professionals, and the law imposes on counselors practicing in all settings the responsibility of knowing how to accurately determine a client's risk of suicide (Bursztajn, Gutheil, Hamm, & Brodsky, 1983; Drukteinis, 1985; Howell, 1988; Knuth, 1979; Perr, 1985). Because the act is done by the client without the counselor being a party to it, courts generally have been reluctant to hold counselors accountable for harm that results from clients who attempt or complete suicide. Lake and Tribbensee (2002), however, in their discussion of liability of colleges and universities for the suicides of adult students, cautioned that current legal trends suggest that mental health professionals on college and university campuses may be held accountable more often in the future for adult student suicides.

Much help is available in the professional literature, including research studies and articles that provide information about warning signs of future suicidal behavior (Berman & Cohen-Sandler, 1982; Cantor, 1976; Daniel & Goldston, 2012; Meneese & Yutrzenka, 1990; Sapyta et al., 2012; Sudak, Ford, & Rushforth, 1984). Today's counselors must know how to make assessments of a client's risk for suicide and must be able to defend their decisions at a later time (Linehan, Comtois, & Ward-Ciesielski, 2012).

The law does not require that counselors always be correct in making their assessments of suicide risk, but it is a legal requirement that counselors make those assessments from an informed position, and that they fulfill their professional obligations to a client in a manner comparable to what other reasonable counselors operating in a similar situation would have done. Because of this standard of care to which counselors are held, the very best action you can take if you are unsure whether a client is at risk for a suicide attempt is to consult with other mental health professionals who are similar to you (Sommers-Flanagan, Sommers-Flanagan, & Lynch, 2001). The *Code of Ethics* (ACA, 2014, §C.2.e.) advises counselors to consult when they have questions regarding their ethical obligations or professional practice. It also is important to look for consensus among your consultants and certainly to follow their advice in making your final decision about what to do in a particular case. Documenting your steps is essential (Boughner & Logan, 1999; Gutheil, 1999). In situations in which you have assessed a client's potential risk for suicide, it is essential that you document carefully, regardless of whether you determine that the client is or is not currently at risk. Essential items to include in your documentation notes include the following:

- What precipitated your concern about the client (such as referral by another person, or something the client said or did)
- Questions you asked the client, and his or her responses
- Individuals you consulted regarding the situation, what you said to them, and how they responded
- Interactions you had with any other persons regarding the situation, from the time you became concerned until you completed your work for the time being regarding the situation

When you make a decision that a client is a danger to self, you must take whatever steps are necessary to prevent the harm, and your actions must be the least intrusive to accomplish that result. Again, consulting with colleagues could be very helpful. Many counselors who have determined that a client may be at risk for suicide require that the client submit to an evaluation by a mental health professional who has expertise in suicide as a condition for continuing to provide counseling services for that individual. For example, you might demand that your client see a psychiatrist on the staff at the facility where you work, if that is an option. Or you might require your client to submit to a mental evaluation at a local hospital where psychiatric services are available. Less intrusive options are available, such as referring the client to a primary care physician if the client is in a health plan that requires that step before gaining access to a specialist, such as a psychiatrist. Of course, you should choose a less intrusive option only if you are sure the client is not at imminent risk.

Because it is so difficult to decide what steps to take in a crisis situation, especially one in which a suicidal client's life may be in danger, we have provided an action plan to follow if you determine that an adult client may be at risk for suicide (see Figure 8-1). If your client is a minor, you must always notify the parents or guardians (Capuzzi, 2002). Responsibilities to minors and their parents or guardians are discussed further in Chapter 11. The steps we suggest are not the only options that counselors have. Rather, we are providing one possible way to manage potentially suicidal clients that hopefully will yield positive results.

If you determine that an adult client has exhibited some behaviors that are related to suicide, but currently does not appear to be at risk for committing suicide . . .

1. If you believe that an adult client may be thinking about suicide or if you have observed or have information that an adult client has exhibited some behaviors that might be interpreted as suicidal, but you do not consider the situation to be an emergency, summarize in your case notes the client's behavior that supports your concern. Do not write that you believe the client may be at risk for suicide. Instead, write that although you do not believe the client may be at risk for suicide, you believe a significant person in his or her life needs to be informed of the behaviors that concern you.
2. If you have consulted with colleagues, experts, or supervisors in reaching your position, document the consultations in your case notes.
3. Tell your client your concerns and, if appropriate, obtain an agreement from the client to inform a significant person in his or her life of your concerns. Tell the client to have that person contact you after being told.
4. If your client is not capable of telling the significant person, or for some other reason asking the client to inform the significant person does not seem like an appropriate course of action, explain to the client that you will be contacting a significant person to share your concern. If you are not in independent private practice, inform your supervisor of the actions you will be taking and follow any directives given.
5. Choose a significant person and inform him or her of the situation. A significant person might be your client's spouse, parent, adult child, other relative, domestic partner, dating partner, or close friend. Choose a person who lives with the client or who is in frequent contact with the client.
6. Document in your case notes all conversations with your client, the client's significant person, and your supervisors.

If you determine that an adult client MAY BE seriously at risk for committing suicide . . .

1. You are dealing with a very serious matter that requires immediate and decisive action. Make the determination that an adult client may be at risk for committing suicide only if the client has made a suicide gesture or attempt, has told you or someone else in a believable fashion that he or she plans to commit suicide, or has engaged in a pattern of behavior that the professional literature suggests is characteristic of a suicidal adult. Follow any agency policies that exist regarding managing suicidal adults. If you are not in an independent private practice, notify your supervisor of the situation and follow any directives given. If policies dictate or if your supervisor directs you to proceed differently from the following steps, follow the policies or the orders of your supervisor.
2. If you have consulted with colleagues, experts, or supervisors in reaching your position, document the consultations in your case notes.
3. Explain to your client that you will have to notify a significant person in his or her life so that the person can help.
4. Assure your client that you will continue to help and that you will disclose only the minimum information necessary to get assistance for the client. Try to calm the client, but do not minimize the seriousness of the situation. Explain what may happen in the next few hours, next few days, and long term.
5. Ensure that your client is not left alone and does not have any opportunity for self-harm before turning the client over to the significant person.
6. Contact a significant person in your client's life and explain that you believe his or her relative, partner, or friend may be at risk for suicide. Give specific details that led to your concern. Insist that the significant person come to pick up the client immediately.
7. If a significant person cannot be found, make sure your client is under the supervision of a responsible person until a significant person is located.

FIGURE 8-1   Steps to follow if you determine that your client may be at risk for suicide

Source: Pearson Education, Inc., Hoboken, NJ.

8. If you cannot contact a significant person and if it is impossible to keep your adult client safe for an extended period of time, call an ambulance and have the client transported to a hospital that has psychiatric services. If you are not in an independent private practice, be sure to inform your supervisor and obtain permission and support for taking this action. If your supervisor directs you to take a different course of action, do so and document in your case notes what you were told and did. Give the ambulance attendant your contact information, and offer to speak with the person at the hospital who will be conducting the evaluation, if requested to do so. Continue to attempt to contact the client's significant person.

9. When you talk to the significant person, ask that person to take possession and responsibility immediately for your client.

10. When the significant person arrives, explain that you believe that your client may be at risk for suicide, give specific details that led to your concern, instruct the significant person what to do next, and ask that a document be signed that acknowledges that the significant person has been informed of your concerns, has been given directions of steps to take next, and has agreed to take responsibility for your client.

11. Have the client sign a form giving you permission to disclose any information you have to mental health professionals who may evaluate or treat the client in the future. If the client refuses or is not capable of signing the form, ask the family member or significant person to sign on your client's behalf.

12. Explain to the significant person that he or she must ensure that your client is not left alone, does not have any opportunities for self-harm, and is taken for an evaluation as soon as possible to determine whether he or she is at risk for suicide.

13. If a significant person refuses to sign the document or communicates to you in some way that he or she will not take the situation seriously, call an ambulance and follow the steps in item 8.

14. As events occur, document in detail in your case notes all the events that transpired in relation to this situation. Be sure to date each entry and indicate the time you wrote it. Make several entries if necessary, and do not delay in writing details in your case notes.

15. When your client returns to you or your agency for services, obtain written permission from your client to contact the professional who determined that your client was not at risk for suicide, or was no longer at risk for suicide.

16. Contact your client's treating physician, psychologist, or mental health provider and explain that the client has returned to you or your agency for services. Ask the treating provider to summarize his or her evaluation and treatment of the client. Inquire as to whether the provider will continue to treat the client, and if so, the details of the planned treatment. Also ask the treating provider the types of counseling services he or she would like for you to provide to the client. Do not agree to provide any counseling services that your position does not allow you to provide. Ask the provider to tell you the circumstances in which you should return the client to him or her for further evaluation or treatment.

17. As soon as possible after you have talked to the provider, document in your case notes details of your conversation. Be sure to date the entry and indicate the time you wrote it.

FIGURE 8-1   (continued)

If you work in an agency, school, hospital, or other organizational setting, you must always follow procedures established by your employer. In many cases, counselors find that their employer does not have guidelines for how to manage potentially suicidal clients. If that is the case, you should consider following the guidelines in Figure 8-1 until such policies are adopted. In addition, you should ask that guidelines be established for the welfare of clients and to protect the counselors who have to make decisions in difficult situations. If your administrative supervisor is present, you must follow his or her directives. The guidelines presented in Figure 8-1 could be adopted by your agency, or you could follow these in the absence of any agency policies or directives from superiors.

As you can see from Figure 8-1, it is assumed that a client you refer for an evaluation will return to you for services. Even if a client is hospitalized, the hospitalization usually is only a few days in duration. Contacting and documenting your consultation with the mental health professional who determined that your client was not at risk for suicide, or was no longer at risk, are vital. You probably will counsel clients who have recently been at risk for suicide. In an interesting study, Paulson and Worth (2002) found that previously suicidal clients described these key therapeutic processes that helped them to overcome suicidal ideation and behaviors: (a) experiencing an affirming and validating relationship as a means of reconnection with others, (b) dealing with the intense emotions surrounding suicidal behavior, and (c) confronting and discarding negative patterns while establishing new, more positive behaviors.

Clients Who May Be at Risk for Harming Others

Counselors are often responsible for violence prevention education (D'Andrea, 2004; Ginter, 2004; Smith & Sandhu, 2004). In addition, there will be situations during your counseling career when you must decide whether a particular client has the potential of harming another person, or perhaps even an individual's property. Making this decision is difficult, as there is no scientific basis for such decisions. If you do determine that a client is a danger to another person, then you must take the steps necessary to prevent harm (Gilbert, 2007; Hermann & Finn, 2002). This may include warning intended victims, whether or not their identity is known. In making these difficult decisions, it is essential to consult with other mental health professionals and to include supervisors to the extent possible.

What began as a legal requirement has now evolved into an ethical duty as well. Standard B.2.a. of the *Code of Ethics* (ACA, 2014) states that the counselor's confidentiality requirement "does not apply when disclosure is required to protect clients or identified others from serious and foreseeable harm." This particular exception to confidentiality has caused considerable confusion and consternation among helping professionals, not only because it involves breaching confidentiality but also because it demands that counselors be able to predict dangerousness. Human behavior is not always predictable, and counselors may find themselves caught on the horns of a dilemma, both ethically and legally, in determining whether to breach a client's confidentiality in order to prevent harm to the client or to others.

8-1 The Case of Todd

Todd is a counselor in a community mental health center. For the last 2 weeks he has been seeing a client named Bill, who is a junior in high school. Bill comes to the center 1 day each week, walking from school to his sessions and then walking home afterward. This afternoon, Bill tells Todd that, after thinking about it for quite some time, he has decided to shoot the assistant principal at his school. Bill says that his father has a rifle collection in their home, and he has access to the guns and to ammunition. Bill explains that he plans to wait outside the assistant principal's home until he walks out in the morning and shoot him as he walks to his car. Because Bill is so calm as he relates all of this information, Todd asks Bill if he is serious. Bill smiles, laughs, and then says, "No, I was only kidding. I would never do anything like that." Because Todd doesn't know Bill very well, he is not sure what to do next. Todd asks Bill to excuse him for a minute and leaves his office to look for his supervisor. He discovers that his supervisor and all the other staff have left for the day. Todd returns to his office and finds Bill standing by a window, looking out with tears in his eyes.

- In these circumstances, what are Todd's options?
- What option would you choose if you were Todd?

Discussion: Todd has a number of options in this situation. He could (a) talk more with Bill and try to assess his potential for harming the assistant principal, (b) call Bill's mother or father and ask her or him to come to the center to pick Bill up, and tell the parents what Bill told him, (c) call the police and ask them to come over to talk with Bill, or (d) call the assistant principal and warn him of the threat against his life.

Todd's best option might be to talk further with Bill. If Todd determines that Bill was not serious, Todd should document what happened in his notes and explain why he reached the conclusion he reached.

Even if Todd determines that Bill might not have been serious, Todd should call Bill's parents and ask them to come over. He should get them to take responsibility for Bill's actions and the assistant principal's safety.

Research indicates that it is impossible to predict whether a particular person is going to harm someone else; yet the law and our ethical standards require counselors to determine whether a client is dangerous. How can this legal and ethical duty be fulfilled? First, it is important to learn as much as you can about the warning signs of persons who commit violent acts against others (Daniels, 2002; Haggard-Grann, 2007; Truscott & Evans, 2001). For example, it appears that the best predictor of violence is past violent behavior (Megargee, 1979; Meloy, 1987; Monahan, 1995; Mulvey & Lidz, 1995; Slovic & Monahan, 1995; Truscott, Evans, & Mansell, 1995). However, you must be careful not to profile, or to assume that a category of persons is prone to violence (Bailey, 2001). Special situations, such as those involving domestic partner violence (Lawson, 2001, 2003) or violence of persons with serious mental disorders, probably require deviations from the general guidelines offered in this chapter.

Once you have determined that a client is indeed dangerous and might harm another person, the law requires that you take whatever steps are necessary to prevent the harm and, further, that the steps you take be the least disruptive (Rice, 1993). You have choices that range from the least intrusive action (obtaining a promise from your client not to harm anyone else) to the most intrusive (having the client involuntarily committed to a psychiatric facility). Numerous possibilities exist between these two extremes, such as notifying the client's family members and getting one of them to take responsibility for keeping the client under control, persuading the client to be voluntarily committed to a residential facility, notifying the police, or calling the client periodically. Certainly, no particular formula of action is necessarily correct when you determine that your client is dangerous. If at all possible, consult with other mental health professionals and use their input in making your decision.

The guidelines in Figure 8-1 regarding managing potentially suicidal clients would work equally well in managing potentially violent clients. You would just need to add the determination of whether to warn intended victims, law enforcement authorities, or both.

DUTY TO WARN INTENDED VICTIMS   Think about how you might react if you were counseling a client who made a threat to harm someone else (Burkemper, 2002). If you were to decide that the client was only venting anger and was not likely to act on the threat, and then later the client carried out the threat, you would have acted ethically in trusting your professional judgment and in preserving confidentiality and the counseling relationship. That would be little solace, however, if someone were killed or seriously injured. Also, the question might arise before an ethics committee or in a court as to whether you could have acted, or should have acted, to avert that harm. On the other hand, if you were to decide that the danger was in fact clear and imminent and you were to issue a warning, no harm would be done to a third party. If the client did not later attempt to harm the possible victim, however, you would have erred in labeling the client dangerous, and your actions probably will have destroyed the counseling relationship. You could be accused of misdiagnosis, defamation of character, or violating confidentiality (*Hopewell v. Adebimpe*, 1982). It is no wonder that counselors view these as no-win situations and might be tempted to simply avoid working with dangerous clients. Yet, it would be ethically questionable to close the doors of the counseling profession to a group of individuals who clearly need our help (Herlihy & Sheeley, 1988).

The duty to warn an identifiable or foreseeable victim of a dangerous client arose out of the landmark *Tarasoff v. Regents of University of California* (1976) court case, which established the following legal concept in California:

> when a psychotherapist *determines*, or pursuant to the standards of his profession *should determine*, that a patient presents a serious danger or violence to others, the therapist incurs an obligation to use reasonable care to protect the foreseeable victim from such danger. (McClarren, 1987, p. 273)

Although the *Tarasoff* doctrine has not been accepted or applied in every jurisdiction in the United States, counselors have chosen to incorporate it into the *Code of Ethics* (ACA, 2014) and generally assume that the concept is a national legal requirement. The only jurisdiction that has specifically rejected the *Tarasoff* duty to warn doctrine is Texas (*Thapar v. Zezulka*, 1999). In Texas, counselors do not have a duty to warn intended victims if their clients threaten to harm another person. As a result, if a mental health professional in Texas did warn an intended victim, the professional might potentially be liable to the client who made the threat for breach of confidentiality.

The facts in the *Tarasoff* case are important in understanding the duty that has been imposed on counselors. Prosenjit Poddar was a 26-year-old graduate student at the University of California at Berkeley. In the course of a session with his counselor, Poddar confided his intention to kill his girlfriend, Tatiana Tarasoff. His counselor was Dr. Lawrence Moore, a psychologist in the university counseling center. Because Moore believed that Poddar might be serious regarding his threat, Moore initiated proceedings to have Poddar committed for a psychiatric evaluation. Moore orally notified two campus police officers of his intentions to commit Poddar and then sent a letter to the police chief requesting assistance from the police department. The police took Poddar into custody, but released him when he promised not to contact Tarasoff. Poddar never went to see Moore again. Neither Moore nor the police notified Tarasoff of Poddar's threat. Two months later, Poddar stabbed and killed Tarasoff on the front porch of her parents' home. Tarasoff's parents sued Moore in a wrongful death action for not confining Poddar and not warning Tarasoff of the threat against her life.

Decisions subsequent to the *Tarasoff* case throughout the United States have interpreted the holding of the case differently. Many courts have limited its application to situations in which the victims are readily identifiable. Other courts, however, have extended the duty to all persons who are endangered by the patient's condition or threats (McClarren, 1987). In *Lipari v. Sears, Roebuck & Co.* (1980), a federal court held that a psychotherapist has a duty to warn and protect unknown victims, as well as those who are readily identifiable. This case extended a counselor's duty to those persons who are foreseeably endangered by a client's conduct.

A Washington state court, following the *Lipari* decision, held that a psychiatrist could possibly be held responsible for injuries sustained by a traffic accident victim. The victim was hurt when a drug-abusing patient, released by the psychiatrist, ran a red light while under the influence of drugs (*Petersen v. State*, 1983). Two California cases expanded the *Tarasoff* doctrine by no longer requiring that a psychotherapist be able to readily identify the patient's victim (*Hedlund v. Superior Court of Orange County*, 1983; *Jablonski v. United States*, 1983).

In a Vermont case, the state supreme court held that a mental health professional has a duty to take reasonable steps to protect a third party from threats of damage to property posed by a patient (*Peck v. Counseling Service of Addison County, Inc.*, 1985). In the *Peck* case, the court found that a counselor could be held responsible for property damage when a client burned down a barn. The client told the counselor he intended to do so, and the counselor did not warn the owners of the barn.

Originally, the *Tarasoff* holding imposed a duty to warn only if the victim was specifically identifiable. Subsequent decisions have extended that duty to include warning persons who are unknown, persons who are unintentionally injured by a patient, whole classes of persons of which the victim is a member, bystanders who might be injured by a patient's negligent act, and individuals whose property a client has threatened to destroy (McClarren, 1987). Fox (2010) has suggested, however, that contemporary courts are tending to limit a mental health practitioner's duty to protect third parties from potentially dangerous clients.

Pabian, Welfel, and Beebe (2009) found that 76.4% of the psychologists in four states were misinformed about their state laws regarding *Tarasoff*-type situations, believing that they had a legal duty to warn intended victims when they did not. Decision making for counselors around the *Tarasoff* legal requirements is complex. One thing is clear, however: Because of the *Tarasoff* case, when you determine that a client might harm an identifiable or foreseeable person, you must directly or indirectly warn that individual of the danger, except in Texas.

CLIENTS WITH HIV   The Centers for Disease Control (CDC; 2013) estimated that 1,144,500 persons aged 13 and older were living with the HIV infection in the United States and approximately 180,900 (15.8%) did not know they were infected. The CDC indicated that gay, bisexual, and other men who have sex with men were the population most profoundly affected by HIV. In 2010, 78% of new HIV infections among males were from this at-risk population. Injection drug users also are more at risk of becoming infected with HIV than the general population. AIDS is the stage of HIV infection that occurs when the immune system is badly damaged and an infected person becomes vulnerable to infections and infection-related cancers called opportunistic illnesses (Centers for Disease Control, 2014).

The advent of HIV/AIDS has placed mental health professionals in a quandary: Do counselors have an ethical duty to warn when a client is HIV confirmed and could be putting others at risk through such behaviors as unprotected sex or needle sharing? According to §B.2.b., *Contagious, Life-Threatening Diseases*, of the *Code of Ethics* (ACA, 2014), "When clients disclose they have a disease commonly known to be both communicable and life threatening, counselors may be justified in disclosing information to identifiable third parties, if the parties are known to be at serious and foreseeable risk of contracting the disease." This standard goes on to say that before making a disclosure of this type, counselors "assess the intent of clients to inform the third parties about their disease or to engage in any behaviors that may be harmful to an identifiable third party." In addition, "Counselors adhere to relevant state laws concerning disclosure about disease status."

Note that, according to ethical guidelines, counselors are *justified* in disclosing, but are not necessarily *required* to disclose, information to a third party who may be *at serious and foreseeable risk*. You will need to weigh a number of factors and determine your own stance regarding arguments that have been offered both for and against breaching confidentiality in working with HIV clients. Due to medical advances, AIDS is no longer routinely fatal, which makes the applicability of this standard open to question. Some writers (Driscoll, 1992; Melton, 1991; Perry, 1989) have made some compelling arguments in favor of maintaining confidentiality. Breaches of confidentiality are especially countertherapeutic when working with clients who have a high level of mistrust due to discrimination against them (for instance, gay men, prostitutes, and intravenous drug users). Exposure to HIV does not carry the same level of risk as a homicidal client who threatens to use a lethal weapon; not every exposure to HIV results in harm. Individuals who have consented to unsafe sex practices or sharing needles that could be contaminated must take responsibility for their own choices. If the client's confidentiality is compromised, the client is likely to discontinue counseling, and the problems that contribute to continuation of high-risk behavior (such as fear of abandonment and loss of control) will be exacerbated.

Other writers have argued for disclosure (Cohen, 1997; Erickson, 1993; Gray & Harding, 1988), pointing out that confidentiality is not an end in itself and that the need to protect someone who may be at risk of contracting a fatal disease creates a higher duty. They suggest that mental health professionals have an obligation to do their part to protect the health and welfare of society at large when HIV clients are putting others at risk. These writers also argue that, although it is an injustice that clients with HIV suffer from discrimination, the protection of others must take precedence over the possibility of discrimination.

It is crucial that you use your clinical judgment in these cases and that you evaluate each HIV confidentiality dilemma on a case-by-case basis (Harding, Gray, & Neal, 1993; Kain, 1989). To be in compliance with the ethical standards, it is imperative that you do not act hastily to breach confidentiality. First, your client must disclose that he or she is infected with HIV, as is required by the *Code of Ethics* (ACA, 2014, §B.2.b.). Often, a consultation with the client's physician is a good option. Because HIV status is a medical condition, informing the client's physician of your concern about the client endangering others may transfer to the physician the obligation of protecting others.

If you believe you must take responsibility because a physician is not available, then you must determine whether your client has already informed the partner or other third party or is intending to do so in the immediate future. It is preferable that clients make their own disclosures, so you might continue to work with the client in exploring the client's willingness to assume this responsibility, or you might involve the partner in the counseling process.

In some jurisdictions, specific statutes have been passed that address the issue of HIV and the duty to warn. When your clients who have HIV refuse to disclose their condition to an endangered third party and you believe that you must do so, you must be aware of any applicable state laws that might restrict or guide your reporting options. Without a doubt, keeping abreast of legal and ethical obligations related to HIV/AIDS will continue to pose real challenges for counselors as more is learned about ways to transmit and prevent the presently incurable disease.

To summarize, your work with clients who are dangerous to themselves or others will be fraught with ethical and legal complexities. It is important to keep up with the literature in this area and to familiarize yourself with guidelines for practice regarding the duty to warn, such as those offered by Costa and Altekruse (1994). Whenever possible, you should consult with fellow professionals (ACA, 2014, §C.2.e.) if you are in doubt about whether you have a duty to warn, protect, or report in a given situation.

A Hypothetical Malpractice Case

To illustrate how a malpractice case might be considered against a counselor, here we analyze a typical situation in which a counselor might be sued. Suppose that a teacher has come to Monica, a high school counselor, with a concern about Mark, an 11th-grade student. Mark has written a paper for English class in which he discusses taking his life because he is upset about his parents' recent divorce. Monica calls Mark into her office and talks with him about the paper. She asks him if he has seriously considered taking his life. After a thorough discussion with Mark, Monica determines that he is not suicidal.

That same day, after school, Mark shoots and kills himself with his father's rifle. Mark's mother, Sheila, finds out about the teacher's referral and files a malpractice lawsuit against Monica, claiming that Monica's incompetence caused her son's death. Sheila's attorney probably would name as respondents in the lawsuit Monica individually, each of her direct supervisors up through the school superintendent, the school board, and any other individuals or groups who might be responsible for Monica's actions or failure to act. If Monica had her own independent professional liability insurance policy, her insurance company would hire a lawyer who would represent Monica individually in the case. If Monica did not have her own liability insurance policy, she probably could not afford to pay an attorney to represent her. She would have to rely for her defense on the school system lawyers, who ultimately represent the school system, not her. The school system would have its lawyers, or the lawyers provided by the school system's liability insurance company, file a legal response to the case. Monica's lawyer, if she had one, and the school system lawyers would work together in defending the lawsuit.

Sheila's attorney, in presenting her case in court, would first have to prove that Monica owed a duty of reasonable care in providing counseling services to Mark. This would not be difficult to prove because Monica is a counselor in the school and called Mark in for a counseling session. When a counselor accepts a person as a client, the counselor then has a duty to provide the client with professional care that meets accepted standards within the profession. Counselors have a fiduciary relationship with clients, which is a relationship that fosters the highest level of trust and confidence (Anderson & Bertram, 2012). Clearly, Monica owed Mark a duty of care.

After establishing that a duty of care was owed to Mark, Sheila's attorney then would have to prove that Monica breached that duty and failed to conform to the required standard of care. Most experts would agree that counselors must assess whether a client is suicidal, even though studies have shown that it is impossible to scientifically predict suicidal behavior (Coleman & Shellow, 1992). If it is determined that the client is in danger, action must be taken to prevent the impending suicide (Ahia & Martin, 1993; Austin, Moline, & Williams, 1990). The question in this situation is whether Monica was reasonable in her assessment of Mark's risk. The only way to prove that Monica made an error in her professional judgment is for Sheila's attorney to bring in one or more expert witnesses who will testify that a competent counselor would not have done what Monica did, or failed to do. The expert witnesses must compare the actions Monica took or did not take to the actions that a reasonable counselor with Monica's same background and preparation, practicing in the same locality, would have taken in the same set of circumstances. This is the legal standard of care to which counselors are held. Monica's attorney would arrange for a different set of experts to testify that Monica did act reasonably in this particular situation. The judge or jury would have to decide which expert witnesses to believe.

After offering evidence through expert witness testimony that Monica breached her duty of care, Sheila's attorney would have to prove that Mark was injured as a result of this breach. It would not be difficult to prove that harm occurred, because Mark killed himself.

Next, Sheila's attorney would have to prove that there was a close causal connection between what Monica did, or failed to do, and Mark's suicide. Sheila's attorney would have to prove that Monica knew or should have known that her actions would result in Mark's death. The attorney would argue that Monica's failure to take action when Mark disclosed that he intended to commit suicide was the proximate cause of Mark's death because she failed to take actions that would prevent him from committing suicide. On the opposing side, Monica's attorney would argue that a number of other intervening factors led to Mark's suicide, and that a reasonable counselor would not and could not have predicted that Mark would take his life, given the circumstances in this situation. Further, Monica's attorney would argue that even if Monica did act negligently in this situation, Mark's suicide cannot be blamed on her failure to take action. Other factors *caused* his suicide—factors such as his father leaving his gun out so that Mark had access to it, no one being at home to supervise him after school, or his distress over his parents' contentious behavior during the divorce. The judge or jury would have to decide whether Monica's failure to act to prevent Mark's suicide was the proximate cause of his death, or whether other factors caused him to take his life.

If Sheila's attorney was successful in convincing the judge or jury that Monica was responsible for Mark's death, then the damage to Sheila, expressed in financial terms, would have to be determined. If a person is damaged with a financial loss, such as a loss in the stock market or investing in a deal that has no value, then it is easy to determine how much money the person needs to be *made whole again.* When a person has a physical injury, however, or loses a loved one through death, then it is very difficult to determine how much money it would take to compensate the person for the loss. In fact, these are losses that cannot be compensated with money, but the law requires financial compensation.

Damages in this situation would be determined by expert witness testimony on Mark's life expectancy, his earning potential, and the anticipated benefit of earnings that would go to his mother, Sheila. Because the loss of a life was involved in this situation, the damages could be hundreds of thousands or several million dollars. Judges or juries have wide discretion in setting the value in these kinds of cases.

If Sheila received a judgment in her favor, the school system's professional liability insurance carrier would most likely pay the judgment. Monica's professional liability carrier might be responsible for paying a portion of the judgment as well. Both the school's and Monica's insurance companies would pay the attorneys' fees and other costs of litigation, which could be as much as several hundred thousand dollars.

At this point, you probably are wondering how often lawsuits are based on client suicide and how often family members prevail and collect judgments. Although client suicide is not the only possible basis for a malpractice lawsuit against counselors, it is undoubtedly one of the most painful types of suits for both plaintiffs and defendants. In the following section, we review some actual cases related to client suicide.

Actual Malpractice Cases

In 1960, a college counselor was sued for the wrongful death of a student who had committed suicide. The student had seen the counselor in a professional capacity (*Bogust v. Iverson*, 1960). The holding in that case was that the college counselor was not a therapist and therefore had no duty to detect or prevent a suicide of a client. Since 1960, however, the counseling profession has evolved substantially, and counselors in all settings are considered mental health professionals. A similar case today would probably have a different result.

A case that is similar to *Bogust v. Iverson* (1960) and the hypothetical case of Monica was decided in Maryland in 1991. In *Eisel v. Board of Education of Montgomery County* (1991), Dorothy Jones and Deidre Morgan, school counselors at Sligo Middle School in Maryland (along with their school board, principal, and superintendent), were sued in a wrongful death action by Stephen Eisel, the father of Nicole Eisel. Nicole Eisel was a 13-year-old student at Sligo Middle School.

Nicole and another 13-year-old girl consummated an apparent murder–suicide pact on November 8, 1988. The complaint filed in the lawsuit was summarized in the case report:

> The amended complaint avers that Nicole became involved in satanism, causing her to have an "obsessive interest in death and self-destruction." During the week prior to the suicide, Nicole told several friends and fellow students that she intended to kill herself. Some of these friends reported Nicole's intentions to their school counselor, Morgan, who relayed the information to Nicole's school counselor, Jones. Morgan and Jones then questioned Nicole about the statements, but Nicole denied making them. Neither Morgan nor Jones notified Nicole's parents or the school administration about Nicole's alleged statements of intent. Information in the record suggests that the other party to the suicide pact shot Nicole before shooting herself. The murder–suicide took place on a school holiday in a public park at some distance from Sligo Middle School. (*Eisel v. Board of Education of Montgomery County,* 1991, pp. 449–450. Court of Appeals of Maryland.)

Attorneys for the school board and its employees argued that school guidance counselors had no duty to recognize or prevent an adolescent's suicide. A motion for summary judgment in favor of the school board and its employees was granted, which means that the court, without even hearing the evidence in the case, found that the counselors were not responsible. Eisel appealed to the Maryland Court of Appeals. The court reversed the summary judgment and required that the case go back to the trial court so that a judge or jury could determine whether the counselors would be held responsible for Nicole Eisel's death.

In coming to this decision, the Maryland Court of Appeals held that "school counselors have a duty to use reasonable means to attempt to prevent a suicide when they are on notice of a child or adolescent student's suicidal intent" (*Eisel v. Board of Education of Montgomery County,* 1991, p. 456. Court of Appeals of Maryland.). The decision noted that the counselors could have determined that Nicole was in danger of committing suicide even though she denied it when asked, that the school board had a policy requiring counselors to notify parents despite any confidentiality concerns, and that the school had a formal suicide prevention program in place. The decision stated, "the relationship of a school counselor and pupil is not devoid of therapeutic overtones" (p. 452). The appeals court did not decide that the two school counselors were responsible for Nicole Eisel's suicide, but it did decide that a judge or jury could determine that the facts were such that the counselors could be held responsible.

It is almost impossible to determine how many lawsuits of a particular nature are filed in court. Most lawsuits are settled without a judgment being rendered or are determined at the trial court level and are not appealed. Only cases that are appealed are reported in case books. From the cases that are appealed, however, it appears that very few lawsuits are filed against counselors due to client suicide, and few of those filed result in judgments against the counselors. Nonetheless, counselors certainly hope to avoid experiencing the double trauma of having a client commit suicide and being named as a defendant in a lawsuit resulting from that suicide. In fact, if you practice competently, the chances are good that you will never have to respond to a malpractice lawsuit.

RESOLVING LEGAL AND ETHICAL CHALLENGES

In Chapter 1, ethical and legal decision making were discussed. A process for ethical decision making was suggested to help you identify key points to consider when you are faced with an ethical dilemma. Reasoning through a dilemma before taking action to resolve it can prevent later problems, such as being accused of improper or unethical behavior. This chapter section, by contrast, focuses on how to deal with suspicions or accusations of unethical or illegal conduct when they do occur.

Chapter 1 also presented a process for identifying legal issues when they arise and ways to request legal advice as an employee or as a counselor in private practice. It is one thing to understand rationally how to recognize legal issues and obtain legal advice, but it is quite another thing to feel the distress of dealing with legal issues when they actually arise.

Legal and Ethical Decision Making

This section of the chapter is aimed at helping you deal with situations that directly involve you in ethical and legal challenges that come before ethics committees, licensure or certification boards, and courts of law. After legal and ethical decision making are briefly reviewed, two kinds of situations are addressed: (a) what to do when you are accused of unethical or illegal behavior and (b) what to do if you suspect that a professional colleague is behaving unethically or illegally. Some guidelines are suggested for avoiding ethical and legal problems and maintaining your professional vitality.

PERSONAL LEGAL DECISION MAKING   It is impossible for counselors to understand all aspects of the law. As a result, you must rely on the advice of attorneys from time to time as you practice. You must make every effort to fully explain a situation to your legal advisors and educate them, to the extent possible, regarding the counseling process and the counseling profession. You can then follow the legal advice you have been given without worrying about whether it is correct. Of course, you should raise questions if you believe you are being given incorrect advice, but you can rely on the advice you have been given. Lawyers are required to stand behind the advice they render. You can sue your lawyers if you are harmed as a result of relying on their incorrect advice. An attorney who has represented mental health professionals when they were sued (Gould, 1998) has stated that the best advice he can give to those who are involved in litigation and are trying to protect themselves from attacks is to listen to their lawyer and do what the lawyer says.

Most legal issues faced by counselors involve acting as witnesses in litigation concerning other people. Unless you are being sued for malpractice or have had a complaint of improper conduct filed against you, it is important to remember that you are not being accused of wrongdoing. Reporting what you know in legal proceedings can be a simple matter if you have been advised by your attorney. It is important to avoid getting emotionally involved in your client's lawsuits or in legal proceedings that affect others. If you lose your objectivity and professional distance, it is easy to get inappropriately involved in legal matters that do not affect you directly.

PERSONAL ETHICAL DECISION MAKING   No doubt it has become evident to you, after reading the previous chapters, that ethical questions rarely have a single, clearly correct answer (Koocher & Keith-Spiegel, 2008). Codes of ethics can be helpful, and certainly they should be consulted. Remember, though, that ethics codes are written in general terms and cannot completely resolve most of the complex ethical dilemmas that arise in practice (Williams, 2001). Often, counselors' ethical problems are existential dilemmas. The decisions they make when attempting to resolve an ethical issue become the right decisions only because they were taken. It is impossible to guarantee in advance that actions, no matter how carefully considered, will have the desired outcome.

Ethical decision making is a complex process, even in the abstract. It can be even more difficult if you must make a decision when you are unsure about the ethics of your behavior or you suspect that a colleague is behaving unethically. Of course, when you have an ethical question, you should consult with fellow counselors, just as counselors who have a legal question should consult with an attorney. As was noted in the previous section, when a counselor asks an attorney for advice, the attorney becomes responsible for the advice given. In a parallel fashion, sometimes a counselor with an ethical question will have a clinical supervisor to whom the responsibility for decisions can be passed. Often, though, this option will not be available. When you have an ethical question, you can—and should—consult with colleagues, but the consultants are not responsible for your decisions or actions. Although an attorney can help you defend your actions later before an ethics committee or a licensing board, if that becomes necessary, an attorney cannot advise you about an ethical dilemma.

Responding to Accusations of Unethical or Illegal Behavior

Neukrug, Milliken, and Walden (2001) asked counselor licensure boards throughout the United States about ethical complaints that had been made against licensees. When the data were collected in 1999, 45 states and the District of Columbia had boards that licensed counselors. Four boards were too new to have processed complaints. Of the remaining 41 boards, 34 (83%) responded. Four of the 34 were not empowered to receive or process ethical complaints against licensees. The 30 remaining boards had received a total of 2,325 complaints in the previous 5 years. Of the 2,325, a total of 1,307 were identified by type of complaint. Of the categorized complaints received by these boards, 24% were for inappropriate dual relationships, 17% were for incompetence, 8% were for practicing without a license or misrepresentation of qualifications, 7% were for having a sexual relationship with a client, 5% were for breach of confidentiality, 4% were for inappropriate fee assessments, 1% were for failure to obtain informed consent, and 1% were for failure to report abuse. This information demonstrates that counselors have complaints filed against them for a variety of reasons. As Keith-Spiegel (2014) has demonstrated, ethics complaints get filed as a result of professionals losing their temper, disclosing personal information, entering into a bartering arrangement, and being involved in a vengeful act. Five times more mental health professionals have licensure board complaints filed against them than have been the target of malpractice lawsuits (Zur, 2011b).

Individuals react in various ways to accusations of unethical or illegal behavior (Warren & Douglas, 2012). Emotions such as fear, panic, and anger are common. It is natural to have a strong reaction, but you must keep your emotions under control so that you can handle the situation effectively. Chauvin and Remley (1996) recommend that you seek personal support by expressing your emotions regarding the accusation to clinical supervisors, family members, friends, or your personal counselor. However, you should avoid talking to them about the facts of the situation.

Despite the denial, embarrassment, or distress you may feel, you should immediately report any threatened or completed accusation of professional misconduct to your immediate administrative supervisor, if you are employed in an agency or institution, and to your personal professional liability insurance carrier. If you fail to notify your insurance company, you could jeopardize the policy's providing legal representation for you or paying off possible judgments. When you tell your supervisor about the accusation, you should ask the supervisor to keep the information confidential and not discuss it with anyone other than the administrative supervisor or the organization's attorney.

In reality, it is not unusual for counselors to be threatened with ethics complaints or malpractice lawsuits. Counselors engage in many activities that could result in ethics claims against them. They must report cases of suspected child abuse, vulnerable adult abuse, or elder abuse, and they often counsel individuals who are embroiled in legal conflicts with others. Sometimes counselors must take actions their clients do not wish them to take, such as informing family members, over a client's objection, if the client is at risk for suicide. As a result, individuals occasionally are angry with counselors and make threats. Diesen (2008) created a new term, *justice obsession syndrome*, to describe individuals who believe that the most important thing in life is to get justice in a personal situation where they firmly believe that an injustice has occurred. An obsession occurs, according to

Diesen, when the importance of retribution is out of proportion to the circumstances. At some point in your counseling practice, you may have a client who feels wronged as a result of what has transpired in counseling sessions with you and becomes obsessed with seeking justice for the perceived wrong. As with other syndromes, the chances of having such a client are not great, but this type of behavior by clients has been known to occur.

Some counselors serve as child custody evaluators. There is always a disappointed—and often angry—parent when a child custody recommendation is made to a judge. Some parents who are upset file ethics complaints against child custody evaluators, accusing them of being biased and unfair.

A counselor who is dealing with an angry client should respond directly to the person making the threat, if that is possible. If you can calm the person down and listen to the concerns, you might be able to resolve the problem immediately or through additional conversations. You should be careful, though, not to admit to wrongdoing and not to say anything you would not want to say under oath or would not want repeated by others in a courtroom later. We advise caution on your part if a client you are counseling has a history of filing lawsuits against other people for any reason. Clients who sue other people may be more inclined to sue their counselors as well. Once a formal complaint or lawsuit has been filed, it is unwise to contact a client and try to talk him or her into withdrawing the complaint (O'Mahony, 2011).

INFORMAL COMPLAINTS   The Introduction to Section I of the *Code of Ethics* (ACA, 2014) states, "Professional counselors behave in an ethical and legal manner. They are aware that client welfare and trust in the profession depend on a high level of professional conduct." This introduction also states, "Counselors incorporate ethical practice into their daily professional work and engage in ongoing professional development regarding current topics in ethical and legal issues in counseling."

Although we hope that you will always do your best to practice within the bounds of professional ethics, even the well-intended counselor occasionally can make mistakes or be accused of wrongdoing, even if no mistake has been made. A fellow counselor might directly observe you do or say something that raises cause for concern, or the concern might have come to your colleague's attention through the report of a client, fellow mental health professional, supervisee, or student. It is important to take the concern seriously, make yourself available to meet and discuss the concern, listen and respond genuinely and nondefensively, and take responsibility for your error if you have made one (Williams, 2001). If the concern can be resolved informally in this way, it is to everyone's advantage.

Formal Complaints

Sometimes clients or other citizens file formal complaints against counselors with licensure boards, certification boards, professional associations, or other entities. When such complaints are filed, it is vital that counselors take them seriously and respond appropriately.

8-2 The Case of Lee

Lee has been licensed by her state board as a counselor for 4 years and is employed as a counselor in a community counseling center. Much to her dismay, Lee received a registered letter at work today informing her that a former client, David, has filed an ethics complaint against her with the licensure board, claiming that he was harmed because Lee is an incompetent counselor. David claims that Lee counseled him for 8 months for depression, during which time she sent him to a psychiatrist for antidepressant medication. David found out recently that he has a brain tumor, which his neurosurgeon has told him causes people to be depressed. David claims that if Lee were competent, she would have advised him to have a physical examination and that the brain tumor would have been discovered earlier. Lee immediately advised her supervisor at the counseling center and called and reported the complaint to her professional liability insurance carrier. After she faxed a copy of the complaint to her insurance carrier, she received a call from an agent telling her that the insurance company wanted Lee to see a local lawyer who would represent Lee. Lee has never heard of the lawyer.

- How should Lee respond to her insurance carrier?
- When Lee meets with her lawyer, how should she conduct herself?

Discussion: Lee should ask her insurance carrier how that lawyer was selected. Usually, lawyers are chosen who have expertise in defending mental health professionals or other professionals in ethics complaints before licensure boards. Insurance companies generally select the best lawyers in the area to represent those they insure.

Lee should agree to meet with the lawyer who has been suggested by the insurance company and accept that lawyer to represent her, unless there is some compelling reason not to. If Lee does not like the suggested lawyer, she can ask the insurance carrier to hire another lawyer whom she prefers, and usually the insurance carrier will agree to do that if the alternative lawyer has expertise in defending suits against mental health professionals.

When Lee meets with her lawyer, she should bring copies of all relevant records with her to the meeting. She should also construct a chronological listing of her relationship with the complaining client that is factual and detailed and bring a copy of that document to give to the lawyer.

Lee should tell the lawyer everything she knows about the situation, even if she is concerned that perhaps she used bad judgment or made some mistakes. The lawyer has a privileged relationship with Lee and cannot tell anyone else what Lee has disclosed. The lawyer needs to know all details (including negative ones) in order to craft an appropriate defense for her.

If you receive notice from a licensure or certification board or from a professional association ethics committee that you have been accused of unprofessional conduct, you need immediate legal counsel (Zur, 2011). The professional liability insurance policy offered to members of ACA provides legal counsel to policyholders who have complaints filed against them. Generally, other professional liability insurance companies provide the same benefit to counselors that they insure. Counselors are advised to make sure the professional liability insurance policy they purchase includes legal representation in the event a formal complaint is filed against them with their licensure board (Zur, 2011). Some policies do not include that benefit and are not the best professional liability insurance options.

Licensure boards, professional association ethics committees, and counselor certification boards have adopted procedures for processing complaints against those who are licensed or certified by their boards or who are members of their association. The procedures used by ACA can be found on the ACA website (www.counseling.org). Each set of procedures is different; however, they have many common steps. The general process that boards and committees use in processing complaints is summarized in the following (Chauvin & Remley, 1996):

- Generally, investigations and the processing of complaints are confidential.
- First, a board will determine whether it has jurisdiction over the counselor against whom the complaint is being made. If the board does not have jurisdiction, it notifies the person making the complaint that it does not have jurisdiction and the case is closed. If the individual is licensed or certified by the board (or is an applicant for a license or certification), then the board generally has jurisdiction.
- Once jurisdiction has been established, the board determines whether the counselor may have violated the board's code of ethics, if the allegations against the counselor are true. If the action (or inaction) of the counselor would not have constituted a violation, the case is closed. When the allegation, if true, might be a violation of the board's code of ethics, the board then begins an investigation of the complaint.
- Investigations might range from actions that are as expensive and complicated as sending investigators to talk to witnesses or the accused counselor, to actions as simple as asking written questions of the accuser or the accused.
- Often, if a violation is found, informal negotiations between the board and accused counselor occur. A settlement of the matter may be reached on a voluntary basis that satisfies both parties.
- If a settlement is not offered by the board or is refused by the counselor, a hearing is generally held. Members of the board (or their designees) sit as a jury. A representative of the board prosecutes the case, and the accused counselor, or the counselor's representative, defends. Usually witnesses are called to testify, including the accuser. Accused counselors usually are allowed to be represented by legal counsel at these hearings.
- After the hearing, the board determines whether the counselor violated the code of ethics. If violations are found, the board may impose sanctions. Sanctions vary but could include a written reprimand only; probation; suspension; or revocation of a license, certification, or association membership.
- If the counselor who has been found in violation of the code of ethics is not satisfied with the result, the counselor can appeal. Usually, there are internal appeals in which the board reviews the case again. Once the internal appeals are exhausted, in most states the counselor can sue the board in a court of law if the counselor believes the treatment was unfair.

If you receive official notice that a malpractice lawsuit has been filed against you, you must notify your employer and your professional liability insurance carrier immediately.

An emotional response to being accused of wrongdoing is natural. It may help to keep in mind that many formal complaints and lawsuits filed against mental health professionals are either dismissed or result in a finding in favor of the professional (Anderson & Swanson, 1994). In a study of complaints against rehabilitation counselors over a 9-year period, Saunders, Barros-Bailey, Rudman, Dew, and Garcia (2007) found that only 71 of the 113 complaints filed accusing rehabilitation counselors of unethical conduct were accepted for investigation. Actions or sanctions were taken against the counselors in only 36 of the 71 cases. It may also be helpful to know that severe sanctions against counselors are rarely imposed by the ACA Ethics Committee; for example, only two members were expelled from the association between 1996 and 2000 (Williams, 2001). In most formal complaint or lawsuit situations, the individuals being accused wish they had done or said some things differently. This is natural as well. To avoid making mistakes that might be detrimental to your case, Chauvin and Remley (1996) and Herlihy and Corey (2015a) have advised that you take the steps in Figure 8-2 if you are accused or sued.

- Maintain composure and respond at all times in a professional and unemotional manner.
- Notify your employer and professional liability insurance carrier immediately.
- Once you have a lawyer, follow the lawyer's advice precisely.
- Respond carefully to the charges. Remember that the members of the board or committee who will be deciding the outcome of the complaint do not know you and will base their decision only on material they have received. Write your response as deliberately and dispassionately as you can, and address each of the specific charges that have been made. For instance, if you have been accused of misapplying a technique, you should submit case notes or other records that show how you deliberated and decided to use the technique, how you were trained to use it, when you consulted about it, and any other steps you took to prevent harm to the client. Do not submit any responses until your attorney has reviewed them.
- Do not agree to speak to a licensure board investigator unless your attorney is present (Zur, 2011).
- Even if you are surprised and hurt that a client or colleague has filed a complaint against you, do not attempt to contact the complainant directly. Doing so could be interpreted as an attempt to coerce or unduly influence the client or colleague (Crawford, 1994).
- Seek emotional support from colleagues, friends, or family members, but focus your interactions on dealing with your emotions. Avoid discussing details of the case except with your attorney.
- Seek professional counseling if being accused results in distress that interferes with your personal or professional functioning.
- If you are guilty of having breached the code of ethics, seek assistance to help you avoid future breaches. This assistance could take the form of professional counseling, continuing education, supervision, or a combination of these resources.

FIGURE 8-2 Steps to take if you are accused of unethical behavior or are sued

Source: Pearson Education, Inc., Hoboken, NJ.

WHEN YOU SUSPECT A COLLEAGUE IS ACTING UNETHICALLY OR ILLEGALLY

Unethical Behavior

The primary purpose of the *Code of Ethics* (ACA, 2014) is to guide our own behavior, not to judge the behavior of others. However, we cannot turn our heads and ignore unethical behavior on the part of others, particularly if such behavior is substantially harming others or has the potential of causing substantial harm. It is each counselor's responsibility to society and to the profession to address in an appropriate manner the behavior of other mental health professionals that appears to be unethical. Generally, mental health professionals have been reluctant to confront the unethical behavior of a colleague (Lowman, 2006). The role of *policeperson* can be very uncomfortable and runs contrary to who we are as counselors and to our commitment to accepting and helping others rather than judging and punishing them. Nonetheless, we must recognize that unless we police our own profession, the courts will step in and do it for us.

The Introduction to Section I of the *Code of Ethics* (ACA, 2014) states, "Counselors strive to resolve ethical dilemmas with direct and open communication among all parties involved and seek consultation with colleagues and supervisors when necessary." This standard clearly communicates to counselors that they should consult when they are unsure whether another counselor is behaving in an unethical manner and should establish *direct and open communication* with the other counselor. When consultation and confrontation do not work, counselors are advised by the *Code of Ethics* (ACA, 2014), in serious cases, to take additional actions.

Standard I.2.a. of the *Code of Ethics* (ACA, 2014) states, "When counselors have reason to believe that another counselor is violating or has violated an ethical standard and substantial harm has not occurred, they attempt to first resolve the issue informally with the other counselor if feasible, provided such action does not violate confidentiality rights that may be involved." Two phrases in this standard require careful consideration. First, what constitutes a *reason to believe*? And second, what constitutes resolution of the issue?

In determining whether you have reason to believe that a colleague is acting unethically, we caution you against making a rush to judgment. You may hear rumors from colleagues that a fellow mental health professional engages in inappropriate behaviors such as sexually harassing clients or billing insurance companies for services that are not actually provided. Although you would be justified in feeling concerned, it would be unwise for you to take on the role of detective and investigate whether the rumors are true. Instead, urge the persons who are telling you the rumors to talk *to* the professional who is supposedly behaving inappropriately rather than talking *about* the individual. At other times, a client might tell you directly about unethical behavior on the part of a former counselor. In these instances, your role can be one of assisting the client to decide whether to take action, if the client has been harmed by the former counselor's behavior. Only when you have direct knowledge of unethical behavior on the part of a fellow mental health professional should you feel obligated to take action.

With respect to what constitutes resolving the issue, as we have noted, the *Code of Ethics* asks counselors to "attempt to first resolve the issue informally with the other counselor if feasible" (ACA 2014, §I.2.b.). It appears that some confusion may exist regarding this ethical obligation. Nearly 30% of the ACA members surveyed by Neukrug and Milliken (2011) believed it was ethical to report a colleague's unethical conduct without first consulting with the colleague. Of course, you will be uncomfortable and anxious if you must confront a counselor about your perception that he or she may have violated an ethical standard. Such feelings are understandable; however, accusing a counselor of wrongdoing is a very serious step, and your anxiety about accusing someone of possible wrongdoing is not a justifiable reason for not attempting to resolve the issue directly with a counselor. It is entirely possible that speaking informally with the other counselor will resolve the problem and thus avoid further discomfort for both parties.

Consider what you might do if you were the counselor in the following scenario.

8-3 The Case of Ramona

Ramona is a counselor educator. At her university, the counseling program is housed within a larger department that includes counseling, educational administration, and school psychology. One day Ramona is visiting an intern at a United Way–funded agency. She notices a flyer on the bulletin board that announces, "John Smith, PhD, will be forming a counseling group for men who are divorced." John is a colleague in her department at the university. He has a master's degree in counseling, but his PhD is in educational administration. She realizes that his advertising himself on the flyer as holding a PhD may be a violation of the *Code of Ethics* (ACA, 2014, §C.4.a. and §C.4.d.).

- Do you think that Ramona can ignore the situation? Or do you think she should do something about this possible ethics violation?
- If Ramona should act, what actions should she take?

Discussion: If Ramona were to decide to report John's behavior to their supervisor, to the state counselor licensure board, or to the ACA Ethics Committee, she would be creating problems—probably unnecessarily—for John and for their ongoing relationship as colleagues. Her first action should be to seek informal resolution by talking directly with John, pointing out that §C.4.a. and §C.4.d. in the *Code of Ethics* (ACA, 2014) are of concern. John may reply that he was unaware of these standards and had no idea that his advertisement might be a breach of the code. Whether or not John's advertisement is an ethics violation is open to question, as a PhD in educational administration could possibly be interpreted by some people as being in a field closely related to counseling. Ramona's goal should be to correct the problem, not to punish John. She can talk with him about what he can do to correct the situation. This might include taking down the flyers and printing new ones or being sure to clarify his credentials during the pregroup screening interview with potential group participants. If John were willing to take the steps agreed upon, Ramona probably would determine that the problem had been satisfactorily resolved.

What if the preceding scenario were different and John, rather than misrepresenting his PhD credential, had been drinking at a bar, encountered a former client and had *come on* to Ramona? What if the client had been uncomfortable seeing John in this situation and had left the bar? We believe that the total situation would dictate Ramona's actions. If Ramona believed this was an isolated incident, and that the client had not been substantially harmed as a result of the relationship, then Ramona should confront John and hopefully obtain agreement that he had made a mistake and a promise not to engage in such actions again. On the other hand, if Ramona believed that John had a history of sexual or romantic relationships with clients or former clients, or had a drinking problem, and if the client in this incident had been substantially harmed, then a confession and promise from John probably would not satisfy Ramona's obligation to the profession and to the public.

You will find that an informal resolution is not always possible when you have knowledge that another counselor may have engaged in unethical practices. The offending colleague may be unwilling to discuss your concern, circumstances may exist that preclude you from confronting your colleague, or you may not be able to raise your concern without violating the confidentiality of an involved party. If the privacy of an involved party is at risk, you should consult with colleagues who are uninvolved and who will not be able to ascertain the identity of the subject of the consultation.

If someone has been substantially harmed or is being substantially harmed by the unethical behavior, and if your consultants agree that you must take action, you must go forward and report the behavior (Smith, 2006). These circumstances will be rare. Standard I.2.b. of the *Code of Ethics* (ACA, 2014) states, "If an apparent violation has substantially harmed or is likely to substantially harm a person or organization and is not appropriate for informal resolution or is not resolved properly, counselors take further action depending on the situation. Such action may include referral to state or national committees on professional ethics, voluntary national certification bodies, state licensing boards, or appropriate institutional authorities. The confidentiality rights of clients should be considered in all actions. This standard does not apply when counselors have been retained to review the work of another counselor whose professional conduct is in question (e.g., consultation, expert testimony)." We suggest that counselors report suspected ethics violations of other counselors to licensure and certification boards, and to association ethics committees, only when the conditions in Figure 8-3 have been met.

- It is impossible to resolve the issue directly with the counselor because of the nature of the circumstances, or because attempts at resolution have been unsuccessful. Being uncomfortable confronting the counselor or your anxiety about accusing someone of wrongdoing is not a justifiable reason for not attempting to resolve the issue directly with the counselor.
- You are certain and have direct knowledge that a serious ethics violation has occurred that is causing substantial harm, or has caused substantial harm.
- Colleagues with whom you have consulted agree that a report must be made.
- You are willing to participate in a hearing and testify against the counselor if a hearing is held.
- You are prepared to defend yourself if you have a counterclaim filed against you.

FIGURE 8-3 Recommended necessary conditions for reporting a colleague for unethical behavior
Source: Pearson Education, Inc., Hoboken, NJ.

The last two items on the list may come as a surprise to many counselors, but they are understandable when the ACA Ethics Committee's policies and procedures for dealing with complaints and the procedures of licensure and certification boards are taken into consideration. For example, the ACA Ethics Committee accepts only written complaints that are signed by complainants. The committee does not accept anonymous complaints. If you believe you must file a complaint, you should write a letter to the Ethics Committee outlining the nature of the complaint, sign it, and send it in an envelope marked *Confidential.* If the person against whom you are making the complaint is an ACA member or was a member when the alleged violation took place, the committee will send you a formal complaint that identifies all the ACA ethical standards that might have been violated, if the accusations are true. You will be asked to sign the complaint (after suggesting modifications, if needed) and a release-of-information form. The accused member then will receive copies of the formal complaint and any evidence or documents you have submitted to support your complaint. (For more complete information, see the ACA Ethics Committee's policies and procedures for processing complaints of ethical violations, which can be found on the ACA website (www.counseling.org).

It is very distressing for counselors to have ethics charges filed against them by professional colleagues. Rarely does an accused counselor simply admit wrongdoing. Instead, the counselor may become defensive and sometimes may even make accusations of unprofessional behavior against the accuser. Usually, a long period of time passes while a complaint is being investigated and considered. The aftermath of the filing of an ethics complaint is stressful for both the accused and the accuser.

If you ever decide to file a complaint, you should request formal complaint forms from appropriate entities and follow precisely the instructions for filing the complaints. It is recommended that, before formally filing a complaint, you consult with an attorney and follow the attorney's advice (Austin, Moline, & Williams, 1990; Crawford, 1994). In many instances, depending on the circumstances and credentials of the counselor being accused, multiple complaints may be appropriate. Complaints may be filed at the same time with all of the following entities:

- All state licensure boards that have licensed the counselor
- All national certification boards that have certified the counselor
- Ethics committees that accept complaints of all professional counseling associations in which the counselor holds active membership
- The counselor's employer

Licensure boards, certification boards, and professional associations will inform individuals who inquire whether an individual comes under their jurisdiction and whether they accept ethics complaints against members. In the counseling profession, complaints are filed with and processed by ACA rather than with local or state chapters. When local chapters, state branches, regions, and divisions of ACA receive ethical complaints against members, they usually refer them to the national ACA Ethics Committee. On the other hand, the National Association of Social Workers and the American Psychological Association (APA) process ethics complaints against members on a local or state level. If an association processes complaints at the local level, information on the proper way to file complaints is available from the association's national office.

Unwarranted Complaints

Standard I.2.e. of the *Code of Ethics* (ACA, 2014) states, "Counselors do not initiate, participate in, or encourage the filing of ethics complaints that are retaliatory in nature or are made with reckless disregard or willful ignorance of facts that would disprove the allegation." This standard provides a foundation for finding counselors in violation of the ACA *Code of Ethics* if they purposefully file a formal ethics complaint against another counselor when they know the complaint is false or if they were not careful to gather and state facts accurately.

Inappropriate Discrimination Against Those Who Have Been Accused

Standard I.2.f. of the *Code of Ethics* (ACA, 2014) attempts to guard against counselors being discriminated against when they have had ethics complaints filed against them, even though the complaints have not yet been resolved. Even the most ethical counselors could have complaints filed against them. All it takes to file a complaint is completing a form and sending it to the proper authorities. In addition, the standard makes an effort to guard against counselors being discriminated against because they have filed complaints against other counselors. This standard states, "Counselors do not deny individuals employment, advancement, admission to academic or other programs, tenure, or promotion based solely on their having made or their being the subject of an ethics complaint. This does not preclude taking action based on the outcome of such proceedings or considering other appropriate information."

Despite this standard, if a complaint against a counselor is pending, employers certainly may conduct their own investigations into alleged wrongdoing and conclude that a counselor has been unethical, even if an ACA complaint still has not been resolved.

Illegal Behavior of Others

Individuals in U.S. society who know of illegal acts by others are not violating any laws if they choose not to report such activities. In the same manner, counselors who know of illegal acts of other counselors generally do not have to report those illegal acts. A citizen in the United States cannot be charged with a crime for refusing or failing to report the criminal act of another person. However, some illegal acts by counselors might also be unethical or might violate state licensure statutes or regulations. The previous section discusses how to proceed if you believe another counselor is acting unethically.

Counselors might become aware of the following illegal activities by other counselors:

- Lying to health care companies so that clients will get reimbursement for the counselors' services
- Purposefully not reporting income to the Internal Revenue Service
- Engaging in a sexual relationship with a minor
- Smoking in a building in which smoking is prohibited
- Speeding while driving a car

Obviously, you might decide to report some of these illegal activities even though you are not legally obligated to do so. Some activities might fall into a gray area, and you would not even think of reporting others.

Although counselors do not have an affirmative duty to report illegal activities of others, if they are questioned by police investigators or subpoenaed, they have to answer questions regarding the matter truthfully. Counselors cannot assist individuals who have broken the law if they are attempting to avoid being questioned, arrested, or convicted of a crime they have committed.

Cases Are Often Complex

In this chapter, you have learned that you have an ethical duty to take appropriate action when you have good reason to believe that a fellow counselor is behaving unethically in a way that could cause substantial harm, and that sometimes you might choose to report an illegal activity. In Chapter 1, some ethical and legal decision-making strategies were offered. Throughout this text, case examples have been provided to help you hone your decision-making skills. You should keep in mind that most real-world ethical and legal problems are very complex and do not lend themselves to easy solutions. The following case example illustrates some of these complications.

8-4 The Case of Bill

Assume that you are a Licensed Professional Counselor in private practice. In April of the past year you were contacted by Bill, a counselor in the local high school. Bill was calling because he wanted to refer Libby, an 18-year-old student. You made an appointment with Libby and met with her in late April. You counseled her for two more sessions. In mid-May, she called to cancel her next session. While on the phone, she told you that she wanted you to understand why she was canceling and terminating the counseling relationship. She also wanted the reassurance that you would not talk with her school counselor.

In response, you reviewed with her the limits of confidentiality and assured her that you would not talk with Bill, but that if she told you of abuse or threatened harm to herself or others, you would have to report it to authorities. Libby then disclosed that she had been having romantic feelings for Bill for nearly a year and that she was upset and confused about the relationship. You stressed to Libby that this would not be a good time to discontinue counseling. Libby promised to think things over and call you back.

Libby returned for one more session in June, soon after she graduated from high school. She told you that she had decided that she and Bill should just be friends. She also disclosed that although she had not had sexual intimacies with Bill, he had talked of being attracted to her. Libby recalled that she had felt confused when Bill first flirted with her, and now felt that her trust had been betrayed. When you asked her for permission to talk with Bill, she adamantly refused. You encouraged her to talk to the school officials, but again she was adamant in refusing, stating that she didn't want to get Bill into trouble. She added that she had never told anyone, including her parents, about what had happened and that she didn't want anyone besides you to know about it.

You know Bill personally, although the two of you are not close friends. You see him at meetings of professional associations and local continuing education workshops. You believe that Libby is telling the truth. At the same time, Bill has always impressed you as a competent professional.

- What are your professional and ethical responsibilities to Libby?
- What are your professional and ethical responsibilities to Bill?

Discussion:
Regarding your responsibilities to Libby:

- You should try to get more information from Libby regarding the exact behaviors of Bill in an effort to determine whether Bill had behaved inappropriately or whether Libby may have misinterpreted his attention.
- You have an obligation to respect Libby's privacy, unless you determine that she may have been subjected to inappropriate romantic overtures from Bill.
- If you have reason to believe that Bill acted inappropriately, you would have an obligation to take some type of action to ensure that he would be held accountable.

Regarding your responsibilities to Bill:

- You should assume that Bill has done nothing wrong until you determine in your mind that he may be guilty of inappropriate behavior with Libby.
- If you decide that Bill may have been inappropriate, you should talk to him directly about the situation and hear his side of the story.
- After talking to Bill, if you believe Libby had been substantially harmed, or that Bill may substantially harm other students, then you should take actions to ensure that Bill is held accountable for his behavior.

There are a number of issues to consider in Libby's case. This situation lends itself well to consultation with others. If you are a student in a graduate course, try consulting with some of your classmates, supervisors, and professors. If you are a practitioner, you might share the case with a colleague. Try to apply the decision-making strategies you have learned.

Guidelines for Avoiding Problems

No matter how carefully you practice or how conscientious you are as a professional, it is always possible that someone will accuse you of unethical or illegal behavior. Guidelines that have been suggested by Chauvin and Remley (1996) for avoiding problem situations follow:

- Restrict your practice of counseling to your areas of competence (Daniluk & Haverkamp, 1993; Gilbert, 1992).
- Do not sue clients for unpaid fees (Woody, 1988a). Those who are sued by you may, in turn, complain about your competency. If you avoid allowing clients to run up bills with you, collecting fees from them will never become an issue.
- Utilize a thorough and complete client disclosure statement in your practice (Beamish, Navin, & Davidson, 1994; Epperson & Lewis, 1987; Hendrick, 1988; Wheeler & Bertram, 2012).
- Never guarantee or imply a guarantee of outcomes (Woody, 1988a).
- Establish and maintain firm professional boundaries between you and your clients.
- Always use supervision for your practice, even if it is peer supervision (Remley, Benshoff, & Mowbray, 1987).

We suggest and briefly discuss a few additional guidelines:

- Stay connected with your fellow mental health professionals. Attend meetings of professional organizations and continuing education workshops. Join a peer consultation group that meets regularly. Isolation can create blind spots (Mascari & Webber, 2006), and counselors who are isolated from their colleagues are more prone to burnout and to inappropriately trying to meet their own needs through their relationships with clients.

- Monitor your self-disclosures made in counseling relationships. Check to make sure that you are self-disclosing for the benefit of your clients rather than to have your own needs met. This is one important way to avoid a subtle slide into blurred boundaries and inappropriate dual relationships.

- Document carefully any circumstances and actions taken in difficult or dangerous client situations (such as abuse or threats to harm self or others; Wheeler & Bertram, 2012).

- Keep current with developments in law and ethics. Ethical standards for the profession are not static, and in every state, laws and rules related to the practice of counseling are constantly changing (Hegarty, 2012). It is vital that you keep abreast of changes in requirements for practice and advances in knowledge in the field.

- To reiterate advice we offer many times throughout this text, when in doubt, consult (Melonas, 2011). As we note, decisions made in isolation are rarely as sound as those made in consultation with others. Choose your consultants wisely—fellow mental health professionals for ethical questions, and attorneys for legal questions—and follow their advice.

- Continually monitor your own effectiveness as a counselor. You have an ethical duty to do this (ACA, 2014, §C.2.e.) as well as a moral responsibility. Recall the discussion of virtue ethics presented in Chapter 1. Virtuous counselors have such an abiding commitment to the ethical values of the profession that they hold themselves accountable even when others do not (Meara, Schmidt, & Day, 1996).

Taylor (1995) has suggested that the following are keys to professional behavior: (a) authentic caring, (b) willingness to examine our own motivations, (c) willingness to tell the truth to ourselves, our peers, and our clients, and (d) willingness to ask for help and to learn. These seem to us to be excellent touchstones for maintaining an ethically and legally sound counseling practice.

A further suggestion is to take care of your own mental and emotional health. In our view, it is often the most conscientious counselors who fall prey to mental and emotional exhaustion. It may help to keep in mind that sound practice is not about achieving perfection; rather, it is about taking responsibility for one's actions and keeping client welfare foremost (Welfel, 2013). At the same time, we believe that there is an ethic of self-care. As Corey et al. (2015) have stated, a key to retaining your vitality as a person and a professional is to realize that you do not have an unlimited capacity to give without replenishing yourself. Attending to your own wellness is fundamental to your ability to assist your clients in achieving emotional health and wellness.

Counselors must take care of themselves legally as well. Professionals who are sued or accused of wrongdoing are not able to function to their maximum potential. We owe it to our clients to protect ourselves legally as we practice, to seek legal advice when it is needed, and to maintain professional liability insurance. By protecting ourselves legally, we are able to help others as professional counselors.

Summary and Key Points

This chapter addresses unfortunate topics related to clients being dissatisfied with the services of counselors. Counselor malpractice is reviewed. In addition, the process whereby counselors are accused of unethical practice is discussed. The following are key points:

- Counselor malpractice is defined as the failure of counselors to render professional services expected in a particular community by a reasonable member of the counseling profession with the result that a recipient of services is harmed. Malpractice can include intentional or unintentional wrongdoing.

- Malpractice lawsuits against counselors are difficult for a client to win because clients must show that counselors were guilty of wrongdoing and that the wrongdoing caused some actual harm to the client.

- Sexual relationships with a client and the suicide of a client are situations in which most counselor malpractice cases are filed.

- Knowing how to proceed when a counselor determines that a client may be at risk for suicide or violence is essential for counselors who practice in all settings.

- Counselors in all states except Texas have a duty to warn known intended victims of their clients. However, state laws vary widely, so it is essential to know the law in the state in which you practice.

- It is very important to consult with attorneys when legal questions arise in your counseling practice.

- On the other hand, other counselors, not lawyers, should be consulted when making difficult ethical or professional decisions.

- If you are accused of unethical practice, you should seek legal advice, avoid talking with others about the accusation, and respond in a professional manner to licensure boards or association ethics committees.

- The first step in addressing what appears to unethical behavior by a colleague is to address the situation directly and to try to resolve the problem through that process. When that fails or in situations where direct interaction with the colleague is impossible, and substantial harm has occurred or is occurring, you should consult with other counselors, and, if necessary, report the situation to employers, licensure boards, or certification entities.

Boundary Issues

FOCUS QUESTIONS

1. How would you define the term *dual relationship*?

2. What are the differences between a friendship and a counseling relationship?

3. Do you think that a sexual relationship between a counselor and a former client is ever acceptable? Why or why not?

4. What would you do if you found that you felt a strong sexual attraction to one of your clients?

Perhaps no ethical and legal issue has caused more controversy among helping professionals than determining the appropriate boundaries of the therapeutic relationship. Boundary issues encompass a wide range of questions that counselors encounter on a daily basis. Just a few such questions are: Is it ethically appropriate to accept a gift from a client? Is it permissible to become friends with a former client after the counseling relationship has ended? Should I ever meet with a client outside the office? Hug a client? Accept a friend of a friend as a client? Attend a community event when a client will also be in attendance?

Although the term *boundary* is part of the everyday language of counseling, it has rarely been defined in the literature (Hermanson, 1997). A *boundary* can be conceptualized as a frame or membrane around the therapeutic dyad that defines a set of roles for the participants in the therapeutic relationship (Smith & Fitzpatrick, 1995). Viewed this way, boundaries help us understand the parameters of the relationship. Although counseling can involve a great deal of emotional intimacy, it is a professional relationship, and therefore it has certain limits that might not apply to a personal relationship. To give some examples, there are limits on physical contact between counselor and client, on time and place for counseling (counseling generally takes place during regularly scheduled appointments and in a particular setting), on the amount and types of self-disclosure made by the counselor, and on the exchange of gifts. Katherine's (1991) definition of a boundary as a "limit that promotes integrity" (p. 3) nicely captures the purpose of setting boundaries. Limits lend structure to the therapeutic relationship, which helps to create a safe space that is "unambiguous, consistent, and reliable" (Jordan & Marshall, 2010, p. 345). Boundaries exist to protect the welfare of clients who are in a vulnerable position in the relationship.

Boundary issues usually have been framed in the literature as questions of dual or multiple relationships. According to Herlihy and Corey (2015b), dual or multiple relationships occur when helping professionals take on two or more roles simultaneously or sequentially with a help seeker. Stated another way, dual or multiple relationships occur whenever helping professionals have another, significantly different relationship with one of their clients, students, or supervisees. Dual relationships can involve combining the role of counselor with another professional relationship (such as teacher, minister, supervisor, employer, or business partner; Smith & Smith, 2001) or combining the counselor role with a personal relationship (such as friend, relative, or lover).

Boundary issues have been a *hot topic* that has generated over 1,500 books, articles, and scholarly works (Pope & Keith-Spiegel, 2008). Historically, dual relationships were generally prohibited or discouraged, but the thinking of our profession has evolved during the twenty-first century. Prohibitions have been replaced by cautions and a recognition that some dual relating can actually be beneficial to clients (Corey, Corey, Corey, & Callanan, 2015). Early versions of the *Code of Ethics* (American Counseling Association [ACA], 2014) cautioned counselors that dual relationships should be avoided, whereas recent versions have reflected a more nuanced understanding of the complexities of boundary issues. In the following section, we discuss some factors that make dual relationships and boundary issues so complicated and difficult to resolve.

THE COMPLEXITIES OF DUAL RELATIONSHIPS

Several characteristics of dual relationships make them problematic for counselors (Herlihy & Corey, 2015b). First, *potential dual relationships can be difficult to recognize*. They can evolve in subtle ways. There is no *danger sign* that marks the point at which a professional relationship crosses the line into behavior that could lead to an inappropriate relationship. It is not difficult for a counselor, or a counselor educator or supervisor, to innocently enter into a form of extraprofessional relationship. A counselor might accept a client's invitation to attend a special event that has meaning for the client. A counselor educator might find a friendship developing with a student whom the educator is mentoring. A supervisor might feel attracted to a supervisee and think about dating the supervisee as soon as the formal supervision is completed.

When dual relationships are sequential rather than simultaneous, it can be particularly difficult to foresee potential problems. Some of the questions with which conscientious professionals struggle are whether a former client can eventually become a friend, how a smooth transition can be made from a supervisory relationship to a collegial relationship once supervision is completed, and what factors must be considered in determining whether a former therapeutic relationship can become a personal relationship of any kind.

A second complicating characteristic is that *the potential outcome of dual relating ranges along a wide continuum from extremely harmful to beneficial to clients*; as can be seen in the following two examples.

9-1 The Case of Gerald

Dorothy, age 23, seeks counseling from Gerald, a Licensed Professional Counselor (LPC) in private practice. Her goal is to work through issues related to the sexual abuse by her stepfather that she had endured when she was a child. After 2 months of counseling, Gerald initiates a sexual relationship with Dorothy. He rationalizes his behavior by telling himself that she can benefit from having a *healthy* sexual relationship. Dorothy feels guilty, confused, and isolated by this betrayal of her trust. She wants to end the sexual relationship but has become so dependent on Gerald that she feels trapped. She begins to have thoughts of suicide.

9-2 The Case of Elizabeth

Fiona has been coming to see Elizabeth, her counselor, for nearly a year. Through counseling, Fiona has gained the self-esteem and confidence to return to college and complete the last four courses she needed in order to graduate. She asks Elizabeth to attend the graduation ceremony. She says that Elizabeth's attendance would mean a great deal to her because she credits the counseling process for making it possible for her to achieve her goal. Elizabeth agrees to attend the ceremony.

- What are the differences between Gerald's motivation and Elizabeth's motivation to cross a boundary?
- What harm do you think might have resulted from Elizabeth attending Fiona's graduation ceremony?

Discussion: The first case illustrates the severe harm to a client that a sexual dual relationship can cause. Gerald's behavior is exploitive, and he is causing harm by revictimizing his client. Gerard's behavior is unethical, and in some jurisdictions it could be criminal as well.

Near the other end of the continuum are situations like Elizabeth's in which a counselor chooses to engage in a form of dual relating in order to benefit a particular client. Elizabeth's choice to attend the graduation ceremony probably has a low risk of causing harm. As the *Code of Ethics* (ACA, 2014) acknowledges in §A.6.b., current counseling relationships are sometimes extended beyond conventional parameters. This standard offers the specific example of attending a formal ceremony such as a wedding/commitment ceremony or graduation. Elizabeth would need to take "appropriate professional precautions" as explained in this standard, which might include consultation and documentation.

You might agree with Elizabeth's decision to attend the graduation ceremony, or you might believe it is not a good idea to make exceptions like this. There is no absolute right answer to this question. You will need to give considered thought to developing your own stance toward boundary issues. Although the risks and benefits of nonprofessional or dual relationships are further discussed later in this chapter, we believe it may be helpful at this point to keep in mind Tomm's (1993) caution that it is not dual relating in itself that creates an ethical problem. Rather, it is the counselor's personal tendency to exploit clients or misuse power. Thus, simply avoiding dual relationships will not prevent exploitation. There are many ways that counselors can misuse their power and influence over clients even when they are not occupying more than one role with them.

A third characteristic that makes boundary issues so complicated is that *some dual relationships are unavoidable*. In rural communities, it may be impossible for counselors to keep their personal lives entirely separate from their professional lives. In addition to working in rural communities, there are a number of situations in which counselors and their clients have shared social communities and in which overlapping roles are inherent. Later in this chapter, we discuss *small worlds* in which some role overlap is inevitable.

Finally, *our traditional ideas of the therapeutic frame are being challenged by developments in the profession and by new, innovative approaches to counseling*. One development is that there is greater cultural diversity among both clients and counselors in our increasingly multicultural society. We agree with Speight (2012), who suggested that cultural competence in counseling requires a different, broader understanding of therapeutic boundaries. She noted that many African Americans place high value on affective expression and sociability. Therefore, African American clients are likely to want counselors to *be real* in the counseling relationship, and they may react negatively to counselors who maintain distance and anonymity. In Latino cultures, where warm, close family and community bonds exist, dual relationships tend to be the norm rather than the exception (Kertesz, 2002, Machuca, 2015). Sometimes, the shared experiences of being members of a marginalized group form a basis for establishing a counseling relationship. For instance, there is some evidence that LGBT counselors, some of whom specialize in counseling LGBT clients, encounter frequent and complicated multiple relationships due to the small size of these communities (Graham & Liddle, 2009). The participation of these counselors in social or political activities in the gay community may be the very reason the clients seek them out.

Some innovative approaches also are challenging the traditional boundaries that existed when counseling usually occurred in an office setting. For example, types of eco-therapy such as adventure-based counseling (Zur, 2007) and *walk and talk* therapy (McKinney, 2011) take place in outdoor settings that are less formal and less structured than in-the-office settings, which could easily lead to a relaxation of boundaries. As a result of all these changes, Jordan and Marshall (2010) have suggested that contemporary counseling practice requires a fluid and flexible frame that is more movable and dynamic than was once assumed.

ETHICAL STANDARDS FOR PROFESSIONAL AND NONPROFESSIONAL RELATIONSHIPS

Because the issues surrounding *dual relationships* or *multiple relationships* are so complex and sometimes confusing, and because dual relationships are not unethical per se, the *Code of Ethics* (ACA, 2014) does not use these terms. Instead, under §§A.5. and A.6 the code provides several standards that address noncounseling roles and relationships as well as professional relationships.

Section A.5. of the *Code of Ethics* (ACA, 2014) identifies the types of noncounseling roles and relationships that are prohibited. Three standards in this section relate to sexual and romantic relationships. Sexual and/or romantic relationships with current clients, their romantic partners, or their families are prohibited (§A.5.a.). Counselors must not engage in electronic sexual or romantic relationship with clients (§A.5.a.). Sexual and/or romantic relationships are also prohibited with former clients, their romantic partners, or their family members for at least 5 years after the last professional contact (§A.5.c.). It is not ethical for counselors to engage in counseling relationships with persons with whom the counselors have had a sexual or romantic relationship in the past (§A.5.b).

Some types of nonprofessional relationships that are not sexual or romantic in nature are also prohibited. Counselors must not engage in counseling relationships with friends or family members with whom they would not be able to remain objective (ACA, 2014, §A.5.d.). They must also avoid engaging in personal virtual relationships (such as becoming *friends* on a social media site) with current clients (§A.5.e.) One additional prohibition is found in §A.6.: "Counselors avoid entering into nonprofessional relationships with former clients, their romantic partners, or their family members when the interaction is potentially harmful to the client." This standard applies to both in-person and electronic interactions.

The *Code of Ethics* (ACA, 2014) does not prohibit *all* nonprofessional relationships. Several standards in Section A.6. provide guidance on managing and maintaining boundaries and professional relationships. These standards clarify that not all such relationships are harmful and that some nonprofessional relationships may be potentially beneficial to clients. The first of these standards addresses the question of whether a counselor may accept as a client an individual the counselor already knows in some capacity. Standard A.6.a. states:

> Counselors consider the risks and benefits of accepting as clients those with whom they have had a previous relationship. These potential clients may include individuals with whom the counselor has had a casual, distant, or past relationship. Examples include mutual or past membership in a professional association, organization, or community.

A second standard addresses extending counseling boundaries with current clients. Standard A.6.b. states:

> Counselors consider the risks and benefits of extending current counseling relationships beyond conventional parameters. Examples include attending a client's formal ceremony (e.g., a wedding/commitment ceremony or graduation), purchasing a service or product provided by a client (excepting unrestricted bartering), and visiting a client's ill family member in the hospital.

In both types of situations—when counselors accept as clients individuals with whom they have had a previous relationship and when counselors extend their boundaries with current clients—the counselors must take appropriate professional precautions such as informed consent, consultation, supervision, and documentation to ensure that judgment is not impaired and no harm or exploitation occurs.

Clearly, the *Code of Ethics* (ACA, 2014) provides extensive guidance with respect to dual relationships and role blending. As we have noted, dual relationships can range along a continuum from extremely harmful to potentially beneficial to clients, and most questions related to professional boundary setting defy easy answers. Thus, it is vital that counselors weigh the risks and benefits of entering into dual relationships, exploring both the potential for harm and the possible benefits to the client. Potential risks and benefits are discussed in the following section.

RISKS AND BENEFITS OF DUAL/MULTIPLE RELATIONSHIPS

The Potential for Harm

Some writers have taken a cautious and conservative stance toward potential dual relationships. St. Germaine (1993) has reminded counselors that the potential for harm is always present in a dual relationship due to the loss of objectivity that accompanies that relationship. Bograd (1993) noted that the power differential between counselor and client makes it impossible for the client to give truly equal consent to an extraprofessional relationship. It is possible that counselors may unintentionally or unconsciously exploit or harm clients who are in a vulnerable position in the relationship. Pope and Vasquez (2010) cautioned that counselors who engage in dual relationships may rationalize their behavior in an attempt to evade their professional responsibility to find acceptable alternatives to dual relationships. Unfortunately, little research has been conducted that explores the impact of violations of nonsexual boundaries on client improvement in counseling (Mathews & Gerrity, 2002).

In determining the risk of harm in a nonprofessional relationship, Kitchener and Harding (1990) suggested that counselors should consider three factors: incompatible expectations, divergent responsibilities, and the power differential. First, the greater the incompatibility of expectations in a dual role, the greater the risk of harm. Second, the greater the divergence of the responsibilities associated with dual roles, the greater the potential for divided loyalties and loss of objectivity. Third, the greater the power differential between the two parties involved in a dual relationship, the greater the potential for exploitation of the individual in the less powerful position. We illustrate each of these factors in the following example.

9-3 The Case of Cora

Cora is the director of a university counseling center, and Eileen is a secretary in the center's main office. Eileen has been an excellent employee for many years, and Cora has come to count on her to help keep the center functioning smoothly. One day Cora comes out of her office and notices that Eileen's eyes are red and puffy and that she seems sad. When Cora expresses her concern, Eileen begins to cry. She tells Cora that she is having some personal problems and adds, "Can I just step into your office for a minute while I pull myself together?" Cora agrees to this request, and they both go into Cora's office and close the door. Eileen begins to tell Cora about her personal problems. Cora listens as Eileen tells her story. After nearly an hour she suggests that Eileen might want to seek counseling. Eileen demurs, saying that she feels better now and thinks she can handle things.

Several weeks go by, during which time Eileen's work is not up to her usual high standards. She makes careless errors and forgets things. Cora calls her into her office twice to address this problem. Each time Cora spends about 30 minutes listening to Eileen's personal problems. At the end of each conversation, Eileen insists that she is "getting a grip on things." When the time comes for Cora to complete her quarterly evaluations of her counseling center staff, she gives Eileen a low rating on a number of the items on the form. When Eileen receives the evaluation, she is hurt and angry. She confronts Cora, saying, "How could you—of all people—do this to me! You know I'm a good employee but am just going through a rough time. You know what's going on in my life. I expected you to understand."

- What do you think caused Eileen's hurt and angry feelings?
- What could Cora have done differently, to avoid this situation?

Discussion: It is likely that Eileen's hurt and anger have resulted from the *incompatible expectations* she held for Cora. On the one hand, Cora has been a caring and sympathetic listener. Even though Cora did not intend to enter into a formal therapeutic relationship with Eileen, she has behaved as a counselor. Eileen has come to expect her to be understanding, accepting, and nonjudgmental while Eileen was working through her personal problems. Given this set of expectations, the evaluation feels like a punishment and a betrayal. On the other hand, she has been a secretary in the center for several years and is accustomed to receiving quarterly evaluations from her supervisor. As an employee, she realizes that her work has not been up to par, and in that role she would expect to receive a fair and accurate evaluation. Her expectations for Cora as a supervisor are incompatible with what she expects from Cora as a sympathetic listener and counselor.

Cora is faced with two *divergent responsibilities* in this situation. Because she has stepped into a counselor role, she needs to be accepting and supportive of Eileen, as well as patient, while Eileen works through her problems. As a supervisor, however, it is Cora's responsibility to evaluate her employees and to do so accurately. It is impossible for Cora to evaluate Eileen and be nonjudgmental at the same time.

Finally, there is a *power differential* in the relationship between Cora and Eileen. Cora is in a position of power because she is Eileen's supervisor who evaluates her work. Eileen is in a less powerful position as an employee and has made herself even more vulnerable by revealing her personal problems. It is Cora's professional responsibility to avoid misusing her power and to ensure that the more vulnerable individual in the relationship is not harmed. Certain characteristics of the therapeutic relationship place counselors in a position of power over clients. When clients come for counseling, they are in an emotionally vulnerable state. In the counseling relationship, the counselor learns much about the client's innermost thoughts and feelings, while the client learns much less about the counselor. This unfortunate problematic situation between Cora and Eileen could have been avoided if Cora had not appeared to assume the role of counselor for Eileen.

Counselors who are asked to counsel individuals with whom they have other relationships are put in a difficult situation, and it happens quite often. When persons with whom you have other relationships (relative, friend, employee, etc.) know that you are a counselor and ask you to counsel them, you need to be prepared to respond in both a caring and professionally appropriate manner. A good approach would be to acknowledge their distress and empathize with them, and then to state that you cannot function as their counselor because of your other relationship with them. Offer to help them locate a good counselor. If you then proceed to listen to their situation, it is wise to remind them periodically that you are listening as a relative, friend, or supervisor rather than as a counselor.

Of course, counselors never *intend* to exploit their clients. Cottone (2005) has urged counselors to think in terms of detriment or harm to clients, rather than in terms of potential exploitation. He notes that the word *exploitive* implies malicious intent, whereas the term *detrimental* focuses on outcome regardless of intent. His point is that counselors need to be held accountable for actions they take that cause harm to clients, regardless of intent.

Potential Benefits

Some scholars have focused on the potential for harm and have urged counselors to avoid entering into dual relationships, and others have argued persuasively that dual relationships can be helpful to clients if they are implemented thoughtfully and with care and integrity. Hedges (1993), presenting a psychoanalytic viewpoint, has argued that there is an essential dual relatedness in psychotherapy in that transference, countertransference, resistance, and interpretation all rest *de facto* on the existence of a dual relationship. Hedges urged counselors to remember that, viewed from this perspective, all beneficial aspects of counseling arise as a consequence of a dual relationship.

Greenspan (2002) described strict adherence to boundaries as a *distance model* that undermines the therapeutic relationship. In a similar vein, Tomm (1993) and Moleski and Kiselica (2005) have suggested that when counselors actively maintain interpersonal distance, they unnecessarily emphasize the power differential and promote an objectification of the therapeutic relationship. Tomm believed that dual relating invites greater authenticity and congruence from counselors and can actually improve their professional judgments because dual relationships make it more difficult for them to hide behind the protection of a professional mask.

Lazarus and Zur (2002) are perhaps the strongest voices among contemporary scholars who take the position that it can be extremely beneficial for counselors to engage in dual relationships with selected clients. They have noted that a power differential in a relationship is not necessarily associated with harm or exploitation. They pointed out that many hierarchical relationships (such as parent–child, teacher–student, and coach–athlete) flourish and contribute to an individual's growth and development. Zur (2007) has argued that rigid adherence to boundaries can actually weaken the therapeutic alliance, and that rigidity, aloofness, and distance are in direct conflict with therapist attributes known to be helpful to clients. Lazarus (2006) has asserted that counselors who selectively transcend certain boundaries actually may provide superior help. In summing up the arguments in favor of flexible boundaries, Moleski and Kiselica (2005) concluded that dual relationships are "not always destined for disaster" (p. 7) and can in fact complement and enhance the counseling relationship.

Unavoidable Dual Relationships

Boundary issues in rural practice have been given a considerable amount of attention. Yet, it is important to recognize that there are other *small worlds* that can exist in a bounded environment or even in an urban environment. Counselors who work in the military face many of the same challenges as rural practitioners (Johnson, Ralph, & Johnson, 2005), as do those who are members of the deaf, religious, corrections and law enforcement, or addictions treatment communities (Glosoff, Corey, & Herlihy, 2006; Lazarus, 2006; Lazarus & Zur, 2002; Schank & Skovholt, 2006). Traditional boundaries do not even exist in some crisis counseling situations, such as large-scale disasters. In the following subsections, we identify some of the boundary questions that can arise in rural, military, pastoral, addictions counseling, and in-home service settings.

RURAL COMMUNITIES   Counselors in isolated, rural communities or very small towns may find it impossible to avoid some overlap among roles (Forester-Miller & Moody, 2015) and may find it much more difficult to maintain clear boundaries than counselors who practice in urban areas (Herlihy & Corey, 2008). Campbell and Gordon (2003) have argued that multiple relationships are inevitable in rural communities due to the limited number of mental health practitioners, access difficulties, characteristics of rural communities, and characteristics of counselors in these communities. Imagine a situation in which the local banker, beautician, auto mechanic, grocery store checkout clerk, and owner of the dry cleaner are all clients of a particular counselor who practices in a small town located a 2-hour drive from a major city. Would you expect that counselor to make a 4-hour round trip to receive all the routine services these clients provide, in order to avoid any possible overlapping of roles?

On the positive side, the fact that nearly every potential client will be an acquaintance of a rural practitioner may present an advantage to the counselor. Forester-Miller and Moody (2015) have suggested that familiarity and trust are necessary ingredients to be an effective counselor in rural areas. On the negative side, rural and small-community practitioners face the additional problem of dealing with the effects that overlapping relationships have on their own families (Schank & Skovholt, 2006). Consider the following scenario.

9-4 The Case of Paula

For several weeks, Marianne has been a client in counseling with Paula. Marianne's husband and Paula's husband both serve on the advisory board for a charitable organization, and the two husbands begin to develop a friendship. They decide that they would like for their wives to meet and that the two couples should go out to dinner together.

- How should Paula respond when her husband suggests this social contact?
- Do you think Marianne should tell her husband that Paula is her counselor and that she would not be comfortable in a social situation with Paula?

Discussion: There is no easy answer to the question of whether Paula should agree to a dinner engagement with her client and her client's husband. Paula will need to consider several factors: Does Marianne's husband know that she is in counseling? Does he know that Paula is her counselor? Is the marriage a relevant issue in counseling? Does Marianne have a high need for privacy? Would Paula feel uncomfortable in the situation if she went to dinner with the client and the client's husband?

An excellent solution to the problem would be for Marianne to tell her husband that she is in counseling with Paula. For now, however, Paula's best approach probably would be to postpone the decision without revealing to her husband her specific reason for doing so. Then she can raise the issue with Marianne during their next session together. If Paula would not be uncomfortable with the two couples having dinner together, then she can be guided by her client's wishes on the matter.

Without question, counselors in rural and small-town practice face dual relationship and role-overlap dilemmas more frequently than do most other practitioners. Counselors in rural practice are aware that the usual *rules* are not always helpful and that they need to adapt creatively to situations as they occur (Corey et al., 2015).

COUNSELING IN THE MILITARY   Counselors who work in the military may find themselves engaged in multiple relationships with clients on a daily basis. These multiple roles are often unavoidable and can be uncomfortable for both the client and the counselor. Johnson (2015) has described the conflicting roles that can exist when a counselor is *embedded* or deployed with a military unit. In this situation, counselors who are also commissioned officers have a legally binding senior–subordinate or subordinate–senior relationship with everyone in the population. Johnson has noted that the military is a rank-conscious culture in which it is difficult to fulfill multiple roles, such as empathic counselor *and* superior officer, or mental health expert *and* direct subordinate. An additional complication is that counselors in embedded or isolated duty stations often cannot refer when role conflicts occur. The counselor may be the only available provider, expected to counsel all service members including personal friends, direct supervisors, and co-workers.

An additional type of role conflict can occur when a counselor is directed to perform a fitness-for-duty or security clearance evaluation on a service member who is also a client. The counseling relationship will almost certainly be jeopardized if the counselor determines that the service member is not fit for deployment or not a good risk for a security clearance.

Johnson (2015) has noted that military counselors are like rural counselors in that they find themselves in nonprofessional contact with many of their clients on a routine basis. "When deployed with a unit, the counselor will find him- or herself eating, sleeping, and carrying out all the mundane tasks of life while (literally!) shoulder-to-shoulder with clients" (p. 255). Thus, military counselors need to be very comfortable with frequent boundary crossings and role blending.

PASTORAL COUNSELING   Pastoral counselors have overlapping relationships with members of their congregations, and they face some unique boundary challenges (Haug, 1999; Lynch, 2002). Boundaries can be particularly difficult to maintain when pastors are expected to provide 24-hour availability, when they often work without direct supervision or in isolation from peers, and when the power differential is exacerbated by the fact that they are idealized by their parishioners (Crisp-Han, Gabbard, & Martinez, 2011; Garland & Argueta, 2012). When Crisp-Han et al. reviewed the cases of 70 pastors who had been referred for mental health treatment, they noted that clergy are expected to perform the multiple, overlapping roles of pastor, counselor, mediator, accountant, CEO, and friend.

Sometimes counselors are not themselves members of the clergy but they provide services to members of a congregation and may have their offices on church premises. These counselors may be particularly challenged to establish and maintain boundaries. They will need to spend considerable effort to ensure that the structure of their practice protects the confidentiality and well-being of their clients and to ensure that members of the church staff do the same (Lyons, 2015).

ADDICTIONS COUNSELING   With the recognition of addictions counseling as an accredited specialty in the 2009 Council for Accreditation of Counseling and Related Education Programs (CACREP) standards, addictions counselors may give increased attention to ethical issues in general and boundary issues in particular (Linton, 2012). At the present time, the education and credentialing of addictions counselors vary widely, and some counselors may not be receiving consistent training in how to manage boundary issues (Veach, 2015). There may also be disparities in how boundary questions are viewed by addictions counselors who are themselves in recovery and those who are not. Hollander, Bauer, Herlihy, and McCollum (2006) found that non-recovering board-certified substance abuse counselors were more likely than recovering counselors to find a variety of multiple relationship behaviors to be ethically problematic.

Some addictions counselors are members of the National Association of Alcoholism and Drug Counselors (NAADAC), which has its own code of ethics (NAADAC, 2011). The NAADAC standards regarding dual relationships differ from those found in the ACA *Code of Ethics*. The NAADAC code takes a more stringent stance, stating that "in rural settings and in small communities, dual relationships are evaluated and avoided as much as possible." Strict adherence to this standard may be particularly difficult for the many substance abuse counselors who are themselves in recovery. What if there is only one 12-step program in the area where a counselor practices? Would you expect that counselor to jeopardize recovery by avoiding the meetings for fear a client might be in attendance? Veach (2015) has noted that addictions counselors encounter some unique boundary issues, particularly related to mutual 12-step group involvement. In her view, addictions counselors would benefit from having written agency guidelines, continuing supervision, and ongoing ethics training.

IN-HOME SERVICES   An increasing number of counselors are providing in-home services to clients who are ill, are not mobile, or do not have the means to travel to an office. Counselors who provide in-home counseling for people with disabilities may find that clients may ask for assistance outside the scope of the counselor's role, such as bringing in the mail or looking for a needed document. In situations like these, it can be a struggle for a counselor to act in a compassionate and humane manner while maintaining appropriate boundaries with clients. Connell (2015) has recommended that guidelines for in-home service provision be clearly set in advance because a natural blurring of boundaries can occur in the home environment.

Boundary Crossings versus Boundary Violations

At this point in your reading of this chapter, you have a feel for some of the complexities of nonprofessional or dual relationships. You may be uncertain regarding your own stance toward some of the issues we have raised. If it is any comfort, many seasoned practitioners are also uncertain. Neukrug and Milliken (2011) surveyed a large sample of ACA members regarding a range of ethical behaviors. The respondents differed in their opinions about several dual relationship behaviors. Hugging a client was judged as ethical by 67% of counselors, whereas 33% thought this was unethical. Despite the existence of specific language in the *Code of Ethics* (ACA, 2014) that allows bartering in certain circumstances (§A.10.e.), 46.6% believed that bartering was unethical. There was nearly an even split in judgment regarding whether a counselor should sell to a client a product related to the counseling relationship (e.g., book, audiotape), with 47.6% deeming it ethical and 53.3% judging it to be unethical. Similar results were obtained on the question of whether it is ethical to become sexually involved with a client at least 5 years after the counseling relationship ended (42.9% ethical, 57.1% unethical). Obviously, experienced counselors disagree as to whether dual relationships with clients are ethical.

Compounding the confusion around nonsexual dual relationships with clients is the fact that counselors may engage in some behaviors with clients from time to time that have a *potential* for creating a dual relationship but are not in themselves dual relationships. These behaviors have been described as *boundary crossings* to distinguish them from ongoing dual relationships.

Several scholars (Gabbard, 1995; Gutheil & Gabbard, 1993; Smith & Fitzpatrick, 1995) have attempted to distinguish between boundary crossings and boundary violations. A boundary crossing is a departure from a commonly accepted practice that occurs to benefit a client. In a crossing, the boundary is shifted to meet the needs of a particular client at a particular moment. By contrast, a violation is a serious breach that causes harm.

An example of a boundary crossing was given earlier in this chapter in the case example involving a counselor (Elizabeth) who decided to attend her client's college graduation ceremony. This counselor's behavior did not constitute an ongoing dual relationship, and arguably it had the potential to enhance the therapeutic relationship. You should be aware, though, that not all counselors would agree with Elizabeth's decision. As Barnett, Wise, Johnson-Greene, and Bucky (2007) have noted, one counselor's intended crossing may be another counselor's perceived violation. We have adapted some of the items in a survey conducted by Borys and Pope (1989) into a questionnaire (see Figure 9-1). We encourage you to complete the questionnaire and then discuss your responses with fellow class members or with colleagues. Think about the rationale you would offer for your responses should a class member or colleague challenge your decisions.

One factor that the survey does not address, and that probably will influence your decisions regarding whether you are willing to engage in occasional boundary crossings in your practice, is that each client is unique. Some clients have generally clear interpersonal boundaries, and an occasional crossing during your relationship with them may have no further repercussions. Other clients present a real challenge to maintaining therapeutic boundaries. Clients with borderline personality traits or who have been diagnosed with the disorder, for example, may be adept manipulators who will try to draw their counselors into a *special* relationship (Gutheil, 1989; Simon, 1989). You will

For each of the following items, place an X in the box that best represents your opinion.					
How ethical is it for a counselor to:	Never Ethical	Rarely Ethical	Sometimes Ethical	Usually Ethical	Always Ethical
1. Barter with a client for goods or services?					
2. Invite a client to a personal party or social event?					
3. Provide counseling to a friend who is in crisis?					
4. Accept a gift from a client if the gift is worth less than $10?					
5. Accept a gift from a client if the gift is worth more than $50?					
6. Accept a client's invitation to a special event?					
7. Go out for coffee with a client after a counseling session?					
8. Become friends with a client after termination of the counseling relationship?					
9. Give a cell number to a client?					
10. Share personal experiences as a member of a self-help group when a client is in attendance?					
11. Occasionally hire a client to baby-sit?					

FIGURE 9-1   Boundary issues survey of opinion

Source: Pearson Education, Inc., Hoboken, NJ.

want to be very firm and consistent in maintaining the therapeutic frame with clients who have poor boundaries in other areas of their lives. Sonne (2005) has urged counselors to exercise extreme care in maintaining boundaries with clients who suffer from any psychological disorder (such as narcissistic personality disorder, delusional disorders, or dissociative disorders) that could impair their ability to understand or negotiate boundaries. Sonne also suggested that the depth of the client's social network outside the counseling relationship should be considered.

In general, from an ethical standpoint, occasional boundary crossings probably can be justified when there is benefit to the client and very little risk of harm. Counselors must take care, however, not to let these crossings become routine. As Herlihy and Corey (2015b) have noted, "Interpersonal boundaries are not static and may be redefined over time as counselors and clients work closely together" (p. 11). These authors cautioned, however, that even seemingly innocent behaviors can, if they become part of a pattern of blurring the professional boundaries, lead to dual relationship entanglements with a real potential for harm. As small, well-intended relaxations of boundaries become more frequent in a therapeutic relationship or in a counselor's practice in general, it has been suggested (Gutheil & Gabbard, 1993; Pope, Sonne, & Holroyd, 1993; Sonne, 1994) that the *slippery slope phenomenon* may come into effect—that is, the gradual erosion of the boundaries of the professional relationship can take counselors down an insidious path toward serious ethical violations. As we discuss next, reasoning about boundary crossings from a legal perspective leads to similar conclusions.

The Legal Perspective on Boundary Crossings

Counselors who are accused of wrongdoing for any reason may have their peers investigate complaints against them, or even may have to defend themselves in an ethics hearing or criminal court (see Chapter 8 on responding to charges of wrongdoing generally). Once you have been accused of having done something wrong, it is too late to undo any small indiscretions from your past. Often in the area of boundary issues, counselors will think, "Well, maybe just this one time it will be all right to ask my client to baby-sit for my daughter" or "This client is particularly mature, so I'm sure we can have lunch together after our session today."

. Unfortunately, these small and seemingly insignificant boundary crossings can be the very evidence that causes an ethics panel, judge, or jury to find against you when you have been accused of having done something wrong. When people judging you consider the small boundary crossings that you have committed, they may come to the conclusion that you are incapable of understanding your profession's prohibition against engaging in multiple relationships that are harmful to clients. Whether you have been falsely accused or even have been accused of something you wish you had not done, it is best if you have very few boundary crossings in your past.

Specific Boundary Issues

In this section, we explore some specific issues that are associated with nonsexual dual relationships and boundaries. These issues include bartering, social and business relationships with clients, accepting gifts from clients, the limits of counselor self-disclosure, and touching or hugging a client.

BARTERING   Bartering with a client for goods or services is not prohibited by the ethical standards of the counseling profession, although it is discouraged as a routine practice. There is no consensus among counseling practitioners as to whether they consider bartering to be ethical. As noted, counselors were divided in their opinion on this issue when surveyed by Neukrug and Milliken (2011). Counselors who enter into bartering arrangements with clients usually are motivated by a desire to provide services to clients whose financial resources are limited and who cannot afford counseling without some sort of alternative arrangement for payment. This intention is admirable, and you may choose to enter into bartering agreements with clients from time to time in your professional career. However, you should be aware of the problems that are inherent in this practice.

One form of bartering involves the exchange of services. For example, a client might be a self-employed interior decorator who is having difficulty paying for continued counseling because his business has been slack lately. His counselor's office suite needs new paint and wallpaper, so they agree to exchange counseling services for redecorating services. It is possible that an arrangement like this could work smoothly, but there are a number of potential pitfalls. For one thing, most services that clients can offer do not have monetary value equal to an hour of counseling (Kitchener & Harding, 1990). Unless clients can devote considerable time each week to holding up their end of the agreement, they are likely to fall further and further behind in the amount owed. They can become trapped in a kind of indentured servitude and come to feel resentful.

In addition to the question of quantity of bartered services, the issue of quality of services provided can be problematic. To take the example of the decorator, what if the counselor thinks the client is doing a sloppy and inferior job of painting and wallpapering the office suite? What if the redecorating work is excellent, but the decorator is not satisfied with the counseling services?

Feelings of resentment that build up in the counselor or in the client are bound to have a negative effect on the counseling relationship.

Another form of bartering involves the exchange of goods for counseling services. For example, a client who is an artist might wish to pay for counseling services by giving the counselor an oil painting. The issues of quality that arise in bartering of services apply to this type of bartering as well. In addition, the issue of how many hours of counseling are equivalent to the value of the painting must be addressed. What criteria should be used to make such a determination?

In the *Code of Ethics* (ACA, 2014), a blanket prohibition against bartering is not made. Instead, the code offers guidelines for counselors to help them determine whether a potential bartering arrangement might be acceptable. The code states that counselors may participate in bartering only if (a) it does not result in exploitation or harm, (b) the client requests it, and (c) such arrangements are an accepted practice among professionals in the community (§A.10.e.).

Diversity Considerations in Bartering. If you establish your practice in a rural community, you may find that bartering is common among local physicians and other professionals. In such a setting, it would be acceptable for you to engage in bartering if your clients initiate the request and if you believe you and the client can work out fair and equitable terms of agreement. We believe it would also be wise for you to consider other alternatives to bartering with clients who cannot pay your full fee. Some of these alternatives, which are further explored in Chapter 13 in a discussion of private practice, might include using a sliding scale fee or providing a set amount of pro bono services.

SOCIAL RELATIONSHIPS WITH CLIENTS Individuals who choose to become professional counselors do not cease to be members of their communities, nor are they expected to forgo their social lives in order to avoid all nonprofessional contacts with clients. As we noted, some social contact with clients is difficult to avoid for counselors who share *small worlds* with their clients. Even when extraprofessional contacts with clients can be avoided with relative ease, however, counselors can find it tempting to develop social relationships and even friendships with their clients.

As Glosoff (2015) has noted, individuals ordinarily look to work as one setting where they can gratify certain psychological and social needs. For many people, their work environment is a place to meet others with whom they can socialize and form friendships. Choosing to become a counselor can limit these opportunities. Almost all counselors will have some clients who are likable and who would make nice friends, but a friendship and a therapeutic relationship cannot exist simultaneously. The therapeutic relationship is like a friendship in that it involves emotional intimacy, but it is different in a significant way. In a therapeutic relationship, the intimacy is one way. Friendships are coequal relationships in which personal disclosures, support, challenge, and other interpersonal dynamics are reciprocal. For a counselor to seek a friendship with a client would be to look for reciprocity in a relationship that is not, by its nature, reciprocal (Hill, 1990).

When counselors blend the roles of friend and counselor, they create a conflict of interest that compromises the objectivity needed for sound professional judgment (Pope & Vasquez, 2010). As professionals, counselors place the interests of their clients foremost, but the dual relationship creates a second set of interests: those of the counselor. For example, a counselor may be reluctant to confront a client who is also a friend, out of fear of jeopardizing the friendship.

Short of an ongoing friendship, there are many possibilities for more limited types of social contact with clients, and a counselor's stance toward these contacts may depend on several factors. The counselor's theoretical orientation might make a difference. Borys (1988) suggested that a psychodynamically oriented counselor might be quite strict about out-of-the-office social contacts with clients, because psychodynamic theory stresses the importance of maintaining the frame of counseling and attention to transference and countertransference issues. In contrast, relationship-oriented counselors or those who espouse systems theory might be more willing to interact with clients outside the therapeutic setting. Another factor may be the nature of the social function. It may be more acceptable to accept a client's invitation to a special occasion, for instance, than to invite a client to a personal party.

Although there has been much debate in the literature, our opinion is that counselors have an ethical obligation to keep their professional and personal or social lives as separate as they reasonably can. Counselors should not get their social needs or personal needs for friendship met through interactions with their clients. ACA members surveyed by Neukrug and Milliken (2011) agreed with this opinion: 95.4% believed it was unethical to engage in a counseling relationship with a friend.

Counselors and clients do, however, meet each other in social contexts without prior planning on either person's part. Therefore, it is essential that counselors discuss with their clients how they might be affected by encountering the counselor outside the office and how these chance meetings should be handled.

A closely related issue that has also been debated in the literature is the question of post-termination friendships with clients. Counselors are often aware of clients' attributes that would make them desirable friends. Clients, for their part, may hope to continue the intimacy they felt and the caring attention they received during the therapeutic relationship. The *Code of Ethics* (ACA, 2014) offers no guidance regarding post-termination friendships with clients, and there is no consensus among helping professionals regarding the advisability of such relationships.

Several risks in postcounseling friendships have been identified. Vasquez (1991) noted that many clients consider reentering counseling with their counselors, and that if a friendship develops this option is closed. Other writers have argued that therapeutic gains are jeopardized when a friendship follows a therapeutic relationship, because a post-termination friendship may disrupt a healthy resolution of transference issues (Gelso & Carter, 1985; Kitchener, 1992). The power differential that existed during the therapeutic relationship is not automatically negated when the counseling is terminated. As Salisbury and Kinnier (1996) have noted, "Unreciprocated knowledge of a former client's most sensitive weaknesses and most intimate secrets can render a client particularly vulnerable" (p. 495) in a friendship with a former counselor.

Despite these risks, there is some evidence that most counselors find the development of friendships with former clients to be ethically acceptable. Fully 70% of counselors surveyed by Salisbury and Kinnier (1996) believed that a postcounseling friendship with a client could be acceptable. Approximately one-third of them actually had engaged in this behavior. The fact that a substantial number of counselors condone or engage in a practice does not necessarily indicate that the practice is appropriate, however. You should avoid a tendency to reflexively accept *prevalence* arguments as a justification for dual relationship behaviors (Pope & Vasquez, 2011).

You should consider a number of factors before pursuing a friendship with a former client. These include the time that has passed since termination, transference and countertransference issues, the length and nature of the counseling, the client's issues and diagnosis, the circumstances of the termination, the client's freedom of choice, whether any exploitation might have occurred in the professional relationship, the client's ego strength and mental health, the possibility of reactivation of counseling, and whether any harm to the client's welfare can be foreseen (Akamatsu, 1988; Kitchener, 1992; Salisbury & Kinnier, 1996). It would be difficult to demonstrate that none of these factors were at play if a counselor were challenged by a licensing board or in court. As a general rule, we believe that counselors would be wise to avoid developing friendships with both current and former clients.

Diversity Considerations in Social Relationships. Cautions against counseling friends or close acquaintances may present difficulties for counselors of color (Herlihy & Watson, 2003). In the African American community, boundaries are permeable, and helpers typically engage in multiple, outside-the-office roles (Parham & Caldwell, 2015). Having a shared primary language with a counselor can be pivotal in the choices of some clients. For instance, there may be only one Spanish-speaking Latino counselor in an elementary school, and that counselor may know and socialize with the families of the Latino students. More generally in Latino cultures, boundaries between social and professional relationships are more flexible than they are in Euro-American cultures. Machuca (2015) noted that in his practice he often received invitations to family events of his clients because "in Latino culture, once you get to know the family secrets you become part of the family" (p. 103).

BUSINESS OR FINANCIAL RELATIONSHIPS WITH CLIENTS Business and financial relationships with clients have received little focused attention in the literature, perhaps because the issues are much the same as those raised by personal and social dual relationships. For instance, counselors who work in rural settings may be more likely to have business-related encounters with clients. Schank and Skovholt (2006) described a situation in which a counselor took his car to a shop to be serviced. He thought the bill was rather high for the services performed but was reluctant to question the charges when he realized that one of his clients had done the work. Of course, such unintended encounters can happen in urban and suburban practice. A counselor might have an electrical or plumbing problem at home and have a client who is employed by the electric company or plumbing contractor show up to do the work. These occurrences, although awkward, might be resolved through an open discussion during the next counseling session.

Anderson and Kitchener (1996) asked counselors to describe critical incidents involving post-counseling relationships with clients. Business or financial relationships were second only to personal or friendship relationships in the frequency with which they were related. Their respondents identified two types of situations that could apply equally to relationships with current clients. The first involved the counselor paying for a client's expertise or assistance. Examples might include hiring a client or former client to perform clerical work or to cater a party at the counselor's home. The second involved a counselor and client joining areas of expertise to produce income, such as going into business together. It appears that counselors regard going into business with a current client as unethical; only 9% of respondents in a survey conducted by Gibson and Pope (1993) rated this behavior as ethical. When the question was one of going into business with a former client, however, the percentage who rated it as ethical rose to 46%.

Other types of dual relating that involve financial considerations occur when a counselor patronizes a client's place of business, or when a counselor sells goods (such as a relaxation tape or a book) to a client. In the former situation, the client could feel pressured to give the counselor a discount or some kind of special services. In the second instance, the client might feel coerced to buy the counselor's product. As was noted, the counselors who responded to the Neukrug and Milliken (2011) survey were divided on the issue of selling a product to a client.

As is true of other types of dual relationships, counselors have differing viewpoints on business relationships with clients, and the same counselor might have differing views in different circumstances. For instance, Sonne (2005) has noted that the degree to which the business relationship is distinct from the counseling relationship could influence a counselor's decision making. Employing a client to work in one's home might be perceived quite differently from employing a client to work in a business in which the counselor has a financial interest but which is located in another town.

Although the practice of entering into business or financial relationships with clients needs further study, our own recommendation is that counselors should avoid entering into these relationships with current or former clients. Whenever a counselor is making a monetary profit from a secondary relationship with a client, that counselor's self-interest is clearly involved.

ACCEPTING GIFTS FROM CLIENTS   When clients offer gifts to their counselors—even small, token gifts—it can make counselors feel uncomfortable. They may be torn between wanting to decline the gift in order to keep the relationship within proper boundaries, yet wanting to accept the gift so that the client will not feel hurt or rejected. The best way to minimize such conflicts is to have a general policy that you do not accept gifts from clients and to include a statement to that effect in your informed consent document. This procedure will not completely solve all potential problems, however. Clients may vary in how they interpret the idea of a gift, or they may forget or choose to ignore that you have a policy. For your part, you probably will not want to interpret your own policy too rigidly. It is difficult to imagine an elementary school counselor refusing to accept a child client's offering of a handmade Valentine, for instance.

The *Code of Ethics* (ACA, 2014) has a standard on accepting gifts from clients. Standard A.10.f. states, "Counselors understand the challenges of accepting gifts from clients and recognize that in some cultures, small gifts are a token of respect and showing gratitude. When determining whether or not to accept a gift from clients, counselors take into account the therapeutic relationship, the monetary value of the gift, a client's motivation for giving the gift, and the counselor's motivation for wanting or declining the gift."

It is certainly possible that a client may offer you a gift at some point. It is wise for you to think through how you plan to handle this event and use the criteria suggested in the *Code of Ethics* (ACA, 2014) to determine whether to accept or refuse a gift.

The monetary value of the gift is one obvious consideration. When you responded to the Boundary Issues Survey in Figure 9-1, did you answer the fourth item differently from how you answered the fifth? If so, a gift's monetary value played some part in your decision-making process. Apparently, many mental health professionals would reason similarly. Over 88% of the counselors who responded to the Neukrug and Milliken (2011) survey thought it was unethical to accept a gift from a client when the value of the gift is more than $25.

It may be useful to consider the client's motivation for offering the gift. A client might offer a small gift as a way of expressing appreciation. This seems different from a gift that the counselor perceives to be a form of manipulation or an attempt to buy loyalty or friendship. Sometimes a client's need to offer gifts can become a useful therapeutic tool. For example, we know of a client who came to each of her first three sessions bringing a small home-baked item, such as a brownie or a loaf of banana bread, saying that she had just finished baking and thought the counselor might like to sample the result. She was an excellent baker, and the counselor accepted the first two offerings with pleasure. When the client came to the third session with a treat, the counselor used this as an entrée to exploring the client's motivations. Through this exploration, the client became aware of her need to *make herself welcome* everywhere she went because she believed that she could not possibly be valued just for herself. This became a very productive session.

It may be equally useful to consider the counselor's motivation for wanting to accept or decline the gift. For example, assume that your client has an extra ticket to a championship sports event and asks you to go along. You are a great sports fan and have been unable to get a ticket to the game. If you find yourself tempted to accept the ticket, keep in mind that you have a fiduciary relationship with your client (see Chapter 4) and that you must not benefit from the relationship. It would also be useful to think about the implicit messages you would be sending to the client, who may think it is now acceptable to call you at home or invite you to future social functions. What if you are not really a sports fan but find yourself thinking that going to the game would be more enjoyable than sitting home alone? In this case, consider your obligation to avoid using clients to meet your own social needs. When you are determining whether to accept a gift from a client, your reasoning must be based on consideration for the client's welfare.

Related to the issue of motivation is the nature or stage of the therapeutic relationship. A client might bring a small gift to a mutually agreed-on termination session as a way of saying "Thank you" to the counselor. Accepting such a gift might not be problematic. By contrast, accepting a gift during the early stages of counseling before a stable therapeutic relationship has been established could set in motion a blurring of boundaries that could become problematic down the road.

Diversity Considerations in Accepting Gifts.   Cultural factors must be considered because gift giving has different meanings in different cultures. For instance, giving gifts is a common practice in many Asian communities as a means of showing gratitude and respect (Bemak & Chung, 2015). Counselors responding from a European American perspective might politely refuse an offered gift without realizing the insult and cultural meaning of their refusal for the client.

Counselors need to take care that their own discomfort at being presented with a gift does not overshadow their sensitivity to what the gift means to the client. Although there is a lack of research examining how accepting or refusing a gift may affect treatment of culturally diverse clients (Hoop, DiPasquale, Hernandez, & Roberts, 2008), we agree with Zur (2007), who urges that gifts should always be evaluated in the context within which they are offered.

SELF-DISCLOSURE   The extent to which counselors engage in self-disclosure depends in large measure on their theoretical orientation and on their skill and comfort in using this technique. Psychodynamically oriented counselors, whose tradition includes Freud's belief that the counselor should remain anonymous, are not likely to engage in much self-disclosure. Counselors who view the therapeutic relationship as more co-equal, such as feminist counselors and existential counselors, place more value on self-disclosure. It appears that most counselors are comfortable with self-disclosure; nearly 87% of the ACA members surveyed by Neukrug and Milliken (2011) deemed self-disclosing to a client to be an ethical behavior.

As a technique, counselor self-disclosure can be a powerful intervention that can strengthen the therapeutic alliance. It is important that you learn the skill of self-disclosure and be able to articulate your rationale for using it in the counseling process. It is equally important that you understand self-disclosure as an ethical issue.

Counselor self-disclosures that are ethically appropriate are done for the client's benefit within the context of the therapeutic process (Smith & Fitzpatrick, 1995). Self-disclosures are considered unethical when they are used to meet the counselor's own needs for intimacy or understanding. It can be difficult for counselors to objectively gauge their motives when their own needs are involved. Pope and Keith-Spiegel (2008) have suggested that counselors who are considering self-disclosing to a client ask themselves two questions: Does this particular disclosure represent a significant departure from my usual practice? If so, why the change?

Counselors in independent private practice may be particularly vulnerable to using self-disclosure as a way to counter feelings of isolation (Glosoff, 2015). Self-disclosure, used improperly or excessively, can lead to a role reversal in which the client becomes the emotional caretaker of the counselor. Topics that are not considered appropriate for counselors to disclose are details of current stressors, personal fantasies or dreams, and their social or financial circumstances (Borys, 1988; Gutheil & Gabbard, 1993; Simon, 1991).

Self-disclosure has become an area of increasing ethical concern as more research has demonstrated that when treatment boundaries become blurred, they usually erode gradually over time. Simon (1991) found that inappropriate counselor self-disclosure, more than any other kind of boundary violation, is likely to precede counselor–client sexual intimacy.

Guidelines for distinguishing appropriate from inappropriate self-disclosure may seem fairly clear as you read about them, but judging what may benefit the client can be very difficult in practice (Smith & Fitzpatrick, 1995). Self-disclosure is a complex issue. You will need to think about whether to self-disclose, and how and when, in working with each of your clients. When you choose to self-disclose, your primary reason must be that you believe the disclosure will benefit the client. It is also important that you take cultural factors into consideration in your decision making.

Diversity Considerations in Self-Disclosure.   In some Asian cultures, self-disclosing to strangers (counselors) is considered a violation of familial and cultural values. Some Asian clients believe that personal matters are best discussed with intimate acquaintances or friends (Bemak & Chung, 2015). Counselor self-disclosure might facilitate the establishment of the close personal relationship that these clients need in order to feel comfortable in sharing their concerns.

Studies have shown mixed results in determining the effects of counselor self-disclosure in counseling African American clients. However, one study provided some empirical support for greater counselor self-disclosure when working with African American clients, regardless of whether the counselor is African American or Caucasian (Cashwell, Shcherbakova, & Cashwell, 2003).

PHYSICAL CONTACT WITH CLIENTS   The boundary question of whether counselors should touch or hug their clients is not easy to resolve. For certain clients, at certain times, a reassuring touch or a gentle hug can be facilitative. Yet, counselors who engage in these behaviors risk having their gestures misinterpreted as sexual advances or as violations of the client's personal space.

Smith and Fitzpatrick (1995) have noted that the issue of therapeutic touch has an interesting history. When talk therapy first began in the Freudian era, physical contact with clients was prohibited because of its presumed negative effect on transference and countertransference. Later, in the 1960s and 1970s, touching became an accepted practice within the human potential movement. One study (Holroyd & Brodsky, 1977) found that 30% of humanistic counselors, as compared to only 6% of psychodynamic counselors, believed that touching could be beneficial to clients. A decade later Pope, Tabachnick, and Keith-Spiegel (1987b) investigated the beliefs of mental health professionals regarding three types of physical contact. Their respondents believed that the most unethical type was kissing a client (with 85% stating that it was never or only rarely ethical), followed by hugging (with 44% disapproval), and finally by handshakes, which were deemed ethical by 94%. The beliefs of today's counselors seem to be quite similar to those reported by Pope et al. (1987b). Of the counselors who responded to the survey conducted by Neukrug and Milliken (2011), 87.5% judged it as unethical to kiss a client as a friendly gesture, and 33% rated hugging a client as unethical. Most (nearly 84%) thought it was acceptable to console a client through touch, such as placing a hand on the client's shoulder.

It appears to us that concerns about the consequences of physical contact with clients are driven more by legal than ethical concerns. Gutheil and Gabbard (1993) related a story of a therapist who was caught by surprise when a client suddenly hugged her on her way out at the end of the counseling session. The therapist felt somewhat uncomfortable about the incident, but left it undocumented and did not engage in further self-reflection. Some weeks later she received a letter from the client's attorney. Probably because such stories are frightening, counselors usually are now trained to be cautious about making physical contact. They are often advised to hug a client only when the client requests it or, at the very least, when the counselor first secures the client's permission. Certainly, professional liability insurance carriers have become concerned that clients might bring suit against their counselors for even well-meaning instances of physical contact. Some applications for malpractice insurance directly ask the question "Do you ever touch a client beyond a routine handshake?" Counselors who answer "yes" must attach an explanation and run the risk of being deemed a risky applicant and having their application for insurance rejected.

Diversity Considerations in Touching Clients.   When you begin to practice as a counselor, you will need to determine your own stance toward physical contact with your clients. Many factors might be considered, such as the age of the client. Routinely hugging elementary school children is probably more acceptable than giving frequent hugs to adult clients. However, counselors who hug clients of the opposite sex run the risk of a sexual impropriety complaint if people report having seen them hugging their young clients. With teens and adults, you will want to assess the likelihood that the client may sexualize or misinterpret your touch. The client's diagnosis and history may also be relevant. For instance, hugging or touching a client who has been sexually abused generally is contraindicated.

Cultures vary widely with respect to the acceptability of touch. For example, people from some European countries routinely kiss each other on both cheeks as a way of greeting, and these clients might think you are cold and distant if you avoid physical contact with them.

The bottom line regarding the issue of therapeutic touch is that it is a matter of professional judgment. There are no definitive guidelines to be found in codes of ethics. In making your own determination about whether to touch a client, you will want to be clear about your motivations for doing so. Zur and Nordmarken (2010) have cautioned against avoiding touch simply out of fear of litigation. If you do use therapeutic touch in your practice, you must be able to demonstrate that touching has served the client's needs and not your own.

Ethical Decision Making

Cultural factors are often important variables in ethical decision making regarding therapeutic boundaries. In this chapter, we have noted that bartering, gift giving, self-disclosure, and therapeutic touch are viewed differently in various cultures. Multiculturally sensitive counselors know that for many minority clients the idea of seeking traditional counseling is foreign, and that these clients are often more comfortable turning to social support systems within their own community. They may be more likely to put their trust in healers who are a part of their culture, such as shamans, folk healers, sangomas, acupuncturists, or curanderos(as). Counselors who work with ethnic minority clients need to be flexible and willing to take on different roles, such as advocate, change agent, advisor, and facilitator of indigenous support systems if they are to effectively assist these clients. They need to balance their understanding of and adherence to their codes of ethics with their understanding of and sensitivity to the values and worldviews of minority clients.

Also, the counselor's own cultural background may contribute to his or her perspective on therapeutic boundaries: In some cultures it is considered polite and respectful to adhere strictly to boundaries of personal space and roles, whereas such behavior is considered rude and rejecting in other cultures. The counselor's religious affiliation is another potentially influencing factor; some religions support and encourage extended relationships among congregants and, as was noted, some clients prefer to work with a counselor who shares their religious affiliation. The counselor's gender may make a difference, as female therapists tend to be more conservative than males in their ethical decision making around boundary issues (Sonne, 2005).

Several writers (Herlihy & Corey, 2015b; Pope & Keith-Spiegel, 2008; Younggren, 2002) have offered decision-making models to assist counselors who are faced with potential dual or multiple relationships. These decision-making models have much in common. They suggest, as a first step, that the counselor should determine whether the potential dual relationship is necessary and whether it is avoidable. Before embarking on or declining to participate in a dual relationship, counselors must judge whether the benefits outweigh the risks or whether the reverse is true. They need to consider the factors that create a potential for harm, including differences in the client's expectations of the counselor in the two roles, the counselor's divergent responsibilities in the two roles, and the power differential in their relationship. Pope and Keith-Spiegel (2008) suggested that counselors imagine what might be the best possible outcome and the worst possible outcome of crossing a boundary or engaging in a dual relationship.

If the counselor believes that the risk of harm to the client is greater than the potential benefits, the counselor should decline to enter the dual relationship and refer if needed. An explanation should be given so the client understands the rationale for not proceeding with the problematic part of the dual relationship.

If the counselor believes that the potential benefits to the client are great and the risk of harm is small, or if the potential dual relationship cannot be avoided, then the dual relationship can be initiated and the following safeguards put in place:

- Secure the client's informed consent to proceed with the dual relationship. The counselor and client should discuss the potential problems and benefits and reach an understanding regarding how they want to handle these problems if they arise. Younggren (2002) has recommended that the client sign an informed consent document, although he also cautions that clients can never give truly informed consent to something that poses a severe risk to them or that violates the prevailing standard of care. For example, even if a client were to sign a consent to enter into a sexual relationship with a counselor, the consent document would not assist the counselor, in either the ethical or legal arena, in a defense of the relationship.
- Seek consultation. Because one of the most intransigent problems in managing dual relationships is the counselor's loss of objectivity, it is important for the counselor to seek ongoing consultation for help in monitoring the relationship and the risk for harm.
- Engage in ongoing discussion with the client. As we discussed in Chapter 4, informed consent is not a one-time matter. The counselor can involve the client in a mutual, ongoing monitoring of the relationship and can discuss any potential problems that they might foresee and attempt to resolve any problems that do arise.
- Document and self-monitor. Although we have heard of instances in which counselors were advised to keep any mention of a dual relationship out of their case notes, we think this is unwise. If a dual relationship ever became an issue in a complaint proceeding before a licensure board or in a court of law, behavior that appears as if the counselor is trying to hide something will not be seen favorably by the parties adjudicating the complaint. It is much better for counselors to be able to demonstrate that they were aware of dualities, that they considered the risks and benefits for the client, and that they took steps to protect the client.
- Obtain supervision. If the risks in a dual relationship seem high, if the relationship is particularly complex, or if the counselor is concerned about the ability to assess the situation objectively, seeking consultation may not be sufficient. In these instances, counselors are wise to engage a fellow mental health professional in ongoing supervision of their work throughout the dual relationship.

In concluding this section, we want to emphasize that boundary issues and dual relationships pose some complex and difficult questions to which there are no easy answers. Each client is unique, each counselor is unique, and each situation is unique and is constantly evolving (Pope & Keith-Spiegel, 2008). Counselors will struggle with boundary setting throughout their professional careers. In the absence of certainties, counselors must think carefully about the consequences of their decisions, have a clear rationale for any boundary crossings, be open to discussing the issues with their clients who are equally affected by any decisions, and consult with colleagues.

SEXUAL DUAL RELATIONSHIPS

The prohibition against sexual intimacies with help seekers is one of the oldest ethical mandates in the health care professions, predating even the Hippocratic Oath. Nonetheless, ethics codes of mental health professions made no mention of this behavior until research began to demonstrate its prevalence and the harm done to clients (Pope & Vasquez, 2010). Although the problem of sexual relationships between counselors and their clients has existed for many decades, it remained unacknowledged in the professional literature through the 1970s. Counselor–client sexual intimacy was the *problem with no name* (Davidson, 1977) because helping professionals were reluctant to confront the issue. The reluctance was so pervasive that Pope (1988) concluded that helping professionals had engaged in *massive denial* (p. 222) of the problem. It was through the pioneering work of a few researchers, such as Gartrell, Herman, Olarte, Feldstein, and Localio (1987) in psychiatry, and Pope (1986, 1988) in psychology and counseling, that helping professionals were made aware that such violations were occurring, and in startling numbers.

Although the limitations of self-report data make it difficult to gauge how commonly counselor–client sexual intimacies actually occur, various studies indicate that approximately 7% of male counselors and 1.6% of female counselors reported sexual relationships with their current or former clients (Akamatsu, 1988; Borys, 1988; Holroyd & Brodsky, 1977; Pope & Bouhoutsos, 1986; Pope et al., 1993; Pope, Tabachnick, & Keith-Spiegel, 1987a; Salisbury & Kinnier, 1996; Thoreson, Shaughnessy, & Frazier, 1995; Thoreson, Shaughnessy, Heppner, & Cook, 1993). It is safe to state that these estimates are probably conservative. When Pope (1986) surveyed patients rather than counselors, as many as 20% of them reported having had sexual contact with their counselors. One hopeful note among these statistics was provided by Anderson and Kitchener (1996). They reviewed studies that had been conducted since 1977 and concluded that the frequency of sexual contact between counselors and current clients is decreasing.

The Offending Mental Health Professional

Mental health professionals who engage in sex with their clients have not been well studied, but the male counselor–female client dyad clearly dominates. It appears that most offenders are repeat offenders. Holroyd and Brodsky (1977) found that 80% of psychologists who reported sexual contact also reported that they had been sexually intimate with more than one client. Pope and Bouhoutsos (1986) described several typical scenarios and rationalizations used by offending counselors:

- In a reversal of roles, the wants and needs of the counselor become the focus of the treatment.
- The counselor claims that sexual intimacy with the client is a valid treatment for sexual or other problems.
- The counselor fails to treat the emotional closeness that develops in counseling with professional attention and respect, claiming that the dual relationship *just got out of hand*.
- The counselor exploits the client's desire for nonerotic physical contact (e.g., a need to be held).

- The counselor fails to acknowledge that the therapeutic relationship continues between sessions and outside the office.
- The counselor creates and exploits an extreme dependence on the part of the client.
- The counselor uses drugs as part of the seduction.
- The counselor uses threat or intimidation.

Although offending counselors do not fit a single profile, the portrait that emerges from the scant literature is one of a professionally isolated male counselor who is experiencing distress or crisis in his personal life (Simon, 1987; Smith & Fitzpatrick, 1995). He shares many characteristics with other impaired professionals, including professional burnout and a pattern of attempting to meet his own personal needs though his clients. Not all offenders will fit this description, however. Golden (1990) and Schoener and Gonsiorek (1988) described a wide range of professionals who become sexually involved with their clients. At one end of the range are those who are naïve and uninformed about ethical standards. At the other extreme are professionals who suffer from sociopathic, narcissistic, or borderline personality disorders and the attendant inability to appreciate the impact of their behavior on others.

It is natural to feel compassion for those naïve offenders who feel remorse for their behavior, but it is important to remember that ignorance is never a valid excuse, nor is blaming the client for being *seductive*. It is always the responsibility of the helping professional to ensure that sexual intimacies do not occur.

Harm to Clients

It has been amply demonstrated that sexual relationships with counselors are extremely detrimental and sometimes even devastating to clients (Moleski & Kiselica, 2005). The harm is deep, lasting, and occasionally permanent. At least 90% of clients who have been sexually involved with a counselor are damaged by the relationship, according to their subsequent counselors (Bouhoutsos, Holroyd, Lerman, Forer, & Greenberg, 1983).

Pope (1988) suggested that clients are likely to suffer from *therapist–patient sex syndrome*, with reactions similar to those of victims of rape, spouse battering, incest, and posttraumatic stress disorder. He described a range of associated symptoms. Clients often experience a deep *ambivalence* toward the offending counselor. They are trapped between extreme dependency on and fear of separation from the counselor and a longing to escape from his power and influence. Like many victims of incest and battering, clients vacillate between wanting to flee from the abuser and wanting to cling to and protect him.

Clients often suffer from feelings of *guilt*, believing that they are to blame for the relationship. They may think that they did something to invite the counselor's behavior. Although they may be deeply angry at the counselor, their rage remains suppressed due to their feelings of ambivalence, their sense of guilt, and the counselor's continuing power. This guilt and rage, when turned inward, leads to an *increased risk of suicide*.

Because the offending counselor insists that the client keep their sexual relationship secret, clients feel *isolated* and cut off from the normal world of human experience. Not surprisingly, many victims manifest a profound *confusion* about their sexuality and about appropriate roles and interpersonal boundaries. When roles are reversed and the client becomes the counselor's emotional caretaker, the client does not know where safe and appropriate boundaries lie.

Counseling involves a high degree of trust, and violation of that trust can have lifelong consequences. Clients' *impaired ability to trust* often prevents them from seeking help from other counselors and may impair their ability to form other close relationships.

In addition, many clients display symptoms similar to those experienced by victims of post-traumatic stress disorder. These symptoms include difficulties with attention and concentration, the reexperiencing of overwhelming emotional reactions when they become involved with a sexual partner, and nightmares and flashbacks.

The harm to clients caused by sexual intimacies with their counselors is now well recognized. The ethical standards of all mental health providers' professional organizations, including the *Code of Ethics* (ACA, 2014), prohibit sexual relationships with clients. There are no credible voices in the profession arguing that sexual relationships with clients should be allowed.

The *Code of Ethics* (ACA, 2014) prohibits counselors from having sexual or romantic interactions or relationships with current clients, their romantic partners, or their family members (§A.5.a.). Romantic or sexual relationships with *former* clients (and their romantic partners or family members) are prohibited for at least 5 years following the last professional contact (§A.5.c.). These prohibitions extend to electronic or on-line interactions.

Typically, codes of ethics for mental health professionals prohibit sexual relationships with former clients for a minimum of 2 years. The *Code of Ethics* (ACA, 2014) specifies a minimum of 5 years. However, it is doubtful a court of law would do the same. Ethical standards reach for the ideal and legal standards define the minimally acceptable behavior society will tolerate from a professional counselor. A board of ethics might find a counselor in violation of the ethical code for having had a harmful romantic relationship with a former client's sister-in-law 4 years after the counseling relationship ended, but it is doubtful that a judge would find that the counselor had committed malpractice for the same behavior. Interestingly, lawyers are still debating whether it is acceptable for attorneys to have sexual relationships with their clients (Buckner & Sall, 2008).

Legal Consequences for Offending Counselors

The harm caused to clients by sexual dual relationships is universally recognized and can have severe legal as well as ethical consequences. As Kaplan et al. (2009) have noted, the fact that sexual relationships with clients are the only exclusion contained in most professional liability insurance policies is an indication of just how harmful these relationships are. Most professional liability policies will provide an attorney to defend a counselor against an accusation of sexual improprieties with a client, but if the counselor is found guilty the insurance company will not pay for damages and will also expect to be reimbursed by the counselor for any legal fees incurred.

CIVIL LAWSUITS Because the impropriety of sexual intimacies with clients is universally recognized, clients who sue counselors for having been sexually involved with them have an excellent chance of winning their lawsuits, if the allegations are true. These lawsuits are civil, which means that one citizen has to sue another for action to be taken against a person who does something wrong.

Clients who were sexually victimized by their counselors and who are ashamed, uneducated, or lacking in self-confidence might choose not to file formal complaints or file civil lawsuits against their perpetrators. When that happens, counselors who violate our ethical standards and violate the rights of their clients are never held accountable. In fact, many believe that the lack of accountability encourages offending counselors to sexually violate other clients. When some counselors observe that others are getting away with having sexual relationships with clients, they may be inclined to do so as well.

Counselors who engage in sexual relationships with their clients may be sued on a number of grounds. Jorgenson (1995) has listed the following causes of action that victimized clients might allege in their lawsuits: malpractice, negligent infliction of emotional distress, battery, intentional infliction of emotional distress, fraudulent misrepresentation, breach of contract, breach of warranty, and spouse loss of consortium (love, companionship, and services). As discussed in Chapter 8, one of the elements a client must prove in a malpractice suit is that a counselor behaved in a manner that breached the standard of care expected or required of counselors.

To encourage clients who are victimized by their mental health professionals to sue, some state legislatures have now passed laws that automatically charge negligence for certain categories of mental health professionals to have sexual relationships with their clients (e.g., Cal. Civ. Code sec. 43.93, West, 1993; Ill. Ann. State. Ch. 70, secs. 801–802, Smith-Hurd, 1992; Minn. Stat. Ann. Sec. 148A, West, 1993; Texas Senate Bill 210, engrossed May 22, 1993; Wis. Stat. Ann. Sec. 895. 70(2), West, 1992). Those who sue must still prove they were harmed as a result of the sexual relationships, but harm can be emotional and financial as well as physical.

Some of these statutes have unusual and forceful components. For example, the Wisconsin statute (Wis. Stat. Ann. sec. 895.70(5), West, 1992) forbids accused mental health professionals from settling their cases without public disclosure. In other words, mental health professionals (or their professional liability insurance companies) who are sued by their clients for having engaged in sex with them cannot agree to an out-of-court settlement that is never reported to the public.

CRIMINALIZATION OF SEX WITH CLIENTS   U.S. society has become so convinced that counselor–client sexual relationships are wrong that some states have now passed statutes that make it a crime for mental health professionals to engage in sex with their clients. Losing a civil lawsuit for having sex with a client can be distressing for counselors, but going to jail for the same thing is a much more dramatic result.

Between 1983 and 1992, 13 states enacted legislation that criminalized sexual relationships between mental health professionals and their clients. Kane (1995) reported that the following states had passed such statutes at the time the review was conducted: California, Colorado, Connecticut, Florida, Georgia, Iowa, Maine, Michigan, Minnesota, New Mexico, North Dakota, South Dakota, and Wisconsin. Each state statute varies in language, but the following professionals have been included in some of the laws: psychotherapists, counselors, marriage and family counselors, clergy, social workers, psychiatrists, and psychologists.

Some of these criminal statutes take unusually tough positions with mental health professionals. For example, the Colorado statute (Colo. Rev. Stat. secs. 12-43-708 [b & c], 1988) permits prosecutors to file injunctions that will put a mental health professional out of business even before the individual has been found guilty, if it can be proven that the professional presents a risk to clients by continuing to practice.

Roberts-Henry (1995), in giving a history of the passage of the Colorado statute, reported that the law was passed in 1988 over a great deal of objection from mental health professionals. Proponents had to compromise and exclude clergy from the bill before it could be passed. Roberts-Henry summarized the law as stating, in essence, that "any psychotherapist who perpetrates sexual penetration or intrusion on a client commits a felony" (p. 340). The law does not allow accused mental health professionals to use consent of the client as a defense.

Although Kane (1995) concluded that the laws criminalizing sexual relationships between mental health professionals and their clients have had a deterrent effect, it appears that they do not totally solve the problem. In Colorado, 8 years after the law had been passed, Roberts-Henry (1995) reported that victims were still treated poorly during the investigation process, and that many prosecutors were unwilling to proceed with cases because they did not understand abuse generally.

Postcounseling Sexual Relationships

Ethical standards of the various mental health professions are divided on the issue of whether it is *ever* ethical for professionals to have sexual relationships with former clients. Social workers are forbidden from ever having a sexual relationship with an individual after a professional relationship has been established (National Association of Social Workers, 1997). However, counselors (American Counseling Association [ACA], 2014) and psychologists (American Psychological Association [APA], 2002) have determined that after a set period of time following termination, sexual relationships may be permissible with former clients. ACA has set 5 years after termination as an acceptable period before a sexual relationship with a former client might be acceptable, and APA has set 2 years. The APA and ACA codes should not be interpreted as blanket permission to engage in post-termination sexual relationships. Counselors who consider entering into romantic or sexual relationships with former clients, even after several years have passed, still have an ethical responsibility to ensure that no harm is done. Not only do all the risk factors for post-termination friendships apply to post-termination sexual relationships, but because of the severity of potential harm, it is even more important to put safeguards in place. The ACA code states that before counselors engage in sexual or romantic interactions or relationships with clients, their romantic partners, or client family members, even after 5 years, counselors must "demonstrate forethought and document (in written form) whether the interaction or relationship can be viewed as exploitive in any way and/or whether there is still potential to harm the former client" (ACA, 2014, §A.5.c.).

Just as professional associations disagree about whether sexual relationships are acceptable after a waiting period, scholars are also divided on the issue. Although Friedman and Boumil (1995) have struggled with the arguments for and against the idea, Simon (1998) has recommended never having a sexual relationship with a former client. Apparently there is no consensus among counseling practitioners, either. In earlier studies that surveyed ACA members, 63.5% of male counselors believed sexual contact with former clients was unethical (Thoreson et al., 1993), and 45% of female counselors believed that this behavior was harmful and constituted misconduct (Thoreson et al., 1995). More recently, 57.1% of the ACA members surveyed by Neukrug and Milliken (2011) deemed it unethical to become sexually involved with a former client even after 5 years have passed since the professional relationship ended. As Herlihy and Corey (2015b) noted, whether sexual relationships with former clients are ever acceptable probably will be a subject of continuing debate for some time to come. In our opinion, sexual relationships with former clients are not appropriate under any circumstances. The risk of harm is far too high; according to one study, 80% of clients who had begun sexual relationships with mental health professionals after counseling ended were found to have been harmed (Pope & Vetter, 1991).

Sexual Attraction to Clients

Although the *Code of Ethics* (ACA, 2014) explicitly forbids sexual relationships with clients, it does not address more subtle ways that sexuality can become part of a counseling relationship. It is not at all unlikely that, at some point in your professional career, you will find that you are sexually attracted to a client. When this happens, it is natural to react with feelings of guilt or self-doubt. Sexual attraction to a client is not aberrant or unusual, however. Research indicates that 70% to 95% of mental health professionals have experienced attraction to at least one client (Bernsen, Tabachnick, & Pope, 1994; Pope, Keith-Spiegel, & Tabachnick, 1986). It is important to remember that *feeling* a sexual attraction to a client is not unethical. What is unethical is to *act* on that attraction.

When you feel a sexual attraction to a client, you have an ethical responsibility to acknowledge and deal with it appropriately. Some useful strategies include consulting with colleagues, carefully considering issues of client welfare, seeking supervision, and self-monitoring to ascertain whether you are feeling particularly needy or vulnerable. If your own needs and issues seem to be causing you to act in ways that are uncharacteristic of you, you will be wise to seek counseling for yourself to resolve those issues.

Sometimes, it will be the client who develops and expresses an attraction to the counselor. The counselor must handle such client disclosures with tact and work to ensure that the client understands that a dating or sexual relationship is not possible.

Counseling Clients Who Have Been Abused by Previous Counselors

In your practice, you should be prepared to counsel clients who report that they have been sexually exploited by a previous counselor. Welfel (2013), after reviewing prevalence studies, concluded that between 22% and 65% of mental health professionals have encountered such clients.

Counselors who provide services to individuals who have been sexually abused by mental health professionals are put in awkward positions. Most counselors feel obligated to take some action to bring attention to the wrongdoing of a fellow mental health professional. These counselors are afraid that if they do not take some action, more clients may be abused.

We caution you, though, if you are ever put in this situation, to be respectful of your client's wishes in the matter. Clients must be willing not only to allege that a mental health professional has abused them, but they must also testify at formal hearings, will probably be cross-examined in a hostile and accusing manner, and must deal with the emotional strain of the process.

Your role, as a counselor, is to assist your client in meeting the counseling goals that the two of you establish together. If the client decides to proceed against the perpetrator in some manner, you can be very helpful in assisting the client to deal with a very difficult situation.

It most likely will do no good for you to file an ethics complaint against another mental health professional if the victim refuses to participate. You would be violating your client's privacy if you disclosed the client's identity without his or her permission. In addition, most licensure boards, criminal prosecutors, or certification groups will not proceed in a case without a witness who was a victim.

Your role as a counselor is not to push your client toward accusing the mental health professional. You must guard against *intrusive advocacy* in your zeal to ensure that the wrong is redressed (Pope, Sonne, & Holroyd, 1993; Wohlberg, 1999). Rather, your job is to provide appropriate counseling services, to avoid imposing your own values, and to assist clients in meeting their personal goals.

It is important to be aware that clients who have been sexually exploited by a previous mental health professional tend to be especially vulnerable to revictimization when their counseling needs are not recognized and addressed. Counseling these clients requires sensitivity and expertise. If you undertake a counseling relationship with such a client, you should read the literature on the topic, get qualified supervision, and be prepared to have strong emotional reactions to the client's disclosures (Welfel, 2013).

To avoid becoming inappropriately involved if a client is trying to decide whether to accuse a former mental health professional of inappropriate sexual activity, you might consider referring the client to an advocacy group. Many such groups are available to assist clients in making the initial decisions and then support them once the process begins. Biele and Barnhill (1995) and Schoener (1989) have listed such advocacy groups in their publications.

Summary and Key Points

Therapeutic boundaries and dual relationships are among the most controversial of all ethical issues. A boundary can be conceptualized as a frame around the therapeutic relationship that defines the participants' roles in that relationship. Counselors enter into dual relationships whenever they take on two or more roles, simultaneously or sequentially, with their clients.

Codes of ethics discourage nonprofessional or dual relationships, except for those relationships that potentially could benefit a client. The only type of dual relationship that is absolutely forbidden is sexual intimacy with a current client, the client's romantic partner, or the client's family members; it is forbidden for at least 5 years with a former client, the client's romantic partner, or the client's family members. Counselors must consider a number of factors when they are contemplating entering into a nonsexual dual relationship, in order to determine the potential for harm to the client.

Most counselors occasionally engage in boundary crossings, which are departures from usual practice that are made to benefit a particular client at a particular time. For instance, a counselor would not routinely meet all clients at out-of-the-office functions but might choose to attend a client's graduation or other special occasion. From a legal perspective, counselors who develop a pattern of frequent boundary crossings are at risk.

Several specific boundary issues were discussed in this chapter. These included bartering, social and business relationships with clients, post-termination friendships, accepting gifts from clients, counselor self-disclosure, and physical contact with clients. Throughout the discussion of these issues, multicultural considerations were highlighted. Guidelines for ethical decision making completed the first section of this chapter. Key points with respect to nonsexual dual relationships are as follows:

- Dual relationship issues are complex and can be difficult to resolve.
- The *Code of Ethics* (ACA, 2014) provides extensive guidance on the types of roles and relationships that must be avoided due to potential harm to clients.
- The ACA *Code of Ethics* also acknowledges that some nonprofessional relationships can potentially be beneficial.
- With the exception of sexual dual relationships, the thinking of the counseling profession has evolved toward more flexibility in determining boundaries.
- Counselors who are considering entering into dual relationships should carefully consider the risks and potential benefits.
- Dual relationships may be unavoidable in some settings, such as rural communities, the military, pastoral counseling, addictions treatment, and in-home counseling.
- A number of counselor behaviors do not by themselves constitute dual relationships, but they have the potential to create dual relationships. These behaviors can be termed *boundary crossings*.
- From both an ethical and a legal perspective, counselors are well advised to avoid developing a pattern of frequent boundary crossings with clients.
- Bartering with a client for goods or services is fraught with potential problems and should generally be avoided.
- Although counselors may be tempted to develop social relationships or even friendships with current or former clients, counselors should not get their own social needs met through their interactions with clients.
- Business or financial relationships with clients should be avoided.
- Although counselors should be cautious about accepting gifts from their clients, there may be instances when accepting a gift is appropriate. Counselors should consider a number of factors when deciding whether to accept or refuse a gift from a client.
- Self-disclosure on the part of counselors is appropriate only when it is done for the benefit of the client.

- The issue of physical contact with clients is difficult to resolve, and many factors must be considered. Today's legal climate tends to discourage counselors from the practice of therapeutic touch.
- Decisions about dual relationships require consideration of cultural variables.

The second section of this chapter focused on sexual dual relationships. Sexual intimacies with clients are probably the most harmful of all types of dual relationships. Pope (1988) has described the harm to clients as a *therapist–patient sex syndrome* that is similar to posttraumatic stress disorder. The following are key points about sexual dual relationships:

- Although estimates of the prevalence of sexual relationships between counselors and their clients seem to vary, it is clear that male counselors are more frequent offenders than are female counselors.
- Legal consequences for offending counselors can be severe. They can be prosecuted in civil court and, in some states, in criminal court as well.
- Although there is universal agreement among mental health professionals that sexual intimacies with current clients are unethical, the question of post-termination sexual relationships is the subject of some debate.
- Counselors who provide services to clients who have been sexually abused by their former counselors face some difficult decisions. They must keep in mind that their role is to assist these clients in meeting goals that are chosen by the clients themselves.

Technology in Counseling

FOCUS QUESTIONS

1. What do you think about counselors providing counseling services to clients through Skype, FaceTime, or some similar type of technology?

2. What are some of the problems clients are bringing to counseling sessions that are directly related to their use of social media or other forms of technology?

3. What steps do counselors need to take to ensure that counseling records that are kept electronically are secure and that client privacy is maintained?

Technological advances in society, especially the Internet, have had a significant impact on the profession of counseling (Hertlein, Blumer, & Mihaloliakos, 2014; Hohenshil, 2000; Kraus, Stricker, & Speyer, 2010; Ziv, 2014). The counseling profession has established a solid presence on the Internet. This offers you abundant opportunities to access virtual libraries for researching the latest information on client problems and effective counseling techniques, as well as to collaborate and consult with other professionals around the world. The National Board for Certified Counselors (NBCC), Council for Accreditation of Counseling and Related Educational Programs (CACREP), and many of the divisions of the American Counseling Association (ACA) have home pages on the World Wide Web, so you can communicate quickly and directly with professional groups that are working to strengthen counseling as a profession. Videoconferencing on the Internet enables you and counselors everywhere to obtain further preparation and even supervision without having to travel great distances. You can subscribe to mailing lists that allow you to share experiences, ask questions, and exchange information and ideas.

Technology is being used today in mental health in ways that were never imagined. Counselors are providing real-time two-way video counseling sessions to clients who are on the other side of the world, clients are presenting with issues related specifically to their social media activities (such as Internet addiction, cyberbullying, and leaving current relationships for ones they found online), and clients with dementia are being tracked with GPS devices (Landau & Werner, 2012). Legal and ethical challenges abound as counselors utilize technology in creative ways in their practices each day.

The various forms of technology that have been developed and are still being developed all have the same basic purpose—to facilitate the transfer of information and enhance the ability to communicate with others. In this transfer and communication process, situations are inevitably created in which sensitive or confidential information might be accessed by inappropriate persons (Welfel & Heinlen, 2001). Every form of technology discussed in this section creates records or recordings of information that, if not treated carefully, could lead to the privacy of clients being compromised.

Certainly, counselors want to maximize their effectiveness by utilizing as many forms of technology as possible (Owen & Weikel, 1999; Sampson & Bloom, 2001). It is also imperative that counselors educate themselves regarding the subtle ways in which their clients' privacy might be affected by the use of technology (Cottone & Tarvydas, 2007). In the ACA *Code of Ethics* (ACA, 2014), an entire new section was added to address technology issues (Section H: Distance Counseling, Technology, and Social Media). Many other standards related to technology issues are found throughout the 2014 *Code*.

The introduction to Section H of the *Code of Ethics* (ACA, 2014), which is devoted to ethical issues related to technology, states that counselors, whether or not they want to, must adapt: "Counselors actively attempt to understand the evolving nature of the profession with regard to distance counseling, technology, and social media and how such resources may be used to better serve their clients. Counselors strive to become knowledgeable about these resources." Standard H.1.a. continues, "Counselors who engage in the use of distance counseling, technology, and/or social media develop knowledge and skills regarding related technical, ethical and legal considerations (e.g., special certifications, additional course work)." So the *Code of Ethics* requires that counselors *actively attempt to understand* the new issues related to technology in counseling, and further, if they engage in the use of technology, they *develop knowledge and skills*.

In the following discussion, we identify a number of areas in which technology is having an impact on the counseling process, and we provide guidelines for ensuring that the privacy of clients is protected. In addition, counselors' personal and professional use of technology is reviewed in relation to ethical and legal obligations.

CLIENT USE OF TECHNOLOGY

Clients use technology in a number of ways. In this section we discuss clients' use of the Internet, the various types of social media, entertainment technology, and technology being used by clients without counselor supervision for self-monitoring and self-improvement.

Social Media

The *Code of Ethics* (ACA, 2014, Glossary) defines *social media* as "technology-based forms of communication of ideas, beliefs, personal histories, etc. (e.g., social networking sites, blogs)." Social media have been categorized by a number of experts, without consensus regarding what is included in social media (Boundless, 2014; Grahl, 2014; White, 2014). According to Grahl (2014), there are six types of social media: (1) social networks, (2) bookmarking sites, (3) social news, (4) media sharing, (5) microblogging, and (6) blog comments and forums. These categories are not discrete, and sometimes they overlap in content and function.

Social networks allow you to connect with other people and usually include a profile and various ways to interact with other users. The most popular social networks are Facebook and LinkedIn.

Bookmarking sites offer services that allow you to save, organize, and manage links to websites and resources on the Internet. The most popular bookmarking sites are Delicious and StumbleUpon.

Social news includes services people use to post various news items or links to articles. Users then vote, and the items receiving the most votes are displayed the most prominently. The most popular social news sites are Digg and Reddit.

Media sharing allows users to upload and share media, including photos and videos. The most popular media sharing sites are YouTube and Flickr.

Microblogging is characterized by short updates that are sent to those who subscribe. The most popular microblogging site is Twitter.

Forums allow members to post messages that are available to other members. Blog comments are similar, except they are attached to blogs and include discussion of the blog. There are too many popular blogs and forums to identify the most popular ones.

Despite the lack of consensus about what is included in social media, everyone agrees that it is very popular and that people of all ages are involved in social media in a variety of formats. As social media began to be developed, some counselors were unsure how they were supposed to respond to their clients' posts. Counselors questioned whether they had an obligation to view what their clients were posting, or perhaps they were not supposed to pry into their clients' social media posts. The *Code of Ethics* (ACA, 2014) takes the position that "Counselors respect the privacy of their clients' presence on social media unless given consent to view such information" (§H.6.c.). As a result of this standard, it generally is not appropriate for counselors to view posts made by their clients. If clients give their permission for their counselors to view their social media posts, however, counselors may look at them.

Many of the problems that clients now bring to counseling are directly related to the relatively new phenomenon of social media. A few of these problems include social media addiction, the fear of missing out (FoMO), social isolation, cyberbullying, and sexting.

Social media addiction occurs when the personal and professional lives of individuals are negatively affected because they cannot stay away from social media sites (Didelot, Hollingsworth, & Buckenmeyer, 2012; Griffiths, 2013). In Germany, Masur, Reinecke, Ziegele, and Quiring (2014) have developed an instrument that measures addiction behavior specifically related to social network site addiction. Hormes, Kearns, and Timko (2014) concluded in a study of undergraduate students that the use of social networking sites is potentially addictive.

People over age 30 may not have heard of FoMO, but youngsters have (White, 2013). FoMO, the fear of missing out, occurs when people are anxious because they believe everyone else is having more fun than they are (Wortham, 2011). A reaction to FoMO is people wanting to stay continually connected to those they know and monitoring what others are doing. Researchers at universities in England (University of Essex, 2013) and the United States have developed a test that allows individuals to determine the extent to which FoMO negatively affects their ability to enjoy what they are doing rather than worrying about what others are up to (Przybylski, Murayama, DeHaan, & Gladwell, 2013). The test can be accessed at www.ratemyfomo.com. Results of studies indicate that those in the age range from 18 to 30 have the highest rates of FoMO.

Social networking sites such as Facebook have been identified as causing social isolation (Parigi & Henson, 2014). However, Grieve, Indian, Witteveen, and Tolan (2013), after completing two studies on the topic, concluded that Facebook use could lead to developing and maintaining relationships, leading to positive psychological outcomes.

Cyberbullying has been identified as a problem that clients bring frequently to counseling sessions (Kowalski, Giumetti, Schroeder, & Lattanner, 2014). McGuckin et al. (2013) have offered suggestions for strategies to help victims cope. Helping youngsters understand that adults need to know when they are being bullied is important in helping victims.

One example of a new area of concern for adolescent problems related to technology is the practice of *sexting*, which involves sending sexual messages or images through text messaging. Despite media attention to sexting (Wolfe, Marcum, Higgins, & Ricketts, 2014), Mitchell, Finkelhor, Jones, and Wolak (2012), in a national study of 1,560 Internet users from ages 10 to 17, found that only about 1% of youth had appeared in or created nude or nearly nude pictures or videos. They concluded that such activity is not widespread among youth, but that there is a need to provide youngsters with information about legal consequences of sexting and advice about what to do if they receive a sexting image. Lunceford (2011) observed that teenagers seem to be unaware of the potential for embarrassment and humiliation when sexts are shared with unintended viewers or even posted on the Internet, despite the highly publicized suicides that have occurred. Although sending pornographic images of minors via the Internet is illegal, lawyers and judges are struggling to determine how to deal with a crime when the victim and perpetrator are the same person. From an ethical perspective, we believe counselors can play a vital role in teaching adolescents to consider the potential for harm involved in activities such as sexting.

Other Technology Used by Clients

In addition to social media, clients use many other forms of technology that affect their relationships with counselors. One developing issue in health care is consumer demand that health care providers communicate with them via texts and e-mail rather than through the traditional telephone method. Cepelewicz (2014) and Tigertext (2014) have cautioned that texts must be secure to protect the health records of patients when health care providers text or e-mail patients. This issue is discussed further later in this chapter.

DISTANCE COUNSELING

The traditional process for counseling involves a counselor and one or more clients meeting face-to-face in a professional office. Since the Internet has come into existence, many counselors have been offering distance counseling. Counseling via teleconference or videoconference has been made possible by downloadable free software programs such as Skype (Reeves, 2011). In addition, counseling is being provided through telephone calls; synchronous online interaction, better known as *chat* (Dowling & Richwood, 2013); and e-mail message exchanges.

10-1 The Case of Abby

Abby specializes in counseling individuals who have experienced the death of a twin brother or sister after reaching adulthood. Abby has written many popular magazine articles about her work and has appeared on national television talk shows. She lives in a small town. She has been getting many requests from all over the United States to counsel clients who have lost an adult twin brother or sister. Abby has never counseled anyone in a distance format, but she has decided to offer distance counseling services for a fee.

- What are some of the ethical and legal considerations Abby should address before beginning to offer distance counseling services?

Discussion: First, Abby should be licensed for independent private counseling practice in the state in which she lives. In addition, she should investigate state laws and regulations in the states in which potential clients whom she wishes to serve are located, to determine if she is eligible to offer residents counseling services without being licensed in that state.

It will be important for Abby to determine whether her present professional liability insurance policy covers distance counseling activities. If not, she should obtain a policy that does.

Abby should also review all of the distance counseling ethical standards in the 2014 ACA *Code of Ethics* to ensure that she is practicing in an ethical manner. These standards are discussed in detail later in this chapter.

Finally, Abby should consider taking continuing education workshops or courses that focus specifically on distance counseling to increase her awareness of the issues and to gain skills in that area. To increase her credibility in a new area of practice, she should consider earning the Distance Credentialed Counselor (DCC) from the Center for Credentialing and Education (www.cce-global.org), an affiliate of the NBCC (www.nbcc.org). For best practice, it would be wise for Abby to seek clinical supervision from an experienced distance counselor when she begins accepting distance counseling clients.

The *Code of Ethics* (ACA, 2014) includes a number of standards related to providing distance counseling to clients. To begin, counselors must ensure that clients understand they have a choice and do not have to engage in distance counseling if they prefer not to (§H.2.a.). This standard also requires that counselors allow clients to determine whether they are willing to use social media or technology within the counseling process.

When distance counseling, social media, or other types of technology are used in counseling, the informed consent obtained from clients must go beyond typical requirements and must include, according to the *Code of Ethics* (ACA, 2014), the following elements: "distance counseling credentials, physical location of practice, and contact information; risks and benefits of engaging in the use of distance counseling, technology, and/or social media; possibility of technology failure and alternate methods of service delivery; anticipated response time; emergency procedures to follow when the counselor is not available; time zone differences; cultural and/or language differences that may affect delivery of services; possible denial of insurance benefits; and social media policy" (§H.2.a.).

The *Code of Ethics* (ACA, 2014) also contains a provision that assumes that electronic records are less secure than paper records. Standard H.2.b. states, "Counselors acknowledge the limitations of maintaining the confidentiality of electronic records and transmissions. They inform clients that individuals might have authorized or unauthorized access to such records or transmissions (e.g., colleagues, supervisors, employees, information technologists)."

Despite a number of concerns regarding distance counseling that are discussed later in this chapter, the practice has become an accepted approach to counseling in the United States. The NBCC (2014), through the Center for Credentialing and Education, offers the Distance Credentialed Counselor (DCC) for counselors who wish to demonstrate their skills in this particular area of counseling (see www.cce-global.org).

Distance counseling presents several advantages, as opposed to face-to-face counseling in the same physical space: (a) increased accessibility of services for those who would otherwise find it difficult to receive services, such as low-income clients; the frail elderly; individuals who are chronically ill or severely physically disabled; rural or isolated individuals; and clients who suffer from agoraphobia, social phobia, extreme introversion, or serious physical illnesses; (b) perceived anonymity may decrease client anxiety, thus encouraging people to ask for help and increasing the extent to which clients are willing to share intimate issues; (c) greater freedom in scheduling; (d) a reduction in lost work time and travel time for clients; and (e) facilitation of improved preparation by allowing better choice of written words over spoken ones (Bouchard et al., 2000; Haberstroh, Dufey, Evans, Gee, & Trepal, 2007; Hamburger & Ben-Artzi, 2000; Heinlen, Welfel, Richmond, & Rak, 2003; Lee, 2010; National Alliance on Mental Illness, 2014; Reeves, 2011; Rummell & Joyce, 2010; Sampson, Kolodinsky, & Greeno, 1997; Schultze, 2006; Shaw & Shaw, 2006; Wilson, Jencius, & Duncan, 1997).

Several researchers have studied clients' reactions and attitudes toward distance counseling. Some scholars have noted positive responses by clients to online counseling services (Cook & Doyle, 2002; Day & Schneider, 2002). Manhal-Baugus (2001) reported that 90% of clients surveyed believed that their online therapists had been helpful to them. Reese, Conoley, and Brossart (2006) found that 58% of 186 survey respondents who had received both distance counseling and physically present face-to-face counseling preferred distance counseling. Further, 96% of their respondents said they would seek distance counseling again, whereas only 63.1% said they would seek face-to-face counseling in the future. The results of this study suggest that some clients prefer distance counseling to face-to-face counseling. Other researchers have found that, although clients were satisfied with distance counseling, they preferred face-to-face counseling (Leibert, Archer, Munson, & York, 2006; Rochlen, Beretvas, & Zack, 2004).

In addition to client satisfaction research, outcome research is beginning to demonstrate the clinical effectiveness of distance counseling (e.g., Barak, Hen, Boniel-Nissim, & Shapira, 2008; Griffiths & Christensen, 2006; Labardee, 2009; Richards & Vigano, 2013). Results of studies suggest that distance counseling is as effective as in-person counseling.

In the *Code of Ethics* (ACA, 2014), §H.4. focuses on *distance counseling relationships* that are delivered through the use of *technology applications in the provision of counseling services*. These applications are listed as including, but not being limited to, "computer hardware and/or software, telephones and applications, social media and Internet-based applications and other audio and/or video communication, or data storage devices or media." This new section of the 2014 *Code* gives counselors guidelines related to boundaries, the ability of clients to use technology, the effectiveness of technology services rendered, access to services, and communication differences when using technology.

Standard H.4.b. of the *Code of Ethics* (ACA, 2014) requires counselors to "discuss and establish professional boundaries with clients regarding the appropriate use and/or application of technology and the limitations of its use within the counseling relationship (e.g., lack of confidentiality, times when not appropriate to use)." It would appear that the boundaries to which this standard is referring might include setting limits on when clients may or may not communicate by e-mail messages or texts, for example.

Counselors are required to *make reasonable efforts* to ensure that clients with whom they use technology understand how to use it and have the capacity to use it (ACA, 2014, *Code of Ethics*, §H.4.c.). This standard requires that counselors "follow up with clients to correct possible misconceptions, discover appropriate use, and assess subsequent steps." Counselors must also provide information regarding gaining access to technology applications when they are being utilized in the counseling relationships.

When counselors or clients determine that distance counseling services are not effective, §H.4.d. of the *Code of Ethics* (ACA, 2014) requires that "counselors consider delivering services face-to-face. If the counselor is not able to provide face-to-face services (e.g., lives in another state), the counselor assists the client in identifying appropriate services."

Standard H.4.f. (ACA, 2014) requires that counselors warn clients about possible misunderstandings when distance counseling is being utilized. This standard states, "Counselors consider the differences between face-to-face and electronic communication (nonverbal and verbal cues) and how these may affect the counseling process. Counselors educate clients on how to prevent and address potential misunderstandings arising from the lack of visual cues and voice intonations when communicating electronically."

The new distance counseling provisions of the 2014 ACA *Code of Ethics* provide ethical guidelines for practice. However, there are many issues in distance counseling that are unresolved and are being discussed in the literature.

A major legal question is whether distance counseling is permitted in states in which counselors must be licensed to practice. A further question arises as to where distance counseling takes place: in the location of the counselor, the location of the client, or both locations. Which laws govern the counseling process related to issues such as reporting abuse is another question. Because distance counseling is still new, these questions will not be resolved until lawsuits are filed for cases in which distance counseling was used. Counselors who expand their practice to distance counseling will need to determine whether their professional liability insurance provides coverage for distance counseling (Reeves, 2011).

Counselors who consider offering counseling services through the Internet should ensure that they are not violating state laws (in the state of the counselor or of the client) that require counselors to be licensed. Standard H.1.b. (ACA, 2014) provides this guidance regarding following legal requirements when using technology in counseling: "Counselors who engage in the use of distance counseling, technology, and social media within their counseling practice understand that they may be subject to laws and regulations of both the counselor's practicing location and the client's place of residence. Counselors ensure that their clients are aware of pertinent legal rights and limitations governing the practice of counseling across state lines or international boundaries."

A potential problem with distance counseling is related to the fact that the field is changing so rapidly. The pace of change will make it difficult for counselors to maintain a full measure of competence in its use. Trepal, Haberstroh, Duffey, and Evans (2007) have suggested that counselor educators prepare counselors to provide distance counseling because it has become so accepted in society. The *Code of Ethics* (ACA, 2014, §H.1.a.) says, "Counselors who engage in the use of distance counseling, technology, and/or social media develop knowledge and skills regarding related technical, ethical, and legal considerations (e.g., special certifications, additional course work)."

Because the use of distance counseling is increasing, some professional associations have issued guidelines to assist counselors and clients who are engaged in the activity (Jencius & Sager, 2001; Rummell & Joyce, 2010; Sampson, 2000; Shaw & Shaw, 2006). These guidelines include *Ethical Standards for Internet Online Counseling* (American Counseling Association [ACA], 2014); *The Practice of Internet Counseling* (National Board for Certified Counselors [NBCC], 2014); *NCDA Guidelines for the Use of the Internet for Provision of Career Information and Planning Services* (National Career Development Association, 2014); *APA Statement on Services by Telephone, Teleconferencing, and Internet* (American Psychological Association [APA], 2015); *Suggested Principles for the Online Provision of Mental Health Services* (International Society for Mental Health Online [ISMHO], 2008); and *ACES Guidelines for Online*

Instruction in Counselor Education (Association for Counselor Education and Supervision [ACES], 1999a).

With distance counseling, there is no reliable method of regulating the services offered, of ensuring the competence of the providers, or of protecting consumers from ill-advised Internet-based services (International Society for Mental Health Online, 2008; Peterson, Hautamaki, & Walton, 2007; Shaw & Shaw, 2006; Wilson, Jencius, & Duncan, 1997). On the other hand, advances are being made in regulating distance counseling services delivered across state lines. A company that helps counselors identify the best technology for online counseling, Behavioral Health Innovation, has reported that 38 state counseling boards now have policies in effect that regulate online counseling for residents of their state (Behavioral Health Innovation, 2014).

Most state counseling boards require that the counselor who is rendering distance counseling services in the state be licensed in that state. After reviewing licensure board rules for professional counselors, marriage and family therapists, psychologists, and social workers, Haberstroh, Barney, Foster, and Duffey (2014) found no rules prohibiting distance counseling and determined that all of the reviewed professions' rules were comparable in addressing online counseling.

Despite the possible advantages of distance counseling and the prevalence of its use, some mental health professionals believe that distance counseling services have multiplied faster than the evidence that such services are safe or effective (Welfel, 2013). A number of concerns have been raised, including the following: (a) the possibility exists that counselors may operate from erroneous assumptions due to the absence of visual and auditory cues, (b) lack of security of communications could lead to breaches of confidentiality, (c) a relationship-building human presence between counselor and client is lacking, (d) effectiveness of counseling non-White clients may be reduced because the counselor may have difficulty attending to the high-context communication style of a population, (e) issues that are interpersonal in nature cannot be addressed effectively using this medium (Wilson et al., 1997), (f) counselors may not be able to discern when a client's condition poses a threat to self or others, (g) counselors may find it difficult to determine an appropriate fee structure for distance counseling, and (h) protecting clients from incompetent or unqualified distance counselors may be difficult. Disadvantages to distance counseling, from the client's perspective, include the absence of personal warmth (Leibert et al., 2006), frustration with the pace of online counseling, and problems with using the technology (Haberstroh et al., 2007).

Shaw and Shaw (2006) completed a comprehensive study in 2001 and 2002 of websites that offer online counseling services. On their checklist to evaluate the ethical intent of such sites, a website could score from 1 to 16, with a higher score indicating that a site complied more fully with ethical standards. Of 88 sites evaluated, only two sites had the highest scores of 16, and the mean score for all sites was 8. Sites had significantly higher scores when they listed an affiliation with a professional association, identified the full name of the counselor or counselors, identified the counselor or counselors as licensed, identified the state in which the service was located, and included an address or telephone number. These researchers found that 38% of the sites provided e-mail contact only; 56% provided e-mail contact along with chat, telephone, or video services; and 7% provided only chat, telephone, or video services. Interestingly, two-thirds of the individuals providing services on these sites identified themselves as licensed, with 13% holding counselor licenses.

Whether clients' health insurance providers reimburse for distance counseling services is an important consideration. Despite problems obtaining insurance reimbursement, Foley and Lardner, LLP (2014) reported that health care providers are actively pursuing distance medical practices, which they term *telemedicine,* because they see that reimbursement will be forthcoming. Behavioral Health Innovation (2014) reported that reimbursement of distance counseling has increased dramatically in the last few years.

COUNSELOR USE OF TECHNOLOGY

In addition to distance counseling, most counselors use technology in rendering counseling and clinical supervision services. Counselors might send clients or supervisees to the Internet to find information or might offer distance clinical supervision services to supervisees.

Counselors regularly use technology in teaching, providing clinical supervision, communicating with clients, communicating with consultants, and keeping records. In addition, some counselors use social media as a part of their practices, and others use technology to help clients monitor their behavior.

Using the Internet to Educate Clients

Counselors sometimes ask clients to read materials relevant to the issues they are discussing in counseling. The explosion of information that is available over the World Wide Web is phenomenal.

Counselors who send their clients or supervisees to the Internet for information must understand the nature of the materials found there (Millner & Kiser, 2002). First, sites on the Internet are not monitored for content or quality. As a result, clients must be cautioned to keep in mind that what they are reading or reviewing may not be accurate or helpful to them. In addition, sites that counselors have reviewed can be changed and may be different by the time they are seen by clients. Counselors who use the Internet to educate their clients should always review beforehand any materials that clients will be reading to ensure accuracy and professionalism.

Communicating with Clients

Traditionally, counselors had little or no communication with clients between counseling sessions. Clients arrived at their counselor's office and met face-to-face with the counselor for 50 minutes, left, and came back the next week. In a typical counseling agency, any communication regarding setting or changing appointments, paying fees, or filing necessary forms was completed through an office manager. With the advent of technology, counselors—much like physicians and other health care providers—are sometimes interacting differently with their clients today, often through e-mail messages or texts.

Many contemporary clients prefer to schedule and change appointments through websites or by using text or e-mail messages. Counselors and their assistants may request insurance information from clients through e-mail messages. Discussions regarding fee payments may take place by e-mail or text messages.

Even though it is controversial, some counselors communicate with their clients regarding their treatment plans or daily coping strategies between appointments using text or e-mail messages. Of course, establishing and maintaining appropriate personal boundaries with clients could become a problem when counselors allow such communications to take place.

When any communication with clients takes place, counselors must ensure the means of communication is secure. The *Code of Ethics* (ACA, 2014, §H.2.d.) states, "Counselors use current encryption standards within their websites and/or technology-based communications that meet applicable legal requirements. Counselors take reasonable precautions to ensure the confidentiality of information transmitted through any electronic means." This standard places the burden on counselors who use communication technology to ensure that their clients' privacy is not compromised. Standard H.2.c. requires that "Counselors inform clients about the inherent limits of confidentiality when using technology."

Taking emergency calls or texts from clients is a practice that could lead to liability for counselors. If an agency employing a counselor has emergency services, clients should be directed to contact the emergency telephone numbers if needed. When no emergency services are available in a counselor's private practice or agency, clients should be informed (in writing) what to do in an emergency. Generally, the best procedure is to have the client contact a hospital emergency room or community emergency service. If counselors allow clients to contact them in emergencies, when counselors do not respond to telephone calls, telephone messages, or text messages, the counselor could be held accountable for harm to a client that results.

Standard H.3. of the *Code of Ethics* (ACA, 2014) states that counselors who communicate with clients through technology applications "take steps to verify the client's identity at the beginning and throughout the therapeutic process. Verification can include, but is not limited to, using code words, numbers, graphics, or other nondescript identifiers." When counselors communicate with consultants or other professionals regarding their clients, §B.3.e. of the *Code of Ethics* (ACA, 2014) states that "Counselors take precautions to ensure the confidentiality of all information transmitted through the use of any medium."

Telephone Use by Counselors

Counselors must be cautious in discussing confidential or privileged information with anyone over a telephone or cell phone. The *Code of Ethics* (ACA, 2014) addresses this need for caution, reminding counselors that they must discuss the private information of clients "only in settings in which they can reasonably ensure client privacy" (§B.3.c.). A second standard, §B.3.e., advises counselors to "take precautions to ensure the confidentiality of all information transmitted through the use of any medium." There is no way to ensure that the person with whom you are talking over the telephone or cell phone is the person he or she claims to be. Also, these conversations can be monitored or intercepted in many ways without you realizing it. As a result of these problems, counselors are advised to be very careful when discussing confidential information over the telephone. Clients who choose to discuss personal information on telephones must be informed regarding the possibility of interception by others.

Many counseling offices in community mental health centers, hospitals, schools, private practices, and other settings use voice mail or answering services to conduct their business. In fact, because of the high cost of secretarial or reception services, most counseling agencies and counselors in private practice use voice mail or answering services.

Counselors must strive to protect the privacy of their clients both when receiving messages and when leaving messages for clients. Counselors who use voice mail or answering services must ensure that access codes to their messages are not disclosed to unauthorized persons. It is unwise to write access codes in personal books that could be misplaced or stolen. It is common practice for counselors to make written notes as they listen to their messages from voice mail or answering services. Such written messages to themselves could contain confidential information and must be handled as carefully as any other confidential record.

Two important factors should be considered when using voice mail. First, a recording is being created that will exist until it is erased or destroyed. Second, there is no way to ensure that the intended person will be the one who retrieves a message that is left, so counselors should avoid revealing anything that is confidential when leaving such messages. Because the fact that a person is a counseling client is itself confidential information, counselors must be very cautious when leaving voice messages for clients.

From a practical perspective, counselors or their assistants often have to reach their clients by telephone. Appointments sometimes have to be canceled or rearranged, forms need to be signed, and other matters come up that need to be handled by telephone. It is wise for counselors who leave

1. Never acknowledge that clients are receiving services or give out information regarding clients to unknown callers. Explain that in respect for the privacy of clients, such information is not given out unless clients first sign authorizations. Explain how authorizations from clients may be obtained.

2. Make efforts to verify that you are talking to the correct person when you receive or make calls in which confidential information will be discussed.

3. Keep in mind the possibility that your conversation is being recorded or monitored by an unauthorized person.

4. If you discuss confidential information regarding a client on the telephone, be professional and cautious throughout the conversation. Avoid becoming friendly or informal, or saying anything *off the record*.

5. Remember that a record will exist at the telephone company that this telephone call was made or received.

6. Do not say anything during the conversation that you would not want your client to hear or that you would not want to repeat under oath in a legal proceeding.

FIGURE 10-1   Guidelines for counselor telephone use

Source: Pearson Education, Inc., Hoboken, NJ.

messages for their clients to identify themselves by name and state their message in such a manner that third persons would not hear anything that the clients would not want them to hear. Remember that clients often have others present when they retrieve their messages.

Because conversations are transmitted by airwaves, there is a chance of a conversation on a cell phone being accidentally or purposefully intercepted by an unauthorized person. In addition, cell phones are carried around wherever individuals go. As a result, persons with cell phones often have conversations in public places or in their automobiles. When talking on a cell phone with a client, it is wise to assume that the person is not in a private place.

Counselors have an ethical obligation to ensure that the staff members in the agency in which they work are educated regarding proper telephone use. Answering service personnel should also be trained to protect the confidentiality of messages. Standard B.3.a. of the *Code of Ethics* (ACA, 2014) states, "Counselors make every effort to ensure that privacy and confidentiality of clients are maintained by subordinates." You should make sure that anyone who works for you is trained to maintain confidentiality of clients, that their actions are monitored, and that corrective action is taken when breaches occur, if necessary. Counselors should follow the guidelines listed in Figure 10-1 when using the telephone and related technologies.

Electronic Mail Communications

Electronic mail, commonly referred to as e-mail, has become the preferred method of communication by those individuals who have access to personal computers in their work or home environments. E-mail messages seem secure because a secret password must be used to send or read messages. Written documents, video images, or audio messages may be attached to e-mail messages that are sent to another person.

Usually, messages are sent between individuals with periods of time passing between communications. This type of interaction resembles a letter-writing exchange. However, it is possible to send and receive messages instantly if both persons are at the computer at the same time. Instant communication by e-mail simulates a conversation and is similar to texting.

10-2 The Case of Amahd

Amahd works as a counselor in a busy community college mental health center. Many of his clients are very adept at electronic communications. As a result, he encourages clients to send him e-mail or text messages if they need to schedule or change appointments or need to communicate with him between appointments for some reason. Amahd had intended all e-mail or text communications with clients to be strictly appointment or business related. Recently, however, several clients have begun to add short personal messages to their e-mail or text notes to him. Mark, a client he has been counseling for 3 months, has even begun to write long notes to Amahd about thoughts and feelings he has been experiencing between counseling sessions. Amahd isn't sure how to handle this situation.

- What problems could you foresee might occur if Amahd allows clients to continue sending him notes and messages like the ones being sent by Mark?
- What advice would you give Amahd?

Discussion: Amahd might experience several problems if he continues to allow clients to send him personal notes and messages. Clients might try to reach him in crisis situations, believing they have instant access at all times to their counselor. Some clients will push personal boundaries and will attempt to continue the counseling relationship by e-mail between sessions. If Amahd does not insist on clients using e-mail or text communications appropriately, he could be accused of unprofessional interactions with his clients. He should tell clients that it is acceptable for them to use e-mail or text messages only for changing appointments or notifying him of an unexpected absence from a session. He should also include guidelines regarding e-mail and text communications in his written client agreement and disclosure statement.

A primary advantage of e-mail is that it is free once access to the Internet is secured through a subscription that may involve a service fee. Many employers provide Internet access to their employees. Today, it is common to have free Internet access at universities, public places such as libraries and government buildings, coffee shops, and restaurants. Other advantages to e-mail over other methods of communication are that individuals can retrieve their messages at their convenience rather than being interrupted by telephone calls, printed copies of messages can be easily created, and replies to messages can be sent quickly and efficiently.

Disadvantages of e-mail communication, when compared to telephone conversations, are the following:

- Communication usually is one-way—it is not interactive.
- Each message is recorded electronically in the memory of the sending computer or other device and perhaps on the server of the e-mail service.
- Communication is not complete until the recipient actually accesses the messages and reads them.
- Once sent, messages cannot be retrieved.
- The quick nature of the communication can lead to sending messages that are not well conceptualized.
- Recipients may misinterpret messages and do not have the benefit of asking for clarification or of noting a person's tone of voice or inflection.

- It is easy to make errors and send messages to the wrong person or to many persons at once.
- Messages can easily be forwarded to others.
- Messages can be altered before being sent on to another person.
- The ease of using e-mail seems to encourage an informality that may not be well suited for professional communications.

The use of e-mail can be deceptive. Those who use e-mail type their message, press a button, and it disappears. Although it appears to be private between the message sender and the receiver, in reality there are a number of opportunities for e-mail messages to be intercepted or read by others.

The primary legal concern for counselors who use e-mail is that a record exists in computers and on servers for every message that is sent or received. Each message is recorded in several computers and can be retrieved. As a result, an e-mail message creates a record that is vulnerable to exposure. Although an e-mail message record is secured by the passwords of the sender and the receiver, it can be retrieved by individuals who operate the computer systems through which the message is sent. As a result of the many ways in which e-mail messages can be accessed or compromised, counselors who use e-mail should be extremely cautious about disclosing confidential information to clients or other professionals through e-mail communications and should warn their clients about the possibility that e-mail messages could be compromised. The *Code of Ethics* (ACA, 2014) includes a number of standards related to informing clients of limitations to privacy, including §§A.2.a., A.2.b., and B.1.d.

Counselors sometimes belong to e-mail communication groups. When a message is sent by an individual, it is received by all persons in the group. Counselors should understand that the increased number of individuals receiving such messages increases the possibility that a message may be sent to others or become public (Berge, 1994; Sampson, 1996). Also, belonging to such groups increases the possibility of mistakes in which a private message intended for an individual is sent instantly to a very large group of people.

Some counselors use listservs and Web-based discussion groups to communicate and exchange ideas with fellow mental health professionals. These can be a convenient means to share information on topics of mutual interest, such as private practice management or dealing with third-party payers. They can also be a resource for obtaining case consultations. If you join into any of these discussions, remember that you must ensure that any client data you share are fully disguised or, if that is not possible, that you have a signed release from the client for this purpose. Keep in mind, too, that you may not know the extent to which any advice you receive is truly expert (Welfel, 2013).

Testing

Some counselors ask clients to complete tests or checklists online. Standard E of the *Code of Ethics* (ACA, 2014) provides guidelines regarding the use of tests in counseling generally.

Some standards in the code are specifically related to the use of technology in testing. Counselors are advised in §E.7.c. to "ensure that technologically administered assessments function properly and provide clients with accurate results." In addition, §H.7.d. states, "Unless the assessment instrument is designed, intended, and validated for self-administration and/or scoring, counselors do not permit unsupervised use."

Technology in Teaching

To assist counselor education programs in ensuring they are teaching the skills that counselors need, the Association for Counselor Education and Supervision (ACES, 1999b) has developed a list of technology competencies that graduate students in counseling should have.

Counselors who teach or offer clinical supervision to trainees or other counselors often use technology. Those who teach use many forms of technology in classrooms, and counselors who provide clinical supervision sometimes provide distance supervision and usually use technology to record sessions with clients for review.

The Introduction to Section F of the *Code of Ethics* (ACA, 2014) acknowledges that counselor supervisors, trainers, and educators use electronic formats in their work. In §F.7.a., counselor educators are reminded, "Whether in traditional, hybrid, and/or online formats, counselor educators conduct counselor education and training programs in an ethical manner and serve as role models for professional behavior." In §F.7.b., counselor educators are expected to be competent in the use of technology when using it to deliver instruction.

Technology in Clinical Supervision

Counselors who provide clinical supervision to counselors in training or to counselors who are working under supervision to gain licensure use technology quite often. Counselors who would like to provide distance clinical supervision to supervisees working toward licensure should check state counselor licensure laws and regulations to determine whether there are any prohibitions against distance clinical supervision or any rules related to the use of technology in clinical supervision.

The *Code of Ethics* (ACA, 2014, § F.2.c.) requires that counselors who use technology in supervision have competency in technology and take precautions to keep client information confidential. The standard states, "When using technology in supervision, counselor supervisors are competent in the use of those technologies. Supervisors take the necessary precautions to protect the confidentiality of all information transmitted through any electronic means."

In §F.7.h. of the code, counselor educators are encouraged to use innovative procedures or techniques (such as the use of technology in supervision), but they are cautioned to explain to supervisees potential risks and ethical considerations.

Social Media Use by Counselors

Some professional counselors use social media to advertise their services or to maintain regular and immediate access to their clients (Birky & Collins, 2011). When they use social media, they must ensure that they are not causing problems related to their work as counselors. Standard H.6.a. of the *Code of Ethics* (ACA, 2014) acknowledges that some counselors use social media themselves and sets the following standard: "In cases where counselors wish to maintain a professional and personal presence for social media use, separate professional and personal web pages and profiles are created to clearly distinguish between the two kinds of virtual presence." It is important that counselors do not mix their personal and professional virtual presence if they use social media.

Thompson (2008) has cautioned that counselors who post personal profile sites may create potential ethical difficulties. Clients might find the counselor's profile and try to communicate with the counselor through the site or add the counselor as a friend, thus blurring professional boundaries. Potentially, clients could learn about aspects of the counselor's personal life. Thus, it is vital that counselors keep their personal digital footprint separate from their professional on-line presence and be diligent about security controls (Jencius, 2015).

In a presentation given at an ACA conference, Keller, Moore, Hamilton, and Terrell (2010) identified ethical standards associated with use of profile sites and offered the following suggestions for ensuring ethical practice: (1) invest the time to ensure that the information remains accurate when you create a profile page for professional use, (2) list all professional licenses and certifications held and provide the links, (3) do not accept clients as *friends*, and do not accept current or former friends as clients, (4) set privacy settings to the highest level to prevent nonprofessional interactions, and (5) establish a method for verifying client identity and for obtaining informed consent before providing any services.

Counselors who use social media for advertising their services must be careful to proceed in an ethical manner. In the *Code of Ethics* (ACA, 2014, §C.3.a.–c.) specific guidelines are provided regarding advertising in situations where social media might be utilized. When counselors advertise, they must ensure whatever they say is accurate and not deceptive in any way (§C.3.a.). The use of testimonials in advertising is a touchy matter and §C.4.b. cautions, "Counselors who use testimonials do not solicit them from current clients, former clients, or any other persons who may be vulnerable to undue influence. Counselors discuss with clients the implications of and obtain permission for the use of any testimonial." The code further advises the following regarding testimonials: "When feasible, counselors make reasonable efforts to ensure that statements made by others about them or about the counseling profession are accurate" (§C.4.c.). Another standard (H.6.d.) indicates that counselors must be careful to avoid disclosing clients' confidential information when counselors use public social media.

Office Security Systems

Many modern offices have security systems designed to protect the individuals who work there. These security systems can include cameras that film each person who enters the building, guards who require identification from visitors, or voice systems that require those who wish to enter to request that a door be unlocked for them. All these measures could compromise the privacy of a counselor's client. Counselors who practice in environments where security measures are used should make efforts to minimize the intrusive nature of these systems. Also, clients should be informed of security measures being used that may not be readily observed.

Electronic Record Keeping

Some potential problems of maintaining counseling records electronically may be resolved as new technologies that increase the security of transmitted messages come into wider use. Maintaining confidentiality of client records will continue to be problematic for some time, however, due to the ease with which unauthorized access can be gained and the unresolved questions regarding the number of individuals, agencies, and government entities that might make a case for having a right to access Internet databases.

Records, once they are created in any form, are never totally secure. It is always possible for an unauthorized person to gain access to records, or for mistakes to occur that cause the privacy of records to be compromised. Just as files filled with papers can be accessed by unauthorized persons, records kept electronically can also be seen by others if not kept secure.

Keeping counseling records electronically has become a common practice. An advantage for counselors is that, by avoiding hard copies of records, they do not have to make storage space available or worry about securing physical files and file cabinets. A disadvantage is that, in some respects, computers have many ways of being compromised, and some counselors are not yet adept at electronic record keeping.

The preferred method of storing information in agencies and offices today is through electronic means. File cabinets and paper copies of documents will eventually become obsolete because computers allow incredible amounts of information to be contained on a storage device. Computers have made business environments more efficient and cost-effective.

Counselors usually think in terms of locks and keys when they consider methods of keeping confidential information secure. With so much data being stored on computers in modern counseling settings, it is important that counselors understand security problems and solutions associated with keeping information on computers (Swenson, 1997). Cloud computing is a significant advance in computing that offers convenient storage and ease of access to files from any computer the counselor is using, but questions remain regarding confidentiality risks and security of client files as well as whether it is advisable to store client data on a system that the counselor does not own or control (International Legal Technology Association, 2010).

Access to confidential computer files is one of the first issues to consider. It is important for counselors to set up their computers so that a password must be used to access sensitive files. One of the problems with using passwords, however, is the danger that the passwords will become known to unauthorized persons. Password holders tend to be anxious about the possibility of forgetting their passwords. As a result, they make notes to themselves with the password on them, and the notes are sometimes seen by others. Some people have even been known to post their password directly on their computer. Offices often will change passwords from time to time to help with security. But, again, this makes computer users nervous about forgetting their passwords, so they record them in a way that leads to their disclosure. Counselors who practice in offices where passwords are used for confidential computer files should be careful not to disclose the passwords to unauthorized persons and not to record the passwords in places where they might be seen by others. In addition, counselors should train office personnel about the importance of password security and alert staff members to the problems that exist in keeping passwords secure.

Printing paper copies of documents from confidential computer files can also cause problems. Printed confidential information should be filed in locked cabinets or destroyed when no longer needed.

Disposing of confidential computer files also is a problem area. Some people believe that when they delete a file in a computer, they have destroyed that information. In reality, most deleted computer files can be retrieved by computer experts. Counselors should understand that all information entered into a computer has the potential to eventually be seen by unauthorized persons, even after the information has been deleted. As in creating any type of record, counselors should assume that what they have written will someday become public information, despite their best efforts to keep records confidential or to delete or destroy them.

Steps should be taken to prevent confidential counseling records kept on computers from being compromised. Listed in Figure 10-2 are some suggestions for counselors who use computers for their records.

Client Behavior and Technology

Counselors have only scratched the surface of what is possible in using technology to monitor and help clients change their behavior. Technology provides excellent tools for counselors when clients want to change their behavior or when the behavior of clients needs to be monitored. Some very savvy counselors are creating innovative ways to assist their clients through the use of cutting-edge technology.

Researchers are investigating using signals from clients that can be tracked electronically to alert clients themselves or their counselors that they are experiencing mental health problems. For example, by electronically tracking speech patterns or facial expressions, mental health professionals might be able to identify clients whose conditions are deteriorating and need assistance with

1. Try to avoid using a computer to which others have access. If this is not possible, store your records in a section that only you and other authorized persons may access.

2. Use passwords for accessing the files in the computer. Keep the passwords secure, limit the number of individuals who know the passwords, and change the passwords periodically.

3. Any time a confidential record is printed from the computer, ensure that it is handled as other confidential materials would be.

4. Avoid placing computers with monitors in public areas where unauthorized persons might accidentally see confidential information.

5. Limit access to computer equipment that is used to enter and retrieve confidential records.

6. Delete computer-stored records on the same basis that traditional records would be destroyed in the agency or office. Keep in mind, though, that deleted files usually can be retrieved by computer experts from a computer's hard drive even after they have been deleted.

7. When information is downloaded from a computer's hard drive to a storage device, or transferred electronically, make sure that confidential material is not accidentally included.

8. Be careful in networking a computer used for confidential information. The more computers that can access information, the greater the chance that confidential information will be compromised.

9. Use a coding system rather than client names on storage device labels so that the client's identity is not obvious to anyone who might see the labels.

10. Regularly update virus protection software.

11. Make a backup copy of all files, and keep them in a location that is secure but separate from the originals.

FIGURE 10-2   Guidelines for computerized records

Source: Pearson Education, Inc., Hoboken, NJ.

their depression or bipolar disorder (Ziv, 2014). Cell phone applications (*apps*) that are available today can do the following amazing things: track mood by asking clients to complete surveys, give tips on breathing or thinking positively, remind clients to take their medications, or create a game out of a cognitive behavioral change treatment program. According to Ziv (2014), these kinds of technological interventions often have not been proven effective through research studies. In addition, many clients are not motivated to use the apps or do not possess enough self-awareness to appreciate their usefulness. Some physiological changes within clients that clients might not be able to identify within themselves, and that are directly related to their mental health, could be tracked with technology. Some examples are increased heart rates in clients who suffer from panic attacks or muscles tightening as a client becomes anxious or angry.

Haniff (2007) has produced an app that presents media designed to lift a person's mood for clients who are depressed. A music program that includes subliminal relaxing music has been used to block out the noise of everyday living. In addition, a computer game has been created that helps to determine a client's triggers for depression.

Coyle, Matthews, Sharry, Nisbet, and Doherty (2005) and Merry and Stasiak (2012) have described computer games designed to provide counseling for adolescents. Young people who are reluctant to talk to counselors can sometimes be convinced to play computer games that are fun, anonymous, and accessible. These games convey advice about their depression or other mental health issues. A clinical trial with one game has shown that such games for adolescents are about as effective as face-to-face counseling.

In today's sophisticated world of technology, counselors may have a tendency to focus on complex gadgets when they think about counseling and technology. Muench (2010) has reminded counselors that some basic technologies are being used regularly to increase access to mental health care. For example, old-fashioned landline telephones are being used in rural areas to provide mental health counseling by connecting clients to counselors who are located thousands of miles away. Internet-based screening tools and interviews also are helping many people to identify and begin the process of change on their own. Text messages can remind or encourage clients to avoid negative behaviors or engage in positive behaviors.

The *Code of Ethics* (ACA, 2014) requires counselors to be competent in the use of technology used in counseling relationships (§H.1.a.) and to ensure clients are agreeable to using technology (§H.2.a). Thus, many responsibilities come with the use of technology in counseling.

Diversity Considerations in the Use of Technology

A major problem with the use of technology in counseling is that technology is not equally available or evenly distributed across cultures in the United States. Statistics published by the U.S. Bureau of the Census (2014) revealed that 83.8% of households reported computer access and 74.4% reported Internet use, with 73.4% reported having a high-speed connection. Computer ownership and Internet use tended to highest among the young, Whites or Asians, the affluent, and the highly educated.

Overall, 83.8% of households reported having a computer. Significant gaps were evident when computer ownership was studied by race/ethnicity and educational attainment:

- Computer ownership was highest for Whites (85.4%) and Asians (92.5%) and lower for Blacks (75.8%) and Hispanics (79.7%).
- Individuals with less than a high school diploma had significantly less access (56.0%).

Overall, 73.4% of households reported having high-speed Internet access. Significant gaps were evident when access was studied by race/ethnicity and educational attainment:

- High-speed Internet access was highest for Whites (76.2%) and Asians (86.0%) and lower for Blacks (60.6%) and Hispanics (65.9%).
- Individuals with less than a high school diploma had significantly less access (42.7%).

Due to this *digital divide*, not all clients will have access to such services as Internet counseling or e-mail communications with their counselors. A legitimate concern is that the poor and underserved will be increasingly left behind as technology in counseling advances. Counselors who use technology in their work with clients should be careful not to assume that clients have access to or expertise in using computer applications. Some clients with disabilities may not have access to assistive devices that allow them to use technology that requires senses such as sight, hearing, or speaking.

On the positive side, technology can be of use to counselors who want to increase their multicultural counseling competence. Numerous websites offer information on various cultures that can be accessed using a search engine. It may be difficult for an individual counselor, however, to assess whether the information is valid. Counselors can also join listservs and discussion groups to gain understanding of different cultures.

Technology undoubtedly will continue to develop at a remarkably rapid pace. Challenges for the counseling profession will include ensuring equal access, addressing differences in culture and learning style inherent in technology, producing outcome research on equitable ways to utilize technology, and including a cultural lens as we continue to develop and assess the uses of technology in counseling (Jencius, 2003).

Summary and Key Points

This chapter presented a discussion of technology and counseling. Advances in technology have had a significant impact on the practice of counseling. Although you certainly will want to use as many forms of technology as you can to maximize your effectiveness, it is important that you adhere to ethical standards, particularly those in the 2014 ACA *Code of Ethics*, Section H: Distance Counseling, Technology, and Social Media.

- Counselors must be aware of client use of social media because it affects their lives in significant ways. Counselors must refrain from looking up, without permission, social media information posted by their clients.
- Clients use other forms of technology, such as texting and e-mail, that also affect their lives and their relationships with their counselors.
- Distance counseling has become a very popular method of delivering counseling services in the United States. Counselors who offer distance counseling must ensure that clients are agreeable to its use, be competent to use the technology, and ensure that the privacy of clients is maintained.
- Counselors are using technology increasingly, some in novel and innovative ways.

- Counselors who use the Web to educate clients must be cautious to ensure that clients understand that not all information on the Web is accurate.
- Communicating with clients using technology has some risky elements, and counselors must ensure that they are professional and responsible when using technology for communication. Even telephone use by counselors requires caution. In addition, e-mail exchanges with clients can lead to problems if clients are given too much latitude.
- Many counselors are using technology for testing, teaching, and clinical supervision.
- When counselors make personal use of social media, they must be careful not to mix personal use with professional use.
- Using technology for record keeping has a number of challenges, but electronic record keeping has become the norm.
- Technology advances are being used by counselors to monitor client behavior and assist clients to achieve their therapeutic goals.
- Some client populations may be disadvantaged by the increasing reliance of counselors on technology.

CHAPTER 11

Counseling Children and Vulnerable Adults

FOCUS QUESTIONS

1. How do you think legal and ethical requirements might come into conflict with each other when counseling minor clients?

2. Why do you think minors under the age of 18 in the United States are not able to assert their legal rights on their own, but instead are required to assert their legal rights in court through their parents or guardians?

3. How can a counselor determine whether an adolescent client's risk-taking behaviors present a sufficiently serious risk for harm to warrant breaching the minor's confidentiality?

4. What is your opinion of laws that make it a crime for a counselor to fail to report cases of suspected abuse of a child, elder, or vulnerable adult?

We stated in the introductory chapter that legal and ethical requirements regarding counseling generally do not conflict with one another. Unfortunately, exceptions to this general rule occur when counselors provide professional services to minor clients or vulnerable adults. Counselors who counsel children and adolescents under the age of 18 or adults who do not have the legal capacity to care for themselves may be more likely than any other counselors to experience conflicts between what they consider to be their ethical or moral obligations and what the law dictates that they must do (Salo, 2015). These conflicts often concern confidentiality of client disclosures made during counseling sessions, or parents or guardians making decisions for dependent children or adult clients with which the clients do not agree. The legal perspective is that counselors are obligated to parents or guardians when counseling minor children. Yet, counselors believe that their primary ethical obligations are to their minor clients. This discrepancy between the legal and the ethical perspectives causes problems, especially in the area of privacy (Orton, 1997).

The *Code of Ethics* (American Counseling Association [ACA], 2014) offers very little guidance that is specific to counseling children (Corr & Balk, 2010); therefore, counselors must rely heavily on their professional judgment in dealing with ethical dilemmas involving minor clients. The numerous areas of conflict between ethical and legal requirements further complicate the work of the counselor. In this chapter, we explore these conflicts between law and ethics and suggest ways to resolve them. Because many of the same issues that arise with minor clients also apply when counseling dependent or vulnerable adults, this chapter includes a discussion about working with these clients as well. Counselors who provide services to minors and to others who lack legal competency must pay attention to the legal rights of parents and guardians. In addition, counselors who counsel clients who may be unable to protect themselves from harm, such as children and vulnerable adults, must take steps to prevent abuse or neglect of these clients.

COUNSELING MINOR CLIENTS

Conflicts between law and ethics occasionally arise very clearly in situations where the client is a minor. One issue that causes tension between law and ethics is whether children should be allowed to enter into counseling relationships without parental knowledge or consent. Also, every child, regardless of age, has a moral right to privacy in the counseling relationship. From a philosophical viewpoint, many counselors would argue that children should have the same rights to confidentiality as adult clients. The legal rights to confidentiality and privilege of minors, however, are more limited. Basically, counselors have an ethical obligation of privacy to minor clients, and a legal obligation to the parents or legal guardians of those same minor clients to keep their children safe and to protect the privacy rights of the parents or guardians.

Counselors who provide counseling services to children must understand the legal rights of parents or guardians and appreciate their ethical obligations to children as well. Balancing these sometimes competing interests can be quite challenging (Lazovsky, 2008). Counselors must contend with the issue of children's access to counseling and with situations in which children may object to their parents being given confidential information they disclosed in counseling sessions. In addition, counselors must decide who has the authority to give permission to disclose confidential information to third parties.

Counselors want to offer an appropriate degree of privacy to children whom they counsel (Isaacs & Stone, 2001). They want children to feel free to disclose aspects of their lives that trouble them, in an atmosphere of trust and confidentiality. It may be helpful for counselors to consider the following facts about children and privacy:

1. Younger children often do not have an understanding of confidentiality or a need for privacy, which is a socially learned concept. Young children may not be nearly as concerned about confidentiality as the counselor is (Huey, 1996) and may not need reassurances of confidentiality (Corr & Balk, 2010).
2. Preadolescents and adolescents may have a heightened desire for privacy that is appropriate to their developmental stage of growth.
3. Some children may not be concerned about their privacy. It is inappropriate to assume that children do not want their parents or guardians to know information they have told counselors.
4. Children sometimes tell an adult about their concerns hoping that the adult will act as an intermediary in telling their parents.
5. The reasoning capacity of children is limited, and because of their age they may not be able to make decisions that are in their own best interest.

Answers to confidentiality questions may vary, depending on the age of the client and on the setting in which the counseling takes place. Very young children are often not very concerned about confidentiality, whereas confidentiality concerns may be paramount for adolescent clients. According to Hendrix (1991), community mental health counselors tend to favor giving minors the same confidentiality rights that adults have, whereas school counselors (particularly those at the elementary school level) feel more oriented toward releasing information to parents.

Legal Status and Rights of Minors

When the United States was established as a country in 1776, the government adopted English common law as its legal foundation. This common law holds that minors must exercise through their parents any legal rights they may have and that minors have no legal standing to contract or bring lawsuits (Kramer, 1994).

The law with respect to minors has seen significant changes since the beginning of the nineteenth century. Before legal reforms, children were treated almost the same way as the property of their parents (especially the father), and the government seldom interfered with parents' control and authority over their children. In Massachusetts during the 1600s, children could be executed if found to be *stubborn and rebellious* (Kramer, 1994). Reforms have included laws that prohibit child labor, require compulsory school attendance, and, more recently, require professionals to report suspected child abuse.

It appears that the legal rights of children include the right to be supported by their parents and the right to not be abused or neglected. Today, even though minors have more governmental protection and are beginning to be recognized by courts as individuals with their own legal rights, the law still favors biological parents' rights over their children. The legal system in the United States usually requires that children assert any legal rights they have through their parents or guardians.

Due to their legal status in our society, children are not able to enter into contracts. Because the counseling relationship is contractual in nature, minors cannot legally agree on their own to be counseled. Thus, minors usually need parental consent before they can receive counseling services. Several exceptions to this requirement, however, have been created by statutes enacted by federal and state legislative bodies.

Clients who cannot comprehend what is being requested in a consent for disclosure or who are unable to make a rational decision are not able to give valid informed consent (Huey, 1996). As a general rule, the law stipulates that clients under the age of 18 are not adults and, therefore, are not competent to make fully informed, voluntary decisions (Davis & Mickelson, 1994). Although counselors may argue that many minor clients are developmentally capable of making these decisions for themselves, the law does not support this belief. The privacy rights of minor clients legally belong to their parents or guardians.

Several writers (Mnookin & Weisberg, 1995; Reppucci, Weithorn, Mulvey, & Monahan, 1984) have taken the position that some children should be able to exercise legal rights on their own, and they have advocated for making 14 the age at which children may legally give their informed consent for counseling or other health-related treatment. In all states (Phillis, 2011), this right is given to mature minors by statute—adolescents over a specified age (usually 16) who are able to understand the nature, risks, and benefits of counseling. Laws in some states allow minors themselves to give informed consent to counseling when there is an emergency situation, or when they need treatment for use of dangerous drugs, sexually transmitted diseases, pregnancy, or birth control (Lawrence & Robinson Kurpius, 2000). A number of states have enacted statutes that lower the legal age for obtaining counseling services, health treatment, or even abortions to an age lower than 18. Some federal laws and statutes also allow minors to consent specifically to counseling services at specified ages prior to age 18.

Phillis (2011) has brought attention to the issue of minors below the age of 18 engaging in sexual activity and choosing to become pregnant. Phillis pointed out that although most states allow minors to consent to sex at age 16, few states allow minors to consent to abortion. Ehrlich (2003) completed a study of minors who had decided to have abortions without first obtaining parental consent and discovered that reasons the girls gave for avoiding parental consent were not because they were rebellious teenagers. Instead she found they did not treat lightly their decision to abort and their decision to not involve their parents. Stone (2002) has warned counselors to be careful to avoid advocating a particular position regarding abortion or assisting a minor in obtaining an abortion when counseling minors. Emancipated minors—who are under the age of 18 but live separately from their parents, manage their own finances, and have been adjudicated legally emancipated by a judge—can enter into a contract for counseling.

With so much variation in state and federal laws and regulations regarding minor clients and informed consent, it is essential for counselors who work with minor clients to know the relevant laws and regulations that apply in settings where they practice. It is important for administrators who supervise counselors to alert them when there are exceptions to the general legal principles that require parent or guardian consent for treatment of minors or give parents or guardians access to confidential information regarding the treatment of their children or wards.

When a minor is the client who will be receiving counseling services, the consent form that is included in Appendix B should be modified to indicate that a minor is the client and that a legal parent or guardian is verifying his or her consent to the counseling relationship. For therapeutic rather than legal purposes, counselors may also want to obtain the minor's signature on the form, depending on the minor's level of development and ability to understand the meaning of the document.

The Rights of Parents

In the *Code of Ethics* (ACA, 2014), several provisions are found that relate to including parents or guardians when counseling minor clients. The wording of §A.2.d. acknowledges the need to balance the rights of minor clients with the rights of their parents or guardians and to include minor clients in decision making, as appropriate. In addition, §B.5.b. advises counselors to "respect the inherent rights and responsibilities of parents/guardians regarding the welfare of their children/charges according to law."

The *Code of Ethics* (ACA, 2014) recognizes that it is often helpful to include parents and other family members when working with minor clients and reinforces the fact that parents can be valuable allies in the counseling process. Standard B.5.b., which encourages counselors to work to establish collaborative relationships with parents and guardians, allows counselors some latitude to use their professional judgment in determining whether and when to involve parents or guardians in the counseling process. Conflicts often can be avoided if counselors approach parents as allies in the counseling process, rather than as adversaries in a struggle over privacy.

Enzer (1985) has said that child psychiatrists are expected by their ethics code to inform children or seek their agreement to activities that affect them even though this is not required by law. Corey, Corey, Corey, and Callanan (2015) have suggested that counselors also have an ethical obligation to provide information to children and adolescents that will help these clients be active partners in their treatment. These authors pointed out that counselors demonstrate respect for client autonomy when they involve minor clients in defining counseling goals and choosing among treatment alternatives. Such an approach is supported by the *Code of Ethics* (ACA, 2014). Standard A.2.d. advises counselors, when working with minors, to seek the assent of minor clients to services and include them in the decision-making process as appropriate. A cooperative approach might also help to minimize some of the reluctance or resentment that minor clients often feel when they are sent to a counselor by their parents, their teachers, or other adults in authority.

Counselors who work with minor clients need to respect parents' rights and responsibilities for their children, yet they also feel the need to honor the confidentiality rights of their clients. Counselors should understand that any time they decide to withhold information from a parent, they assume responsibility for harm caused if that information later leads to injuries for the client. Examples of such potentially injurious information include minors disclosing that they are using controlled substances, engaging in sexual activity, breaking laws, or engaging in other risky behavior that their parents do not know about.

Parents or guardians probably have a legal right to know the contents of their children's counseling sessions, although a court may hold otherwise because of specific state or federal statutes or regulations, or due to legal precedent from case law in that jurisdiction. Of course, it would be complicated and expensive for parents to enforce their rights, but given the state of the law regarding parent and child relationships, they probably do have the right.

To avoid situations in which parents demand information and minor clients refuse to authorize counselors to provide it, it is wise to establish a thorough understanding with all parties regarding the issue of confidentiality before the counseling relationship is initiated. The use of written informed consent agreements among counselors, their minor clients, and the parents of minors would be helpful to avoid misunderstandings. Counselors must balance the ethical rights of clients to make choices, their capacity to give consent or assent to counseling, and the rights and responsibilities of parents or families to protect minor clients and make decisions on their behalf (ACA, 2014, §A.2.d.).

Responding to Parents Who Demand Confidential Counseling Information

Many professionals who counsel children report that they have never faced situations in which a parent or guardian demanded to know the contents of counseling sessions and the child felt strongly that the parent or guardian should not be told. Other counselors, however, have had to deal with such situations (Mitchell, Disque, & Robertson, 2002). If you are ever presented with such a challenge and decide that the child's desire for the parent or guardian to not be told is reasonable, we suggest you consider following these steps:

1. Discuss the inquiry with the minor and see if the minor is willing to disclose the content of the counseling session to the adult. Sometimes counselors are more concerned about privacy than a child is. If that doesn't work, go to step 2.
2. Try to persuade the adult that the child's best interests are not served by revealing the information. Attempt to educate the inquiring adult about the nature of the counseling relationship, and assure the adult that information will be given if the child is in danger. If that doesn't work, go to step 3.
3. Schedule a joint session with the adult and the minor. Assume the role of a mediator at this session. Hope that the adult's mind will be changed about wanting the information or that the minor will be willing to disclose enough information to satisfy the adult. If that doesn't work, choose step 4 or step 5.
4. Inform the child ahead of time and then disclose the content of the session to the inquiring adult. If the adult is not a parent or guardian, inform the parent or guardian before disclosing the information. Remember that the adult may have a legal right to the information.
5. Refuse to disclose the information to the inquiring adult. Secure approval from your direct administrator before doing this. Remember that the adult may have a legal right to the information.

RIGHTS OF NONCUSTODIAL PARENTS   Counselors who provide services to children often counsel minors whose parents are separated, going through a divorce, or are divorced. Special challenges for counselors occur when parents attempt to pull counselors into their custody disputes.

A typical challenge presents itself when one parent wants the counselor to take his or her side in a court proceeding related to child custody. We recommend that counselors of children of divorce focus on their role of counseling the child and consulting with parents as necessary for the benefit of the child, avoiding in the process becoming embroiled in custody battles.

Counselors should refuse to support one parent over the other in a child custody controversy. The reasons are many: (a) the counselor must be able to maintain working relationships with both parents to be an effective counselor for the child, (b) counselors of children know very little about what goes on in a home or in a marriage, so it would be inappropriate for counselors to support one parent over the other, and (c) child custody evaluators, not the children's counselors, should be giving advice to judges related to custody matters. Counselors could be child custody evaluators, but they cannot serve in that role when they are a child's counselor as well. See Chapter 7 for a discussion of counselors as expert witnesses.

If counselors of children are subpoenaed to court to testify in a child custody hearing after expressing their position that they do not want to become involved in that controversy, the counselors must be careful how they conduct themselves in the legal proceedings. Any time counselors receive a subpoena, they should obtain legal advice (see Chapter 6). Generally, in child custody situations, one parent waives the privacy of the counselor–child relationship, so counselors must provide information through depositions or testimony in hearings or trials. When counselors are in such situations, they should answer any factual questions asked of them. If they are asked opinion questions, especially regarding the fitness of a parent, they should decline to give an opinion, maintaining that they do not have enough information to form a judgment on that matter, which is true. Counselors know only what is told to them. They do not have in-depth knowledge regarding the parents of their child clients.

Wilcoxon and Magnuson (1999) have argued that it usually is in the child's best interest to include the noncustodial parent in the counseling process. Children's counselors generally have a responsibility to provide requested information to noncustodial parents. Some states, however, do not require health care providers to provide noncustodial parents with information regarding the treatment of their children. If there is a controversy over whether a noncustodial parent should have information about the counseling of his or her child, counselors are advised to seek and follow legal advice that is based on the laws in their state.

Children at Risk for Harm to Self or Others

As noted, a minor client's confidentiality might need to be breached due to parental demands. At other times, it will be the counselor who determines that parents or guardians must be given information that a child has disclosed in counseling sessions. If counselors determine that a child is at risk of harm (to self or others), they must inform the child's parents. School counselors must also consider whether they should report student risk-taking behaviors to an administrative superior (usually the school principal; Moyer, Sullivan, & Growcock, 2012). See Chapter 8 for a detailed discussion of the responsibilities of counselors when their clients may be at risk of endangering themselves or others. When a child client is at risk of suicide, a counselor's duty to notify the parents is clear. Much less clear are instances when children and adolescents engage in self-injuring behaviors (such as delicate cutting). Because there does seem to be a relationship between suicide and self-injury, counselors need to know how to assess for suicidal risk (Hoffman & Kress, 2010). Because deciding whether a child is at risk can be a difficult judgment to make, consultation with other counselors is recommended. If a counselor tells parents every time a child engages in any risky behavior, children will not be willing to disclose important information to that counselor. On the other hand, if a counselor decides not to inform a parent when a child is engaged in risky behavior, that counselor could be held legally accountable if the child is later harmed or harms someone else (Gilbert, 2002; Hermann & Finn, 2002; Hermann & Remley, 2000).

When situations arise in which counselors do have to inform parents or guardians of potential harm to their children or others, counselors should make efforts to maintain the counseling relationship with their child clients. Steps that might help in that regard would be having the children tell their parents themselves, telling parents with the children present, or—at a minimum—informing the child before telling the parents. If you were Mary's counselor in the following case example, would you tell Mary's parents about her marijuana use?

11-1 The Case of Benjamin

Mary, age 14, reveals to Benjamin, her school counselor, that she once smoked marijuana with her friends on a weekend. She states that she has never tried any other drugs and insists that she knows better than to "get hooked on marijuana or even try the hard stuff." Mary also insists that the counselor must not tell her parents and that to do so would be a betrayal of her trust.

- What are the arguments for and against Benjamin informing Mary's parents of her one-time marijuana use?
- What factors should Benjamin consider in making his decision?

Discussion: Of course, if his school system has a policy that parents must be informed in situations like this, Benjamin would be unwise to ignore the policy.

If no such policy exists, however, Benjamin must weigh the risks to Mary and to himself. How serious is the danger involved in the one-time use of marijuana? Is it better to honor the client's wishes and not tell the parents in the hope of maintaining a trusting counseling relationship in which the problem can be further explored? Or is informing the parents a wiser choice?

Benjamin should consider several factors in making his decision. First, he should check out any values issues of his own that might be involved: Is his decision-making process being influenced by his own liberal attitudes toward marijuana use, for instance? What are the prevailing standards and attitudes in the community?

He should also consider factors such as the age and maturity of the student involved, his judgment about whether the parents' response would harm the student if the parents were told, the student's willingness to consider informing her parents in the near future, any applicable school policies, and any relevant ethical standards and laws.

If Benjamin decides that the parents must be informed, he should let Mary know that he cannot keep this particular secret and try to negotiate a procedure for informing the parents that will be acceptable to her.

This case is an example of a situation that requires a counselor to make a judgment call about informing parents. There are no easy answers to these questions. Benjamin would be well advised to consult with other school counselors who are likely to have dealt with situations like this one.

Release of Records

Ethically conscientious counselors work hard to respect the rights of minor clients to control access to personal information divulged during counseling, to the extent that is possible. It is important to remember that confidentiality is not absolute for clients of any age. As has been noted, a legal consideration that limits the confidentiality of minors is that confidentiality and freedom of choice are both predicated on the ability of the client to give voluntary, informed consent.

Minor clients should have some control over the release of information that results from their choosing to engage in the counseling process (Huey, 1996). However, parents or guardians must exercise any legal rights children have up until they reach the age of 18 (unless a statute allows a younger age) or until the child is emancipated by a court of law. As was discussed in Chapter 6, parents do not have access to counseling case notes kept in the sole possession of the maker on demand under Family Educational Rights and Privacy Act (FERPA; 1974), but parents would have access to such notes under a subpoena or specific court order.

Generally, a parent or guardian has a legal right to assert the privilege that would belong to a minor. In some circumstances, however, courts have found that parents did not have the best interests of the child in mind and have refused to allow the parents to assert a child's privilege (*People v. Lobaito,* 1984). Courts have also appointed a *guardian ad litem* to determine the best interests of a child related to privilege (*Nagle v. Hooks*, 1983).

Confidentiality in School Counseling

Unless there is a federal or state statute to the contrary, school counselors do not have a legal obligation to obtain parental permission before counseling students. When parents enroll their children in school, they know or should know that their children will be participating in a number of obligatory and optional services, and one of those optional services is counseling in most schools. School systems or school principals who require counselors to obtain parental permission to counsel students are imposing that requirement because they feel it is an appropriate or *politically correct* thing to do, not because it is required by law. These administrators may be concerned that community support for the school and its counselors would be negatively affected if parents believed that the counselors were withholding information regarding the fact that their child is being counseled (Glosoff & Pate, 2002).

Because most counseling services are not required of all school students, however, parents who object to their child's participation in counseling probably have a right to do so. In extreme circumstances, school counselors should think about whether a child might be a victim of abuse or neglect when the parents object to their child's participation in counseling. However, counselors are cautioned to avoid jumping to the conclusion that parents or guardians have something to hide because they object to their child being counseled. Counselors should entertain the suspicion that a child might be at risk for abuse or neglect only if there is some compelling evidence that abuse is occurring.

School counselors routinely encounter situations that call on their professional judgment to decide whether student risk-taking behaviors are of sufficient intensity, frequency, and duration to warrant breaching a student's confidentiality (Moyer & Sullivan, 2008). After reviewing the approach that various federal court districts have taken in determining whether minors have a legal right to keep information, such as a pregnancy, secret from their parents, Gilbert (2007) concluded that district court judges should take into account whether requiring disclosure to parents by health care providers would keep minors from seeking help. Prober (2005) has argued against school districts enacting requirements that school health personnel notify parents when minors report pregnancies to them so that students will continue to seek assistance from adults in the school environment. According to Prober (2005), such rules requiring mandatory reporting to parents are illegal and unconstitutional.

Results of one survey of school counselors (Isaacs & Stone, 1999) indicated that school counselors would breach confidentiality for the following issues: impending suicide or suicide pact, violent retaliation for victimization, use of crack cocaine, sexual intercourse with multiple partners when HIV positive, armed robbery, and signs of serious depression. Isaacs and Stone (1999) also found that the age of the child was the most significant variable that counselors considered in their decision making. Younger children were seen as more dependent and in need of protection, whereas high school students were viewed as being more capable of giving informed consent and making mature decisions. Moyer and Sullivan (2008) also surveyed school counselors to determine whether they would breach confidentiality to report risk-taking behaviors of student clients. They found that only one behavior (suicidal behavior) was perceived almost unanimously as posing an immediate threat, and that there was little consensus regarding a range of other risk-taking behaviors.

Many misunderstandings can be avoided if counselors take proactive steps to inform students, parents, and school personnel about confidentiality and its limits (Huss, Bryant, & Mulet, 2008; Keim & Cobia, 2010). Counselors in schools might consider publishing information about their services in the documents given to parents when they enroll their child in the school. A modified version of the information addressed to students might be published in student handbooks as well. Glosoff and Pate (2002) offered the reminder that there are many stakeholders in the school counseling program. They recommended that counselors conduct in-service programs for teachers and administrators, make presentations at PTA meetings, and visit classrooms early in the school year. All of these activities have the goal of educating interested parties about the role of the school counselor and the parameters of confidentiality.

Confidentiality in Working with Minors in Nonschool Settings

The work setting of counselors often determines the types of confidentiality issues they encounter in working with minor clients (Salo, 2015). Counselors in private practice may encounter fewer issues around confidentiality because parents usually have given legal consent for the counselor to work with the client and because the number of people involved in the counseling process may be limited to the counselor, the minor client, and the parents or guardians.

By contrast, children who are being counseled in an inpatient facility will likely have been placed there by a parent or by children's protective services. These minors, regardless of their age, usually are considered incapable of making important decisions for themselves (Salo, 2015), as the caregivers are assumed to be operating in the minor client's best interest. Parents may be consulted over the course of the minor client's stay in the facility, and treatment teams will also be involved in determining the treatment plans.

Confidentiality in Consultations

Many counselors who provide services for children work in schools, treatment facilities, or social services agencies. Staff members often must consult with each other for the benefit of the children being served. It is important for counselors to educate other non–mental-health staff members that they must keep confidential any personal information they learn about children as a result of their professional positions. If professionals disclose confidential information outside the institution and the reputations of parents or guardians are damaged, they could have the basis for a lawsuit.

School counselors, in particular, are in a precarious position because they have responsibilities as consultants to other educators. Because teachers and administrators may not have the same obligations to uphold student privacy, school counselors must constantly balance the potential benefits to a student of divulging private information to teachers or administrators duri versus the potential harm that might be caused by sharing that information (Isaacs

Reporting Suspected Child Abuse or Neglect

Every state now has a statute that requires counselors and other professionals to report cases of suspected child abuse or neglect to a governmental agency (Jones, 1996; Kemp, 1998).

Although the *Code of Ethics* (ACA, 2014) does not specifically address child abuse reporting, we have seen that counselors do have a general ethical duty to protect vulnerable persons from harm (§B.2.a.). McEachern, Aluede, and Kenny (2008), for example, have discussed the responsibility of school counselors to include discussion of the problem of emotional abuse in their classroom guidance lessons. It appears that many mental health professionals do not routinely report child abuse or neglect and that confidentiality is the crucial variable that causes them to fail to make such reports (Corey et al., 2015; MacNair, 1992). Counselors may be reluctant to report for several reasons, including their desire to avoid betraying a child's trust, fear that a child protective services investigation will be poorly handled, fear of retaliation from the alleged perpetrator, or hope of maintaining the counseling relationship with the family so that the abusing adults can be helped to learn more appropriate parenting skills. Conti (2011) has suggested that mental health professionals who are working with attorneys representing their counseling clients in a legal action should be exempt from making mandatory suspected child abuse reports. Conti's rationale for this suggestion is that lawyers are not allowed to make such reports because reporting would violate the attorney–client privilege. Nonetheless, in cases of child abuse or neglect, the need for absolute confidentiality in counseling has been determined by state legislators to be less important than the need to protect children.

STATUTORY REQUIREMENTS Because all states and U.S. jurisdictions now have mandatory reporting statutes of some type in the area of child abuse and neglect, and the statutes vary in their wording, it is vital for counselors to know the exact language of statutes that require them to make reports of suspected abuse or neglect. All states, the District of Columbia, American Samoa, Guam, the Northern Mariana Islands, Puerto Rico, and the Virgin Islands have enacted statutes that require certain categories of professionals to report suspected child abuse or neglect (Child Welfare Information Gateway, 2014). Mandatory child abuse or neglect reporting statutes for each state and U.S. possession can be found at childwelfare.gov.

Counselors must know which categories of professionals must make reports of suspected abuse or neglect, and whether reports must be made only for suspected current abuse or for suspected past abuse as well. Reporting statutes protect mandatory reporters from lawsuits that might be filed against them by those who have been reported, but sometimes only if the report is mandated by law. If reports of suspicions of past abuse are not mandated by law, then counselors making such reports may not be protected. Furthermore, if state statutes require that reports be made when the perpetrator is the child's caretaker and a report is made when the suspected perpetrator is not the caretaker, again, counselors making such reports may not be protected. Where counselors work, their job titles, their licensing status, and other such factors may determine whether they are mandated by statute to make suspected abuse reports.

The protective clauses of mandatory abuse reporting laws protect counselors who make reports in *good faith*. In other words, as long as counselors sincerely believe that child abuse or neglect may have occurred or is occurring, they will be protected from lawsuits that might be filed against them by individuals who have been reported. This means that lawsuits against a counselor for defamation of character or some other type of tort would not prevail as long as the counselor genuinely believed that abuse or neglect might have occurred, even if it was later proven that no abuse or neglect had existed. In a 2011 New York case (*Cox v. Warwick Valley Central School District*, 2010), courts supported a middle school principal who was sued by parents after they were reported for suspected abuse in the course of suspending the student from school for submitting an essay in English class that included violence. Despite the ruling in *Cox*, if a counselor has been involved in a conflict on some other matter with a suspected perpetrator, it would be wise to ask another professional to gather evidence of the suspected abuse directly and make the report. Otherwise the suspected perpetrator might be able to convince others that the counselor made the report in *bad faith*: that the counselor knew that the report was untrue but made it to cause problems for the suspected perpetrator because of the previous conflict regarding another matter.

The language of the statute in your state tells you who must make an actual suspected child abuse or neglect report and where and how the report must be filed. In some states, counselors can fulfill their legal obligation by telling their supervisors that they suspect child abuse or neglect, and then it is the supervisors' legal obligation to file the report. In other states, the counselor who suspects child abuse or neglect has the legal obligation to personally file the report. Some statutes require oral reports only; others demand that written reports be filed; still others require reports to be filed within certain time frames. You are encouraged to locate and read carefully the mandatory child abuse and neglect reporting statutes in your jurisdiction, and then to ask for interpretations from an attorney if there is something you do not understand.

Important language in the statutes includes the following: (a) who must make the report to the governmental agency (the person with the suspicion or the supervisor), (b) when the report must be made (immediately, within 24 hours, 48 hours, or some other time frame), (c) whether the oral report must be followed by a written report, (d) what specific information is required when the report is made (such as age of the child, name and address of the child, specifics of cause of suspicion, name and address of parents), (e) whether past abuse must be reported, and (f) whether specific categories of suspected perpetrators must be reported (parents or guardians only, caretakers, siblings, other), whereas other categories of suspected perpetrators do not have to be reported. In situations where only specified categories of suspected perpetrators must be reported (for example, only caretakers must be reported), counselors may still report other categories of suspected perpetrators (such as neighbors or relatives).

Statutes vary in reporting requirements for past child abuse when the victim is no longer in danger. The statute may say specifically that past abuse must be reported, or that only currently abusive situations must be reported, or the statute may be silent on the issue. Laws are constantly changing with respect to reporting child abuse, and existing laws are being interpreted. For example, in May 2012 the attorney general of Texas issued an opinion that the state child abuse reporting statute does not require professionals to report abuse or neglect that occurred during the childhood of an adult client. Some statutes mandate that only suspected abuse by parents or guardians must be reported. However, all statutes allow nonmandated reports to be made as well. Statutes that require only caretakers to be reported leave counselors in doubt as to whether to report issues such as sibling or peer (or even neighbor) child abuse (Phillips-Green, 2002). The problems associated with sibling abuse have been highlighted by Kiselica and Morrill-Richards (2007). In the event that more than one person suspects that abuse is occurring and that all of those involved are mandated reporters, the person making the report should indicate that the report is being made on behalf of others as well and ask that their names also be recorded as reporters.

Singley (1998) has argued that mandatory suspected child abuse reporters should be given civil good faith immunity for failing to report suspected abuse, just as they are given immunity in state statutes for good-faith reporting of suspected abuse. Singley has suggested that changing the laws would significantly reduce the number of unnecessary reports of suspected child abuse that are made out of fear of civil liability. At this point, however, mandated reporters can be sued by injured children or their parents if the mandated reporters fail to make reports of suspected abuse when they are required to do so by law.

DETERMINING WHETHER A REPORT MUST BE MADE   The duty to report suspected physical, sexual, or emotional child abuse or neglect is a legal requirement (Mitchell & Rogers, 2003). This reporting obligation is clear, but counselors still must exercise clinical judgment in making a determination that a child has been or is currently being abused or neglected.

Before counselors determine that they have a legal obligation to file a report, they must form a clinical opinion that a possibility exists that a child has been or is being abused or neglected. Suspicion regarding abuse or neglect might arise as the result of something a counselor observes, such as seeing marks on a child, observing behavior that indicates abuse, or noticing something a child says in a counseling session. Also, clients may make verbal or written statements that they have been abused or that they have perpetrated abuse on others. If you are unsure whether you have enough information to form a suspicion that child abuse or neglect is involved, consult with colleagues.

Counselors must first exercise their judgment as to whether they suspect that abuse or neglect might be occurring or might have occurred in the past. Responsible counselors would consider the following factors in exercising their judgment: (a) the credibility of the alleged victim, (b) prevailing standards for discipline in the community, and (c) information that is known about the alleged victim and alleged perpetrator.

11-2 The Case of Leslie

As a result of a play counseling session, Leslie, an elementary school counselor, has come to suspect that Arielle, a second-grader, is being physically abused by her father. Leslie realizes that the law in her state requires her to report the suspected abuse within 24 hours. Leslie is hesitant to do so, however, because her experience with the local child protective services agency is that it is ineffective in responding to such reports. Leslie fears that the agency social worker will visit Arielle's home but take no further immediate action. Her concern is that the father will escalate the abuse, placing Arielle in even greater danger.

- What should Leslie do when she believes following the dictates of the reporting abuse statute might endanger her child client?
- What problems could occur if Leslie decides not to make a report?

Discussion: Even though Leslie believes filing a report might endanger Arielle, she should consider the importance of compliance with the law that requires her to report. Leslie should think about actions she might take to help ensure the child's safety. These might include enlisting the assistance of the child's mother or other relatives or teaching the child self-protection strategies.

She might also emphasize her concerns for the child's safety to the child protective services personnel and request that they take steps to protect the child. Leslie should document her contact with the agency and should inform her principal (or other immediate supervisor) of the situation.

She should talk with Arielle further after the report has been made to determine what happened thereafter. She should make additional reports if she believes the abuse has continued. If Leslie decides not to make a report and if Arielle is harmed by further abuse and it is learned that Leslie knew about but did not report the abuse, Leslie could face legal repercussions. Leslie could also face disciplinary action by her school administrator.

Leslie would have to deal with her feelings, which could include regret and guilt, if Arielle were harmed when a different decision on Leslie's part might have prevented the harm.

MAKING THE REPORT   In addition to adhering to statutory requirements in making mandatory suspected child abuse or neglect reports, counselors also must follow any procedures in effect in their employment setting. For example, a school district might require that a building principal be notified and a written report be filed before a report is made to state authorities, even when the counselor is mandated by law to make the report personally. Although school or agency policies cannot interfere with a counselor's obligation to make a report, policies can specify that school or agency administrators be notified simultaneously or after a report has been made. An employed counselor should always inform the supervisor before or immediately after making a report, even if supervisor notification is not required by policy.

It is important that counselors not forget their professional obligations to clients in fulfilling their legal obligations to make suspected child abuse or neglect reports (Remley & Fry, 1993). Child abuse or neglect reports are very disruptive to families. The lives of victims, perpetrators, and family members can be changed significantly when such reports are made. Although making a report of suspected child abuse or neglect may end your legal duties, your ethical and professional responsibilities as a counselor in the situation may continue for a long time after a mandatory report has been made.

Although most statutes allow suspected abuse reports to be made anonymously, professionals should give their names when they make reports. In addition, to protect themselves, reporters should always make a note to themselves indicating the date and time they made the oral report and the name of the person who took the report, along with a written summary of what was said when the report was made.

AFTER A REPORT HAS BEEN MADE   The procedural aspects of making suspected child abuse or neglect reports are important from a legal perspective. However, counselors always must exercise their professional judgment before and after making such reports. Reporters should have several goals in mind: (a) maintaining, to the extent possible, any counseling relationship they have with the parties involved, (b) being concerned about the welfare of the alleged victim before and after the report (Remley & Fry, 1993), (c) helping the parties deal with the process that follows reports, and (d) fulfilling their statutory legal obligations.

After making a report, counselors must again exercise their professional judgment in determining whether to tell the alleged victim that a report has been made; whether to tell the alleged perpetrator; and how to interact with the alleged victim, parents or guardians, and the alleged perpetrator after the report has been made.

State agency personnel or police officers may contact the reporter to gather further information after a report has been made. These individuals have investigatory powers and a right to question witnesses. Agency personnel or police officers need to determine whether a child abuse or neglect report reflects actual abuse or neglect and the degree to which a child may be in danger (Kemp, 1998). Counselors should not discuss the case with unknown persons on the telephone.

They should ask to see credentials of investigators, and they should be cooperative with state child protection agency investigators or police officers. Counselors may request that interviews be scheduled at times that are convenient for them. If investigators want to speak to alleged victims, the director of the agency or principal of the school should respond to such requests. Some states have specific statutory language that governs interviews with possible child abuse or neglect victims in school settings.

State agencies that investigate suspected abuse reports often are inundated with reports and may be understaffed. They must decide which cases are the most severe, and they usually pay particular attention to those situations. Whenever counselors are frustrated because they do not believe the state agency handles investigations properly or they believe children are put at risk after reports are made, they should report additional incidents and should request a meeting with governmental agency representatives to discuss the perceived problems.

School Violence

Multiple incidences of shootings and other acts of violence in schools have highlighted the need for school personnel to intervene to prevent students from causing harm to others (Hermann & Finn, 2002; Hermann & Remley, 2000; Sandhu, 2000). In response to the problem of widespread school violence, some school districts have created policies that require counselors to report students' destructive impulses or contemplation of illegal acts (Sandhu, 2000). These policies sometimes can put school counselors in a difficult position. If students, particularly adolescents, know that counselors will routinely be reporting any disclosures of their thoughts about hurting someone, they may decide not to reveal that information to their counselors. This, in turn, could reduce the opportunity to address the risk of violence (Welfel, 2013). School counselors need to work with administrators to ensure that school policies do not create a barrier to access to counseling services for students who are at risk for committing violent acts.

On a day-to-day level, school counselors also have an ethical obligation to work to prevent bullying (Espelage, Bosworth, & Simon, 2000; Hazler, 2001; Neufeld, 2002; Renshaw, 2001; Roberts & Morotti, 2000) and harassment of students by other students (King, Tribble, & Price, 1999). Counselors can address this duty through classroom guidance activities aimed at helping students understand the effects of bullying, intimidation, and harassment. A helpful resource in dealing with school violence is a guide to safe schools entitled *Early Warning, Timely Response: A Guide to Safe Schools* (U.S. Department of Education, 1998).

Dual or Multiple Relationships

Ethical dilemmas can be created by the job description and work environment of school counselors (Huey, 1996). School counselors play multiple roles, and there are inherent conflicts in some of these roles. Sometimes counselors are expected to serve, along with teachers, in duty assignments such as bathroom monitor, lunchroom supervisor, or chaperone at extracurricular events. If counselors must carry out the disciplinary functions that accompany these duties, this will compromise their ability to function effectively as personal counselors with their students. It would be unreasonable to expect students to trust and confide in a counselor who assigned them to detention or reported their misbehavior to the principal.

School counselors sometimes voluntarily take on additional roles, such as coach for an athletic team or club sponsor. Counselors can justifiably argue that these extra roles provide them with opportunities to know their student clients better outside the formal setting of the counselor's office. They should also be cognizant, however, that there is potential for misunderstandings and conflicts because these roles involve evaluation and supervision.

Occasionally, school policies exist that impinge on counselor effectiveness. If policies require counselors to inform parents about details of counseling sessions involving issues of birth control, pregnancy, abortion, sexually transmitted diseases, or other sensitive matters, some students will avoid discussing these issues with their counselors (Herlihy & Corey, 2015b).

School counselors, especially those who work in small towns and rural communities, are likely to have friends who are teachers as well as friends who are parents. Both of these situations can lead to uncomfortable dual-role conflicts. Friendships between teachers and counselors seem inevitable, given their shared interest in children's welfare, their daily contacts, and the fact that some school counselors were teachers before they became counselors. Teachers are accustomed to the sharing that occurs among colleagues, and they value open communication with other school personnel regarding students with whom they all work. Counselors, on the other hand, come from a position of honoring the confidentiality of their child clients. This *clash of cultures* complicates the work of the school counselor (Welfel, 2013).

School counselors are equally likely to have friends who are parents, and it is possible that a friend's child might also be a student client of the counselor. In such instances, counselors must be careful to keep boundaries around the professional relationship with the child and the personal relationship with the child's parents. This can pose difficult challenges (Herlihy & Corey, 2015b).

In addition, there is great potential for dual-role conflicts when counselors deal with child abuse. Counselors are required to report suspected abuse, yet their role is rarely limited to that of reporter. They are often asked to perform many other functions, including that of school system employee; court witness; liaison with social services; and counselor to the victim, perpetrator, or family (Remley & Fry, 1993). Because most children are left in their parents' custody after a report is made, the school counselor is likely to have the ongoing task of providing counseling for the child. Treatment of abuse victims is an intense and lengthy process that can strain a counselor's resources during a period when the counselor must also remain involved with the court system. The counselor will need to work with caseworkers from the children's protective services agency, with police and prosecutors, and perhaps with other attorneys. These simultaneous, multiple roles can severely test a counselor's ability to handle conflicting demands.

It is a challenge for caring counselors to maintain appropriate professional boundaries when they work with children who have been abused or who, for other reasons, are clearly in need of help. The counselor in the following example is a case in point.

11-3 The Case of Jeffrey

Jeffrey is a high school counselor who is well liked and respected by his student clients. He has a reputation among his students for being willing to go out of his way to help them. One morning at 2:00 a.m., 16-year-old Edmund, who is a member of one of the counseling groups that Jeffrey conducts at school, shows up at Jeffrey's home. Edmund claims that he has been kicked out of the house by his parents and that he has nowhere else to go. It is raining, and Edmund is soaking wet. He begs Jeffrey to let him stay there for just one night and promises that he will call his parents in the morning.

- What would happen if Jeffrey were to allow Edmund to spend the night and later Edmund accused Jeffrey of making sexual advances toward him during the night he stayed at Jeffrey's home?

- What would be the wisest things for Jeffrey to say and do in this situation?

Discussion: If Jeffrey allowed Edmund to spend the night and later Edmund accused Jeffrey of making sexual advances toward him during the night, Jeffrey might face the following problems:

- Jeffrey would appear to have been unprofessional in allowing a student to spend the night with him.
- No matter what Jeffrey said or did in response to Edmund's claims, people would still wonder whether Edmund was telling the truth.
- Jeffrey might get fired from his job for allowing Edmund to spend the night with him.
- The school district probably would deny any responsibility for what happened that night because Jeffrey was at home and not on duty.

Jeffrey should consider the following steps:

- Jeffrey could take Edmund in and give him a towel to dry off with and require Edmund to stay in the public parts of his home, such as the kitchen or front porch.
- He could call Edmund's parents and ask them to pick Edmund up. Other relatives, such as grandparents or aunts or uncles, might also be called to intervene.
- If Jeffrey determines that he should not call the parents, he could call the police and ask them to come and pick Edmund up.

Diversity Considerations with Minors

Working with children requires specialized knowledge and skills. Counselors who counsel minor clients must have a thorough understanding of child and adolescent development so that they can design interventions to match a child's developmental level (Lawrence & Robinson Kurpius, 2000). This knowledge base includes a solid grounding in the development of gender role, racial identity, and sexuality. Counselors must be careful not to impose their own values onto minor clients regarding gender, race or ethnicity, or sexual orientation, especially during adolescence when young people are forming their own unique identities.

Bemak and Chung (2007) have noted that school counselors are uniquely positioned to address the societal inequities and injustices that affect many poor students and students of color in U.S. schools. They have suggested that school counselors, serving as advocates for students, can play a significant role in reducing the academic achievement gap.

School counselors must be cognizant that female students and gay and lesbian students are likely to be subjected to sexual harassment and violence in the school environment. A solid body of research indicates that gay and lesbian students experience high rates of verbal and physical assault (Comstock, 1991; McFarland & Dupuis, 2001; Pilkington & D'Augelli, 1995). Barber and Mobley (1999), Little (2001), and Welfel (2013) have offered several strategies that school counselors can employ when counseling gay youth. Welfel has suggested the use of inclusive, nonsexist language; challenging antigay and antifemale comments made by students and school personnel, educating students and staff about sexual harassment and homophobia, and having a repertoire of appropriate referral resources for students and families who need them. School counselors can serve as advocates for other stigmatized groups of students as well, including children who are HIV-positive, whose parents are imprisoned, who are grossly overweight, or who have experienced a family suicide (Corr & Balk, 2010; Lee, 2001).

In working with parents and families of child clients, it is important for school counselors to have an understanding of systems theories. Often, a child's behavioral, social, or academic problems are reflective of family dysfunction. In addition, it is crucial for counselors to have an awareness of cultural differences in child-rearing practices. Some of the most complex and difficult situations that counselors encounter in their work with clients involve a convergence of the *duty to warn* exceptions to confidentiality and privilege with questions of counselor values and cultural diversity. An issue that can be particularly problematic in this regard is child abuse reporting.

In determining whether to make a report of child abuse, it is important to keep in mind that norms regarding acceptable child-rearing practices and punishment vary by culture (Fontes, 2002). The following case example illustrates this point.

11-4 The Case of Tonya

Tonya, a Licensed Professional Counselor (LPC) in a community counseling agency, has begun counseling the Hernandez family. The parents, Guillermo and Anabella, emigrated from Guatemala 6 years ago. They are experiencing some family conflict in their relationships with their three children: two teenage girls and a 7-year-old boy. Today, as Tonya is walking down the hallway to the reception area to greet the Hernandezes, she sees Guillermo grab the young boy roughly by the arm and slap him across the face. She is alarmed to see this abusive behavior and thinks she may have to report it to Child Protective Services.

- Do you believe that child-rearing practices that are acceptable in a subculture should be tolerated by the U.S. legal system?
- What do you think Tonya should do in this situation?

Discussion: Within the concept of *familismo*, family is a source of pride in Latino cultures, and it is very important for children to be well-behaved and represent the family well in public. When children misbehave publicly, Latino parents may respond immediately with physical punishment, which places them at greater risk for reports to child protection agencies. Knowing this information may make a difference in whether Tonya believes that what she saw was child abuse.

If Tonya believes, after considering cultural values, that what she saw Guillermo do (roughly grab his son by the arm and slap him in the face) constitutes child abuse, she is legally obligated to make a report. She should explain to him that, by law, she has to make a report.

If Guillermo cannot understand or speak English very well, Tonya should obtain an interpreter. She should explain to him that although his behavior might be common and acceptable in his native country of Guatemala, it may not be acceptable by law in the United States.

She could explain to him how American parents might discipline their children in public in a way that is culturally acceptable here and help him understand how his behavior might be viewed by the majority culture. If she makes a report, she should explain to him what might happen after she does so, and she should make a sincere attempt to continue her counseling relationship with him and his family.

Tonya may decide that what she saw did not constitute child abuse. If she makes that determination, she will not make a report.

Counselors who provide professional services to culturally diverse populations of children and adolescents must continually examine their own values in determining the most appropriate actions when confronted with risk-taking behaviors. They must be clear about their own stances toward such issues as drug and alcohol use, premarital sex, abortion, and appropriate discipline, and they must be cognizant of community standards.

VULNERABLE ADULTS

All of the issues related to minor clients apply equally to any adult clients who have been legally adjudicated mentally incompetent or who have had legal guardians appointed based on their diminished capacity. Just as counselors have an ethical and legal obligation to protect children when there is suspicion of abuse or neglect, they have a duty to protect adult clients who are vulnerable to maltreatment due to diminished capacity to protect themselves from harm. Adults who might be considered vulnerable include developmentally disabled, severely mentally ill, elderly, and physically disabled individuals. In 2006 it was reported that all 50 states, the District of Columbia, Guam, Puerto Rico, and the Virgin Islands had enacted statutes that provided protective and social services for victims of elder abuse (Stiegel & Klem, 2006). The statutes vary widely regarding the definition of elder abuse; the age of protected elders; the types of abuse, neglect, and exploitation that are covered; whether abuse is a criminal or civil offense; and the remedies for abuse. State elder abuse reporting laws and updates have been collected by the Stetson University College of Law (2014).

Elder or Vulnerable Adult Maltreatment

Numerically, the elderly are by far the largest group of adults who are vulnerable to abuse or neglect. Elder maltreatment is a growing but underrecognized problem in our society. The population of citizens over the age of 65 has grown twice as fast as all other age groups (Welfel, Danzinger, & Santoro, 2000). In 2009, 12.9% of the U.S. population was 65 years or older, and by 2030 this group is expected to comprise 19% of the population (Administration on Aging, 2014).

Although many older adults continue to enjoy good health and function independently, beginning at age 75 the risk steadily increases for developing diseases and disorders that compromise functioning, including cognitive impairments. Older people who suffer from dementia, physical decline, or chronic diseases that limit their ability to live independently are at the greatest risk for maltreatment.

It is difficult to estimate the incidence of elder maltreatment because it so often goes unreported. It is possible that as few as 1 in 14 cases is reported (Quinn & Tomita, 1997). According to some estimates, it is likely that as many as 10 million older adults suffer abuse or neglect every year (Schwiebert, Myers, & Dice, 2000).

The National Center on Elder Abuse (2014) has estimated that about two-thirds of all elder abuse perpetrators are family members; most are the victim's adult child or spouse. According to the Center, abusers in many instances are financially dependent on the elder's resources, often have alcohol or drug problems, have mental or emotional illnesses, and feel burdened by their caregiving responsibilities.

The National Center on Elder Abuse (2014) has provided data that show that abused elders are at higher risk of health problems and have been shown to have a 300% higher risk of death when compared to those who had not been abused. Comijs, Penninx, Knipscheer, and van Tilburg (1999) found that victims of elder abuse had significantly higher levels of psychological distress and lower perceived self-efficacy than older adults who had not been victimized. Clearly, there is a role for professional counselors both in prevention of maltreatment and in assisting victims to recover from its effects, which can include depression; posttraumatic stress symptomology; learned helplessness; and feelings of isolation, alienation, and mistrust.

Welfel et al. (2000) identified several forms of elder maltreatment. *Neglect*, defined as failure to provide essential physical or mental care for an older person, is the most common form. Neglect can be intentional or unintentional, or even self-inflicted. Self-neglect can occur when elderly people forget to take their medications or take them incorrectly, skip meals, use alcohol to self-medicate against depression or loneliness, or fail to maintain personal hygiene. Because self-neglect is often associated with depression (Quinn & Tomita, 1997), counselors are particularly well equipped to treat this problem.

Physical violence, another fairly common type of elder maltreatment, can take many forms, including slapping, pinching, withholding medication or overmedicating, misuse of physical restraints, and force feeding. Persons with dementia are particularly vulnerable to physical abuse by caregivers (Welfel et al., 2000). Psychological abuse, likewise, occurs in a variety of ways. Among the more frequently reported manifestations are verbal berating, threats to institutionalize the elder individual, and threats of abandonment, intimidation, or humiliation.

Financial exploitation is nearly as prevalent as psychological abuse, and it is estimated that there are 5 million cases of elder financial abuse each year (National Center on Elder Abuse, 2014). This form of abuse occurs when someone (often a caretaker) misuses an older person's income or resources for his or her own personal gain. Abusers may deny elderly adults things to which they are entitled, steal their possessions or money, or coerce them into signing contracts that are not in their best interest.

The following case example illustrates a situation in which more than one form of elder abuse is present.

11-5 The Case of Marjorie

Jerome is 89 years old and lives with his 58-year-old son, Tyler. Tyler is an accountant whose wife divorced him after many years of attempting to get him to kick his cocaine habit. Jerome suffers from mild dementia and is partially paralyzed as a result of a stroke. He needs assistance with bathing and dressing, but he is able to get around the house using a walker. Tyler often leaves for work before Jerome awakens in the morning, which results in Jerome being forced to spend the day unbathed and in his pajamas. It is not uncommon for Tyler to fail to come home after work because he is out looking to buy cocaine. On several such occasions, Jerome has burned himself while trying to cook his dinner. Tyler cashes Jerome's Social Security checks for him, but more often than not he spends the money to buy drugs. When Jerome tries to discuss these problems with his son, Tyler yells at him and threatens to put him into a nursing home. Jerome is so terrified by this possibility that he withdraws into silence.

Marjorie is a home visit counselor from the local mental health center. The first time she visits Jerome in his home, she is disturbed by his grooming and physical condition. Very reluctantly, Jerome tells Marjorie about some of Tyler's behaviors. Marjorie becomes even more concerned about Jerome's welfare.

- What should Marjorie say to Jerome?
- What do you think Marjorie should do?

Discussion: Marjorie should inform Jerome that he does not have to endure the conditions in which he is living. She should assure him there are alternatives that he might find acceptable and explain to him what those alternatives are.

Marjorie should consider taking the following actions:

- If her state law requires counselors to report cases of suspected elder abuse, Marjorie should make the report.

- If there is no statutory requirement, then Marjorie should decide whether it is in Jerome's best interest to report the suspected abuse to authorities even though there is no legal requirement to do so.
- Marjorie should try to arrange an appointment with Tyler to determine whether she can be of assistance in helping him care for his father and perhaps persuade him to seek treatment for his drug addiction.

If you will be counseling older adults or families whose concerns including caretaking elderly relatives, you should be aware that elder abuse is difficult to detect. As is true in the case example just described, the perpetrator is usually a family member, and neither the victim nor members of the family want to reveal the problem. If you are alert to the possibility, however, you may find yourself confronted with the question of what to do when you suspect elder maltreatment. You must consider both your legal and your ethical obligations.

All states have enacted some form of legislation aimed at reducing elder maltreatment (Tatara, 1996). In many ways the laws are similar to child abuse reporting statutes, but they are different in that not every state mandates that professionals report suspected abuse to authorities. Another difference is that elder abuse reporting statutes usually allow older adults to refuse protective services if they do not want them (Welfel et al., 2000). To compound the problem, there is little uniformity across the states in elder abuse reporting statutes. Statutes vary with respect to age requirements for qualifying as *elderly*, types of abuse that are reportable, procedures for reporting, and whether counselors and other mental health professionals are considered to be mandated reporters. Obviously, you will need to learn the specific requirements of the relevant statutes in the state and community where you will be practicing.

As an ethical obligation, reporting of elder maltreatment arises from the principles of nonmaleficence and beneficence. When counselors suspect that a vulnerable person is being harmed in some way, they have a duty to intervene to prevent the harm from continuing and to promote client welfare. Welfel et al. (2000) offered the following guidelines for counselors faced with situations of elder maltreatment:

- Remember to consider the possibility of elder maltreatment when working with older clients who are dependent on family or others for their care.
- Interview family members separately to increase the likelihood of honest disclosures about the situation. Often, older adults feel intimidated by the presence of family members or embarrassed over the nature of the information.
- Provide an empathic and supportive environment in which clients will feel safe to reveal information that they may find shameful, humiliating, or acutely distressing. Ask nonjudgmental questions, like "Do you feel safe in your home?" or "Do you feel in control of your finances?"
- Focus on helping the older clients and their families or caregivers to improve the quality of care. Educate clients and families about the services available in their communities to assist them, such as advocacy groups and respite care facilities.
- Know the risk factors related to elder abuse. These include, for an older person, poor physical health, cognitive impairment, sufficient frailty to make independent living impossible, and a tendency to act disruptively. Risk factors for caregivers include a history of mental disorders, substance abuse problems, and a history of using violence to resolve conflict. Family characteristics that increase risk include social isolation and inadequate financial resources to assist with caregiving.

If, after careful exploration, you believe that you must make a report, you will want to try to accomplish this in a way that will not destroy the counseling relationship. You should involve the client in the reporting process, discuss thoroughly the logistical and emotional consequences of the report, report only essential information to preserve confidentiality to the extent possible, and follow up to ensure that needed services are being offered (Welfel et al., 2000).

Other Issues in Counseling Older Adults

Schwiebert et al. (2000) identified two issues, in addition to abuse or neglect, that pose difficult ethical questions for counselors who work with older adults. When older adults have cognitive impairments, for example, questions regarding informed consent arise. If a client begins counseling during the early stages of a progressive deteriorating disease such as Alzheimer's, at what point is that client no longer able to consent to continued counseling? Can the counselor continue to work with the client, or must the counselor wait until permission is granted by a legal guardian?

A second circumstance that can present agonizing dilemmas for counselors arises when clients have a terminal illness. Counselors are confronted with ethical and legal quandaries when these clients want to end their suffering by hastening their own deaths. The *Code of Ethics* (ACA, 2014), §B.2.b., is related to end-of-life decisions of clients. The standard states, "Counselors who provide services to terminally ill individuals who are considering hastening their own deaths have the option to maintain confidentiality, depending on applicable laws and the specific circumstances of the situation and after seeking consultation or supervision from appropriate professional and legal parties." Bennett and Werth (2006) have concluded that these types of ethical guidelines provide counselors with more latitude when counseling terminally ill clients who have a desire to die. Werth and Crow (2009) have offered the opinion that, due to the guidelines in the *Code of Ethics,* counselors are in the safest ethical and legal position of all mental health professionals with respect to working with clients on end-of-life decision making. The issue of counseling terminally ill clients was discussed briefly in Chapter 4 as it relates to value conflicts. That topic is discussed in more detail in the following section.

END-OF-LIFE DECISIONS   Due in large part to the aging of the U.S. population and to continuing developments in life-saving and life-sustaining medical technology, death in U.S. society now commonly occurs at an advanced age or after a prolonged illness. Thus, it is likely that increasing numbers of individuals will consider making a request for aid-in-dying through physician-assisted suicide. As a result, counselors will be called on more frequently to work with clients who are considering this action, and with their families and significant others (Herlihy & Watson, 2004).

At the present time, Oregon, Vermont, and Washington are the only states that have legalized physician-assisted suicide through legislation. Montana allows physician-assisted suicide as the result of a court ruling (Euthanasia.procon.org, 2014). In other states, physician-assisted suicide is a criminal act, or the law is ambiguous (Crawford, 1999). In 2014, 39 states had statutes explicitly criminalizing assisted suicide, and in three additional states assisted suicide was criminalized through common law. In four states, the law was unclear on the legality of physician-assisted suicide (Euthanasia.procon.org, 2014). After reviewing the results of officially sanctioned physician-assisted suicide in Oregon and the Netherlands in the context of laws and statutes, Stern and DiFonzo (2007) concluded that there is still much to be learned about palliative care, societal beliefs about dying, and laws that eventually might be passed related to this topic. They stated that physicians need to take an unambiguous stand on physician-assisted suicide to avoid uninformed legislators enacting laws that are not in the best interests of those who are dying.

In 1997, the U.S. Supreme Court considered the legality of assisted suicide. The Court heard appeals to two circuit court decisions that had struck down criminal prohibitions against assisted suicide in the states of New York and Washington. The Court held unanimously in both cases that there is not a constitutional right to physician-assisted suicide, leaving it up to individual states to determine whether to allow the practice (Werth & Gordon, 2002). Even though the *Code of Ethics* (ACA, 2014) reflects support for a person's right to choose the time and manner of ending suffering caused by terminal illness, and support for counselor involvement in such decision making, you must decide for yourself whether you are able and willing to work with these clients. This will entail carefully examining your beliefs and values about living and dying, quality of life, and the right to die (Herlihy & Watson, 2004; Jamison, 2012). Do you believe that people have the right to hasten their own death? If so, in what circumstances? When they have a terminal illness? If so, must death be imminent? When their condition is not terminal but their lives are filled with pain and suffering and there is no hope for improvement? In some circumstances, such as when clinical depression is clouding a client's judgment or when a client is being pressured by others to consider physician-assisted suicide, you may need to invoke your duty to warn and protect that client (see Chapter 5 for a discussion of this duty).

You must also be aware of cultural issues, as some scholars have asserted that if physician-assisted suicide were more broadly legalized, it would have the greatest effect on the most vulnerable members of our society—those whose autonomy is already compromised by poverty, lack of access to quality medical care, advanced age, or membership in a stigmatized group (New York State Task Force on Life and the Law, 1994). Thus, if you counsel terminally ill clients considering physician-assisted suicide, you will need to carefully self-monitor to guard against making assumptions based on the client's race, socioeconomic status, religious and spiritual beliefs, or age. Consider the following case example:

11-6 The Case of Karen

Karen is a counselor who works in a hospital, and her job is to counsel patients and families while they are hospitalized. Weldon is a 73-year-old widower with a grown daughter. Although Weldon has been diagnosed with terminal cancer, his doctors tell him that he might expect to live more than another year with further surgery and chemotherapy. Weldon wants to request physician-assisted suicide, stating that he doesn't want to die a lingering death or to consider hospice care. He adds that he doesn't want to be a burden to his daughter, who is a single mother and works long hours to support her two children. He insists that he would find it humiliating to be cared for by strangers in a hospice. He doesn't want to involve his daughter in his decision-making process because she would never accept the idea of a hastened death for him and because he wants her memories of him to be happy ones.

- How should Karen proceed in her counseling relationship with Weldon?
- Do you believe that other states should follow the example of Oregon, Vermont, and Washington and pass laws that permit physician-assisted suicide? Why or why not?

Discussion: Karen's first action should be to determine whether her state allows physician-assisted suicides. If they are allowed in her state, Karen should learn as much as possible about the requirements for a person to choose that option. If she feels competent to counsel Weldon regarding physician-assisted suicide, she can use her counseling skills to help him review his options and make his final decisions. Karen might assist Weldon by helping him to examine his motives for wanting physician-assisted suicide and to explore other alternatives. She also could work to facilitate an open dialog between him and his daughter.

Arguments for physician-assisted suicide laws include the following:

- Persons should have a right to choose to die with dignity.
- It is inhumane to keep people alive when their quality of life has diminished beyond reason.
- Physicians have been assisting people with dying throughout history. It is time now to make it legal.

Arguments against such laws include the following:

- It is impossible to know whether a person who wants to commit suicide is able to make such a choice.
- Vulnerable individuals would be at the mercy of others who might want them to die.
- Only God should decide when a person will die.

Counselors are well qualified to assist terminally ill clients with end-of-life decision making and may be called on more frequently to provide services, particularly if other states follow the example of Oregon, Vermont, and Washington in enacting *death with dignity laws*. Bennett and Werth (2006) have advised counselors who work with clients making end-of-life decisions to take several steps to ensure that clients receive quality care. First, counselors should determine whether they have the competency and training to work with such clients. Second, they should conduct a thorough assessment of the client, or refer the client to a competent provider. Third, it is wise to consult with other professionals. Fourth, counselors should document carefully the assessment, consultations, and treatment options that were considered and chosen.

Diversity Considerations in Counseling Older Adults

In working with older adults, counselors must guard against clinician age bias. Stereotyping and discrimination against older people appears to be a significant problem among mental health counselors. Danzinger and Welfel (2000) reviewed the research and found evidence that counselors are reluctant to work with older people, tend to view them as having poorer prognoses, and see them as being more set in their ways and less able to change. Clients who suffer from Alzheimer's disease or other cognitive impairments are as deserving of respect for their autonomy in decision making as are any other clients. When counseling with an older person, or a client with a pervasive developmental disability or severe mental illness, counselors must take care to avoid the paternalistic assumption that others (including the counselor) know what's best for the client.

Clients Who Have Been Declared Legally Incompetent

All of the legal issues that apply to children and elderly persons also apply to individuals who have been declared incompetent by courts. Although very few individuals are declared by courts to be legally incompetent, adults who are developmentally disabled, critically ill, seriously injured, mentally ill, or elderly could be declared incompetent by a court. If such individuals are declared incompetent, the court appoints a legal guardian who has the same legal powers over the individual that a biological parent or a legal guardian would have over a child.

Counselors must be careful to distinguish between adult clients who have actually been declared incompetent and those who still maintain their legal rights but are dependent on others.

Dependent adults maintain their legal rights until a court, upon a petition filed by some party, declares them incompetent and appoints a guardian.

The *Code of Ethics* (ACA, 2014) addresses the informed consent and confidentiality rights of clients who have been declared legally incompetent. Standard A.2.d. reminds counselors to seek the assent of clients to counseling services and to include them in the decision-making process as appropriate. Standard B.5.a. requires counselors to protect the confidentiality of clients who lack the capacity to give voluntary, informed consent.

Summary and Key Points

This chapter focuses on legal and ethical considerations in working with children and vulnerable adults. There are discrepancies between legal and ethical perspectives regarding certain issues in counseling minors, such as privacy and confidentiality rights. These discrepancies pose some difficult challenges for counselors. Many of the same issues that arise in working with minor clients also apply when providing services to vulnerable adults.

Some of the key points made in this chapter about counseling children include the following:

- Minor clients have an ethical right to privacy and confidentiality in the counseling relationship, but the privacy rights of minors legally belong to their parents or guardians.
- Counselors should not automatically assume that all minor clients do not want their parents to know information they have shared with their counselors. The stance that minor clients take toward privacy will vary according to their age, developmental stage, and motivation for sharing information with the counselor.
- The *Code of Ethics* (ACA, 2014) allows counselors latitude to use their professional judgment in determining whether and when to involve parents or guardians in the counseling process.
- Generally, clients under the age of 18 are not considered legally competent to give informed consent to counseling, although there are exceptions to this rule.
- Parents or guardians probably have the legal right to know the contents of counseling sessions with their children.

- Noncustodial parents have certain rights and might be included in the counseling process if it is in a child's best interest.
- Counselors can follow a sequence of steps in resolving a situation in which a parent or guardian demands information and the minor client feels strongly that the information should not be divulged to the parent or guardian.
- Counseling is a contractual relationship into which minors cannot legally enter on their own. Nonetheless, school counselors do not have a legal obligation to obtain parent permission before counseling student clients. On the other hand, parents who object to their child's participation in counseling probably have the legal right to demand that services be discontinued.
- For legal purposes, informed consent to counsel a minor should be obtained from the parents. As an ethical matter, the child client should be actively involved in giving consent and determining treatment goals and strategies.
- Counselors are required by law to report suspected child abuse or neglect. Counselors need to be very familiar with reporting requirements in the state where they practice, because statutes vary considerably from state to state.
- The reporting of suspected child abuse requires counselors to exercise their professional judgment before and after making a report. A host of factors must be taken into consideration throughout the process.
- School violence has become an increasing concern that raises questions for counselors regarding reporting threats and how to prevent bullying and harassment of children.

- School counselors often play multiple roles. Conflicts can occur between the role of counselor and other roles such as bathroom or lunchroom monitor, coach or club sponsor, and friend to teachers and parents of student clients. Difficult challenges are posed by the need to maintain appropriate boundaries around dual professional roles or simultaneous personal and professional roles.

Counseling vulnerable adults and clients who have been legally declared incompetent was also addressed in this chapter. Key points include the following:

- Counselors have an ethical and legal obligation to protect adult clients who are vulnerable to abuse or neglect due to a diminished capacity to protect themselves.
- Elder abuse and neglect are underreported and are common problems in today's society.
- As the U.S. population ages, counselors will be confronted more often with requests to assist clients in their end-of-life decision making.
- All of the legal issues that apply to minor clients apply to individuals who have been declared by courts to be legally incompetent. Counselors need to be careful to distinguish between legally incompetent clients and clients who are dependent on others but who retain their legal rights.

Counseling Families and Groups

FOCUS QUESTIONS

1. How is confidentiality different when counseling couples, families, or groups, as opposed to counseling an individual client?

2. Why do you think marriage and family counselors end up embroiled in their clients' lawsuits so often?

3. What should counselors tell potential counseling group members to ensure adequate informed consent?

E thical and legal issues can be complex when counselors work with more than one client at a time, as they do in family counseling and group counseling. Many of the same issues apply as when counseling individuals, but they often are more complicated and difficult to resolve when more than one client is involved.

This chapter begins with a focus on counseling families. Ethical concerns that are particularly challenging when counseling families are competence, consent, confidentiality, competing interests (Koocher, 2008), protecting client welfare, and the potential for imposition of counselor values. These familiar topics are revisited from a family systems orientation. This first section also examines some special considerations that often arise in family counseling such as preserving a marriage versus facing divorce, child custody, family secrets, and ethical questions posed by domestic violence.

The second portion of this chapter focuses on group work. The issues of client welfare and informed consent, protecting clients from harm, privacy and confidentiality, dual relationships, counselor values, and counselor competence take on new dimensions when applied to group counseling. Additional ethical and legal rights and responsibilities must be addressed when conducting group counseling, such as freedom to exit a group, screening potential members, protecting confidentiality with minors in groups, and dealing with outside-of-group socializing among group members.

FAMILY COUNSELING

Family counselors use a systems perspective in working with their clients. From this viewpoint, the family provides the context for understanding its individual members and their problems. Family counselors believe that actions taken by any family member will influence the other members and that their reactions in turn will have a reciprocal effect on the individual (Corey, Corey, Corey, & Callanan, 2015). Counselors often work with couples, parents and children, nuclear families, families of origin, extended families, and nontraditional families. Therefore, the first question that the counselor needs to answer is "Who is the client?" Although family counselors see the entire family system as their client, the answer to this seemingly basic question is not that simple. If the counseling goals of one family member are different from or even antithetical to the wishes of another member, whose interests does the counselor serve? Family counselors need to consider their responsibilities to each of the parties involved in the counseling process (Fisher, 2009). Balancing the interests and fostering the well-being of everyone in the family is one of the most challenging ethical mandates for family counselors (Corey et al., 2015).

Counselors who provide services to couples or families on a regular basis should consult two specialized codes of ethics that have been developed by the International Association of Marriage and Family Counselors (IAMFC), a division within the American Counseling Association (ACA); and the American Association for Marriage and Family Therapy (AAMFT). The IAMFC code, the *Ethical Code for the International Association of Marriage and Family Counselors* (Hendricks, Bradley, Southern, Oliver, & Birdsall, 2011), can be found at www.iamfconline.org. The 2012 *AAMFT Code of Ethics* can be found at www.aamft.org.

Sometimes counseling begins as individual work, and the family is included later. The ACA *Code of Ethics* (ACA, 2014) encourages counselors to recognize that families are usually important forces in clients' lives. The code says that counselors "consider enlisting the support, understanding, and involvement of others," including family members, when appropriate and with client consent (§A.1.d.). When counseling begins with an individual client and then includes family members, to whom does the counselor have primary responsibility—the individual family member who originally sought counseling or the family as a whole? Standard A.6.d. states that when changing from individual to relationship or family counseling, or vice versa, counselors obtain informed consent from the client and "explain the right of the client to refuse services related to the change." This standard further advises that clients must be fully informed of any anticipated consequences of counselor role changes. Therefore, when counselors begin counseling with an individual client and then change the focus to family counseling, they will need to revisit issues related to goals, informed consent, parameters of confidentiality, and treatment planning.

Problems can arise when these questions are not resolved at the beginning of the counseling relationship. Standard A.8. of the *Code of Ethics* (ACA, 2014) states that counselors clarify at the outset "which person or persons are clients and the nature of the relationships the counselor will have with each involved person." The standard provides guidance in the event the counselor is called upon to perform conflicting roles and requires that, in such circumstances, "the counselor will clarify, adjust, or withdraw from roles appropriately." In addition, "Counselors seek agreement and document in writing such agreement among all involved parties regarding the confidentiality of information." (§B.4.b.).

Because the law and the counseling profession have different perspectives on the family, the two are sometimes in conflict. Family counselors often view the family system as their client and treat the family, as opposed to treating individual members of a family. The law, on the other hand, always views family members as having separate and distinct rights and responsibilities that are individual in nature. To further complicate the situation, the law states that any minor or legally incompetent family member can exercise rights only through parents or legal guardians. This poses problems when one family member wants a family counselor to uphold confidentiality and another family member demands that the counselor reveal in court conversations what took place during counseling sessions. A family counselor generally favors the family member who wants privacy, whereas the law usually favors the family member who wants the information revealed. This problem is discussed in greater depth later in this chapter.

Informed Consent

When working with families, the issue of informed consent is complicated. The counselor must attempt to ensure that consent to counseling is given freely after clear and sufficient information has been provided and must also address the following questions:

- Who gives consent on behalf of the family?
- Who in the family is seeking counseling, and are any participants reluctant to participate? Can family members who feel pressured to join in the counseling process give truly free consent?
- What happens when one of the adults in the family refuses to give consent for family counseling?
- How capable are potential participants—particularly children—of understanding what they are getting into?
- How can counselors adequately address the reality that there will be changes in the family system, as well as in individual members, as a result of counseling?

Obtaining informed consent from all members of a family sometimes is not possible. In marriage and family counseling, the desired procedure is to have all adults and legally competent family members give consent to counseling. A difficult situation arises if one such individual refuses to do so. Kenneth, the counselor in the following scenario, is faced with this situation.

12-1 The Case of Kenneth

Kenneth is a private practitioner who is licensed as a professional counselor and as a marriage and family therapist. He receives a telephone call from Mr. Marquez, who wants to make an appointment for himself and his two children, ages 10 and 12. He states that he and his wife have been having serious marital difficulties, which are taking their toll on the children, who are beginning to act out both at home and at school. He adds that his wife is supportive of their wish to seek counseling but that she refuses to participate in the process because she believes the marital problems are entirely his fault.

- How do you think Kenneth should respond to this request from Mr. Marquez?
- If Kenneth begins counseling with Mr. Marquez and his two children, what issues should he keep in mind?

Discussion: Kenneth might agree to see the family members who are willing to engage in counseling. If he does so, he should explain to Mr. Marquez the problems that exist when one family member is unwilling to participate. If Kenneth begins counseling with Mr. Marquez and his children, he will need to be careful to avoid allowing the three attending family members to blame the absent wife/mother for problems that are occurring in the family. He should, instead, keep the focus on helping Mr. Marquez and each child examine their own behavior and how it contributes positively and negatively to the family dynamics.

The issue of what to do about nonparticipating family members raises some difficult ethical questions. A controversial procedure used by some family counselors is to withhold services until all family members agree to participate in counseling. The problem with this practice is that the counselor thereby cooperates with the resistant family member by keeping the rest of the family from receiving counseling. Willing family members are then put in an unfair position of being denied services (Haas & Alexander, 1981; Wilcoxon, Remley, & Gladding, 2013). Of course, coercion of reluctant family members would be unethical, but some family counselors are comfortable exerting some pressure on a resistant family member to participate in one or two sessions. These counselors hope that the resistance can be overcome when members see that they are not going to be scapegoated or blamed for the family's problems (Welfel, 2013). Other strategies that have been suggested include inviting the reluctant family member to attend one individual session to explain the counseling process and address any fears the person may have, referring the willing family members to individual counseling with other providers until the entire family is ready to enter into counseling, and sending the nonparticipating member a letter explaining the family counseling process and changes that might occur as a result of counseling (Wilcoxon & Fennel, 1983).

Another point of view is that when individual family members refuse to participate, counseling still should be made available for those who desire counseling. Counseling should also be made available to family members who are mandated by courts to attend counseling.

Although children cannot legally give informed consent, counselors are wise to involve them in the decision-making process. It is hard to imagine that family counseling would be successful if it included a resistant, resentful teenager who felt left out of the decision to engage in the process. Counselors must be able to communicate with adolescents and children in a way that enables them to understand their role in the family counseling process, and then request their consent to participate (Goldenberg & Goldenberg, 1996).

Just as counselors have an ethical obligation to alert individual clients to life changes that might occur as a result of counseling, family counselors must describe potential changes in family relationships as well as adaptations that individual family members might make in conjunction with shifts in the family system (Herlihy & Corey, 2015a). It can be very difficult to anticipate directions that these reciprocal changes might take, and it is possible that counseling outcomes viewed as desirable by one participant, such as a wife's decision to divorce, might be seen as disastrous by another participant (Wilcoxon et al., 2013). Nonetheless, family counselors have an obligation to explain that the family system will be the focus of the counseling process and that no one family member will be treated as the *identified patient* who is the source of the family's problems (Corey, Corey, Corey, & Callanan, 2015).

Client Welfare

Family counseling gives priority to the good of the family and, thus, may not be in the best interests of an individual in the family. Ethical practice demands that family counselors make every effort to minimize the risks to individuals. One way to accomplish this is to encourage family members to question how counseling relates to their needs and goals as well as to those of the family. This kind of discussion should take place as part of the informed consent process and throughout counseling, as needed.

Although family counselors may consider the family as a whole to be their client, the law would demand that all clients within a family group be able to rely on the counselor to act in a manner that furthers their best interest and protects them from harm. Legal problems might arise, for example, if a client in family counseling were financially harmed after a counselor encouraged the family to make decisions that excluded the family member from the financial support of the family.

The changing nature of families raises another legal concern for family counselors. Few families seeking counseling today consist of a biological mother and father, and their children. Instead, families reflect a number of societal trends: single parents are raising children; a stepparent is in the family; single parents have partners to whom they are not married living with the family; close friends are intimately involved with the family; extended family members such as grandparents (Bradley, Whiting, Hendricks, & Wheat, 2010), adult siblings, uncles, aunts, or cousins reside with the family and may be responsible for raising the children; and gay and lesbian couples are raising children. Family counselors must keep in mind, when working with nontraditional families, that only biological parents or court-appointed guardians have legal rights of control and authority over children. Often, one or more biological parents who are not present in a family have legal rights that must be considered when family decisions regarding children are made.

One-third of the children in the United States live in some type of stepparenting situation. Stepparents, nonmarried partners, grandparents, other relatives, and friends have no legal rights to confidential information or other privileges held by biological parents. In the event that a counselor wants a person other than a biological parent to have confidential information regarding a child client, a simple solution is to have a biological parent sign a form allowing the counselor to disclose information to the other person.

Risky Techniques

Any time counselors use techniques that are out of the ordinary, they must ensure that clients are protected. If a client is harmed as a result of a nontraditional or unusual technique, the client or the counselor's colleagues could claim that the counselor was operating outside the scope of accepted practices in the field.

Family members often enter counseling feeling vulnerable and fragile, and they may relinquish some of their own authority and allow the counselor to be very influential (Manfrini, 2006). The ethical obligation to reduce client dependency and foster autonomy can be particularly problematic in marriage and family therapy because, in most marriage and family therapy approaches, the counselor is seen as an active and directive agent of change (Nichols & Schwartz, 2004; Wilcoxon et al., 2013). Family counselors sometimes become quite active in directing family members to take, or refrain from taking, certain actions. Directives given by counselors are sometimes called *prescriptions* (Carlson, Sperry, & Lewis, 1997). A professional who prescribes behavior must ensure that no one is harmed as a result of the directives.

One controversial technique used by some family counselors is known as *paradoxical directives* or *interventions*. The concept behind the technique is that if authorities instruct persons to do things that are against their best interests, they will defy the counselor and correct the behavior on their own (Goldenberg & Goldenberg, 1998). When paradoxical directives are used in the strategic family counseling model, according to Carlson et al. (1997), "The therapist assigns tasks in which success is based on the family defying instructions or following them to an extreme point and ultimately recoiling, thus producing change" (p. 63). As an example, assume that a teenage daughter is in an inappropriate role reversal situation with her parent. The parent is acting like a teenager, and the daughter is acting like a disapproving parent. The family counselor tells the daughter to work harder at correcting her parent's irresponsible behavior and to take on even more household responsibilities. In this situation, the counselor would hope that the daughter would recoil, defy the counselor's directive, and recognize that she was taking on a parenting role that was inappropriate for her.

Ethical concerns regarding this technique have been raised. One objection to paradoxical directives is that they are manipulative and deceptive. Even though the counselor may ultimately debrief the target of the intervention (the daughter in the previous example), the counselor delivers the intervention without revealing these intentions. Haley (1987) has argued that such a procedure is a *benevolent lie*, but many writers question whether techniques that involve deception can ever be considered ethically permissible (Lakin, 1994; Welfel, 2013).

A second concern involves the risk of negative outcomes. Some applications of this technique that are potentially dangerous are (a) a parent who is overly strict is told to become more strict in disciplining the children and (b) an employee who is frantically worried about not performing up to an employer's expectations is told to be more concerned about pleasing the boss. In these two examples, it is clear how problems could manifest themselves. The parent could physically harm the children, and the employee could become so distressed as to lose the job.

Paradoxical techniques are not the only type of powerful intervention used in family counseling. Family sculpting, a psychodrama technique, also can have powerful and unpredictable effects. Other interventions that evoke strong feelings or uncover feelings that have been kept secret in the family can leave clients vulnerable to harm. As a result, family counselors must carefully consider the ramifications of such interventions (Welfel, 2013) and ensure that no one is harmed.

Family Violence

Lawson (2003) has pointed out that 50% to 60% of couples seeking counseling services have reported at least one incidence of violence in their relationship. In 1987, Arias, Samios, and O'Leary found that intimate partner violence was more common in dating couples and among women about to be married than in married couples. In addition, men and women were almost equally violent toward one another in terms of frequency, as reported by Straus (1999) and Straus and Gelles (1992).

Some scholars, and feminist counselors in particular, have been critical of the idea of applying systems theory to abusive relationships. They note that 95% of victims of physical abuse are women, and they assert that blaming the relationship or relationship dynamics for the abuse is inexcusable. They believe strongly that the male abuser must be held responsible for his behavior.

Welfel (2013) has described the difficulties inherent in attempting to conduct family counseling with couples when abuse is occurring in their relationship. When one partner in a relationship is being abused by the other, the foundation for successful counseling is absent. The partner being abused cannot express feelings honestly in counseling sessions or risk behavior change. The perpetrator can evade personal responsibility when the problem is framed as a family issue. For these reasons, most writers recommend that family counselors see the partners individually, at least initially. Of course, some counselors believe that couples counseling is an appropriate approach when dealing with some physically abusive relationships. Haddock (2002) has addressed the need for counselors to be prepared to assess for partner abuse and provide counseling to the couple. There is no empirical evidence that one approach is more effective than the other.

Wilcoxon et al. (2013) have presented a thoughtful discussion of ethical dilemmas that counselors face when intimate partner violence is present in the relationship of a couple in counseling. For example, if counselors encourage the victim to leave or insist that the victim leave a violent relationship, are the counselors imposing their own values and infringing on the client's right to autonomy in decision making? On the other hand, *not* encouraging a victim to leave a dangerous situation would seem to violate the moral principle of *do no harm*. We caution counselors not to encourage a victim to leave a violent relationship until a safety plan is in place to ensure that this individual does not come to further harm.

Privacy, Confidentiality, and Privileged Communication

Challenges to confidentiality increase exponentially when counselors counsel more than one person at the same time (Kleist & Bitter, 2009). Counselors can guarantee confidentiality only on their own parts. They must encourage confidentiality but make it clear that it cannot be guaranteed on the part of family members. You might review the statement regarding privacy in family situations that is included in the client information and agreement found in Appendix B to see how this might be accomplished.

The legal counterpart to the ethic of confidentiality is privileged communication. The general rule regarding privileged communication is that privilege is waived if a third party is present (Knapp & VandeCreek, 1987). Most licensed counselors practice in jurisdictions where privilege exists between counselors and their clients, but where there is no specific guarantee of privilege for family situations. In these circumstances, clients who wish to bring family members into counseling sessions must be told that the privilege that normally would exist between the counselor and the client probably would be lost.

Some privilege statutes have been enacted more recently that specifically grant privilege to family members individually and to their counselor (Arthur & Swanson, 1993; Huber & Baruth, 1987; Kearney, 1984). In these situations, an individual client could prevent a counselor from being forced to testify as to what occurred in the sessions, but there is a question as to whether the client would be able to prevent other family members from testifying if they were inclined to do so. As a result, counselors who practice in states where privilege does exist in family counseling situations should assure clients that they would not willingly disclose information from their sessions, but they also should inform clients that other family members may not have the same obligation to keep the relationship confidential (Jacobs, Masson, & Harvill, 1998).

In *Perez v. City of Chicago* (2004), a federal court found that family members had a right to demand that their private information revealed in family counseling sessions be kept private even when a family member who was a party in a lawsuit had waived his privilege. The court noted that it would be very impractical for a counselor to redact information from family counseling notes to preserve the privacy of the family and therefore held that the family counseling records did not have to be produced in response to a subpoena. This is an unusual result, but it demonstrates how privacy rights unexpectedly will be preserved by courts.

Counselors who provide professional services for married persons are often confronted with a problem related to privileged communication and married couples. In a typical scenario, the couple comes to the counselor because they are experiencing problems in their marriage. In the course of the counseling relationship, a number of stressful topics are discussed, and either the husband or the wife admits engaging in negative behaviors such as excessive drinking, infidelity, abusive behavior, or violent acts. Later, the couple decides to divorce. One of the parties wants the counselor to repeat in a legal deposition or hearing the admissions the other party made in the course of the counseling sessions. The other party, for obvious reasons, wants the counselor to keep the information confidential.

12-2 The Case of Sanjeev

Sanjeev recently began counseling a couple, Margaret and Jason, who were having marital problems after 3 years of marriage. They have one child, a daughter who is 1 year old. During the first two sessions, Jason tearfully admitted to having had an extramarital affair with one of Margaret's good friends during their first year of marriage. The affair lasted 6 months. Margaret had suspected that Jason was romantically involved with her friend, but she was not sure about it until Jason admitted it in the counseling session. Before the third counseling session occurred, Margaret told Jason that she could no longer live with him because of his affair with her friend and that she was filing for divorce, alimony, and child support. Jason called and canceled the third session and reported to Sanjeev what Margaret had said to him.

Now, 1 year later, Margaret's attorney has subpoenaed Sanjeev to attend a deposition to discuss Jason's admission of the affair in the counseling session. Yesterday, Sanjeev received a call from Jason saying that he did not want Sanjeev to reveal what he had said in the counseling sessions because what he said was confidential and privileged.

- What should Sanjeev do now?
- If Sanjeev does attend the deposition, how should he respond to questions?

Discussion: Sanjeev should obtain legal advice immediately. An important question with which his attorney can help him is whether a statute exists in Sanjeev's state that extends privilege to family counseling situations. If there is such a statute, Sanjeev's attorney will tell him he cannot reveal confidential information at the deposition. If there is no statute, the law may require him to reveal what Jason said. Sanjeev's attorney will attempt to preserve Jason's privacy if Sanjeev asks the lawyer to do that. How Sanjeev conducts himself in the deposition depends on how his attorney has advised him. He should ask his attorney to accompany him to the deposition.

The situation described here occurs frequently. When counselors find themselves in such dilemmas, they must consult an attorney where they are employed or a private practice lawyer if they are private practitioners. If the counselor refuses to testify at a deposition after a subpoena has been issued, and the spouse who made the negative admissions has legally waived privilege under state law, the counselor could be held in contempt of court. If, on the other hand, the counselor does testify and the relationship with the spouse who made the negative admissions was privileged under state law, the counselor could be legally accountable to that person for violating the spouse's privacy. Reading the state statute on privilege is not sufficient because legal arguments could be made for and against disclosure whether or not a privilege statute exists and regardless of the wording in the statute. This is a situation in which counselors must seek legal counsel and must follow the advice of their attorneys. Of course, counselors should tell their attorneys whether they want to testify and their reasons for feeling that way. This will help the attorney review the situation from the counselor's perspective.

Confidentiality of records can be a problematic issue when counseling couples or families. Adams (2010) has raised the question of what happens to records when the original counseling relationship is altered, either by the addition of a spouse or partner to a previously individual counseling relationship or when a couple are seen separately as individuals for some but not all sessions. The *Code of Ethics* (ACA, 2014) in §B.6.e. states, "In situations involving multiple clients, counselors provide individual clients with only those parts of records that relate directly to them and do not include confidential information related to any other client."

Family Secrets

A confidentiality issue that emerges frequently in family counseling is how to deal with family secrets: information that one family member has shared with the counselor but has withheld from a spouse, children, or other family members (Brendel & Nelson, 1999). There has been considerable debate over whether counselors should keep such revelations in confidence (Kuo, 2009; Margolin, 1982). One position is that secrets should be kept. A rationale for this stance is that the counselor, by agreeing to uphold the confidentiality of individual family members, will be more likely to obtain honest and complete information. This will help the counselor better understand family dynamics and conduct an accurate assessment.

A differing position is that counselors should refuse to keep secrets. Butler, Rodriguez, Roper, and Feinauer (2010), in a survey of relationship mental health professionals, found that most believed that healing and attachment security were best achieved through disclosure and supported facilitated disclosure of infidelity. In this view, secrets are seen as being counterproductive to the open and honest communication that is necessary for family counseling to be successful. In addition, by refusing to keep secrets, the counselor can prevent triangulation. Triangulation is a kind of subgrouping created when the counselor and the family member with the secret collude in withholding information from the other family member(s). Some family counselors make it a policy to refuse to see family members individually to avoid becoming recipients of secrets (Dattilio, 2009).

Still others have argued a third, middle-ground position. They stress the need for flexibility and propose that counselors should exercise their professional judgment, divulging or maintaining a confidence in accordance with the greatest benefit for the family. They argue that the criterion should be the effect on therapeutic progress and family welfare.

One type of secret that has received a great deal of attention is marital infidelity. Snyder and Doss (2005) have suggested that conflicts of interest may be unavoidable for counselors, who must work to ensure that improvement in one spouse does not occur at the expense of the other. When one partner in a relationship discloses an affair that remains unknown to the other, effective counseling may be impossible (Whitman & Wagers, 2005). Counselors have several choices regarding how to deal with a disclosure of infidelity: they can inform the couple in the initial session that anything revealed outside of conjoint session becomes a part of the couple's therapy; they can treat the information as confidential on a temporary basis but insist that the individual who committed the infidelity disclose to the partner; or they can keep the revelation confidential (Snyder & Doss, 2005).

The *Code of Ethics* (ACA, 2014) allows counselors some discretion in how to deal with family secrets. Standard B.4.b. says that counselors first clearly define who is considered *the client*, and the standard states, "Counselors seek agreement and document in writing such agreement among all involved parties regarding the confidentiality of information. In the absence of an agreement to the contrary, the couple or family is considered to be the client." If you believe that no secrets should be allowed within the context of family counseling, you could include a policy in your disclosure statement that each individual gives permission to the counselor to disclose to other family members anything said in any interactions between family members and the counselor.

You should keep in mind that your promise to uphold confidentiality is not absolute. When securing informed consent from family members, tell them that if you learn about activities going on in the family that put family members in danger (such as spouse battering, child abuse, or incest), you may need to take steps to prevent further harm. You must also let your family clients know that you must breach confidentiality when you are required by law to do so.

Divorce and Child Custody

Because it appears that about half of the marriages in the United States end in divorce and the divorce rates of second marriages is even higher (American Psychological Association, 2014), many children are affected by divorce. An increasing number of children are born in the United States today to parents who are not married. DeParle and Tarvernise (2012) have reported that the majority of children born to women under 30 in the United States are born to women who are not married. Fathers of children who are not married to the mothers of their children have the same legal responsibilities and rights as men who father children within marriages. A new area of counseling that is quite challenging is coparent counseling (Fridhandler & Lehmer, 2014), in which counselors work with both separated or divorced parents as they try to raise their children.

It is important for counselors to understand the nature of child custody so that they will not be tempted to involve themselves inappropriately in custody battles. The Children's Rights Council (2014) provides information regarding custody and parenting that is helpful to parents and those who help parents. Some basic information regarding custody is offered here to give you some sense of the difficulties involved in trying to make decisions regarding your role.

Generally, a custody order by a court defines the nature of the rights and responsibilities of two parents who are separated or divorced, in relation to a child or children. Pruett and DiFonzo (2014), in distinguishing between physical and legal custody have indicated that legal custody is focused on parental decision making, whereas physical custody is related to time spent with a minor child. Physical custody dictates living arrangements for a minor child and determines which parent is responsible for day-to-day decisions regarding the child. When the parent who was not granted legal custody has physical possession of a child, that parent usually has the authority to make decisions concerning the child's welfare.

The primary components of a custody order specifically define which parent has physical possession of a child at which times and orders child support payments when appropriate. Unless a parental right is specifically altered, modified, or terminated in a custody order, a parent maintains that right, even without the right to physical custody. As a result, noncustodial parents might have a right to receive correspondence that schools send to parents, to review their child's school record, to contract for counseling for the child, to demand that a child discontinue counseling services, and to take other actions that a custodial parent would have a right to take.

Whether a child's preferences will be considered in making custody decisions varies greatly from court to court. Appellate courts have done everything from allowing judges to base custody decisions entirely on the expressed preferences of the child to allowing judges to disregard those preferences entirely. Most judges will consider the wishes of a child regarding custody, particularly if the child is older (Kramer, 1994).

Generally, courts give custody preference to natural parents over others who have an interest in obtaining custody. If a caretaker who is not a biological parent wants to obtain custody over the objections of a natural parent, usually a court would have to find the natural parent unfit (Kramer, 1994).

There are many forms of child custody, including sole custody, split custody (one parent is awarded custody of some children, and the other parent receives custody of the remaining children), divided custody (each parent is awarded custody for part of the year), and joint custody. Awarding joint custody to both parents is a controversial practice, yet all but seven states in the United States have statutory provisions that allow joint custody as an option (Children's Rights Council, 2014). Some experts believe that joint custody is a positive concept in that it allows natural parents to participate equally in raising their children. Others believe that joint custody is usually detrimental to children because children suffer when parents disagree and no one seems to be in charge. A Nebraska court has said that joint custody is not favored and should be avoided (*Petrashek v. Petrashek*,

1989), whereas a court in Montana has determined that joint custody is in the best interests of a child (*In re marriage of Kovash*, 1993). Roy (2008) has reported that parenting plans have replaced legal primary and secondary parent status in Florida, following models that had been adopted already in Oregon and New Mexico.

It is difficult for nonlawyers, including counselors, to determine whether a parent has a legal right to possession of a child at any given moment. Parents often agree to modify the times that they have possession. Some custody orders even stipulate that the parties may mutually agree to modifications. If parents are in conflict over who should have possession of a child, counselors should insist that administrators, lawyers, or even the police become involved in resolving the dispute, rather than trying to resolve it themselves.

Courts sometimes, though rarely, issue an order terminating parental rights. This order severs the legal relationship between a child and the biological or legal parent. Custody and termination of parent rights orders vary greatly in their structure and language and must be drafted to comply with state law. Court orders should always be interpreted by attorneys if there is a question regarding their meaning.

When a divorce has been contentious and child custody has been disputed, parents sometimes make demands that put school counselors in an awkward position. The following scenario is a case in point.

12-3 The Case of David

Mrs. Jones brings her 12-year-old daughter to school and enrolls her midyear. As she is enrolling her daughter, Mrs. Jones produces a legal document that she says gives her full legal custody of her daughter and terminates all of her husband's parental rights. She instructs David, the school counselor, that if her former husband inquires about his daughter, the school should give him no information and certainly should not allow him to see or pick up her daughter from the school.

- How should David respond to Mrs. Jones's request?
- What should the school officials do in this case?

Discussion: David should not try to deal with this matter; he should refer Mrs. Jones to the school principal. The principal should read the court order to determine what the language actually says about the custody rights of Mrs. Jones and her former husband. If the language is unclear, the principal should ask the school district attorney to interpret it. The principal would also be wise to ask the lawyer how to handle the situation if the former husband shows up at the school and demands to see or take his daughter from school.

Counselor Competence

Marriage and family counseling is based on a theoretical perspective that is philosophically quite different from the foundations of individual counseling (Cottone, 1992) and as a result, skills and techniques different from those of individual counselors are required (Rappleyea, Harris, White, & Simon, 2009). Thus, Warnke (2001) has suggested that developing competence in marriage and family counseling requires more than the completion of one or two specialized courses. The AAMFT (AAMFT, 2015) has established educational requirements that are quite extensive and include, in addition to academic training, supervised experience in working with couples and families, work in one's own family of origin, and personal therapy. In addition, the AAMFT has adopted core competencies for family therapists (Perosa & Perosa, 2010). The Council for Accreditation of Counseling and Related Educational Programs (CACREP, 2014) has also promulgated a set of core competencies that are considered necessary for counselors who hold themselves out as specialists in marriage and family counseling.

There is debate among helping professionals as to whether marriage and family counseling is a separate discipline or a specialty area of counseling. Marriage and family counselors in most states have succeeded in getting separate licensure bills passed that set them apart from licensed professional counselors. This diversity of opinion is reflected in the ethics arena. The AAMFT has a code of ethics (AAMFT, 2012), as does the International Association for Marriage and Family Counseling (IAMFC; Hendricks et al., 2011) which is a division of ACA. We recommend that you familiarize yourself with both of these specialized codes for family counselors. They provide guidance more specific to working with couples and families than does the ACA code, which is focused primarily on individual counseling. For example, the AAMFT code (AAMFT, 2012) explicitly states that counselors must clearly advise their clients that decisions on marital status are the responsibility of the client. The *Code of Ethics* (ACA, 2014) does not address the issue of whether counselors can ethically advocate for the preservation of a marriage or for divorce.

We believe that counselors who are trained generically as professional counselors can appropriately include family counseling in their practices. Specific training in marriage and family counseling is recommended. Additional training could include specific coursework, supervised experience, and some personal work on understanding one's own family of origin issues. The potential for countertransference reactions intensifies when counselors have unresolved family of origin issues (Corey et al., 2015). The bottom line is that professional counselors must stay within the boundaries of their competence in providing services to couples and family clients.

Counselor Values

The personal values of counselors undeniably have an influence on how they conduct individual counseling. The role of counselor values may be particularly critical in the practice of marriage and family counseling (Corey et al., 2015; Huber, 1994; Yakunina, Weigold, & McCarthy, 2011). Very few family counselors deliberately attempt to impose their own values on clients. Yet, it is impossible for counselors to avoid using their influence in subtle ways—sometimes without being aware that they are doing so. Marriage and family counseling often deals with some of the most value-laden issues in our society. Just a few examples are offered in Figure 12-1.

- Cohabitation, marriage, and divorce
- Marital fidelity and extramarital affairs
- Parenting and disciplining of children
- Birth control, abortion, and adoption
- Relationships between couples of different races or cultures
- Gay and lesbian relationships
- Sex roles and gender roles
- Unorthodox sexual practices, such as sadomasochism, partner swapping, or fetish arousal

---

FIGURE 12-1 Value-laden issues in marriage and family counseling

Source: Pearson Education, Inc., Hoboken, NJ.

Counseling is never value free, and all family counselors have their own definitions of healthy and dysfunctional families, effective and ineffective ways of communicating, and affirming and destructive relationships. As Welfel (2013) has so aptly pointed out, no therapeutic work could take place without these definitions. It is not unusual for couples and family clients to espouse values different from those of the counselor, and it is in these instances that counselors are the most challenged to avoid imposing their own agendas. To illustrate, as you read the following case example, try to be aware of the assumptions and values that have entered your thinking about the case.

12-4 The Case of Charlotte

George and Victor are a gay couple who have sought counseling from Charlotte to help them decide whether to make a big change in their lives. A number of years ago, George was married and had a son with his wife. He has been divorced and in a committed relationship with Victor for 5 years. George has been thinking about seeking joint custody of his son, who is now 13 years old and with whom he has maintained a parental relationship, although his son has not lived with him. Victor is generally supportive of the idea but admits to some apprehension about having to help parent a teenage son, having to deal with George's ex-wife, and having to share George's affection and attention.

- What assumptions do you think Charlotte might hold that could influence how she works with George and Victor?
- What if you were George and Victor's counselor? Do you hold certain ideas about the morality of homosexuality? About how enduring homosexual and heterosexual relationships are likely to be? About what makes a *healthy* role model for a 13-year-old boy? About the impact that a homosexual or heterosexual partner's jealousy or possessiveness might have on child rearing?

Discussion: Charlotte might be assuming that gay men cannot parent effectively, that they would not be good role models for a teenage boy, or that homosexuality is morally wrong. It is important for counselors to give careful thought to their own values and assumptions around such issues so they are better prepared to counsel LGBT clients and less likely to impose their own values.

One issue of counselor values that has received increased attention in recent years is gender bias. Feminist counselors in particular have contended that family counselors are far from immune to the sex role stereotyping that exists in our society. When counselors do not challenge traditional assumptions about gender roles, they are likely to expect women to be the ones to change in counseling (Nixon, 1993). Counselors also may be vulnerable to certain other biases, such as (a) placing less importance on the demands of a woman's career than on those of a man, (b) encouraging couples to accept the belief that raising children is primarily the mother's responsibility, (c) seeing a woman's extramarital affair as more serious than a man's, and (d) assuming that marriage is the best choice for a woman (Guterman, 1991; Margolin, 1982; Sekaran, 1986). On the other hand, feminists have been accused of having their own biases when they encourage counselors to help women define themselves rather than be defined by others, to set their own standards rather than try to meet the expectations of others, and to nurture themselves as much as they nurture others. Some have criticized feminist counselors for rejecting stereotypical but societally endorsed roles of men and women, even though many individuals have consciously chosen those roles.

Family counselors must work to achieve a balance with respect to gender and therapeutic change. They are likely to cause harm to both partners in a relationship if they urge change in gender-prescribed roles solely because they believe such changes are needed. Conversely, it is equally irresponsible to condone through silence emotional abuse or intimidation (Wendorf & Wendorf, 1992). Of course, we are exposing our own biases when we suggest that some goals worth striving for, in your work with couples and families, might include the following: (a) practicing in a gender-aware manner, (b) being open to nontraditional roles and relationships, (c) helping family members identify ways that their views on gender roles may be contributing to their problems, and (d) continually monitoring your own behavior for unintended bias, such as looking more at the wife when discussing child rearing and more at the husband when discussing financial issues.

Today gay and lesbian couples are much more visible in our society, especially since marriage between persons who have the same gender has become legal. Bigner and Wetchler (2012) have produced a handbook that offers insight into counseling gay and lesbian couples and families. According to Benson (2013), this handbook by Bigner and Wetchler reviews current research, provides information regarding transgender populations, and summarizes recent legal changes that have an impact on gay and lesbian individuals and families.

You probably have identified some of your values and assumptions as you reflected on the issues we have raised in this section. Over the course of your career as a counselor, you will inevitably encounter couple and family clients whose values, lifestyles, and choices are very different from your own. It will be important for you to be aware of your own values and biases and keep clearly in mind that it is not your role to decide how couples or families should change. You will be better able to make informed ethical decisions when you know your own values and understand and respect the values of the families with whom you are working.

GROUP COUNSELING

Most of the ethical and legal issues that were discussed in relation to family counseling apply to group counseling as well. A primary difference between family counseling and group counseling is that group members usually do not know each other and do not have personal relationships with each other outside the group counseling environment.

This portion of the chapter addresses the issues of informed consent, screening, client welfare and protection from harm, privacy and confidentiality, dual relationships, socializing among members, counselor values, and competence as they pertain to group work. Included in the discussion are some ethical and legal considerations unique to group counseling, such as freedom to exit a group and screening potential members. The Association for Specialists in Group Work (ASGW) is the division of the American Counseling Association (ACA) that addresses professional issues in group counseling. ASGW has published two documents that can be very helpful to counselors who provide group counseling services: the *Best Practice Guidelines* (ASGW, 2007) and the *Professional Standards for the Training of Group Workers* (ASGW, 2000).

Informed Consent

Potential members of a counseling group have the same rights to informed consent as do prospective clients who are seeking individual counseling. See Chapter 4 for a review of these rights.

Because the group format differs in some significant ways from individual counseling, counselors need to address additional elements of informed consent for group participation, preferably in a pre-group interview. According to Corey (2011), elements that participants have a right to understand before they make a decision to join a group include the following:

- The purpose of the group, and its format, procedures, and ground rules
- The psychological risks involved in group participation
- What services can and cannot be provided within the group setting
- The division of responsibility between leader and participants
- The rights and responsibilities of group members
- Confidentiality and its limits
- Ways the group process may or may not be congruent with the participant's cultural values
- Freedom to leave the group if it does not turn out to be what a member wants or needs

The purpose of counseling is an issue that must be addressed in individual as well as group counseling, but clients in a group setting have less freedom to determine the topics or process of counseling. Typically, group leaders have already established a general theme or purpose for the group, such as adjustment to divorce, assertiveness training, or succeeding in college. Therefore, the aim in discussing the group's purpose is to help prospective members determine whether their goals in seeking counseling have a reasonable chance of being met within a group context, and if so, whether the particular group is compatible with their goals and needs.

There are psychological risks involved in individual counseling as well as in group participation, but in group counseling the risks are increased because the group leader has less situational control over events. Therefore, informed consent must include a full discussion of this topic. Group pressure or coercion is one such risk that has received considerable attention from specialists in group work. Risks are discussed further in a later section on client welfare.

Although group workers consider it an ethical imperative to give members the freedom to exit a group at any time during the life of the group, they have debated the delicate matter of how such an event should be handled. When a member drops out of a group, it can cause disruptions in the process for the remaining members. If members are concerned that they have said or done something to cause the departure, the trust and cohesion of the group will be affected. For this reason, many group leaders believe that members who are considering leaving the group should be encouraged to raise the matter in a group session rather than simply notify the leader of their decision to withdraw. Corey (2011) has stated that group members have a responsibility to the leaders and to other members to explain why they want to leave. The member who wants to exit the group may feel pressured or coerced to remain, however, rather than have to submit to such a process. The ethical question in these situations is whether the comfort and wishes of the individual member or of the group as a whole should take precedence.

Although clients in voluntary groups have the freedom to withdraw from participation, this freedom is abridged when counseling is court ordered. Mandated clients must be informed that prematurely exiting a group could place them in a compromised legal position, possibly including being remanded to jail (Herlihy & Flowers, 2010).

Both counselor and client must fulfill certain responsibilities in order for counseling to be successful. In a group setting, regular attendance and being on time for sessions are particularly important client responsibilities, because other members and the group as a unit are negatively affected when an individual does not meet these obligations. In individual counseling, clients can choose to share information they have discussed in sessions, but in group counseling they have a responsibility to maintain the confidences of other members. Taking interpersonal risks and giving feedback to others are further responsibilities that pertain to group counseling participants.

When group members are minors, obtaining informed consent raises some of the same issues discussed in Chapter 11 on working with minors individually. Whether the minor or the parent has the right to make the decision for a minor to participate in a group is a thorny issue. There are potential problems with either requiring or not requiring parental consent. It is possible that parents might not give consent for their children to participate in some groups, such as groups for children of alcoholics (COAs) or abused children. However, if parental consent is not sought and parents later are upset to learn that their child has been participating in such a group, this also could present problems. In schools, group counseling programs are part of the counseling program delivered on a regular basis, so there is no requirement that school counselors obtain parental permission for students to participate in groups. However, some school districts or school principals require parental permission anyway.

Screening

Leaders should secure informed consent of potential group members prior to implementing a counseling group. They should also screen potential members to determine whether any of them should be excluded (Hines & Fields, 2002; Ritchie & Huss, 2000). The *Code of Ethics* (ACA, 2014) requires that counselors screen prospective group participants and do their best to select members whose needs and goals are compatible with the goals of the group. Counselors should select members whose well-being will not be jeopardized by the group experience and who will not impede the group process (§A.9.a.). The primary criteria for inclusion should be whether potential members are likely to contribute to the group and whether they are likely to be compatible with each other.

Unless the group has a very specific purpose, it is much easier to decide whom to exclude than it is to decide whom to include. Prospective participants who generally should be excluded are those who are likely to dominate or monopolize group time, are hostile or aggressive in their style of interacting with others, are in a state of severe crisis, are suicidal, are lacking in ego strength, are acutely psychotic, and are highly suspicious or paranoid (Corey, 2011). Individuals diagnosed with certain personality disorders, such as narcissistic or antisocial, are considered poor candidates for group counseling (Yalom, 2005).

Generally, highly motivated clients who have interpersonal problems will profit most from a group experience (Yalom, 2005). Of course, the purpose of the group will be an important factor in determining whether prospective members will be included or excluded.

Some additional issues must be considered when recruiting and screening minor clients for groups in school settings. If counselors ask teachers to refer potential members for groups on topics such as children of divorce, COAs, or attention deficit hyperactivity disorder (ADHD) or disruptive classroom behaviors, they run the risk of labeling such students as well as violating their privacy. Some school counselors do not give their groups a name that would label children or imply a diagnosis and allow students to come see the counselor at their own discretion to discuss their interest in participating in a group (Ritchie & Huss, 2000).

Client Welfare and Protection from Harm

Participating in a counseling group, like any catalyst for personal change, can pose psychological risks. Group counselors have an ethical responsibility to take precautions to protect group members "from physical, emotional, or psychological trauma" (ACA, 2014, §A.9.b.). They need to have a solid understanding of the forces that operate in groups and how to mobilize those forces in a constructive manner (Corey, 2011). Four potential dangers to which group leaders need to be alert are scapegoating of members, the subjection of members to undue pressure, the misuse of confrontation, and injury resulting from group exercises or activities that involve physical contact.

Sometimes an individual member of a group is singled out as a scapegoat, and this person is made the object of the group's frustration or hostility. When this happens, it is the responsibility of the group leader to take firm steps to stop this behavior. Group counselors have an ethical responsibility to avoid coercing participants into changing in directions that are not chosen by the participants themselves, and to intervene when members use undue pressure or coercion.

Confrontation is a valuable and powerful tool in a group, but it can be misused by members who have not developed the skill of confronting constructively. When members are inappropriately confrontational, it is the group counselor's responsibility to intervene. It is critical that group counselors model appropriate confrontation.

Although the possibility of a group member physically harming another group member is remote, it could happen with some populations and in particular settings. Counselors who conduct group counseling sessions are expected to ensure the safety of members. Group members who have the potential for harming others either should be excluded from group sessions or should be monitored carefully. Warning signs for potentially dangerous clients were outlined in Chapter 8.

Some group counseling approaches involve group members interacting with each other physically. The law of assault and battery requires that individuals not be touched or put in apprehension of being touched without their permission (Swenson, 1997). Counselors who use group exercises that involve touching should explain in their disclosure statements to clients that touching among members will take place. They should avoid touching that might be considered offensive or sexual, and they should not use any activity that might result in a physical injury.

Privacy and Confidentiality

As noted, counselors can guarantee only their own behavior with respect to upholding confidentiality. Counselors must inform clients that they cannot guarantee confidentiality on the parts of group members. It is possible that counselors do not clearly understand how confidentiality promises in group work differ from those that can be offered in individual counseling. Of the ACA members surveyed by Neukrug and Milliken (2011), nearly 37% thought it was ethical to guarantee confidentiality for group members.

It is important for group counselors to communicate to group members the importance of keeping information shared in groups private and to explain the limits of confidentiality. Some group counseling situations bring special challenges regarding confidentiality. For example, imagine how complicated it would be to provide privacy when conducting group play therapy (Ware & Dillman Taylor, 2014).

Confidentiality with Minors

The ethical and legal complexities of conducting groups with minors are highlighted when a group member discloses some risky behavior that his or her parents should know about. There is no answer as to how such situations should be handled. The counselors must assess each unique situation, given all that is known about the minor and his or her family and what is known about the risky activity in which the minor is involved. Consultation with other counselors before making a decision is always the best course of action for counselors.

12-5 The Case of Shadiqua

Shadiqua, a high school counselor, is conducting a group for sophomore girls. The purpose of the group is to foster self-esteem and to help in making wise choices. During the fifth session, the topic is boyfriends and whether to *just say no* to sex. Megan, a 15-year-old, shares that she and her 15-year-old boyfriend are sexually active and that she thinks it's okay because they are really in love. Megan adds that her parents *would kill* her boyfriend if they found out and would throw her out of the house.

- Do you think Megan's parents must be notified? Or can Shadiqua keep Megan's disclosure in confidence?
- If Shadiqua breaches Megan's confidentiality, what are the risks to her relationship with Megan and with the group?

Discussion: Because Megan is a minor, Shadiqua should talk privately with Megan to see if she can persuade Megan to tell her parents. Shadiqua can remind Megan that the limits of confidentiality had been discussed at the beginning of and throughout the group, and she can remind Megan of those discussions. It is possible that, despite Shadiqua's previous explanations of confidentiality limits, Megan and other group members will feel betrayed and the effectiveness of the group will be compromised if Shadiqua decides to tell Megan's parents. If Shadiqua does not inform Megan's parents and Megan is harmed in some way due to being sexually active and the parents find out that Shadiqua knew and didn't inform them, of course the parents would be upset and might accuse Shadiqua of unethical practice. On the other hand, Shadiqua might choose to take the risk of not telling the parents because she does not believe Megan is endangering herself through her sexual activity with her boyfriend.

Cases in which parents may need to be told information points up the importance, when working with minors, of discussing confidentiality and its limits before the group begins and throughout the life of the group. If counselors reiterate confidentiality limits whenever sensitive topics are broached during group sessions, they will have a better chance of avoiding such difficult dilemmas.

Privileged Communication

Privileged communication may exist for relationships between counselors and clients in your jurisdiction, but this privilege generally is considered to be waived when you are counseling more than one person. A few privileged communications statutes grant privilege to individual group counseling members and their counselor (Arthur & Swanson, 1993: Huber & Baruth, 1987; Kearney, 1984). Read and understand provisions of the privileged communication statute in your state to determine whether group counseling situations are covered.

Dual Relationships

Although dual relationships between counselors and their clients, including members of counseling groups, are generally to be avoided, relationships between group members and leaders will vary somewhat depending on context. When task groups are held within a work environment, for instance, casual contact between leaders and group members may be inevitable. In counseling groups, however, outside-of-group contact between leaders and individual members can be inappropriate and counterproductive for the group as a whole (Gladding, 2012).

If the group counselor has a personal or social relationship with one of the members, this can lead to charges of favoritism. The counselor might avoid confronting this member or might be reluctant to explore in group some interpersonal issues that are problematic in the social relationship with the member. Group counselors should not use group clients to meet their personal needs for social relationships or friendships. The role of group counselors is to help members meet their goals, not to help counselors meet their own needs.

Just as group counselors should not develop friendships with group members, they should not admit friends or close acquaintances to counseling groups they are conducting. In the same way that preexisting personal relationships are problematic in a group context, prior professional relationships can cause difficulties. Some counselors make it a routine practice to form their groups largely from their former clients in individual counseling (Herlihy & Corey, 2015a). This is not unethical, although there are potential problems. Members of a group who have been counseled individually and who are accustomed to having the counselor's full attention for the entire session may find it difficult to share their counselor with other group members. In addition, members who are not former individual clients of the counselor may feel disadvantaged because they have not had the same opportunity to form a bond with their group counselor.

There are limits to counselor self-disclosure in group counseling as well as in individual counseling. As a group leader, you must monitor your self-disclosures so that you are aware of what you are saying and your rationale for sharing any personal information. Although it is not your role to use group time to work on your own issues, you can self-disclose appropriately in several ways. You can let members know that you are personally affected by what they are sharing, you can express your persistent reactions to members and offer feedback, and you can model appropriate and timely self-disclosure by expressing how you are affected in the moment by what is going on in the group (Herlihy & Corey, 2015a).

Socializing Among Members

Group work specialists have taken varying positions on the question of whether socializing among group members facilitates or hinders the group process. As is true of leader–member contact outside of group sessions, much depends on the context in which the group occurs. In 12-step groups, socializing among members outside the meetings is common, and one member might serve as another member's sponsor. In hospitals, schools, and other institutional settings, it is inevitable that members will encounter one another between sessions. Many group leaders avoid making strict rules about socializing and personal relationships among members because these rules are impossible to enforce (Jacobs, Harvill, & Masson, 1994).

Although the group counselor cannot control members' lives outside the group, there are some good reasons for discouraging the members from forming friendships or social relationships with each other during the group's duration. If cliques or subgroups form, this is detrimental to the group process. If some group members meet outside the group context and discuss matters that are best dealt with in group sessions, hidden agendas will develop and impede group progress. Members who meet outside the group in this way have a responsibility to bring information about their meetings into the group, but they may avoid doing so. Yalom (2005) has made the point that counseling groups teach people how to form intimate relationships but do not provide these relationships. Thus, group leaders have a responsibility to discuss with members the reasons why it is inadvisable for them to socialize between group sessions. If members recognize the pitfalls and understand the rationale for avoiding outside-of-group socializing, they are more likely to honor the counselor's request to refrain from this activity.

Counselor Competence

Because many, if not most, counselors will conduct group work as part of their professional practices, training standards are written to ensure that counselors have adequate knowledge and experience in leading groups. CACREP (2009) requires that graduate programs in counseling include training in group work that incorporates the study of group dynamics, group leadership, theories of group counseling, methods of group counseling, types of group work, and ethical considerations. The CACREP standards also require the development of group work skills under supervision as part of the requirements for practicum and internship training.

ASGW has published *Professional Standards for the Training of Group Workers* (2000) that describes two levels of competencies for group counseling. The first level specifies core knowledge and skill knowledge that provide a foundation for specialized training.

According to ASGW (2000), after counselors in training have mastered the core knowledge and skills, they can develop a group work specialization in one or more of the following areas: (a) task/work group facilitation, (b) group psychoeducation, (c) group counseling, and (d) group psychotherapy. Developing competence in both the basic and the specialized levels of practice requires participation in planning and supervising small groups and clinical experience in leading groups under careful supervision.

Different groups require various leader competencies. For example, a counselor may be qualified to facilitate adolescent groups but be ill prepared to conduct reminiscence groups for elderly residents of a nursing home. You will need to continually evaluate the match between the types of groups you are considering conducting and your level of training and experience. As you prepare to include group work in your professional practice, you will find that you need specific training and supervised experience for each type of group you intend to lead (Corey, 2011).

It is equally important that you continue to update and expand your skills and knowledge. As is true with all counseling specialties, counselors who work with groups need to continually update their knowledge and skills, particularly in new and emerging areas. Counselors who engage in group work are urged to familiarize themselves with ASGW's *Multicultural and Social Justice Competence Principles for Group Workers* (2012).

Lakin (1994) has expressed concern that many counselors fail to monitor their own competence in the wide range of group modalities and varied clientele to be served. Both continuing education and peer supervision can be useful in this regard. Gladding (2012) has suggested that peer supervision groups can be particularly helpful for increasing one's knowledge as well as one's awareness of even minor misjudgments in group leadership.

Diversity and Values Considerations in Group Counseling

It is not at all unusual for value-laden issues—such as divorce, sexuality, religion, family of origin issues, and honesty versus deceit in relationships—to be brought into a group. Corey (2011) has noted that a group can be an ideal place for members to assess the degree to which their interpersonal behavior is consistent with their values, through receiving feedback from others. The group counselor's role in this process is to make the group a safe place where members can feel free to explore values issues that are troubling to them.

Multicultural and Social Justice Competence Principles for Group Workers (ASGW, 2012) reminds group counselors of the importance of sensitivity to cultural differences. It is crucial that you, as a group leader, are aware of how your own cultural background, attitudes, values, and beliefs influence the way you work with a group. You must be alert to issues of oppression, sexism, and racism as you work with diverse group members. You should not impose your values on group members or operate as though all members share your world view or cultural assumptions. If the group is based on values that are alien to some group members, the counselor is likely to encounter resistance from those members. You will want to understand and respect the roles of family and community, religion and spirituality, and ethnicity and culture in the lives of group members. It is also important for group counselors to develop skills for working with clients from other countries. Yakunina, Wiegold, and McCarthy (2011) have noted that groups can be very effective in helping foreign students deal with issues of acculturative stress, language difficulties, cultural misunderstandings, racial and ethnic discrimination, and loss of proximity to support systems such as family and friends.

Group counselors need to be prepared to address issues of social justice in their work with clients. Burnes and Ross (2010) have expressed concern that counselors are unprepared to address the impact of privilege and oppression on the group process. Counselors should seek out training to become more prepared, as groups can be very effective for empowerment at the systemic as well as the individual level (Hays, Arredondo, Gladding, & Toporek, 2010). Ratts, Anthony, and Santos (2012) have offered a model for transforming traditional group work into a socially just framework.

Certain values are inherent in the group process, such as self-disclosure, risk-taking behaviors, communicating openly and directly, and increasing awareness and autonomy. Group counselors must be cognizant that some of these values may run counter to the values of group members. For example, striving for personal autonomy may be an alien concept for group members who come from certain cultures (Herlihy & Corey, 2015a).

Summary and Key Points

When counselors work with multiple clients, as they do in family and group counseling, ethical and legal issues can be more complicated to resolve. Family counselors often work from a systems perspective that is quite different from the theoretical underpinnings of individual counseling. They view the entire family system, rather than its individual members, as their client.

Key points with respect to family counseling include the following:

- The issue of informed consent in family counseling presents some unique challenges, such as determining who in the family gives consent and how to deal with situations in which one family member is reluctant to participate or refuses to participate in the process.

- When one adult, legally competent individual in the family refuses to give consent for the family to participate, counseling cannot take place with all family members.
- Although reluctant family members cannot be forced or coerced into participating in family counseling, some family counselors encourage these resistant members to attend one or two sessions.
- Children cannot give legal informed consent; nonetheless, they should be included in the process.
- Counselors must be aware of legal questions created by the changing nature of families, particularly with respect to the rights of biological parents versus other family members who may wish to be involved in family counseling.

- Family counseling involves some powerful techniques. One such technique about which ethical concerns have been expressed is paradoxical directives. Such techniques must be used with caution so that no harm is caused.
- Whether family counseling should be avoided when there is ongoing abuse in the family should be carefully considered.
- Counselors must make it clear to family clients that there are special limits to confidentiality; counselors can guarantee confidentiality only on their own parts.
- Privileged communication generally is waived if a third party is present in the counseling situation.
- Some more recently enacted privileged communication statutes extend privilege to family clients and group member clients. Counselors should consult with an attorney regarding how to interpret these statutes.
- Family counselors take differing positions on how to handle the issue of family secrets.
- Divorce and child custody issues can be particularly problematic for counselors, and counselors should take care to avoid involving themselves inappropriately in custody disputes.
- Counselor values have a strong impact on how counselors conduct family counseling. Counselors must be vigilant so that they do not inadvertently impose their own values and assumptions, particularly regarding culture and gender roles.
- Developing competence in family counseling requires specialized coursework, supervised experience, and experience in the counselor's own family of origin work.

Group counseling is another modality that involves multiple clients. Ethical and legal issues have different implications in the group context than they do in individual counseling. Key points regarding group counseling include the following:

- Informed consent to participate in group counseling involves a number of issues in addition to the standard elements of informed consent for individual counseling.
- Group leaders must balance the rights of the individual against the needs of the group when a member wants to exit the group prematurely.
- It is good practice to screen potential members of a group to exclude those who are unlikely to benefit from the experience, and to select those who are most likely to contribute to the group and be compatible with each other.
- Group counselors have a responsibility to protect group members from harm and to be alert to the dangers inherent in scapegoating, undue pressure, inappropriate confrontation, and injury resulting from activities that involve physical contact.
- As is true in family counseling, confidentiality is difficult to enforce in group settings, and counselors should make a special effort to ensure that group members understand the importance of confidentiality and how to avoid inadvertent breaches.
- Privileged communication may not exist in group counseling situations unless the state statute specifically extends privileged communication to group counselors and their clients individually.
- There are additional limitations to confidentiality when groups are composed of clients who are minors.
- Group counselors should make every effort to avoid dual relationships with members of their counseling groups.

CHAPTER 13

Professional Relationships, Private Practice, and Health Care Plans

FOCUS QUESTIONS

1. What types of interactions and relationships do counselors have with other mental health professionals who practice in their community?

2. What kind of help does a counselor need in order to set up a private practice?

3. How would you respond if you were a provider of counseling services for a managed care organization and you believed your client needed additional counseling sessions, but the case manager told you that no more counseling sessions would be provided?

PROFESSIONAL RELATIONSHIPS

Counselors who practice in all settings interact regularly with other professionals (Edwards, Patterson, & Grauf-Grounds, 2001). Mental health professionals communicate and collaborate in several ways. They confer, consult, coordinate client care, engage in teamwork, and refer clients to each other (Glosoff, 2001). *Conferring*, the least structured of these types of communication, may be defined as an informal comparing of observations. For example, a school counselor might confer with a teacher to determine whether a child's classroom behavior has improved as a result of counseling for impulse control.

Consulting (discussed in detail in Chapter 15) occurs when one professional solicits the opinion or advice of another professional. The consultation could focus on many possible issues, from determining the most efficacious treatment for a client's problem to resolving an ethical dilemma that the consultee may be facing.

Coordination of services usually refers to procedures put in place to ensure that all service providers are working from the same treatment plan and goals and are aware of each other's roles and functions in serving a client. For instance, a school counselor might work with the school psychologist, principal, school nurse, and teachers to implement and monitor a child's individualized educational plan (IEP). *Teamwork*, the most structured form of collaboration, often takes place in inpatient settings where various professionals provide a range of services to a client such as individual counseling, group counseling, art therapy, medication monitoring, case management, and family therapy. Members of treatment teams tend to have formalized roles and responsibilities and work together over time—for example, for the duration of a client's stay in a psychiatric hospital (Linville, Hertlein, & Lyness, 2007).

Finally, *referrals* occur when professionals determine that a type of expertise they do not possess is needed to assist a client. For example, a counselor might refer a client to a psychiatrist to assess whether psychotropic medication is indicated.

Counselors must be able to establish and maintain appropriate relationships with mental health and other professionals (such as physicians, law enforcement officials, and teachers) in order to render quality mental health care services to their clients (American Counseling Association [ACA], 2014, *Code of Ethics*, §D). They must also be alert to ethical and legal considerations that relate to their interactions with other professionals.

Just as it is essential to establish appropriate personal boundaries with clients, students, and supervisees, it is equally important to establish appropriate boundaries with other professionals. Counselors must continually determine their precise role when they are interacting with other professionals. This role depends on the circumstances. Therefore, counselors must understand that they have many roles and responsibilities and often must clarify their position to others with whom they interact. Two examples may help to illustrate this point.

EXAMPLE ONE   A psychiatrist in private practice has diagnosed a patient as suffering from a mental disorder and has prescribed medication. The psychiatrist refers the person for counseling services to a counselor in private practice. In this situation, the psychiatrist and counselor function as co-equal partners in treating the individual. They consult and relate to each other in that fashion.

EXAMPLE TWO   A psychiatrist is employed as director of a public mental health center. The psychiatrist assigns a client to a staff counselor for treatment and specifies that the counselor should have five sessions with the client related to proper parenting skills development. The psychiatrist is the counselor's administrative supervisor, and the counselor is in the role of an employee carrying out the directives of a superior. Of course, the counselor has an obligation to exercise judgment in the case, but the dynamics between the two professionals will be much different from those in the first situation.

The ethical and legal issues that are important to counselors as they interact with other professionals include the following: (a) employer/employee relationships, (b) confidential information, (c) referrals, and (d) respect for other professionals.

Employer/Employee Relationships

Most counselors practice their profession as employees of agencies and entities such as schools, hospitals, mental health centers, and rehabilitation agencies. At some time in their careers, most counselors also supervise others in organizational settings, which requires them to function in the role of employer.

As a result, it is important that counselors understand the basic legal principles of employment law. Counselors also need to be prepared to address some of the tensions experienced by professionals who have obligations both to clients and to employers.

COUNSELORS AS EMPLOYEES   When a counselor applies for, is offered, and accepts a job, the counselor then becomes an employee and must function within the legal framework that guarantees certain rights to employees and also imposes on them a number of obligations.

Employed counselors have a legal right guaranteed by the U.S. Constitution or federal statutes (e.g., Title VII of the Civil Rights Act of 1964; Age Discrimination in Employment Act of 1967; Title I of the Americans with Disabilities Act of 1990) to be free in the workplace of discrimination based on race, color, sex, religion, national origin, age, and disabilities (Belton & Avery, 1999). In some states or localities, discrimination based on other traits, such as sexual orientation, may be prohibited by statute as well.

Also, employees do not have to submit to any supervisor's directive that constitutes a crime. If a directive is unethical, it might also be illegal. However, most ethical issues are debatable. Therefore, in order for a court to support a professional who refused to follow a supervisor's directive because the employee believed the directive was unethical, a directive probably would have to be clearly unethical and put clients at substantial risk.

Although a few employees have detailed contracts with their employers, most employees work without contracts. This means that they are employed at the pleasure of their employer and that the employer may terminate the arrangement at any point without giving a reason.

Originally, under the common law that the United States inherited from England, employees worked for employers under what is known as the *at will doctrine*. According to Perritt (2013), this concept held that employers could fire employees "at any time for a good reason, a bad reason, or for no reason at all" (p. 3). The pure at will doctrine has eroded over time in the United States; however, there is still a general concept in law that employees do not have a right to employment, and a presumption that employers have a right to dismiss employees without giving any reasons.

When employees who do not have employment contracts are fired, the legal burden is on them to prove that their dismissal was wrongful and should be overturned by a court (Perritt, 2013). Three legal theories might lead courts to conclude that a dismissal was wrongful: (a) The employer promised that the employee would have employment security, (b) the dismissal offends some important public policy, or (c) the termination was *unfair* or done *in bad faith*.

In many large businesses and governmental settings, policies and procedures exist that govern employer/employee relationships without contracts being signed. When such policies and procedures exist, they must be followed.

Labor unions generally negotiate employment contracts for their members. Unions provide leverage for employees that they would not normally have when disputes arise between employee and employer. If an employment contract has been negotiated either individually by an employee or by a union, then the exact terms of the contract will dictate the employer/employee relationship.

When disputes arise between employees and employers, the law generally favors the employer (Perritt, 2013). Individuals are not forced to work, and certainly they do not have to work for a particular employer. Because employees are free to resign from their jobs if they are dissatisfied, employers cannot be forced to comply with the preferences of an employee.

By accepting a job, an employee agrees to perform the tasks assigned. These tasks can be any that the employer wishes, unless there is an employment contract or internal policies and procedures to the contrary. If an employee refuses to carry out the directives of a supervisor, this constitutes insubordination, for which an employee can be legally dismissed. The only defenses to refusing to carry out the directives of a supervisor would probably be that a directive (a) was in violation of an employment contract, (b) was in violation of internal policies or procedures, (c) illegally discriminated against a protected category of individuals, or (d) constituted a crime.

Many counselors who are also employees are concerned about being in a situation in which they believe they have an ethical obligation to act or refrain from acting, and their employer issues a directive to the contrary. The *Code of Ethics* (ACA, 2014) does not require counselors to *fall on their swords* and resign if they believe an organization demands actions that pose a conflict with the code. Instead, they should address their concerns directly with their employer and work toward change in the organization (§D.1.h. and §I.2.d.). Standard D.1.h. provides a number of alternative actions for counselors who believe they are working for an employer who has inappropriate policies or practices, including "referral to appropriate certification, accreditation, or state licensure organizations, or voluntary termination of employment." Counselors should bear in mind, though, that licensure and certification boards accept ethical complaints only against individuals and will not accept complaints against organizations. Although counselors may be uncomfortable working in a conflictual situation, it is acceptable from both an ethical and a practical standpoint for them to secure employment elsewhere before resigning their position.

Most employers understand that licensure laws and codes of ethics guide the behavior of the professionals they employ, even though the employers may not be members of the same profession. Nonetheless, there are many disagreements among experts and professionals regarding what constitutes ethical and unethical behavior (Sperry, 2007). Most often, when disputes arise in ethical areas between professionals and their employers, it is because the parties disagree as to what is ethical and unethical.

Following are some examples of situations in which professionals and their employers might disagree about an ethical issue:

- A physician believes that an operation would be in a patient's best interest, but the health maintenance organization determines that a different, less expensive form of treatment is acceptable.
- An attorney who is an associate in a law firm believes that a potential client has no chance of winning a lawsuit against a former employer because of the facts and the law. The attorney recommends that the firm decline to represent the potential client, but a senior partner directs the associate to take the case and to pursue it vigorously.
- A psychologist who is employed by a prison believes that many of the inmates who are evaluated are in need of medical care due to their mental conditions. The supervisor, who is a psychiatrist, disagrees and says that the psychologist should just conclude that the inmates do not need medical care.

These situations illustrate that any professional who is employed could face problems of ethical decision making. The following case describes a counselor who has a disagreement with an employer regarding an ethical issue.

13-1 The Case of Jason

Jason has been a counselor in a community mental health center for 2 years. A new director, Sofia, has been hired recently. Sofia holds a master's degree in business, and she has never worked in a mental health facility before. Other counselors tell the director, Sofia, that Jason is an ineffective counselor, that he becomes inappropriately involved in the personal lives of clients, and that he does not follow center policies. Sofia wants to ensure that Jason is performing his job responsibilities adequately. Therefore, she directs Jason to show her his case notes at the end of each day and to summarize his work with each of his clients. Jason refuses, based on his ethical requirement to keep his conversations with his clients confidential. Sofia fires Jason.

- If you had been advising Sofia regarding this problem situation with Jason, what would you have advised her to do differently?
- If you had been advising Jason regarding this situation, what would you have advised him to do differently?

Discussion: A better approach for the supervisor would have been to assign another, perhaps senior, mental health professional to supervise Jason's work for a period of time. On the other hand, Jason could have responded differently and perhaps saved his job. He could have engaged in a conversation with Sofia to determine why she was concerned about his job performance and could have presented his side of the story. He could have offered to be supervised by a senior counselor for a period of time to assure his supervisor of his competency.

Jason could have tried to accommodate his supervisor's concerns in some way and at the same time preserve the privacy of his clients. For example, he could have removed identifying information from his records. Trying to work with a supervisor is much better than defying the supervisor's order.

This situation describes a difficult problem for counselors and for those who supervise mental health professionals but are not mental health professionals themselves. Sofia, the counseling center director in this case example, certainly has an obligation to ensure that her employees are performing their jobs adequately. The director is legally responsible for the work of her employees. On the other hand, professionals have a confidentiality obligation to clients.

At some time in your professional career, you may be faced with a situation in which you and your employer disagree about what is ethical. We recommend that you take these steps if you believe your employer is forcing you to act in what you consider to be an unethical manner:

1. Avoid discussing the situation with co-workers in casual conversations or in staff meetings. Consult with outside experts and colleagues in a confidential manner regarding the issue, and ask them to keep your conversations confidential. If there is a consensus that the action is unethical, go to step 2. If time allows, a request could be made to the ACA Ethics Committee for an interpretation of the *Code of Ethics* (ACA, 2014). There is a formal process for requesting interpretations (see Chapter 8), and it might take a number of months to receive an interpretation. If experts and colleagues do not agree that the action is unethical, you could argue internally for change but should follow the directives of your supervisor. If you have professional liability insurance, you might have the benefit of consulting with a legal advisor regarding a situation such as the one you are facing.
2. Schedule an appointment with your supervisor to discuss the matter. Tell your supervisor which provisions in the *Code of Ethics* (ACA, 2014) you believe are being violated, and ask that you not be directed to act in what you consider to be an unethical manner. If your supervisor requests additional information or support for your position, offer to provide it to the extent possible.

3. If step 2 does not lead to a satisfactory resolution of the issue, you must decide whether to stay in the organization and work toward change or whether to look for a different job that does not force you to compromise your beliefs about your ethical obligations. If you decide to stay in the organization, go to step 4. If you decide to leave, update your résumé and begin your search. For practical purposes, if possible, keep your present job while you are searching. Many employers are suspicious that unemployed professionals may be poor employees, and many employers do not favor applicants who left previous jobs because of disputes with their employers.

4. Ask your supervisor to schedule a three-way appointment with you and his or her supervisor to discuss the situation. If your supervisor refuses, inform your supervisor that you are going to talk with his or her supervisor. Then, ask that supervisor directly for an appointment to discuss the matter.

5. If step 4 does not resolve the issue (and you still have your job), determine whether organizational policies could be created or changed that would resolve the dilemma in a manner that would be ethically acceptable to you. If so, suggest that a policy or procedure be created or changed following the procedure used to make suggestions within your organization (ACA, 2014, §D.1.h.). To try to preserve your working relationship, inform your supervisor of your activities, if possible. Try to avoid the appearance that this issue is a struggle between you and your boss that one of you will win and the other will lose. Instead, present the issue as important to the organization and to your profession and advocate for change in a professional manner.

COUNSELORS AS EMPLOYERS   Counselors who are in private practice or who own their own businesses naturally will hire employees from time to time to assist them with their work. In addition, counselors who become supervisors in the agencies in which they are employed become members of the management team and agents of their employer. Such supervisor–counselors function as employers as well.

The *Code of Ethics* (ACA, 2014) states that counselors "hire for professional counseling positions only individuals who are qualified and competent for those positions" (§C.2.c.). This standard suggests that counselors should not agree to hire in counseling positions individuals who are not qualified through education and experience. Standard D.1.f., which states, "Counselors select competent staff and assign responsibilities compatible with their skills and experience," reinforces the concept that counselors who hire must ensure that their employees are capable of providing quality counseling services.

Employed counselors should realize that they must assume the role of employer any time they have one or more persons who report to them administratively. Sometimes administrative lines within organizations are blurred. It is vital for counselors to clarify, if they are unsure, whether they are the administrative supervisors for individuals with whom they work. Generally, an administrative supervisor assigns work responsibilities to another employee and evaluates that person's performance. In addition, administrative supervisors generally make final decisions or final recommendations about whom to hire for positions that report to them. Administrative supervisors also have significant influence and responsibility in disciplining and dismissing employees who report to them.

Employed counselors may have clerical or professional staff members who report to them. Employees want their supervisors to be clear in communicating expectations and directives. All counselors—whether they are in a supervisory, subordinate, or collegial relationship with employers and employees—have an ethical obligation to make expectations clear and to establish working agreements that are known to all parties.

Employees also want their supervisors to be fair and just in dealing with them. Counselors do not commit or condone practices that are inhumane, illegal, or unjustifiable in hiring or promotion.

They do not discriminate on the basis of "age, culture, disability, ethnicity, race, religion/spirituality, gender, gender identity, sexual orientation, marital/partnership status, language preference, socioeconomic status, immigration status, or any basis proscribed by law" (ACA, 2014, §C.5.).

It is very important that counselors who supervise others avoid favoritism or the appearance of favoritism among employees. Consider what could happen if a friendship or personal relationship developed between a supervisor and a supervisee. When the supervisor later disciplined or dismissed another employee or gave some type of benefit or promotion to the friend, the supervisor would be vulnerable to a complaint of favoritism, or perhaps even illegal discrimination.

As a result, it is recommended that counselors who supervise others maintain a personal distance between themselves and those they supervise. Organizational environments, however, often promote employee friendships through a friendly climate or social gatherings that sometimes even extend to family members. If a friendship or personal relationship does develop between a supervisor and employee, the counselor should be careful to avoid personal interactions with the employee at work and must self-monitor carefully to ensure that the employee is not being given favorable treatment. See additional discussions of multiple relationships in Chapter 9. Consider the following case.

13-2 The Case of Margaret

When Margaret was promoted to director of the local mental health center, one of the first personnel decisions she made was to hire one of her best friends, Beth, as a staff counselor. Margaret knew that Beth was an excellent counselor with many years of experience who would perform well as an employee for the center. Now, after a year, Beth has indeed performed her job in an exemplary manner. However, Beth is very focused on work and is highly productive in the work environment, and she has alienated most of the other employees at the center. They see her as unfriendly, abrupt in interpersonal communications, and self-centered. Margaret and Beth have maintained their friendship and frequently socialize together on the weekends. A unit supervisor has recently resigned, and Margaret must appoint someone to take his place. The two top candidates for the job are Beth and another staff counselor who is very popular among his peers. However, in Margaret's opinion, he is not as capable as an administrator. Margaret wants to promote Beth to the supervisory position, but she is worried that other staff members will be very upset with her if she does.

- What could Margaret have done to make this situation less difficult than it is?
- Whom do you think Margaret should promote?

Discussion: Perhaps Margaret should not have hired her best friend in the first place. However, once she did hire Beth, she should have ensured that her friendship with Beth was not evident in the workplace. If Margaret promotes Beth, surely most of her staff members will believe she is biased and promoted Beth because of their personal friendship. If Margaret promotes the other staff member instead of Beth, Margaret will worry that she is being unfair to Beth and to the organization. There is no easy solution to a problem like this. No matter what she decides, Margaret should work with Beth to help Beth improve her interpersonal relationships with other staff members. However, Margaret's attempt to do that may have a negative effect on her personal relationship with Beth. To avoid situations such as this, it is best to avoid personal relationships with supervisees, if possible.

Employed counselors who serve as administrative supervisors must thoroughly familiarize themselves with the policies and procedures of the organization and with the contract terms of any-one employed through either a personal or a union contract. It is essential that administrative supervisors follow, in detail, all written procedures. A common problem for administrative supervisors is having their decisions overturned either within the organization or by courts because they have failed to follow written procedures. Administrative supervisors who disapprove of organizational policies, organizational procedures, or contract clauses should work within proper channels to get them changed. Supervisors must follow such policies and procedures or contract clauses precisely while they are still in effect.

Confidential Information

In the context of relationships with other professionals, counselors must often share information about clients that is confidential or even privileged. In Chapter 5, sharing information with other professionals was identified as an exception to confidentiality and privileged communication requirements. Consistent with informed consent requirements, counselors should inform clients in advance if they plan to share confidential information with other professionals.

It is best to obtain written permission from clients to transfer private information to others. Although written permission generally is not a legal requirement, the federal Health Insurance Portability and Accountability Act (HIPAA) law as well as state licensure laws or regulations for counselors could require that permission be in writing. Also, the *Code of Ethics* (ACA, 2014) requires that written permission be obtained to transfer records (§B.6.g.). A model client waiver form is included in Appendix C.

The *Code of Ethics* (ACA, 2014) also requires counselors to try to ensure that receivers of their records are sensitive to the confidential nature of the records (§B.6.g.). Counselors are not expected to conduct an investigation of the policies and procedures for maintaining confidentiality of every individual, agency or institution that receives their records. What good practice dictates is that counselors ensure that the client's fully informed consent has been given to transfer the records and that they clearly mark as *confidential* any records that they send. Only information that is pertinent to the purpose of sharing records should be disclosed. The federal HIPAA law that applies to most counseling agencies has strict requirements in these areas (see Chapters 5 and 6).

Referrals

The practice of making referrals to other professionals is associated with a number of ethical responsibilities. Because counselors have an obligation to practice only within the boundaries of their competence, they refer clients whom they are unable to assist (ACA, 2014, §A.11.a.). The concept that counselors should refer clients if they do not believe they are qualified or competent to serve them effectively has caused concern within the counseling profession. As was discussed in Chapter 4, we believe this standard should not be interpreted in a way that would allow a counselor to refuse to counsel clients based on gender identity, sexual orientation, or any other basis that would constitute discrimination. The update of the *Code of Ethics* (ACA, 2014) added new language to address such concerns. Standard A.11.b. states, "Counselors refrain from referring prospective and current clients based solely on the counselor's personally held values, attitudes, beliefs, and behaviors. Counselors respect the diversity of clients and seek training in areas in which they are at risk of imposing their values onto clients, especially when the counselor's values are inconsistent with the client's goals or are discriminatory in nature."

The responsibility to protect client welfare also may lead to a referral. Counselors are cautioned to avoid abandoning clients and "assist in making appropriate arrangements for the continuation of treatment, when necessary, during interruptions such as vacations, illness, and following termination" (ACA, 2014, §A.12.). Standard A.11.a. states that counselors "are knowledgeable about culturally and clinically appropriate referral resources and suggest these alternatives." However, counselors should discontinue counseling relationships if referrals by clients are rejected (§A.11.a.). Counselors recommend other service providers when they terminate a counseling relationship "when it becomes reasonably apparent that the client no longer needs assistance, is not likely to benefit, or is being harmed by continued counseling" (§A.11.c.). Finally, "when counselors refer clients to other practitioners, they ensure that appropriate clinical and administrative processes are completed and open communication is maintained with both clients and practitioners" (§A.11.d.).

Counselors are prohibited from using their places of employment or institutional affiliation to recruit or gain clients, supervisors, or consultees for their private practice (ACA, 2014, §C.3.d.). The law regarding referrals is based on professionals' fiduciary responsibilities to their clients. The law requires that professionals not do anything that would benefit themselves at the expense of a client or that would harm a client in any way. Obviously, counselors would benefit if they referred clients to their own practice, which is why §C.3.d. exists.

Many counselors are concerned about the propriety of referring a client to a particular counselor. This practice is neither unethical nor illegal. There is a misperception among counselors that referrals to only one specified individual are wrong because many agencies, particularly agencies that are publicly funded, have policies either prohibiting referrals to specific practitioners altogether or requiring that counselors refer to a specified minimum number of individuals. Agencies have developed these policies in an attempt to avoid furthering the business interests of some mental health professionals to the detriment of other mental health professionals who practice in the community. To avoid complaints from professionals that others are being favored by the agency, many agencies adopt policies that require multiple referrals.

Ethical guidelines require counselors to be knowledgeable about culturally and clinically appropriate referral resources so that they can suggest alternatives to clients (ACA, 2014, §A.11.a.). Perhaps it is the use of the plural *alternatives* that has led some counselors to believe mistakenly that they must always provide clients with more than one referral source. The intent of this standard is to stress that counselors need to be familiar with the resources in their community that provide mental health and related services. If a counselor believes that a client would be well served by a referral to any of a number of other professionals, then it is good practice to give all these choices to the client. If a counselor believes that a client would be best served by a particular mental health professional whose specialty area matches the client's needs, then the counselor should feel free to recommend that particular resource (unless agency or organizational rules require multiple referrals or no referrals to specific individuals).

Generally, a counselor would not be held accountable for the malpractice of a professional to whom an individual had been referred. However, if the counselor making the referral had some reason to know or should have known that a particular professional had a notoriously negative reputation in the professional community, then the counselor might be held accountable for harm suffered by the person who was referred.

Sometimes clients who seek counseling services are already being seen by another mental health professional. For example, a person who is receiving psychotropic medication from a psychiatrist might also seek counseling. In these instances, counselors should obtain client consent to contact and work with the other professional to establish positive and collaborative professional relationships (ACA, 2014, §A.3.).

Respecting Other Professionals

The introduction to Section D of the *Code of Ethics* (ACA, 2014) emphasizes the importance of developing and maintaining positive, collaborative working relationships with other mental health and non–mental health professionals. The quality of services to clients is enhanced when counselors develop positive relationships and communication systems with colleagues. Non–mental health professionals might include ministers (Kane, 2013), attorneys, physicians, and others who may be serving the same clients.

Counselors have a responsibility to become knowledgeable about related mental health professionals and to be "respectful of approaches that are grounded in theory and/or have an empirical or scientific foundation but may differ from their own" and "Counselors acknowledge the expertise of other professional groups and are respectful of their practices" (ACA, 2014, §D.1.a.). They "work to develop and strengthen relationships with colleagues from other disciplines to best serve clients" (§D.1.b.). A collaborative approach is particularly vital when counselors serve as members of interdisciplinary treatment teams that deliver multifaceted services to clients.

Counselors must be aware that their opinions regarding other professionals, particularly other mental health professionals, carry considerable weight with the general public. Counselors must be respectful of other professionals even if they personally have negative feelings about their approaches to practice. Our relationships with fellow mental health professionals should be based on respect, honesty, and fairness (Welfel, 2013). We noted in Chapter 2, in our discussion of professional identity, that counselors sometimes have philosophical and practical differences regarding therapeutic approaches, as well as turf wars, with other mental health professionals. A counselor and a psychologist might find themselves, on Monday, testifying at the state legislature on opposite sides of a mental health provider issue. On Tuesday, they might meet as members of a treatment team to work for the best interests of their shared clients. The key to managing such situations is to keep professional disagreements in the political and philosophical realms and to stringently avoid bringing them into our work with clients.

Glosoff (2001) raised an important point in noting that, when we focus on differences and disagreements, our attitude toward fellow mental health professionals tends to be one of tolerance rather than appreciation for how these differences can help us to better serve our clients. Rather than believing that our point of view is the only valid one, we need to keep in mind that interprofessional collaboration is an important resource for meeting the complex psychological, emotional, social, economic, physical, and spiritual needs of our clients. Counselors who have a strong professional identity and can clearly articulate their perspectives will be better able to establish and maintain collegial relationships with other mental health professionals (Glosoff, 2001).

From a legal perspective, counselors must be careful to avoid saying or writing comments that might damage the reputation of another professional. If counselors repeat rumors that are inaccurate, or purposefully make false oral or written statements, such actions could damage the reputations of other professionals, and those individuals could sue for libel or slander. *Libel* refers to false, defamatory, or malicious *written* statements; *slander* refers to such statements that are *spoken*. Generally, the law of libel and slander requires that persons who believe they were harmed by the words of another prove *special harm* (Robertson, Powers, Anderson, & Wellborn, 2011). Injured persons usually have to prove actual pecuniary loss, as opposed to humiliation or general harm to their reputations. However, accusing persons of being unfit for their profession falls under the category of libel or slander per se, which means that *special harm* does not have to be proven. Because professional reputation is so important to a career, it is assumed in law that persons are harmed if their reputation is damaged by lies or deceit.

Schwartz, Kelly, and Partlett (2010) have listed the following defenses to accusations of libel or slander: truth, retraction, absolute privilege, and qualified privilege. If you were accused of defaming another person, you could argue that what you said or wrote was true. You also could publicly retract what you said or wrote. Judges have absolute privilege and cannot be sued for what they say in their official capacity. If you are defending yourself, you have a *qualified privilege* to repeat what you have heard if you must do so to protect yourself.

PRIVATE PRACTICE

Many counselors-in-training idealize private practice and have a goal of owning their own independent counseling practice someday. They may not have considered that by owning a private practice they will be running a business and that opening a practice involves all the promises and pitfalls of starting any small business. Most counselors do not have training or experience in business administration, so it is important that they consider many important issues before deciding whether to go into private practice.

The Small Business Administration (SBA, 2014) has suggested that small business owners evaluate themselves to determine whether entrepreneurship is for them. To be successful, entrepreneurs must be comfortable taking risks, independent, persuasive, able to negotiate, creative, and supported by others. To help counselors determine whether starting a private practice is a good idea for them, the SBA asks them to answer 20 questions that include, among others, "Am I prepared to spend the time and money needed to get my business started?" and "How long do I have before I start making a profit?" These sobering questions (and their answers) could be very helpful to counselors who are considering opening a private practice. To see how you measure up to the Small Business Administration's ideas about running a business of your own, visit the agency's website at www.sba.gov.

Taxes and Business Licenses

If counselors generate any income at all outside of their salary, they are in business and have a private practice. Depending on the state statute and the nature of the services rendered, counselors may need to be licensed by their state counselor licensing board. In some states, a license is required to provide counseling services in a private practice, whereas in other states a license is optional. Also, in some states counselors may conduct educational workshops, produce written professional products, and engage in other counseling-related activities that produce an income without being licensed. Whether a license in counseling is required depends entirely on the wording of the state counselor licensure statute.

Counselors who generate income outside of wages or salaries must file a separate federal income tax form for income produced from a business. In states that have income taxes, similar forms sometimes must be filed at the state level as well.

Numerous federal, state, and local requirements must be addressed when counselors open their private practices. Haynsworth (1986) has listed the following possible steps that a counselor might need to take:

- Obtain a federal tax identification number if there are any employees.
- In some states, obtain a professional license.
- Apply for and obtain a business license.
- Purchase workers' compensation insurance or unemployment compensation insurance.
- If required, obtain employee bonds.

- Purchase liability, property damage, or other types of insurance.
- Comply with a fictitious or assumed name statute.
- Fulfill other public filing requirements that may exist.

Counselors with businesses must purchase a business license from their local jurisdiction's office, which is usually located in a city hall or county courthouse (Alberty, 2014). Purchasing a business license involves listing a business address. In most jurisdictions, zoning laws prohibit or limit in some way clients (or customers) coming to a residence. So, if a residence is listed as the place of business, the counselor must indicate that no clients or customers come there for services. For example, a counselor might provide counseling services only on-line or might provide services at another counselor's place of business or in the homes of clients. Each year, when a business license is renewed, counselors must report the amount of their gross income and pay a tax to the city or county. This tax is minimal until substantial income is generated. Although few jurisdictions actively pursue those who violate business license laws, violations could become important if a counselor were accused of wrongdoing at some point.

Counselors who generate income and fail to report it on federal and state income tax forms, or who fail to purchase and renew business licenses each year, are committing crimes. A number of counselors who are unaware of tax and business license requirements are in violation of these laws. Ignorance of legal requirements does not excuse those who violate them.

Business Form

Businesses are structured in a number of ways. Most professional private practices are known in law as sole proprietorships. The individual professional owns the private practice and no other professional has a financial interest in it. This is the simplest form of business ownership and the one chosen by most private practitioners in counseling. In our opinion, it is usually the best option for counselors who engage in private practice.

The second most popular business form for counselors is a partnership. Generally, partnerships should be chosen only if a partnership is required to obtain financing for a new business or if there is a significant advantage in the commercial market for a partnership over a sole proprietorship.

Many counselors seem to choose partnerships because they are anxious about beginning a business venture on their own, or because they want the social benefits of affiliating with friends or colleagues. These are not good reasons for forming a partnership. There are many arguments against forming partnerships that should be carefully considered: (a) Total agreement on all business decisions is required; (b) each partner is fully liable for the acts or omissions of the other partner; (c) there is a presumption of equality of partners regarding liabilities and profits; (d) personal assets are not protected from business debts; and (e) dissolutions of partnerships can be contentious and very expensive if problems cannot be resolved amicably and one or more partners hire lawyers to represent their interests.

A corporation is a third possible business form. Generally, individuals are motivated to form corporations if the business involved is very risky and if the owner has substantial personal assets (Alberty, 2014). Most states have what is known as *professional corporations*, in which individual professionals essentially incorporate their individual private practices. Although professional corporations were very popular in the past, tax advantages have been reduced through legislation (Hamilton, Macey, & Moll, 2012). Corporations are complicated and difficult to keep current, and as a result, professional corporations have fallen out of favor. However, according to Weil (1983), some individuals still form professional corporations which offer the following advantages: (a) accumulation of capital, (b) transferability of ownership, (c) flexible fiscal year, (d) employee benefits, (e) some reduction in liability, and (f) management structure.

A professional's primary motivation for choosing any type of corporate form for a private practice would be to protect personal assets in the event that the business failed or a judgment was rendered against it. A reason for not forming a corporation, however, is that adequate professional liability insurance can be purchased to avoid losing the business and personal assets because of a lawsuit or judgment. Other problems with corporations include the following: (a) They are very expensive to form, (b) meetings must be held periodically and annual reports filed or the corporation will cease to exist legally, (c) income is taxed to the corporation and is taxed again when it is distributed to owners, and (d) accountants and lawyers must be retained on a continuous basis to ensure that the corporation is functioning properly.

Some counselors choose to form nonprofit corporations as the basis of their practice. Essentially, counselors form a nonprofit corporation and then pay themselves a salary from the proceeds of the entity. Such corporations have favorable tax laws (Hamilton, Macey, & Moll, 2012) and might be eligible for certain grants. The significant problem with nonprofit corporations is that the counselor does not own or control them. To qualify as a nonprofit corporation, the charter of the entity must include a board of directors. Although counselors might originally form boards that will support them as directors, it is possible that board members may begin to assert themselves or that replacement board members may not support the counselor. A nonprofit corporation board has the authority to remove the counselor as the director and to take over the business entity.

Fees for Services

Counselors in private practice must set fees for their services, and they struggle with establishing their fee structures (Newlin, Adolph, & Kreber, 2004). They are in business, so they must generate enough income to cover their business expenses. In addition, if their private practice is their only source of income, they want to generate enough income above expenses to allow them to have a comfortable lifestyle. Steele (2012) and Truffo (2007) have suggested that counselors can achieve significant wealth if they manage their private practices effectively. However, counselors know that if their fees are too high, clients will go elsewhere for services. If their fees are too low, clients may not value the services they are receiving, or they may choose a practitioner who charges higher fees in the belief that the fee reflects the quality of services offered. Although most professionals seek to establish the highest fee that the market will tolerate, counselors, like lawyers, are in a fiduciary relationship with clients. Therefore, they must set fees within a framework of basic fairness (Smith & Mallen, 1989).

The *Code of Ethics* (ACA, 2014, §A.10.c.) states that in establishing fees, counselors should consider the *financial status of clients and locality*. The standard probably was intended to encourage counselors to set fees that reflect the economy in the locality. However, it could be misinterpreted to mean that counselors should charge clients according to their ability to pay, which could result in problems for counselors in private practice. Legally, counselors and other professionals may set any fees that they wish for their services. They can even charge different clients different amounts for the same service as long as they do not discriminate based on constitutionally protected categories of persons. Standard A.10.c. also states, "If a counselor's usual fees create undue hardship for the client, the counselor may adjust fees, when legally permissible, or assist the client in locating comparable, affordable services." If a potential client cannot afford to pay the fee you have established for your services in your private counseling practice, then you may adjust your fees, or you may help that client by providing him or her with referrals where counseling services may be free or available at rates below those you charge.

Some counselors establish the same *sliding scale* fee structure in their private practices that is used by counseling centers supported by public funds or private charitable funds. A sliding scale fee structure sets the fee for services based on objective criteria such as amount of income and size of family. With sliding scales, individuals with more income and less financial burden pay more for the same services than those with less income and more financial burden. Although a sliding scale seems more appropriate for a nonprofit agency than it does for a private practice from a business perspective, counselors in private practice could adopt this method, too.

An important part of charging fees is the process of collecting them (Barnett & Walfish, 2012). Many counselors are uncomfortable taking money from their clients, but collecting fees is a necessary part of maintaining a successful private practice. Counselors who avoid the collection of fees probably should consider working in an agency where they do not have to collect client fees rather than operating a private practice.

The trend today is for all professionals to collect fees as services are rendered. In other words, counseling clients probably should be expected to pay for each session at the time the session is held. An exception, of course, would be clients whose payments will be made by another entity, such as an indemnity health insurance company, preferred provider organization, employee assistance program, or governmental agency. Counselors in private practice should develop clear policies regarding fee payment, and these policies should be spelled out specifically in the counselor's disclosure statement (see Appendix B). It is unwise to make any exceptions. If unanticipated problems arise regarding payment, it is best to address these problems immediately with the client (Knapp & VandeCreek, 2008).

Standard A.10.d. of the *Code of Ethics* (ACA, 2014) states, "If counselors intend to use collection agencies or take legal measures to collect fees from clients who do not pay for services as agreed upon, they include such information in their informed consent documents and also inform clients in a timely fashion of intended actions and offer clients the opportunity to make payment." Although this standard suggests that counselors do sue their clients for unpaid fees, we recommend against this practice. In the event that a counselor does allow a client to develop a large bill for services, the counselor should never threaten a client in any way if payment is not made, and certainly should never sue the client. If a counselor demanded payment from a former client for past services rendered, the former client could take the position that the services were inferior and could countersue or file a complaint with the counselor's licensure board, certifying agency, or professional association (Smith & Mallen, 1989). In our opinion, it is better just to forget client bills that are never paid and, in the future, to avoid allowing any bills to develop.

Attorney and Accountant Services

Counselors who are employed can expect their employer to provide them with legal consultation when requested. Counselors in private practice must pay for the services of attorneys when they are needed. Employed counselors are not required to keep business financial records, but counselors in private practice must retain the services of an accountant on an ongoing basis.

As a counselor in private practice, you will need the services of attorneys for a variety of issues (Pope & Vasquez, 2005). Some of the more common situations are as follows:

- You are considering forming a partnership and must know the legal implications.
- You have been presented with a lease to sign for your office space, and you do not know much about leases.
- You receive a subpoena for a client's records, and the client tells you not to release them.
- Staff members from a health insurance company notify you that they are denying claims made by one of your clients because they do not believe you rendered the services you said you provided.

- An investigator for a suspected child abuse case you reported is very aggressive in dealing with you.
- You and your partner have decided to dissolve a partnership, and your partner is being very unreasonable.

Legal issues arise regularly in a private practice, as this list illustrates. Advice regarding identifying and establishing a relationship with an attorney is provided in Chapter 1.

Most counselors in private practice do not have the expertise or time to handle all the financial obligations of their business. As a counselor in private practice, you would be wise to retain an accountant or an accounting firm to perform the following tasks for you:

- Set up a system for recording income and expenses
- Develop a retirement program for you and your employees
- Handle your payroll, including deducting income taxes and Social Security payments
- File annual tax returns for you

The expenses for the services of attorneys and accountants are substantial and are part of the overhead for a counselor's private practice. Avoiding legal or financial advice because of the expense involved can lead to substantial problems later.

Professional Liability Insurance

Professional liability insurance is essential for counselors in private practice. There are numerous ethical challenges particular to private practices (Barnett, Zimmerman, & Walfish, 2014; Hammer & Kessler, 2012; Woody, 2011). In addition, if a counselor's private practice accumulates debts that exceed the assets of the practice, which could happen if a counselor were sued, a counselor's personal assets might be taken. A counselor's personal assets are always at risk when a private practice is opened. Even if the practice is incorporated, personal assets can sometimes be accessed in a lawsuit.

Therefore, it is essential that counselors purchase professional liability insurance for their practices. Counselors in private practice should purchase the best professional liability insurance available to them and should request the maximum coverage available. If possible, a policy should be purchased that pays for attorneys' fees and judgments; legal representation if an ethics complaint is filed against the counselor; claims made for actions that occurred during the time the policy was in effect; and claims against supervisees, partners, or employees.

Counselors in private practice also need insurance that covers injuries that might occur on their office premises (Schutz, 1990), acts or omissions by employees that they may be supervising, and any other claim that may arise as a result of their business. This type of insurance is relatively inexpensive.

Making the Transition

Typically, counselors who go into private practice begin their professional careers by working in an agency or organization for several years to gain experience and to complete the hours of supervised practice required for licensure. Later, when they are considering going into private practice, they should assess their ability to handle financial uncertainties. These include an initial period of struggle that may last 3 to 5 years while the practice is getting established, financial losses incurred by cancellations and no-shows, and income that fluctuates from month to month. Personal stressors, such as isolation and dealing with suicidal clients, should also be given some thought. For counselors who can manage the stressors and who enjoy the independence that self-employment allows, private practice can be very rewarding.

A counselor who establishes a part-time private practice while employed as a counselor in an agency must be careful not to accept clients for a fee in the private practice who could receive the same services from the counselor in the employment setting (ACA, 2014, §A.10.a.). If an agency does allow its counselors to accept agency clients in their private practices, then the standard says that clients are informed of other options in addition to being counseled by a staff member in his or her private practice.

An issue that seems to be emerging in the realm of private practice is restrictive covenants, usually called noncompetition agreements. A *noncompetition agreement* prohibits an employee from practicing the profession for a specified time or within a geographic region when the employee leaves the organization. Although these types of agreements have been common in professions such as law, medicine, architecture, and dentistry, they present unique problems for counselors. Three issues that could have an effect on client welfare are informed consent, transfer of clients, and solicitation of clients (Wyatt & Daniels, 2000). Counselors who are planning to leave an employing agency need to inform clients regarding their choices. Will the client be transferred to another counselor within the agency, or can the client choose to follow the counselor to the counselor's private practice? If the client has the choice, the counselor must be careful not to exercise undue influence on the client's decision.

As you have seen after reading this section of the chapter, starting your own private practice is a complex process. According to Gilabert (2014), 80% of all new businesses fail in the first 18 months. The Small Business Administration (2014) has indicated the following top reasons for business failures that could be associated with counseling private practices: insufficient start-up capital (money), lack of experience, personal use of business funds, competition, and low sales.

Most counselor preparation programs do not offer courses in establishing and maintaining private counseling practices (Green, Baskind, Mustian, Reed, & Taylor, 2007). As a result, counselors who plan to open private practices should attend workshops on the topic and read materials that have been developed to help them achieve success (Diana, 2010; Grodzki, 2000; Hunt, 2004; Paterson, 2011; Rowell & Green, 2003; Stout & Grand, 2006; Truffo, 2007; Walfish & Barnett, 2009). The American Counseling Association offers its members access to valuable and detailed private practice information provided by an experienced private practitioner, Anthony Centore (American Counseling Association, n.d.). The information is one of the benefits of ACA membership.

Counselors in both private practice and in agency or other community settings must deal effectively with third-party payers, or health care insurance companies, if they are to serve the majority of clients who seek counseling services. In our observation, counselors in private practice struggle to a great extent with issues related to receiving reimbursement from third-party payers (Rowell & Green, 2003). In the following section, we discuss some realities of managed care that counselors need to understand.

HEALTH CARE PLANS

Health care plan assistance is a necessity for many individuals who receive mental health care services; they could not afford the services without this help. It is important for counselors to have a basic understanding of how health care plans function, particularly in the area of providing mental health care services.

In many countries, citizens pay taxes to the government, and the government then provides health care services for no cost. In the United States, individuals pay for health care plans because the federal government does not provide health care services and the cost of some of their health care needs could easily exceed the individual's financial resources. When people enter into contracts with health care companies, the health care plan agrees to provide them with health care in return for a premium they pay on a regular basis.

As a fringe benefit, employers in the United States often provide health care plans for their employees free of charge or, more commonly, they subsidize the cost of the plans for their employees. Individuals who are unemployed, who own their own businesses, or who work for employers who do not provide health care plans must purchase their own. Indigent persons or disabled individuals who cannot purchase their own insurance may receive health care assistance in the form of Medicaid (42 U.S.C. §1396, 1982) from the government. Older persons receive Medicare from the federal government if they qualify due to having paid into Medicare when they were working.

Unfortunately, a number of persons in the United States have no health care plan at all. These individuals must pay for medical services as they are rendered to them, or they simply do not receive medical care. Howe (1999) has suggested that most of the people who do not have health care plans belong to the *working poor*. These are people who produce income that exceeds the eligibility limits for Medicaid, have jobs that do not provide health care plans as a fringe benefit, and cannot afford to purchase health care plans on their own. There are millions of individuals in the United States who do not have health care plans to assist them in paying for mental health care services. In addition, many of the health care plans that people do have pay for no mental health care services or for services that are extremely limited.

On March 23, 2010, the Affordable Care Act took effect in the United States. The goal of the Act is for every U.S. citizen to have health care. Every citizen was required to have a health insurance plan by 2014 if they could afford one and if their religious beliefs allowed health care, and those who do have a health care plan may be assessed. Many health care providers are concerned that mental health care services are not covered under the new federal plans to the same extent that physical health care services are provided (Flaskerud, 2009).

State Insurance Laws

Each state or jurisdiction in the United States has different laws governing health care plan contracts that may be sold in that state. These laws require that health care plan companies offer certain health benefits in order to be allowed to sell plans in that state. In addition to benefits that are mandated by state law, health care companies can offer additional benefits as an incentive for individuals to purchase plans from them rather than from other companies.

A state may also mandate by statute which categories of professionals are eligible to render the health care services that are reimbursable. Physicians are always listed as acceptable providers of health care services. State legislation can require that other health care providers, such as chiropractors, nurses, or physical therapists, be eligible to provide health care services under all insurance plans sold in the state. This type of statute is called *freedom of choice* legislation. It allows consumers of health care services to choose the providers they prefer, rather than allowing health care companies to limit categories of approved providers, thereby excluding other providers. In some states, freedom of choice statutes exist that require allowing licensed counselors to provide mental health care services if those services are reimbursed by health care companies. In other states, where such legislation does not exist, health care companies can determine for themselves whether they will reimburse for services if they are rendered by licensed counselors.

In most circumstances, health care companies will voluntarily reimburse their plan members for the reimbursable mental health care services of licensed counselors. If health care companies refuse to allow licensed counselors to provide mental health care services to their plan holders and there is no statute in that state to the contrary, plan members or licensed counselors cannot force them to allow licensed counselors to be providers. See Chapter 2 for a review of how counselors can become active in legislative issues affecting their profession.

Managed Care

Managed health care is a relatively new concept that has had a significant impact on mental health care services (Rupert & Baird, 2004). Basically, managed care means that people are not given all health care services that they want or that their provider wants for them. Instead, health plan members are given the services that the health care plan company has determined are appropriate and necessary. The idea is to lower the cost to the company for health care by *managing* the care provided.

These companies have policies regarding the type of care they will provide for preventive procedures or for various illnesses. They also use a procedure known as *utilization review*, in which a physician or panel of physicians reviews requests for services from the treating service providers to determine whether the services will be allowed (*Wickline v. State of California*, 1986). If plan members or their providers want services that exceed those allowed under a managed care system, they must request exceptions from the company.

A controversy regarding managed care revolves around whether health care companies are indeed containing health care costs appropriately by eliminating unnecessary procedures and limiting allowable services, or they are simply increasing their profits at the expense of health care recipients. Many health care providers are dissatisfied with managed care systems because administrators make decisions about health care services that professionals believe they should make themselves. Two-thirds of the mental health counselors in one study stated that they believed managed care had had a negative impact on their counseling relationships (Danzinger & Welfel, 2001).

Most health care companies today limit the number of outpatient visits for mental health concerns that members are allowed each year. The idea of limiting counseling services to a set number of visits is objectionable to many mental health care providers. They would rather have health care companies allow clients as many visits as the professional believes are necessary to resolve a mental health concern. Of course, clients who are plan members could have more visits than their health care plan allows, but they would have to pay the fees themselves.

Types of Health Care Plans

Health care companies offer many different types of plans to the public. The most common kinds available today include health maintenance organizations (HMOs), preferred provider organizations (PPOs), and traditional indemnity health insurance policies. Of course, many other types of health care plans exist, such as exclusive provider organizations (EPOs; Carabillo, 1986), managed care organizations (MCOs), and individual practice associations (IPAs; Randall, 1994). Combinations of two or more types are occasionally formed, and sometimes what appears to be an HMO is actually a preferred provider organization (PPO).

When individuals purchase health care plans from an HMO, they agree to go to the HMO for all their health care needs, and they agree to accept the provider of the health care services assigned to them by the HMO. Although most HMOs offer some flexibility in choosing providers within the organization, members cannot go outside the organization for their health care. HMOs hire providers of health care. Members do not pay for services and then get reimbursed. Instead, they receive health care services from the HMO for no fee or for co-payments that they have agreed to in their contracts.

Individuals who purchase health care plans from a PPO agree to go to providers who have been preapproved by the organization for all of their health care needs. PPO policy members can choose their providers, but only from the list of approved providers given to them by the PPO plan.

PPOs do not hire providers of health care. The approved providers on their list usually are in private practice or work for a separate health care agency. PPO providers collect co-pays and deductibles and bill insurers, but members are responsible for what the insurer does not cover.

Indemnity insurance works something like a PPO, but individuals who purchase indemnity health insurance do not have to go to providers who have been preapproved by the organization. Policyholders can choose their health care provider, as long as the provider is in a category of providers that the insurance company recognizes. Health care providers collect co-pays and deductibles and bill insurers, and persons insured by indemnity health insurance companies are responsible for what the insurer does not cover.

Counselors as Service Providers

Some counselors or counseling agencies refuse to accept clients who intend to use their health care plan to assist with fees. The position of these counselors and agencies is that dealing with health care plans or insurance companies is too time consuming or is objectionable philosophically. The clients of such counselors and agencies are directly responsible for any fees charged for the services rendered to them. Of course, such clients must have the financial resources to be able to afford the services. Thus, the counselors in these practices counsel only individuals who have the financial means to afford their services.

In contrast, many agencies that employ counselors require that they become providers for health care plans. In addition, most counselors in private practice find that they must become providers in order to have enough paying clients to maintain their businesses.

Becoming a provider for a PPO is not an easy process. Counselors must first determine which PPOs exist in their community and then apply to become a provider separately for each one. Sometimes the application process is difficult and time consuming. PPOs purposefully limit their lists of preferred providers. Not all eligible mental health professionals in the community will be accepted by a PPO. They can accept or reject any application they receive, as long as they do not illegally discriminate against a professional. In order to become a provider for a particular PPO, a counselor may have to apply many times over a long period. Despite these difficulties, counselors do seem to be succeeding at becoming providers—60% of the counselors in one study reported that they were approved providers for at least one managed care organization (Danzinger & Welfel, 2001). Once a counselor has been accepted by a PPO as a provider, or when a counselor has accepted a client who has indemnity health insurance that will reimburse the client for the counselor's services, it is important that the counselor complete health plan forms in an appropriate and professional manner.

Most health care plans demand accountability from their providers. Plans may require counselors to submit detailed justifications for their diagnoses. In addition, most health care plans expect providers of mental health care services to develop objective and measurable goals as a part of each client's treatment plan. Some plans even send auditors to providers' offices to determine whether the provider is offering a professional setting for rendering services, is keeping confidential information secure, is accessible to clients for services, and is keeping records appropriately. If providers do not comply with a health care plan's requirements, the plan has the option of removing them as providers. In fact, to avoid liability, health care plans must remove providers from their lists who are ineffective professionally (Corcoran, 1989).

It is vital for counselors to request detailed information from each health care plan for which they provide services regarding the plan's expectations from providers. Each plan is unique and requests various types of information in a multitude of formats. In order to maintain provider status, counselors must comply with the requirements of each health care plan. Counselors must be "accurate, honest, and objective in reporting their professional activities and judgments to appropriate third parties, including courts, health insurance companies, those who are the recipients of evaluation reports, and others" (ACA, 2014, §C.6.b.).

Counselors who serve as providers must be prepared to deal with a number of ethical and legal issues that are unique to managed care and other types of health plans (Lawless, Ginter, & Kelly, 1999). Trudeau, Russell, de la Mora, and Schmitz (2001) found that mental health professionals from various disciplines generally are dissatisfied with managed care programs. Issues with which counselors must contend in managed care environments include client privacy, proper diagnosis, informed consent, receiving payment for services, continuing treatment and denial of services, and avoiding fraud. Welfel (2013) has pointed out that counselors who work with managed care companies must deal with a conflict of interest in that they must avoid alienating the company from whom they need referrals and must be advocates for quality care for their clients at the same time.

Federal Health Care Plans

Counselors have been politically active in each state to become recognized as mental health care providers by health care companies under state laws. Counselors have also had a number of successes in being recognized as providers under federal health care plans.

The National Board for Certified Counselors (2014) has summarized federal programs in which counselors have already been officially accepted as mental health care providers. These programs include the Medicare program, the Department of Veterans Affairs, the Military Health Systems, and the Indian Health Service. In addition, a federal occupational series for counselor has been created.

Client Privacy

When clients contract with health care plans, they sign forms that give health care providers permission to provide information regarding their health care to their health care plan administrators. Clients, in the past, believed that they had to agree that service providers could release any information regarding their treatment that the administrators requested. However, the Health Insurance Portability and Accountability Act (HIPAA) has changed that situation significantly. Under HIPAA, insurance companies are limited in the types of information they may request, and they are not allowed to disallow claims if clients refuse to provide them with certain types of information, such as psychotherapy notes. See Chapter 6 for a thorough discussion of the provisions of HIPAA.

Many mental health professionals feel uneasy about providing detailed information regarding their clients' diagnoses and treatment to administrators who usually are not mental health professionals. Their discomfort is compounded by the fact that they have no control over what happens to the information after it is released to the provider (Danzinger & Welfel, 2001). Yet if counselors wish to be providers, they must provide this information. When counselors become providers for PPOs, they should request a copy of the privacy waivers that PPO members routinely sign. If a counselor is ever unsure about whether a client wants the counselor to provide information requested from a health care plan administrator, it would be best to ask the client to sign a waiver giving permission for the information to be sent.

In our opinion, it is fruitless for an individual counselor to challenge the idea that health care providers inappropriately invade the privacy of their clients. If a counselor believes that a health care plan policy should be changed, the counselor should communicate directly with a company representative regarding the policy. Counselors who believe that laws or regulations should be changed should work through the state or national counseling association to seek legislative changes. ACA belongs to a coalition of mental health organizations working to influence national legislation. Glosoff (1998) has suggested that counselors might take additional steps, such as increasing their role in the decision-making processes of managed care companies and working with companies to establish clearly structured appeals processes. Knapp and VandeCreek (2008) have reminded counselors that they have an ethical obligation to advocate for clients by informing policy makers about problems with the present health care system.

Diagnosis

In Chapter 7, we noted that using the *Diagnostic and Statistical Manual (DSM)* creates conflicts for counselors who espouse a wellness or developmental orientation. Most managed care organizations require that mental health professionals assign a *DSM* diagnosis to their clients in order to qualify for reimbursement of services. Most companies limit in some way the diagnoses for which they will pay benefits. Some companies will not reimburse for V-code conditions, typical developmental transitions, personality disorder diagnoses, adjustment disorders, or family or couples counseling.

Counselors are sometimes caught in a conflict because they want to promote client welfare by helping clients receive reimbursement and, at the same time, to provide accurate diagnoses. Given the choice between an honest diagnosis without insurance reimbursement and a deceptive diagnosis with third-party payment, some counselors may succumb to playing a game of *diagnosing for dollars*, in which diagnoses are tied to the chance of being reimbursed by health care companies (Wylie, 1995). Rather than yield to these temptations, counselors can improve the chances that their treatment plans will be approved by assessing thoroughly, setting realistic treatment goals, and complying with health care companies' recommended treatment protocols (Hoyt, 1995). Counselors are ethically obligated to "take special care to provide proper diagnosis of mental disorders" (ACA, 2014, *Code of Ethics*, §E.5.a.).

Informed Consent

Managed care can complicate informed consent procedures in several ways. Because managed care plans typically limit treatment options and the number of sessions for which they will reimburse, counselors must address these limitations with clients at the outset of the counseling relationship (Daniels, 2001). In addition, counselors must be alert to whether contracts they may sign with managed care organizations include *gag* clauses stipulating that counselors cannot discuss with their clients alternative treatments that fall outside the boundaries of plan-approved services (Wineburgh, 1998). These clauses in contracts run contradictory to the principle of client autonomy and have been challenged in court (Danzinger & Welfel, 2001). Informed consent also includes ensuring that clients know what information their managed care organization requires the counselor to disclose, as well as the implications of any diagnosis that might be assigned (ACA, 2014, *Code of Ethics*, §A.2.b.).

Receiving Payment for Services

Most PPOs pay providers directly for services rendered to the PPO members. These fees are sent to providers after they have completed necessary forms that document the services rendered. This arrangement means that counselors often receive payment long after services have been rendered.

When counselors provide services to indemnity health insurance policyholders, counselors can handle payment in one of two ways. Counselors may require that the client pay for services as they are rendered and then file for reimbursement. Counselors may also allow clients to assign their reimbursement to the counselors so that the payment comes to the counselor from the insurance company. With either method, counselors must verify to the insurance company that they provided services for the client and must provide all the information regarding the services requested by the insurance company.

Usually, both PPOs and health insurance companies require clients to pay a portion of the counselor's fees directly. This amount is called a *co-payment*. It is vital that counselors collect co-payments from clients when such payments are a requirement of the PPO or indemnity health insurance company.

After counselors have succeeded in becoming approved providers under managed care plans, they confront some ethical issues. Most managed care companies approve only brief mental health treatment as a cost containment measure. Thus, counselors must be prepared to provide brief therapy for many of their clients who want their health care plans to pay for services. Many counselors have not been trained in the brief therapies. Only recently have counselor training programs recognized the need to teach not only the traditional approaches but also the brief therapy models. Programs are just beginning to prepare students to meet the clinical and ethical challenges created by managed care. Therefore, practitioners whose training did not adequately prepare them must seek continuing education in the brief therapies and seek supervision and consultation while developing their competencies (Glosoff, 1998; ACA, 2014, §C.2.b.).

Counselors who participate in managed care plans must be able to assess which clients will be well served in a time-limited context. They must be knowledgeable about referral resources for clients whose needs cannot be met under the limitations of their health care plans. Because counselors have an ethical obligation to be advocates for their clients (ACA, 2014, §A.6.a.), they must also be skilled at appealing health care companies' decisions to deny reimbursement when clients need more sessions than their plan allows.

Continuing Treatment and Denial of Services

Although counselors may do their best to accept clients who can be well served by time-limited therapy, inevitably there will be clients who will need more sessions than their health care plan allows or approves. In these situations, counselors may be caught between the need to uphold their ethical standards and their need to remain financially viable in private practice. They have ethical obligations to avoid abandoning clients (ACA, 2014, §A.12.), to ensure appropriate termination (§A.11.c.), and to help clients find alternative resources for continued treatment (§A.11.d.).

Christensen and Miller (2001) found that mental health professionals continually faced issues of abandonment when they had to terminate clients before they believed they should have. It is not ethical to discontinue counseling services for lack of payment when the client is in a state of crisis or emergency. In such situations, counselors must continue providing treatment until the emergency is resolved or appropriate alternative care can be arranged (Welfel, 2013). At the same time, counselors cannot be expected, except in emergency situations, to continue indefinitely to counsel clients without receiving payment for their services (ACA, 2014, §A.11.c.).

Lawsuits have been filed when patients suffered injuries after their health plans refused to cover services that were requested (*Wickline v. State of California*, 1986; *Wilson v. Blue Cross*, 1990). In these cases, the health plans argued that their denial of payment or reimbursement for services was not a denial of care. They argued that the treating health care provider had the final responsibility for appropriate care. The courts in these cases held that health plans could be held liable if they were negligent in denying health care services that were necessary to avoid a patient being injured. In *Wickline*, the court also found that the physician involved in the case should have protested the health plan's denial of care that he requested. It was the court's position that a health care provider is not liable if a health plan refuses to provide necessary care but that the provider does have a responsibility to protest if the recommendation for care is not accepted.

Mental health care services under managed care probably present more challenges to providers than do physical health care services. First, mental health care often is limited to levels that seem inappropriate to mental health care providers. For example, a health care plan may allow only five reimbursed counseling sessions a year; or worse, the plan may require that a member have a diagnosis of a serious mental or emotional disorder, while severely limiting the services that may be provided under the plan.

The court cases discussed previously provide a foundation for making some recommendations to counselors providing services to clients covered by managed health care companies. These recommendations will help you protect yourself from legal liability:

- If you believe that a client requires counseling services beyond what has been approved by a managed health care company, request the additional services on behalf of the client. If the request is denied, file a written protest or complaint with the company.
- Instruct the client regarding the right to appeal a decision that denies additional services (Hilliard, 1998).
- If the client is a danger to self or others or is in a crisis and cannot afford to pay for your services directly, continue providing services for the client until care can be transferred to another professional or to a facility that provides mental health care.

Anderson (2000), who is a counselor and also has been a managed care case manager, has offered suggestions to counselors about how to deal constructively with managed care companies. He has suggested that counselors avoid treating managed care case managers as the enemy but, instead, establish a positive relationship with them for the benefit of clients. Anderson has recommended to counselors that they emphasize good treatment plans in their practices, use proper code numbers in submitting claim forms, and use empirical research results to support exceptions to decisions that have been made.

Avoiding Fraud

Counselors who complete the forms required by PPOs or health insurance companies must be careful to avoid fraudulent practices. Fraud occurs when counselors misrepresent to health care companies any facts regarding their services so their clients will receive payment or reimbursement for the counselors' services. If fraudulent practices are discovered, and because fraud is a crime, health care companies can file civil lawsuits to recover payments or reimbursements made inappropriately and can even cause prosecutors to file criminal charges against counselors.

Mayfield (1996) found that many counselors do not know what constitutes health care fraud. It is possible for counselors to commit fraud without realizing they are doing so if they do not understand which practices are fraudulent. New counselors should be careful not to pattern their behavior after that of seasoned practitioners because some actions that mental health professionals have been taking for years are actually fraudulent. Substantial numbers of the mental health counselors surveyed by Danzinger and Welfel (2001) had changed or would change treatment plans based on managed care limitations (60%), had terminated or would terminate with clients before they were ready because of these limits (46%), and had changed or would change a client's diagnosis to receive additional reimbursement (44%).

We believe that counselors sometimes engage in health care fraud activities because they are motivated to help their clients receive mental health care services that are paid for or reimbursed by health plans. Counselors report inaccurate information to health care plans so that their clients will be able to begin or continue counseling. Unfortunately, counselors also benefit from fraudulent practices in that health plans pay for their services based on inaccurate information they have provided. Therefore, it appears to outside observers that counselors are being very self-serving when they give false information to health care plans. Consider the following situation.

13-3 The Case of Danny

Danny has just been licensed as a professional counselor and has decided to open a private practice. He knows from talking to other licensed counselors in his state that a few of the major PPOs and health insurance companies in the state do not pay or reimburse clients for the services of licensed counselors. Danny's good friend, Monique, is a licensed clinical psychologist. Monique's clients do receive payment or reimbursement for her services. Monique agrees to sublease office space to Danny for his private practice. In addition, Monique agrees to sign off on PPO and health insurance forms, indicating that she is the client's therapist, even though Danny is the one seeing the clients. Monique and Danny meet weekly and review each of Danny's cases to ensure that Monique is comfortable with his treatment of clients. All clients are told that Monique is supervising Danny. In exchange for Monique's assistance, Danny agrees to give Monique 25% of all fees he collects from PPO and health insurance clients.

• What is the major problem with this arrangement?
• What do you think would happen if Monique indicated on the insurance forms that Danny provided the mental health care services and that Monique supervised him in providing those services?

Discussion: This arrangement between Danny and Monique appears to be one that serves everyone's purposes well. Monique is helping out her friend and realizing extra income through subleasing her office space, supervising Danny, and receiving 25% of the PPO and health insurance client fees that Danny collects. Danny is able to see clients who normally would not be able to see him because their health care plans will pay or reimburse as long as Monique continues to supervise him and sign off. Clients are pleased that their health care plans are paying for their counseling services. This may *seem* like a perfectly reasonable arrangement, and mental health practitioners have long been involved in these kinds of arrangements.

The problem is that Monique and Danny are fraudulently misrepresenting their services to the PPOs and health insurance companies. Although it may seem unfair that health care plans do not reimburse licensed counselors for their services, health care plans in their state do have the right to refuse to pay for the services of licensed counselors. If a health care company discovers what they are doing, the company could sue Monique, Danny, and Danny's clients for fraud, and perhaps collect all of the fees they paid out to them plus other damages. In addition, the company could request that the local prosecutor file criminal fraud charges against all the parties and might also file ethics complaints against Monique and Danny with their licensure boards.

Actually, there is nothing wrong with licensed counselors affiliating with other mental health professionals, such as licensed psychologists or licensed physicians. If the counselor is going to provide the direct service to clients, then PPO and insurance forms must be completed to reflect the actual situation. For example, in the previous case example, no fraud would have been involved if

Monique had indicated on forms that Danny, a licensed counselor, was providing the direct service, and she, the licensed psychologist, was supervising Danny's work. A PPO or health insurance company might have refused to pay or reimburse for services provided under such an arrangement (which it would have a legal right to do), but possibly payment or reimbursement would have been approved. Then the entire arrangement between Danny and Monique would have been acceptable. There is nothing illegal or unethical about fee splitting under arrangements such as theirs as long as there are no misrepresentations to PPOs or health insurance companies.

Listed in the following section are a number of fraudulent practices in which mental health professionals sometimes engage that could lead to serious trouble. Counselors commit fraud when they report the following to PPOs or health insurance companies:

- An approved professional is providing direct services to a client, when the services actually are being provided by a counselor who is not approved for payment or reimbursement.
- A client has a *DSM* diagnosis that is approved for payment or reimbursement, when the counselor actually does not believe the diagnosis is accurate.
- The counselor is seeing a client for individual counseling that is reimbursable, when actually the counselor is providing couples, family, or group counseling that is not reimbursable.
- The counselor is collecting a required co-payment from a client, when actually the counselor is waiving the co-payment.
- Counseling services were rendered on a specific date, when actually the client missed the session but the counselor billed for the missed session anyway.
- The counselor appears to be a physician by signing forms in the space marked *physician's signature*, without noting that the counselor is a licensed counselor rather than a physician.
- The counselor is beginning a counseling relationship with a client for the first time, when actually they are involved in an ongoing counseling relationship, because health care providers often will not pay or reimburse for *preexisting conditions*.
- The client is requesting payment or reimbursement from only one health care plan, when the counselor knows that the client is requesting payment for the same services from two or more plans.

As discussed in Chapter 7, counselors who are willing and properly trained to diagnose emotional and mental disorders have an ethical and legal obligation to diagnose according to accepted standards in the mental health field (ACA, 2014, §E.5.a.). If a counselor determines that a client does not have a *DSM* disorder for which a health care plan will pay or reimburse, then the counselor must not assign such a disorder just to allow a client to obtain health care plan financial assistance.

Changing Nature of Health Care Plans

We have summarized the current types of health care plans available and the issues they raise for mental health care providers. Health care plans have changed substantially over the past decade and are expected to continue to change as legislators and the public discuss and change health care delivery systems in the United States. It is important for counselors who provide services for clients with health care plans to constantly monitor changes in the health care industry. What may be an acceptable practice today may be prohibited tomorrow.

Diversity Considerations

As noted, some people in the United States do not have health care insurance. Unfortunately, many of these individuals are the very people who can ill afford to pay out of pocket for mental health care services. Wilcoxon, Magnuson, and Norem (2008) have urged counselors to confront the business paradigm of the health care industry and have suggested that counselors should advocate for changing corporate approaches to client care that further disadvantage those who already are disadvantaged. Counselors in private practice grapple with conflicts between their desire to assist these individuals and their need to generate sufficient income to maintain their practices. Private practitioners are encouraged to provide some *pro bono* service—that is, service for which there is little or no financial return (ACA, 2014, Section A Introduction). Knapp and VandeCreek (2008) have pointed out, though, that decisions about pro bono and reduced cost services should be made only after careful consideration of possible ramifications. For example, will the client devalue the worth of the services if the services are free?

13-4 The Case of Isabelle

Isabelle has been in private practice for 10 years. She has an office in an affluent part of town, and all of her clients either have insurance that pays for her services or are wealthy enough to pay her from their personal funds. Isabelle feels some guilt, however, because she entered the counseling profession to be of help to individuals and to society. She also is aware that the *Code of Ethics* (ACA, 2014) encourages counselors to provide some services pro bono. Isabelle is wondering how she should provide free services to some clients.

- If Isabelle decides to see some clients for free or at a reduced rate in her private practice, what problems might that cause?
- How else might Isabelle meet her pro bono obligations?

Discussion: If Isabelle were to accept some clients into her private practice who pay nothing, she would need to have clear criteria regarding how clients could qualify for the services. If her other clients were to somehow learn that she was serving some clients pro bono and they did not understand how she came to that decision, they might feel resentful even if they can afford her full fee. Perhaps a better option for Isabelle to fulfill her pro bono obligation would be to volunteer her counseling services in a community agency for a period of time each week, or to provide free workshops in the community.

Summary and Key Points

This chapter focuses on three related topics—professional relationships, private practice, and health care plans. Counselors who practice in any setting interact regularly with other professionals and must conduct themselves in an ethically and legally appropriate manner. Although private practice is idealized by many counselors in training, private practice is a business that carries associated risks and requires knowledge of business practices.

Key points regarding professional relationships include the following:

- Counselors will take different roles depending on the circumstances of their interactions with other professionals.
- Because most counselors function at various times as employees and as employers, it is important that they understand the basic principles of employment law.

- Counselors as employees have the right to be free of discrimination in the workplace and to refuse to follow a supervisor's directive if it constitutes a crime.
- Counselors as employees do not have a right to employment, and in all but limited circumstances they can be dismissed from their jobs.
- Counselors and their employers sometimes disagree about what is ethical, and several steps can be taken to attempt to resolve these disagreements.
- Counselors as employers need to be clear about their roles and their expectations of those whose work they supervise.
- Counselors as employers should avoid close personal relationships or friendships with their employees.
- Counselors should obtain client permission and must work to preserve client confidentiality when transferring private information about clients.
- Although counselors cannot make referrals in ways that might benefit the counselors themselves, they may make referrals to other professionals as dictated by client welfare or the policies of their employers.
- Relationships between counselors and other mental health professionals are characterized by respect, honesty, and fairness.
- Counselors must avoid making statements about other professionals that could be libelous or slanderous.

Private practice is a business. Counselors who wish to start their own practices need to understand certain aspects of business practice. Key points regarding private practice include the following:

- Counselors who wish to start their own practices must be knowledgeable about taxes; business licenses; and the various forms of businesses, including sole proprietorships, partnerships, and corporations.
- Private practitioners must set fees that are reasonable by community standards.

- Counselors must understand the appropriate and inappropriate uses of a sliding scale fee.
- Counselors should collect payment at the time they render their services.
- Counselors in private practice need the services of attorneys and accountants to assist them in managing their businesses.
- It is vitally important that counselors carry adequate professional liability insurance.
- Private practice is not for every counselor. The risks and benefits must be carefully weighed before a decision to enter private practice is made.

Most individuals today have some type of health insurance that is paid for or subsidized by their employers or by the government. Several types of insurance plans raise complex issues for counselors who wish to become approved providers of mental health care services. Key points regarding health insurance include the following:

- Each state in the United States has different laws that govern which health care plan contracts may be sold in that state.
- There are a number of types of health care plans, including HMOs, PPOs, and traditional indemnity plans.
- Managed care has been a controversial development that has had a significant impact on mental health care services.
- With some perseverance, counselors often can become providers for managed care companies.
- Ethical and legal issues raised by managed care and other types of health plans include maintaining client privacy, rendering appropriate diagnoses, ensuring informed consent of clients, receiving payment for services, continuing treatment after benefits end, problems caused by denial of services, avoiding insurance fraud, and meeting the needs of individuals who do not have mental health insurance.

CHAPTER **14**

Issues in Counselor Education

FOCUS QUESTIONS

1. What kinds of information do prospective students need to receive about a counselor training program so that they can make an informed decision regarding whether to apply?

2. What do you think you should do if you know that a classmate is struggling and does not seem to be learning the skills, behaviors, and dispositions needed to become a competent counselor?

3. What kinds of relationships outside the classroom between counselor education professors and students are appropriate?

I n this chapter and the next chapter, we explore ethical and legal issues that arise in counselor training, supervision, and consultation. All three of these functions involve relationships that are tripartite—that is, they involve at least three parties. Professionals who serve as counselor educators, supervisors, or consultants share common concerns in that they are responsible for the welfare of counseling clients, but indirectly. These professionals have obligations to students, supervisees, and consultees, but at the same time they are responsible to the clients who are being served by those they educate and supervise and with whom they consult. These multiple responsibilities can complicate ethical, legal, and professional decision making. This chapter focuses on issues in counselor education.

COUNSELOR EDUCATION PROGRAMS

Informed Consent

Just as clients have the right to know what they are getting into when they come for counseling, students have the right to know what will be expected of them before they choose to enter a graduate program in counseling. In keeping with the spirit of informed consent, prospective students need enough information to enable them to make wise choices about their graduate studies.

In the American Counseling Association's *Code of Ethics* (ACA, 2014), §F.8.a. lists quite explicitly the information that must be provided to prospective students before they enter a program. This information includes the following:

- The values and ethical principles of the profession
- The type and level of skill and knowledge acquisition required for successful completion of the training program
- Technology requirements
- Program training goals, objectives, and mission, and subject matter that will be covered
- Bases for evaluation
- Training components that encourage self-growth or self-disclosure as part of the training process
- The type of supervision settings and requirements of the sites for required clinical field experiences
- Student and supervisee evaluation and dismissal policies and procedures
- Up-to-date employment prospects for graduates

Application materials must include all of these elements. Many prospective students search for program information on university websites, so website materials should be thorough and current.

You learned in Chapter 4 that informed consent is a legal as well as an ethical matter. The law of informed consent requires that individuals be properly *informed* before their *consent* is valid. Before graduate students can appropriately agree to enter a program into which they have been accepted and subsequently meet the program's requirements for graduation, they must be informed of all of the requirements. In addition, the program's requirements for graduation must be presented in sufficient detail to allow entering students to fully understand their obligations.

Perhaps the most important goal of informed consent in admissions is to ensure that prospective students understand that becoming a counselor involves more than acquiring knowledge. Counseling students are expected to engage in a variety of learning experiences that differ from those that are required in most other disciplines (Pease-Carter & Barrio Minton, 2012). Applicants should be made aware that their training will challenge them on the personal as well as the academic level (Herlihy & Corey, 2015a).

Admissions

Counselor educators want to admit into training programs individuals who are likely to succeed at developing the knowledge, skills, and characteristics needed to become effective counselors (Stone & Hanson, 2002). Academic ability is one important criterion, and relevant work experience might also be considered. Some graduate programs list minimum criteria for admission, which might include a minimum Graduate Record Examination (GRE) score or Miller Analogy Test (MAT) score, a minimum undergraduate or graduate grade point average (GPA), or a minimum number of years of work experience. Swank and Smith-Adcock (2014) found that 70%

of counselor education programs use standardized test scores and 95% use GPA as criteria for admission into master's degree programs. Smaby, Maddux, Richmond, Lepkowski, and Packman (2005) have cautioned counselor educators to avoid relying excessively on admissions test scores that have not proven to be accurate in predicting graduate student success or the development of counseling knowledge or counseling skills.

Demonstrated academic ability is a relatively straightforward criterion to apply. Admissions decisions become more difficult when we consider that learning to be a counselor involves more than mastery of academic content. Counselor educators must attempt to ensure that students have the emotional stability and temperament to succeed as counselors (Welfel, 2013). As we noted in Chapter 7 on competence, it is possible for a student to have strong intellectual abilities and still not possess the personal and interpersonal characteristics to be an effective counselor. A significant number of individuals who are attracted to careers in counseling seem to have personality or adjustment problems that would negatively affect their ability to develop the competencies needed to become effective counselors (Foster & McAdams, 2009). Therefore, counselor educators attempt to screen applicants carefully and select students for training programs who possess characteristics that have been shown to be associated with counseling effectiveness. As you can imagine, it is difficult for counselor educators to assess whether program applicants have these personal and interpersonal attributes. Many programs attempt to gather some information by requiring applicants to submit letters of reference or a personal statement or essay. According to Swank and Smith-Adcock (2014), 96% of programs gather information about master's program applicants by requiring them to submit letters of reference, 89% require a personal statement or essay, and 82% also require a personal interview. Leverett-Main (2004) found that counselor educators perceived personal interviews of applicants as the most effective screening measure they used when selecting individuals to admit to their programs.

Admissions decisions for applicants are usually based on a review of several factors. These are considered in relation to the number of individuals that the program can accommodate and the credentials of other applicants. Counseling graduate programs should make it clear that they make admissions decisions in this manner. University administrators and judges generally would not substitute their judgment for that of faculty members unless it was clear that an applicant had been unfairly discriminated against or that the faculty had failed to follow procedures that they had established.

Counselor education programs cannot legally discriminate against prospective students who are in any category of students that is protected by the U.S. Constitution or federal statutes and their implementing regulations. These categories include race, sex, disability, age, residence, and alien status (Kaplin & Lee, 1995). Counselor education programs must be careful to avoid discriminating against students with disabilities. Rothstein (1997) has warned that programs which exclude students with mental disabilities must ensure that the disability is directly related to students' ability to perform the functions of counseling.

Programs can give special consideration to applicants whose characteristics are underrepresented in the program or in the profession of counseling. Affirmative action is an attempt to consider how past discrimination may have negatively affected a category of individuals and to give them special consideration when they apply to a graduate program. Although it appears that the government has the right to refuse to implement affirmative action programs, universities still may apply affirmative action principles to their admissions process if they choose to do so (*Bakke v. Regents of the University of California*, 1978; *DeFunis v. Odegaard*, 1973, 1973, 1974; *DeRonde v. Regents of the University of California*, 1981; *McDonald v. Hogness*, 1979). Nondiscrimination is an ethical mandate as well as a legal consideration. Counselor educators have an ethical responsibility to ensure that counselor education programs reflect the cultural diversity of our society. According to the *Code of Ethics* (ACA, 2014):

> Counselor educators actively attempt to recruit and retain a diverse student body. Counselor educators demonstrate commitment to multicultural/diversity competence by recognizing and valuing diverse cultures and types of abilities students bring to the training experience. Counselor educators provide appropriate accommodations that enhance and support diverse student well-being and academic performance. (§F.11.b.)

For some counselor education programs that are located in geographical areas where the population is not very diverse, recruiting a diverse student body can be a challenge. Even when diverse students can be attracted to a program, a recursive situation may occur in which a program continues to admit and ultimately lose students who are members of marginalized societal groups because the students are always entering programs in which most of the students are members of the dominant culture (Shin, 2008). Admissions materials that emphasize the program's commitment to diversity and social justice may help to attract more diverse applicants (Pack-Brown, Thomas, & Seymour, 2008). Recruiting, promoting, and retaining diverse faculty also has been correlated with an increase in the diversity of the student body (Bemak & Chung, 2007). Shin (2008) has suggested that programs use flexible admissions criteria to increase student diversity, rather than continue to rely on GPA and GRE scores, which are less reliable predictors of success for racially and ethnically diverse applicants.

Curriculum Issues

In Chapter 2, we discussed in some detail the curricular components that a counselor education program must contain in order to be accredited by the Council for Accreditation of Counseling and Related Educational Programs (CACREP). CACREP standards (CACREP, 2014) are generally accepted by the profession as a model curriculum for master's-level preparation of counselors. Here, we highlight some of the ethical responsibilities of counselor educators in delivering the curriculum and explore one of the most ethically sensitive components of training—self-growth experiences.

TEACHING ETHICS, MULTICULTURAL COUNSELING, AND SOCIAL JUSTICE   Counselor educators must make students aware of the ethical standards of the counseling profession and their responsibilities to the profession (ACA, 2014, §F.7.e.). In some programs, ethics is taught as a separate course (Jordan & Stevens, 2001), whereas in others it is not. Lambie, Hagedorn, and Ieva (2010) found that participation in ethics courses significantly increased students' ethical and legal knowledge, but that social–cognitive development and ethical decision-making ability did not change significantly. The researchers hypothesized that ethical reasoning abilities may develop slowly. Yet, ethical decision-making skills are essential; experts polled by Herlihy and Dufrene (2011) identified helping students develop these skills as the most important ethical issue in counselor preparation. Ametrano (2014) has described how an ethics course can teach ethical decision making, increase tolerance for ambiguity, and enhance student awareness of how values influence decision making in the wake of the *Ward v. Wilbanks* (2010) legal case (described in detail in Chapter 4).

We recommend that ethical and legal issues be infused throughout the training process when students are at different developmental levels. Students who are just beginning their studies in this area may look at these issues one way. Later, as they encounter a variety of situations during their practicum and internship, their views are likely to evolve (Corey, Corey, Corey, & Callanan, 2015). Counselor educators have strengthened their focus on multicultural pedagogy in recent years (Hall, Barden, & Conley, 2014) in response to a growing recognition that multicultural competence is essential to ethical practice. As was noted in Chapter 3, today it is almost a certainty that counselors will encounter clients whose cultural backgrounds are different from their own. This reality presents a challenge for counselor educators who must determine how to best prepare counselors who are multiculturally competent. Counselor educators are obligated to "infuse material related to multicultural/diversity into all courses and workshops for the development of professional counselors" (ACA, 2014, §F.7.c.). In addition, counselor educators infuse multicultural/diversity competency in their training and supervision practices, and "train students to gain awareness, knowledge, and skills in the competencies of multicultural practice" (§F.11.c.). Despite these mandates, some evidence suggests that graduates feel unprepared to work effectively with culturally diverse clients (Bidell, 2012; Rock, Carlson, & McGeorge, 2010), perhaps because counselor educators have tended to emphasize knowledge acquisition over skill development in teaching multicultural counseling courses (Priester et al., 2008). Several instructional practices may be more effective in increasing students' multicultural competency, including the use of theory and varied pedagogical strategies, exposure to diverse groups, and exploration of student biases (Malott, 2010). Hall, Barden, and Conley (2014) have suggested integrating elements of relational–cultural theory such as world view, power, and mutual empathy into more traditional models to enhance students' skill development.

Social justice, a growing force within the counseling profession, is creating a shift in how prospective counselors are being prepared for the profession (Chang, Crethar, & Ratts, 2010). Pack-Brown et al. (2008) have highlighted the importance of infusing issues related to multiculturalism and social justice into all counselor education courses. Students often believe they are inadequately prepared in social justice and advocacy, and counselor educators are responding by implementing pedagogical strategies such as exploring the dynamics of privilege and oppression, engaging students in the development of critical consciousness, using experiential activities, and engaging students in service learning projects to move learning beyond the classroom (Manis, 2012; Steele, Bischof, & Craig, 2014).

TEACHING THEORIES AND TECHNIQUES   Counselor educators have an ethical responsibility to teach current theories and techniques that are effective for the populations that students will be counseling. This obligation is articulated in the *Code of Ethics* (ACA, 2014), which states that counselor educators "provide instruction based on current information and knowledge available in the profession" (§F.7.b.). This means that counselor education programs must expose students to a wide range of counseling theories and encourage students to develop their own theoretical stances. Before the 1960s, models of counseling that were taught were almost exclusively those developed by Euro-American males. It was generally assumed by counselor educators that these models had universal application. Today's counselor educators are aware that traditionally taught theories may be inadequate to address the needs of diverse clientele. They also give emphasis to multicultural, feminist, ecological, and other systemic approaches that may be more applicable to diverse client populations.

Counselor educators "promote the use of techniques/procedures that are grounded in theory and/or have an empirical or scientific foundation" (ACA, 2014, §F.7.h.). When counselor educators introduce students to techniques or modalities that are developing or innovative, they must explain to students the potential risks and ethical considerations of using them. The intent of this standard is not to discourage innovation; it serves to remind counselor educators and students of the importance of intentionality in selecting techniques and as a caution against implementing techniques that may be risky for clients if those techniques are not well proven.

INFUSING TECHNOLOGY   The *Code of Ethics* (ACA, 2014) contains an entire section (Section H) devoted to distance counseling, technology, and social media (see Chapter 10 for a full discussion of technologies). Counselor educators are ethically obligated to ensure that students develop these competencies as part of their training, particularly because the potential for unethical misuse of technology is great. For instance, DiLillo and Gale (2011) found that the vast majority of graduate students had searched for information about their clients by surfing the Internet.

Some counselor education programs are delivering courses or even their entire curriculum via distance learning, and most counselor educators make use of technologies (such as e-mail, videoconferencing, and discussion boards) to enhance classroom instruction (Trepal, Haberstroh, Duffey, & Evans, 2007). Vaccaro and Lambie (2007) have noted that, in order to ethically infuse technologies into the curriculum, counselor education programs and students must have the necessary equipment and must be trained to use the technologies and to understand their benefits and limitations.

Newer technologies, including social networking websites such as Facebook and MySpace, have become increasingly popular and have raised new ethical issues related to privacy and dual relationships. For example, a student might ask a professor to be a *friend*, and an unfair power dynamic would be created within the class if the professor were to accept the invitation. In addition, if privacy settings are not managed carefully, faculty and students may have access to each other's personal information. Because of these concerns, Hartig, Terry, and Turman (2011) have recommended that counselor education programs develop policies regarding their expectations of student conduct on social networking websites.

EXPERIENTIAL LEARNING   Counselor education programs, whether they are offered in a traditional or on-line format, must integrate academic study and supervised practice (ACA, 2014, §F.7.d.). Typically, training programs present students with a graduated series of opportunities to practice the skills they are learning, beginning with an introductory skills or techniques course and progressing through a supervised practicum and internship.

Self-growth experiences in counselor education programs have been the subject of considerable debate, particularly among educators who teach group counseling courses and skills classes in which students practice counseling with each other (Merta, Wolfgang, & McNeil, 1993; Pierce & Baldwin, 1990; Schwab & Neukrug, 1994). The issue is how counselor educators can balance students' rights to privacy against the need to provide effective training that helps students increase their understanding of interpersonal dynamics and their awareness of self and others.

Until the mid-1980s, professors who had any administrative, supervisory, or evaluative authority over students were prohibited from offering students self-growth experiences, and counselor education programs were required to offer students alternatives to self-growth experiences without penalty or prejudice. These guidelines, which certainly protected students' privacy rights, allowed for the possibility that a student could go through an entire training program without participating in a self-growth experience. In recent decades, there has been a shift in thinking about self-growth experiences. The current *Code of Ethics* (ACA, 2014) clarifies that self-growth is an expected component of counselor training. Standard F.8.c. states that counselor educators are "mindful of ethical principles when they require students to engage in self-growth experiences." Counselor educators inform students that they have a right to decide what information about themselves they will share or withhold in class. Evaluation has to be independent from the student's self-disclosure—that is, students cannot be graded on their level of self-disclosure. In addition, counselor educators may require students to seek professional help to address any personal concerns that have the potential to affect their professional competence (§F.8.d.).

DEVELOPING AND EVALUATING COUNSELING SKILLS   Effective counseling requires counselors to apply techniques and behaviors that are accepted as effective in the professional literature. In addition, they must know when to engage in which behaviors, and how to acknowledge the unique personalities of the counselor and the client in the counseling process. Counseling includes scientific principles that are artfully applied. Students may be uneasy about being evaluated on their skill development because criteria are less objective than in tests of academic performance that have scores or numbers.

Counselor educators who teach counseling skills must define effective counseling in specific and concrete terms so that students can become proficient in their skill development. Students who are not performing well in counseling skills classes have a right to know their deficiencies so that they can take steps to improve their performance.

If an evaluation or grade is challenged, counselor educators have to explain to peers, and later perhaps to a judge or jury, the criteria they used to evaluate a student's counseling skills performance. Steps that counselor educators should take to help students understand their requirements in a counseling skills course include the following:

- Indicate the skills to be learned in the course in terms that are as specific and behavioral as possible.
- Give students periodic, specific feedback regarding the development of those skills.
- Develop methods of transferring evaluations into numbers or grades that can be justified.

What do you think would be the outcome of the appeal made by Naomi, the graduate student in the following scenario?

14-1 The Case of Naomi

Naomi is a first-semester master's student in a counselor education program. Over the course of the semester, she does excellent work in her courses in counseling theories and human growth and development, earning an A in both courses. Naomi is also enrolled in the beginning counseling techniques class. During the first half of the semester, she is evaluated twice by the instructor on her skill development as demonstrated in role-play counseling sessions with classmates. After she receives a grade of *unacceptable* on her first evaluation, she makes an appointment with the professor, who gives her specific feedback regarding areas of performance she needs to improve. At midterm, she shows very little improvement, and the instructor asks her to make another appointment to receive individualized feedback. Naomi does not follow up on this request. After observing Naomi's counseling performance for the third time, the instructor takes her aside after class and explains that Naomi is at risk for failing the course if she continues to be unable to demonstrate the basic active listening skills required. Together, they develop a growth plan with specific, behavioral objectives. For the remainder of the semester, Naomi is so anxious about performance evaluations that she *freezes up* and makes no progress. She ignores the instructor's suggestion that she seek counseling to deal with her performance anxiety. At the end of the semester, she does not receive a passing grade, which means, by program policy, that she cannot continue in the program. Naomi files an appeal, asserting that she is an excellent student as evidenced by her A grades in her other two courses.

- Why do you think a graduate student in counseling, such as Naomi, might make grades of A in two courses and a failing grade in her counseling techniques course?
- What might Naomi have done differently to improve her chances of receiving a passing grade?

Discussion: Naomi has very little chance of succeeding with her appeal. She received feedback throughout the semester and was given specific instructions regarding what she needed to do to improve her performance. In addition, she failed to respond to the instructor's requests to make a second appointment or to take steps to deal with her performance anxiety. There is no evidence that the instructor violated procedures or was unfair in evaluating Naomi. This case illustrates the effort required to evaluate students on their skill development. This course instructor devoted much more time and effort in working with Naomi than would have been required had the course been a traditional, didactic course in which grades were based on performance on objective tests.

Evaluation issues can be very complex for educators who teach skills courses, particularly for those who teach group counseling courses. Among counselor educators the consensus is that students learn best when didactic instruction is accompanied by experiential learning about group process and dynamics (Spargo, Orr, & Chang, 2010). Generally, the course instructor avoids serving as the facilitator of the experiential component of the class, because this dual role creates ethical dilemmas when evaluating students for continuation in the program. Although students are informed about the limits of confidentiality at the outset of the group experience, a level of trust can develop in the group that fosters personal risk taking. Student self-disclosures may allow course instructors to have knowledge about a student that might cause educators to have concerns about the student's fitness for the profession. The counselor educators would then be caught on the horns of a dilemma, not wanting to violate the student's confidentiality but also feeling a need to fulfill their gatekeeper role. Because of these dual role conflicts, counselor education programs have developed a number of alternative methods for delivering the experiential component of a group counseling class (Furr & Barret, 2000). Some of these alternative methods include the following:

- Skilled counselors could be contracted to provide the experiential component of the course.
- Advanced students could lead their fellow students in group experiences.
- Students could be sent off-campus to participate in group experiences.
- Actors could be employed to play the roles of group members (Fall & Levitov, 2002).
- Videos could be used to engage students in observational learning.
- A *fishbowl technique* could be used to combine observational and experiential learning (Spargo et al., 2010).

EVALUATIONS OF FIELD EXPERIENCE PERFORMANCE Just as evaluating the development of counseling skills can be difficult, evaluating students' performance in their practicum and internship experiences is an area in which evaluation can be challenging. It is important for counselor education programs to have specific and understandable procedures for entering and completing field experiences. Developing practicum and internship sites, communicating with on-site supervisors, and orienting everyone involved are complex tasks for counselor educators, yet these responsibilities are clearly delineated in the *Code of Ethics* (ACA, 2014). According to §F.7.i., counselor educators must develop clear policies regarding field placement and other clinical experiences, and they must provide clearly stated roles and responsibilities for students, site supervisors, and program supervisors. Counselor educators must also confirm that site supervisors are qualified to provide supervision and are informed of their ethical and professional responsibilities as supervisors.

During field experiences, graduate students are evaluated by a number of professors and on-site supervisors. If a student's performance is evaluated negatively, counselor educators must ensure that the evaluations are fair. To avoid having negative evaluations successfully challenged, counselor educators must follow all the procedures that have been established by the program for field placements.

PERSONAL AND PROFESSIONAL DEVELOPMENT   Because there is a well-established relationship between clinical competence and personal and professional development, counselor educators have an ethical obligation to evaluate student development in areas other than academic performance and skills acquisition (Lamadue & Duffey, 1999). Duba, Paez, and Kindsvatter (2010) found that master's-level counseling students were most frequently evaluated on the criteria of interpersonal interactions in academic or professional settings, personality, and professionalism. CACREP accreditation standards (CACREP, 2014) and the Association for Counselor Education and Supervision ethical guidelines (ACES, 1993) require counselor educators to assess students' professional and personal growth and development. Characteristics that have been deemed to be crucial to personal and professional development were discussed in Chapter 7.

When student development proceeds according to faculty expectations, problems are unlikely to arise. However, sometimes students struggle in their personal and professional development. Historically, counselor educators have shown a preference for using informal means to address these problems (Foster & McAdams, 2009). Counselor educators are aware that there is a great deal of subjectivity involved in such evaluations and may be reluctant to negatively evaluate students along these dimensions because of concern about being unfair, a hope that the problems will self-correct with further training, or fear that the students will bring lawsuits against them (Frame & Stevens-Smith, 1995; Gaubatz & Vera, 2002). Despite this possible reluctance, however, counselor educators recognize the need to be clear and specific in evaluating personal and professional development and to communicate their expectations to students. Most programs have developed written assessment forms that include criteria for personal and professional growth. Foster and McAdams (2009) have noted that these types of evaluation can be anxiety provoking for students, and that students who are not familiar with the programs' assessment policies and procedures may consider the policies to be punitive.

Brown-Rice and Furr (2013) have noted that classmates often are aware of peers who are having problems with professional competency and that the learning of all students is affected by these problems. Students may be concerned about a classmate. Generally, students understand the importance of intervention for the sake of the classmate's future clients as well as the profession (Foster, Leppma, & Hutchinson, 2014), but they may be uncertain as to whether or how they should take action. Brown-Rice and Furr (2013) and Parker et al. (2014) have recommended that counselor educators develop, implement, and inform students about formal procedures that provide an opportunity for students to approach a faculty member when a peer is struggling.

Gatekeeping

As we noted in Chapter 7, competence in counseling is hard to define. Nonetheless, counselor educators are gatekeepers to the profession and must evaluate students to determine whether they should be allowed to progress through and graduate from their counselor preparation programs. It would be unfair to the public if incompetent or unprepared students were allowed to graduate (Hensley, Smith, & Thompson, 2003). At the same time, it would be unfair to students if this evaluation process were not ongoing and systematic and conscientiously communicated. Therefore, counselor educators must clearly state to students the level of competency expected, their appraisal methods, and the timing of evaluations (ACA, 2014, §F.9.a.). They provide students with ongoing feedback regarding their performance throughout the training program.

Counselor educators share a strong commitment to giving students every possible opportunity to succeed in their studies and to keeping students informed of their progress. They hope that students will use this feedback to build on their strengths and to remediate problem areas or deficiencies.

Sometimes, however, students are not able to achieve the needed counseling competencies. When this happens, counselor educators have an ethical obligation to exercise their gatekeeping responsibilities. The *Code of Ethics* (ACA, 2014) advises counselor educators to (a) assist students in securing remedial assistance, (b) seek consultation from other professionals and document their decision to dismiss or refer students for assistance, and (c) ensure that students know in a timely manner that problems exist and provide them with due process (§F.9.b.).

REMEDIATION   Gatekeeping began to be discussed in the professional literature after a counseling student was dismissed from a public university in 2005 on the grounds of deficient professional performance. The student brought a lawsuit against the counseling program faculty and the university (*Plaintiff v. Rector and Board of Visitors of The College of William and Mary*, 2005). The focus of the gatekeeping literature was on dismissing students rather than on remediation (Henderson & Dufrene, 2011) until recent years, when the remediation process began to receive more attention. Dufrene and Henderson (2009) defined remediation as "a documented, procedural process that addresses perceived inabilities in trainees' performance with the intent to provide trainees with specific means to remedy their inabilities" (p. 151). McAdams and Foster (2007) described remediation procedures that were developed by the counselor education faculty at The College of William and Mary as an outgrowth of the lawsuit that was filed against them. In addition, Dufrene and Henderson (2009) and Kress and Protivnak (2009) have described the steps involved in developing and implementing an Individualized Remediation Plan or Professional Development Plan that is a behaviorally focused contract between the faculty and student. Henderson and Dufrene (2011) identified strategies for remediation intervention, including personal counseling, increased supervision, repetition of coursework, and restricting some form of student participation in the program (e.g., a leave of absence). Remediation continues to be a problematic issue, however. Although personal counseling may be recommended or required, there have been no studies that demonstrate the effects of required counseling on the professional performance of remediated students (Prosek, Holm, & Daly, 2013). Further, Brown (2013) found that counselor education programs are inconsistent in the terms they use to describe problematic student behavior, and that programs continue to rely on subjective means to assess such problems. Rust, Raskin, and Hill (2013) also found a lack of standardization across programs and noted that little is known about how cultural differences may factor into how problematic behavior is defined. These researchers recommended that counselor education programs develop formal assessment tools, including qualitative and quantitative methods, and publish specific criteria for assessing problematic behaviors (Brown, 2013; Rust, Raskin, & Hill, 2013).

DISMISSAL DECISIONS   The remediation process does not always work as desired. Sometimes, even after counselor educators have identified problems and have assisted a student in securing remedial assistance, the student is still unable to demonstrate mastery of the required skills, knowledge, or dispositions. When efforts at remediation fail, counselor educators are obligated to dismiss from the preparation program students who are unable to provide competent counseling services (Kerl, Garcia, McCullough, & Maxwell, 2002).

In other disciplines in which skills must be mastered by students, such as medicine and nursing, courts defer to the judgment of professors, unless established procedures are violated or professors are clearly unfair in rendering their evaluations (*Connelly v. University of Vermont*, 1965;

Dutile, 2001). In *Connelly*, the judges explained that courts defer to professors on academic matters because, in matters of scholarship, the school authorities are uniquely qualified by training and experience to judge the qualifications of a student, and efficiency of instruction depends in no small degree on the school faculty's freedom from interference from other noneducational tribunals. It is only when the school authorities abuse this discretion that a court may interfere with the decision to dismiss a student.

A U.S. Supreme Court case, *Horowitz v. Board of Curators of the University of Missouri* (1978), has established that professional programs have the right to dismiss students who have excellent academic records but poor performance in applied areas. In *Horowitz*, a medical student who had excellent grades on written examinations was dismissed for deficiencies in the areas of clinical performance, peer and patient relations, and personal hygiene.

In the realm of counselor education, a student at The College of William and Mary brought suit against the university and the counselor education faculty who dismissed her. McAdams and Foster (2007) and McAdams, Foster, and Ward (2007) have described in detail the lengthy legal process that ensued, which resulted in a decision in favor of the counseling program faculty and university. These authors concluded that dismissal decisions in counselor education programs are likely to be legally justified but only after faculty have provided a student with fair and just opportunities to remediate any identified deficiencies.

As was discussed in Chapter 4, lawsuits were brought by students who were dismissed from their counseling graduate programs at Eastern Michigan University and Augusta State University in Georgia. The faculty at those institutions determined that the two students were deficient in multicultural competence after the students refused to counsel LGBT clients regarding same-sex relationships. Both students were dismissed only after they failed to meet the requirements of remediation plans offered to them. These cases are likely to have an impact on the criteria and process by which dismissal decisions are made. Hutchens, Block, and Young (2013) concluded that the decisions in *Ward* and *Keeton* reinforce the importance of counselor education programs ensuring that all faculty members agree on policies and how they are implemented, and that policies and procedures are applied uniformly to all students, well documented, and readily available to students. Dugger and Francis (2014) reflected on lessons learned from their involvement as defendants in *Ward v. Wilbanks*. They reiterated the importance of having and adhering to policies and procedures for dismissal decisions and noted that it is also vital to have a concrete process for responding to a lawsuit, assume all communications will be subpoenaed, and seek support throughout the process.

Counselor educators never take lightly a decision to dismiss a student from a preparation program. The care that is taken in such decisions is reflected in the ethical standards, which state that counselor educators must use ongoing evaluation to become aware of and address the inability of some students to achieve counseling competencies (ACA, 2014, §F.9.b.). When limitations are identified, counselor educators seek professional consultation and document their decisions to refer students for assistance or dismiss them from the program. Students must have recourse to address such decisions and be provided with due process (§F.9.b.). The CACREP standards also address the issue of dismissal of students for nonacademic reasons. These standards require that when evaluations indicate that a student is inappropriate for a counseling program, faculty assist in facilitating the student's transition out of the program and into a more appropriate area of study, if that is possible (CACREP, 2014). The case of Naomi in this chapter is a good example of how a student can be academically competent but deficient in counseling skill development. The program faculty can assist Naomi, if she is willing, to find a different area of graduate study that may be more compatible with her competencies.

No hearing is required if a student is dismissed for academic reasons. However, if a student is dismissed for misconduct, a hearing is required. Due process probably requires that a student be informed of inadequacies and of their consequences on academic standing (Kaplin & Lee, 1995). As a result, it is important for faculty members to avoid mixing misconduct charges with academic or performance reasons if they discipline or dismiss students (*Horowitz v. Board of Curators of the University of Missouri*, 1978; *Regents of the University of Michigan v. Ewing*, 1985).

ENDORSEMENT   Professional preparation programs such as medicine, nursing, and counseling have a responsibility to society to ensure not only that graduates have the knowledge necessary to practice successfully but also that they have the ability to apply that knowledge in a manner that leads to effective professional practice.

Although negative decisions or recommendations can be difficult to make, counselor educators should not endorse a student for employment or for any credential (such as a graduate degree, certification, or licensure) if they believe that the student is not qualified (ACA, 2014, §F.6.d.). Remember that counselor educators are gatekeepers to the profession, and they have responsibilities not only to their students but also to the future clients of their students and to the profession as a whole.

FACULTY AND STUDENT ISSUES

Faculty Competence

Competence is an issue that applies to counselor educators as well as students. Counselor educators must also be able to provide competent services. The *Code of Ethics* (ACA, 2014, §F.7.a.) requires counselor educators to be skilled as teachers and practitioners. They must be knowledgeable regarding the ethical, legal, and regulatory aspects of the profession, and they have an obligation to make students aware of their responsibilities. They conduct counselor education programs in an ethical manner and serve as role models for the profession.

As role models, counselor educators must practice what they preach and make ongoing efforts to ensure their own continuing competence. Reading and attending workshops and conferences to stay up to date on developments in the field, working a few hours a week at a counseling agency in the community to keep their skills as practitioners sharp, paying serious attention to student evaluations of their teaching and courses and implementing recommended improvements, and conducting and publishing their own research are just a few of the strategies counselor educators might use to keep themselves on their *growing edge*.

A requirement that is new in the most recent *Code of Ethics* (ACA, 2014) is §F.7.b., which addresses counselor educator competence directly. This standard requires counselor educators to provide instruction that is both based on current information and knowledge available to the profession and is within their areas of knowledge and competence. Some counselor education programs may have a practice of allowing the most experienced professors to choose the courses they want to teach, which leaves new and inexperienced faculty members teaching the courses that no one else wants to teach (Kaplan & Martz, 2014). Continuing this practice could put new professors in the position of being in violation of the *Code of Ethics* (ACA, 2014).

Diversity Considerations

Counselor education programs have an ethical responsibility to recruit and retain not only culturally diverse students but also diverse faculty (ACA, 2014, §F.11.a. & §F.11.b.). Although Schweiger, Henderson, McCaskill, Clawson, and Collins (2011) observed a trend toward attempting to hire faculty who are diverse both theoretically and culturally in order to give students a more diverse set of perspectives, the counselor education professorate remains predominantly White. Constantine, Smith, Redington, and Owens (2008) reported that African American faculty members continue to experience racial microaggressions (subtle negative messages), feelings of invisibility or being *spotlighted*, and lack of mentoring. Although women are well represented in the ranks of counselor educators, Hill, Leinbaugh, Bradley, and Hazler (2005) found that female counselor educators' life satisfaction was negatively influenced by toxic faculty environments, office politics, and being overcontrolled by others, as well as by lack of mentors. Counselor education programs must address racism and sexism, develop and implement strategies to increase the number of ethnic/racial minority faculty, and facilitate the progress of minority and women faculty through the ranks. Until such efforts are successful, there will continue to be a dearth of mentors and role models for racial or ethnic minority students who aspire to become counselor educators.

Student–Faculty Research Collaboration

Counselor educators are often subject to the same pressures felt by their colleagues in other disciplines when they work in a *publish or perish* environment. These pressures may tempt counselor educators to become overly concerned about the number of their publications and to neglect considerations of quality or their actual contributions to a study (Welfel, 2013). Do you think this may have been the case in the following scenario?

14-2 The Case of Lakiesha

Lakiesha was elated when she was accepted into a doctoral program in counselor education. During her first semester she worked very hard at her studies. Dr. Wilks, one of her professors, was particularly impressed with one of the papers she wrote and suggested to her that she should consider publishing it. Lakiesha made several attempts to seek out Dr. Wilks for guidance on how to publish, but he was always too busy working on his own research and writing, so she let the matter drop. Over the next 2 years, she continued to be a diligent student and found other professors to mentor her. She completed her formal course work and was preparing to sit for the general examination that, once passed, would admit her into all but dissertation (ABD) status. Dr. Wilks was one of the professors on her general examination committee. Lakiesha was shocked and angry when she came across a published article by Dr. Wilks that was based largely on the paper she had written for him 2 years ago. She wanted to confront him but was afraid that such an action might negatively affect his evaluation of her examination. She thought about talking to one of the other professors who had been a helpful mentor but was reluctant to put him in an awkward position. In the end, she didn't say anything to anyone.

- What might have been a good course of action for Lakiesha to take to address this situation?
- Can you think of any justifications that Dr. Wilks might have for his actions?

Discussion: It appears that Dr. Wilks may have violated his ethical obligation to give credit to this student who contributed to his article in a manner that was in accordance with her contributions. Standard G.5.f. of the *Code of Ethics* (ACA, 2014) states that manuscripts that are substantially based on a student's course paper, project, dissertation, or thesis must be used only with the student's permission and must list the student as lead author. If the contributions of Lakiesha's paper to Dr. Wilks's article were less substantial, she would still merit an acknowledgment (§G.5.d.).

To avoid misunderstandings, it is wise for a student and professor who wish to undertake a collaborative research project to carefully work out, *in advance*, the arrangements regarding their respective contributions, deadlines, and publication credit for the completed work (§G.5.e.). Ethically conscientious counselor educators are careful to avoid exploiting their students who may be eager to contribute to a professor's research study or who may feel honored to be asked to assist.

Personal Relationships Between Counselor Educators and Students

Counselor educators are obligated to clearly define and maintain ethical, professional, and social relationship boundaries with their students. They should not seek to meet their personal needs for affiliation, friendship, or sex through relationships with students. In Chapter 9 we examined issues surrounding dual relationships between counselors and clients. The relationships between counselor educators and students are both similar to and different from the relationships between counselors and clients.

A similarity is that both dyads involve a power differential in an inherently unequal relationship in which one person is seeking a service: counseling or education. Throughout a graduate degree program, and even after a degree is earned, faculty members must evaluate students. Evaluative responsibilities create a power differential. The power of educators goes far beyond grades; counselor educators can provide students with introductions that create networking opportunities; sponsorship to professional associations; opportunities for research experience and publications; and letters of recommendation for scholarships, assistantships, internships, and jobs (Moore, 1997).

Faculty–student relationships are different from counselor–client relationships in some significant ways. Although students can differ considerably in levels of maturity and this has implications for how faculty relate to them (Biaggio, Paget, & Chenoweth, 1997), faculty–student relationships are usually characterized by multiple and overlapping roles (Scarborough, Bernard, & Morse, 2006). The roles in the relationship between counselor and client are fixed in that the client never becomes the counselor, nor does the counselor become the client. Whether these roles must continue after termination of a therapeutic relationship is a subject of debate. Some counselors believe *"Once a client, always a client."* It is not true, however, that *"Once a student, always a student."* The roles in the educator–student relationship are always in transition as students progress through the program, first as beginning students, next as advanced students and interns, then as graduates, and finally as colleagues and professional peers of their trainers. On the other hand, professors have a degree of power over former students for a long time. Professors are asked throughout the careers of former students for recommendations for jobs, certifications, and licenses.

It has been argued that students are in an even more vulnerable position than are clients with respect to dual relationships. Whereas clients can terminate their relationships with their counselors, students do not have the same option. Furthermore, students engaged in dual relationships with educators risk damage not only to themselves personally but also to their professional careers (Blevins-Knabe, 1992; Keith-Spiegel & Koocher, 1985). Kolbert, Morgan, and Brendel (2002) discovered that counseling graduate students were more concerned than were faculty about the ability of faculty members to maintain objectivity and avoid student exploitation while engaged in dual relationships with students. These researchers concluded that faculty members may be unaware of students' concerns regarding the fairness of dual relationships and the negative impact these dual relationships can have on the student group as a whole within a counselor education program.

Relationship boundaries in counselor education are somewhat fluid because good teaching at the graduate level often involves mentoring and opportunities for faculty and students to interact in professional and social settings such as colloquiums, receptions, and special events (Keith-Spiegel, 1994). Mentoring is typically viewed in the literature as a positive kind of dual relationship that is encouraged in academia because of its potential benefits to students. Nonetheless, even mentoring involves potential risks, such as personal disillusionment with the relationship, professional repercussions when the mentoring relationship falters, and the possible sexualization of the relationship, which is particularly associated with the male mentor–female protégée dyad (Gilbert & Rossman, 1992; Haring-Hidore & Paludi, 1989; Kitchener & Harding, 1990; Rosenbach, 1993).

Despite these complicating factors, counselor educators can take some steps to maintain healthy boundaries with students. The *Code of Ethics* (ACA, 2014) contains several standards that describe these steps under §F.10: *Roles and Relationships Between Counselor Educators and Students*. These standards are summarized as follows:

- Counselor educators are prohibited from having sexual or romantic interactions or relationships with students currently enrolled in a counseling program and over whom they have power and authority. This prohibition applies to electronic as well as in-person interactions (§F.10.a.).
- Counselor educators do not condone or subject students to sexual harassment (§F.10.b.). Sexual harassment is illegal as well as unethical; Title IX of the Education Amendments of 1972 prohibits sexual harassment, which occurs when students are pressured by unwanted sexual overtures or acts.
- Nonprofessional relationships with former students are not prohibited, but counselor educators must be aware of the power differential that continues to exist. Whenever counselor educators consider engaging in social, sexual, or other intimate relationships with a former student, they must discuss the potential risks with the former student (§F.10.c.).
- Counselor educators avoid nonacademic relationships with students in which there is a risk of potential harm to the student or which may compromise the training experience or grades assigned (§F.10.d.).
- If a counselor educator believes a nonprofessional relationship may be beneficial to a student, the educator should take precautions similar to those taken by counselors when working with clients. In addition, counselor educators should "discuss with students the rationale for such interactions, the potential benefits and drawbacks, and the anticipated consequences for the student," "clarify the specific nature and limitations of the additional role(s) they will have with the student prior to engaging in a nonprofessional relationship," and have only nonprofessional relationships that are "time-limited and/or context specific and initiated with student consent" (§F.10.f.).

SEXUAL OR ROMANTIC RELATIONSHIPS   Although the *Code of Ethics* (ACA, 2014) prohibits sexual relationships between counselor educators and current students, consensual sexual relationships between adult students and professors generally are not prohibited by law. Whether such sexual relationships should be allowed has been debated in the professional legal literature (Chamallas, 1988; DeChiara, 1988; Keller, 1988). Those who believe they should be prohibited have argued that because of the differential in power between students and professors, truly consensual sexual relationships could never be possible. Those who argue that such relationships should be allowed have contended that prohibiting such relationships would infringe on constitutional rights of free association, would inappropriately invade the privacy of faculty and students, or would infantilize or disempower adult students by denying them the right to make their own choices. Historically, concern about the harm caused by sexual relationships has been a concern primarily of faculty in counseling and psychology programs, but there is some indication that this concern is spreading. Several universities have implemented policies that forbid all professors and administrators from dating students they teach, mentor, or supervise (James, 1996; Leatherman, 1993).

Lawsuits brought by students against college and university professors because of consensual personal relationships probably would not be successful because these relationships are not prohibited by law. However, because teaching counseling skills requires personal reflection on the part of students and requires counselor educators to assess students in personal as well as academic areas, an argument could be made that professor–student personal relationships in counseling programs have more potential for harm than such relationships in other academic disciplines (Kress & Dixon, 2007). In addition, the specific sections in the *Code of Ethics* (ACA, 2014) that prohibit sexual relationships with students (§F.10.a.) or sexual harassment of students (§F.10.b.) would seem to give students a foundation for prevailing in a lawsuit when they believe they have been harmed by a professor who had a personal relationship with them.

The question of whether a sexual relationship between a counselor educator and student can truly be consensual and noncoercive takes on some new dimensions when viewed from an ethical framework. Most of the research studies that have examined faculty–student sexual relationships have focused on psychology students and professors and have found that sexual contact occurs most frequently between male professors and female graduate students. Studies of sexual intimacies between counselor educators and students have also found that the male professor–female student is the predominant dyad (Miller & Larrabee, 1995; Thoreson, Morrow, Frazier, & Kerstner, 1990). Studies also indicate that the attitudes of women who have been involved in these relationships change over time. Although they may have believed that the relationship was truly consensual at the time, in retrospect they view the experiences as more coercive, more of a hindrance to the working relationship, and more damaging to their professional careers (Glaser & Thorpe, 1986; Miller & Larrabee, 1995). These studies challenge the argument that adult students are able to consent freely to such relationships and raise questions about how prepared the students were to deal with the ethics of such intimacies at the time.

NONSEXUAL RELATIONSHIPS   Although counselor educators should not enter into formal, therapeutic relationships with students, the very nature of counselor training presents many opportunities for professors to get to know students at a personal level. Students may self-disclose personal issues during a live demonstration of counseling, a dyadic practice session in which one student is serving as the counselor and the other as a client, or an experiential component of a group counseling course. This could also happen when a counselor educator is exploring a practicum student's difficulties in working with a particular client, or in courses in which students are encouraged to explore any personal biases, prejudices, or values that might interfere with their ability to counsel effectively. Students who engage in self-exploration do so in the belief that their professors will not violate their trust. Thus, counselor educators have a special responsibility to be trustworthy recipients of the knowledge they gain about students' personal lives, and personal and interpersonal struggles. This trustworthiness is as important in the student–educator relationship as it is in the client–counselor relationship.

It is clear that certain kinds of dual relationships are inevitable in counselor training programs. There is no universal agreement regarding how these situations can best be handled. Bowman, Hatley, and Bowman (1995) suggested that dual relationships should be evaluated in terms of how the faculty member and student *behave* in the relationship, rather than assume that the very existence of a dual role is unethical. Welfel (2013) and Lloyd (1992) have expressed similar sentiments, arguing that when faculty take a rigid stance against all forms of dual relationships with students, they are probably overreacting to the risks. They may also be sidestepping their obligation to confront the struggles of making responsible decisions that will foster maximum student development. Because new issues related to dual relationships are continually emerging, such as participation of faculty and students on social networking sites (Hartig, Terry, & Turman, 2011), it is important for counselor educators to have a thoughtfully considered model for decision making about such issues.

Biaggio, Paget, and Chenoweth (1997) have suggested guidelines for maintaining ethical relationships between faculty and students. First, the professor's position of power and authority over students must be acknowledged, and dual relationships should be carefully monitored. Second, a flexible frame that includes a core set of norms for ethical relationships should be utilized to evaluate dual relationships between faculty and students. Finally, a climate for ethical behavior should be fostered. The importance of an ethical climate cannot be overemphasized. Counselor educators function as role models for the profession. Studies have indicated that dual relationships between educators and students increase the likelihood that students will later judge dual relationships between counselors and clients as being ethical, and thus foster the continued occurrence of unethical behaviors (Moore, 1997; Pope, Levinson, & Schover, 1979; Vasquez, 1988). Students learn about dual relationships not only from explicit ethics education but also from their own experiences. Counselor educators have a crucial responsibility to model ethical management of relationships with students if they hope to foster ethical attitudes and behaviors in students (Herlihy & Corey, 2015b).

Blevins-Knabe (1992) has suggested some questions that are helpful when trying to determine whether a dual relationship between a faculty member and a student is appropriate. You might ask yourself the following questions when considering having a dual relationship with a counselor educator:

- Has my professor fully discussed with me the potential risks and benefits of our dual relationship? Do we have a clear working agreement?
- What am I learning in this relationship? Am I becoming more competent, or more dependent on a *special* relationship?
- What are my fellow students learning? Are they learning about equitable treatment, or about special privilege?
- Do I have a choice? Do I feel the freedom to refuse requests the professor might make or to withdraw from the relationship without penalty?
- Do I believe the professor has maintained the capacity to evaluate me objectively?

Diversity Considerations in Faculty–Student Relationships

Mentoring is the one form of role blending that is almost universally viewed as positive and important to the professional development of counselor trainees. Mentors serve as role models, advisers, sources of support, and sponsors into the profession upon graduation. Doctoral students who have opportunities to conduct collaborative research, teaching, and professional services are enriched by the experience and are better prepared to enter the professorate.

Because there are so few counselor educators who are non-White, it may be difficult for graduate students who are persons of color to find a mentor with whom they identify and feel comfortable in the close and complex mentoring relationship. Thus, it is essential that counselor educators are effective cross-cultural mentors (Brinson & Kottler, 1993). Counselor education faculty can also encourage experienced doctoral students to mentor doctoral students new to the program as well as master's-level students.

Relationships Among Students

In courses in which counseling techniques are taught, students are sometimes asked to be clients for their fellow students as they practice their counseling skills. To avoid unrealistic role playing, students sometimes are asked by course instructors to discuss real issues with which they are struggling. This practice can put students in awkward situations. Students who are the clients may feel hesitant or uneasy in self-disclosing personal information in front of instructors and their peers. In addition, students who are the counselors may be unsure how much to probe, wanting to be sensitive to the privacy of their fellow classmates. Counselor educators who ask students to be clients for other students in counseling skills courses should give clear guidelines as to what kinds of issues should be discussed (issues they do not mind others knowing about), should caution all course members to maintain confidentiality regarding issues discussed in class, and should intervene if student clients appear uneasy or distressed.

When counselor education programs offer the doctorate degree as well as the master's degree, doctoral students frequently are involved in supervising the skills development of beginning students. The doctoral students, in turn, receive supervision of their supervision by faculty. This practice, known as layered supervision, offers many advantages. When motivated and enthusiastic doctoral students assist with supervision, master's students receive more supervision and high-quality supervision. Doctoral students may have more focused energy and effort to devote to supervision, compared with faculty members who have many other responsibilities. Students learn to give and receive corrective feedback and to manage multiple roles (Remley et al., 1998). At the same time, this practice places some complex demands on doctoral students, who must move in and out of the multiple roles of student, supervisee, supervisor, mentor, protégé, and peer/classmate (Dickens, 2014). They are in a position of authority over their master's student supervisees but may not feel empowered in that role because of the pressures they feel as students (Scarborough et al., 2006). The *Code of Ethics* (ACA, 2014) addresses these concerns by saying that counselor educators make efforts to ensure the rights of students are not compromised when their peers lead experiential counseling activities (§F.7.g.). Counselor educators need to impress upon students who lead groups composed of other students, or who supervise other students, that they have the same ethical obligations that counselor educators, trainers, and supervisors have. Faculty must carefully supervise student group leaders or student supervisors to help them understand that multiple relationships in counselor education programs are normative (Scarborough et al., 2006) and to help them navigate these relationships and resolve problems that occur. What are your reactions to the situation in which a doctoral student, Luis, finds himself in the following scenario?

14-3 The Case of Luis

Luis, age 26, received his master's degree a year ago. He immediately applied for admission and was accepted into the doctoral program in counselor education at the same university. He has been assigned to supervise Ella, a 45-year-old master's-degree student, as she begins her counseling internship. Luis and Ella were in two classes together when he was still in the master's program, although they did not know each other very well. Despite Luis's best efforts to establish a supervisory alliance, Ella becomes increasingly resistant to supervision. Luis shares his difficulties with his faculty supervisor and wonders whether Ella should be assigned to a different doctoral student supervisor.

- What are some reasons Ella may be resistant to being supervised by Luis?
- What do you think the faculty supervisor should do in this circumstance?

Discussion: Ella may be finding it difficult to accept the fact that Luis, who is someone she has known as a peer and who is much younger than she, is now in a supervisory capacity over her. Luis's faculty supervisor might suggest that Luis address this dynamic directly with Ella. If her resistance to supervision continues, the faculty member should intervene and try to do so in a way that will make this into a positive learning experience for both Ella and Luis.

Responsibilities of Students

Reading this chapter has made you aware that students have many rights. For example, you are entitled, under the law, to due process and freedom from discrimination. Section F of the *Code of Ethics* (ACA, 2014) contains numerous standards concerning the duties of counselor educators to ensure that your welfare is safeguarded. Along with your rights come certain responsibilities. According to the *Code of Ethics*, students preparing to become counselors must adhere to the code and have the same obligations to clients as do counselors who have already completed their training (§F.5.a.). You must be familiar with codes of ethics; lack of knowledge or misunderstanding of an ethical responsibility is not a defense against a charge of unethical conduct (§I.1.a.).

Just as practicing counselors have an ethical responsibility to refrain from providing counseling services when they are impaired, counselors in training also refrain from offering or providing counseling services when their physical, mental, or emotional problems are likely to harm a client or others (ACA, 2014, §F.5.b.). You are ethically obligated to remain alert to signs of impairment, seek assistance (including personal counseling) for problems, and notify your program supervisors when you are aware that you are unable to provide effective services (§F.5.b.). Therefore, it is essential that you are open to receiving feedback from your professors and supervisors when they express concern that your personal issues or problems are interfering with your ability to provide effective counseling services, and that you take steps to address any problems that may exist.

It is crucial that you practice ethical behaviors and decision making while you are still a student. Your time as a graduate student can be well spent by developing good professional habits, such as carefully handling client records, and consulting when you are uncertain about how to deal with a situation. Following are some strategies to enhance the development of your professional identity and learn more about your legal, ethical, and professional responsibilities:

- Join and actively participate in student organizations such as Chi Sigma Iota, if your university has a chapter of this honorary society for counselors, or other campus organizations for counseling students.
- Join professional organizations such as ACA and its divisions that represent your specialty interests, as well as your state and local counseling organizations. Student membership rates are generally much lower than are regular dues.
- Attend professional workshops and conferences that deal with ethical, legal, and professional issues.

Summary and Key Points

This chapter explores a number of complex ethical and legal issues that arise in the counselor training process. Counselor educators' ethical and legal responsibilities to students begin before students enter a graduate program and continue even after students graduate. Students have many rights—to give informed consent to enter a program, to expect admissions decisions to be equitable, to receive high-quality training, to be able to count on fair evaluations and opportunities to remediate deficiencies, to receive credit for their contributions to research, and to have appropriate boundaries maintained in their relationships with faculty and peers. With these rights come a number of concomitant responsibilities.

Some of the key points in this chapter include the following:

- Students have the right to know what will be expected of them before they select a graduate program in counseling. Counselor education programs have a responsibility to provide students with enough information to make wise decisions.
- Admissions criteria for counselor education programs typically include demonstrated academic ability as well as more subjective measures. These are designed to assess whether applicants possess personal and interpersonal characteristics associated with the ability to counsel effectively.
- Counselor educators are responsible for making students aware of the ethical standards of the counseling profession. Students have the same obligations to uphold standards for ethical behavior as do counselors who have already completed their training.
- Counselor educators must be competent and must provide students with current information about theories, techniques, and approaches that are effective for the client populations the students will be counseling.
- Counselor education programs integrate academic study and supervised practice. Self-growth experiences that involve student self-disclosure are an integral part of the training process. Counselor educators strive to balance students' rights to privacy against the need to provide effective training.
- It is difficult to assess the development of a student's counseling skills and to evaluate field experiences. Although evaluation may be subjective, courts defer to professors on academic matters.
- Students who are unable to demonstrate required competencies must be given opportunities to remediate their deficiencies as well as the opportunity to appeal the decision.
- Counselor educators, as gatekeepers to the profession, must ensure that students who are unable to provide competent counseling services are not graduated from the program or endorsed for any professional credential. Counselor educators never take lightly a decision to dismiss a student from a training program.
- Relationship boundary issues in counselor training are complex. Faculty–student relationships are characterized by multiple and overlapping roles. Counselor educators are responsible for maintaining healthy boundaries with students by avoiding sexual harassment and sexual intimacies with students, by providing informed consent to students with whom they engage in multiple roles, by remaining cognizant of the power differential, and by maintaining a thoughtful awareness of their potency as role models for students.
- Because there are so few counselor educators who are persons of color, counselor educators must be skilled as cross-cultural mentors.

CHAPTER 15

Supervision and Consultation

FOCUS QUESTIONS

1. How are counseling, supervision, and consultation similar? How are they different from each other?

2. What would you do if you believed your clinical supervisor was not competent to provide you with quality supervision services?

3. As a beginning counselor, in what circumstances do you think you might seek consultation? In what circumstances do you think others might come to you for consultation?

This chapter discusses legal, ethical, and professional issues that occur in supervision and consultation. During your career as a counselor, you will almost certainly be involved in each of these activities, in both the learner or help-seeker role (as supervisee or consultee) and the expert or help-provider role (as supervisor or consultant).

Supervision has been practiced for as long as counseling and psychotherapy have been in existence. Only in recent decades, however, has supervision been given much attention as a process that is distinct from education, counseling, and consultation. The term *supervision* can involve a number of processes, ranging from one counselor having direct control and authority over another to a counselor simply giving input to a colleague involving a specific case. Bernard and Goodyear (2014) have defined clinical supervision as an intervention provided by a senior or experienced member of a profession to a junior or aspiring member or members of that same profession. Supervision also has been described as an attachment process that involves the development of a bond or working alliance that is gradually loosened as the end of supervision nears (Nelson, Oliver, Reeve, & McNichols, 2010). Clinical supervision involves multiple roles, including teacher, mentor, coach, evaluator, adviser, and consultant. Supervision also involves multiple responsibilities. Supervisors usually are responsible not only for the welfare of their supervisees but also, in an indirect way, for the welfare of their supervisees' clients. In addition, a supervisor may have an obligation to the agency or other setting where the supervised practice occurs to ensure that quality services are provided. Also, supervisors, like counselor educators, serve as gatekeepers to the profession.

Consultation, like supervision, involves a tripartite relationship among at least three parties: the consultant, the consultee, and the consultee's client or client system. Consultation has become increasingly common among mental health professionals in community agencies, schools, and other settings (Dinkmeyer, Carlson, & Dinkmeyer, 1994; Dougherty, 2014). Dougherty's (2014) definition of consultation is widely accepted. He describes consultation thus:

> An indirect process in which a human services professional assists a consultee with a work-related (or caretaking-related) problem with a client system, with the goal of helping both the consultee and the client system in some specified way. (p. 8)

Counselors frequently are the recipients of services from consultants, and they often function in the role of consultant. When consulting, they apply their professional expertise to the questions, needs, or concerns of those who have sought their services.

Many of the issues we raised regarding counselor education in Chapter 14 are equally pertinent to supervision and consultation. In this chapter, we discuss them as they apply to the specific triad involved (supervisor–supervisee–client or consultant–consultee–client or client system).

SUPERVISION

The professional literature in mental health supervision recognizes two basic types of supervision for counselors—administrative and clinical (Borders & Leddick, 1987). Administrative supervision occurs when direct-line administrators give direction, or supervision, to counselors who are their employees. Clinical supervision, on the other hand, is the process whereby the work of counselors is reviewed by other mental health professionals, usually with the goal of increasing the counselors' effectiveness. Within counselor education programs, supervision has the dual purpose of monitoring the services provided by counselors-in-training and monitoring the welfare of clients who are receiving services from these trainees (American Counseling Association [ACA], 2014, §F.1.a.).

The purpose of administrative supervision is to ensure that counselors who are employed are performing their jobs appropriately. Administrative supervisors usually have direct control and authority over those who are being supervised. Generally, the purpose of clinical supervision is to help counselors increase their skills and ensure that they are serving their clients appropriately. Clinical supervisors usually have no direct control and authority over the counselors they supervise, unless they happen to be the counselors' administrative supervisor as well. Counselors who are receiving clinical supervision often are completing field experiences for their graduate program, or post-master's supervised experience for state licensure or national certification (Magnuson, Norem, & Wilcoxon, 2000). In some instances, an administrative supervisor also serves as a counselor's clinical supervisor, and this arrangement has positive aspects and usually is not problematic (Tromski-Klingshirn & Davis, 2007). Most of our discussion in this chapter focuses on clinical supervision rather than on administrative supervision. Keep in mind, though, that the law treats the relationships differently because the purposes of the two types of supervision generally are quite different. When there is a legal question regarding supervision, the issue of whether the supervisor has direct control and authority is important.

Fair Evaluation

Fair evaluation in supervision has to do with supervisee rights. Legal due process rights derive from the Fourteenth Amendment to the U.S. Constitution. Supervisees who work in public institutions and those who work in private organizations that have policies stipulating due process rights can expect to be protected from unfair or arbitrary decisions that affect them negatively. According to Bernard and Goodyear (2014), the most blatant violations of supervisees' fair evaluation rights occur when a supervisee is given a negative final evaluation or is dismissed from an internship or job without having been given warning that performance was inadequate along with reasonable opportunity to improve.

What this means for supervisors is that they need to provide supervisees with ongoing feedback, periodic evaluation, and opportunities to correct their deficiencies. When evaluation is negative, the changes that the supervisee must make should be communicated in specific, behavioral terms. Bernard and Goodyear (2014) have suggested that supervisees should be given a specific description of what constitutes inadequate performance, what behaviors constitute improvement, and what degree of improvement is expected. The *Code of Ethics* (ACA, 2014) contains some provisions to ensure that supervisee rights are protected when supervisors believe that supervisee limitations are impeding performance. Supervisors assist supervisees in securing remedial assistance when needed, seek consultation and document their decisions to dismiss or refer supervisees for assistance, and ensure that supervisees are aware of options available to them to address such decisions (§F.6.b.).

Counselors who supervise sometimes create problems because they are uncomfortable with evaluation and avoid giving clear feedback to a supervisee about deficiencies they observe. Supervisees will then be justifiably upset and angry when they receive a negative final evaluation or when the supervisor declines to endorse them for licensure or another professional credential. Supervisors should provide formative as well as summative feedback to supervisees. Formative feedback is designed to help supervisees improve their skills, whereas summative feedback serves the purpose of evaluating the performance of supervisees. Evaluation must be ongoing, and formal evaluation sessions must be scheduled throughout the supervisory relationship (ACA, 2014, §F.6.a.). Feedback should be given both orally and in writing.

Informed Consent

Informed consent for supervision should be obtained both from the client and from the supervisee. *Clients* of supervisees need to know that their counselor is working under supervision and need to understand what this supervision will mean for them. For instance, will their sessions be observed, or audio- or videotaped? Who will be involved in supervision? Will the client's case be discussed with a supervision group? What does this all mean in terms of the client's confidentiality? These questions must be clearly addressed with clients, and clients need to provide written consent before they agree to enter into the counseling relationship. Best practice requires that counselors provide clients with specific information regarding supervisory relationships.

Clients have the right to be aware that their counselors are working under supervision, and they have the right to know the supervisee's identity and qualifications to provide counseling services (ACA, 2014, §F.5.c.). Sometimes counselors who are being supervised will minimize the need for supervision and gloss over the details of the arrangement in an attempt to make themselves and their clients more comfortable. As a counselor working under supervision, you may be concerned that your clients will not believe you are competent to provide services and may not develop trust and confidence in you. These concerns should not inhibit you from fully informing your clients about supervision, however. If a client expresses reservations about a third party being privy to sensitive information that might be shared, a solution might be to arrange for the client to meet the supervisor face-to-face and raise any concerns directly with the supervisor. If some clients refuse to allow you to tape sessions or discuss their cases during supervision sessions and your supervisor requires the opportunity to supervise your counseling sessions with these clients, you may have to terminate your relationship with these clients and transfer them to another counselor.

Just as the supervisee has a responsibility to secure the client's informed consent, the supervisor is obligated to ensure that the *supervisee* understands and consents to the conditions of supervision. Several points should be discussed between the supervisor and the supervisee before they enter into a formal working relationship. These points are included in Figure 15-1. The *Code*

- *Purposes of supervision.* The purposes of supervision are varied. The goal of a supervision arrangement could be to foster the supervisee's professional development and protect the welfare of clients while a supervisee is in the process of developing the competence to work independently. Although an important benefit of supervision could be that the supervisee accrues the supervised hours to fulfill requirements for an internship or licensure, simply acquiring a certain number of hours is not the purpose of supervision. When a supervisor and supervisee undertake their relationship with the intent of having the supervisor sign off on the required hours, there is little chance that supervision will be a growth-producing experience for the supervisee.

- *The logistics of supervision.* An understanding should be reached regarding how frequently the supervisor and supervisee will meet, where they will meet, and for how long. If the supervisee is under the direct control and authority of the supervisor in a work setting, the supervisee should know how to contact the supervisor, who to contact in case of an emergency, and what to do if the supervisor or the designee is unavailable. Supervisors and supervisees should discuss the various forms of documentation required by licensing boards—or in the case of student interns, by the university and the internship site—and who will be responsible for completing the paperwork.

- *Information about the supervisor.* Supervisees need to know that their supervisors are qualified by training, experience, or credentials to provide them with competent supervision. Supervisors should provide prospective supervisees with information regarding their credentials. To help supervisors and supervisees determine whether there are any differences in perspective that might need to be negotiated, supervisors should explain their theoretical orientations and describe their supervisory styles to potential supervisees.

- *Expectations, roles, and responsibilities.* These should be made clear for each party in the relationship. For instance, is the supervisee expected to bring audio- or videotapes to the supervisory sessions, present cases for discussion, or prepare in some other specific way? If the supervisor is charging a fee, what are the arrangements for payment? What is the nature of the supervisory relationship, and how does it differ from a counseling relationship or a consulting relationship? What are the boundaries of the relationship?

- *Evaluation.* It is best practice to explain in detail to supervisees the processes and procedures for evaluating their performance.

- *Ethical and legal practice.* Supervisors should not simply assume that supervisees have been instructed and that they know all they need to know about legal and ethical issues. Supervisors protect themselves and safeguard the welfare of their supervisees and the supervisees' clients when they ascertain at outset of the supervisory relationship areas of ethical and legal practice in which the supervisee may need further instruction or clarification.

FIGURE 15-1 Topics to be discussed before supervision begins

Source: Pearson Education, Inc., Hoboken, NJ.

of Ethics (ACA, 2014) addresses informed consent for supervision, requiring supervisors to incorporate into their supervision the principles of informed consent and participation and inform supervisees of their policies and procedures and the mechanisms for due process appeal of their supervisory actions (§F.4.a.).

Supervision Agreements

Written agreements are recommended for counselor–client relationships, and these agreements are also important for supervisory relationships. Generally, written agreements are not necessary in administrative supervision because such relationships are dictated by the job descriptions of both the supervisor and the supervisee. The types of supervisory arrangements in clinical supervision vary substantially among dyads. Whereas one clinical supervisor may require payment for services and weekly audiotapes of sessions, another clinical supervisor may not charge a fee and may prefer to observe sessions. A written agreement can articulate a supervisory relationship in detail to avoid later misunderstandings. It can also serve to formalize the relationship, educate the supervisee regarding the nature of supervision, provide a model of how to approach informed consent with clients, and provide security for both parties by structuring the relationship (McCarthy et al., 1995).

An example of a supervision agreement is included in Appendix F. This particular agreement is designed for a licensed counselor to provide supervision for a counselor who is accruing post-master's supervised experience required for licensure. Sections of this agreement could be modified easily to fit a number of other clinical supervision situations. This agreement covers very important understandings between the supervisor and the supervisee. Note that the clinical supervisor gives deference to the administrative or on-site supervisor, and that the agreement includes several statements meant to limit the clinical supervisor's responsibilities for the counselor's day-to-day activities.

Supervisor Competence

Being a competent counselor does not necessarily mean that one is also a competent supervisor (Muratori, 2001). In fact, being a skilled counseling practitioner is only one prerequisite for competence as a supervisor. It also requires specific training in the knowledge and skills involved in supervision. Licensure boards in some states (e.g., California, Ohio, Louisiana, Texas) now require those who supervise candidates to be not only trained and licensed as counselors but also approved by the boards as supervisors. The Center for Credentialing and Education, a National Board for Certified Counselors (NBCC) corporate affiliate, offers a national supervisory credential that may be used to verify one's expertise in supervision of counselors. More information about this credential may be found at cce-global.org.

The *Code of Ethics* (ACA, 2014) states that "prior to offering clinical supervision services, counselors are trained in supervision methods and techniques" (§F.2.a.). The Association for Counselor Education and Supervision (ACES) *Standards for Counseling Supervisors* (1990) provides a detailed description of the characteristics and competencies of effective supervisors. Briefly, the standards that represent best practice (Storm, Todd, Sprenkle, & Morgan, 2001) state that competent supervisors:

- Are effective counselors themselves.
- Have attitudes and traits consistent with the supervisory role, such as sensitivity to individual differences, motivation and commitment to supervision, and comfort with the authority inherent in the supervisory role.

- Are familiar with and can skillfully apply the ethical, legal, and regulatory dimensions of supervision.
- Understand the professional and personal nature of the supervisory relationship and the impact of supervision on the supervisee.
- Understand the methods and techniques of supervision.
- Appreciate the process of counselor development and how it unfolds in supervision.
- Are skilled in case conceptualization and management.
- Can evaluate a supervisee's counseling performance fairly and accurately and provide feedback to facilitate growth.
- Are knowledgeable about oral and written reporting and recording.
- Have a solid grasp of the rapidly expanding body of theory and research concerning counseling and counselor supervision.

Supervisors must be cognizant of the need for continuing education. According to the *Code of Ethics* (ACA, 2014), clinical supervisors "regularly pursue continuing education activities, including both counseling and supervision topics and skills" (§F.2.a.). This task can be enormous for supervisors, as they need to keep current in their own specialty areas as well as be aware of advances that are being made in the general area of clinical supervision (Bernard & Goodyear, 2014). Research has demonstrated that experienced supervisors can benefit from competency training. The clinical supervisors who participated in a study by Tebes et al. (2011) reported significant increases in their perceived ability to manage supervisory relationships, manage supervisee job performance, and promote supervisee professional development.

Supervisees sometimes want to gain experience working in specialty areas or with client populations in which the supervisor has limited training or experience. In these cases, supervisors must decide whether they have the necessary skills to adequately supervise. Supervisors should be clear about the kinds of cases they would not supervise (such as substance abuse, genetic counseling, or sexual abuse), the kinds of settings that are outside their scope of expertise (e.g., an agency counselor who works with adults not feeling competent to supervise an elementary school counselor), and the kinds of cases they would supervise only when they are working under supervision themselves or in conjunction with a consultant. In fact, because supervision is such a complex and demanding responsibility, supervisors would be wise to have a consultant or consultation group with whom they meet regularly to monitor their performance.

Confidentiality Concerns

When you are working as a counselor under supervision, you can expect your supervisor to inform you about client rights, including the protection of client privacy and confidentiality in the counseling relationship (ACA, 2014, §F.1.c.). You will need to provide your clients with disclosure information that informs them of how the supervision process influences the limits of confidentiality, and let them know who will have access to their records. You will have access to sensitive information about clients that must be kept confidential. In some circumstances, this information may be privileged by statute. At the same time, you will be required to share information about your clients with your supervisor. As a general rule, sharing confidential and privileged information with professionals who have a need to know for professional purposes, such as supervision, is acceptable and does not destroy legal privilege (Cleary, 1984). You must know how to apply the general principles of confidentiality to your specific situation. If you are working in a community agency, the agency is likely to have policies and regulations regarding release of client information, and you must know and abide by these regulations.

What would happen if your site supervisor were to inappropriately disclose confidential or privileged information? Because you may have had no control over who would be your supervisor, you probably would not be held accountable. Nonetheless, you do have a professional and legal responsibility to address concerns you may have regarding an untrustworthy supervisor. This can be extremely difficult, because you are in a vulnerable position. If you are a practicum student or intern in a counselor training program, you should bring your concern to the attention of your university supervisor, who will help you determine how to proceed. If possible, it is best for you to resolve the concern directly with the site supervisor involved. Counselors who have graduated from a training program and are working under supervision toward their licensure should also attempt first to resolve the concern directly with the supervisor. If this approach is not feasible or is unsuccessful, they should consult with their supervisor's administrative supervisor.

The use of technology in supervision is burgeoning, and supervisors are challenged to keep current with all the innovations. The use of videoconferencing as a means of providing supervision is increasing because of its time and cost efficiency (Jencius, Baltimore, & Getz, 2010). However, because even encryption-protected telecommunications systems are highly vulnerable to intrusion, supervisors need to carefully weigh the benefits of providing distance supervision against the potential threats to confidentiality (Jencius, 2015; McAdams & Wyatt, 2010).

Supervisory Relationships

Supervision occurs at multiple levels and involves a number of parties, including a client, a counselor/ supervisee, and one or more supervisors. Within a counselor training program, both a university supervisor and a site supervisor typically oversee the work of the student who is completing a field-based practicum or internship. In counselor education programs that have doctoral as well as master's programs, doctoral students sometimes supervise master's-level interns, in a structure called *layered supervision*. What makes this type of supervision layered is that the doctoral student supervisor will be supervised as well. Master's-level interns can benefit from this arrangement. Fernando (2013) found that supervisees of doctoral students reported significantly higher self-efficacy and satisfaction than did students who were supervised by faculty. When relationships involve clients, a supervisee, a university supervisor, a site supervisor, a supervisor who is a doctoral student, and the supervisor of the doctoral student supervisor, sorting out the roles and responsibilities can be a daunting task.

Supervision also occurs at the post-master's level. The counselor licensure movement has produced another group of supervisors—those who work with licensure applicants (Borders, Cashwell, & Rotter, 1995). Obviously, there are multiple roles and relationships to consider in supervision.

All of the guidelines in the *Code of Ethics* (ACA, 2014) regarding nonprofessional relationships between counselor educators and students apply equally to the supervisory relationship. Boundaries in supervisory relationships must be carefully managed because supervisors have considerable power in the relationship. In their gatekeeping function, they hold the key to the supervisee's entrance into the profession. Their supervisees look to them as models of professional behavior. In addition, because the supervisory relationship can involve a strong emotional connection, transference and countertransference reactions are common. Skilled supervisors are aware of (and address in supervision) the phenomenon of parallel process, which occurs when counselors unconsciously identify with their clients and then present to their supervisors in a similar fashion (Giordano, Clarke, & Borders, 2013).

Supervision is a complex process that can be further complicated when supervisors have multiple roles with their supervisees, such as teacher, clinical supervisor, and administrative supervisor. If possible, these roles should be divided among several supervisors.

The *Code of Ethics* (ACA, 2014; §F.3.a.) cautions supervisors to clearly define and maintain ethical professional, personal, and social relationships with supervisees, and to consider the risks and benefits when they consider extending current supervisory relationships beyond conventional parameters. Although supervisors will probably encounter their supervisees in social settings and community activities, such as workshops or meetings of professional associations, socializing or friendships with supervisees could make it difficult, if not impossible, for the supervisor to conduct an objective evaluation. As we noted in Chapter 14, counselor educators and supervisors can be tempted to relax the boundaries as students near completion of their training programs. As supervisees make the transition to becoming their supervisors' professional peers, their interactions take on an increasingly collegial tone. Nonetheless, supervisors must remember that their position requires them to evaluate their supervisees and perhaps recommend them for licensure or future employment.

Supervisors play multiple roles. Three roles often discussed in the literature are teacher, counselor, and consultant. Sometimes supervisors function more like teachers, especially when they are working with beginning supervisees. Sometimes they function more like peers or consultants, usually with advanced supervisees. Although supervision is also similar to counseling, there are important differences. In counseling, the relationship sometimes *is* the intervention, whereas if supervision consisted only of the supervisory relationship, the supervisee would not learn new and needed skills. A second important difference is that counseling is nonjudgmental, whereas supervision always has an evaluative component (Goodyear, Arcinue, & Getzelman, 2001).

Just as counselor educators should not become counselors to their students, a supervisor should not establish a therapeutic relationship with a supervisee as a substitute for supervision. The *Code of Ethics* (ACA, 2014) states clearly that "supervisors do not provide counseling services to supervisees" (§F.6.c.). Supervisors address interpersonal competencies in terms of the impact of these issues on clients, the supervisory relationship, and professional functioning (§F.6.c.). The distinctions between the therapeutic aspects of the supervisor's role and the role of the counselor are not always clear. Herlihy and Corey (2015a) have argued that when supervisors are overly cautious in trying to avoid the counselor role, they may do their supervisees a disservice. Effective supervision includes a focus on the impact of the counselor on the counseling process, and when supervision focuses exclusively on client cases or problem-solving strategies for working with clients, opportunities for supervisee growth may be lost. Research studies have indicated that supervisees value and feel comfortable in sessions that focus on their personal issues (Sumerel & Borders, 1996); supervisees experience less role conflict when the emotional bond between supervisor and supervisee is strong (Ladany & Friedlander, 1995); and counselors prefer a supervisor who is collegial and relationship oriented over one who is task oriented (Usher & Borders, 1993). At the same time, a personal-issues focus should not slide beyond appropriate boundaries and become a therapeutic relationship. When supervisors become counselors to their supervisees, these dual relationships model inappropriate behaviors that the supervisees may later perpetuate in their counseling relationships or when they become supervisors themselves (Tyler & Tyler, 1994).

There is a delicate balance to be maintained in the supervisory relationship. In your work as a practicum student or intern, your own unresolved personal issues occasionally may be triggered by a client, and this may interfere with your counseling effectiveness. You can expect your supervisor to help you identify what is occurring and to understand the issues involved. Your supervisor might even suggest that you seek counseling to help resolve the issues, but the focus of your supervisory sessions should remain on your work and should not become personal therapy sessions for you. These guidelines are applicable to the situation in which Dr. Jones finds herself in the following scenario.

15-1 The Case of Dr. Jones

Dr. Jones has been supervising Marla's work as a practicum student. Marla has demonstrated very good skills thus far in her first semester of counseling real clients. Dr. Jones has just watched one of Marla's sessions from behind the one-way mirror at the practicum clinic and was surprised to see Marla falter midway through the session and continue to give a poor performance. After the session, Dr. Jones sits down with Marla for a supervision session and shares her surprise that Marla's counseling skills in the session had fallen so far short of her usual abilities. Marla responds by bursting into tears and stating that her personal life is falling apart and she is under incredible stress.

- How should Dr. Jones react to this situation?
- Why is it inappropriate for a clinical supervisor to provide professional counseling services to a supervisee?

Discussion: Dr. Jones certainly will want to be supportive and empathic toward Marla, but without slipping into a counselor role. Dr. Jones might use active listening skills to allow Marla to vent her feelings, discuss how Marla's personal problems are affecting her professional performance, and perhaps suggest that Marla seek counseling. If Dr. Jones were to provide counseling services to Marla, this would constitute an inappropriate dual relationship and would make it very difficult for both of them when the time comes for Dr. Jones to evaluate Marla's practicum performance.

SEXUAL RELATIONSHIPS BETWEEN SUPERVISORS AND SUPERVISEES   There is clear consensus in the counseling profession regarding the impropriety of sexual dual relationships between supervisors and their supervisees. The *Code of Ethics* (ACA, 2014, §F.3.b.) states that sexual intimacies between supervisors and supervisees are unethical. Bowman, Hatley, and Bowman (1995) conducted a survey of faculty and graduate students in programs accredited by the Council on Accreditation of Counseling and Related Educational Programs (CACREP), which included a scenario depicting a romantic relationship between a practicum student and the professor who was supervising her. All faculty and 99% of students believed this situation was unethical. Despite this belief system, sexual relationships still do occur in supervision. One survey (Miller & Larrabee, 1995) found that about 6% of female ACES members reported sexual experiences with educators or supervisors during their graduate training. Less than one-third of these encounters, however, were with supervisors.

Although sexual intimacies seem to occur in only a small percentage of relationships between supervisors and supervisees, it is probably much more common for feelings of sexual attraction to develop between them. When this happens, several actions could be taken to resolve the problem. It is important to remember that when sexual attraction takes place in a supervisory relationship, the supervisor has the obligation, as the person with the power in the relationship, to manage the attraction in an appropriate and ethical manner. The supervisee could be transferred to a different supervisor, if this could be done without having a negative impact on the supervisee's clients or the supervisee's professional growth. If circumstances prevent a transfer, the supervisory relationship should be carefully documented by both the supervisor and the supervisee. The supervisor should, at a minimum, request regular consultation and obtain a second opinion when evaluating the supervisee's abilities. It would be prudent to involve another supervisor who would monitor the supervisory relationship.

The manner in which issues of sexual attraction are handled by a supervisor can have a potent modeling effect for the supervisee. Feelings of sexual attraction to a client are likely to occur for the first time when counselors are still novices working under supervision. Therefore, supervisors must do more than admonish their supervisees to avoid sexual intimacies with clients. They must create an ethical climate for supervisee self-exploration (Bartell & Rubin, 1990). It is crucial that the supervisor develop a relationship of trust that encourages supervisees to honestly discuss their feelings of sexual attraction to a client without fear of being judged negatively.

Accountability and Responsibility

Supervisors have a number of parties to whom they are directly and indirectly accountable. Although their primary responsibilities are to facilitate the growth of supervisees and to protect clients, they also have a larger scope of responsibility that includes parties who are indirectly involved.

The supervisor is indirectly responsible to the field setting in which the supervisee is working to ensure that clients who are served by the supervisee receive quality care. Community agencies, schools, hospitals, and other settings that accept and provide site supervision to practicum students and interns take on an additional responsibility that requires considerable time and effort. In return, university supervisors feel an obligation to ensure that these students make a positive contribution to the setting and do so in a professional manner.

Supervisors, like counselor educators, serve as gatekeepers to the profession. If supervisee incompetence is not addressed, the counseling program's reputation in the community will suffer, and the counseling profession itself will be diminished. Supervisors must not endorse supervisees for graduation from a training program or for a professional credential if the supervisees are not able to provide effective counseling services (ACA, 2014, §F.6.d.). In a broad sense, the supervisor functions to protect future consumers of counseling services. Figure 15-2 depicts the multiple layers of responsibility and accountability of supervisors.

Increased supervision is often prescribed as an intervention when supervisees are not making sufficient progress in their competency development (Henderson & Dufrene, 2011). After reviewing

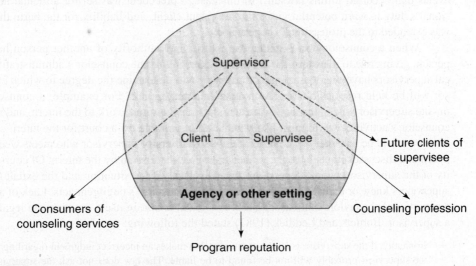

FIGURE 15-2 Multiple layers of supervisor responsibility

Source: Pearson Education, Inc., Hoboken, NJ.

the literature, Nelson et al. (2010) concluded that a therapeutic supervisory stance is the most crucial variable in working with problematic supervisees. They emphasized the importance of creating a trusting relationship and safe environment before evaluating supervisee performance. Recent research evidence supports this conclusion. Ladany, Mori, and Mehr (2013) found that the most effective supervisors facilitated open communication, and Mehr, Ladany, and Caskie (2014) found that supervisees were more willing to disclose when the supervisory working alliance was strong. Herlihy and Corey (2015a) have noted that supervisees sometimes are reluctant to openly discuss with their supervisors mistakes they may have made in their clinical work. It is critical, however, that supervisees feel safe to discuss their doubts and fears if they are to rectify their mistakes and learn from them.

Supervisors are not only accountable for the work of their supervisees in an ethical and professional sense, but they can also be held legally liable for supervisee incompetence. This legal responsibility, which occurs under the principle of vicarious liability, is discussed next.

Vicarious Liability

The legal principle known as *respondeat superior*, or *vicarious liability*, holds that individuals who have control and authority over others will be held accountable for their negligence (Christie, Meeks, Pryor, & Sanders, 1997). Generally, an employer will be held accountable for the negligence of an employee who is acting within the scope of employment (*John R. v. Oakland Unified School District*, 1989; *Lisa M. v. Henry Mayo Newhall Memorial Hosp.*, 1995). *Respondeat superior*, originally a Latin term meaning "Let the master answer," is the basis for an English legal concept known as *master/servant*. The legal reasoning has been that one who has the authority to direct the activities of another (the *master*) should be held accountable for the negligence of the person who has submitted to such authority (the *servant*). In the mental health arena, counselors who work for others or who volunteer their services, such as they usually do in an internship, would be the *servants*. The administrative supervisor would be the counselor's *master*. From a practical standpoint, a person who has been injured by a servant (or employee) has a better chance of being compensated by a master (or employer) because masters tend to have more resources than servants.

The principle of vicarious liability was applied to the mental health professions in the famous *Tarasoff v. Regents of University of California* (1976) case. (See Chapter 7 for a review of the events that occurred in this lawsuit.) In this case, a precedent was set for a mental health professional's duty to warn potential victims of a violent client, and liability for the harm that was done was extended to the professional's supervisor.

When a counselor who is under the control and authority of another person harms a third person, giving rise to a lawsuit, the amount of control that the counselor's administrative and clinical supervisors have over the counselor probably will determine the degree to which each supervisor will be held responsible for the counselor's negligence. For example, a counselor intern's on-site supervisor who is physically present each day, assigns work to the intern, and monitors the counselor's activities would most likely be held accountable by a court for the intern's negligence. A court would be less likely to hold responsible a university supervisor who meets weekly with the intern and discusses issues brought to the supervisor's attention by the intern. Of course, the liability of the supervisors would depend on the exact facts in the situation and the extent to which the supervisors knew or should have known about the counselor's negligent acts. Lack of awareness of a supervisee's behaviors that caused harm to a client is not, in itself, an adequate legal defense for a supervisor. Borders and Leddick (1987) stated the following:

> Ironically, if the supervisor is aware of the case, but makes an incorrect judgment regarding the case, the supervisor probably will not be found to be liable. The law does not ask the supervisor to be infallible, but rather, to be involved. (p. 55)

Obviously, supervision can be a risky undertaking. Snider (1985) has offered some guidelines for supervisors to help them reduce their likelihood of being named as a co-defendant in a malpractice lawsuit. These guidelines offer protection to supervisees as well. First, it is important to maintain a trusting relationship in which supervisees feel comfortable in sharing their doubts and concerns. Second, supervisors must keep up to date with legal issues that affect supervision and mental health practice in general. Third, supervisors must recognize the need for competent legal advice and ensure that an attorney is available to provide legal support. In addition, both supervisors and supervisees should carry professional liability insurance.

Supervisors are advised to document their supervisory sessions, not only because of the liability issues involved, but also to improve evaluation and to monitor client care. This documentation should include (a) meeting date and time, (b) a listing of cases discussed, (c) notes regarding client progress, (d) recommendations made to the supervisee, (e) issues to be followed up in future meetings, and (f) a plan for remediating any significant supervisee deficiencies that are identified (Harrar, VandeCreek, & Knapp, 1990; Welfel, 2013). Although documentation of supervisory sessions may constitute best practice, our observation is that not all supervisors actually take notes related to their supervision sessions.

Supervisor and Supervisee Rights and Responsibilities

It should be evident from your reading thus far that supervision is a serious responsibility that is not undertaken lightly by your supervisor. For the process to facilitate your maximum professional growth, both you and your supervisor must understand your roles and responsibilities and work conscientiously to fulfill them.

You have the right to expect certain behaviors from your supervisor. Your supervisor will work to ensure that you are aware of professional and ethical standards and legal responsibilities (ACA, 2005, §F.4.c.). You can expect your supervisor to provide you with regular face-to-face supervision. If you are a student in a CACREP-accredited training program, you will receive a minimum of 1 hour per week of individual supervision and 1.5 hours per week of group supervision during your practicum and internship. Your supervisor may require you to bring audio- or videotapes to your supervisory sessions, or may even wish to have direct interaction with clients. Simply reviewing your case notes is not a viable alternative to these direct activities, although it may be a fairly common practice (Navin, Beamish, & Johanson, 1995).

You can expect supervisors to give you their full attention during your agreed-on supervision time. Your supervisory sessions should be reasonably free from interruptions, and your supervisor should not have taken on an excessive number of supervisees. Although some agencies have policies limiting the number of supervisees for whom their employees may be responsible, not all state licensure boards stipulate a maximum number of supervisees (Welfel, 2013). Your supervisor has a responsibility to ensure that you are able to contact him or her in emergencies or, if the supervisor is unavailable, to provide you with alternative on-call supervisors to assist you in handling crises (ACA, 2014, §F.4.b.).

You can expect your supervisor to thoroughly explain the supervision process to you and secure your informed consent, to possess the competencies described earlier in this chapter, to be skilled at managing the boundaries of the supervisory relationship, to provide you with ongoing feedback about your performance, and to safeguard the confidentiality of information exchanged.

For your part, it is important that you are open to receiving feedback and are willing to work to implement suggestions that will help you improve your effectiveness as a counselor. Although you may be hesitant at times to admit your uncertainties, confusion, or lack of knowledge about various aspects of your professional functioning, it is much better that you bring your concerns to your supervisory sessions and ask for assistance. Remember that supervision is a developmental process. Each time you master a new skill or add new knowledge and understanding to your repertoire, you become more competent to one day practice independently.

Technology Issues in Supervision

Technologies have been infused extensively into the clinical supervision of counselors and have facilitated communication and improved the quality of supervision in myriad ways. Supervisees benefit from immediate, in-session learning when supervisors communicate feedback through bug-in-the-ear, phone-in, monitor-text, computer-based live supervision, or other synchronous methods. E-mail, instant messaging (IM) and texting, and teleconferencing all have increased the ease and speed with which supervisee and supervisor can communicate with each other. Asynchronous video conferencing and digital video recording have made it possible for supervisors to review supervisees' counseling sessions without traveling to the site where the supervisee is working (Jencius, Baltimore, & Getz, 2010).

Distance supervision that uses various technologies has revolutionized counselor supervision and is proving to be an effective means of providing supervision services (Chapman, Baker, Nassar-McMillan, & Gerler, 2011). Distance supervision offers many benefits, including lower costs to supervisees, flexibility in scheduling, supervision opportunities for those who live in isolated or rural communities, immediate access to a supervisor in crisis situations, and real-time supervision from experts on specific clinical issues (McAdams & Wyatt, 2010). Vaccaro and Lambie (2007) have noted that ethical issues must always be addressed in supervision, regardless of how it is delivered. These authors reviewed issues of confidentiality, liability, and technological competencies that arise in distance supervision. They reminded supervisors and supervisees that (a) they must be specifically trained in using the needed technologies, (b) measures must be taken to ensure the security of computer-based communications, (c) informed consent documents should explicitly discuss the limits of computer-based supervision, and (d) counselor education programs that use distance supervision should have adequate liability coverage and provide technical support. Problematic aspects of distance supervision that remain to be addressed include the potential for miscommunications between supervisor and supervisee due to restricted nonverbal cues, and understanding the regulations that pertain to distance supervision. McAdams and Wyatt (2010) found that regulations were in place for technology-assisted distance supervision in 6 states, were under development or discussion in 18 states, but were prohibited as illegitimate activities in 19 states. Uneven regulation can make it difficult to determine whether distance supervision is acceptable when the supervisee and supervisor are communicating from different states. See Chapter 10 for a full discussion of distance supervision.

Diversity Considerations in Supervision

Addressing cultural diversity issues in supervision is essential to helping supervisees become multiculturally competent counselors (Ancis & Marshall, 2010; Colistra & Brown-Rice, 2011). If supervisors are not attuned to diversity issues in supervision, they are likely to inadvertently reinforce the biased attitudes and behaviors of their supervisees. Supervisors must remain aware that their world views are likely to influence the therapeutic choices made by their supervisees (Brown & Landrum-Brown, 1995). Effective cross-cultural supervisors are aware of and address the role of multiculturalism/diversity in the client–supervisee and supervisor–supervisee relationships (ACA, 2014, §F.2.b.). Supervisors must themselves be multiculturally competent if they are to foster the development of such competence in their supervisees. Wong, Wong, and Ishiyama (2013) found that the supervisor's multicultural competence was a significant factor in cross-cultural supervision dyads.

Research has shown that discussing diversity issues in supervision can increase supervisee satisfaction with supervision (Duan & Roehlke, 2001; Estrada, Frame, & Williams, 2004), increase supervisees' perceptions of their own multicultural competence (Toporek, Ortega-Villalobos, & Pope-Davis, 2004), and lead to more positive outcomes for clients (Ancis & Marshall, 2010). There is consensus that it is the responsibility of supervisors to initiate discussions of cultural differences with their supervisees (Bernard & Goodyear, 2014; Corey, Haynes, Moulton, & Muratori, 2010). If the supervisor is silent on this issue, the supervisee will get the message that cultural diversity is a taboo subject in supervision.

It is likely that you will become a supervisor to at least one counselor or counselor trainee during your career. It is also likely that your supervisee will be culturally different from you in some ways. Although you may feel uncomfortable about broaching the issue of cultural differences with your supervisee, it is necessary to break the taboo about talking about racial, gender, or cultural differences (Corey et al., 2010). When you become a supervisor, it will be your responsibility to be aware of the complex ways in which culture and gender interact between client, counselor, and supervisor and present multiple challenges to communication and understanding (Nelson et al., 2006). Your initial supervisory sessions with your supervisees present opportunities to establish an open dialogue regarding multicultural issues.

Once the supervisory alliance is established, you can promote multicultural competence in your supervisees by incorporating multicultural case conceptualization into supervision. You can do this by helping your supervisees analyze the impact of their client's race or ethnicity, gender role socialization, social class, sexual orientation, and other salient cultural variables on the client's problems. It is also important that you promote culturally appropriate interventions, which may include teaching supervisees how to advocate for their clients.

A cultural variable that is often overlooked is that mental health professionals of different disciplines (including psychology, social work, marriage and family therapy, and psychiatry) often supervise someone with a different background, training, and theoretical orientation to practice. These differences must also be addressed at the outset of the supervisory relationship to avoid misunderstandings and conflicts (Campbell, 2000).

CONSULTATION

Counselors must assume a variety of roles as they perform their work responsibilities, and each role demands different perspectives, attitudes, and behaviors. The professional role that counselors engage in at any given moment determines their behavior and, in many instances, their responsibilities to the individual with whom they are interacting. Consultant and consultee are two roles that counselors take on regularly.

Counselors regularly consult with others for the benefit of their clients and to further their knowledge of a particular area of counseling. Counselors use the following consultants: other mental health professionals when making clinical or ethical judgments; other professionals, such as physicians, social workers, nurses, and psychologists, who are also treating their client; family members, friends, and significant others in the clients' lives, for the benefit of clients; administrators in their employment setting, regarding their job responsibilities or when seeking direction in difficult situations; and attorneys, when they have legal questions. The very best step a counselor can take when faced with a difficult ethical decision or with a legal question is to consult (Gottlieb, 2006; Knapp & VandeCreek, 2006; Woody, 2013). Consulting with peers and other mental health professionals is best for ethical dilemmas. Consulting with supervisors and attorneys is necessary for legal problems.

Counselors also find themselves in the role of consultant in a number of situations. A fellow counselor may be having difficulty making a clinical or ethical decision. Another professional who is treating one of their clients may request a consultation. In all of these examples, the consultation takes place between two individuals (a consultant and a consultee) for the benefit of a third person (a client). These consultation relationships are not formalized and generally are limited to a single discussion or a brief series of discussions. We refer to this type of consultation as *peer consultation*. By contrast, counselors sometimes function as consultants to organizations such as businesses, agencies, or schools. These consultation relationships are usually more long term and are formalized in some manner, often through a contract. This type of consultation is known as *organizational consultation*. Both peer and organizational consultations are primarily aimed at work-related concerns as opposed to the consultee's personal problems.

Accountability

In most situations, consultants do not have control and authority over the person who is receiving the benefit of their consultation. Consultants essentially are giving advice. Once individuals receive advice from a consultant, they are free to accept or ignore the advice they have been given. When consultants have no control over the actions taken by individuals who have received their advice, they cannot be held accountable legally for an individual's negligence even if they give inaccurate or wrong information or give bad advice.

Exceptions exist when a consultant is a counselor's administrative or clinical supervisor. As explained in this chapter, a supervisor who has control over a counselor's actions probably has some degree of legal liability for the negligence of the counselor. Also, it is possible that an individual who retains a consultant may have a legal cause of action based on contract principles against a consultant who gives wrong or poor advice that the consultee relies on.

Counselors who are asked to consult with colleagues sometimes are concerned about whether they might be held responsible for advice they give as consultants. This is the case with Allison in the following scenario.

15-2 The Case of Allison

Raymond, a counselor in a mental health center, approaches Allison, another counselor at the center who has no administrative authority over him, and asks her to consult with him regarding a client with whom he is having some difficulty. As Raymond describes his work with the client, Allison has a hunch that the client may have borderline personality traits that Raymond has not recognized. She is hesitant to enter into a consultation with him, however, because she knows that clients diagnosed with borderline personality disorder can be difficult to counsel. Allison wonders to herself, "What if Raymond doesn't do an adequate job in working with this client? If I give him advice, can I be held accountable?"

- What do you think Allison should do?
- If Allison does agree to consult with Raymond, how can she be helpful to him in working with his client?

Discussion: Allison should realize that Raymond will make the final decisions regarding how to counsel his client, and he will be responsible for his actions. A consultant who has no administrative authority over another counselor cannot be held accountable for what the counselor/consultee ultimately does. Allison should listen carefully to Raymond's concerns, and she might choose to give him her best advice depending on how she understands the situation. She will need to set boundaries to maintain her consultant role. She should not meet with the client herself to evaluate the client, and to avoid taking on a supervisory role, she should not meet regularly with Raymond regarding his counseling of the client.

After you have begun your counseling practice and you need to consult, you should choose consultants carefully with the understanding that you, as the individual who is seeking advice, will be held accountable. You should choose consultants who are knowledgeable, trustworthy, and reputable.

Power

Although consultants generally have no legal accountability for the actions of their consultees, it is important to remember that the power, or ability to influence, is not evenly distributed in consulting relationships. Because the consultant is viewed as an expert, there is potential for misuse or abuse of power. Even if the power differential is more perceived than real, consultants may have considerable influence on the outcome and process of a consultation. Therefore, consultants have an ethical responsibility to avoid misusing their power (Simpson & Glowiak, 2012).

Consultation Contracts

In organizational consulting and in some other situations, consultants enter into long-term agreements with others to provide advice in a particular manner. A clinical supervisor who provides supervision over a 2-year period for a counselor who is gathering experience for licensure or certification is also a consultant. Just as a supervision agreement is recommended for supervisory relationships, a written contract is recommended for counselors who consult.

The following recommendations have been offered for contracts that are prepared by consultants:

- Clearly specify the work to be completed by the consultant.
- Describe in detail any work products expected from the consultant.
- Establish a time frame for the completion of the work.
- Establish lines of authority and the person to whom the consultant is responsible.
- Describe the compensation plan for the consultant and the method of payment.
- Specify any special agreements or contingency plans agreed on by the parties (Remley, 1993).

Counselors who take on consulting roles need to understand the legal principles involved in accountability and contracts and to fulfill those roles in an ethical manner. Unlike counselors who function as supervisors (who have the ACA *Code of Ethics* to assist them), consultants are at somewhat of a disadvantage. There is no code of ethics specifically for consultants, and the ACA *Code of Ethics* (ACA, 2014) contains few standards (§B.7.a., §D.2.a., and §D.2.b.) that address consultation directly. This paucity of ethical standards, along with the fact that not all counselors are adequately trained in consultation (Brown, 1993; Newman, 1993), raises some cause for concern that counselors may not be well prepared to resolve the ethical dilemmas they encounter when they are functioning as consultants. Dougherty (2014) has identified several ethical issues that consultants frequently face. These include (a) consultant competence, (b) safeguarding consultee and client rights, (c) the consultation relationship, and (d) the role of values and diversity in consultation.

Consultant Competence

Competence to provide services is an important ethical issue in consultation, just as it is in counseling and supervision. Before counselors agree to enter into a consultation relationship, they must assess whether their personal and professional competence is adequate for the task (Dougherty, 2014). When you become an experienced counselor and are asked to consult with peers, you should ask for a description of the potential consultee's problem and then determine whether you possess the expertise needed to be of assistance. For example, if you have worked for several years in a clinic that specializes in treating individuals with eating disorders, you will probably feel confident that you can serve as a consultant to a high school counselor who is wondering whether one of her student clients suffers from anorexia. By contrast, assume that you are approached by another counselor in the clinic where you work. She tells you that she needs a consultation because she is concerned that one of her teenage clients' parents might sue her for malpractice. This colleague has a legal problem, and you should refer her to the clinic supervisor. Being asked to consult is always a compliment, but you should not always agree to such a request. Gottlieb (2006) has suggested several questions that counselors might ask themselves before making a decision whether to consult, including the following: Am I qualified? Can I be objective with this colleague? Are there any potential conflicts of interest? Do I have the time to give this request the attention it deserves?

When counselors are asked to perform organizational consultation, they should present their professional qualifications clearly to avoid misrepresenting themselves. Before entering into an agreement to provide services, they should ensure that they have the resources and competencies to provide the needed assistance (ACA, 2014, §D.2.a.). It is essential that consultants know their own limitations, and they should make an appropriate referral when they are unable to provide the requested services. The ability to carefully self-monitor one's own boundaries of competence is particularly critical because so few counselors have received formal training in consultation. Organizational consultation can be particularly complex because multiple parties are involved, both directly and indirectly. Because this can complicate the ethical and legal considerations, it is important that the consultant clarify who is the client before agreeing to enter into the consultative relationship (Fuqua, Newman, Simpson, & Choi, 2012).

Welfel (2013) has stated that counselors tend to make the same mistake regarding competence to consult as they make regarding competence to supervise: they assume that counseling skills are sufficient. She cautions counselors that when they present themselves as skilled consultants, they must be prepared to demonstrate the sources of their knowledge and to be ethically responsible for any harm their interventions might cause. Without a contract, consultants may not be legally responsible for the outcomes of interventions they suggest, but they do have a professional and ethical obligation to carefully consider the implications of actions that may be taken based on their advice.

Safeguarding Consultee and Client Rights

Due to the triadic nature of consultation, the client does not employ the consultant or sometimes even know that a consultant is involved. Welfel (2013) reminds counselors who consult to be attuned to the ramifications of their work for these rather invisible participants. Newman (1993) has raised a similar caution, noting that consultants must be sensitive to the effects of their work on all parties involved and to avoid situations in which their work could be used to the detriment of clients or client systems. The following scenario illustrates such an event.

15-3 The Case of Jerry

Jerry was hired by an administrator in a large organization to conduct a series of conflict resolution workshops with an employee group. Part of the agreement was that Jerry would conduct a pre- and post-assessment of the participants' conflict resolution skills to assess what they had learned. Jerry included the results of these assessments in his final report to the administrator. Later, the administrator used this information as one basis for determining which of the employees would be let go when the organization downsized.

- How did Jerry err as a consultant? How did the organization administrator err?

- What do you think Jerry can do to ensure that such problems do not occur again in his work as a consultant?

Discussion: Jerry violated the privacy of the employees when he provided the administrator with their specific scores. It appears that he failed to clarify with the administrator exactly what his role as consultant would entail and what would be contained in the report. The administrator erred by using the information Jerry inappropriately gave him to make management decisions. He violated the trust of his employees by using that information. In the future, Jerry should develop a clear and detailed contract with any organization before he agrees to serve as a consultant to that organization.

This scenario raises two crucial ethical issues: informed consent and confidentiality. Obviously, Jerry failed to negotiate how his report would be used by the administrator who hired him. The unfortunate outcome could have been avoided if Jerry had adhered to his ethical obligation to "inform all parties involved about the purpose of the service to be provided, relevant costs, potential risks and benefits, and the limits of confidentiality" (ACA, 2014, §D.2.b.).

Informed consent is an important consultee right that also extends to clients and client systems involved. In peer consultation, informed consent is a relatively straightforward matter. As we have suggested in other chapters, it is sound ethical practice for counselors to inform a client that they plan to consult about the client's case, explain their rationale, and obtain consent to proceed. Standard D.2.d. of the *Code of Ethics* (ACA, 2014) advises counselors functioning as consultants to review, both verbally and in writing, "the rights and responsibilities of both counselors and consultees."

Informed consent is much more complicated in organizational consulting. Often, administrators or executives hire consultants and make decisions about the work they want the consultant to do. Employee-clients may have little or no input into this decision, and the consultation process will be negatively affected if they feel coerced to participate. Therefore, consultants must be sensitive to the hierarchical nature of organizations and work skillfully with all the parties involved to make consent as informed and voluntary as possible (Welfel, 2013). Consultants must discuss the goals and purposes of the consultation, potential benefits and risks, and desired outcomes with those who will be affected by the consultation. Dougherty (2014) suggests that consultants should mentally put themselves in the consultees' position and ask themselves what they would like to know at the outset. Consultants must also remember that informed consent is an ongoing process, so these issues may need to be revisited periodically.

The *Code of Ethics* (ACA, 2014) offers these guidelines for protecting confidentiality in consultation: (a) information is discussed for professional purposes only; (b) reports present only data germane to the purposes of the consultation; and (c) every effort is made to protect client identity and avoid undue invasion of privacy (§B.7.a.). In addition, counselors who consult with colleagues do not disclose confidential information that reasonably could lead to the identification of a client or other person or organization unless they have obtained prior consent or the disclosure cannot be avoided (§B.7.b.). In peer consultations, confidentiality issues are not particularly difficult to manage. It is usually possible for a counselor to consult without revealing the identity of the client who is the subject of the consultation. Even if the consultant were to ascertain the client's identity, the consultant understands the professional obligation to keep information confidential.

In organizational consulting, it is important that those who participate in the process have a clear understanding of the limits of confidentiality. Consultants have an ethical responsibility to ensure that the participants understand what information will be gathered, how it will be used, with whom it will be shared, and for what purpose (Simpson & Glowiak, 2012). Managing confidentiality is particularly complicated when consultation is aimed at organizational change (Newman, 1993). If disgruntled employees share information about their boss with the consultant, will the consultant keep their disclosures confidential? Dougherty (2014) has suggested that employing the concept of anonymity—sharing the information but protecting its source—might be a useful strategy in such situations. He also suggests that complex questions about confidentiality should be posed at the outset of consultation, consensus on the answers reached, and the consensus publicized.

The Consultation Relationship

Because the consultant–consultee–client relationship is very complex, consultants must be particularly careful to maintain appropriate boundaries. Because counseling, supervision, and consultation are alike in several ways and there is some role overlap, it can be easy for counselors to confuse these activities with each other. Similarities and differences are outlined in the following paragraphs.

Consultation and *counseling* are similar in that both usually are voluntary in nature and each is a temporary process aimed at assisting the help seeker to function independently, without the helper, in the future. Both counseling and consultation are collaborative relationships, but they are not relationships between equals. In each relationship one participant is assumed to have greater expertise that can be brought to bear on the problem. Consultation and counseling are different in that counseling is a dyadic relationship in which a direct service is provided to a client, whereas consultation involves a triadic relationship in which an indirect service is provided to someone who works directly with a client. Counseling generally focuses on personal problems, whereas consultation focuses on work-related problems.

Consultation and *supervision* are similar in that both relationships are tripartite; the person who provides assistance to the client does so indirectly through a third party (the consultee or the supervisee). In both relationships, the goal is to increase the help seeker's skills and ability to function independently. They are different in that supervision is not always voluntary, and in a supervisory relationship the person in the help-seeker role may not be free to decline the helper's advice or recommendations without penalty. Supervision is a hierarchical relationship, whereas consultation is a collaborative relationship: consultants have no direct authority over the help seeker. Also, supervision is generally ongoing or long term, whereas peer consultation is usually temporary and of brief duration.

The focus of the consultation relationship should be on work-related problems, not on the personal problems of the consultee. As is the case in supervisory relationships, there is a fine line to be drawn, and it can be difficult to distinguish between professional concerns and personal issues. For example, assume you are a school counselor who has been approached by a teacher who wants help in dealing with a difficult student. During the consultation, the teacher says, "You're helping me see that the student's behavior isn't all that much out of line. If I weren't in the midst of a painful divorce, he wouldn't be getting under my skin this way." You must be careful to avoid converting the consultation into a counseling relationship that centers on the teacher's personal problems.

Dual relationships in consultation create conflicts of interest as well as role conflicts. The two most common dual roles in consultation are combining the role of consultant with that of counselor or supervisor (Dougherty, 2014). The blurring of boundaries that leads consultants into the counselor role often occurs when a consultant determines that the basis for a work-related concern resides more in the consultee than in the client. In these instances, the consultant should refer the consultee for assistance.

When a consultant has supervisory or administrative experience, it can be easy to incorporate supervision into a consulting relationship. This is inappropriate because consultation is essentially a peer relationship, whereas supervision involves evaluation and a power differential. Dougherty (2014) has noted that the use of supervision in consultation allows the consultant to build an illegitimate power base, creates potential conflicts of interest, and violates the consultation contract. Dual relationships in consultation should be avoided.

Freedom of choice is the final important relationship issue to consider in consultation. Consultees should feel comfortable that they have the freedom to do whatever they choose to do with the consultant's recommendations. Freedom of choice is diminished when a dependency on the consultant is created. Consultants must avoid coercing, pressuring, or manipulating consultees into taking actions that the consultant might advocate. Having a clear understanding at the outset about the parameters of the relationship can help prevent later problems caused by blurred boundaries.

The Role of Values and Diversity in Consultation

Consultants, like counselors, must be aware of the ways in which their values and world views influence the process and outcomes of their work. As Newman (1993) has stated, "To ignore or deny the central role of values in the practice of consultation is naive at best, and from an ethical perspective, dangerous" (p. 151). The consultant, consultee, and client or members of the client system all have values formed by their life experiences, and these values will have a mutual influence in the consulting process. Therefore, consultants must possess a reflective understanding of their values and how they influence the process of consultation and make a commitment not to impose them on consultees (Dougherty, 2014). In addition, consultants must understand diverse world views and be aware of differences in reasoning and communication patterns. They must be aware of how their own culture and gender affect their work as consultants.

Value conflicts may be inevitable in organizational consulting because the process involves multiple parties who have diverse and often competing interests and priorities. Conflicts can occur in peer consultations as well, particularly when the consultant and consultee have differing world views. For example, Pete, a Native American counselor, has asked Judy, a traditionally trained Anglo counselor, to consult with him regarding a client with whom he is working. Pete believes that the client would be well served by bringing members of the client's family into the counseling process. Judy disagrees, believing that this would diminish the client's autonomy and violate the client's confidentiality. In this case, the consultant and consultee have very different ideas, formed by their world views, regarding how the client can best be helped. Judy is operating from Euro-American notions of individualism and autonomy. For Pete, including the client's family would be consistent with the tradition of honoring the wisdom of tribal elders, which is part of his cultural background. Consultants must be honest with themselves in determining whether they can be objective enough to work with a consultee whose values or world views differ significantly from their own.

Increasingly, consultants are providing their services during crisis and disaster situations. Consultants need knowledge and skills that are unique to these situations, including how to conduct a lethality assessment, familiarity with organizational crisis policies and procedures, crisis intervention skills, and knowledge of how to develop a disaster plan (Corey, Corey, Corey, & Callanan, 2015).

Summary and Key Points

Supervision and consultation are two types of tripartite relationships that involve complex ethical considerations. Legal issues in supervision and consultation have to do primarily with fair evaluation, accountability, and contracts. Supervision is an intervention that an experienced member of a profession provides to a novice member of that profession. Consultation is a process in which a counselor assists a consultee with a work-related problem related to a client or client system.

Key points regarding supervision include the following:

- There are two types of supervision—administrative and clinical—that differ in the amount of control or authority that the supervisor has over the supervisee.
- Supervisors must be sensitive to the due process rights of their supervisees, especially with respect to the obligation to provide ongoing feedback and evaluation of supervisee performance.
- Informed consent for supervision must be obtained from both the client and the supervisee.
- Points that should be discussed between a supervisor and a supervisee before they enter into a working relationship include the purposes of supervision; the logistics of supervision; information about the supervisor's qualifications and supervisory style; the expectations, roles, and responsibilities of both parties; evaluation; and ethical and legal practice.

- Written supervision agreements are recommended to avoid misunderstandings and to articulate the nature of the supervisory relationship.
- The requirements to keep client information confidential in counseling relationships apply equally to supervision relationships.
- Boundaries in the supervisory relationship must be managed carefully. Supervisors should not engage in close personal or social relationships with their supervisees, nor should they establish a counseling relationship as a substitute for supervision. Of course, sexual intimacies between supervisors and supervisees are unethical.
- Supervisors have a large scope of responsibility and a number of parties to whom they are accountable. Under the legal principle of *vicarious liability*, to the extent that supervisors have direct control and authority over their supervisees, they may be held liable for their negligence.
- Both the supervisor and the supervisee have certain rights and responsibilities in the relationship. It is crucial that both parties understand these rights and responsibilities in order for supervision to work in facilitating supervisee growth while protecting client welfare.

Counselors frequently take on the roles of consultant and consultee. Two types of consultation discussed in this chapter are peer consultation and organizational consultation. Key points regarding consultation include the following:

- Because consultants generally do not have direct control and authority over those who receive their services, they cannot be held accountable legally for the negligence of the consultee.
- When counselors enter into long-term agreements to provide consultation services, they should negotiate a written contract for the services.
- Consultants must be aware of the ways in which their values and their cultural backgrounds influence the consulting process and outcomes.

- Counselors must ensure that they have the needed competencies before they agree to take on a consulting role with a peer or with an organization.
- Consultants must take care to safeguard the informed consent and confidentiality rights of consultees and clients.
- Consultation focuses on work-related problems, not on the personal problems, of the consultee. Maintaining this work-related focus, avoiding the dual relationship problems that are created by blending consultation with counseling or supervision, and ensuring consultee freedom of choice are all important consultant obligations.

CHAPTER 16

Professional Writing, Conducting Research, and Publishing

FOCUS QUESTIONS

1. What is plagiarism, and why do you think so many college students get into trouble because they plagiarize?

2. Why do you think it is important for master's-level counselors to understand research?

3. Why do you think the U.S. government has required universities and other organizations that conduct research to establish institutional review boards that review research proposals to ensure that human subjects are protected from harm?

This chapter explores ethical and legal issues involved when graduate students, counselors, or counselor educators engage in the scholarly activities of professional writing, research, and publication. Issues of academic integrity arise in many situations. Students in counselor preparation programs are expected to perform in an honest manner as they write term papers, complete course assignments, take tests, and prepare tapes of counseling sessions during practicum and internship. Counseling supervisees are required to report to their supervisors, in an accurate manner, counseling-related tasks they perform. Professors who teach and supervise counseling students and supervisees expect information to be reported to them in an honest fashion.

Wester (2007, 2011) has noted that little has been written about research integrity in counseling and has called upon professional counselors who conduct research to better inform themselves regarding their ethical obligations. If you are a full-time counseling practitioner or a master's-level graduate student, you may be thinking that a discussion of research or scholarship has only minimal relevance to what you do or intend to do. It is true that counseling practitioners, traditionally, have not engaged in research or even read much research (Tracey, 1991). Even today, counselors tend to view research and publication as activities that are performed by their professors, by doctoral-level graduate students, or by counselors whose employment depends on governmental or private funding sources that demand research to show that grant or contract dollars are well spent. You should be aware, however, that current economic and societal trends are challenging the assumptions that practitioners do not need to involve themselves in research activities (Watts, 2015; Welfel, 2013).

Counselors in schools and agencies' are experiencing increased demands for accountability (Eschenauer & Chen-Hayes, 2005; Gysbers, 2004). More and more, counselors are being required to demonstrate that they are making a difference in the lives of children and adults (Erford et al., 2011). They are being asked to show that their services are having an effect on societal concerns such as school shootings, teen suicide, school failure and dropping out, unemployment, and the spread of sexually transmitted diseases (Lancaster, Balkin, Garcia, & Valarezo, 2011). Managed care companies are demanding accountability from counselors as well. They are requiring counselors whose services they are reimbursing to demonstrate that their treatments are effective with the clients served. Although Sexton (2001) has suggested that *best practice* in counseling must be *evidence based,* Ray et al. (2011) found in a review of articles from 1998 to 2007 in American Counseling Association division-affiliated journals that only 6% of counseling research articles explored effectiveness of counseling interventions. In recent years, articles focused on evidence and best practice (Choate & Gintner, 2011; Miller, Short, Garland, & Clark, 2010; Whiston, Tai, Rahardja, & Eder, 2011) are appearing more frequently. External pressures suggest that more counselors will be involved in conducting research and disseminating the results in the future (Crane & Law, 2002). Perhaps this involvement will help to close the gap between what researchers discover and the way in which counselors practice (Murray, 2009).

Many practicing counselors collect data and write reports. In addition, doctoral-level counseling graduate students and university counselor educators are heavily involved in research. Davis, Wester, and King (2008) have found that questionable research practices do exist within the counseling profession. This chapter highlights some of the important ethical, legal, and professional issues in writing, conducting research, and publishing.

PROFESSIONAL WRITING

Writing often is a significant part of the professional activities of counselors. Counselors in all settings are required to create a multitude of documents, including notes from client sessions, evaluations of clients, reports regarding counseling programs, correspondence among counseling staff members, and letters to individuals outside the setting where counselors work.

Graduate students in counselor preparation programs write many term papers and reports that are submitted to professors. The general principles regarding academic integrity apply to the writing activities of counseling graduate students, practicing counselors, supervisors, and counselor educators alike. The following discussion, however, is intended primarily to assist graduate students, whom we often see struggle with the needs to avoid plagiarism and to master APA style.

Academic Integrity

Although the vast majority of counseling students are diligent in their efforts to practice academic integrity, instances of academic dishonesty do occur. Some scholars have studied motivation to engage in academic dishonesty. Williams, Craig, and Paulhus (2010) conducted a series of three studies in an effort to predict academic dishonesty and to better understand why students cheat. In past studies (Cizek, 1999; Stern & Havlicek, 1986), two-thirds of students surveyed have reported cheating, and in a more recent study (Robinson, Amburgey, Swank, & Faulker, 2004), up to 80% reported having been academically dishonest. A number of research studies have suggested that cheating might be predicted based on gender, subject matter being studied, ethnicity, or personality traits, but those findings are inconclusive. A popular belief is that technology and the Internet have changed the way in which students define academic dishonesty, especially plagiarism (Baird & Dooey, 2014; Lee, 2011). Gabriel (2010) reported that scholars and professors around the United States are saying that many students do not believe that lifting the writing of others and claiming it as their own is wrong for a number of reasons. Many students note that Web pages often do not include author information; some see much information on the Web as *common knowledge*; many have downloaded music (perhaps illegally) without even a thought that doing so might be wrong or illegal; and some argue that the ideas of originality and author ownership are outmoded in today's technological world. In addition, digital technology makes copying and pasting written information from the Internet very easy (Isaacs, 2011).

Although it is understood why modern students may believe that plagiarism is acceptable, the ACA *Code of Ethics* (American Counseling Association, 2014) specifically prohibits plagiarism; most universities have strict honor codes or academic rules that prohibit plagiarism; and copyright laws in the United States provide legal protections of original works by authors. One major problem in dealing with the issue of plagiarism is that many students (and many professors as well) are not sure of exactly what constitutes plagiarism. According to §G.5.b. of the ACA *Code of Ethics* (ACA, 2014), counselors must not plagiarize, which is defined as presenting another person's work as one's own. The *Publication Manual of the American Psychological Association* (APA, 2010) includes similar prohibitions against plagiarism. Watts (2015) has pointed out that some guidelines regarding plagiarism can be confusing and difficult to interpret. First, the *Code of Ethics* (ACA, 2014) requires counselors to give credit to previous work on a topic by others *or self* (§G.5.c). This means that authors do not present their own work as if it were not previously published. Students may wonder whether this means that they must cite their own work if they turn in a paper containing material that builds on a previously submitted paper. Second, the *Publication Manual of the American Psychological Association* (APA, 2010) states that the practice of presenting the work of others as if it were one's own work can extend to *ideas* as well as written words. It is difficult to know where many ideas originated. Because plagiarism is so difficult to understand, teaching students about plagiarism and giving them strategies for avoiding it are vitally important tasks (Elander, Pittam, Lusher, Fox, & Payne, 2010; Wester, 2011).

Universities and legal authorities impose severe sanctions for plagiarism. In universities, students found guilty of plagiarism could be given a failing grade on an assignment, issued an academic warning, suspended, or even expelled. In courts of law, those who plagiarize might have to pay monetary damages to the original author for having stolen his or her ideas or words.

A number of websites exist today where professors or editors of journals or texts may enter what has been written by someone else and check to see if the phrases, sentences, paragraphs, or passages are plagiarized (Lee, 2011). Examples of such websites include turnitin.com, plagiarism-checker.com, articlechecker.com, plagiarismdetect.org, and doccop.com. The existence of these websites is testimony to the fact that many academics are aggressive about exposing individuals who plagiarize, with some demanding that they be punished. Our position is that, generally, punishment should not be the first alternative considered when plagiarism is detected. Rather, the offender should be educated regarding the inappropriateness of plagiarizing. However, individuals who

- It is acceptable and common in academic writing to use ideas, direct quotations, or paraphrased information from others. The key is to always give credit to other authors when you do that.

- Always give a citation to another author's work when you quote or paraphrase what the other author has said.

- Generally, in academic writing, paraphrasing is valued more highly than using direct quotations. Usually, direct quotations should be used when it is impossible to communicate what another writer has said without using his or her exact words. It is always essential to give credit to other authors when paraphrasing what they have said.

- When introducing the ideas of another author, use phrases such as "According to Smith . . ." or "Jones said . . ." or "In his 1987 study, Robinson found. . . ."

- Always put quotation marks around direct words, phrases, sentences, or excerpts when another author's direct words are quoted.

- If you paraphrase information from another author, look back over what you have written and what the other author wrote to ensure that you have not used any exact phrases used by the other author. If it is important to use exact phrases from another author, put those phrases inside quotation marks.

- Read examples of good paraphrasing and poor paraphrasing so you can understand how to paraphrase appropriately.

- You do not have to give a source for information that is considered *common knowledge*. For example, it is generally agreed that Christopher Columbus discovered America in 1492, that the boiling point of water is 100 degrees Celsius, and that Mark Twain wrote *Huckleberry Finn*. As a result of common knowledge, you do not have to attribute such generally accepted information to a source. However, if some other person has given a unique interpretation to common knowledge facts, then you would have to give that person credit for his or her unique perspective. If you are in doubt as to whether a particular piece of information is common knowledge, it is always a good idea to provide a citation to an authority who has stated the knowledge.

- If one author quotes another, it is always best to find the original author's statement rather than rely on the second author's interpretation of what the first author said. If you do quote one author's quotation of another, make it clear in your writing that is what you are doing.

- All instances of plagiarism are unacceptable, even if they are unintentional, small, or seemingly unimportant.

FIGURE 16-1   Tips for avoiding plagiarism

Source: Pearson Education, Inc., Hoboken, NJ.

repeatedly plagiarize and purposefully steal the ideas and writing of others should not be allowed to continue to do so.

A helpful tutorial on plagiarism that students can access is provided by Indiana University, and many other universities and organizations have provided guidelines to writers for avoiding plagiarism (Empire State College, 2011; Fowler, 2003; Office of Research Integrity, 2011; Roig, 2009; The Writing Place, 2005). The tips for avoiding plagiarism in Figure 16-1 were created from their suggestions.

16-1 The Case of Sylvia

Sylvia is a first-year master's-degree student in a counselor education program. She was required to write a term paper in her counseling theories course. While she was collecting information to put in her paper, she kept a careful record of the APA citations of texts, text chapters, and professional journal articles she read. Each time she read a professional source, she jotted down notes about what she had read so she could include the information in her term paper. Occasionally, she wrote down direct quotes from an author and put quotation marks around the materials and indicated the page number where the quote appeared when she did so.

Unfortunately, at one point Sylvia forgot to put quote marks around a few sentences that were a direct quote, and she later thought she had written the information herself. So she copied the sentences into her term paper, thinking they expressed thoughts she had created herself.

Sylvia's theories course professor, Dr. Adams, routinely submitted all student papers to an Internet service that checked for plagiarism. The sentences Sylvia had written in her paper were identified as direct quotes from an article Sylvia had cited in her paper, but Sylvia had not attributed the quotes to the author of the article.

Dr. Adams recently had dealt with several other instances of serious plagiarism in her classes, so she submitted Sylvia's paper and evidence of Sylvia's plagiarism to the Office of Judicial Affairs at her university and filed a formal complaint alleging that Sylvia had plagiarized.

- What other actions could Dr. Adams have taken?
- Do you think Sylvia should be punished for having plagiarized?

Discussion: The actions described in this case study are clearly an example of a situation in which a student who plagiarized should be educated rather than punished. Dr. Adams could have met with Sylvia, showed Sylvia the evidence of her plagiarism, and asked Sylvia to explain what had happened. Dr. Adams would have then learned of Sylvia's mistake and could have helped Sylvia avoid similar mistakes in the future. Of course, Sylvia is responsible for the errors she made, and if Dr. Adams believed a consequence was warranted, she might have deducted points on Sylvia's paper or given her a lower grade. Putting Sylvia through an extended ordeal with the university's Office of Judicial Affairs could have been avoided if Dr. Adams had reacted differently.

Proper citation of sources is essential to avoid plagiarism. Generally, professors require graduate students to write their research papers and to cite using APA style. The sixth edition of the *Publication Manual of the American Psychological Association* (APA, 2010) is an indispensable resource, and further assistance can be accessed at apastyle.org. Purdue University also has established several websites to assist students with professional writing; these can be found by typing *Purdue Owl* into a search engine.

CONDUCTING RESEARCH

Conducting research in an ethical manner is essential (Wester, 2011). Perhaps the first question that should be addressed in a discussion of research procedures is this: Who conducts a research study, and who is responsible for ensuring that it is carried out in an ethical and legally appropriate manner?

Research Roles

The American Psychological Association (APA, 1982) has described several roles in research. The first is the *principal investigator*, who conceptualizes, designs, and plans the study. If the principal investigator carries out the research alone, of course, the ethical and legal responsibilities fall to this one individual. The Code of Ethics (ACA, 2014) specifies that the ultimate responsibility for ethical research practice lies with the principal researcher (§G.1.f.).

More often, though, the principal investigator has one or more persons who assist in the data collection, statistical analysis, or other components of the research study. In these instances, a second role is that of *research assistant*. In academia, students often play this role when they assist their professors with research. When this is the case, both the principal investigator and the research assistant(s) are responsible for proper behavior, but the principal investigator, as the supervisor, has the ultimate responsibility for any breaches of ethics or law that might occur.

A third role is that of *research supervisor*. This person advises and oversees the research of someone else. In an academic setting, this typically would be a professor who supervises the doctoral dissertation or master's thesis research of a student. These relationships are based on mutual respect and are more co-equal because graduate students are knowledgeable researchers who have been trained in research procedures and in ethics.

A discussion of roles raises the issue of potential dual relationships. Professors who supervise thesis or dissertation research often have other relationships with the students involved. They may be simultaneously supervising students' clinical work in an internship, teaching them in formal courses, mentoring them toward their transition into the world of work, co-presenting with them at professional conferences, interacting with them as peers at meetings of local professional organizations, and writing letters of recommendation for their future employment. Most of these roles have an evaluative component, thus giving the professor considerable power over the student who is conducting the research.

Because of this power differential and the resultant potential for exploitation, counselor educators must attend carefully to ethical issues when they involve their students as research subjects or research assistants. Students' participation as research subjects should be voluntary. Certainly, professors should not require students to participate in their research as part of the student's grade or evaluation. Beyond that minimal requirement, they also must realize that students can feel pressured or even coerced to serve as subjects for professors' research.

When students volunteer or are asked to serve as research assistants, a full discussion must take place before the students agree to participate. In this discussion, the counselor educator should provide (a) assurance that there will be no penalty to students who decline to participate, (b) a clarification of expectations regarding who will do which parts of the work, (c) a timeline for completion of the various tasks, (d) an agreement about the type of acknowledgment that the students will receive when the research is published (including whether they will be listed as co-authors), and (e) an agreement about the process that will be followed if any problems or misunderstandings should occur. The Association for Counselor Education and Supervision (ACES) has published guidelines for research mentorship that provide thorough guidance on professor–student research collaboration (Borders et al., 2012).

Research Design

The overarching goal of all counseling research is, in a global sense, to identify interventions that will facilitate positive changes in clients and in their lives (Szymanski & Parker, 2001). Research studies must be rigorously and carefully designed.

Even when research is of high quality, experimental design raises some ethical considerations. Some researchers use a control group that does not receive the potential benefits of the treatment being investigated. If a delay in receiving treatment increases subject discomfort, or if the emotional conditions of control group members deteriorate while they are participating in the study, client welfare is at issue. The conundrum is that whether the experimental treatment is indeed beneficial cannot be known without conducting the study. One way to reduce risk to control group participants is to compare the experimental treatment with other treatments known to be effective, if such an option is available and viable. If the experimental treatment is found to be effective, the researcher has an ethical obligation to offer it to control group participants as soon as possible after the experiment is completed.

The ethical issues discussed thus far apply to quantitative research, which was once the predominant method of conducting research in the social sciences. A relatively recent development in counseling research is the burgeoning of qualitative research (Hays & Wood, 2011). Unlike quantitative research—which uses statistics to control, explain, and predict—qualitative research uses words to create rich descriptions to understand the experiences of people who have *lived* a particular phenomenon. Qualitative research is particularly well suited to the counseling field (Hunt, 2011), as it acknowledges the diversity of experience and honors "both empirical data and the power of personal narrative" (Paisley, 1997, p. 4).

DIVERSITY CONSIDERATIONS IN RESEARCH DESIGN   Designing research studies in counseling is an incredibly challenging process. Being sensitive to diversity issues means taking into consideration the complexity of variables involved in research with human beings. Szymanski and Parker (2001) have stated that contextual variables include client characteristics (such as gender, race or ethnicity, age, socioeconomic status, attitudes and values, and world views), counselor variables (including all of the same individual characteristics that apply to clients, plus training, experience, and theoretical orientation), and counseling process variables (interactional and reciprocal aspects of counseling) It is impossible to control for all these factors, yet any variance must be explained.

To give just a few examples of the importance of contextual variables, researchers should not generalize their results to populations not represented in their sample. If a study's participants were only men, the researcher cannot make generalizations to both genders. If the participants were primarily White and middle class, the researcher must acknowledge the generalizability limitations of the study with respect to race, ethnicity, and socioeconomic status.

The *Code of Ethics* (ACA, 2014) states that counselors "minimize bias and respect diversity in designing and implementing research" (Section G, Introduction). Several difficulties present themselves in conducting research with ethnic minority groups and women (Kurasaki, Sue, Chun, & Gee, 2000). First, counseling practices based on Western theories or treatment modalities may be culturally inappropriate for some members of minority groups. Thus, studies that measure the effectiveness of traditional approaches may not produce valid results with minority research participants. Second, researchers often have difficulty finding an appropriate sample to study, due to the small size of some minority populations and the unwillingness of some groups (such as illegal immigrants) to become research participants. Third, because race or ethnicity and gender are closely linked to other variables such as socioeconomic status, researchers must account for these other variables before attributing any differences to race or gender. Fourth, as we noted in Chapter 7, many standardized tests have questionable validity when used with minority group research participants. Despite all these obstacles, however, a growing body of culture-sensitive research (e.g., Arenas & Paz Sandin, 2009; Nagayama-Hall, 2001; Ojeda, Flores, Meza, & Morales, 2011; Smith, 2010) is making contributions to our understanding.

Protecting Research Participants from Harm

In every research project that involves human subjects, there is some risk to the participants. Although counseling research rarely poses physical risks, there may be psychological risks because participation can cause discomfort, stress, anxiety, or distress. The ACA ethical standards (ACA, 2014) remind counselors who conduct research that they are responsible for the participants' welfare and should "take reasonable precautions to avoid causing injurious psychological, emotional, physical, or social effects" to the participants (§G.1.e.). Three ways to minimize risks to participants are to (a) ensure that participation is voluntary, (b) secure participants' informed consent, and (c) protect the confidentiality of participants.

VOLUNTARY PARTICIPATION   Ethical standards encourage researchers to make participation in their research voluntary. When counselors conduct research involving clients, the counselors must make it clear to clients that they are free to choose whether to participate (ACA, 2014, §G.2.c.).

16-2 The Case of Clay

Clay is a counselor educator interested in conducting a research study related to older students' success in college. He plans to study whether individual mentoring of older college students helps them succeed academically. At his university, there is a program for at-risk students whose grade point averages were below 2.0 the previous semester. To continue at the university, these students must participate in an at-risk student program that requires them to attend study skills classes and meet with an academic support group each week. The director of the program has agreed to allow Clay to include as participants in the study all students in the program who are above the age of 40. The director has offered to tell these students that participating in Clay's study is a requirement of the at-risk program. Clay is wondering whether it would be ethical for the director to require students to participate in his study.

- Do you think requiring the students to participate would be ethical? Why or why not?
- What might Clay do to ensure that students who participate in his study are not harmed in any way?

Discussion: Such an arrangement is not unethical. Although it is best if participation in a study is voluntary, researchers do not always have to study only those who volunteer to participate. Clay should inform participants that they can discontinue participation at any time they wish, and he should follow up with any students who drop out to determine whether they need assistance for any reason. Another method of addressing this situation would be, after the data have been collected, to ask students whether they are agreeable to having Clay utilize their data in the study. In that way, all students would have participated in the program, but only those who agreed would have their data included in the study.

Researchers must be particularly careful to protect the rights of participants who may not be participating voluntarily or who may be vulnerable to abuse, such as prisoners, hospital patients, residents of institutions, or individuals who are not competent to give consent. Children should be given the opportunity to assent to participation, although legally their parents or guardians must give informed consent (Welfel, 2013).

INFORMED CONSENT   The ACA (2014) ethical standards go into great detail regarding what informed consent for research should entail (§G.2.a.). Participants have a right to receive a full explanation of the following, in language that they understand:

- The purpose of the research and procedures to be followed (Researchers must explain to participants what they will be expected to do and how long it will take.)
- Any procedures that are experimental or relatively untried
- Discomforts and risks involved, and the power differential that exists between researchers and participants
- Benefits or changes in individuals or organizations that might be expected (There are many possible benefits, but basically, they can be considered to be external, such as money, or internal, such as learning something new or making a contribution to science.) (Wilkinson & McNeil, 1996)
- Appropriate alternative procedures that might be advantageous for participants
- Their right to have their questions answered regarding the procedures
- Any limitations on confidentiality (For example, if a participant showed signs of suicidal ideation, confidentiality concerns would be secondary to concerns for ensuring the person's safety.)
- The format and target audiences for dissemination of the research findings
- Their freedom to withdraw their consent and discontinue their participation at any time, without penalty

A troublesome issue in informed consent is that of concealment or deception. There can be some very good reasons for researchers to withhold certain information from participants. For example, if participants know the goals of the study, their desire to perform in socially desirable and helpful ways can skew the data. Some measure of concealment can often be justified. After data are collected, however, researchers must provide participants with information that will "remove any misconceptions participants have regarding the research" (ACA, 2014, §G.2.g.).

Deception is a more difficult matter. Researchers should be cautious about deliberately misinforming participants about the purpose of the study. The ethical guidelines for psychologists are explicit about deception. They specify that researchers never deceive participants about significant aspects that would affect their willingness to participate, such as physical risks, discomfort, or unpleasant emotional experiences. In addition, any deception must be explained to participants as early as feasible, preferably at the conclusion of their participation but not later than at the conclusion of the research. During the explanation, the researcher is obligated to try to correct any misperceptions that participants may have (APA, 2012).

CONFIDENTIALITY   The third consideration in minimizing risks to research participants is confidentiality. Information obtained about research participants during the course of a study must be kept confidential (ACA, 2014, §G.2.d.). Researchers can ensure confidentiality in several ways. During data collection or in scoring protocols, a coding system rather than participants' names can be used. Any material collected (such as written reports, test scores, or audiotaped interviews) that includes identifying information about participants must be kept securely in a locked file or in computer files protected by passwords to which only the investigators and their assistants have access.

The *Code of Ethics* (ACA, 2014) also addresses relationships between researchers and research participants. When researchers consider extending the boundaries of the relationship beyond conventional parameters, they consider the risks and benefits and document any unusual actions taken (§G.3.a.). Sexual or romantic relationships (both in-person and electronic) with current research participants are prohibited (§G.3.b.), and research participants are not sexually harassed (§G.3.c.).

When results are reported, participants' names are not used. The *Code of Ethics* (ACA, 2014) requires researchers to protect the confidentiality of participants (§G.2.d.). When reporting case studies or other descriptive information about research participants, all identifying details must be disguised. People who participate in research studies have a right to expect to have their anonymity or confidentiality protected.

Institutional policies often require researchers to guarantee anonymity to participants when their informed consent is obtained. Once a researcher has guaranteed that a participant's identity will not be revealed, the researcher must take care to avoid disclosure (Wilkinson & McNeil, 1996). If a lawsuit were filed claiming damages for disclosure of a research participant's identity, courts probably would try to determine whether the researcher had made reasonable efforts to ensure anonymity after promising to do so. Careless disclosure of research participants' identities could cause legal problems for those who engage in counseling research.

Welfel (2013) has raised an ethical concern about research that does not involve the actual participation of clients but instead reviews client records. Securing the informed consent of the clients may seem unnecessary because they are not put at risk or inconvenienced, but it would be ethically questionable to proceed on such an assumption. Unless the clients were told when they entered counseling that their records would be utilized in a research study, Welfel believes that the researcher should attempt to contact the clients and request their permission to review the records. If this is not feasible, the counselors who produced the records might eliminate any identifying data from the records before giving the researcher access to them. Other researchers would argue that it would not be necessary to obtain consent from former clients to collect data from records as long as the researcher did not disclose the names of clients to others and did not identify the clients in reporting the study's results.

Institutional Review Boards

Many of the ethical mandates regarding the protection of research participants are legal requirements as well. The National Research Act of 1974 requires institutions that receive any federal funds to establish committees to review research proposals to ensure that human participants are protected (Maloney, 1984). National Research Act of 1974 regulations have been developed with specific requirements for researchers (45 Code of Federal Regulations 46). The penalty for violation of the requirements would be removal of federal funds from the institution, which would be devastating for both public and private institutions because almost all receive substantial federal support.

Universities and other research institutions have institutional review boards (IRBs) that approve and oversee research involving human subjects. All investigators connected with an institution must have their research approved by an IRB, also sometimes called a *human subjects committee*. This applies to graduate students who conduct research as well as to faculty. IRBs, which have considerable power, typically require researchers to submit detailed proposals describing informed consent procedures, the voluntary nature of participation, and the protection of confidentiality of information collected (Welfel, 2013).

If you plan to conduct research during your graduate studies, your university will have a standard protocol for submitting your proposed research to its IRB. You will need to obtain this protocol, complete it carefully, and have it reviewed by your major professor before you begin your research study. If you are collecting data from more than one source (e.g., students at several universities), you may be required to obtain approval from all of the IRBs. When you apply for approval to conduct a research project, you must guarantee to the IRB that you will take a number of steps to protect human participants. If you fail to do the things you have promised, you could be held legally accountable by the institution and by any participant who was harmed.

Reporting Results

Once researchers have collected and analyzed the data from a study, they have four additional ethical obligations. According to the *Code of Ethics* (ACA, 2014), they need to honor their commitments to research participants (§G.2.f.), explain the nature of the study to remove any misconceptions (§G.2.g.), report their results honestly and accurately (§G.4.a., G.4.b., G.4.c.), and make available sufficient original research data to qualified professionals who may wish to replicate their study (§G.4.e.).

Commitments to Participants

When researchers make a commitment to research participants before their participation in the project, then those commitments must be honored after the project is completed (ACA, 2014, §G.2.g.). Often researchers offer to give participants feedback regarding the study after the research project has ended. In research parlance, the process of providing feedback is sometimes called *debriefing*. Some evidence seems to suggest that providing feedback may be a frequently neglected commitment. McConnell and Kerbs (1993) found that more than 30% of researchers failed to provide participants with the feedback they had promised. When this happens, the participants not only are left hanging with respect to the particular study but also are likely to be less enthusiastic about participating in future research studies.

If you plan to conduct research, you must consider (a) when you will offer to give feedback to your participants, (b) how you will give it, and (c) what you will tell them. In terms of timing, if you offer to give feedback, it should be given as soon as is feasible after the data are collected. You must also decide how much information you want to share about such aspects as the research purpose, hypotheses or research questions, the sample, and the contribution you hope the study will make. Carmen, the graduate student in the following case example, needs some help in deciding how to provide feedback.

16-3 The Case of Carmen

Carmen, a doctoral student in a counselor education program, is designing her dissertation study, which involves surveying Licensed Professional Counselors (LPCs) regarding their attitudes toward counseling men who batter. She intends to send her potential participants a survey, along with a cover letter explaining her study that also includes informed consent information. Carmen plans to utilize an on-line survey service to collect her data. She wants to protect participant confidentiality, so she plans to ask recipients to return the survey anonymously. She wants to offer to provide participants with a summary of her study's results but is unsure how to obtain their names and addresses without compromising their confidentiality. She asks her dissertation director for advice.

- What suggestions might her dissertation adviser offer?
- Why do you think participants should be provided with a summary of the study once it is completed, if they want one?

Discussion: Most on-line survey services allow for respondents to ask for feedback in such a way that their identity is not tied to their survey responses. Carmen's dissertation adviser might instead suggest that Carmen ask participants who want to receive the results summary to send her their names and addresses via e-mail. Of course, Carmen will need to follow up and send the summary to those who request it, and do so in a timely manner. Another option would be to publish the results in the newsletter of the LPC board, which all participants receive. A third option might be for Carmen to inform participants that the results will be posted on a website URL given to them.

Participants need to be provided with a summary of the study, if they want one, for the following reasons:

- It is respectful, after asking individuals to participate, to give them the results at a later date.
- Participants have a right to know the outcome of a study in which they have participated.
- Individuals who receive follow-up information might be more willing to participate in studies in the future.

Honest and Accurate Reporting of Results

Counselors are responsible for reporting research accurately and in a manner that minimizes the possibility that results will be misleading. They are prohibited from engaging in fraudulent research, distorting or misrepresenting data, or deliberately biasing their results (ACA, 2014, §G.4.a.).

Unfortunately, these practices may not be uncommon (Swenson, 1997). In the academic setting, pressures to *publish or perish* can be strong for assistant professors who are nearing their tenure decisions. Sometimes doctoral students, having become emotionally invested in producing a study with significant results, are tempted to ignore contrary findings or manipulate data to fit their expectations. The push for productivity can also be strong in research environments where continued funding depends on demonstrating that grant funds are being well spent. Miller and Hersen's (1992) text on research fraud cites numerous examples of the kinds of research misconduct that occur when a researcher's self-interest takes precedence over ethical standards.

The *Code of Ethics* (2014) provides some specific guidance regarding the full and accurate reporting of research results. First, ethical counselors do not ignore findings that run contrary to their hopes or expectations. They do not distort or misrepresent data or deliberately bias their results and describe the extent to which results are applicable for diverse populations (§G.4.a.). They must communicate the results of any research judged to be of professional value, even if it reflects unfavorably on institutions, programs, services, prevailing opinions, or vested interests (§G.4.b.). If they discover significant errors in their published research, they take reasonable steps to correct those errors (§G.4.c.).

Cooperating with Other Researchers

The ultimate aim of research in counseling is to improve the practice of the profession. As a body of evidence accumulates about the effectiveness of a counseling process or treatment strategy, it will be more widely applied, and more clients will be better served. Replication studies are one vital process through which this goal is accomplished. Thus, counselors have an ethical duty to "make available sufficient original research data to qualified professionals who may wish to replicate or extend the study" (ACA *Code of Ethics*, 2014, §G.4.e.).

What this means for you, as a researcher, is that you have an obligation to keep your raw data for a number of years so that other researchers can have access to it. As Welfel (2013) has pointed out, this is not such an onerous duty now that voluminous data can be stored on computer disks. If you receive a request for your data, you would be wise to follow the dictates of the APA *Ethical Principles* (APA, 2012), which require you to release the data if other researchers are conducting studies to verify your results (§8.14).

PUBLICATIONS

Ethical issues related to publication include giving credit to others for their work and following appropriate procedures for submitting work for publication consideration. Giving credit to others is a legal as well as an ethical issue. Other legal issues that are important to counselors who engage in all types of scholarly activities include observing copyright laws, signing contracts, and reporting income derived from research, presentations, or publications.

Giving Credit to Contributors

Earlier we mentioned the pressure to *publish or perish* that can exist among university faculty. This pressure can affect the behavior of professors and can also have a negative impact on their students.

The practice of evaluating professors for tenure, promotion, and merit pay increases based largely on their records of scholarly publications has fostered an atmosphere that is more competitive and self-interested than would be ideal. Sometimes counselor educators who are outstanding teachers are denied tenure for lack of sufficient publications and are forced to leave their university positions, to the dismay of their students and the professors themselves. Others are challenged to uphold their scholarly integrity under reward systems that give more credit for sole authorship than for cooperative research endeavors, for being listed as first author on a publication, and for producing publications in quantity with little consideration for quality. These factors, although they do not excuse inappropriate behavior, probably do contribute to such practices among professors as publishing student work under their own names or usurping first authorship for work that was more the student's than their own.

The *Code of Ethics* (ACA, 2014) addresses these practices in several ways. First, in publishing, counselors are familiar with and give recognition to previous work on a research topic and give full credit to those who deserve it (§G.5.c.). Second, they must give credit through "joint authorship, acknowledgment, footnote statements, or other appropriate means to those who have contributed significantly" to their work, in accordance with such contributions (§G.5.d.). Third, guidelines exist for determining the order and types of acknowledgment to be given when more than one person has contributed to research (Moore & Griffin, 2007). The principal contributor is listed first, whereas minor technical or professional contributions are acknowledged in notes or introductory statements (§G.5.d.). A student is listed as the principal author on an article that is substantially based on the student's course paper, project, dissertation, or thesis (§G.5.f.). This standard arose because students sometimes have felt taken advantage of by their professors.

It is important for you to be familiar with these guidelines if you are involved or are planning to be involved in research activities during your graduate studies. The professor with whom you are collaborating or whom you are assisting should have a conversation with you before you begin the research endeavor regarding the work you will do and the type of acknowledgment you will receive. If you will be contributing substantially to the project, your professor should discuss with you and any other co-authors the order in which names will appear, because the first author listed is generally assumed to have contributed the most to a collaborative project, and the last author listed is assumed to have contributed the least. The order of names should be open to negotiation throughout the project, and all authors must be in agreement by the time the product is published. If your professor does not offer to have a discussion with you about these matters, you should feel free to request it. In a study that included over 1,000 participants, Welfare and Sackett (2011) surveyed doctoral students and faculty members in education-related disciplines regarding how they made decisions related to journal article authorship. They found that respondents believed authorship decisions should be made before beginning work together and then evaluated throughout the project. In addition, respondents indicated that doctoral students should initiate authorship discussions to the same degree as faculty members do. However, the results indicated that faculty members usually decided independently who received credit for authoring manuscripts. To what extent do you think proper procedures were followed in the next case scenario?

16-4 The Case of Singh

Singh, a master's student in a counselor education program, wrote a term paper for Dr. Martinez's class that greatly impressed the professor. Dr. Martinez suggested to Singh that his paper could be published, with some modifications. Singh, although flattered and excited, admitted to Dr. Martinez that he didn't know anything about how to get published. The professor offered to help him. They met and established an agenda that described the needed additional research and revisions to the manuscript, divided the workload equally between them, and established timelines and a meeting schedule. They completed their task and submitted the manuscript for publication, with Singh listed as the senior (first named) author.

- Do you think it was appropriate that the professor was listed as a co-author of the article?
- How would you feel if one of your professors offered to help you publish a paper you had written?

Discussion: If the professor's contributions were substantial enough that they might eventually lead to the paper's publication, the professor being listed as an author is warranted. The paper will look much different when it is submitted for publication than it did when the student wrote it. The differences will be a result of the professor's advice.

Usually, students are excited when a professor offers to help them publish a paper they have written and are pleased to list their professor as a co-author. The process followed by Singh and Dr. Martinez seems to have met ethical guidelines. As you will see, when you read the following section, Singh may have several more time-consuming tasks to perform before his manuscript is published.

We turn now to the legal arena as it applies to the issue of giving credit to others. One source of litigation involves conflicts among multiple authors of scholarly work. Because individuals legally own the ideas that are reflected in written materials, multiple authors may argue over who owns which ideas.

Counselors who contribute to a scholarly work have legal rights regarding that work. When more than one person is involved, each author has some independent legal rights and some legal rights that require full agreement of all the involved authors (Leaffer, 1989). Each joint author has the full right to use the work or to allow others to reproduce it. However, agreement among all the joint authors is required to grant exclusive rights to the work or to transfer ownership rights of the work to a non-author. Authors also must agree on an equitable manner of sharing income derived from the product.

Financial compensation for written works usually occurs in conjunction with a contract signed by the author(s) and a publisher. The terms of such contracts vary substantially and should always specify the amount of compensation that will be paid to each author individually.

Problems occur in multiple authorship of scholarly works when counselors do not discuss issues such as percentage of ownership, order of listing of author names, and other joint authorship matters. If one of the authors believes that he or she has not received adequate recognition or financial compensation, the individual may have legal ownership rights that could be pursued.

Submitting Work for Publication Consideration

The primary ethical standard regarding the process of submitting work for publication has to do with duplicate submission. Counselors should submit their manuscripts for publication consideration to only one journal at a time (ACA, 2014, §G.5.g.). Other fields (such as law) allow multiple submissions of a manuscript to several refereed journals at one time, so the social sciences rule requiring submission to only one journal at a time can be frustrating for authors. Because the time that elapses between the original submission and the publication of a manuscript can be lengthy, there is always concern that the material will be outdated by the time it is published or that someone else may publish something similar in the interim. There is no alternative to this system, however. Turnaround time from submission to publication is improving in refereed journals due to advances in the use of technology.

If you conduct research with your professors, you will experience the frustrations of *the waiting game*. It is likely that you will need to rewrite and resubmit your manuscript, maybe more than once, or it may be rejected by the first journal to which you have submitted it. You and your professor will then need to rewrite it and submit it to another journal. This process takes many months, at best, and can take years. Patience is a necessary virtue if you intend to be active in conducting and publishing research.

The *Code of Ethics* (ACA, 2014) includes a lengthy standard to guide the activities of counselors who serve as editorial board members of refereed journals or who review manuscripts written by others. This standard states:

> Counselors who review materials submitted for publication, research, or other scholarly purposes respect the confidentiality and proprietary rights of those who submitted it. They make publication decisions based on valid and defensible standards. Counselors review article submissions in a timely manner and based on their scope and competency in research methodologies, and make every effort to only review materials that are within their scope of competency and use care to avoid personal biases. (§G.5.h.)

This standard was added to address questionable activities by some reviewers. Unfortunately, situations have occurred in which reviewers have stolen ideas from authors and used them as their own before the author's ideas were published, have been biased in their reviews of materials, have been dilatory in completing reviews, and have agreed to review materials that they were not qualified to comment on. Fortunately, these negative practices are unusual.

Copyright Laws

Counselors involved in research, presentations, or publishing need to be aware of basic legal principles involving copyright. Essentially, a copyright acknowledges legally that individuals *own* ideas once they have created them.

Authors of original written materials have a copyright immediately when the documents are produced (General Revision of the Copyright Law, 1999). Materials do not have to be registered with the U.S. Copyright Office to be protected from infringement. However, individuals who do register their materials might qualify for an award of attorney's fees and substantial statutory damages if someone *steals* their ideas (Patry, 1986).

Authors who wish to announce that they are protective of their work usually insert at the end of the document either the symbol © or the abbreviation *Copr.* followed by the year of first publication, with the author's name listed underneath. The © symbol indicates that authors are aware that their work is protected legally but does not necessarily indicate that the work has been registered (Henn, 1991).

Most written materials are legally protected from the time they are created until 50 years after the author's death. In the case of multiple authors, the copyright lasts until 50 years after the death of the last author. Copyright protection of tests, corporate products, or anonymous works lasts for 75 years from the date of first publication or 100 years from its date of creation, whichever date expires first.

When authors publish their work in a text or journal, they often assign or transfer their copyright to the publisher. As a result, a publisher, rather than the authors themselves, may own a copyright to a particular written work. The fact that a publication may no longer be available for purchase, or may be *out of print*, does not affect the author's or publisher's legal copyright protection. Permission to reproduce the work must still be obtained from the copyright owner.

Some publishers have become rather aggressive in protecting their copyrighted materials. Publishers sell for a profit the materials they produce, so they are naturally concerned when individuals duplicate their published materials and they lose income as a result. Cases against businesses that duplicate materials (Henn, 1991) have demonstrated that some publishers will bring lawsuits to protect their copyrighted materials.

Counselors who are involved in scholarly activities generally do not register their written materials with the U.S. Copyright Office because of the time and expense involved. However, when you produce materials that are unique, have a potential for a high commercial value, or might be susceptible to being illegally duplicated, you may wish to consider paying the required fees and registering them.

Counselors also must ensure that they do not infringe on the legal rights of others by duplicating protected materials without permission. Before duplicating any material, you should obtain permission from the copyright owner, either the author or the publisher (Johnson & Roark, 1996), and give credit to the author of the material. Most duplicating businesses, university printing operations, and publishers are familiar with the process of obtaining permission to duplicate copyrighted materials.

The extent to which individuals can use the copyrighted work of others is sometimes difficult to determine. The Reporters Committee for Freedom of the Press (2008) has developed guidelines to assist individuals in avoiding copyright infringement, which can be found at rcfp.org.

Contracts

Counselors who engage in scholarly activities sometimes enter into contracts with publishers, entities that fund research projects, or organizations that pay for presentations. Generally, when there are no financial dealings involved, such as pay, honoraria, or reimbursement of expenses, no contract is signed by the parties. When counselors benefit in some way financially from the scholarly activity in which they are engaged, a contract often is signed by all of the parties involved. Letters of agreement that are signed by two parties usually are legal contracts as well.

The legal assumption made when a contract is signed by two or more parties is that the written contract represents an agreement reached among the individuals involved after they have carefully considered all the options and after open negotiations have occurred. Another important assumption regarding contracts is that the written document covers all the issues that were important to the parties. These two assumptions generally are not true when counselors sign contracts related to their scholarly work, and this can cause problems for counselors at a later time.

The reality is that counselors generally sign, without questioning, contracts that are presented to them by the entities with whom they will be working. Most entities that contract with counselors for services use preprinted contract forms that usually have been prepared by the attorneys representing the entities. They are the result of years of experience in contracting with authors, presenters, and researchers. Specific terms are filled on blank lines. Attorneys who prepare contract forms naturally include terms that are favorable to their clients. As a result, such contract forms protect the rights of the entities who are buying the counselors' services, but they do not favor the counselors who will be signing them.

A further reality is that most counselors who produce scholarly works and who contract with entities for their services do not believe they have the financial resources to have contracts reviewed by their own attorneys. In addition, counselors may not have a favorable position in the negotiations process. The entities contracting with them can often go to other counselors for the same services if they cause problems in the negotiations process. These entities may be unwilling to alter their contract form for one individual.

The result is that most counselors engaged in writing, presenting, or conducting research usually sign the contract presented to them and hope for the best. Sometimes the only area that can be successfully negotiated with preprinted contracts is the amount of compensation or reimbursement. Most counselors sign very few contracts and have neither the position nor the resources to do anything more than read contracts presented to them, ask for clarification of terms they do not understand, negotiate basic financial matters, and finally sign them.

Of course, counselors who have unique credentials or talents have more negotiating power and can be more aggressive in the contract negotiations process. If substantial compensation is involved or if the publications could have a significant impact on their careers, they probably should hire an attorney to either negotiate contracts for them or at least advise them as they negotiate contracts for themselves. Beren and Bunnin (1983) have developed a guide for authors that includes advice on locating attorneys who specialize in publications law.

When a counselor is employed and the contract for a research project is between the institution and the funding entity, the contract usually is negotiated directly between the institution's representatives and the funding entity. A counselor may apply for external funding, but the contract goes to the counselor's employer.

When counselors receive funding that is external to their institution, it is important that they comply with the terms of their funding contract. The person who applies for a grant and receives the funding usually is responsible for ensuring that the money is spent properly.

The funded project's manager must sign all expenditure authorizations. Occasionally project managers engage in fraudulent practices that can lead to civil and criminal charges against them. Diverting project funds to other purposes, falsifying reimbursement requests, and failing to follow required bidding for service procedures are some of the fraudulent practices that may cause problems.

Reporting Income

When counselors receive any payment for their services, they must report it for income tax purposes. It does not matter whether the payment is called a fee, charge, payment, or even an honorarium. It is considered income by the Internal Revenue Service and must be reported.

In fact, counselors who receive income for their scholarly activities are in *private practice* and should conform to all of the legal requirements for private practices that are discussed in Chapter 13. A city or county business license should be purchased, and professional liability insurance should be secured.

Generally, the type of practice can be listed as *consultant*, and counselors are not required to be licensed as mental health professionals by their state to engage in many types of scholarly activities, such as writing, presenting workshops, or conducting research. State laws should be consulted to determine whether a license is required.

Summary and Key Points

This chapter deals with ethical and legal considerations that are important for counselors who write, who conduct research, and who report their findings in scholarly publications.

All counselors write when they are graduate students and later when they practice professionally. In addition, counselors who are professors and supervisors often must evaluate the writing of other counselors. There are ethical and legal implications regarding the writing activities of counselors, especially about plagiarism.

Some key points regarding writing include the following:

- Counselors in training must write many papers during their academic programs. Counselors in practice write reports, case notes, and other documents related to their jobs.
- Researchers have found that the majority of students admit to cheating or academic dishonesty.
- Some scholars have suggested that students today, because of the technological world we live in, are more comfortable incorporating the ideas or work of others as their own because it is so easy to cut and paste information from the Web and because there is less respect among young people for original creative works.
- Plagiarism is prohibited by ethical codes and laws in the United States.
- The *Publication Manual of the American Psychological Association* (APA, 2010) specifies that plagiarism is unacceptable and explains that plagiarism occurs when individuals present the work of others as their own.

- Counselors who plagiarize are punished by universities and in courts of law.
- Guidelines have been developed to assist counselors to avoid plagiarism.

Due to current demands for accountability of counselors in all settings, more counselors than ever before will probably be involved in conducting research and publishing their findings. The process of conducting research involves understanding the various roles that are involved, knowing how to design good studies, and protecting participants from harm. The process of reporting the results entails giving feedback to participants, reporting honestly and accurately, and cooperating with other researchers.

Some key points regarding research include the following:

- The principal investigator conceptualizes, designs, and plans a research study and has the primary responsibility for seeing that ethical and legal requirements are followed.
- Students sometimes serve as research assistants when they help with a professor's research project.
- The professor who supervises the master's thesis or doctoral dissertation of a graduate student is the research supervisor who shares ethical and legal responsibilities with the student investigator.
- Counselor educators must carefully manage dual roles with their students who are involved with them in research projects.
- Poorly designed research is actually unethical because it wastes the time of participants and

erodes the esteem in which research is generally held.

- Good research pays attention to issues of cultural diversity.
- Participating in a research study involves some level of risk to human participants; therefore, they must be protected from harm.
- Ways to protect participants are to ensure that their participation is voluntary, secure their fully informed consent to participate, and protect their confidentiality.
- Proposed research studies must be approved by institutional review boards, which are quite rigorous in evaluating research that involves human subjects.
- After a study is completed, researchers must debrief or give feedback to everyone who participated in the study.
- Despite the existence of many pressures to publish, counselors must report the results of their studies with complete honesty and accuracy.
- Researchers are required to keep their raw data and make them available to other researchers who might want to replicate the study.

Both ethical and legal issues exist in writing and publishing. One ethical issue is knowing the procedures for submitting one's work for publication. Legal issues include observing copyright laws, signing contracts, and reporting income. The issue of giving credit to others who have contributed to a research study has both ethical and legal dimensions. Some key points regarding publications include the following:

- Pressures to "publish or perish" that exist in academia can make it challenging for counselor educators to uphold their scholarly integrity.
- When publishing research, authors must give credit to all others who have contributed to the study, in accordance with their level of contribution.
- Counselors who produce scholarly works have legal rights regarding those works; when legal problems occur, they are usually due to multiple authorship.
- Counselors must not submit manuscripts for publication consideration to more than one social sciences journal at a time.
- Counselors must know the basic principles of copyright law.
- Counselors generally are not very adept at understanding contracts, although they may enter into contracts with publishers, entities that fund research, and organizations that pay them for giving presentations.
- All income received for scholarly activities must be reported to the Internal Revenue Service.

APPENDIX A

ACA *Code of Ethics*

MISSION

The mission of the American Counseling Association is to enhance the quality of life in society by promoting the development of professional counselors, advancing the counseling profession, and using the profession and practice of counseling to promote respect for human dignity and diversity.

ACA CODE OF ETHICS PREAMBLE

The American Counseling Association (ACA) is an educational, scientific, and professional organization whose members work in a variety of settings and serve in multiple capacities. Counseling is a professional relationship that empowers diverse individuals, families, and groups to accomplish mental health, wellness, education, and career goals.

Professional values are an important way of living out an ethical commitment. The following are core professional values of the counseling profession:

1. enhancing human development throughout the life span;
2. honoring diversity and embracing a multicultural approach in support of the worth, dignity, potential, and uniqueness of people within their social and cultural contexts;
3. promoting social justice;
4. safeguarding the integrity of the counselor–client relationship; and
5. practicing in a competent and ethical manner.

These professional values provide a conceptual basis for the ethical principles enumerated below. These principles are the foundation for ethical behavior and decision making. The fundamental principles of professional ethical behavior are

- *autonomy*, or fostering the right to control the direction of one's life;
- *nonmaleficence*, or avoiding actions that cause harm;
- *beneficence*, or working for the good of the individual and society by promoting mental health and well-being;
- *justice*, or treating individuals equitably and fostering fairness and equality;
- *fidelity*, or honoring commitments and keeping promises, including fulfilling one's responsibilities of trust in professional relationships; and
- *veracity*, or dealing truthfully with individuals with whom counselors come into professional contact.

ACA CODE OF ETHICS PURPOSE

The *ACA Code of Ethics* serves six main purposes:

1. The *Code* sets forth the ethical obligations of ACA members and provides guidance intended to inform the ethical practice of professional counselors.
2. The *Code* identifies ethical considerations relevant to professional counselors and counselors-in-training.
3. The *Code* enables the association to clarify for current and prospective members, and for those served by members, the nature of the ethical responsibilities held in common by its members.
4. The *Code* serves as an ethical guide designed to assist members in constructing a course of action that best serves those utilizing counseling services and establishes expectations of conduct with a primary emphasis on the role of the professional counselor.
5. The *Code* helps to support the mission of ACA.
6. The standards contained in this *Code* serve as the basis for processing inquiries and ethics complaints concerning ACA members.

The *ACA Code of Ethics* contains nine main sections that address the following areas:

> Section A: The Counseling Relationship
>
> Section B: Confidentiality and Privacy
>
> Section C: Professional Responsibility
>
> Section D: Relationships With Other Professionals
>
> Section E: Evaluation, Assessment, and Interpretation
>
> Section F: Supervision, Training, and Teaching
>
> Section G: Research and Publication
>
> Section H: Distance Counseling, Technology, and Social Media
>
> Section I: Resolving Ethical Issues

Each section of the *ACA Code of Ethics* begins with an introduction. The introduction to each section describes the ethical behavior and responsibility to which counselors aspire. The introductions help set the tone for each particular section and provide a starting point that invites reflection on the ethical standards contained in each part of the *ACA Code of Ethics*. The standards outline professional responsibilities and provide direction for fulfilling those ethical responsibilities.

When counselors are faced with ethical dilemmas that are difficult to resolve, they are expected to engage in a carefully considered ethical decision-making process, consulting available resources as needed. Counselors acknowledge that resolving ethical issues is a process; ethical reasoning includes consideration of professional values, professional ethical principles, and ethical standards.

Counselors' actions should be consistent with the spirit as well as the letter of these ethical standards. No specific ethical decision-making model is always most effective, so counselors are expected to use a credible model of decision making that can bear public scrutiny of its application. Through a chosen ethical decision-making process and evaluation of the context of the situation, counselors work collaboratively with clients to make decisions that promote clients' growth and development. A breach of the standards and principles provided herein does not necessarily constitute legal liability or violation of the law; such action is established in legal and judicial proceedings.

The glossary at the end of the *Code* provides a concise description of some of the terms used in the *ACA Code of Ethics*.

SECTION A: THE COUNSELING RELATIONSHIP

Introduction

Counselors facilitate client growth and development in ways that foster the interest and welfare of clients and promote formation of healthy relationships. Trust is the cornerstone of the counseling relationship, and counselors have the responsibility to respect and safeguard the client's right to privacy and confidentiality. Counselors actively attempt to understand the diverse cultural backgrounds of the clients they serve. Counselors also explore their own cultural identities and how these affect their values and beliefs about the counseling process. Additionally, counselors are encouraged to contribute to society by devoting a portion of their professional activities for little or no financial return (*pro bono publico*).

A.1. Client Welfare

A.1.a. PRIMARY RESPONSIBILITY   The primary responsibility of counselors is to respect the dignity and promote the welfare of clients.

A.1.b. RECORDS AND DOCUMENTATION   Counselors create, safeguard, and maintain documentation necessary for rendering professional services. Regardless of the medium, counselors include sufficient and timely documentation to facilitate the delivery and continuity of services. Counselors take reasonable steps to ensure that documentation accurately reflects client progress and services provided. If amendments are made to records and documentation, counselors take steps to properly note the amendments according to agency or institutional policies.

A.1.c. COUNSELING PLANS   Counselors and their clients work jointly in devising counseling plans that offer reasonable promise of success and are consistent with the abilities, temperament, developmental level, and circumstances of clients. Counselors and clients regularly review and revise counseling plans to assess their continued viability and effectiveness, respecting clients' freedom of choice.

A.1.d. SUPPORT NETWORK INVOLVEMENT   Counselors recognize that support networks hold various meanings in the lives of clients and consider enlisting the support, understanding, and involvement of others (e.g., religious/spiritual/community leaders, family members, friends) as positive resources, when appropriate, with client consent.

A.2. Informed Consent in the Counseling Relationship

A.2.a. INFORMED CONSENT   Clients have the freedom to choose whether to enter into or remain in a counseling relationship and need adequate information about the counseling process and the counselor. Counselors have an obligation to review in writing and verbally with clients the rights and responsibilities of both counselors and clients. Informed consent is an ongoing part of the counseling process, and counselors appropriately document discussions of informed consent throughout the counseling relationship.

A.2.b. TYPES OF INFORMATION NEEDED Counselors explicitly explain to clients the nature of all services provided. They inform clients about issues such as, but not limited to, the following: the purposes, goals, techniques, procedures, limitations, potential risks, and benefits of services; the counselor's qualifications, credentials, relevant experience, and approach to counseling; continuation of services upon the incapacitation or death of the counselor; the role of technology; and other pertinent information. Counselors take steps to ensure that clients understand the implications of diagnosis and the intended use of tests and reports. Additionally, counselors inform clients about fees and billing arrangements, including procedures for non-payment of fees. Clients have the right to confidentiality and to be provided with an explanation of its limits (including how supervisors and/or treatment or interdisciplinary team professionals are involved), to obtain clear information about their records, to participate in the ongoing counseling plans, and to refuse any services or modality changes and to be advised of the consequences of such refusal.

A.2.c. DEVELOPMENTAL AND CULTURAL SENSITIVITY Counselors communicate information in ways that are both developmentally and culturally appropriate. Counselors use clear and understandable language when discussing issues related to informed consent. When clients have difficulty understanding the language that counselors use, counselors provide necessary services (e.g., arranging for a qualified interpreter or translator) to ensure comprehension by clients. In collaboration with clients, counselors consider cultural implications of informed consent procedures and, where possible, counselors adjust their practices accordingly.

A.2.d. INABILITY TO GIVE CONSENT When counseling minors, incapacitated adults, or other persons unable to give voluntary consent, counselors seek the assent of clients to services and include them in decision making as appropriate. Counselors recognize the need to balance the ethical rights of clients to make choices, their capacity to give consent or assent to receive services, and parental or familial legal rights and responsibilities to protect these clients and make decisions on their behalf.

A.2.e. MANDATED CLIENTS Counselors discuss the required limitations to confidentiality when working with clients who have been mandated for counseling services. Counselors also explain what type of information and with whom that information is shared prior to the beginning of counseling. The client may choose to refuse services. In this case, counselors will, to the best of their ability, discuss with the client the potential consequences of refusing counseling services.

A.3. Clients Served by Others

When counselors learn that their clients are in a professional relationship with other mental health professionals, they request release from clients to inform the other professionals and strive to establish positive and collaborative professional relationships.

A.4. Avoiding Harm and Imposing Values

A.4.a. AVOIDING HARM Counselors act to avoid harming their clients, trainees, and research participants and to minimize or to remedy unavoidable or unanticipated harm.

A.4.b. PERSONAL VALUES Counselors are aware of—and avoid imposing—their own values, attitudes, beliefs, and behaviors. Counselors respect the diversity of clients, trainees, and research participants and seek training in areas in which they are at risk of imposing their values onto clients, especially when the counselor 's values are inconsistent with the client's goals or are discriminatory in nature.

A.5. Prohibited Noncounseling Roles and Relationships

A.5.a. SEXUAL AND/OR ROMANTIC RELATIONSHIPS PROHIBITED Sexual and/or romantic counselor–client interactions or relationships with current clients, their romantic partners, or their family members are prohibited. This prohibition applies to both in-person and electronic interactions or relationships.

A.5.b. PREVIOUS SEXUAL AND/OR ROMANTIC RELATIONSHIPS Counselors are prohibited from engaging in counseling relationships with persons with whom they have had a previous sexual and/or romantic relationship.

A.5.c. SEXUAL AND/OR ROMANTIC RELATIONSHIPS WITH FORMER CLIENTS Sexual and/or romantic counselor–client interactions or relationships with former clients, their romantic partners, or their family members are prohibited for a period of 5 years following the last professional contact. This prohibition applies to both in-person and electronic interactions or relationships. Counselors, before engaging in sexual and/or romantic interactions or relationships with former clients, their romantic partners, or their family members, demonstrate forethought and document (in written form) whether the interaction or relationship can be viewed as exploitive in any way and/or whether there is still potential to harm the former client; in cases of potential exploitation and/or harm, the counselor avoids entering into such an interaction or relationship.

A.5.d. FRIENDS OR FAMILY MEMBERS Counselors are prohibited from engaging in counseling relationships with friends or family members with whom they have an inability to remain objective.

A.5.e. PERSONAL VIRTUAL RELATIONSHIPS WITH CURRENT CLIENTS Counselors are prohibited from engaging in a personal virtual relationship with individuals with whom they have a current counseling relationship (e.g., through social and other media).

A.6. Managing and Maintaining Boundaries and Professional Relationships

A.6.a. PREVIOUS RELATIONSHIPS Counselors consider the risks and benefits of accepting as clients those with whom they have had a previous relationship. These potential clients may include individuals with whom the counselor has had a casual, distant, or past relationship. Examples include mutual or past membership in a professional association, organization, or community. When counselors accept these clients, they take appropriate professional precautions such as informed consent, consultation, supervision, and documentation to ensure that judgment is not impaired and no exploitation occurs.

A.6.b. EXTENDING COUNSELING BOUNDARIES Counselors consider the risks and benefits of extending current counseling relationships beyond conventional parameters. Examples include attending a client's formal ceremony (e.g., a wedding/commitment ceremony or graduation), purchasing a service or product provided by a client (excepting unrestricted bartering), and visiting a client's ill family member in the hospital. In extending these boundaries, counselors take appropriate professional precautions such as informed consent, consultation, supervision, and documentation to ensure that judgment is not impaired and no harm occurs.

A.6.c. DOCUMENTING BOUNDARY EXTENSIONS   If counselors extend boundaries as described in A.6.a. and A.6.b., they must officially document, prior to the interaction (when feasible), the rationale for such an interaction, the potential benefit, and anticipated consequences for the client or former client and other individuals significantly involved with the client or former client. When unintentional harm occurs to the client or former client, or to an individual significantly involved with the client or former client, the counselor must show evidence of an attempt to remedy such harm.

A.6.d. ROLE CHANGES IN THE PROFESSIONAL RELATIONSHIP   When counselors change a role from the original or most recent contracted relationship, they obtain informed consent from the client and explain the client's right to refuse services related to the change. Examples of role changes include, but are not limited to

1. changing from individual to relationship or family counseling, or vice versa;
2. changing from an evaluative role to a therapeutic role, or vice versa; and
3. changing from a counselor to a mediator role, or vice versa.

Clients must be fully informed of any anticipated consequences (e.g., financial, legal, personal, therapeutic) of counselor role changes.

A.6.e. NONPROFESSIONAL INTERACTIONS OR RELATIONSHIPS (OTHER THAN SEXUAL OR ROMANTIC INTERACTIONS OR RELATIONSHIPS)   Counselors avoid entering into nonprofessional relationships with former clients, their romantic partners, or their family members when the interaction is potentially harmful to the client. This applies to both in-person and electronic interactions or relationships.

A.7. Roles and Relationships at Individual, Group, Institutional, and Societal Levels

A.7.a. ADVOCACY   When appropriate, counselors advocate at individual, group, institutional, and societal levels to address potential barriers and obstacles that inhibit access and/or the growth and development of clients.

A.7.b. CONFIDENTIALITY AND ADVOCACY   Counselors obtain client consent prior to engaging in advocacy efforts on behalf of an identifiable client to improve the provision of services and to work toward removal of systemic barriers or obstacles that inhibit client access, growth, and development.

A.8. Multiple Clients

When a counselor agrees to provide counseling services to two or more persons who have a relationship, the counselor clarifies at the outset which person or persons are clients and the nature of the relationships the counselor will have with each involved person. If it becomes apparent that the counselor may be called upon to perform potentially conflicting roles, the counselor will clarify, adjust, or withdraw from roles appropriately.

A.9. Group Work

A.9.a. SCREENING   Counselors screen prospective group counseling/therapy participants. To the extent possible, counselors select members whose needs and goals are compatible with the goals of the group, who will not impede the group process, and whose well-being will not be jeopardized by the group experience.

A.9.b. PROTECTING CLIENTS   In a group setting, counselors take reasonable precautions to protect clients from physical, emotional, or psychological trauma.

A.10. Fees and Business Practices

A.10.a. SELF-REFERRAL   Counselors working in an organization (e.g., school, agency, institution) that provides counseling services do not refer clients to their private practice unless the policies of a particular organization make explicit provisions for self-referrals. In such instances, the clients must be informed of other options open to them should they seek private counseling services.

A.10.b. UNACCEPTABLE BUSINESS PRACTICES   Counselors do not participate in fee splitting, nor do they give or receive commissions, rebates, or any other form of remuneration when referring clients for professional services.

A.10.c. ESTABLISHING FEES   In establishing fees for professional counseling services, counselors consider the financial status of clients and locality. If a counselor's usual fees create undue hardship for the client, the counselor may adjust fees, when legally permissible, or assist the client in locating comparable, affordable services.

A.10.d. NONPAYMENT OF FEES   If counselors intend to use collection agencies or take legal measures to collect fees from clients who do not pay for services as agreed upon, they include such information in their informed consent documents and also inform clients in a timely fashion of intended actions and offer clients the opportunity to make payment.

A.10.e. BARTERING   Counselors may barter only if the bartering does not result in exploitation or harm, if the client requests it, and if such arrangements are an accepted practice among professionals in the community. Counselors consider the cultural implications of bartering and discuss relevant concerns with clients and document such agreements in a clear written contract.

A.10.f. RECEIVING GIFTS   Counselors understand the challenges of accepting gifts from clients and recognize that in some cultures, small gifts are a token of respect and gratitude. When determining whether to accept a gift from clients, counselors take into account the therapeutic relationship, the monetary value of the gift, the client's motivation for giving the gift, and the counselor's motivation for wanting to accept or decline the gift.

A.11. Termination and Referral

A.11.a. COMPETENCE WITHIN TERMINATION AND REFERRAL   If counselors lack the competence to be of professional assistance to clients, they avoid entering or continuing counseling relationships. Counselors are knowledgeable about culturally and clinically appropriate referral resources and suggest these alternatives. If clients decline the suggested referrals, counselors discontinue the relationship.

A.11.b. VALUES WITHIN TERMINATION AND REFERRAL   Counselors refrain from referring prospective and current clients based solely on the counselor's personally held values, attitudes, beliefs, and behaviors. Counselors respect the diversity of clients and seek training in areas in which they are at risk of imposing their values onto clients, especially when the counselor's values are inconsistent with the client's goals or are discriminatory in nature.

A.11.c. PROPRIATE TERMINATION Counselors terminate a counseling relationship when it becomes reasonably apparent that the client no longer needs assistance, is not likely to benefit, or is being harmed by continued counseling. Counselors may terminate counseling when in jeopardy of harm by the client or by another person with whom the client has a relationship, or when clients do not pay fees as agreed upon. Counselors provide pretermination counseling and recommend other service providers when necessary.

A.11.d. APPROPRIATE TRANSFER OF SERVICES When counselors transfer or refer clients to other practitioners, they ensure that appropriate clinical and administrative processes are completed and open communication is maintained with both clients and practitioners.

A.12. Abandonment and Client Neglect

Counselors do not abandon or neglect clients in counseling. Counselors assist in making appropriate arrangements for the continuation of treatment, when necessary, during interruptions such as vacations, illness, and following termination.

SECTION B: CONFIDENTIALITY AND PRIVACY

Introduction

Counselors recognize that trust is a cornerstone of the counseling relationship. Counselors aspire to earn the trust of clients by creating an ongoing partnership, establishing and upholding appropriate boundaries, and maintaining confidentiality. Counselors communicate the parameters of confidentiality in a culturally competent manner.

B.1. Respecting Client Rights

B.1.a. MULTICULTURAL/DIVERSITY CONSIDERATIONS Counselors maintain awareness and sensitivity regarding cultural meanings of confidentiality and privacy. Counselors respect differing views toward disclosure of information. Counselors hold ongoing discussions with clients as to how, when, and with whom information is to be shared.

B.1.b. RESPECT FOR PRIVACY Counselors respect the privacy of prospective and current clients. Counselors request private information from clients only when it is beneficial to the counseling process.

B.1.c. RESPECT FOR CONFIDENTIALITY Counselors protect the confidential information of prospective and current clients. Counselors disclose information only with appropriate consent or with sound legal or ethical justification.

B.1.d. EXPLANATION OF LIMITATIONS At initiation and throughout the counseling process, counselors inform clients of the limitations of confidentiality and seek to identify situations in which confidentiality must be breached.

B.2. Exceptions

B.2.a. SERIOUS AND FORESEEABLE HARM AND LEGAL REQUIREMENTS The general requirement that counselors keep information confidential does not apply when disclosure is required to protect clients or identified others from serious and foreseeable harm or when legal requirements demand that confidential information must be revealed. Counselors consult with other professionals when in doubt as to the validity of an exception. Additional considerations apply when addressing end-of-life issues.

B.2.b. CONFIDENTIALITY REGARDING END-OF-LIFE DECISIONS   Counselors who provide services to terminally ill individuals who are considering hastening their own deaths have the option to maintain confidentiality, depending on applicable laws and the specific circumstances of the situation and after seeking consultation or supervision from appropriate professional and legal parties.

B.2.c. CONTAGIOUS, LIFE-THREATENING DISEASES   When clients disclose that they have a disease commonly known to be both communicable and life threatening, counselors may be justified in disclosing information to identifiable third parties, if the parties are known to be at serious and foreseeable risk of contracting the disease. Prior to making a disclosure, counselors assess the intent of clients to inform the third parties about their disease or to engage in any behaviors that may be harmful to an identifiable third party. Counselors adhere to relevant state laws concerning disclosure about disease status.

B.2.d. COURT-ORDERED DISCLOSURE   When ordered by a court to release confidential or privileged information without a client's permission, counselors seek to obtain written, informed consent from the client or take steps to prohibit the disclosure or have it limited as narrowly as possible because of potential harm to the client or counseling relationship.

B.2.e. MINIMAL DISCLOSURE   To the extent possible, clients are informed before confidential information is disclosed and are involved in the disclosure decision-making process. When circumstances require the disclosure of confidential information, only essential information is revealed.

B.3. Information Shared With Others

B.3.a. SUBORDINATES   Counselors make every effort to ensure that privacy and confidentiality of clients are maintained by subordinates, including employees, supervisees, students, clerical assistants, and volunteers.

B.3.b. INTERDISCIPLINARY TEAMS   When services provided to the client involve participation by an interdisciplinary or treatment team, the client will be informed of the team's existence and composition, information being shared, and the purposes of sharing such information.

B.3.c. CONFIDENTIAL SETTINGS   Counselors discuss confidential information only in settings in which they can reasonably ensure client privacy.

B.3.d. THIRD-PARTY PAYERS   Counselors disclose information to third-party payers only when clients have authorized such disclosure.

B.3.e. TRANSMITTING CONFIDENTIAL INFORMATION   Counselors take precautions to ensure the confidentiality of all information transmitted through the use of any medium.

B.3.f. DECEASED CLIENTS   Counselors protect the confidentiality of deceased clients, consistent with legal requirements and the documented preferences of the client.

B.4. Groups and Families

B.4.a. GROUP WORK   In group work, counselors clearly explain the importance and parameters of confidentiality for the specific group.

B.4.b. COUPLES AND FAMILY COUNSELING   In couples and family counseling, counselors clearly define who is considered "the client" and discuss expectations and limitations of confidentiality. Counselors seek agreement and document in writing such agreement among all involved parties regarding the confidentiality of information. In the absence of an agreement to the contrary, the couple or family is considered to be the client.

B.5. Clients Lacking Capacity to Give Informed Consent

B.5.a. RESPONSIBILITY TO CLIENTS   When counseling minor clients or adult clients who lack the capacity to give voluntary, informed consent, counselors protect the confidentiality of information received—in any medium—in the counseling relationship as specified by federal and state laws, written policies, and applicable ethical standards.

B.5.b. RESPONSIBILITY TO PARENTS AND LEGAL GUARDIANS   Counselors inform parents and legal guardians about the role of counselors and the confidential nature of the counseling relationship, consistent with current legal and custodial arrangements. Counselors are sensitive to the cultural diversity of families and respect the inherent rights and responsibilities of parents/guardians regarding the welfare of their children/charges according to law. Counselors work to establish, as appropriate, collaborative relationships with parents/guardians to best serve clients.

B.5.c. RELEASE OF CONFIDENTIAL INFORMATION   When counseling minor clients or adult clients who lack the capacity to give voluntary consent to release confidential information, counselors seek permission from an appropriate third party to disclose information. In such instances, counselors inform clients consistent with their level of understanding and take appropriate measures to safeguard client confidentiality.

B.6. Records and Documentation

B.6.a. CREATING AND MAINTAINING RECORDS AND DOCUMENTATION   Counselors create and maintain records and documentation necessary for rendering professional services.

B.6.b. CONFIDENTIALITY OF RECORDS AND DOCUMENTATION   Counselors ensure that records and documentation kept in any medium are secure and that only authorized persons have access to them.

B.6.c. PERMISSION TO RECORD   Counselors obtain permission from clients prior to recording sessions through electronic or other means.

B.6.d. PERMISSION TO OBSERVE   Counselors obtain permission from clients prior to allowing any person to observe counseling sessions, review session transcripts, or view recordings of sessions with supervisors, faculty, peers, or others within the training environment.

B.6.e. CLIENT ACCESS   Counselors provide reasonable access to records and copies of records when requested by competent clients. Counselors limit the access of clients to their records, or portions of their records, only when there is compelling evidence that such access would cause harm to the client. Counselors document the request of clients and the rationale for withholding some or all of the records in the files of clients. In situations involving multiple clients, counselors provide individual clients with only those parts of records that relate directly to them and do not include confidential information related to any other client.

B.6.f. ASSISTANCE WITH RECORDS ·When clients request access to their records, counselors provide assistance and consultation in interpreting counseling records.

B.6.g. DISCLOSURE OR TRANSFER   Unless exceptions to confidentiality exist, counselors obtain written permission from clients to disclose or transfer records to legitimate third parties. Steps are taken to ensure that receivers of counseling records are sensitive to their confidential nature.

B.6.h. STORAGE AND DISPOSAL AFTER TERMINATION   Counselors store records following termination of services to ensure reasonable future access, maintain records in accordance with federal and state laws and statutes such as licensure laws and policies governing records, and dispose of client records and other sensitive materials in a manner that protects client confidentiality. Counselors apply careful discretion and deliberation before destroying records that may be needed by a court of law, such as notes on child abuse, suicide, sexual harassment, or violence.

B.6.i. REASONABLE PRECAUTIONS   Counselors take reasonable precautions to protect client confidentiality in the event of the counselor's termination of practice, incapacity, or death and appoint a records custodian when identified as appropriate.

B.7. Case Consultation

B.7.a. RESPECT FOR PRIVACY   Information shared in a consulting relationship is discussed for professional purposes only. Written and oral reports present only data germane to the purposes of the consultation, and every effort is made to protect client identity and to avoid undue invasion of privacy.

B.7.b. DISCLOSURE OF CONFIDENTIAL INFORMATION   When consulting with colleagues, counselors do not disclose confidential information that reasonably could lead to the identification of a client or other person or organization with whom they have a confidential relationship unless they have obtained the prior consent of the person or organization or the disclosure cannot be avoided. They disclose information only to the extent necessary to achieve the purposes of the consultation.

SECTION C: PROFESSIONAL RESPONSIBILITY

Introduction

Counselors aspire to open, honest, and accurate communication in dealing with the public and other professionals. Counselors facilitate access to counseling services, and they practice in a nondiscriminatory manner within the boundaries of professional and personal competence; they also have a responsibility to abide by the *ACA Code of Ethics*. Counselors actively participate in local, state, and national associations that foster the development and improvement of counseling. Counselors are expected to advocate to promote changes at the individual, group, institutional, and societal levels that improve the quality of life for individuals and groups and remove potential barriers to the provision or access of appropriate services being offered. Counselors have a responsibility to the public to engage in counseling practices that are based on rigorous research methodologies. Counselors are encouraged to contribute to society by devoting a portion of their professional activity to services for which there is little or no financial return (*pro bono publico*). In addition, counselors engage in self-care activities to maintain and promote their own emotional, physical, mental, and spiritual well-being to best meet their professional responsibilities.

C.1. Knowledge of and Compliance With Standards

Counselors have a responsibility to read, understand, and follow the *ACA Code of Ethics* and adhere to applicable laws and regulations.

C.2. Professional Competence

C.2.a. BOUNDARIES OF COMPETENCE Counselors practice only within the boundaries of their competence, based on their education, training, supervised experience, state and national professional credentials, and appropriate professional experience. Whereas multicultural counseling competency is required across all counseling specialties, counselors gain knowledge, personal awareness, sensitivity, dispositions, and skills pertinent to being a culturally competent counselor in working with a diverse client population.

C.2.b. NEW SPECIALTY AREAS OF PRACTICE Counselors practice in specialty areas new to them only after appropriate education, training, and supervised experience. While developing skills in new specialty areas, counselors take steps to ensure the competence of their work and protect others from possible harm.

C.2.c. QUALIFIED FOR EMPLOYMENT Counselors accept employment only for positions for which they are qualified given their education, training, supervised experience, state and national professional credentials, and appropriate professional experience. Counselors hire for professional counseling positions only individuals who are qualified and competent for those positions.

C.2.d. MONITOR EFFECTIVENESS Counselors continually monitor their effectiveness as professionals and take steps to improve when necessary. Counselors take reasonable steps to seek peer supervision to evaluate their efficacy as counselors.

C.2.e. CONSULTATIONS ON ETHICAL OBLIGATIONS Counselors take reasonable steps to consult with other counselors, the ACA Ethics and Professional Standards Department, or related professionals when they have questions regarding their ethical obligations or professional practice.

C.2.f. CONTINUING EDUCATION Counselors recognize the need for continuing education to acquire and maintain a reasonable level of awareness of current scientific and professional information in their fields of activity. Counselors maintain their competence in the skills they use, are open to new procedures, and remain informed regarding best practices for working with diverse populations.

C.2.g. IMPAIRMENT Counselors monitor themselves for signs of impairment from their own physical, mental, or emotional problems and refrain from offering or providing professional services when impaired. They seek assistance for problems that reach the level of professional impairment, and, if necessary, they limit, suspend, or terminate their professional responsibilities until it is determined that they may safely resume their work. Counselors assist colleagues or supervisors in recognizing their own professional impairment and provide consultation and assistance when warranted with colleagues or supervisors showing signs of impairment and intervene as appropriate to prevent imminent harm to clients.

C.2.h. COUNSELOR INCAPACITATION, DEATH, RETIREMENT, OR TERMINATION OF PRACTICE   Counselors prepare a plan for the transfer of clients and the dissemination of records to an identified colleague or records custodian in the case of the counselor's incapacitation, death, retirement, or termination of practice.

C.3. Advertising and Soliciting Clients

C.3.a. ACCURATE ADVERTISING   When advertising or otherwise representing their services to the public, counselors identify their credentials in an accurate manner that is not false, misleading, deceptive, or fraudulent.

C.3.b. TESTIMONIALS   Counselors who use testimonials do not solicit them from current clients, former clients, or any other persons who may be vulnerable to undue influence. Counselors discuss with clients the implications of and obtain permission for the use of any testimonial.

C.3.c. STATEMENTS BY OTHERS   When feasible, counselors make reasonable efforts to ensure that statements made by others about them or about the counseling profession are accurate.

C.3.d. RECRUITING THROUGH EMPLOYMENT   Counselors do not use their places of employment or institutional affiliation to recruit clients, supervisors, or consultees for their private practices.

C.3.e. PRODUCTS AND TRAINING ADVERTISEMENTS   Counselors who develop products related to their profession or conduct workshops or training events ensure that the advertisements concerning these products or events are accurate and disclose adequate information for consumers to make informed choices.

C.3.f. PROMOTING TO THOSE SERVED   Counselors do not use counseling, teaching, training, or supervisory relationships to promote their products or training events in a manner that is deceptive or would exert undue influence on individuals who may be vulnerable. However, counselor educators may adopt textbooks they have authored for instructional purposes.

C.4. Professional Qualifications

C.4.a. ACCURATE REPRESENTATION   Counselors claim or imply only professional qualifications actually completed and correct any known misrepresentations of their qualifications by others. Counselors truthfully represent the qualifications of their professional colleagues. Counselors clearly distinguish between paid and volunteer work experience and accurately describe their continuing education and specialized training.

C.4.b. CREDENTIALS   Counselors claim only licenses or certifications that are current and in good standing.

C.4.c. EDUCATIONAL DEGREES   Counselors clearly differentiate between earned and honorary degrees.

C.4.d. IMPLYING DOCTORAL-LEVEL COMPETENCE   Counselors clearly state their highest earned degree in counseling or a closely related field. Counselors do not imply doctoral-level competence when possessing a master's degree in counseling or a related field by referring to themselves as "Dr." in a counseling context when their doctorate is not in counseling or a related field. Counselors do not use "ABD" (all but dissertation) or other such terms to imply competency.

C.4.e. ACCREDITATION STATUS   Counselors accurately represent the accreditation status of their degree program and college/university.

C.4.f. PROFESSIONAL MEMBERSHIP   Counselors clearly differentiate between current, active memberships and former memberships in associations. Members of ACA must clearly differentiate between professional membership, which implies the possession of at least a master's degree in counseling, and regular membership, which is open to individuals whose interests and activities are consistent with those of ACA but are not qualified for professional membership.

C.5. Nondiscrimination

Counselors do not condone or engage in discrimination against prospective or current clients, students, employees, supervisees, or research participants based on age, culture, disability, ethnicity, race, religion/spirituality, gender, gender identity, sexual orientation, marital/partnership status, language preference, socioeconomic status, immigration status, or any basis proscribed by law.

C.6. Public Responsibility

C.6.a. SEXUAL HARASSMENT   Counselors do not engage in or condone sexual harassment. Sexual harassment can consist of a single intense or severe act, or multiple persistent or pervasive acts.

C.6.b. REPORTS TO THIRD PARTIES   Counselors are accurate, honest, and objective in reporting their professional activities and judgments to appropriate third parties, including courts, health insurance companies, those who are the recipients of evaluation reports, and others.

C.6.c. MEDIA PRESENTATIONS   When counselors provide advice or comment by means of public lectures, demonstrations, radio or television programs, recordings, technology-based applications, printed articles, mailed material, or other media, they take reasonable precautions to ensure that

1. the statements are based on appropriate professional counseling literature and practice,
2. the statements are otherwise consistent with the *ACA Code of Ethics*, and
3. the recipients of the information are not encouraged to infer that a professional counseling relationship has been established.

C.6.d. EXPLOITATION OF OTHERS   Counselors do not exploit others in their professional relationships.

C.6.e. CONTRIBUTING TO THE PUBLIC GOOD (*Pro Bono Publico*)   Counselors make a reasonable effort to provide services to the public for which there is little or no financial return (e.g., speaking to groups, sharing professional information, offering reduced fees).

C.7. Treatment Modalities

C.7.a. SCIENTIFIC BASIS FOR TREATMENT   When providing services, counselors use techniques/procedures/modalities that are grounded in theory and/or have an empirical or scientific foundation.

C.7.b. DEVELOPMENT AND INNOVATION   When counselors use developing or innovative techniques/procedures/modalities, they explain the potential risks, benefits, and ethical considerations of using such techniques/procedures/modalities. Counselors work to minimize any potential risks or harm when using these techniques/procedures/modalities.

C.7.c. HARMFUL PRACTICES   Counselors do not use techniques/procedures/modalities when substantial evidence suggests harm, even if such services are requested.

C.8. Responsibility to Other Professionals

C.8.a. PERSONAL PUBLIC STATEMENTS   When making personal statements in a public context, counselors clarify that they are speaking from their personal perspectives and that they are not speaking on behalf of all counselors or the profession.

SECTION D: RELATIONSHIPS WITH OTHER PROFESSIONALS

Introduction

Professional counselors recognize that the quality of their interactions with colleagues can influence the quality of services provided to clients. They work to become knowledgeable about colleagues within and outside the field of counseling. Counselors develop positive working relationships and systems of communication with colleagues to enhance services to clients.

D.1. Relationships With Colleagues, Employers, and Employees

D.1.a. DIFFERENT APPROACHES   Counselors are respectful of approaches that are grounded in theory and/or have an empirical or scientific foundation but may differ from their own. Counselors acknowledge the expertise of other professional groups and are respectful of their practices.

D.1.b. FORMING RELATIONSHIPS   Counselors work to develop and strengthen relationships with colleagues from other disciplines to best serve clients.

D.1.c. INTERDISCIPLINARY TEAMWORK   Counselors who are members of interdisciplinary teams delivering multifaceted services to clients remain focused on how to best serve clients. They participate in and contribute to decisions that affect the well-being of clients by drawing on the perspectives, values, and experiences of the counseling profession and those of colleagues from other disciplines.

D.1.d. ESTABLISHING PROFESSIONAL AND ETHICAL OBLIGATIONS   Counselors who are members of interdisciplinary teams work together with team members to clarify professional and ethical obligations of the team as a whole and of its individual members. When a team decision raises ethical concerns, counselors first attempt to resolve the concern within the team. If they cannot reach resolution among team members, counselors pursue other avenues to address their concerns consistent with client well-being.

D.1.e. CONFIDENTIALITY   When counselors are required by law, institutional policy, or extraordinary circumstances to serve in more than one role in judicial or administrative proceedings, they clarify role expectations and the parameters of confidentiality with their colleagues.

D.1.f. PERSONNEL SELECTION AND ASSIGNMENT   When counselors are in a position requiring personnel selection and/or assigning of responsibilities to others, they select competent staff and assign responsibilities compatible with their skills and experiences.

D.1.g. EMPLOYER POLICIES   The acceptance of employment in an agency or institution implies that counselors are in agreement with its general policies and principles. Counselors strive to reach agreement with employers regarding acceptable standards of client care and professional conduct that allow for changes in institutional policy conducive to the growth and development of clients.

D.1.h. NEGATIVE CONDITIONS   Counselors alert their employers of inappropriate policies and practices. They attempt to effect changes in such policies or procedures through constructive action within the organization. When such policies are potentially disruptive or damaging to clients or may limit the effectiveness of services provided and change cannot be affected, counselors take appropriate further action. Such action may include referral to appropriate certification, accreditation, or state licensure organizations, or voluntary termination of employment.

D.1.i. PROTECTION FROM PUNITIVE ACTION   Counselors do not harass a colleague or employee or dismiss an employee who has acted in a responsible and ethical manner to expose inappropriate employer policies or practices.

D.2. Provision of Consultation Services

D.2.a. CONSULTANT COMPETENCY   Counselors take reasonable steps to ensure that they have the appropriate resources and competencies when providing consultation services. Counselors provide appropriate referral resources when requested or needed.

D.2.b. INFORMED CONSENT IN FORMAL CONSULTATION   When providing formal consultation services, counselors have an obligation to review, in writing and verbally, the rights and responsibilities of both counselors and consultees. Counselors use clear and understandable language to inform all parties involved about the purpose of the services to be provided, relevant costs, potential risks and benefits, and the limits of confidentiality.

SECTION E: EVALUATION, ASSESSMENT, AND INTERPRETATION

Introduction

Counselors use assessment as one component of the counseling process, taking into account the clients' personal and cultural context. Counselors promote the well-being of individual clients or groups of clients by developing and using appropriate educational, mental health, psychological, and career assessments.

E.1. General

E.1.a. ASSESSMENT   The primary purpose of educational, mental health, psychological, and career assessment is to gather information regarding the client for a variety of purposes, including, but not limited to, client decision making, treatment planning, and forensic proceedings. Assessment may include both qualitative and quantitative methodologies.

E.1.b. CLIENT WELFARE Counselors do not misuse assessment results and interpretations, and they take reasonable steps to prevent others from misusing the information provided. They respect the client's right to know the results, the interpretations made, and the bases for counselors' conclusions and recommendations.

E.2. Competence to Use and Interpret Assessment Instruments

E.2.a. LIMITS OF COMPETENCE Counselors use only those testing and assessment services for which they have been trained and are competent. Counselors using technology-assisted test interpretations are trained in the construct being measured and the specific instrument being used prior to using its technology-based application. Counselors take reasonable measures to ensure the proper use of assessment techniques by persons under their supervision.

E.2.b. APPROPRIATE USE Counselors are responsible for the appropriate application, scoring, interpretation, and use of assessment instruments relevant to the needs of the client, whether they score and interpret such assessments themselves or use technology or other services.

E.2.c. DECISIONS BASED ON RESULTS Counselors responsible for decisions involving individuals or policies that are based on assessment results have a thorough understanding of psychometrics.

E.3. Informed Consent in Assessment

E.3.a. EXPLANATION TO CLIENTS Prior to assessment, counselors explain the nature and purposes of assessment and the specific use of results by potential recipients. The explanation will be given in terms and language that the client (or other legally authorized person on behalf of the client) can understand.

E.3.b. RECIPIENTS OF RESULTS Counselors consider the client's and/or examinee's welfare, explicit understandings, and prior agreements in determining who receives the assessment results. Counselors include accurate and appropriate interpretations with any release of individual or group assessment results.

E.4. Release of Data to Qualified Personnel

Counselors release assessment data in which the client is identified only with the consent of the client or the client's legal representative. Such data are released only to persons recognized by counselors as qualified to interpret the data.

E.5. Diagnosis of Mental Disorders

E.5.a. PROPER DIAGNOSIS Counselors take special care to provide proper diagnosis of mental disorders. Assessment techniques (including personal interviews) used to determine client care (e.g., locus of treatment, type of treatment, recommended follow-up) are carefully selected and appropriately used.

E.5.b. CULTURAL SENSITIVITY Counselors recognize that culture affects the manner in which clients' problems are defined and experienced. Clients' socioeconomic and cultural experiences are considered when diagnosing mental disorders.

E.5.c. HISTORICAL AND SOCIAL PREJUDICES IN THE DIAGNOSIS OF PATHOLOGY   Counselors recognize historical and social prejudices in the misdiagnosis and pathologizing of certain individuals and groups and strive to become aware of and address such biases in themselves or others.

E.5.d. REFRAINING FROM DIAGNOSIS   Counselors may refrain from making and/or reporting a diagnosis if they believe that it would cause harm to the client or others. Counselors carefully consider both the positive and negative implications of a diagnosis.

E.6. Instrument Selection

E.6.a. APPROPRIATENESS OF INSTRUMENTS   Counselors carefully consider the validity, reliability, psychometric limitations, and appropriateness of instruments when selecting assessments and, when possible, use multiple forms of assessment, data, and/or instruments in forming conclusions, diagnoses, or recommendations.

E.6.b. REFERRAL INFORMATION   If a client is referred to a third party for assessment, the counselor provides specific referral questions and sufficient objective data about the client to ensure that appropriate assessment instruments are utilized.

E.7. Conditions of Assessment Administration

E.7.a. ADMINISTRATION CONDITIONS   Counselors administer assessments under the same conditions that were established in their standardization. When assessments are not administered under standard conditions, as may be necessary to accommodate clients with disabilities, or when unusual behavior or irregularities occur during the administration, those conditions are noted in interpretation, and the results may be designated as invalid or of questionable validity.

E.7.b. PROVISION OF FAVORABLE CONDITIONS   Counselors provide an appropriate environment for the administration of assessments (e.g., privacy, comfort, freedom from distraction).

E.7.c. TECHNOLOGICAL ADMINISTRATION   Counselors ensure that technologically administered assessments function properly and provide clients with accurate results.

E.7.d. UNSUPERVISED ASSESSMENTS   Unless the assessment instrument is designed, intended, and validated for self-administration and/or scoring, counselors do not permit unsupervised use.

E.8. Multicultural Issues/Diversity in Assessment

Counselors select and use with caution assessment techniques normed on populations other than that of the client. Counselors recognize the effects of age, color, culture, disability, ethnic group, gender, race, language preference, religion, spirituality, sexual orientation, and socioeconomic status on test administration and interpretation, and they place test results in proper perspective with other relevant factors.

E.9. Scoring and Interpretation of Assessments

E.9.a. REPORTING   When counselors report assessment results, they consider the client's personal and cultural background, the level of the client's understanding of the results, and the impact of the results on the client. In reporting assessment results, counselors indicate reservations that exist regarding validity or reliability due to circumstances of the assessment or inappropriateness of the norms for the person tested.

E.9.b. INSTRUMENTS WITH INSUFFICIENT EMPIRICAL DATA Counselors exercise caution when interpreting the results of instruments not having sufficient empirical data to support respondent results. The specific purposes for the use of such instruments are stated explicitly to the examinee. Counselors qualify any conclusions, diagnoses, or recommendations made that are based on assessments or instruments with questionable validity or reliability.

E.9.c. ASSESSMENT SERVICES Counselors who provide assessment, scoring, and interpretation services to support the assessment process confirm the validity of such interpretations. They accurately describe the purpose, norms, validity, reliability, and applications of the procedures and any special qualifications applicable to their use. At all times, counselors maintain their ethical responsibility to those being assessed.

E.10. Assessment Security

Counselors maintain the integrity and security of tests and assessments consistent with legal and contractual obligations. Counselors do not appropriate, reproduce, or modify published assessments or parts thereof without acknowledgment and permission from the publisher.

E.11. Obsolete Assessment and Outdated Results

Counselors do not use data or results from assessments that are obsolete or outdated for the current purpose (e.g., noncurrent versions of assessments/instruments). Counselors make every effort to prevent the misuse of obsolete measures and assessment data by others.

E.12. Assessment Construction

Counselors use established scientific procedures, relevant standards, and current professional knowledge for assessment design in the development, publication, and utilization of assessment techniques.

E.13. Forensic Evaluation: Evaluation for Legal Proceedings

E.13.a. PRIMARY OBLIGATIONS When providing forensic evaluations, the primary obligation of counselors is to produce objective findings that can be substantiated based on information and techniques appropriate to the evaluation, which may include examination of the individual and/or review of records. Counselors form professional opinions based on their professional knowledge and expertise that can be supported by the data gathered in evaluations. Counselors define the limits of their reports or testimony, especially when an examination of the individual has not been conducted.

E.13.b. CONSENT FOR EVALUATION Individuals being evaluated are informed in writing that the relationship is for the purposes of an evaluation and is not therapeutic in nature, and entities or individuals who will receive the evaluation report are identified. Counselors who perform forensic evaluations obtain written consent from those being evaluated or from their legal representative unless a court orders evaluations to be conducted without the written consent of the individuals being evaluated. When children or adults who lack the capacity to give voluntary consent are being evaluated, informed written consent is obtained from a parent or guardian.

E.13.c. CLIENT EVALUATION PROHIBITED Counselors do not evaluate current or former clients, clients' romantic partners, or clients' family members for forensic purposes. Counselors do not counsel individuals they are evaluating.

E.13.d. AVOID POTENTIALLY HARMFUL RELATIONSHIPS Counselors who provide forensic evaluations avoid potentially harmful professional or personal relationships with family members, romantic partners, and close friends of individuals they are evaluating or have evaluated in the past.

SECTION F: SUPERVISION, TRAINING, AND TEACHING

Introduction

Counselor supervisors, trainers, and educators aspire to foster meaningful and respectful professional relationships and to maintain appropriate boundaries with supervisees and students in both face-to-face and electronic formats. They have theoretical and pedagogical foundations for their work; have knowledge of supervision models; and aim to be fair, accurate, and honest in their assessments of counselors, students, and supervisees.

F.1. Counselor Supervision and Client Welfare

F.1.a. CLIENT WELFARE A primary obligation of counseling supervisors is to monitor the services provided by supervisees. Counseling supervisors monitor client welfare and supervisee performance and professional development. To fulfill these obligations, supervisors meet regularly with supervisees to review the supervisees' work and help them become prepared to serve a range of diverse clients. Supervisees have a responsibility to understand and follow the *ACA Code of Ethics.*

F.1.b. COUNSELOR CREDENTIALS Counseling supervisors work to ensure that supervisees communicate their qualifications to render services to their clients.

F.1.c. INFORMED CONSENT AND CLIENT RIGHTS Supervisors make supervisees aware of client rights, including the protection of client privacy and confidentiality in the counseling relationship. Supervisees provide clients with professional disclosure information and inform them of how the supervision process influences the limits of confidentiality. Supervisees make clients aware of who will have access to records of the counseling relationship and how these records will be stored, transmitted, or otherwise reviewed.

F.2. Counselor Supervision Competence

F.2.a. SUPERVISOR PREPARATION Prior to offering supervision services, counselors are trained in supervision methods and techniques. Counselors who offer supervision services regularly pursue continuing education activities, including both counseling and supervision topics and skills.

F.2.b. MULTICULTURAL ISSUES/DIVERSITY IN SUPERVISION Counseling supervisors are aware of and address the role of multiculturalism/diversity in the supervisory relationship.

F.2.c. ONLINE SUPERVISION When using technology in supervision, counselor supervisors are competent in the use of those technologies. Supervisors take the necessary precautions to protect the confidentiality of all information transmitted through any electronic means.

F.3. Supervisory Relationship

F.3.a. EXTENDING CONVENTIONAL SUPERVISORY RELATIONSHIPS Counseling supervisors clearly define and maintain ethical professional, personal, and social relationships with their supervisees. Supervisors consider the risks and benefits of extending current supervisory relationships in any form beyond conventional parameters. In extending these boundaries, supervisors take appropriate professional precautions to ensure that judgment is not impaired and that no harm occurs.

F.3.b. SEXUAL RELATIONSHIPS   Sexual or romantic interactions or relationships with current supervisees are prohibited. This prohibition applies to both in-person and electronic interactions or relationships.

F.3.c. SEXUAL HARASSMENT   Counseling supervisors do not condone or subject supervisees to sexual harassment.

F.3.d. FRIENDS OR FAMILY MEMBERS   Supervisors are prohibited from engaging in supervisory relationships with individuals with whom they have an inability to remain objective.

F.4. Supervisor Responsibilities

F.4.a. INFORMED CONSENT FOR SUPERVISION   Supervisors are responsible for incorporating into their supervision the principles of informed consent and participation. Supervisors inform supervisees of the policies and procedures to which supervisors are to adhere and the mechanisms for due process appeal of individual supervisor actions. The issues unique to the use of distance supervision are to be included in the documentation as necessary.

F.4.b. EMERGENCIES AND ABSENCES   Supervisors establish and communicate to supervisees procedures for contacting supervisors or, in their absence, alternative on-call supervisors to assist in handling crises.

F.4.c. STANDARDS FOR SUPERVISEES   Supervisors make their supervisees aware of professional and ethical standards and legal responsibilities.

F.4.d. TERMINATION OF THE SUPERVISORY RELATIONSHIP   Supervisors or supervisees have the right to terminate the supervisory relationship with adequate notice. Reasons for considering termination are discussed, and both parties work to resolve differences. When termination is warranted, supervisors make appropriate referrals to possible alternative supervisors.

F.5. Student and Supervisee Responsibilities

F.5.a. ETHICAL RESPONSIBILITIES   Students and supervisees have a responsibility to understand and follow the *ACA Code of Ethics*. Students and supervisees have the same obligation to clients as those required of professional counselors.

F.5.b. IMPAIRMENT   Students and supervisees monitor themselves for signs of impairment from their own physical, mental, or emotional problems and refrain from offering or providing professional services when such impairment is likely to harm a client or others. They notify their faculty and/or supervisors and seek assistance for problems that reach the level of professional impairment, and, if necessary, they limit, suspend, or terminate their professional responsibilities until it is determined that they may safely resume their work.

F.5.c. PROFESSIONAL DISCLOSURE   Before providing counseling services, students and supervisees disclose their status as supervisees and explain how this status affects the limits of confidentiality.

Supervisors ensure that clients are aware of the services rendered and the qualifications of the students and supervisees rendering those services. Students and supervisees obtain client permission before they use any information concerning the counseling relationship in the training process.

F.6. Counseling Supervision Evaluation, Remediation, and Endorsement

F.6.a. EVALUATION   Supervisors document and provide supervisees with ongoing feedback regarding their performance and schedule periodic formal evaluative sessions throughout the supervisory relationship.

F.6.b. GATEKEEPING AND REMEDIATION   Through initial and ongoing evaluation, supervisors are aware of supervisee limitations that might impede performance. Supervisors assist supervisees in securing remedial assistance when needed. They recommend dismissal from training programs, applied counseling settings, and state or voluntary professional credentialing processes when those supervisees are unable to demonstrate that they can provide competent professional services to a range of diverse clients. Supervisors seek consultation and document their decisions to dismiss or refer supervisees for assistance. They ensure that supervisees are aware of options available to them to address such decisions.

F.6.c. COUNSELING FOR SUPERVISEES   If supervisees request counseling, the supervisor assists the supervisee in identifying appropriate services. Supervisors do not provide counseling services to supervisees. Supervisors address interpersonal competencies in terms of the impact of these issues on clients, the supervisory relationship, and professional functioning.

F.6.d. ENDORSEMENTS   Supervisors endorse supervisees for certification, licensure, employment, or completion of an academic or training program only when they believe that supervisees are qualified for the endorsement. Regardless of qualifications, supervisors do not endorse supervisees whom they believe to be impaired in any way that would interfere with the performance of the duties associated with the endorsement.

F.7. Responsibilities of Counselor Educators

F.7.a. COUNSELOR EDUCATORS   Counselor educators who are responsible for developing, implementing, and supervising educational programs are skilled as teachers and practitioners. They are knowledgeable regarding the ethical, legal, and regulatory aspects of the profession; are skilled in applying that knowledge; and make students and supervisees aware of their responsibilities. Whether in traditional, hybrid, and/or online formats, counselor educators conduct counselor education and training programs in an ethical manner and serve as role models for professional behavior.

F.7.b. COUNSELOR EDUCATOR COMPETENCE   Counselors who function as counselor educators or supervisors provide instruction within their areas of knowledge and competence and provide instruction based on current information and knowledge available in the profession. When using technology to deliver instruction, counselor educators develop competence in the use of the technology.

F.7.c. INFUSING MULTICULTURAL ISSUES/DIVERSITY   Counselor educators infuse material related to multiculturalism/diversity into all courses and workshops for the development of professional counselors.

F.7.d. INTEGRATION OF STUDY AND PRACTICE In traditional, hybrid, and/or online formats, counselor educators establish education and training programs that integrate academic study and supervised practice.

F.7.e. TEACHING ETHICS Throughout the program, counselor educators ensure that students are aware of the ethical responsibilities and standards of the profession and the ethical responsibilities of students to the profession. Counselor educators infuse ethical considerations throughout the curriculum.

F.7.f. USE OF CASE EXAMPLES The use of client, student, or supervisee information for the purposes of case examples in a lecture or classroom setting is permissible only when (a) the client, student, or supervisee has reviewed the material and agreed to its presentation or (b) the information has been sufficiently modified to obscure identity.

F.7.g. STUDENT-TO-STUDENT SUPERVISION AND INSTRUCTION When students function in the role of counselor educators or supervisors, they understand that they have the same ethical obligations as counselor educators, trainers, and supervisors. Counselor educators make every effort to ensure that the rights of students are not compromised when their peers lead experiential counseling activities in traditional, hybrid, and/or online formats (e.g., counseling groups, skills classes, clinical supervision).

F.7.h. INNOVATIVE THEORIES AND TECHNIQUES Counselor educators promote the use of techniques/procedures/modalities that are grounded in theory and/or have an empirical or scientific foundation. When counselor educators discuss developing or innovative techniques/procedures/modalities, they explain the potential risks, benefits, and ethical considerations of using such techniques/procedures/modalities.

F.7.i. FIELD PLACEMENTS Counselor educators develop clear policies and provide direct assistance within their training programs regarding appropriate field placement and other clinical experiences. Counselor educators provide clearly stated roles and responsibilities for the student or supervisee, the site supervisor, and the program supervisor. They confirm that site supervisors are qualified to provide supervision in the formats in which services are provided and inform site supervisors of their professional and ethical responsibilities in this role.

F.8. Student Welfare

F.8.a. PROGRAM INFORMATION AND ORIENTATION Counselor educators recognize that program orientation is a developmental process that begins upon students' initial contact with the counselor education program and continues throughout the educational and clinical training of students. Counselor education faculty provide prospective and current students with information about the counselor education program's expectations, including

1. the values and ethical principles of the profession;
2. the type and level of skill and knowledge acquisition required for successful completion of the training;
3. technology requirements;
4. program training goals, objectives, and mission, and subject matter to be covered;
5. bases for evaluation;

6. training components that encourage self-growth or self-disclosure as part of the training process;
7. the type of supervision settings and requirements of the sites for required clinical field experiences;
8. student and supervisor evaluation and dismissal policies and procedures; and
9. up-to-date employment prospects for graduates.

F.8.b. STUDENT CAREER ADVISING Counselor educators provide career advisement for their students and make them aware of opportunities in the field.

F.8.c. SELF-GROWTH EXPERIENCES Self-growth is an expected component of counselor education. Counselor educators are mindful of ethical principles when they require students to engage in self-growth experiences. Counselor educators and supervisors inform students that they have a right to decide what information will be shared or withheld in class.

F.8.d. ADDRESSING PERSONAL CONCERNS Counselor educators may require students to address any personal concerns that have the potential to affect professional competency.

F.9. Evaluation and Remediation

F.9.a. EVALUATION OF STUDENTS Counselor educators clearly state to students, prior to and throughout the training program, the levels of competency expected, appraisal methods, and timing of evaluations for both didactic and clinical competencies. Counselor educators provide students with ongoing feedback regarding their performance throughout the training program.

F.9.b. LIMITATIONS Counselor educators, through ongoing evaluation, are aware of and address the inability of some students to achieve counseling competencies. Counselor educators do the following:

1. assist students in securing remedial assistance when needed,
2. seek professional consultation and document their decision to dismiss or refer students for assistance, and
3. ensure that students have recourse in a timely manner to address decisions requiring them to seek assistance or to dismiss them and provide students with due process according to institutional policies and procedures.

F.9.c. COUNSELING FOR STUDENTS If students request counseling, or if counseling services are suggested as part of a remediation process, counselor educators assist students in identifying appropriate services.

F.10. Roles and Relationships Between Counselor Educators and Students

F.10.a. SEXUAL OR ROMANTIC RELATIONSHIPS Counselor educators are prohibited from sexual or romantic interactions or relationships with students currently enrolled in a counseling or related program and over whom they have power and authority. This prohibition applies to both in-person and electronic interactions or relationships.

F.10.b. SEXUAL HARASSMENT Counselor educators do not condone or subject students to sexual harassment.

F.10.c. RELATIONSHIPS WITH FORMER STUDENTS Counselor educators are aware of the power differential in the relationship between faculty and students. Faculty members discuss with former students potential risks when they consider engaging in social, sexual, or other intimate relationships.

F.10.d. NONACADEMIC RELATIONSHIPS Counselor educators avoid nonacademic relationships with students in which there is a risk of potential harm to the student or which may compromise the training experience or grades assigned. In addition, counselor educators do not accept any form of professional services, fees, commissions, reimbursement, or remuneration from a site for student or supervisor placement.

F.10.e. COUNSELING SERVICES Counselor educators do not serve as counselors to students currently enrolled in a counseling or related program and over whom they have power and authority.

F.10.f. EXTENDING EDUCATOR–STUDENT BOUNDARIES Counselor educators are aware of the power differential in the relationship between faculty and students. If they believe that a nonprofessional relationship with a student may be potentially beneficial to the student, they take precautions similar to those taken by counselors when working with clients. Examples of potentially beneficial interactions or relationships include, but are not limited to, attending a formal ceremony; conducting hospital visits; providing support during a stressful event; or maintaining mutual membership in a professional association, organization, or community. Counselor educators discuss with students the rationale for such interactions, the potential benefits and drawbacks, and the anticipated consequences for the student. Educators clarify the specific nature and limitations of the additional role(s) they will have with the student prior to engaging in a nonprofessional relationship. Nonprofessional relationships with students should be time limited and/or context specific and initiated with student consent.

F.11. Multicultural/Diversity Competence in Counselor Education and Training Programs

F.11.a. FACULTY DIVERSITY Counselor educators are committed to recruiting and retaining a diverse faculty.

F.11.b. STUDENT DIVERSITY Counselor educators actively attempt to recruit and retain a diverse student body. Counselor educators demonstrate commitment to multicultural/diversity competence by recognizing and valuing the diverse cultures and types of abilities that students bring to the training experience. Counselor educators provide appropriate accommodations that enhance and support diverse student well-being and academic performance.

F.11.c. MULTICULTURAL/DIVERSITY COMPETENCE Counselor educators actively infuse multicultural/diversity competency in their training and supervision practices. They actively train students to gain awareness, knowledge, and skills in the competencies of multicultural practice.

SECTION G: RESEARCH AND PUBLICATION

Introduction

Counselors who conduct research are encouraged to contribute to the knowledge base of the profession and promote a clearer understanding of the conditions that lead to a healthy and more just society. Counselors support the efforts of researchers by participating fully and willingly whenever possible. Counselors minimize bias and respect diversity in designing and implementing research.

G.1. Research Responsibilities

G.1.a. CONDUCTING RESEARCH   Counselors plan, design, conduct, and report research in a manner that is consistent with pertinent ethical principles, federal and state laws, host institutional regulations, and scientific standards governing research.

G.1.b. CONFIDENTIALITY IN RESEARCH   Counselors are responsible for understanding and adhering to state, federal, agency, or institutional policies or applicable guidelines regarding confidentiality in their research practices.

G.1.c. INDEPENDENT RESEARCHERS   When counselors conduct independent research and do not have access to an institutional review board, they are bound to the same ethical principles and federal and state laws pertaining to the review of their plan, design, conduct, and reporting of research.

G.1.d. DEVIATION FROM STANDARD PRACTICE   Counselors seek consultation and observe stringent safeguards to protect the rights of research participants when research indicates that a deviation from standard or acceptable practices may be necessary.

G.1.e. PRECAUTIONS TO AVOID INJURY   Counselors who conduct research are responsible for their participants' welfare throughout the research process and should take reasonable precautions to avoid causing emotional, physical, or social harm to participants.

G.1.f. PRINCIPAL RESEARCHER RESPONSIBILITY   The ultimate responsibility for ethical research practice lies with the principal researcher. All others involved in the research activities share ethical obligations and responsibility for their own actions.

G.2. Rights of Research Participants

G.2.a. INFORMED CONSENT IN RESEARCH   Individuals have the right to decline requests to become research participants. In seeking consent, counselors use language that

1. accurately explains the purpose and procedures to be followed;
2. identifies any procedures that are experimental or relatively untried;
3. describes any attendant discomforts, risks, and potential power differentials between researchers and participants;
4. describes any benefits or changes in individuals or organizations that might reasonably be expected;
5. discloses appropriate alternative procedures that would be advantageous for participants;
6. offers to answer any inquiries concerning the procedures;
7. describes any limitations on confidentiality;
8. describes the format and potential target audiences for the dissemination of research findings; and
9. instructs participants that they are free to withdraw their consent and discontinue participation in the project at any time, without penalty.

G.2.b. STUDENT/SUPERVISEE PARTICIPATION Researchers who involve students or supervisees in research make clear to them that the decision regarding participation in research activities does not affect their academic standing or supervisory relationship. Students or supervisees who choose not to participate in research are provided with an appropriate alternative to fulfill their academic or clinical requirements.

G.2.c. CLIENT PARTICIPATION Counselors conducting research involving clients make clear in the informed consent process that clients are free to choose whether to participate in research activities. Counselors take necessary precautions to protect clients from adverse consequences of declining or withdrawing from participation.

G.2.d. CONFIDENTIALITY OF INFORMATION Information obtained about research participants during the course of research is confidential. Procedures are implemented to protect confidentiality.

G.2.e. PERSONS NOT CAPABLE OF GIVING INFORMED CONSENT When a research participant is not capable of giving informed consent, counselors provide an appropriate explanation to, obtain agreement for participation from, and obtain the appropriate consent of a legally authorized person.

G.2.f. COMMITMENTS TO PARTICIPANTS Counselors take reasonable measures to honor all commitments to research participants.

G.2.g. EXPLANATIONS AFTER DATA COLLECTION After data are collected, counselors provide participants with full clarification of the nature of the study to remove any misconceptions participants might have regarding the research. Where scientific or human values justify delaying or withholding information, counselors take reasonable measures to avoid causing harm.

G.2.h. INFORMING SPONSORS Counselors inform sponsors, institutions, and publication channels regarding research procedures and outcomes. Counselors ensure that appropriate bodies and authorities are given pertinent information and acknowledgment.

G.2.i. RESEARCH RECORDS CUSTODIAN As appropriate, researchers prepare and disseminate to an identified colleague or records custodian a plan for the transfer of research data in the case of their incapacitation, retirement, or death.

G.3. Managing and Maintaining Boundaries

G.3.a. EXTENDING RESEARCHER–PARTICIPANT BOUNDARIES Researchers consider the risks and benefits of extending current research relationships beyond conventional parameters. When a nonresearch interaction between the researcher and the research participant may be potentially beneficial, the researcher must document, prior to the interaction (when feasible), the rationale for such an interaction, the potential benefit, and anticipated consequences for the research participant. Such interactions should be initiated with appropriate consent of the research participant. Where unintentional harm occurs to the research participant, the researcher must show evidence of an attempt to remedy such harm.

G.3.b. RELATIONSHIPS WITH RESEARCH PARTICIPANTS Sexual or romantic counselor–research participant interactions or relationships with current research participants are prohibited. This prohibition applies to both in-person and electronic interactions or relationships.

G.3.c. SEXUAL HARASSMENT AND RESEARCH PARTICIPANTS Researchers do not condone or subject research participants to sexual harassment.

G.4. Reporting Results

G.4.a. ACCURATE RESULTS Counselors plan, conduct, and report research accurately. Counselors do not engage in misleading or fraudulent research, distort data, misrepresent data, or deliberately bias their results. They describe the extent to which results are applicable for diverse populations.

G.4.b. OBLIGATION TO REPORT UNFAVORABLE RESULTS Counselors report the results of any research of professional value. Results that reflect unfavorably on institutions, programs, services, prevailing opinions, or vested interests are not withheld.

G.4.c. REPORTING ERRORS If counselors discover significant errors in their published research, they take reasonable steps to correct such errors in a correction erratum or through other appropriate publication means.

G.4.d. IDENTITY OF PARTICIPANTS Counselors who supply data, aid in the research of another person, report research results, or make original data available take due care to disguise the identity of respective participants in the absence of specific authorization from the participants to do otherwise. In situations where participants self-identify their involvement in research studies, researchers take active steps to ensure that data are adapted/changed to protect the identity and welfare of all parties and that discussion of results does not cause harm to participants.

G.4.e. REPLICATION STUDIES Counselors are obligated to make available sufficient original research information to qualified professionals who may wish to replicate or extend the study.

G.5. Publications and Presentations

G.5.a. USE OF CASE EXAMPLES The use of participants', clients', students', or supervisees' information for the purpose of case examples in a presentation or publication is permissible only when (a) participants, clients, students, or supervisees have reviewed the material and agreed to its presentation or publication or (b) the information has been sufficiently modified to obscure identity.

G.5.b. PLAGIARISM Counselors do not plagiarize; that is, they do not present another person's work as their own.

G.5.c. ACKNOWLEDGING PREVIOUS WORK In publications and presentations, counselors acknowledge and give recognition to previous work on the topic by others or self.

G.5.d. CONTRIBUTORS Counselors give credit through joint authorship, acknowledgment, footnote statements, or other appropriate means to those who have contributed significantly to research or concept development in accordance with such contributions. The principal contributor is listed first, and minor technical or professional contributions are acknowledged in notes or introductory statements.

G.5.e. AGREEMENT OF CONTRIBUTORS Counselors who conduct joint research with colleagues or students/supervisors establish agreements in advance regarding allocation of tasks, publication credit, and types of acknowledgment that will be received.

G.5.f. STUDENT RESEARCH Manuscripts or professional presentations in any medium that are substantially based on a student's course papers, projects, dissertations, or theses are used only with the student's permission and list the student as lead author.

G.5.g. DUPLICATE SUBMISSIONS Counselors submit manuscripts for consideration to only one journal at a time. Manuscripts that are published in whole or in substantial part in one journal or published work are not submitted for publication to another publisher without acknowledgment and permission from the original publisher.

G.5.h. PROFESSIONAL REVIEW Counselors who review material submitted for publication, research, or other scholarly purposes respect the confidentiality and proprietary rights of those who submitted it. Counselors make publication decisions based on valid and defensible standards. Counselors review article submissions in a timely manner and based on their scope and competency in research methodologies. Counselors who serve as reviewers at the request of editors or publishers make every effort to only review materials that are within their scope of competency and avoid personal biases.

SECTION H: DISTANCE COUNSELING, TECHNOLOGY, AND SOCIAL MEDIA

Introduction

Counselors understand that the profession of counseling may no longer be limited to in-person, face-to-face interactions. Counselors actively attempt to understand the evolving nature of the profession with regard to distance counseling, technology, and social media and how such resources may be used to better serve their clients. Counselors strive to become knowledgeable about these resources. Counselors understand the additional concerns related to the use of distance counseling, technology, and social media and make every attempt to protect confidentiality and meet any legal and ethical requirements for the use of such resources.

H.1. Knowledge and Legal Considerations

H.1.a. KNOWLEDGE AND COMPETENCY Counselors who engage in the use of distance counseling, technology, and/or social media develop knowledge and skills regarding related technical, ethical, and legal considerations (e.g., special certifications, additional course work).

H.1.b. LAWS AND STATUTES Counselors who engage in the use of distance counseling, technology, and social media within their counseling practice understand that they may be subject to laws and regulations of both the counselor's practicing location and the client's place of residence. Counselors ensure that their clients are aware of pertinent legal rights and limitations governing the practice of counseling across state lines or international boundaries.

H.2. Informed Consent and Security

H.2.a. INFORMED CONSENT AND DISCLOSURE Clients have the freedom to choose whether to use distance counseling, social media, and/or technology within the counseling process. In addition to the usual and customary protocol of informed consent between counselor and client for face-to-face counseling, the following issues, unique to the use of distance counseling, technology, and/or social media, are addressed in the informed consent process:

- distance counseling credentials, physical location of practice, and contact information;
- risks and benefits of engaging in the use of distance counseling, technology, and/or social media;
- possibility of technology failure and alternate methods of service delivery;
- anticipated response time;
- emergency procedures to follow when the counselor is not available;
- time zone differences;
- cultural and/or language differences that may affect delivery of services;
- possible denial of insurance benefits; and
- social media policy.

H.2.b. CONFIDENTIALITY MAINTAINED BY THE COUNSELOR Counselors acknowledge the limitations of maintaining the confidentiality of electronic records and transmissions. They inform clients that individuals might have authorized or unauthorized access to such records or transmissions (e.g., colleagues, supervisors, employees, information technologists).

H.2.c. ACKNOWLEDGMENT OF LIMITATIONS Counselors inform clients about the inherent limits of confidentiality when using technology. Counselors urge clients to be aware of authorized and/or unauthorized access to information disclosed using this medium in the counseling process.

H.2.d. SECURITY Counselors use current encryption standards within their websites and/or technology-based communications that meet applicable legal requirements. Counselors take reasonable precautions to ensure the confidentiality of information transmitted through any electronic means.

H.3. Client Verification

Counselors who engage in the use of distance counseling, technology, and/or social media to interact with clients take steps to verify the client's identity at the beginning and throughout the therapeutic process. Verification can include, but is not limited to, using code words, numbers, graphics, or other nondescript identifiers.

H.4. Distance Counseling Relationship

H.4.a. BENEFITS AND LIMITATIONS Counselors inform clients of the benefits and limitations of using technology applications in the provision of counseling services. Such technologies include, but are not limited to, computer hardware and/or software, telephones and applications, social media and Internet-based applications and other audio and/or video communication, or data storage devices or media.

H.4.b. PROFESSIONAL BOUNDARIES IN DISTANCE COUNSELING Counselors understand the necessity of maintaining a professional relationship with their clients. Counselors discuss and establish professional boundaries with clients regarding the appropriate use and/or application of technology and the limitations of its use within the counseling relationship (e.g., lack of confidentiality, times when not appropriate to use).

H.4.c. TECHNOLOGY-ASSISTED SERVICES   When providing technology-assisted services, counselors make reasonable efforts to determine that clients are intellectually, emotionally, physically, linguistically, and functionally capable of using the application and that the application is appropriate for the needs of the client. Counselors verify that clients understand the purpose and operation of technology applications and follow up with clients to correct possible misconceptions, discover appropriate use, and assess subsequent steps.

H.4.d. EFFECTIVENESS OF SERVICES   When distance counseling services are deemed ineffective by the counselor or client, counselors consider delivering services face-to-face. If the counselor is not able to provide face-to-face services (e.g., lives in another state), the counselor assists the client in identifying appropriate services.

H.4.e. ACCESS   Counselors provide information to clients regarding reasonable access to pertinent applications when providing technology-assisted services.

H.4.f. COMMUNICATION DIFFERENCES IN ELECTRONIC MEDIA   Counselors consider the differences between face-to-face and electronic communication (nonverbal and verbal cues) and how these may affect the counseling process. Counselors educate clients on how to prevent and address potential misunderstandings arising from the lack of visual cues and voice intonations when communicating electronically.

H.5. Records and Web Maintenance

H.5.a. RECORDS   Counselors maintain electronic records in accordance with relevant laws and statutes. Counselors inform clients on how records are maintained electronically. This includes, but is not limited to, the type of encryption and security assigned to the records, and if/for how long archival storage of transaction records is maintained.

H.5.b. CLIENT RIGHTS   Counselors who offer distance counseling services and/or maintain a professional website provide electronic links to relevant licensure and professional certification boards to protect consumer and client rights and address ethical concerns.

H.5.c. ELECTRONIC LINKS   Counselors regularly ensure that electronic links are working and are professionally appropriate.

H.5.d. MULTICULTURAL AND DISABILITY CONSIDERATIONS   Counselors who maintain websites provide accessibility to persons with disabilities. They provide translation capabilities for clients who have a different primary language, when feasible. Counselors acknowledge the imperfect nature of such translations and accessibilities.

H.6. Social Media

H.6.a. VIRTUAL PROFESSIONAL PRESENCE   In cases where counselors wish to maintain a professional and personal presence for social media use, separate professional and personal web pages and profiles are created to clearly distinguish between the two kinds of virtual presence.

H.6.b. SOCIAL MEDIA AS PART OF INFORMED CONSENT   Counselors clearly explain to their clients, as part of the informed consent procedure, the benefits, limitations, and boundaries of the use of social media.

H.6.c. CLIENT VIRTUAL PRESENCE   Counselors respect the privacy of their clients' presence on social media unless given consent to view such information.

H.6.d. USE OF PUBLIC SOCIAL MEDIA   Counselors take precautions to avoid disclosing confidential information through public social media.

SECTION I: RESOLVING ETHICAL ISSUES

Introduction

Professional counselors behave in an ethical and legal manner. They are aware that client welfare and trust in the profession depend on a high level of professional conduct. They hold other counselors to the same standards and are willing to take appropriate action to ensure that standards are upheld. Counselors strive to resolve ethical dilemmas with direct and open communication among all parties involved and seek consultation with colleagues and supervisors when necessary. Counselors incorporate ethical practice into their daily professional work and engage in ongoing professional development regarding current topics in ethical and legal issues in counseling. Counselors become familiar with the ACA Policy and Procedures for Processing Complaints of Ethical Violations[1] and use it as a reference for assisting in the enforcement of the *ACA Code of Ethics*.

I.1. Standards and the Law

I.1.a. KNOWLEDGE   Counselors know and understand the *ACA Code of Ethics* and other applicable ethics codes from professional organizations or certification and licensure bodies of which they are members. Lack of knowledge or misunderstanding of an ethical responsibility is not a defense against a charge of unethical conduct.

I.1.b. ETHICAL DECISION MAKING   When counselors are faced with an ethical dilemma, they use and document, as appropriate, an ethical decision-making model that may include, but is not limited to, consultation; consideration of relevant ethical standards, principles, and laws; generation of potential courses of action; deliberation of risks and benefits; and selection of an objective decision based on the circumstances and welfare of all involved.

I.1.c. CONFLICTS BETWEEN ETHICS AND LAWS   If ethical responsibilities conflict with the law, regulations, and/or other governing legal authority, counselors make known their commitment to the *ACA Code of Ethics* and take steps to resolve the conflict. If the conflict cannot be resolved using this approach, counselors, acting in the best interest of the client, may adhere to the requirements of the law, regulations, and/or other governing legal authority.

I.2. Suspected Violations

I.2.a. INFORMAL RESOLUTION   When counselors have reason to believe that another counselor is violating or has violated an ethical standard and substantial harm has not occurred, they attempt to first resolve the issue informally with the other counselor if feasible, provided such action does not violate confidentiality rights that may be involved.

---

[1]See the American Counseling Association web site at http://www.counseling.org/knowledge-center/ethics

I.2.b. REPORTING ETHICAL VIOLATIONS   If an apparent violation has substantially harmed or is likely to substantially harm a person or organization and is not appropriate for informal resolution or is not resolved properly, counselors take further action depending on the situation. Such action may include referral to state or national committees on professional ethics, voluntary national certification bodies, state licensing boards, or appropriate institutional authorities. The confidentiality rights of clients should be considered in all actions. This standard does not apply when counselors have been retained to review the work of another counselor whose professional conduct is in question (e.g., consultation, expert testimony).

I.2.c. CONSULTATION   When uncertain about whether a particular situation or course of action may be in violation of the *ACA Code of Ethics*, counselors consult with other counselors who are knowledgeable about ethics and the *ACA Code of Ethics*, with colleagues, or with appropriate authorities, such as the ACA Ethics and Professional Standards Department.

I.2.d. ORGANIZATIONAL CONFLICTS   If the demands of an organization with which counselors are affiliated pose a conflict with the *ACA Code of Ethics*, counselors specify the nature of such conflicts and express to their supervisors or other responsible officials their commitment to the *ACA Code of Ethics* and, when possible, work through the appropriate channels to address the situation.

I.2.e. UNWARRANTED COMPLAINTS   Counselors do not initiate, participate in, or encourage the filing of ethics complaints that are retaliatory in nature or are made with reckless disregard or willful ignorance of facts that would disprove the allegation.

I.2.f. UNFAIR DISCRIMINATION AGAINST COMPLAINANTS AND RESPONDENTS   Counselors do not deny individuals employment, advancement, admission to academic or other programs, tenure, or promotion based solely on their having made or their being the subject of an ethics complaint. This does not preclude taking action based on the outcome of such proceedings or considering other appropriate information.

I.3. Cooperation With Ethics Committees

Counselors assist in the process of enforcing the *ACA Code of Ethics*. Counselors cooperate with investigations, proceedings, and requirements of the ACA Ethics Committee or ethics committees of other duly constituted associations or boards having jurisdiction over those charged with a violation.

GLOSSARY OF TERMS

Abandonment—the inappropriate ending or arbitrary termination of a counseling relationship that puts the client at risk.

Advocacy—promotion of the well-being of individuals, groups, and the counseling profession within systems and organizations. Advocacy seeks to remove barriers and obstacles that inhibit access, growth, and development.

Assent—to demonstrate agreement when a person is otherwise not capable or competent to give formal consent (e.g., informed consent) to a counseling service or plan.

Assessment—the process of collecting in-depth information about a person in order to develop a comprehensive plan that will guide the collaborative counseling and service provision process.

Bartering—accepting goods or services from clients in exchange for counseling services.

Client—an individual seeking or referred to the professional services of a counselor.

Confidentiality—the ethical duty of counselors to protect a client's identity, identifying characteristics, and private communications.

Consultation—a professional relationship that may include, but is not limited to, seeking advice, information, and/or testimony.

Counseling—a professional relationship that empowers diverse individuals, families, and groups to accomplish mental health, wellness, education, and career goals.

Counselor Educator—a professional counselor engaged primarily in developing, implementing, and supervising the educational preparation of professional counselors.

Counselor Supervisor—a professional counselor who engages in a formal relationship with a practicing counselor or counselor-in-training for the purpose of overseeing that individual's counseling work or clinical skill development.

Culture—membership in a socially constructed way of living, which incorporates collective values, beliefs, norms, boundaries, and lifestyles that are cocreated with others who share similar worldviews comprising biological, psychosocial, historical, psychological, and other factors.

Discrimination—the prejudicial treatment of an individual or group based on their actual or perceived membership in a particular group, class, or category.

Distance Counseling—The provision of counseling services by means other than face-to-face meetings, usually with the aid of technology.

Diversity—the similarities and differences that occur within and across cultures, and the intersection of cultural and social identities.

Documents—any written, digital, audio, visual, or artistic recording of the work within the counseling relationship between counselor and client.

Encryption—process of encoding information in such a way that limits access to authorized users.

Examinee—a recipient of any professional counseling service that includes educational, psychological, and career appraisal, using qualitative or quantitative techniques.

Exploitation—actions and/or behaviors that take advantage of another for one's own benefit or gain.

Fee Splitting—the payment or acceptance of fees for client referrals (e.g., percentage of fee paid for rent, referral fees).

Forensic Evaluation—the process of forming professional opinions for court or other legal proceedings, based on professional knowledge and expertise, and supported by appropriate data.

Gatekeeping—the initial and ongoing academic, skill, and dispositional assessment of students' competency for professional practice, including remediation and termination as appropriate.

Impairment—a significantly diminished capacity to perform professional functions.

Incapacitation—an inability to perform professional functions.

Informed Consent—a process of information sharing associated with possible actions clients may choose to take, aimed at assisting clients in acquiring a full appreciation and understanding of the facts and implications of a given action or actions.

Instrument—a tool, developed using accepted research practices, that measures the presence and strength of a specified construct or constructs.

Interdisciplinary Teams—teams of professionals serving clients that may include individuals who may not share counselors' responsibilities regarding confidentiality.

Minors—generally, persons under the age of 18 years, unless otherwise designated by statute or regulation. In some jurisdictions, minors may have the right to consent to counseling without consent of the parent or guardian.

Multicultural/Diversity Competence—counselors' cultural and diversity awareness and knowledge about self and others, and how this awareness and knowledge are applied effectively in practice with clients and client groups.

Multicultural/Diversity Counseling—counseling that recognizes diversity and embraces approaches that support the worth, dignity, potential, and uniqueness of individuals within their historical, cultural, economic, political, and psychosocial contexts.

Personal Virtual Relationship—engaging in a relationship via technology and/or social media that blurs the professional boundary (e.g., friending on social networking sites); using personal accounts as the connection point for the virtual relationship.

Privacy—the right of an individual to keep oneself and one's personal information free from unauthorized disclosure.

Privilege—a legal term denoting the protection of confidential information in a legal proceeding (e.g., subpoena, deposition, testimony).

Pro bono publico—contributing to society by devoting a portion of professional activities for little or no financial return (e.g., speaking to groups, sharing professional information, offering reduced fees).

Professional Virtual Relationship—using technology and/or social media in a professional manner and maintaining appropriate professional boundaries; using business accounts that cannot be linked back to personal accounts as the connection point for the virtual relationship (e.g., a business page versus a personal profile).

Records—all information or documents, in any medium, that the counselor keeps about the client, excluding personal and psychotherapy notes.

Records of an Artistic Nature—products created by the client as part of the counseling process.

Records Custodian—a professional colleague who agrees to serve as the caretaker of client records for another mental health professional.

Self-Growth—a process of self-examination and challenging of a counselor's assumptions to enhance professional effectiveness.

Serious and Foreseeable—when a reasonable counselor can anticipate significant and harmful possible consequences.

Sexual Harassment—sexual solicitation, physical advances, or verbal/nonverbal conduct that is sexual in nature; occurs in connection with professional activities or roles; is unwelcome, offensive, or creates a hostile workplace or learning environment; and/or is sufficiently severe or intense to be perceived as harassment by a reasonable person.

Social Justice—the promotion of equity for all people and groups for the purpose of ending oppression and injustice affecting clients, students, counselors, families, communities, schools, workplaces, governments, and other social and institutional systems.

Social Media—technology-based forms of communication of ideas, beliefs, personal histories, etc. (e.g., social networking sites, blogs).

Student—an individual engaged in formal graduate-level counselor education.

Supervisee—a professional counselor or counselor-in-training whose counseling work or clinical skill development is being overseen in a formal supervisory relationship by a qualified trained professional.

Supervision—a process in which one individual, usually a senior member of a given profession designated as the supervisor, engages in a collaborative relationship with another individual or group, usually a junior member(s) of a given profession designated as the supervisee(s) in order to (a) promote the growth and development of the supervisee(s), (b) protect the welfare of the clients seen by the supervisee(s), and (c) evaluate the performance of the supervisee(s).

Supervisor—counselors who are trained to oversee the professional clinical work of counselors and counselors-in-training.

Teaching—all activities engaged in as part of a formal educational program that is designed to lead to a graduate degree in counseling.

Training—the instruction and practice of skills related to the counseling profession. Training contributes to the ongoing proficiency of students and professional counselors.

Virtual Relationship—a non–face-to-face relationship (e.g., through social media).

APPENDIX B

Counseling Disclosure and Agreement Forms

CLIENT INFORMATION AND AGREEMENT FOR COUNSELORS IN PRIVATE PRACTICE
_____, M.Ed., NCC
Licensed Professional Counselor (LPC)

I am pleased you have chosen me as your counselor. This document is designed to inform you about my background and to ensure that you understand our professional relationship.

I am licensed as a Professional Counselor by the _____ Board of Examiners for Licensed Professional Counselors. Only licensed mental health professionals may provide counseling services in this state. In addition, I am certified by the National Board of Certified Counselors, a private certifying agency that recognizes counselors who have distinguished themselves through meeting the board's standards for education, knowledge, and experience.

I hold a master's degree (M.Ed.) in counseling from the University of _____. The graduate program I completed is accredited by the Council for Accreditation of Counseling and Related Educational Programs (CACREP). I have been a counselor since _____. My counseling practice is limited to adolescents and adults and includes career, personal, couples, marriage, and group counseling. I also am available for divorce mediation.

I provide services for clients in my private practice who I believe have the capacity to resolve their own problems with my assistance. A counseling relationship between a Professional Counselor and client is a professional relationship in which the Professional Counselor assists the client in exploring and resolving difficult life issues. I believe that as people become more accepting of themselves, they are more capable of finding happiness and contentment in their lives. Self-awareness and self-acceptance are goals that sometimes take a long time to achieve. While some clients may need only a few counseling sessions to feel complete, others may require months or even years of counseling. Clients are in complete control and may end our counseling relationship at any point, and I will be supportive of that decision. If counseling is successful, clients should feel that they are able to face life's challenges in the future without my support or intervention.

My counseling services are limited to the scheduled sessions we have together. In the event you feel your mental health requires emergency attention or if you have an emotional crisis, you should report to the emergency room of a local hospital and request mental health services.

Although our sessions will be very intimate, it is important for you to realize that we have a professional, rather than a personal, relationship. Our contact will be limited to the paid sessions you have with me. Please do not invite me to social gatherings, offer gifts, or ask me to relate to you in any way outside our counseling sessions. You will be best served if our relationship stays strictly professional and if our sessions concentrate exclusively on your concerns. You will learn a great deal about me as we work together during your counseling experience. However, it is important for you to remember that you are experiencing me only in my professional role.

I will keep confidential anything you say to me with the following general exceptions: you direct me to tell someone else, I determine you are a danger to yourself or others, or I am ordered by a court to disclose information.

In the event you are dissatisfied with my services for any reason, please let me know. If I am not able to resolve your concerns, you may report your complaints to the State of _____ Licensed Professional Counselors Board of Examiners (address, telephone number). I hold license # _____.

In return for a fee of $ _____ per session, I agree to provide counseling services for you. Sessions are 50 minutes in duration. It is impossible to guarantee any specific results regarding your counseling goals. However, I assure you that my services will be rendered in a professional manner consistent with accepted ethical standards.

The fee for each session will be due and must be paid at the conclusion of each session. Cash or personal checks are acceptable forms for payment. I will provide you with a monthly receipt for all fees paid.

In the event you will not be able to keep an appointment, you must notify me 24 hours in advance. If I do not receive such advance notice, you will be responsible for paying for the session you missed.

If you are a member of an HMO, PPO, or some type of managed health care plan, I can tell you if I am an authorized provider of services under that plan. If I am an authorized provider, services will be provided to you under the terms of that plan's contract. Fees will be billed and collected according to the requirements of that plan. If I am not an authorized provider, you may still receive services from me for a fee, but your plan will not reimburse you for the cost of any of my services. Plans often will reimburse for only a limited number of visits per year. If you exceed that limit, you may still receive services from me, but your plan will not reimburse you for the cost of services that exceed its maximum number of visits.

If you wish to seek reimbursement for my services from your health insurance company, I will be happy to complete any necessary forms related to your reimbursement provided by you or the insurance company. Since you will be paying each session for my services, any later reimbursement from the insurance company should be sent directly to you. Please do not assign any payments to me.

Most health insurance companies will reimburse clients for my counseling services, but some will not. Those that do reimburse usually require that a standard amount be paid by you before reimbursement is allowed and usually only a percentage of my fee is reimbursable. You should contact a company representative to determine whether your insurance company will reimburse you and the schedule of reimbursement that is used.

Health insurance companies usually require that I diagnose your mental condition and indicate that you have an illness before they will agree to reimburse you. In the event a diagnosis is required, I will inform you of the diagnosis I plan to render before I submit it to the health insurance company.

If you have any questions, feel free to ask. Please sign and date both copies of this form. You keep one and give the other copy to me.

_____   _____
Your Signature   Your Client's Signature

_____   _____
Date   Date

CLIENT INFORMATION AND AGREEMENT FOR COUNSELORS EMPLOYED IN AN AGENCY

_____ Community Mental Health Center
address
city, state, zip
telephone number
_____, M.Ed., NCC
Licensed Professional Counselor (LPC)

_____ Community Mental Health Center will be providing counseling services to you, and I have been assigned as your counselor. This document is designed to inform you about the services provided by this agency and my background.

_____ Community Mental Health Center offers a variety of services, which include the following: _____. All residents of _____ County are eligible for services.

I am licensed as a Professional Counselor by the _____ Board of Examiners for Licensed Professional Counselors. In addition, I am certified by the National Board of Certified Counselors, a private certifying agency that recognizes counselors who have distinguished themselves through meeting the board's standards for education, knowledge, and experience.

I hold a master's degree (M.Ed.) in counseling from the University of _____. The graduate program I completed is accredited by the Council for Accreditation of Counseling and Related Educational Programs (CACREP). I have been a counselor since _____. My counseling practice is limited to adolescents and adults and includes career, personal, couples, marriage, and group counseling. I also am available for divorce mediation.

A counseling relationship between a Professional Counselor and client is a professional relationship in which the Professional Counselor assists the client in exploring and resolving difficult life issues. I believe that as people become more accepting of themselves, they are capable of finding happiness and contentment in their lives. Self-awareness and self-acceptance are goals that sometimes take a long time to achieve. While some clients may need only a few counseling sessions to feel complete, others may require months or even years of counseling. Clients are in complete control and may end our counseling relationship at any point, and I will be supportive of that decision. If counseling is successful, clients should feel that they are able to face life's challenges in the future without my support or intervention. My counseling services are limited to the scheduled sessions we have together. In the event you feel your mental health requires emergency attention or if you have an emotional crisis, you should report to the emergency room of a local hospital and request mental health services.

Although our sessions will be very intimate, it is important for you to realize that we have a professional, rather than a personal, relationship. Our contact will be limited to the paid sessions you have with me. Please do not invite me to social gatherings, offer gifts, or ask me to relate to you in any way outside our counseling sessions. You will be best served if our relationship stays strictly professional and if our sessions concentrate exclusively on your concerns. You will learn a great deal about me as we work together during your counseling experience. However, it is important for you to remember that you are experiencing me only in my professional role.

I will keep confidential anything you say to me with the following general exceptions: you direct me to tell someone else, I determine you are a danger to yourself or others, or I am ordered by a court to disclose information.

In the event you are dissatisfied with my services for any reason, please let me know. If I am not able to resolve your concerns, you may report your complaints to _____, my supervisor here at the _____ Community Mental Health Center.

The general fee for services at _____ Community Mental Health Center is $_____ per session. However, if you apply for a reduction in fees for services based on your family's income, you may be eligible for a reduction in fees. If you are granted a reduction in fees, United Way, a local charitable organization, pays the portion of the fees that you cannot afford. Based on your application for a reduction in fees for services, your fees have been established at $_____ per session.

Sessions are 50 minutes in duration. It is impossible to guarantee any specific results regarding your counseling goals. However, I assure you that my services will be rendered in a professional manner consistent with accepted ethical standards.

The fee for each session will be due and must be paid at the conclusion of each session. Cash or personal checks are acceptable forms for payment. I will provide you with a monthly receipt for all fees paid. In the event you will not be able to keep an appointment, you must notify me 24 hours in advance. If I do not receive such advance notice, you will be responsible for paying for the session you missed.

If you are a member of an HMO, PPO, or some type of managed health care plan, I can tell you if this agency is an authorized provider of services under that plan. If this agency is an authorized provider, services will be provided to you under the terms of that plan's contract. Fees will be billed and collected according to the requirements of that plan. If this agency is not an authorized provider, you may still receive services from me for a fee, but your plan will not reimburse you for the cost of any of my services. Plans often will reimburse for only a limited number of visits per year. If you exceed that limit, you may still receive services from me, but your plan will not reimburse you for the cost of services that exceed its maximum number of visits.

If you have any questions, feel free to ask. Please sign and date both copies of this form. You keep one and give the other copy to me.

_____   _____
Your Signature   Your Client's Signature

_____   _____
Date   Date

CLIENT INFORMATION AND AGREEMENT
FOR COUNSELORS WHO EVALUATE INDIVIDUALS

The purpose of our relationship is for me to gather information from you and to evaluate you so that I will be able to render an opinion regarding the best custody situation for your minor child. This process will work best if you are cooperative in providing me with the information I need and if we maintain a professional relationship throughout the evaluation.

Nothing that we discuss will be confidential. I will be required to give a written opinion to the judge who appointed me to your case. I may use in that report any information that you give to me during the duration of our relationship. In addition, I may be required to testify under oath at legal proceedings regarding interactions we have had and opinions I have rendered.

I guarantee you that I will be fair and unbiased in rendering my opinions in this case. The best interest of your child will guide my decisions.

In the event you feel I am acting in an unfair or biased manner, please have your attorney notify the judge who is presiding in this case and request that the judge determine whether my actions have been unprofessional.

Although I am a Licensed Professional Counselor in this state, I am not serving as your counselor. In the event you feel a need for counseling, I will be happy to refer you to agencies or individuals who might be able to assist you.

If you have any questions, feel free to ask. Please sign and date both copies of this form. You keep one and give the other copy to me.

_____

Your Signature

_____   Signature of the Person
                                                            Being Evaluated

_____

Date   _____

                                                            Date

CLIENT INFORMATION AND AGREEMENT FOR COUNSELORS EMPLOYED
IN AN AGENCY WHO ARE COUNSELING INVOLUNTARY CLIENTS

_____ Community Mental Health Center

address

city, state, zip

telephone number

_____, M.Ed., NCC

Licensed Professional Counselor (LPC)

_____ Community Mental Health Center will be providing counseling services to you, and I have been assigned as your counselor. This document is designed to inform you about the services provided by this agency and my background.

_____ Community Mental Health Center offers a variety of services, which include the following: _____. All residents of _____ County are eligible for services.

You have been required to obtain counseling sessions from this agency by the judge who is handling your criminal case. As your counselor, I will be required to report to your probation officer whether you attended counseling sessions, whether you paid for services received, and whether I believe that you are benefiting from our counseling sessions. As a result, you must understand that anything you say to me in counseling may be transmitted to your probation officer and that I may be required to testify regarding the contents of our sessions at court proceedings regarding your case.

I am licensed as a Professional Counselor by the _____ Board of Examiners for Licensed Professional Counselors. In addition, I am certified by the National Board of Certified Counselors, a private certifying agency that recognizes counselors who have distinguished themselves through meeting the board's standards for education, knowledge, and experience.

I hold a Master's (M.Ed.) degree in counseling from the University of _____. The graduate program I completed is accredited by the Council for Accreditation of Counseling and Related Educational Programs (CACREP). I have been a counselor since _____. My counseling practice is limited to adolescents and adults and includes career, personal, couples, marriage, and group counseling. I also am available for divorce mediation.

A counseling relationship between a Professional Counselor and client is a professional relationship in which the Professional Counselor assists the client in exploring and resolving difficult life issues. I believe that as people become more accepting of themselves, they are more capable of finding happiness and contentment in their lives. Self-awareness and self-acceptance are goals that sometimes take a long time to achieve. While some clients may need only a few counseling sessions to feel complete, others may require months or even years of counseling. If counseling is successful, clients should feel that they are able to face life's challenges in the future without my support or intervention.

My counseling services are limited to the scheduled sessions we have together. In the event you feel your mental health requires emergency attention or if you have an emotional crisis, you should report to the emergency room of a local hospital and request mental health services.

Although our sessions will be very intimate, it is important for you to realize that we have a professional, rather than a personal, relationship. Our contact will be limited to the paid sessions you have with me. Please do not invite me to social gatherings, offer gifts, or ask me to relate to you in any way outside our counseling sessions. You will be best served if our relationship stays strictly professional and if our sessions concentrate exclusively on your concerns. You will learn a great deal about me as we work together during your counseling experience. However, it is important for you to remember that you are experiencing me only in my professional role.

In the event you are dissatisfied with my services for any reason, please let me know. If I am not able to resolve your concerns, you may report your complaints to _____, my supervisor here at the _____ Community Mental Health Center.

The general fee for services at _____ Community Mental Health Center is $_____ per session. However, if you apply for a reduction in fees for services based on your family's income, you may be eligible for a reduction. If you are granted a reduction in fees, United Way, a local charitable organization, pays the portion of the fees that you cannot afford. Based on your application for a reduction of fees for services, your fees have been established at $_____ per session.

Sessions are 50 minutes in duration. It is impossible to guarantee any specific results regarding your counseling goals. However, I assure you that my services will be rendered in a professional manner consistent with accepted ethical standards.

The fee for each session will be due and must be paid at the conclusion of each session. Cash or personal checks are acceptable forms for payment. I will provide you with a monthly receipt for all fees paid.

In the event you will not be able to keep an appointment, you must notify me 24 hours in advance. If I do not receive such advance notice, you will be responsible for paying for the session you missed.

If you are a member of an HMO, PPO, or some type of managed health care plan, I can tell you if this agency is an authorized provider of services under that plan. If this agency is an authorized provider, services will be provided to you under the terms of that plan's contract. Fees will be billed and collected according to the requirements of that plan. If this agency is not an authorized provider, you may still receive services from me for a fee, but your plan will not reimburse you for the cost of any of my services. Plans often will reimburse for only a limited number of visits per year. If you exceed that limit, you may still receive services from me, but your plan will not reimburse you for the cost of services that exceed its maximum number of visits.

_____ Community Mental Health Agency does not participate in any type of health insurance reimbursement. If you have a health insurance policy that reimburses you for mental health services, it is suggested that you seek a provider who is qualified to render those services to you. If you receive services from me at this agency, you will be responsible for the fees for all services received.

If you have any questions, feel free to ask. Please sign and date both copies of this form. You keep one and give the other copy to me.

_____   _____
Your Signature   Your Client's Signature

_____   _____
Date   Date

CLIENT INFORMATION AND AGREEMENT FOR COUNSELORS EMPLOYED IN A SCHOOL

Include a statement similar to the one below in a letter to parents at the beginning of the year, orientation materials, and so on. The statement could be easily modified to be addressed to students themselves and included in a student handbook.

"I'm Your Child's School Counselor"

The counseling program at _____ (school) is designed to assist your child to make the most of his or her educational experiences. As your child's counselor, I am concerned about his or her emotional well-being, academic progress, and personal and social development.

I have a master's degree (M.Ed.) in school counseling from the University of _____. My graduate program is accredited by the American Counseling Association's Council for the Accreditation of Counseling and Related Educational Programs (CACREP), the nationally recognized accrediting agency for counseling graduate programs. I am a National Certified Counselor (NCC), National Certified School Counselor (NCSC), and a Licensed Professional Counselor (LPC) in _____. In addition, I am certified as a school counselor by the state of _____. Before beginning my duties as a counselor at _____ (school), I held the following positions: _____. I currently serve as _____.

The following specific activities are offered by the counseling program:
1. Periodic classroom lessons related to positive personal growth and development
2.
3.
(etc.)

Reasons that I might contact parents regarding their child include, but are not limited to, the following:
1. Assistance is needed from parents in specific areas to help their children achieve success in school
2.
etc.

Unfortunately, I am not able to provide the following services to your child or to parents:
1. Testifying in court in child-custody matters.
2. Providing intensive long-term counseling services when they are needed by a child.
3.
(etc.)

Your child will be participating in the school counseling program on a regular basis. In the event you have questions about the counseling program, please call me at _____. I sincerely look forward to working with you in the coming year to help your child have a successful experience in our school.

_____

Your Signature

_____

Date

APPENDIX C

Client Request Form to Transfer Records

[This form was constructed to meet HIPAA requirements. In the event an agency or practice is not subject to HIPAA requirements, such a form could be simpler.]

    I, _____ (fill in name of client), hereby request that copies of my counseling records as described below be transferred to the following individual or institution:

_____

                    (name and address to where records should be transferred)

    Only copies of records will be sent that are necessary to fulfill the purpose for which you are requesting this transfer. With that in mind, what is the purpose for requesting that copies of your records be sent? _____

    Generally, notes made by your counselor after each session (known as psychotherapy notes) are not transferred. Would you like for copies of these psychotherapy notes to be sent also?

_____ Yes

_____ No

    Generally, copies of your records are sent one time only as soon as possible, and you would have to complete and sign a form again for additional requests. If you would like to alter this general procedure in any way, please indicate your preferences:

    To the best of your knowledge, when did you begin and end counseling services at this agency?

_____ Date Counseling Services Began
_____ Date Counseling Services Ended

_____   _____
Client Signature   Date

APPENDIX D

Client Permission Form to Record
Counseling Session
for Supervision Purposes

I, _____ [fill in name of client], hereby give my permission for my counselor, _____
[fill in your name], to audiotape/videotape our counseling session on _____ [fill in date, or if
over a period of time, fill in inclusive dates].

   I understand that the purpose of this recording is for the clinical supervision of my counselor's
work. I understand that only my client's clinical supervisor, _____ [fill in name of supervisor],
will review the tape and that the tape will be erased after the supervisor has reviewed it.

_____   _____
Client's Signature   Date

APPENDIX E

Guidelines for Counseling Case Notes*

1. Write any case notes that assist you in being a more effective counseling practitioner. Do not hesitate to keep case notes if they help you in being a better counselor.
2. There is no general legal duty to keep case notes, but because maintaining case notes is a standard procedure in the counseling profession, it could be considered unusual if a counselor did not have case notes for a particular case.
3. Always assume that any notes you write will someday be read in open court with you and your client present, along with newspaper, radio, and television reporters.
4. Separate your notes into at least two distinct sections: *objective* and *subjective*.
5. In the objective section, record precisely what the client said, what you said, and what you observed. Do not draw any conclusions or enter any speculations at this point. You might entitle this section "Observations."
6. In the subjective section, record any thoughts that you will need for the future: impressions of the client, speculations about the reasons for the client's problems, reminders to yourself of your present thoughts, or plans for the next session would all be acceptable. You might entitle this section "Impressions."
7. Keep case notes in locked file drawers, and ensure that only clerical assistants and you have access to your notes. If notes are kept in a computer, be sure they are not accessible to others.
8. There is no general legal principle regarding the length of time you need to keep case notes once they are recorded. However, there are federal statutes that cover certain federally funded projects, hospital and counseling center accreditation standards, and particular agency procedures that require that case notes be kept for certain periods of time. Of course, such statutes, standards, and procedures should be followed if they apply to your case.
9. Regularly destroy your case notes. When you destroy them, be sure no identifying information remains. It is best to shred, burn, or in some other manner totally destroy the records.
10. Because there are no requirements in work settings regarding the length of time for retention, keep case notes as long as you think you might need them. However, you should destroy case notes on a systematic basis. For example, some counselors destroy case notes of terminated clients 6 months after termination, 1 year after termination, or 3 years after termination. It is a good idea to destroy notes only one or two days each year, for example, on every December 31.
11. When destroying your case notes, do not include those notes in which you have documented steps you have taken to protect yourself in the event you are accused of wrongdoing. Keep these case notes for longer periods of time, perhaps indefinitely.
12. Never, under any circumstances, destroy case notes after you receive a subpoena or if you think you might be receiving a subpoena in the future. Such acts could be interpreted as obstruction of justice, and you could be held in contempt of court.

*Composed by T. Remley

APPENDIX F

Clinical Supervision Model Agreement

I, (your name), agree to provide supervision for you for the purposes of becoming a Licensed Professional Counselor (change title if necessary) in the state of (your state).

I am licensed by the state of (your state) as a Professional Counselor (change title if necessary). I am also licensed as a Professional Counselor in (list other states, if applicable). I hold (list your degrees) degrees in counseling from the (list your university). I am a National Certified Counselor (NCC). In the past, I have served as (tailor this to your résumé) a high school counselor, community college counselor, university career counselor, counselor educator, community mental health center counselor, and counselor in private practice. My areas of counseling expertise include (tailor this to your résumé) personal and social adjustment, relationship issues, career decision making, work adjustment, divorce mediation, anger management, and serious mental illnesses.

It is your responsibility to obtain the degree necessary, meet the specific course content requirements, and complete the required practicum and internship necessary to register our supervision with the (your state) Licensed Professional Counselors Board of Examiners (LPC Board) (change title of board if necessary) so that you may obtain beginning supervision for the purpose of becoming licensed. You must complete the necessary LPC Board forms and include all attachments. I will complete the section of the form for the supervisor, will provide you with a copy of my "Declaration of Practice and Procedures," and will sign where necessary. You must then submit the forms to the LPC Board for approval.

The supervision I provide for you will be individual supervision. You will meet with me 1 hour each week during the time you are completing your required (insert number of hours required in your state) hours of supervised experience as a counselor intern. The hourly fee for my services is $_____, which has been set according to a fee schedule based on the income of you and your spouse or partner. This fee schedule will be reviewed annually and adjusted as appropriate. Fees are payable by check before each supervision session begins. In the event you must reschedule a session for some reason, you must notify me 24 hours in advance. If such notice is not received, you must pay the full fee for the missed session plus the fee for the current session prior to the next scheduled session. If you miss a session for circumstances beyond your control and were unable to contact me prior to missing the session, no fee will be charged.

Once our supervision relationship has been approved by the licensure board, our supervision meetings will begin. Our professional relationship will be limited to the formal scheduled hours we have agreed to for your supervision. In the event situations occur in your role as counselor for which you need direction and advice, you should consult your immediate supervisor at the site where you are providing counseling services and follow his or her direction. My regular hourly fee for supervision must be paid by you for any telephone or face-to-face consultation requested by you outside our regularly scheduled supervision sessions.

My philosophy of supervision is that my role as your clinical supervisor is to assist you in practicing counseling in the most effective manner possible, given your choice of counseling theories, approaches, and interventions. I will review your work and give you my impressions of your strengths and weakness and will assist you in improving your skills as a counselor. In addition, I will evaluate your work on a continuing basis.

It is your responsibility to notify your administrative supervisor at the site or sites where you are collecting your hours of experience that you are receiving clinical supervision from me. You should explain the nature of our supervisory relationship. If your administrative supervisor wishes to consult with me regarding your work, ask him or her to contact me.

In order for me to supervise you, you must be able to audiotape or videotape one counseling session each week. You must follow any requirements your site or sites may impose regarding these tapes. Before each meeting we have, you will provide me with a new tape. You will transfer the tape to me electronically in the secure fashion we agree upon, and I shall ensure no one else has access to the tape. I will keep information revealed in the tape confidential. I will review the tape before our next meeting and will permanently delete the tape after I have reviewed it.

During the time I am serving as your clinical supervisor, I will make every effort to review with you cases that you choose to bring to my attention for consultation. In addition, I will review the tapes of counseling sessions that you provide to me. My duty to you is to provide you with professional clinical supervision. However, I will not be responsible for your day-to-day activities as a counselor. Your administrative supervisor or supervisors at your site or sites will be responsible for your ongoing counseling activities.

Because I must evaluate your professional performance as a counselor, we will not have a personal friendship during the time I am serving as your supervisor. While we may have a congenial and collegial professional relationship and may attend social functions together, we should not include each other in social interactions one of us has initiated. Please do not offer me gifts or invite me to your home or nonprofessional social events you are hosting during the time I am serving as your clinical supervisor.

You must complete a total of (insert the required number) hours of supervised experience. When you have completed the first 1,000 hours, I will provide you with a written evaluation of your progress and performance, including my determination of whether you are progressing satisfactorily toward your goal of becoming a Licensed Professional Counselor. I will provide you with another written evaluation at the end of the second 1,000 hours. At the end of your total number of hours of supervised experience, I will verify the supervision I have provided to you to the LPC Board and will either recommend or not recommend you for licensure as a Professional Counselor.

I agree to provide clinical supervision to you of your counseling responsibilities in a professional manner to the extent described within this agreement. Our relationship is limited to the terms and conditions set forth herein. Either of us, with a 2-week written notice to the other, may cancel this agreement for any reason. In the event the agreement is canceled by either of us, you agree to notify the LPC Board immediately.

By signing below, I am agreeing to provide you with clinical supervision according to the terms of this agreement, and you are agreeing to pay my fee and comply with the terms of this agreement as well.

_____   _____   _____   _____
Supervisor's Signature   Date   Supervisee's Signature   Date

REFERENCES

Abbott, A. (1988). *The system of professions: An essay on the division of expert labor.* Chicago: University of Chicago Press.

Abraham, S. C. (1978). *The public accounting profession: Problems and prospects.* Lexington, MA: Lexington Books.

Adams, S. A. (2010). Who is my client? Maintaining paperwork when the client changes. *The Family Journal, 18,* 70–72.

Adkison-Bradley, C. (2013). Counselor education and supervision: The development of the CACREP Doctoral Standards. *Journal of Counseling & Development, 91,* 44–49. doi: 10.1002/j.1556-6676.2013.00069.x

Adarand Constructors, Inc. v. Pena, 515 U.S. 200, 115 S.Ct. 2097, 132 L.Ed.2d 158 (1995).

Administration on Aging. (2014). *Aging Statistics.* Retrieved from http://www.aoa.acl.gov

Age Discrimination in Employment Act of 1967, 29 U.S.C. §621 et seq. (1999).

Ahia, C. E., & Martin, D. (1993). *The danger-to-self-or-others exception to confidentiality.* Alexandria, VA: American Counseling Association.

Akamatsu, T. J. (1988). Intimate relationships with former clients: National survey of attitudes and behavior among practitioners. *Professional Psychology: Research and Practice, 199,* 454–458.

Alberty, S. C. (2014). *Advising small business.* New York: Thomson Reuters.

Allen, M., Burt, K., Bryan, E., Carter, D., Orsi, R., & Durkan, L. (2002). School counselors' preparation for and participation in crisis intervention. *Professional School Counseling, 6,* 96–102.

Allison v. Patel, 211 Ga. App. 376, 438 S.E.2d 920 (1993).

American Association for Marriage and Family Therapists. (2012). *Code of ethics.* Alexandria, VA: Author.

American Association for Marriage and Family Therapists. (2015). *Commission on Accreditation for Marriage and Family Education.* Retrieved from http://www.aamft.org

American Association of State Counseling Boards. (2014). Retrieved from http://www.aascb.org

American Board of Psychiatry and Neurology. (2014). *Application materials.* Retrieved from http://www.abpn.com/ifas.htm

American Counseling Association. (n.d.). *Anthony Centore.* Retrieved from www.counseling.org/news/blog/authors/anthony-centore

American Counseling Association. (2005). *2005 ACA Code of Ethics.* Retrieved from http://ethics.iit.edu/ecodes/node/4192

American Counseling Association. (2014). *2014 ACA Code of Ethics.* Retrieved from http://www.counseling.org

American Psychiatric Association. (2013). *Diagnostic and statistical manual of mental disorders, 5th edition (DSM-5).* Washington, DC: Author.

American Psychological Association. (1982). *Ethical principles in the conduct of research with human participants.* Washington, DC: Author.

American Psychological Association. (2006). Strategies for private practitioners coping with subpoenas or compelled testimony for client records or test data. *Professional Psychology: Research and Practice, 37,* 215–222. doi: 10.1037/0735-7028.37.2.215

American Psychological Association. (2007). Record keeping guidelines. *American Psychologist, 62,* 993–1004.

American Psychological Association. (2010). *Publication manual of the American Psychological Association, Sixth edition.* Washington, DC: Author.

American Psychological Association. (2012). *Ethical principles of psychologists and code of conduct including 2010 amendments.* Retrieved from http://www.apa.org

American Psychological Association. (2014). *Marriage and divorce.* Retrieved from http://www.apa.org/topics/divorce

American Psychological Association. (2015). *APA Statement on Services by Telephone, Teleconferencing, and Internet.* Retrieved from http://www.apa.org/ethics/education/telephone-statement.aspx

American Psychological Association Commission on Accreditation. (2014). *Guidelines and principles for accreditation of programs in professional psychology.* Retrieved from http://www.apa.org

Americans with Disabilities Act of 1990, Pub. L. 101–336, 104 Stat. 328 (1990).

Ametrano, I. M. (2014). Teaching ethical decision making: Helping students reconcile personal and professional values. *Journal of Counseling & Development, 92,* 154–161.

Amnesty International. (2001). *Crimes of hate, conspiracy of silence.* Oxford, UK: Alden Press.

Ancis, J. R., & Marshall, D. S. (2010). Using a multicultural framework to assess supervisees' perceptions of culturally competent supervision. *Journal of Counseling & Development, 88,* 277–284.

Anderson, A. M. N., & Bertram, B. (2012). *The counselor and the law* (6th ed.). Alexandria, VA: American Counseling Association.

Anderson, C. E. (2000). Dealing constructively with managed care: Suggestions from an insider. *Journal of Mental Health Counseling, 22,* 343–353.

Anderson, D., & Freeman, L. T. (2006). Report of the ACA Ethics Committee: 2004–2005. *Journal of Counseling & Development, 84,* 225–227.

Anderson, D., & Swanson, C. D. (1994). *Legal issues in licensure.* Alexandria, VA: American Counseling Association.

Anderson, S. K., & Kitchener, K. S. (1996). Nonromantic, nonsexual post-therapy relationships between psychologists and former clients: An exploratory study of critical incidents. *Professional Psychology: Research and Practice, 27,* 59–66.

Aponte, J. F., & Wohl, J. (2000). *Psychological intervention and cultural diversity.* Boston: Allyn & Bacon.

Applebaum, P. (1993). Legal liability and managed care. *American Psychologist, 48,* 251–257.

Appelbaum, P. S., Lidz, C. W., & Meisel, A. (1987). *Informed consent: Legal theory and clinical practice.* New York: Oxford University Press.

Appleby, G. (Ed.). (2001). *Working class gay and bisexual men.* New York: Harrington Park Press.

Application of Striegel, 92 Misc2d 113, 399 N.Y.S.2d 584 (1977).

Arenas, M. A., & Paz Sandin, M. (2009). Intercultural and cross-cultural communication research: Some reflections about culture and qualitative methods. *Forum: Qualitative Social Research, 10,* 15–19.

Armstrong, K. L. (2007). Advancing social justice by challenging socioeconomic disadvantage. In C. C. Lee (Ed.), *Counseling for social justice* (2nd ed., pp. 15–30). Alexandria, VA: American Counseling Association.

Arredondo, P., & Aricniega, G. M. (2001). Strategies and techniques for counselor training based on the multicultural counseling competencies. *Journal of Multicultural Counseling and Development, 29,* 263–273.

Arredondo, P., Toporek, R., Brown, S. P., Jones, J., Locke, D., Sanchez, J., & Stadler, H. A. (1996). Operationalization of the multicultural counseling competencies. *Journal of Multicultural Counseling and Development, 24,* 42–78.

Arthur, G. L., Jr., & Swanson, C. D. (1993). *Confidentiality and privileged communication.* Alexandria, VA: American Counseling Association.

Association for Counselor Education and Supervision. (1990). Standards for counseling supervisors. *Journal of Counseling & Development, 69,* 30–32.

Association for Counselor Education and Supervision. (1993). *Ethical guidelines for counseling supervisors.* Retrieved from http://files.acesonline.net/doc/ethical_guidelines.htm

Association for Counselor Education and Supervision. (1999a). *ACES guidelines for online instruction in counselor education.* Retrieved from http://files.acesonline.net/doc/1999_guidelines_for_online_instruction.htm

Association for Counselor Education and Supervision. (1999b). *Technical competencies for counselor education students: Recommended guidelines for program development.* Retrieved from http://www.acesonline.net/competencies.htm

Association for Lesbian, Gay, Bisexual & Transgender Issues in Counseling. (2009). *Competencies for counseling transgender individuals.* Retrieved from http://www.algbtic.org

Association for Lesbian, Gay, Bisexual & Transgender Issues in Counseling. (2012). *Competencies for counseling LBGQQIA individuals.* Retrieved from http://www.algbtic.org

Association for Specialists in Group Work. (2000). *Professional standards for the training of group workers.* Alexandria, VA: Author.

Association for Specialists in Group Work. (2007). *Best practice guidelines 2007 revisions.* Alexandria, VA: Author. Retrieved from http://asgw.org

Association for Specialists in Group Work. (2012). *Multicultural and social justice competency principles for group workers.* Alexandria, VA: Author.

Atkinson, D. R., & Hackett, G. (2004). *Counseling diverse populations* (3rd ed.). Madison, WI: Brown and Benchmark.

Atkinson, D. R., Thompson, C. E., & Grant, S. K. (1993). A three-dimensional model for counseling racial/ethnic minorities. *The Counseling Psychologist, 21,* 257–277.

Auerbach, R. S. (2006). New York's immediate need for a psychotherapist-patient privilege encompassing psychiatrists, psychologists, and social workers. *Albany Law Review, 69,* 889–892.

Austin, K. M., Moline, M. E., & Williams, G. T. (1990). *Confronting malpractice: Legal and ethical dilemmas in psychotherapy.* Newbury Park, CA: Sage.

Axelson, J. A. (1993). *Counseling and development in a multicultural society* (2nd ed.). Pacific Grove, CA: Brooks/Cole.

Bailey, K. A. (2001). Legal implications of profiling students for violence. *Psychology in the Schools, 38,* 141–155.

Baird, C., & Dooey, P. (2014). Ensuring effective support in higher education alleged plagiarism cases. *Innovative Higher Education, 39,* 387–400.

Baird, K. A., & Rupert, P. A. (1987). Clinical management of confidentiality: A survey of psychologists in seven states. *Professional Psychology: Research and Practice, 18,* 347–352.

Bakke v. Regents of the University of California, 438 U.S. 265 (1978).

Baldo, T. D., Softas-Nall, B., & Shaw, S. F. (1997). Student review and retention in counselor education: An alternative to Frame and Stevens-Smith. *Counselor Education and Supervision, 36,* 245–253.

Barak, A., Hen, L., Boniel-Nissim, M., & Shapira, N. (2008). A comprehensive review and meta-analysis of the effectiveness of Internet-based psychotherapeutic interventions. *Journal of Technology in Human Services, 26,* 109–160.

Barber, J. S., & Mobley, M. (1999). Counseling gay adolescents. In A. M. Horne & M. S. Kiselica (Eds.), *Handbook of counseling boys and adolescent males* (pp. 161–178). Thousand Oaks, CA: Sage.

Barnett, J. (2008). Impaired professionals: Distress, professional impairment, self-care, and psychological wellness. In M. Hersen & A. M. Gross (Eds.), *Handbook of clinical psychology* (Vol. 1; pp. 857–884). Hoboken, NJ: John Wiley.

Barnett, J. E., & Johnson, W. B. (2011). Integrating spirituality and religion into psychotherapy: Persistent dilemmas, ethical issues, and a proposed decision-making process. *Ethics & Behavior, 2,* 147–164.

Barnett, J. E., & Johnson, W. B. (2015). *Ethics desk reference for counselors* (2nd ed.). Alexandria, VA: American Counseling Association.

Barnett, J. E., & Walfish, S. (2012). *Billing and collecting for your mental health practice: Effective strategies and ethical practice.* Washington, DC: American Psychological Association.

Barnett, J. E., Wise, E. H., Johnson-Greene, D., & Bucky, S. F. (2007). Informed consent: Too much of a good thing or not enough? *Professional Psychology: Research and Practice, 38,* 179–186. doi: 10.1037/0735-7028.38.2.179

Barnett, J. E., Zimmerman, J., & Walfish, S. (2014). *The ethics of private practice: A practical guide for mental health clinicians.* New York: Oxford University Press.

Barrett, K. A., & McWhirter, B. T. (2002). Counselor trainees' perceptions of clients based on client sexual orientation. *Counselor Education and Supervision, 41,* 219–232.

Barsky, A. E., & Gould, J. W. (2002). *Clinicians in court: A guide to subpoenas, depositions, testifying, and everything else you need to know.* New York: Guilford Press.

Bartell, P. A., & Rubin, L. J. (1990). Dangerous liaisons: Sexual intimacies in supervision. *Professional Psychology: Research and Practice, 21,* 442–450.

Beamish, P. M., Navin, S. L., & Davidson, P. (1994). Ethical dilemmas in marriage and family therapy: Implications for training. *Journal of Mental Health Counseling, 16,* 129–142.

Beck, E. S. (1999). Mental health counseling: A stakeholder's manifesto. *Journal of Mental Health Counseling, 21,* 203–214.

Becker, R. F. (1997). *Scientific evidence and expert testimony handbook: A guide for lawyers, criminal investigators and forensic specialists.* Springfield, IL: Charles C Thomas.

Behavioral Health Innovation. (2014). *Telemental health therapy comparisons.* Retrieved from http://www.telementalhealthcomparisons.com

Belton, R., & Avery, D. (1999). *Employment discrimination law* (6th ed.). St. Paul, MN: West.

Bemak, F., & Chung, R. C. (2007). Training social justice counselors. In C. C. Lee (Ed.), *Counseling for social justice* (pp. 239–258). Alexandria, VA: American Counseling Association.

Bemak, F., & Chung, R. C. (2015). Cultural boundaries, cultural norms: Multicultural and social justice perspectives. In B. Herlihy & G. Corey, *Boundary issues in counseling* (3rd ed., pp. 84–89). Alexandria, VA: American Counseling Association.

Bennett, A. G., & Werth, J. L. (2006). Working with clients who may harm themselves. In B. Herlihy & G. Corey, *ACA Ethical Standards Casebook* (6th ed., pp. 223–228). Alexandria, VA: American Counseling Association.

Bennett, B. E., Bricklin, P. M., Harris, E. I., Knapp, S., VandeCreek, L., & Younggen, J. N. (2006). *Assessing and managing risk in psychological practice: An individualized approach*. Rockville, MD: The Trust.

Benshoff, J. M., & Paisley, P. O. (1996). The Structured Peer Consultation Model for school counselors. *Journal of Counseling & Development, 74,* 15–30.

Benson, K. (2013). Review of Handbook of LGBT-affirmative couple and family therapy. *Journal of Marital and Family Therapy, 39,* 403–404.

Beren, P., & Bunnin, B. (1983). *Author law and strategies.* Berkeley, CA: Nolo Press.

Berge, Z. L. (1994). Electronic discussion groups. *Communication Education, 43,* 102–111.

Bergman, D. M. (2013). The role of government and lobbying in the creation of a health profession: The legal foundations of counseling. *Journal of Counseling & Development, 91,* 61–67. doi: 10.1002/j.1556-6676.2013.00072.x

Berlin, I. N. (1987). Suicide among American Indian adolescents: An overview. *Suicide & Life-Threatening Behavior, 17,* 218–232.

Berman, A. L., & Cohen-Sandler, R. (1982). Suicide and the standard of care: Optimal v. acceptable. *Suicide and Life-Threatening Behavior, 12,* 114–122.

Bernard, J. M., & Goodyear, R. K. (2014). *Fundamentals of clinical supervision* (5th ed.). Boston: Allyn & Bacon.

Berner, M. (1998). Informed consent. In L. E. Lifson & R. I. Simon (Eds.), *The mental health practitioner and the law* (pp. 23–43). Cambridge, MA: Harvard University Press.

Bernsen, A., Tabachnick, B. G., & Pope, K. S. (1994). National survey of social workers' sexual attraction to their clients: Results, implications, and comparison to psychologists. *Ethics & Behavior, 4,* 369–388.

Bevacqua, F., & Kurpius, S. E. R. (2013). Counseling students' personal views and attitudes toward euthanasia. *Journal of Mental Health Counseling, 35,* 172–188.

Biaggio, M., Paget, T. L., & Chenoweth, M. S. (1997). A model for ethical management of faculty-student dual relationships. *Professional Psychology: Research and Practice, 28,* 184–189.

Bidell, M. P. (2012). Examining school counseling students' multicultural and sexual orientation competencies through a cross-specialization comparison. *Journal of Counseling & Development, 90,* 200–207.

Biele, N., & Barnhill, E. (1995). The art of advocacy. In J. C. Gonsiorek (Ed.), *Breach of trust: Sexual exploitation by health care professionals and clergy* (pp. 317–332). Thousand Oaks, CA: Sage.

Bienvenu, C., & Ramsey, C. J. (2006). The culture of socioeconomic disadvantage: Practical approaches to counseling. In C. C. Lee (Ed.), *Multicultural issues in counseling: New approaches to diversity* (3rd ed., pp. 345–353). Alexandria, VA: American Counseling Association.

Bieschke, K. J., McClanahan, M., Tozer, E., Grzegorek, J. L., & Park, J. (2000). Programmatic research on the treatment of lesbian, gay, and bisexual clients: The past, the present, and the course for the future. In R. M. Perez, K. A. DeBord, & K. J. Bieschke (Eds.), *Handbook of counseling and psychotherapy with lesbian, gay, and bisexual clients* (pp. 309–335). Washington, DC: American Psychological Association.

Bigner, J. J., & Wetchler, J. L. (Eds.). (2012). *Handbook of LGBT-affirmative couple and family therapy.* New York: Routledge.

Birky, I., & Collins, W. (2011). Facebook: Maintaining ethical practice in the cyberspace age. *Journal of College Student Psychotherapy, 25,* 193–203.

Blakely, T. J., Smith, K., & Swenson, M. (2004). The electronic record as infrastructure. *Psychiatric Rehabilitation Journal, 27,* 271–274. doi:10.2975/27.2004.271.274

Blevins-Knabe, B. (1992). The ethics of dual relationships in higher education. *Ethics and Behavior, 2,* 151–163.

Bobby, C. L. (2013). The evolution of specialties in the CACREP Standards: CACREP's role in unifying the profession. *Journal of Counseling & Development, 91,* 35–43. doi: 10.1002/j.1556-6676.2013.00068.x

Bograd, M. (1993, January/February). The duel over dual relationships. *The California Therapist,* 7–16.

Bogust v. Iverson, 10 Wisc.2d 129, 102 N.W.2d 228 (1960).

Bok, S. (1983). *Secrets: On the ethics of concealment and revelation.* New York: Vintage Books.

Boling v. Superior Court. 105 Cal. App.3d 430, 164 Cal. Rptr. 432 (App. 1980).

Borders, L. D. (1991). A systematic approach to peer group supervision. *Journal of Counseling & Development, 69,* 248–252.

Borders, L. D., Cashwell, C. S., & Rotter, J. C. (1995). Supervision of counselor licensure applicants: A comparative study. *Counselor Education and Supervision, 35,* 54–69.

Borders, L. D., & Leddick, G. R. (1987). *Handbook of counseling supervision.* Alexandria, VA: Association for Counselor Education and Supervision.

Borders, L. D., Wester, K. L., Granello, D. H., Chang, C. Y., Hays, D. G., Pepperell, J., & Spurgeon, S. L. (2012). Association for

Counselor Education and Supervision guidelines for research mentorship: Development and implementation. *Counselor Education & Supervision, 51,* 162–175.

Borsari, B., & Tevyaw, T. O. (2005). Stepped care: A promising treatment strategy for mandated students. *NASPA Journal, 42,* 381–397.

Borys, D. S. (1988). *Dual relationships between therapist and client: A national survey of clinicians' attitudes and practices.* Unpublished doctoral dissertation, University of California, Los Angeles.

Borys, D. S., & Pope, K. S. (1989). Dual relationships between therapist and client: A national study of psychologists, psychiatrists and social workers. *Professional Psychology: Research and Practice, 20,* 283–293.

Bouchard, S., Payeur, R., Rivard, V., Allard, M., Paquin, B., & Renaud, P. (2000). Cognitive behavior therapy for panic disorder with agoraphobia in videoconference: Preliminary results. *Cyberpsychology & Behavior, 3,* 999–1007.

Boughner, S. R., & Logan, J. P. (1999). Robert H. Woody: Legal issues in couple and family counseling. *The Family Journal, 7,* 302–310.

Bouhoutsos, J., Holroyd, J., Lerman, H., Forer, B., & Greenberg, M. (1983). Sexual intimacy between psychologists and patients. *Professional Psychology, 14,* 185–196.

Boumil, M. M., Freitas, F. F., & Freitas, C. F. (2012). Waiver of the psychotherapist-patient privilege: Implications for child custody litigation. *Case Western Reserve University Health Matrix: Journal of Law-Medicine, 22,* 1–31. Retrieved from http://www .lexisnexis.com

Boundless. (2014, June 27). *What is social media? Boundless Marketing.* Retrieved from http://www .boundless.com

Bowerbank, J. E. (2006). Do's and don'ts about a nonparty's response to federal and state court deposition subpoenas involving civil litigation. *Orange County Lawyer, 48,* 38–41.

Bowman, V. E., Hatley, L. D., & Bowman, R. L. (1995). Faculty–student relationships: The dual role controversy. *Counselor Education and Supervision, 34,* 232–242.

Braaten, E. E., Otto, S., & Handelsman, M. M. (1993). What do people want to know about psychotherapy? *Psychotherapy, 30,* 565–570.

Bradley, L. J., Whiting, P. P., Hendricks, B., & Wheat, L. S. (2010). Ethical imperatives for intervention with elder families. *The Family Journal, 18,* 215–221. doi: 10.1177/1066480710364507

Bradley, R. W., & Cox, J. A. (2001). Counseling: Evolution of the profession. In D. C. Locke, J. E. Myers, & E. L. Herr (Eds.), *The handbook of counseling* (pp. 27–41). Thousand Oaks, CA: Sage.

Braun, S. A., & Cox, J. A. (2005). Managed mental health care: Intentional misdiagnosis of mental disorders. *Journal of Counseling & Development, 83,* 425–433.

Bray, B. (2013, May 13). CACREP degree to be required for counselor licensure in Ohio. *Counseling Today.* Alexandria, VA: American Counseling Association. Retrieved from http://ct.counseling.org

Bray, J. H., Shepherd, J. N., & Hays, J. R. (1985). Legal and ethical issues in informed consent to psychotherapy. *American Journal of Family Therapy, 13,* 50–60.

Brendel, J. M., & Nelson, K. W. (1999). The stream of family secrets: Navigating the islands of confidentiality and triangulation involving family therapists. *The Family Journal, 7,* 112–117.

Brinson, J., & Kottler, J. (1993). Cross-cultural mentoring in counselor education. *Counselor Education & Supervision, 32,* 241–254.

Brodsky, S. L., & Terrell, J. J. (2011). Testifying about mitigation: When social workers and other mental health professionals face aggressive cross-examination. *Journal of Forensic Social Work, 1,* 73–81.

Brott, P. E., & Myers, J. E. (1999). Development of professional school counselor identity: A grounded theory. *Professional School Counseling, 2,* 339–348.

Broverman, I. K., Broverman, D., Clarkson, F. E., Rosencrantz, P., & Vogel, S. (1970). Sex role stereotypes and clinical judgments of mental health. *Journal of Consulting and Clinical Psychology, 34,* 1–7.

Brown, D. (1993). Training consultants: A call to action. *Journal of Counseling & Development, 72,* 139–143.

Brown, M. (2013). A content analysis of problematic behavior in counselor education programs. *Counselor Education & Supervision, 52,* 179–192.

Brown, M. T., & Landrum-Brown, J. (1995). Counselor supervision: Cross-cultural perspectives. In J. C. Ponterotto, J. M. Casas, L. A. Suzuki, & C. M. Alexander (Eds.), *Handbook of multicultural counseling* (pp. 263–286). Thousand Oaks, CA: Sage.

Brown-Rice, K. A., & Furr, S. (2013). Preservice counselors' knowledge of classmates' problems of professional competency. *Journal of Counseling & Development, 91,* 224–233.

Bruff v. North Mississippi Health Services, 244 F.3d 495 (5th Cir. 2001).

Buckner, C. J., & Sall, R. K. (2008). Ethically speaking: Point/counterpoint—Sex with clients: Prohibition or permission? *Orange County Lawyer, 50,* 38.

Burkemper, E. M. (2002). Family therapists' ethical decision-making processes in two duty-to-warn situations. *Journal of Marital and Family Therapy, 28,* 203–211.

Burn, D. (1992). Ethical implications in cross-cultural counseling and training. *Journal of Counseling & Development, 70,* 578–583.

Burnes, T. R., & Ross, K. L. (2010). Applying social justice to oppression and marginalization in group process: Interventions and strategies for group workers. *Journal for Specialists in Group Work, 35,* 169–176.

Bursztajn, H., Gutheil, T. G., Hamm, R. M., & Brodsky, A. (1983). Subjective data and suicide assessment in the light of recent legal developments. Part II: Clinical uses of legal standards in the interpretation of subjective data. *International Journal of Law and Psychiatry, 6,* 331–350.

Butler, M. H., Rodriguez, M. A., Roper, S. O., & Feinauer, L. L. (2010). Infidelity secrets in couple therapy: Therapists' views on the collision of competing ethics around relationship-relevant secrets. *Sexual Addiction & Compulsivity, 17,* 82–105. doi: 10.1080/10720161003772041

Butler, S. F. (1998). *Assessment preparation and practices reported by mental health and related professionals.* Unpublished doctoral dissertation, University of New Orleans.

Calamari, J. D., Perillo, J. M., & Bender, H. H. (1989). *Cases and problems on contracts* (2nd ed.). St. Paul, MN: West.

Calmes, S. A., Piazza, N. J., & Laux, J. M. (2013). The use of touch in counseling: An ethical decision-making model. *Counseling and Values, 58,* 59–68. doi: 10.1002/j.2161-007X.2013.00025.x

Campbell, C. D., & Gordon, M. C. (2003). Acknowledging the inevitable: Understanding multiple relationships in rural practice. *Professional Psychology: Research and Practice, 34,* 430–434.

Campbell, J. M. (2000). *Becoming an effective supervisor: A workbook for counselors and psychotherapists.* Philadelphia: Accelerated Development.

Canterbury v. Spence, 464 F.2d 772 (D.C. Cir 1972).

Caplow, T. (1966). The sequence of professionalization. In H. M. Vollmer & D. L. Mills (Eds.), *Professionalization* (pp. 19–21). Upper Saddle River, NJ: Prentice-Hall.

Capuzzi, D. (2002). Legal and ethical challenges in counseling suicidal students. *Professional School Counseling, 6,* 36–45.

Capuzzi, D., & Golden, L. (Eds.). (1988). *Preventing adolescent suicide.* Muncie, IN: Accelerated Development, Inc.

Carabillo, J. A. (1986). Liability for treatment decisions: How far does it extend? In C. M. Combe (Ed.), *Managed health care: Legal and operational issues facing providers, insurers, and employers* (pp. 341–407). New York: Practicing Law Institute.

Carlson, J., Sperry, L., & Lewis, J. A. (1997). *Family therapy: Ensuring treatment efficacy.* Pacific Grove, CA: Brooks/Cole.

Caron, C. (1996). Making meaning out of the experiences of our lives. *Contemporary Women's Issues Database, 12,* 22–25.

Casas, J. M., Park, Y. S., & Cho, B. (2010). The multicultural and internationalization counseling psychology movements: When all is said and done, it's all multicultural, isn't it? In J. G. Ponterotto, J. M. Casas, L. A. Suzuki, & C. M. Alexander (Eds.), *Handbook of multicultural counseling* (3rd ed., pp. 189–200). Thousand Oaks, CA: Sage.

Cashwell, C. C., Shcherbakova, J., & Cashwell, T. H. (2003). Effect of client and counselor ethnicity on preference for counselor self-disclosure. *Journal of Counseling & Development, 81,* 196–201.

Center for Credentialing & Education. (2014). Retrieved from http://www.cce-global.org

Centers for Disease Control. (2013). *HIV in the United States: At a Glance.* Retrieved from http://www.cdc.gov

Centers for Disease Control. (2014). *About HIV/AIDS.* Retrieved from http://www.cdc.gov

Cepelewicz, B. B. (2014, May 23). Text messaging with patients: Steps physicians must take to avoid liability. *ModernMedicine Network.* Retrieved from http://medicaleconomics.modernmedicine.com

Chafee, Z. (1943). Privileged communications: Is justice served or obstructed by closing the doctor's mouth on the witness stand? *Yale Law Journal, 52,* 607–612.

Chamallas, M. (1988). Consent, equality and the legal control of sexual conduct. *Southern California Law Review, 61,* 777–862.

Chang, C. Y., Crethar, H. C., & Ratts, M. J. (2010). Social justice: A national imperative for counselor education and supervision. *Counselor Education & Supervision, 50,* 82–87.

Chapman, R. A., Baker, S. B., Nassar-McMillan, S. C., & Gerler, E. R. (2011). Cybersupervision: Further examination of synchronous and asynchronous modalities in counseling practicum supervision. *Counselor Education & Supervision, 50,* 298–313.

Chauvin, J. C., & Remley, T. P., Jr. (1996). Responding to allegations of unethical conduct. *Journal of Counseling & Development, 74,* 563–568.

Child Welfare Information Gateway. (2014). *Mandatory reporters of child abuse and neglect: State Statutes Search.* Washington DC: U.S. Department of Health and Human Services. Retrieved from http://www.childwelfare.gov

Children's Rights Council. (2014). *Home.* Lanham, MD: Author. Retrieved from http://www .crckids.org

Childress-Beatty, L., & Koocher, G. P. (2013). Dealing with subpoenas. In G. P. Koocher, J. C. Norcross, & B. A. Greene (Eds.), *Psychologists' desk reference* (3rd ed., pp. 564–567). New York: Oxford University Press.

Choate, L. H. (2012). Counseling adolescents who engage in non-suicidal self-injury: A dialectical behavior therapy approach. *Journal of Mental Health Counseling, 34,* 56–70.

Choate, L. H., & Gintner, G. G. (2011). Prenatal depression: Best practice guidelines for diagnosis and treatment. *Journal of Counseling & Development, 89,* 373–382.

Christensen, L. L., & Miller, R. B. (2001). Marriage and family therapists evaluate managed mental health care: A qualitative inquiry. *Journal of Marital and Family Therapy, 27,* 509–514.

Christie, G. C., Meeks, J. E., Pryor, E. S., & Sanders, J. (1997). *Cases and materials on the law of torts* (3rd ed.). St. Paul, MN: West.

Chronister, K. M., & McWhirter, E. H. (2003). Applying social cognitive career theory to the empowerment of battered women. *Journal of Counseling & Development, 81,* 418–425.

Chung, R. C., & Bemak, F. (2002). The relationship of culture and empathy in cross-cultural counseling. *Journal of Counseling & Development, 80,* 154–159.

Cizek, G. J. (1999). *Cheating on tests: How to do it, detect it, and prevent it.* Mahwah, NJ: Erlbaum.

Claim of Gerkin, 106 Misc.2d 643, 434 N.Y.S.2d 607 (1980).

Clausen v. Clausen, 675 P.2d 562 (Utah, 1983).

Cleary, E. (Ed.). (1984). *McCormick's handbook on the law of evidence* (3rd ed.). St. Paul. MN: West.

Cohen, E. D. (1997). Ethical standards in counseling sexually active clients with HIV. In *Ethics in therapy* (pp. 211–233). New York: Hatherleigh.

Cohen, R. J., & Mariano, W. E. (1982). *Legal guidebook in mental health.* New York: The Free Press.

Coleman, P., & Shellow, R. A. (1992). Suicide: Unpredictable and unavoidable—Proposed guidelines provide rational test for physician's liability. *Nebraska Law Review, 71,* 643–693.

Colistra, A., & Brown-Rice, K. (2011). *When the rubber hits the road: Applying multicultural competencies in cross-cultural supervision.* Retrieved from http://www.counselingoutfitters .com/vistas/vistas11/Article_43 .pdf

Collison, B. B. (2001). Professional associations, standards, and credentials in counseling. In D. C. Locke, J. E. Myers, & E. L. Herr (Eds.), *The handbook of counseling* (pp. 55–68). Thousand Oaks, CA: Sage.

Comer, R. J. (2007). *Abnormal psychology* (6th ed.). New York: Worth.

Comijs, H. C., Penninx, B. W. J. H., Knipscheer, K. P. M., & van Tilburg, W. (1999). Psychological distress in victims of elder mistreatment: The effects of social support and coping. *Journal of Gerontology, 54,* 240–245.

Commission on Rehabilitation Counselor Certification. (2014). Retrieved from http://www .cce-global.org

Commonwealth ex rel. Platt v. Platt, 404 A.2d 410 (Pa. Super. 1979).

Comprehensive Alcohol Abuse and Alcoholism Prevention, Treatment and Rehabilitation Act of 1972, 42 U.S.C.A. §290dd-2 (West, 1997).

Comstock, G. D. (1991). *Violence against lesbians and gay men.* New York: Columbia University Press.

Conarton, S., & Kreger-Silverman, L. (1988). Feminine development through the life cycle. In M. Dutton-Douglas & L. E. A. Walker (Eds.), *Feminist psychotherapies: Integration of therapeutic and feminist systems.* Westport, CT: Ablex.

Connell, A. (2015). Boundary issues and in-home counseling for clients with disabilities. In B. Herlihy & G. Corey, *Boundary issues in counseling* (3rd ed., pp. 271–272). Alexandria, VA: American Counseling Association.

Connelly v. University of Vermont, 244 F.Supp. 156 (D.Vt. 1965).

Constantine, M. G. (2001). Addressing racial, ethnic, gender, and social class issues in counselor training and practice. In D. B. Pope-Davis & H. L. K. Coleman (Eds.), *The intersection of race, class and gender in multicultural counseling* (pp. 341–350). Thousand Oaks, CA: Sage.

Constantine, M. G. (2002). The intersection of race, ethnicity, gender, and social class in counseling: Examining selves in cultural contexts. *Journal for Multicultural Counseling and Development, 30,* 210–215.

Constantine, M. G., Smith, L., Redington, R. M., & Owens, D. (2008). Racial microaggressions against Black counseling and counseling psychology faculty: A central challenge in the multicultural counseling movement. *Journal of Counseling & Development, 86,* 348–355.

Conti, S. (2011). Student note: Lawyers and mental health professionals working together: Reconciling the duties of confidentiality and mandatory child abuse reporting. *Family Court Review, 49,* 388–396. Retrieved from http://www.lexisnexis.com

Conyne, R. K., & Horne, A. M. (2001). The current status of groups being used for prevention. *The Journal for Specialists in Group Work, 3,* 289–292.

Cook, J. E., & Doyle, C. (2002). Working alliance in online therapy: Preliminary results. *Cyberpsychology and Behavior, 5,* 95–105.

Corcoran, M. E. (1989). Managing the risks in managed care. In M. E. Corcoran (Ed.), *Managed health care 1989* (pp. 7–70). New York: Practicing Law Institute.

Corey, G. (2011). *Theory and practice of group counseling* (8th ed.). Pacific Grove, CA: Brooks/Cole.

Corey, G., Corey, M. S., Corey, C., & Callanan, P. (2015). *Issues and ethics in the helping professions with 2014 ACA codes* (9th ed.). Stamford, CT: Cengage Learning.

Corey, G., Haynes, R., Moulton, P., & Muratori, M. (2010). *Clinical supervision in the helping professions: A practical guide* (2nd ed.). Alexandria, VA: American Counseling Association.

Corr, C. A., & Balk, D. E. (2010). *Children's encounters with death, bereavement, and coping.* New York: Springer.

Costa, L., & Altekruse, M. (1994). Duty-to-warn guidelines for mental health counselors. *Journal of Counseling & Development, 72,* 346–350.

Cottle, M. (1956). Witnesses—Privilege-communications to psychotherapists. *University of Kansas Law Review, 4,* 597–599.

Cottone, R. R. (1985). The need for counselor licensure: A rehabilitation counseling perspective. *Journal of Counseling & Development, 63,* 625–629.

Cottone, R. R. (1992). *Theories and paradigms of counseling and psychotherapy.* Needham Heights, MA: Allyn & Bacon.

Cottone, R. R. (2005). Detrimental therapist-client relationships—Beyond thinking of "dual" or "multiple" roles: Reflections on the 2001 *AAMFT Code of Ethics. American Journal of Family Therapy, 33,* 1–17.

Cottone, R. R., & Tarvydas, V. M. (2007). *Counseling ethics and decision making* (3rd ed.). Upper Saddle River, NJ: Pearson Merrill Prentice-Hall.

Council for Accreditation of Counseling and Related Educational Programs. (2009). *2009 Standards.* Retrieved from http://www.cacrep.org

Council for Accreditation of Counseling and Related Educational Programs. (2014). *2014 Standards.* Retrieved from http://www.cacrep.org

Council on Rehabilitation Education. (2014). Retrieved from http://www.core-rehab.org

Council on Social Work Education. (2014). *Educational policy and accreditation standards.* Retrieved from http://www.cswe.org

Coyle, D., Matthews, M., Sharry, J., Nisbet, A., & Doherty, G. (2005). Personal investigator: A therapeutic 3D game for adolescent psychotherapy. *Journal of Interactive Technology & Smart Education, 2,* 73–88.

Cox v. Warwick Valley Central School District, 2010 U.S. Dist. LEXIS 142734 (S.D.N.Y., Aug. 16, 2010).

Cramton, R. C. (1981). Incompetence: The North American experience. In L. E. Trakman & D. Watters (Eds.), *Professional competence and the law* (pp. 158–163). Halifax, Nova Scotia, Canada: Dalhousie University.

Crane, D. R., & Law, D. D. (2002). Conducting medical offset research in a health maintenance organization: Challenges, opportunities, and insights. *Journal of Marital and Family Therapy, 28,* 15–19.

Crawford, R. (1999). Counseling a client whose family member is planning a suicide. *The Family Journal, 7,* 165–169.

Crawford, R. L. (1994). *Avoiding counselor malpractice.* Alexandria, VA: American Counseling Association.

Crisp-Han, H., Gabbard, G. O., & Martinez, M. (2011). Professional boundary violations and mentalizing in the clergy. *Journal of Pastoral Care and Counseling, 65,* 1–11.

Croteau, J. M., Talbot, D. M., Lance, T. S., & Evans, N. J. (2002). A qualitative study of the interplay between privilege and oppression. *Journal for Multicultural Counseling and Development, 30,* 239–258.

Culver, L. M. (2011). *Counselor perceptions of the efficacy of training and implementation of self-care strategies related to trauma work.* Unpublished dissertation, University of New Orleans.

Curd, T. (1938). Privileged communications between the doctor and his patient—An anomaly of the law. *West Virginia Law Review, 44,* 165–174.

Curran, D. F. (1987). *Adolescent suicidal behavior.* Washington, DC: Hemisphere Publishing.

Currie, C. L., Kuzmina, M. V., & Nadyuk, R. I. (2012). The counseling profession in Russia: Historical roots, current trends, and future perspectives. *Journal of Counseling & Development, 90,* 488–493. doi: 10.1002/j.1556-6676.2012.00060.x

Cynthia B. v. New Rochelle Hospital, 86 A.D.2d 256, 449 N.Y.S.2d 755 (App. Div. 1982).

Dailey, S. F., Gill, C. S., Karl, S. L., & Barrio Minton, C. A. (2014a). Historical underpinnings, structural alterations and philosophical changes: Counseling practice implications of the DSM-5. *The Professional Counselor, 4,* 166–178. doi: 10.15241/sfd.4.3.166

Dailey, S. F., Gill, C. S., Karl, S. L., & Barrio Minton, C. A. (2014b). *DSM-5: Learning companion for counselors.* Alexandria, VA: American Counseling Association.

D'Andrea, M. (2004). Comprehensive school-based violence prevention training: A developmental-ecological training model. *Journal of Counseling & Development, 82,* 277–286.

D'Andrea, M., & Foster Heckman, E. (2008). A 40-year review of multicultural counseling outcome research: Outlining a future research agenda for the multicultural counseling movement. *Journal of Counseling & Development, 86,* 356–363.

Daniel, S. S., & Goldston, D. B. (2012). Hopelessness and lack of connectedness to others as risk factors for suicidal behavior across the lifespan: Implications for cognitive-behavioral treatment. *Cognitive and Behavioral Practice, 19,* 288–300. doi: 10.1016/j.cbpra.2011.05.003

Daniels, J. A. (2001). Managed care, ethics, and counseling. *Journal of Counseling & Development, 79,* 119–122.

Daniels, J. A. (2002). Assessing threats of school violence: Implications for counselors. *Journal of Counseling & Development, 80,* 215–218.

Daniluk, J. C., & Haverkamp, B. E. (1993). Ethical issues in counseling adult survivors of incest. *Journal of Counseling & Development, 72,* 16–22.

Danzinger, P. R., & Welfel, E. R. (2000). Age, gender, and health bias in counselors: An empirical analysis. *Journal of Mental Health Counseling, 22,* 135–149.

Danzinger, P. R., & Welfel, E. R. (2001). The impact of managed care on mental health counselors: A survey of perceptions, practices, and compliance with ethical standards. *Journal of Mental Health Counseling, 23,* 137–150.

Dattilio, F. M. (2009). *Comprehensive cognitive-behavior therapy with couples and families.* New York: Guilford.

Davidson, V. (1977). Psychiatry's problem with no name: Therapist–patient sex. *American Journal of Psychoanalysis, 37,* 43–50.

Davis, J. L., & Mickelson, D. J. (1994). School counselors: Are you aware of ethical and legal aspects of counseling? *The School Counselor, 42,* 5–13.

Davis, M. S., Wester, K. L., & King, B. (2008). Narcissism, entitlement, and questionable research practices in counseling: A pilot study. *Journal of Counseling & Development, 86,* 200–210.

Davis, P. A. (1983). *Suicidal adolescents.* Springfield, IL: Charles C Thomas.

Day, S. X., & Schneider, P. (2002). Psychotherapy using distance technology: A comparison of face-to-face, video, and audio treatment. *Journal of Counseling Psychology, 49,* 499–503.

Day-Vines, N. L. (2007). The escalating incidence of suicide among African Americans: Implications for counselors. *Journal of Counseling & Development, 85,* 370–377.

Dean, L. A., & Meadows, M. E. (1995). College counseling: Union and intersection. *Journal of Counseling & Development, 74,* 139–142.

DeChiara, P. (1988). The need for universities to have rules on consensual sexual relationships between faculty members and students. *Columbia Journal of Law and Social Problems, 21,* 137–162.

Dedden, L., & James, S. (1998, Summer). A comprehensive guide to free career counseling resources on the Internet. *The ASCA Counselor, 17,* 19.

Defense of Marriage Act (DOMA), Pub. L. 104–199, 110 Stat. 2419 (1996); 1 U.S.C. § 7; 28 U.S.C. § 1738C.

DeFunis v. Odegaard, 507 P.2d 1169 (Wash. 1973), dismissed as moot, 416 U.S. 312 (1973), on remand, 529 P.2d 438 (Wash. 1974).

Delphin, M. E., & Rowe, M. (2008). Continuing education in cultural competence for community mental health practitioners. *Professional Psychology: Research and Practice, 39,* 182–191.

DeParle, J., & Tavernise, S. (2012, February 17). For women under 30, most births occur outside of marriage. *New York Times.* Retrieved from http://www.nytimes.com

DeRonde v. Regents of the University of California, 625 P.2d 220 (Cal. 1981).

Deutsch, C. J. (1985). A survey of therapists' personal problems and treatment. *Professional Psychology: Research and Practice, 16,* 305–315.

Diana, D. P. (2010). *Marketing for the mental health professional: An innovative guide for practitioners.* Hoboken, NJ: John Wiley.

Dickens, K. N. (2014). *Counselor education doctoral students' experiences with multiple roles and relationships.* Unpublished doctoral dissertation, University of New Orleans.

Didelot, M. J., Hollingsworth, L., & Buckenmeyer, J. A. (2012). Internet addiction: A logotherapeutic approach. *Journal of Addictions and Offender Counseling, 33,* 18–33. doi: 10.1002/j. 2161-1874.2012.00002.x

Diesen, C. (2008). Therapeutic jurisprudence at the conference of the International Association of Law and Mental Health in Padua, Italy: The justice obsession syndrome. *Thomas Jefferson Law Review, 30,* 487. Retrieved from http://www.lexisnexis.com

DiLillo, D., & Gale, E. B. (2011). To Google or not to Google: Graduate students' use of the Internet to access personal information about clients. *Training and Education in Professional Psychology, 5,* 160–166.

Dinkmeyer, D., Jr., Carlson, J., & Dinkmeyer, D. (1994). *Consultation: School mental health professionals as consultants.* Muncie, IN: Accelerated Development.

Doll, B., Strein, W., Jacob, S., & Prasse, D. P. (2011). Youth privacy when educational records include psychological records. *Professional Psychology: Research and Practice, 42,* 259–268. doi: 10.1037/a0023685

Dollarhide, C. T., Gibson, D. M., & Moss, J. M. (2013). Professional

identity development of counselor education doctoral students. *Counselor Education and Supervision, 52,* 137–150. doi: 10.1002/j.1556-6978.2013.00034.x

Dorken, H., & Webb, J. T. (1980). 1976 third-party reimbursement experience: An interstate comparison by insurance carrier. *American Psychologist, 35,* 355–363.

Dorre, A., & Kinnier, R. T. (2006). The ethics of bias in counselor terminology. *Counseling and Values, 51,* 66–79.

Dougherty, A. M. (2014). *Psychological consultation and collaboration in school and community settings* (6th ed.). Belmont, CA: Cengage Brooks/Cole.

Dowling, M., & Richwood, D. (2013). Online counseling and therapy for mental health problems: A systematic review of individual synchronous interventions using chat. *Journal of Technology in Human Services, 31,* 1–21. doi: 10.1080/15228835.2012.728508

Downing, N. E., & Roush, K. L. (1985). From passive acceptance to active commitment: A model of feminist identity development. *Counseling Psychologist, 13,* 695–709.

Draine, J. (2013). Introduction: Mental health, mental illness, poverty, justice, and social justice. *American Journal of Psychiatric Rehabilitation, 16,* 87–90.

Driscoll, J. M. (1992). Keeping covenants and confidence sacred: One point of view. *Journal of Counseling & Development, 70,* 704–708.

Drukteinis, A. M. (1985). Psychiatric perspectives on civil liability for suicide. *Bulletin of American Academy of Psychiatry Law, 13,* 71–83.

Drummond, R. J., & Jones, K. D. (2010). *Assessment procedures*

for counselors and helping professionals (7th ed.). Boston: Pearson.

Duan, C., & Roehlke, H. (2001). A descriptive "snapshot" of cross-racial supervision in university counseling center internships. *Journal of Multicultural Counseling and Development, 29,* 131–146.

Duba, J. D., Paez, S. B., & Kindsvatter, A. (2010). Criteria of nonacademic characteristics used to evaluate and retain community counseling students. *Journal of Counseling & Development, 88,* 154–162.

Dufrene, R., & Henderson, K. L. (2009). A framework for remediation plans for counseling trainees. In G. R. Walz, S. C. Bleuer, & R. K. Yep (Eds.), *Compelling counseling images: The best of VISTAS 2009* (pp. 149–159). Alexandria, VA: American Counseling Association.

Dugan, W. E. (1965). Preface. In J. W. Loughary, R. O. Stripling, & P. W. Fitzgerald (Eds.), *Counseling, a growing profession* (pp. i–iii). Alexandria, VA: American Counseling Association.

Dugger, S. M., & Francis, P. C. (2014). Surviving a lawsuit against a counseling program: Lessons learned from *Ward v. Wilbanks. Journal of Counseling & Development, 92,* 135–141.

Durodoye, B. A. (2013). Ethical issues in multicultural counseling. In C. C. Lee (Ed.), *Multicultural issues in counseling: New approaches to diversity* (4th ed., pp. 295–308). Alexandria, VA: American Counseling Association.

Dutile, F. N. (2001). Students and due process in higher education: Of interests and procedures. *Florida Coastal Law Journal, 2,* 243–255.

Dworkin, S. H., & Yi, H. (2003). LGBT identity, violence, and social justice: The psychological is political. *International Journal for the Advancement of Counseling, 25,* 269–279.

Edwards, D. C. (2006). Duty-to-warn—Even if it may be hearsay? The implications of a psychotherapist's duty-to-warn a third person when information is obtained from someone other than his patient. *Indiana Health Law Review, 3,* 171–179.

Edwards, T. M., Patterson, J. E., & Grauf-Grounds, C. (2001). Psychiatry, MFT, and family medicine collaboration: The Sharp Behavioral Health Clinic. *Families, Systems, & Health, 19,* 25–35.

Ehrlich, J. S. (2003). Grounded in the reality of their lives: Listening to teens who make the abortion decision without involving their parents. *Berkeley Women's Law Journal, 18,* 61–179. Retrieved from http://www.lexisnexis.com

Eisel v. Board of Education of Montgomery County, 597 A.2d 447 (Md. 1991).

Elander, J., Pittam, G., Lusher, J., Fox, P., & Payne, N. (2010). Evaluation of an intervention to help students avoid unintentional plagiarism by improving their authorial identity. *Assessment & Evaluation in Higher Education, 35,* 157–171. doi: 10.1080/02602930802687745

Ellis v. Ellis, 472 S.W.2d 741 (Tenn. App. 1971).

Emener, W. G., & Cottone, R. R. (1989). Professionalization, deprofessionalization, and reprofessionalization of rehabilitation counseling according to criteria of professions. *Journal of Counseling & Development, 67,* 576–581.

Emerson, S., & Markos, P. A. (1996). Signs and symptoms of the impaired counselor. *Journal of Humanistic Education and Development, 34,* 108–117.

Empire State College. (2011). *Plagiarism and how to avoid it (guidelines for students).* Rochester, NY: Author. Retrieved from http://www7.esc.edu/hshapiro /writing_program/Orientation /main/plagiarism.htm

Engels, D. W., Minor, C. W., Sampson, J. P., Jr., & Splete, H. H. (1995). Career counseling specialty: History, development, and prospect. *Journal of Counseling & Development, 74,* 134–138.

Enns, C. Z. (2004). Counseling girls and women: Attitudes, knowledge, and skills. In D. R. Atkinson & G. Hackett (Eds.), *Counseling diverse populations* (pp. 285–307). Boston: McGraw-Hill.

Enzer, N. B. (1985). Ethics in child psychiatry—An overview. In D. H. Schetky & E. P. Benedek (Eds.), *Emerging issues in child psychiatry and the law* (pp. 3–21). New York: Brunner/Mazel.

Epperson, D. L., & Lewis, K. N. (1987). Issues of informed entry into counseling: Perceptions and preferences resulting from different types and amounts of pretherapy information. *Journal of Counseling Psychology, 34,* 266–275.

Erford, B. T., Erford, B. M., Lattanzi, G., Weller, J., Schein, H., Wolf, E., Hughes, M., Darrow, J., Savin-Murphy, J., & Peacock, E. (2011). Counseling outcomes from 1990–2008 for school-aged youth with depression: A meta-analysis. *Journal of Counseling & Development, 89,* 439–458.

Erickson, S. (1993). Ethics and confidentiality in AIDS counseling: A professional dilemma. *Journal of Mental Health Counseling, 15,* 118–131.

Erickson, K. P., & McAuliffe, G. J. (2003). A measure of counselor competency. *Counselor Education and Supervision, 43,* 120–133.

Erickson, K. P., & McAuliffe, G. J. (2006). Constructive development and counselor competence. *Counselor Education and Supervision, 45,* 180–192.

Eschenauer, R., & Chen-Hayes, S. F. (2005). The transformative individual school counseling model: An accountability model for urban school counselors. *Professional School Counseling, 8,* 244–248.

Espelage, D. L., Bosworth, K., & Simon, T. R. (2000). Examining the social context of bullying behaviors in early adolescence. *Journal of Counseling & Development, 78,* 326–333.

Estrada, D., Frame, M. W., & Williams, C. (2004). Cross-cultural supervision: Guiding the conversation toward race and ethnicity. *Journal of Multicultural Counseling and Development, 32,* 307–319.

Etzioni, A. (1969). *The semi-professions and their organization.* New York: The Free Press.

Euthanasiaprocon.org. (2014). *State-by-state guide to physician-assisted suicide. Assisted suicide laws state by state.* Retrieved from euthanasia.procon.org

Even, T. A., & Robinson, C. R. (2013). The impact of CACREP accreditation: A multiway frequency analysis of ethics violations and sanctions. *Journal of Counseling & Development, 91,* 26–34. doi: 10.1002/j. 1556-6676.2013.00067.x

Fabian, E. S. (2007). Counselor advocacy for access: Addressing the challenges of disability. In C. C. Lee (Ed.), *Counseling for social justice* (2nd ed., pp. 75–94). Alexandria, VA: American Counseling Association.

Fall, K. A., Levitov, J. E., Jennings, M., & Eberts, S. (2000). The public perception of mental health professions: An empirical examination. *Journal of Mental Health Counseling, 22,* 122–134.

Family Educational Rights and Privacy Act of 1974, 20 U.S.C.A. §1232g (West, 1997).

Farber, B. A., & Heifetz, L. J. (1982). The process and dimensions of burnout in psychotherapists. *Professional Psychology, 13,* 293–301.

Feisthamel, K. P., & Schwartz, R. C. (2009). Differences in mental health counselors' diagnoses based on client race: An investigation of adjustment, childhood, and substance-related disorders. *Journal of Mental Health Counseling, 31,* 47–59.

Fernando, D. M. (2013). Supervision by doctoral students: A study of supervisee satisfaction and self-efficacy, and comparison with faculty supervision outcomes. *The Clinical Supervisor, 32,* 1–14.

Finn, S. E., & Tonsager, M. E. (1992). Therapeutic effects of providing MMPI-2 test feedback to college students awaiting therapy. *Psychological Assessment, 4,* 278–287.

Fisher, C. B., Cea, C. D., Davidson, P. W., & Fried, A. (2006). Capacity of persons with mental retardation to consent to participate in randomized clinical trials. *American Journal of Psychiatry, 163,* 1–8.

Fisher, C. B., & Oransky, M. (2008). Informed consent to psychotherapy: Protecting the dignity and respecting the autonomy of patients. *Journal of Clinical Psychology: In Session, 64,* 576–588.

Fisher, M. A. (2008). Protecting confidentiality rights: The need for an ethical practice model. *American Psychologist, 63,* 1–13.

Fisher, M. A. (2009). Replacing "who is the client?" with a different ethical question. *Professional Psychology: Research and Practice, 40,* 1–7.

Fisher, R. M. (1964). The psychotherapeutic professions and the law of privileged communications. *Wayne Law Review, 10,* 609–654.

Flaskerud, J. H. (2009). The "human right" to mental health care. *Issues in Mental Health Nursing, 30,* 796–797. doi: 10.3109/01612840903019740

Foley & Lardner, LLP. (2014). *2014 telemedicine survey: Executive summary.* Retrieved from http://www.foley.com

Fong, M. L., & Silien, K. A. (1999). Assessment and diagnosis of DSM-IV anxiety disorders. *Journal of Counseling & Development, 77,* 209–217.

Fontes, L. A. (2002). Child discipline in immigrant Latino families: Reducing violence and misunderstandings. *Journal of Counseling & Development, 80,* 31–40.

Forester-Miller, H., & Moody, E. E. (2015). Rural communities: Can dual relationships be avoided? In B. Herlihy & G. Corey, *Boundary issues in counseling* (3rd ed., pp. 251–253). Alexandria, VA: American Counseling Association.

Foster, J. M., Leppma, M., & Hutchinson, T. S. (2014). Students' perspectives on gatekeeping in counselor education: A case study. *Counselor Education & Supervision, 53,* 190–203.

Foster, V. A., & McAdams, C. R. (2009). A framework for creating a climate of transparency for professional performance assessment: Fostering student investment in gatekeeping. *Counselor Education & Supervision, 48,* 271–284.

Fowler, J. E. (2003). *Avoiding plagiarism: A student survival guide.* Starkville, MS: Mississippi State University. Retrieved from http://www.ece.msstate.edu/~fowler/Classes/plagiarism.pdf

Fox, P. K. (2010). Commentary: So the pendulum swings—Making sense of the duty to protect. *Journal of the American Academy of Psychiatry and the Law, 38,* 474–478.

Fox, R. E. (1994). Training professional psychologists for the twenty-first century. *American Psychologist, 49,* 200–206.

Frame, M. S., & Stevens-Smith, P. (1995). Out of harm's way: Enhancing monitoring and dismissal processes in counselor education programs. *Counselor Education & Supervision, 35,* 118–129.

Francis, P. C. (2015). Evolution of the ACA ethical standards and the casebook. In B. Herlihy & G. Corey, *ACA ethical standards casebook* (7th ed., pp. 4–12). Alexandria, VA: American Counseling Association.

Francis, P. C., & Dugger, S. M. (2014). Professionalism, ethics, and values-based conflicts in counseling: An introduction to the special section. *Journal of Counseling & Development, 92,* 131–134.

Fridhandler, B., & Lehmer, M. (2014). Ethical issues in coparent counseling. *Journal of Child Custody: Research, Issues, and Practices, 11,* 139–158. doi.: 10.1080/15379418.2014.921590

Friedman, J., & Boumil, M. M. (1995). *Betrayal of trust: Sex and power in professional relationships.* Westport, CT: Praeger.

Friedson, E. (1983). The theory of professions: State-of-the-art. In R. Dingwall & P. Lewis (Eds.), *The sociology of the professions.* New York: St. Martin's Press.

Fulero, S. M., & Wilbert, J. R. (1988). Record-keeping practices of clinical and counseling psychologists: A survey of practitioners. *Professional Psychology: Research and Practice, 19,* 1988, 658–660. doi: 10.1037/0735-7028.19.6.658

Fuqua, D. R., Newman, J. L., Simpson, D. B., & Choi, N. (2012, April). Who is the client in organizational consultation? *Consulting Psychology Journal: Practice and Research.* [No pagination specified]. doi: 1037/a0027722

Furr, S. R., & Barret, B. (2000). Teaching group counseling skills: Problems and solutions. *Counselor Education & Supervision, 40,* 94–105.

Gabbard, G. O. (1995, April). What are boundaries in psychotherapy? *The Menninger Letter, 3,* 1–2.

Gabriel, T. (2010, August 1). Plagiarism lines blur for students in digital age. *New York Times.* Retrieved from http://www .nytimes.com

Gale, A. U., & Austin, B. D. (2003). Professionalism's challenges to professional counselors' collective identity. *Journal of Counseling & Development, 81,* 3–10.

Garcia, J., Glosoff, H. L., & Smith, J. L. (1994). Report of the ACA Ethics Committee: 1993–1994. *Journal of Counseling & Development, 73,* 253–256.

Garcia, J., Salo, M., & Hamilton, W. M. (1995). Report of the ACA Ethics Committee: 1994–1995. *Journal of Counseling & Development, 72,* 221–224.

Garcia, J. G., Cartwright, B., Winston, S. M., & Borzuchowska, B. (2003). A transcultural integrative model for ethical decision making in counseling. *Journal of Counseling & Development, 81,* 268–277.

Garfield, S. L. (1994). Research on client variables in psychotherapy. In A. E. Bergen & S. L. Garfield (Eds.), *Handbook of psychotherapy and behavior change* (4th ed., pp. 190–228). New York: Wiley.

Garland, D. R., & Argueta, C. (2012). How clergy sexual misconduct happens: A qualitative study of first-hand accounts. *Social Work and Christianity, 37,* 5.

Garner, B. A. (Ed.). (2014). *Black's law dictionary* (10th ed.). New York: Thomson West.

Garnets, L., Hancock, K. A., Cochran, S. D., Goodchilds, J., & Peplau, L. A. (1991). Issues in psychotherapy with lesbians and gay men. *American Psychologist, 46,* 964–972.

Gartrell, N., Herman, J., Olarte, S., Feldstein, M., & Localio, R. (1987). Reporting practices of psychologists who knew of sexual misconduct by colleagues. *American Journal of Orthopsychiatry, 57,* 287–295.

Gaubatz, M. D., & Vera, E. M. (2002). Do formalized gatekeeping procedures increase programs' follow-up with deficient trainees? *Counselor Education and Supervision, 41,* 294–305.

Gaubatz, M. D., & Vera, E. M. (2006). Trainee competence in master's-level counseling programs: A comparison of counselor educators' and students' views. *Counselor Education and Supervision, 46,* 32–43.

Gelso, C. J., & Carter, J. A. (1985). The relationship in counseling and psychotherapy: Components, consequences, and theoretical antecedents. *The Counseling Psychologist, 13,* 155–243.

General Revision of the Copyright Law, 17 U.S.C. 101 et seq. (1999).

Genia, V. (2000). Religious issues in secularly based psychotherapy. *Counseling and Values, 44,* 213–222.

Gerstein, J. (2012). Another court finds Defense of Marriage Act unconstitutional. *Politico,* February 22, 2012. Retrieved from http://www.politico.com /blogs/under-the-radar/2012/02 /another-court-finds-defense-of-marriage-act-unconstitutional-115243.html

Gibson, R. L., & Mitchell, M. H. (2008). *Introduction to counseling and guidance* (7th ed.). Upper Saddle River, NJ: Merrill/Prentice-Hall.

Gibson, W. T., & Pope, K. S. (1993). The ethics of counseling: A national survey of certified counselors. *Journal of Counseling & Development, 71,* 330–336.

Gilabert, K. (2014). *Top five reasons 80% of all new businesses fail.* Washington, DC: Small Business Administration. Retrieved from www.sba.gov

Gilbert, H. L. (2007). Minors' constitutional right to informational privacy. *University of Chicago Law Review, 74,* 1375–1397.

Gilbert, L. A., & Rossman, K. M. (1992). Gender and the mentoring process for women: Implications for professional development. *Professional Psychology: Research and Practice, 23,* 233–238.

Gilbert, M. L. (2002). "Time-out" for student threats?: Imposing a duty to protect on school officials. *UCLA Law Review, 49,* 917.

Gilbert, S. P. (1992). Ethical issues in the treatment of severe psychopathology in university and college counseling centers. *Journal of Counseling & Development, 71,* 330–336.

Gilligan, C. (1982). *In a different voice: Psychological theory and women's development.* Cambridge, MA: Harvard University Press.

Ginter, E. J. (1999). David K. Brooks' contribution to the developmentally based lifeskills approach. *Journal of Mental Health Counseling, 21,* 191–202.

Ginter, E. J. (2001). Private practice: The professional counselor. In D. C. Locke, J. E. Myers, & E. L. Herr (Eds.), *The handbook of counseling* (pp. 355–372). Thousand Oaks, CA: Sage.

Ginter, E. J. (2004). JCD's special section on school violence: Reactions and thoughts of a counselor. *Journal of Counseling & Development, 82,* 310–312.

Giordano, A., Clarke, P., & Borders, L. D. (2013). Using motivational interviewing techniques to address parallel process in supervision. *Counselor Education & Supervision, 52,* 15–29.

Gladding, S. T. (2012). *Groups: A counseling specialty* (6th ed.). Upper Saddle River, NJ: Pearson/ Merrill/Prentice Hall.

Glaser, R. D., & Thorpe, J. S. (1986). Unethical intimacy: A survey of sexual contact and advances between psychology educators and female graduate students. *American Psychologist, 41,* 43–51.

Glickhauf-Hughes, C., & Mehlman, E. (1996). Narcissistic issues in therapists: Diagnostic and treatment considerations. *Psychotherapy, 32,* 213–221.

Glosoff, H. L. (1998). Managed care: A critical ethical issue for counselors. *Counseling and Human Development, 31,* 1–16.

Glosoff, H. L. (2001). Ethical issues related to interprofessional communication. In E. R. Welfel & R. E. Ingersoll (Eds.), *Mental health desk reference* (pp. 419–426). New York: Wiley.

Glosoff, H. L. (2015). Multiple relationship issues in private practice. In B. Herlihy & G. Corey, *Boundary issues in counseling* (3rd ed., pp. 229–236). Alexandria, VA: American Counseling Association.

Glosoff, H. L., Corey, G., & Herlihy, B. (2006). Avoiding detrimental multiple relationships. In B.

Herlihy & G. Corey (Eds.), *ACA Ethical Standards Casebook* (6th ed., pp. 209–215). Alexandria, VA: American Counseling Association.

Glosoff, H. L., Garcia, J., Herlihy, B., & Remley, T. P., Jr. (1999). Managed care: Ethical considerations for counselors. *Counseling and Values, 44,* 8–16.

Glosoff, H. L., Herlihy, B., & Spence, B. (2000). Privileged communication in the counselor–client relationship. *Journal of Counseling & Development, 78,* 454–462 http://onlinelibrary. wiley.com/doi/10.1002/ j.1556-6676.2000.tb01929.x/ abstract John Wiley & Sons.

Glosoff, H. L., Herlihy, S., Herlihy, B., & Spence, B. (1997). Privileged communication in the psychologist–client relationship. *Professional Psychology: Research and Practice, 28,* 573–581.

Glosoff, H. L., & Pate, R. H. (2002). Privacy and confidentiality in school counseling. *Professional School Counseling, 6,* 20–28.

Golden, L. (1990, March 1). In Schafer, C. Ethics: Dual relationships come under scrutiny. *Guidepost, 1,* 3, 16.

Goldenberg, H., & Goldenberg, I. (1998). *Counseling today's families* (3rd ed.). Pacific Grove, CA: Brooks/Cole.

Goldenberg, I., & Goldenberg, H. (1996). *Family therapy: An overview* (4th ed.). Pacific Grove, CA: Brooks/Cole.

Goldman, S., & Beardslee, W. R. (1999). Suicide in children and adolescents. In D. G. Jacobs (Ed.), *Guide to suicide assessment and intervention* (pp. 417–442). San Francisco: Jossey-Bass.

Gomez, A., & Knight, S. C. (2013). Disclosure of mental health records in court-mandated outpatient treatment proceedings and the Health Insurance Portability

and Accountability Act (HIPAA). *Journal of the American Academy of Psychiatry and the Law, 41,* 460–461.

Goodyear, R. K. (2000). An unwarranted escalation of counselor-counseling psychologist professional conflict: Comments on Weinrach, Lustig, Chan, and Thomas (1998). *Journal of Counseling & Development, 78,* 103–106.

Goodyear, R. K., Arcinue, F., & Getzelman, M. (2001). Counseling supervision: Essential concepts and practices. In E. R. Welfel & R. E. Ingersoll (Eds.), *Mental health desk reference* (pp. 490–496). New York: Wiley.

Gostin, L. O. (1995). Informed consent, cultural sensitivity, and respect for persons [Editorial]. *Journal of the American Medical Association, 274,* 844–845.

Gottlieb, M. C. (2006). A template for peer ethics consultation. *Ethics & Behavior, 16,* 151–162.

Gould, D. (1998). Listen to your lawyer. In L. E. Lifson & R. I. Simon (Eds.), *The mental health practitioner and the law* (pp. 344–356). Cambridge, MA: Harvard University Press.

Gould, J. W. (1998). *Conducting scientifically crafted child custody evaluations.* Thousand Oaks, CA: Sage.

Grabois, E. W. (1997/1998). The liability of psychotherapists for breach of confidentiality. *Journal of Law and Health, 12,* 39. Retrieved from http://seg802.ocs. lsu.edu:2077/universe/document?_m=582c9eaa09083fd41b9 2e849a2f4baf8&_docnum= 9&wchp=dGLbVzz-zSkVb&_ md5=db8f2cb26af0c898d724e65c a80ee62b

Graham, S. R., & Liddle, B. J. (2009). Multiple relationships encountered by lesbian and bisexual psychotherapists: How close is too close? *Professional Psychology: Research and Practice, 40,* 15–21. doi: 10.1037/a0013904

Grahl, T. (2014). *The 6 types of social media.* Out:think. Retrieved from http://outthinkgroup.com

Granello, D. H., Kindsvatter, A., Granello, P. F., Underfer-Babalis, J., & Moorhead, H. J. H. (2008). Multiple perspectives in supervision: Using a peer consultation model to enhance supervisor development. *Counselor Education & Supervision, 48,* 32–46.

Granello, P. F., & Hanna, F. J. (2003). Incarcerated and court-involved adolescents: Counseling an at-risk population. *Journal of Counseling & Development, 81,* 11–18.

Gray, L., & Harding, A. (1988). Confidentiality limits with clients who have the AIDS virus. *Journal of Counseling & Development, 65,* 219–226.

Gray, S. W. (2011). *Competency-based assessments in mental health practice.* Hoboken, NJ: Wiley.

Green, R. G., Baskind, F. R., Mustian, B. E., Reed, L. N., & Taylor, H. R. (2007). Professional education and private practice: Is there a disconnect? *Social Work, 52,* 151–159.

Greenburg, S. L., Lewis, G. J., & Johnson, J. (1985). Peer consultation groups for private practitioners. *Professional Psychology: Research and Practice, 16,* 437–447.

Greenspan, M. (2002). Out of bounds. In A. A. Lazarus & O. Zur (Eds.), *Dual relationships and psychotherapy* (pp. 425–431). New York: Springer.

Grieve, R., Indian, M., Witteveen, G. A., & Tolan, J. M. (2013). Face-to-face or Facebook: Can social connectedness be derived online? *Computers in Human Behavior,* 29, 604–609. doi:10.1016/j.chb.2012.11.017

Griffiths, K. M., & Christensen, H. (2006). Review of randomized controlled trials of Internet interventions for mental disorders and related conditions. *Clinical Psychologist, 10,* 16–19.

Griffiths, M. D. (2013). Social networking addiction: Emerging themes and issues. *Addiction Research & Therapy, 4.* doi: 10.4172/2155-6105.1000e118

Grodzki, L. (2000). *Building your ideal private practice: A guide for therapists and other healing professionals.* New York: W. W. Norton.

Grosch, W. N., & Olsen, D. C. (1994). *When helping starts to hurt.* New York: Norton.

Grover, S. (2005). Reification of psychiatric diagnoses as defamatory: Implications for ethical clinical practice. *Ethical Human Psychology and Psychiatry, 7,* 77–86.

Gumper, L. L. (1984). *Legal issues in the practice of ministry.* Minneapolis, MN: Ministers Life Resources.

Guo, Y., Wang, S., Combs, D. C., Lin, Y., & Johnson, V. (2013). Professional counseling in Taiwan: Past to future. *Journal of Counseling & Development, 91,* 331–335. doi: 10.1002/j.1556-6676.2013.00101.x

Guterman, M. (1991). Working couples: Finding a balance between family and career. In J. M. Kummerow (Ed.), *New directions in career planning and the workplace* (pp. 167–193). Palo Alto, CA: Consulting Psychologists Press.

Gutheil, T. G. (1989). Borderline personality disorder, boundary violations, and patient–therapist sex: Medicolegal pitfalls. *American Journal of Psychiatry, 146,* 597–602.

Gutheil, T. G. (1999). Liability issues and liability prevention in suicide. In D. G. Jacobs (Ed.), *The Harvard Medical School guide to suicide assessment and intervention* (pp. 561–578). San Francisco: Jossey-Bass.

Gutheil, T. G., & Drogin, E. Y. (2013). *The mental health professional in court.* Arlington, VA: American Psychiatric Association.

Gutheil, T. G., & Gabbard, G. O. (1993). The concept of boundaries in clinical practice: Theoretical and risk-management dimensions. *American Journal of Psychiatry, 150,* 188–196.

Guttmacher, M., & Weihofen, H. (1952). Privileged communications between psychiatrist and patient. *Indiana Law Journal, 28,* 32–44.

Gysbers, N. C. (2004). Comprehensive guidance and counseling programs: The evolution of accountability. *Professional School Counseling, 8,* 1–14.

Haas, L. J., & Alexander, J. R. (1981). *Ethical and legal issues in family therapy.* Paper presented at the meeting of the American Psychological Association, Los Angeles.

Haas, L. J., & Cummings, N. A. (1991). Managed outpatient mental health plans: Clinical, ethical, and practical guidelines for participation. *Professional Psychology: Research and Practice, 22,* 45–51.

Haas, L. J., & Malouf, J. L. (1995). *Keeping up the good work: A practitioner's guide to mental health ethics* (2nd ed.). Sarasota, FL: Professional Resource Exchange.

Haberstroh, S., Barney, L., Foster, N., & Duffey, T. (2014). The ethical and legal practice of online counseling and psychotherapy: A review of mental health professions. *Journal of Technology in*

Human Services, 32, 149–157. doi: 10.1080/15228835. 2013.872074

Haberstroh, S., Dufey, T., Evans, M., Gee, R., & Trepal, H. (2007). The experience of online counseling. *Journal of Mental Health Counseling, 29,* 269–282.

Haddock, S. A. (2002). Training family therapists to assess for and intervene in partner abuse: A curriculum for graduate courses, professional workshops, and self-study. *Journal of Marital and Family Therapy, 28,* 193–202.

Hafen, B. Q., & Frandsen, K. J. (1986). *Youth suicide: Depression and loneliness.* Provo, UT: Behavioral Health Associates.

Hagan, M. A. (1997). *Whores of the court: The fraud of psychiatric testimony and the rape of American justice.* New York: Regan Books.

Haggard-Gran, U. (2007). Assessing violence risk: A review and clinical recommendations. *Journal of Counseling & Development, 3,* 294–301.

Halbert, C. H., Bary, F. K., Weathers, B., Delmoor, E., Coyne, J., Wileyto, O., et al. (2007). Differences in cultural beliefs and values among African American and European American men with prostate cancer. *Cancer Control, 14,* 277–284.

Haley, J. (1987). *Problem solving therapy* (2nd ed.). San Francisco: Jossey-Bass.

Hall, C. R., Dixon, W. A., & Mauzey, E. (2004). Spirituality and religion: Implications for counselors. *Journal of Counseling & Development, 82,* 504–507.

Hall, K. G., Barden, S., & Conley, A. (2014). A relational-cultural framework: Emphasizing relational dynamics and multicultural skill development. *The Professional Counselor, 4,* 71–83.

Hamburger, Y. A., & Ben-Artzi, E. (2000). The relationship between extraversion and neuroticism and the different uses of the Internet. *Computers in Human Behavior, 16,* 441–449.

Hamilton, R. W., Macey, J. H., & Moll, D. X. (2012). *Cases and materials on corporations including partnerships and limited liability companies* (11th ed.). St. Paul, MN: West.

Hammer, S., & Kessler, K. H. (2012). Ethical and legal aspects of private practice. In C. E. Stout (Ed.), *Getting better at private practice* (pp. 52–68). Hoboken, NJ: John Wiley.

Handelsman, M. M. (2001). Accurate and effective informed consent. In E. R. Welfel & R. E. Engersoll (Eds.), *The mental health desk reference* (pp. 453–458). New York: Wiley.

Handler, J. F. (1990). *Law and the search for community.* Philadelphia: University of Pennsylvania Press.

Haniff, D. (2007). Mental health issues and pervasive computing. In D. Ramduny-Ellis & D. Rachovides (Eds). *BCS-HCI '07 Proceedings of the 21st British HCI group annual conference on people and computers: HCI ... but not as we know it* (vol. 2; pp. 171–172). Swindon, England: British Computer Society.

Hanjorgiris, W. F., & O'Neill, J. H. (2006). Counseling people with disabilities: A sociocultural minority group perspective. In C. C. Lee (Ed.), *Multicultural issues in counseling: New approaches to diversity* (3rd ed., pp. 321–342). Alexandria, VA: American Counseling Association.

Hansen, J. T. (2003). Including diagnostic training in counseling curricula: Implications for professional identity development.

Counselor Education and Supervision, 43, 96–107.

Hansen, J. T. (2005). The devaluation of inner subjective experiences by the counseling profession: A plea to reclaim the essence of the profession. *Journal of Counseling & Development, 83,* 406–415.

Hansen, J. T. (2006). Is the best practices movement consistent with the values of the counseling profession? A critical analysis of best practices ideology. *Counseling and Values, 50,* 154–160.

Hansen, J. T. (2007). Should counseling be considered a health care profession? Critical thoughts on the transition to a health care ideology. *Journal of Counseling & Development, 85,* 286–293.

Hansen, J. T. (2012). Extending the humanistic vision: Toward a humanities foundation for the counseling profession. *The Journal of Humanistic Counseling, 51,* 133–144. doi: 10.1002/ j.2161-1939.2012.00011.x

Hansen, J. T., Speciale, M., & Lemberger, M. E. (2014). Humanism: The foundation and future of professional counseling. *The Journal of Humanistic Counseling, 53,* 170–190.

Harding, A., Gray, L., & Neal, M. (1993). Confidentiality limits with clients who have HIV: A review of ethical and legal guidelines and professional policies. *Journal of Counseling & Development, 71,* 297–305.

Haring-Hidore, M., & Paludi, M. A. (1989). Sexuality and sex in mentoring and tutoring: Implications for women's opportunities and achievement. *Peabody Journal of Education, 64,* 164–172.

Harley, D. A., Jolivette, K., McCormick, K., & Tice, K. (2002). Race, class, and gender: A constellation of positionalities with implications for counseling. *Journal of Multicultural Counseling and Development, 30,* 216–238.

Harrar, W. R., VandeCreek, L., & Knapp, S. (1990). Ethical and legal aspects of clinical supervision. *Professional Psychology: Research and Practice, 21,* 37–41.

Harris, A. D. (1997). *Licensing requirements* (2nd ed.). Alexandria, VA: American Counseling Association.

Hartig, N. A., Terry, K. P., & Turman, A. M. (2011). *Social networking websites and counselors-in-training: Ethical and professional issues.* Retrieved from http://www.counselingoutfitters.com/vistas/vistas11/Article_64.pdf

Haug, I. E. (1999). Boundaries and the use and misuse of power and authority: Ethical complexities for clergy psychotherapists. *Journal of Counseling & Development, 77,* 411–417.

Haynsworth, H. J. (1986). *Organizing a small business entity.* Philadelphia: American Law Institute–American Bar Association Committee on Continuing Professional Education.

Hays, D. G., Arredondo, P., Gladding, S. T., & Toporek, R. L. (2010). Integrating social justice in group work: The next decade. *Journal for Specialists in Group Work, 35,* 177–206.

Hays, D. G., & Wood, C. (2011). Infusing qualitative traditions in counseling research designs. *Journal of Counseling & Development, 89,* 288–295.

Hazler, R. J. (2001). Bullying: Counseling perpetrators and victims. In D. C. Locke, J. E. Myers, & E. L. Herr (Eds.), *Handbook of multicultural counseling* (pp. 191–198). Thousand Oaks, CA: Sage.

Healey, A. C., & Hays, D. G. (2012). A discriminant analysis of gender and counselor professional identity development. *Journal of Counseling & Development, 90,* 55–62. doi: 10.1111/j.1556-6676.2012.00008.x

Hedges, L. E. (1993, July/August). In praise of dual relationships. Part II: Essential dual relatedness in developmental psychotherapy. *The California Therapist,* 42–46.

Hedlund v. Superior Court of Orange County, 34 Cal. 3d 695, 669 P.2d 41, 194 Cal. Rptr. 805 (1983).

Hegarty, W. (2012). Snapshot. In D. H. Granello & M. E. Young, *Counseling today: Foundations of professional identity* (p. 399). Boston: Pearson.

Heinlen, K. T., Welfel, E. R., Richmond, E. N., & Rak, C. F. (2003). The scope of WebCounseling: A survey of services and compliance with NBCC standards for the ethical practice of WebCounseling. *Journal of Counseling & Development, 81,* 61–69.

Heller, M. S. (1957). Some comments to lawyers on the practice of psychiatry. *Temple Law Quarterly, 30,* 401–407.

Helms, J. E., & Cook, D. A. (1999). *Using race and culture in counseling and psychotherapy: Theory and practice.* Boston: Allyn & Bacon.

Henderson, K. L. (2010). *The remediation of students in counseling graduate programs: Behavioral indicators, terminology, and interventions.* Unpublished dissertation, University of New Orleans.

Henderson, K. L., & Dufrene, R. L. (2011). *Student remediation: Practical considerations for counselor educators and supervisors.* Retrieved from http://counselingoutfitters.com/vistas/vistas11/Article_45.pdf

Hendrick, S. S. (1988). Counselor self-disclosure. *Journal of Counseling & Development, 66,* 419–424.

Hendricks, B. E., Bradley, L. J., Southern, S., Oliver, M., & Birdsall, B. (2011). Ethical code for the International Association of Marriage and Family Counselors. *The Family Journal, 19,* 217–224. doi: 10.1177/1066480711400814

Hendrix, D. H. (1991). Ethics and intrafamily confidentiality in counseling with children. *Journal of Mental Health Counseling, 13,* 323–333.

Henn, H. G. (1991). *Henn on copyright law: A practitioner's guide.* New York: Practicing Law Institute.

Hensley, L. G., Smith, S. L., & Thompson, R. W. (2003). Assessing competencies of counselors in training: Complexities in evaluating personal and professional development. *Counselor Education & Supervision, 42,* 219–230.

Herlihy, B., & Corey, G. (2008). Boundaries in counseling: Ethical and clinical issues. *Ethical Issues in Professional Counseling, 11,* 13–23.

Herlihy, B., & Corey, G. (2015a). *ACA ethical standards casebook* (7th ed.). Alexandria, VA: American Counseling Association.

Herlihy, B., & Corey, G. (2015b). *Boundary issues in counseling: Multiple roles and responsibilities* (3rd ed.). Alexandria, VA: American Counseling Association.

Herlihy, B., & Dufrene, R. L. (2011). Current and emerging ethical issues in counseling: A Delphi study of expert opinions. *Counseling and Values, 56,* 10–24.

Herlihy, B., & Flowers, L. (2010). Group work: Ethical/legal considerations. In D. Capuzzi & M. Stauffer (Eds.), *Introduction to group work* (5th ed., pp. 191–217). Denver: Love.

Herlihy, B., James, A., & Taheri, K. (In press). Social justice and counseling ethics. In C. C. Lee (Ed.),

Counseling for social justice (3rd ed.). Alexandria, VA: American Counseling Association.

Herlihy, B., & Remley, T. P., Jr. (2001). Legal and ethical challenges in counseling. In D. C. Locke, J. E. Myers, & E. L. Herr (Eds.), *The handbook of counseling* (pp. 69–89). Thousand Oaks, CA: Sage.

Herlihy, B., & Sheeley, V. L. (1988). Counselor liability and the duty to warn: Selected cases, statutory trends, and implications for practice. *Counselor Education and Supervision, 27,* 203–215.

Herlihy, B., & Watson, Z. E. (2003). Ethical issues and multicultural competence in counseling. In F. D. Harper & J. McFadden (Eds.), *Culture and counseling: New approaches* (pp. 363–378). Boston: Allyn & Bacon.

Herlihy, B., & Watson, Z. E. (2004). Ethical issues in assisted suicide. In D. Capuzzi (Ed.), *Suicide across the life span.* Alexandria, VA: American Counseling Association.

Herlihy, B., & Watson, Z. E. (2006). Social justice and counseling ethics. In C. C. Lee (Ed.), *Counseling for social justice.* Alexandria, VA: American Counseling Association.

Herlihy, B., Watson, Z. E., & Patureau-Hatchett, M. (2008). Ethical concerns in diagnosing culturally diverse clients. *Ethical Issues in Professional Counseling, 11,* 25–33.

Hermann, M. A. (2001). *Legal issues in counseling: Incident preparation and consultation.* Unpublished doctoral dissertation, University of New Orleans, Louisiana.

Hermann, M. A., & Finn, A. (2002). An ethical and legal perspective on the role of school counselors in preventing violence in schools.

Professional School Counseling, 6, 46–54.

Hermann, M. A., & Remley, T. P., Jr. (2000). Guns, violence, and schools: The results of school violence—Litigation against educators and students—Shedding more constitutional rights at the school house gate. *Loyola Law Review, 46,* 389–439.

Hermann, M. A., Remley, T. P., Jr., & Huey, W. C. (Eds.). (2011). *Ethical and legal issues in school counseling* (3rd ed.). Alexandria, VA: American School Counselor Association.

Hermanson, G. L. (1997). Boundaries and boundary management in counselling: The never-ending story. *British Journal of Guidance and Counselling, 25,* 133–146.

Hermon, D. A., & Hazler, R. J. (1999). Adherence to a wellness model and perceptions of psychological well-being. *Journal of Counseling & Development, 77,* 339–343.

Hershenson, D. B., & Berger, G. P. (2001). The state of community counseling: A survey of directors of CACREP-accredited programs. *Journal of Counseling & Development, 79,* 188–193.

Hershenson, D. B., Power, P. W., & Waldo, M. (1996). *Community counseling: Contemporary theory and practice.* Boston: Allyn & Bacon.

Hertlein, K. M., Blumer, M. L. C., & Mihaloliakos, J. H. (2014). Marriage and family counselors' perceived ethical issues related to online therapy. *The Family Journal: Counseling and Therapy for Couples and Families,* 1–8. doi: 10.1177/1066480714547184

Hill, M. (1990). On creating a theory of feminist therapy. *Women and Therapy, 91,* 53–65.

Hill, N. R., Leinbaugh, T., Bradley, C., & Hazler, R. (2005). Female

counselor educators: Encouraging and discouraging factors in academia. *Journal of Counseling & Development, 83,* 374–380.

Hilliard, J. (1998). Termination of treatment with troublesome patients. In L. E. Lifson & R. I. Simon (Eds.), *The mental health practitioner and the law* (pp. 216–221). Cambridge, MA: Harvard University Press.

Hines, P. L., & Fields, T. H. (2002). Pregroup screening issues for school counselors. *Journal for Specialists in Group Work, 27,* 358–376.

Ho, E. Y., D'Agostine, T. A., Yadegar, V., Burke, A., & Bylund, C. (2012). Teaching patients how to talk with biomedical providers about their complementary and alternative medicine use. *Patient Education and Counseling, 89*(3), 405–410. doi: 10.1016/j.pec.2012.03.009

Hoffman, R. M., & Kress, V. E. (2010). Adolescent nonsuicidal self-injury: Minimizing client and counselor risk and enhancing client care. *Journal of Mental Health Counseling, 32,* 342–353.

Hogan, D. B. (1979). *The regulation of psychotherapists.* Cambridge, MA: Ballinger Publishing.

Hohenshil, T. H. (1996). Editorial: Role of assessment and diagnosis in counseling. *Journal of Counseling & Development, 75,* 64–67.

Hohenshil, T. H. (2000). High tech counseling. *Journal of Counseling & Development, 78,* 365–368.

Hohenshil, T. H., Amundson, N. E., & Niles, S. G. (Eds.). (2013). *Counseling around the world: An international handbook.* Alexandria, VA: American Counseling Association.

Holcomb-McCoy, C. C., & Mitchell, N. A. (2007). Promoting ethnic/racial equality through empowerment-based counseling. In C. C.

Lee (Ed.), *Counseling for social justice* (2nd ed., pp. 137–157). Alexandria, VA: American Counseling Association.

Holcomb-McCoy, C. C., & Myers, J. E. (1999). Multicultural competence and counselor training: A national survey. *Journal of Counseling & Development, 77,* 294–302.

Hollander, J. T., Bauer, S., Herlihy, B., & McCollum, V. (2006). Beliefs of Board Certified Substance Abuse Counselors regarding multiple relationships. *Journal of Mental Health Counseling, 28,* 84–94.

Holroyd, J. C., & Brodsky, A. M. (1977). Psychologists' attitudes and practices regarding erotic and nonerotic physical contact with patients. *American Psychologist, 32,* 843–849.

Hoop, J. G., DiPasquale, T., Hernandez, J. M., & Roberts, L. W. (2008). Gay and lesbian social justice: Strategies for social advocacy. *Ethics and Behavior, 18,* 353–372.

Hopewell v. Adebimpe, 130 Pitt. L. J. 107 (1982).

Hopkins, W. E. (1997). *Ethical dimensions of diversity.* Thousand Oaks, CA: Sage.

Hormes, J. M., Kearns, B., & Timko, C. A. (2014). Craving Facebook? Behavioral addiction to online social networking and its association with emotion regulation deficits. *Addiction, 109,* 2079–2088. doi: 10.1111/add.12713

Horowitz v. Board of Curators of the University of Missouri, 435 U.S. 78 (1978).

Hospital and Community Psychiatry. (1979). Virginia court ruling stirs concern about confidentiality protections in group therapy. *Hospital and Community Psychiatry, 30,* 428.

Howe, G. E. (1999, April 19). *Safety net critical for health care of working poor.* Retrieved from http://www.bizjournals.com/milwaukee/stories/1999/04/19/editorial4.html

Howell, J. A. (1988). Civil liability for suicide: An analysis of the causation issue. *Arizona State Law Journal,* 573–615.

Hoyt, M. F. (1995). *Brief therapy and managed care: Readings for contemporary practice.* San Francisco: Jossey-Bass.

Huber, C. H. (1994). *Ethical, legal, and professional issues in the practice of marriage and family therapy* (2nd ed.). Upper Saddle River, NJ: Merrill/Prentice Hall.

Huber, C. H., & Baruth, L. G. (1987). *Ethical, legal and professional issues in the practice of marriage and family therapy.* Upper Saddle River, NJ: Merrill/Prentice Hall.

Huey, W. C. (1996). Counseling minor clients. In B. Herlihy & G. Corey (Eds.), *ACA ethical standards casebook* (5th ed., pp. 241–245). Alexandria, VA: American Counseling Association.

Hughes, E. C. (1965). Professions. In K. S. Lynn (Ed.), *The professions in America* (pp. 1–14). Boston: Houghton Mifflin.

Hughes, G. (2014). *Competence and self-care in counselling and psychotherapy.* New York: Routledge.

Hunt, B. (2011). Publishing qualitative research in counseling journals. *Journal of Counseling & Development, 89,* 296–300.

Hunt, B., Matthews, C., Milsom, A., & Lammel, J. A. (2006). Lesbians with physical disabilities: A qualitative study of their experiences with counseling. *Journal of Counseling & Development, 84,* 163–174.

Hunt, H. (2004). *Essentials of private practice.* New York: W. W. Norton.

Huss, S. N., Bryant, A., & Mulet, S. (2008). Managing the quagmire

of counseling in a school: Bringing the parents on board. *Professional School Counseling, 11,* 362–367. doi: 10.5330/PSC.n.2010-11.362

Hussain, S. A., & Vandiver, K. T. (1984). *Suicide in children and adolescents.* New York: SP Medical and Scientific Books.

Hutchins, A. M. (2006). Counseling gay men. In C. C. Lee (Ed.), *Multicultural issues in counseling: New approaches to diversity* (3rd ed., pp. 269–289). Alexandria, VA: American Counseling Association.

Hutchens, N., Block, J., & Young, M. (2013). Counselor educators' gatekeeping responsibilities and students' First Amendment rights. *Counselor Education & Supervision, 52,* 82–95.

Ibrahim, F. A., & Arredondo, P. (1990). Ethical issues in multicultural counseling. In B. Corey & G. Corey (Eds.), *ACA ethical standards casebook* (4th ed., pp. 137–145). Alexandria, VA: American Counseling Association.

Ideal Publishing Corp. v. Creative Features, 59 A.2d 862, 399 N.Y.S.2d 118 (1977).

In re marriage of Kovash, 858 P.2d 351 (Mont. 1993).

In the Matter of Miguel M. v. Barron, 950 N.E.2d 107 (N.Y. 2011).

Ingersoll, R. E., Bauer, A., & Burns, L. (2004). Children and psychotropic medication: What role should advocacy counseling play? *Journal of Counseling & Development, 82,* 337–342.

International Legal Technology Association. (2010). The ethics and security of cloud computing. Retrieved from http://www.iltanet.org

International Society for Mental Health Online. (2008). *Suggested principles for the online provision of mental health services.*

Retrieved from http://www
.ismho.org

International Test Commission.
(2001). International guidelines
for test use. *International Journal
of Testing, 1,* 93–114.

Irish, D. P. (1993). Multiculturalism
and the majority population. In D.
P. Irish, K. F. Lundquist, & V. J.
Nelson (Eds.), *Ethnic variations
in dying, death, and grief: Diver-
sity in universality* (pp. 1–12).
Washington, DC: Taylor &
Francis.

Isaacs, D. (2011). Plagiarism is not
OK. *Journal of Pediatrics and
Child Health, 47,* 159. doi:
10.1111/j.1440-1754.2011.
02050.x

Isaacs, M. L., & Stone, C. (1999).
School counselors and confidentiality: Factors affecting professional choices. *Professional
School Counseling, 2,* 258–266.

Isaacs, M. L., & Stone, C. (2001).
Confidentiality with minors:
Mental health counselors' attitudes toward breaching or preserving confidentiality. *Journal of
Mental Health Counseling, 23,*
342–356.

Israel, T. (2004). What counselors
need to know about working with
sexual minority clients. In D. R.
Atkinson & G. Hackett (Eds.),
Counseling diverse populations
(3rd ed., pp. 347–364). Boston:
McGraw-Hill.

Ivey, A., Ivey, M., Myers, J., &
Sweeney, T. (2005). *Developmental counseling and therapy: Promoting wellness over the lifespan.*
Boston: Houghton Mifflin.

Ivey, A. E., D'Andrea, M., Ivey, M.
B., & Simek-Morgan, L. (2007).
*Theories of counseling and psy-
chotherapy: A multicultural per-
spective* (6th ed.). Boston: Allyn
& Bacon.

Ivey, A. E., & Ivey, M. B. (1998).
Reframing *DSM-IV*: Positive

strategies from developmental
counseling and therapy. *Journal
of Counseling & Development,
76,* 334–350.

Ivey, A. E., & Ivey, M. B. (1999).
Toward a developmental diagnostic and statistical manual: The
vitality of a contextual framework. *Journal of Counseling &
Development, 77,* 484–490.

Jablonski v. United States, 712 F.2d
391 (9th Cir. 1983).

Jacobs, D. G., Brewer, M., & Klein-
Benheim, M. (1999). Suicide
assessment: An overview and recommended protocol. In D. G.
Jacobs (Ed.), *The Harvard Medical School guide to suicide
assessment and intervention*
(pp. 3–39). San Francisco:
Jossey-Bass.

Jacobs, E. E., Harvill, R. L., &
Masson, R. L. (1994). *Group
counseling: Strategies and skills*
(2nd ed.). Pacific Grove, CA:
Brooks/Cole.

Jacobs, E. E., Masson, R. L., &
Harvill, R. L. (1998). *Group
counseling: Strategies and skills*
(3rd ed.). Pacific Grove, CA:
Brooks/Cole.

Jaffee v. Redmond et al., 1996 WL
314841 (U.S. June 13 1996).

James, J. (1996, May 11). University
to adopt rules that put limits on
dating. *Register-Guard* (Eugene,
OR), pp. 1, 6A.

Jamison, S. (2012). Legalized physician-assisted suicide would
improve treatment of the terminally ill. In N. Merino (Ed.),
*Assisted suicide: Current contro-
versies* (pp. 115–121). San Francisco: Jossey-Bass.

Janson, G. R., & Steigerwald, F. J.
(2002). Family counseling and
ethical challenges with gay, lesbian, bisexual, and transgendered
(GLBT) clients: More questions
than answers. *The Family
Journal, 10,* 415–418.

Jencius, M. (2003). Applications of
technological advances for multi-
cultural counseling professionals.
In F. D. Harper & J. McFadden
(Eds.), *Culture and counseling:
New approaches* (pp. 350–362).
Boston: Pearson.

Jencius, M. (2015). Technology,
social media, and online counseling. In B. Herlihy & G. Corey,
ACA ethical standards casebook
(7th ed., pp. 245–254). Alexandria, VA: American Counseling
Association.

Jencius, M., Baltimore, M. L., &
Getz, H. G. (2010). Innovative
use of technology in clinical
supervision. In J. R. Culbreth &
L. L. Brown (Eds.), *State of the
art in clinical supervision*
(pp. 63–86). New York:
Routledge.

Jencius, M., & Sager, D. E. (2001).
The practice of marriage and fam-
ily counseling in cyberspace. *The
Family Journal, 9,* 295–301.

Jencius, M., & West, J. (2003). Traditional counseling theories and
cross-cultural implications. In F.
D. Harper & J. McFadden (Eds.),
*Culture and counseling: New
approaches* (pp. 339–349).
Boston: Pearson.

Jilek-Aall, L. (1988). Suicidal behavior among youth: A cross-cultural
comparison. *Transcultural
Psychiatry Research Review, 25,*
86–105.

John R. v. Oakland Unified School
District, 48 Ca.3d 438, 256 Cal.
Rptr. 766, 769 P.2d 948 (1989).

Johnson, S. J. (2000). Promoting professional identity in an era of educational reform. *Professional
School Counseling, 4,* 31–40.

Johnson, S. W., & Maile, L. J.
(1987). *Suicide and the schools: A
handbook for prevention, intervention, and rehabilitation.*
Springfield, IL: Charles C
Thomas.

Johnson, W. B. (2015). Multiple relationships in military mental health counseling. In B. Herlihy & G. Corey, *Boundary issues in counseling* (3rd ed., pp. 254–259). Alexandria, VA: American Counseling Association.

Johnson, W. B., Barnett, J. E., Elman, N. S., Forrest, L., & Kaslow, N. J. (2012). The competent community: Toward a vital reformulation of professional ethics. *American Psychologist, 67,* 557–569.

Johnson, W. B., Ralph, J., & Johnson, S. J. (2005). Managing multiple roles in embedded environments: The case of aircraft carrier psychology. *Professional Psychology: Research and Practice, 36,* 73–81.

Johnson, W. K., & Roark, D. B. (1996). *A copyright sampler.* Chicago: American Library Association.

Jones, P. A. (1996). Interstate testimony by child protective agency workers in the child custody context. *Vermont Law Review, 21,* 633–675.

Jordan, K., & Stevens, P. (2001). Teaching ethics to graduate students: A course model. *The Family Journal, 9,* 178–184.

Jordan, M., & Marshall, H. (2010). Taking counseling and psychotherapy outside: Destruction or enrichment of the therapeutic frame? *European Journal of Psychotherapy & Counselling, 12,* 345–359.

Jorgenson, L. M. (1995). Sexual contact in fiduciary relationships. In J. C. Gonsiorek (Ed.), *Breach of trust: Sexual exploitation by health care professionals and clergy* (pp. 237–283). Thousand Oaks, CA: Sage.

Kain, C. D. (Ed.). (1989). *No longer immune: A counselor's guide to AIDS.* Alexandria, VA: American Counseling Association.

Kane, A. W. (1995). The effects of criminalization of sexual misconduct by therapists. In J. C. Gonsiorek (Ed.), *Breach of trust: Sexual exploitation by health care professionals and clergy* (pp. 317–332). Thousand Oaks, CA: Sage.

Kane, M. N. (2013). Catholic priests' knowledge of pastoral codes of conduct in the United States. *Ethics & Behavior, 23,* 199–213. doi: 10.1080/10508422. 2012.737690

Kaplan, D., & Martz, E. (2014, July). An overview of the revised ACA Code of Ethics. *Counseling Today,* 20–21.

Kaplan, D. M., Kocet, M. M., Cottone, R. R., Glosoff, H. L., Miranti, J. G., et al. (2009). New mandates in the revised ACA Code of Ethics. *Journal of Counseling & Development, 87,* 241–256.

Kaplan, D., & Martz, E. (2014, November). Raising the bar for counselor educators. *Counseling Today, 57*(5), 26–27.

Kaplan, D. M., Tarvydas, V. M., & Gladding, S. T. (2014). 20/20: A vision for the future of counseling: The new consensus definition of counseling. *Journal of Counseling & Development, 92,* 366–372. doi: 10.1002/ j.1556-6676.2014.00164.x

Kaplin, W. A., & Lee, B. A. (1995). *The law of higher education* (3rd ed.). San Francisco: Jossey-Bass.

Katherine, A. (1991). *Boundaries: Where you end and I begin.* New York: Simon & Schuster.

Katz, A. D., & Hoyt, W. T. (2014). The influence of multicultural counseling competence and anti-Black prejudice on therapists' outcome expectancies. *Journal of Counseling Psychology, 61,* 299–305.

Kearney, M. (1984). Confidentiality in group psychotherapy. *Psychotherapy in Private Practice, 2,* 19–20.

Keeton v. Anderson-Wiley, et al., U.S. Court of Appeals, 11th Circuit, 664 F3d 865; 2011 U.A. App. LEXIS 25007; 23 Fla. L. Weekly Fed. C 647 (2011).

Keim, M. A., & Cobia, D. (2010). Legal and ethical implications of working with minors in Alabama: Consent and confidentiality. *Alabama Counseling Association Journal, 35,* 28–34.

Keith-Spiegel, P. (1994). Teaching psychologists and the new APA ethics code: Do we fit in? *Professional Psychology: Research and Practice, 25,* 362–368.

Keith-Spiegel, P. (2014). *Red flags in psychotherapy: Stories of ethics complaints and resolutions.* New York: Routledge.

Keith-Spiegel, P., & Koocher, G. P. (1985). *Ethics in psychology: Professional standards and cases.* New York: Random House.

Keller, A., Moore, E., Hamilton, D., Terrell, D., & Hahn, L. (2010, March). *Facebook: Implications for counselor education students, faculty and practitioners.* Paper presented at the American Counseling Association Conference.

Keller, E. (1988). Consensual amorous relationships between faculty and students: The constitutional right to privacy. *Journal of College and University Law, 15,* 21–42.

Kemp, A. (1998). *Abuse in the family: An introduction.* Pacific Grove, CA: Brooks/Cole.

Kennedy, J. A. (2003). *Psychiatric treatment planning* (2nd ed.). Arlington, VA: American Psychiatric Publishing.

Kerl, S. B., Garcia, J. L., McCullough, S., & Maxwell, M. E. (2002). Systematic evaluation of professional performance: Legally supported procedure and process. *Counselor Education and Supervision, 41,* 321–334.

Kertesz, R. (2002). Dual relationships in psychotherapy in Latin America. In A. A Lazarus & O. Zur (Eds.), *Dual relationships and psychotherapy* (pp. 329–334). New York: Springer.

Kett, J. F. (1968). *The formation of the American medical profession: The role of institutions, 1780–1860.* New Haven, CT: Yale University Press.

Kinch, S., & Kress, V. E. (2012). The creative use of chain analysis techniques in counseling clients who engage in nonsuicidal self-injury. *Journal of Creativity in Mental Health, 7,* 343–354.

King, J. H., & Anderson, S. M. (2004). Therapeutic implications of pharmacotherapy: Current trends and ethical issues. *Journal of Counseling & Development, 82,* 329–336.

King, K. A., Tribble, J. L., & Price, J. H. (1999). School counselors' perceptions of nonconsensual sexual activity among high school students. *Professional School Counseling, 2,* 286–290.

Kiracofe, N. M., & Wells, L. (2007). Mandated disciplinary counseling on campus: Problems and possibilities. *Journal of Counseling & Development, 85,* 269–268.

Kiselica, M. S. (1999). Confronting my own ethnocentrism and racism: A process of pain and growth. *Journal of Counseling & Development, 77,* 14–17.

Kiselica, M. S., & Morrill-Richards, M. (2007). Sibling maltreatment: The forgotten abuse. *Journal of Counseling & Development, 85,* 148–161.

Kiselica, M. S., & Robinson, M. (2001). Bringing advocacy counseling to life: The history, issues, and human dramas of social justice work in counseling. *Journal*

of *Counseling & Development, 79,* 387–397.

Kitchener, K. S. (1992). Posttherapy relationships: Ever or never? In B. Herlihy & G. Corey (Eds.), *Dual relationships in counseling* (pp. 145–148). Alexandria, VA: American Association for Counseling and Development.

Kitchener, K. S., & Harding, S. S. (1990). Dual role relationships. In B. Herlihy & L. Golden (Eds.), *Ethical standards casebook* (4th ed., pp. 145–148). Alexandria, VA: American Association for Counseling and Development.

Kitzrow, M. A. (2002). Survey of CACREP-accredited programs: Training counselors to provide treatment for sexual abuse. *Counselor Education and Supervision, 42,* 107–118.

Kleist, D., & Bitter, J. R. (2009). Virtue, ethics, and legality in family practice. In J. R. Bitter, *Theory and practice of family therapy and counseling* (pp. 43–65). Washington, DC: American Psychological Association.

Knapp, S., & VandeCreek, L. (1987). *Privileged communications in the mental health professions.* New York: Van Nostrand Reinhold.

Knapp, S. & VandeCreek, L. (2006). *Practical ethics for psychologists: A positive approach.* Washington, DC: American Psychological Association.

Knapp, S., & VandeCreek, L. (2008). The ethics of advertising, billing, and finances in psychotherapy. *Journal of Clinical Psychology: In Session, 64,* 613–625.

Knuth, M. O. (1979). Civil liability for causing or failing to prevent suicide. *Loyola of Los Angeles Law Review, 12,* 965–991.

Kolbert, J. B., Morgan, B., & Brendel, B. (2002). Faculty and student perceptions of dual relationships within counselor

education: A qualitative analysis. *Counselor Education and Supervision, 41,* 193–206.

Koocher, G. P. (2008). Ethical challenges in mental health services to children and families. *Journal of Clinical Psychology: In Session, 64,* 1–12.

Korman, M. (1974). National conference on levels and patterns of professional training in psychology: Major themes. *American Psychologist, 13,* 615–624.

Kottler, J. (1993). *On being a therapist.* San Francisco, CA: Jossey-Bass.

Kottler, J. A., & Schofield, M. (2001). When therapists face stress and crisis: Self-initiated coping strategies. In E. R. Welfel & R. E. Ingersoll (Eds.), *The mental health desk reference* (pp. 426–432). New York: Wiley.

Kowalski, R. M., Giumetti, G. W., Schroeder, A. N., & Lattanner, M. R. (2014). Bullying in the digital age: A critical review and meta-analysis of cyberbullying research among youth. *Psychological Bulletin, 140,* 1073–1137. doi: 10.1037/a0035618

Kramer, D. T. (1994). *Legal rights of children* (2nd ed.). New York: McGraw-Hill.

Kraus, R., Stricker, G., & Speyer, C. (Eds.). (2010). *Online counseling: A handbook for mental health professionals* (2nd ed.). Burlington, MA: Academic Press.

Kress, V. E., & Dixon, A. (2007). Consensual faculty-student sexual relationships in counselor education: Recommendations for counselor educators' decision making. *Counselor Education and Supervision, 47,* 110–122.

Kress, V. E., Hoffman, R. M., & Eriksen, K. (2010). Ethical dimensions of diagnosing: Considerations for clinical mental health counselors. *Counseling and Values, 55,* 101–112.

Kress, V. E., & Protivnak, J. T. (2009). Professional development plans to remedy problematic counseling student behaviors. *Counselor Education and Supervision, 48*, 154–166.

Kress, V. E. W. (2003). Self-injurious behaviors: Assessment and diagnosis. *Journal of Counseling & Development, 81*, 490–496.

Kulic, K. R., Dagley, J. C., & Horne, A. M. (2001). Prevention groups with children and adolescents. *The Journal for Specialists in Group Work, 26*, 211–218.

Kunkel, M. A., & Williams, C. (1991). Age and expectations about counseling: Two methodological perspectives. *Journal of Counseling & Development, 70*, 314–320.

Kuo, F. (2009). Secrets or no secrets: Confidentiality in family therapy. *American Journal of Family Therapy, 37*, 351–354.

Kurasaki, K. S., Sue, S., Chun, C., & Gee, K. (2000). Ethnic minority intervention and treatment research. In J. E. Aponte & J. Wohl (Eds.), *Psychological intervention and cultural diversity* (pp. 234–249). Boston, MA: Allyn & Bacon.

Kutchins, H., & Kirk, S. (1987, May). *DSM-IIIR* and social work malpractice. *Social Work*, 205–211.

Labardee, L. (2009, Summer). Online counseling crosses the chasm. *EAP Digest*, 12–20.

Ladany, N., & Friedlander, M. L. (1995). The relationship between the supervisory working alliance and trainees' experience of role conflict and role ambiguity. *Counselor Education and Supervision, 34*, 220–231.

Ladany, N., Mori, Y., & Mehr, K. E. (2013). Effective and ineffective supervision. *The Counseling Psychologist, 41*, 28–47.

LaFountain, R. M., & Baer, E. C. (2001). Increasing CACREP's name recognition: The effect of written correspondence on site supervisors' awareness level. *Journal of Counseling & Development, 79*, 194–199.

Lake, P., & Tribbensee, N. (2002). The emerging crisis of college student suicide: Law and policy responses to serious forms of self-inflicted injury. *Stetson Law Review, 32*, 125. Retrieved from http://seg802.ocs.lsu.edu:2077/universe/document?_m=7db3c69cd06df1980a9838e79cf1b8e0&_docnum=3&wchp=dGLbVzz-zSkVb&_md5=52e3fdd ac81fc559f5e59a15e2dc7d63

Lakin, M. (1994). Morality in group and family therapies: Multiperson therapies and the 1992 ethics code. *Professional Psychology: Research and Practice, 25*, 344–348.

Lamadue, C. A., & Duffey, T. H. (1999). The role of graduate programs as gatekeepers: A model for evaluating student counselor competence. *Counselor Education & Supervision, 39*, 101–109.

Lambert, M. J., & Cattani-Thompson, K. (1996). Current findings regarding the effectiveness of counseling: Implications for practice. *Journal of Counseling & Development, 74*, 601–608.

Lambie, G. W., Hagedorn, W. B., & Ieva, K. P. (2010). Social-cognitive development, ethical and legal knowledge, and ethical decision making of counselor education students. *Counselor Education & Supervision, 49*, 228–246.

Lancaster, C., Balkin, R. S., Garcia, R., & Valarezo, A. (2011). An evidence-based approach to reducing recidivism in court-referred youth. *Journal of Counseling & Development, 89*, 488–492.

Landau, R., & Werner, S. (2012). Ethical aspects of using GPS for tracking people with dementia: Recommendations for practice. *International Psychogeriatrics, 29*, 358–366. doi: 10.1017/S1041610211001888

Langer, E. J., & Abelson, R. P. (1974). A patient by any other name … : Clinician group differences and labeling bias. *Journal of Consulting and Clinical Psychology, 42*, 4–9.

Lassiter, P. S., & Barret, B. (2007). Gay and lesbian social justice: Strategies for social advocacy. In C. C. Lee (Ed.), *Counseling for social justice* (2nd ed., pp. 31–50). Alexandria, VA: American Counseling Association.

Lat, D. (2010). Breaking: Defense of Marriage Act (DOMA) held unconstitutional. *Above the Law, 08 July 2010*. Retrieved from http://abovethelaw.com/2010/07/breaking-defense-of-marriage-act-doma-struck-down

Laux, J. M. (2002). A primer on suicidology: Implications for counselors. *Journal of Counseling & Development, 80*, 380–383.

Lawless, L. L., Ginter, E. J., & Kelly, K. R. (1999). Managed care: What mental health counselors need to know. *Journal of Mental Health Counseling, 21*, 50–65.

Lawrence, G., & Robinson Kurpius, S. E. (2000). Legal and ethical issues involved when counseling minors in nonschool settings. *Journal of Counseling & Development, 78*, 130–137.

Lawson, D. M. (2001). The development of abusive personality: A trauma response. *Journal of Counseling & Development, 79*, 505–509.

Lawson, D. M. (2003). Incidence, explanations, and treatment of partner violence. *Journal of*

Counseling & Development, 81, 19–32.

Lawson, G. (2007). Counselor wellness and impairment: A national survey. *Journal of Humanistic Counseling, Education and Development, 46,* 20–34.

Lawson, G., & Myers, J. E. (2011). Wellness, professional quality of life, and career-sustaining behaviors: What keeps us well? *Journal of Counseling & Development, 89,* 163–171.

Lazarus, A. A. (2006). Transcending boundaries in psychotherapy. In B. Herlihy & G. Corey (Eds.), *Boundary issues in counseling: Multiple roles and responsibilities* (2nd ed., pp. 16–19). Alexandria, VA: American Counseling Association.

Lazarus, A. A., & Zur, O. (Eds.). (2002). *Dual relationships and psychotherapy.* New York: Springer.

Lazovsky, R. (2008). Maintaining confidentiality with minors: Dilemmas of school counselors. *Professional School Counseling, 11,* 235–245.

Leaffer, M. A. (1989). *Understanding copyright law.* New York: Matthew Bender.

Leahy, M. J., & Szymanski, E. M. (1995). Rehabilitation counseling: Evolution and current status. *Journal of Counseling & Development, 74,* 163–166.

Leatherman, C. (1993). In the debate over faculty-student dating, the talk turns to ethics, sex, even love. *Chronicle of Higher Education, 24,* A15–A17.

Lee, C. C. (2001). Defining and responding to racial and ethnic diversity. In D. C. Locke, J. E. Myers, & E. L. Herr (Eds.), *Handbook of multicultural counseling* (pp. 581–588). Thousand Oaks, CA: Sage.

Lee, C. C. (2013). The CACREP site visit process. *Journal of Counseling & Development, 91,* 50–54. doi: 10.1002/j.1556-6676.2013.00070.x

Lee, C. C. (Ed.). (2007). *Counseling for social justice* (2nd ed.). Alexandria, VA: American Counseling Association.

Lee, C. C. (Ed.). (2013). *Multicultural issues in counseling: New approaches to diversity* (4th ed.). Alexandria, VA: American Counseling Association.

Lee, C. C. (Ed.). (2015). Social justice and counseling across cultures. In B. Herlihy & G. Corey, *ACA ethical standards casebook* (7th ed., pp. 155–162). Alexandria, VA: American Counseling Association.

Lee, C. C., & Kurilla, V. (1997). Ethics and multiculturalism: The challenge of diversity. In *The Hatherleigh guide to ethics in therapy* (pp. 235–248). New York: Hatherleigh Press.

Lee, S. (2010). Contemporary issues of ethical e-therapy. *Journal of Ethics in Mental Health, 5,* 1–5.

Lee, S. M., Suh, S., Yang, E., & Jang, Y. J. (2012). History, current status, and future prospects of counseling in South Korea. *Journal of Counseling & Development, 90,* 494–499. doi: 10.1002/j.1556-6676.2012.00061.x

Lee, Y. (2011). Understanding anti-plagiarism software adoption: An extended protection motivation theory perspective. *Decision Support Systems, 50,* 361–369. doi: 10.1016/j.dss.2010.07.009

Leibert, T., Archer, J., Munson, J., & York, K. (2006). An exploratory study of client perceptions of Internet counseling and the therapeutic alliance. *Journal of Mental Health Counseling, 28,* 69–83.

Leppma, M., & Jones, K. D. (2013). *Multiple assessment methods and sources in counseling: Ethical considerations.* Retrieved from http://www.counseling.org/knowledge-center/vistas/vistas-2013

Leverett-Main, S. (2004). Program directors' perceptions of admission screening measures and indicators of student success. *Counselor Education and Supervision, 43,* 207–219.

Levitt, D. H., & Moorhead, H. J. H. (Eds.). (2013). *Values and ethics in counseling: Real-life ethical decision making.* New York: Routledge.

Levy, J., Galambos, G., & Skarbek, Y. (2014). The erosion of psychiatrist-patient confidentiality by subpoenas. *Australasian Psychiatry, 22,* 332–336. doi: 10.1177/1039856214536241

Lewis, J. A. (2007). Challenging sexism: Promoting the rights of women in contemporary society. In C. C. Lee (Ed.), *Counseling for social justice* (2nd ed., pp. 95–110). Alexandria, VA: American Counseling Association.

Lewis, J. A., Ratts, M. J., Paladino, J., & Toporek, R. (2011). Social justice counseling and advocacy: Developing new leadership roles and competencies. *Journal for Social Action in Counseling and Psychology, 3,* 5–16.

Liaison Committee on Medical Education. (2014). *LCME accreditation standards.* Retrieved from http://www.lcme.org

Linehan, M. M., Comtois, K. A., & Ward-Ciesielski, E. F. (2012). Assessing and managing risk with suicidal individuals. *Cognitive and Behavorial Practice, 19,* 218–232. doi: 10.1016/j.cbpra.2010.11.008

Linton, J. M. (2012). Ethics and accreditation in addictions counselor training: Possible field placement issues for CACREP-accredited addictions counseling programs. *Journal of Addictions and Offender Counseling, 33,* 48–61. doi: 10.1002/j.2161-1874.2012.0004.x

Linville, D., Hertlein, K. M., & Lyness, A. M. P. (2007). Medical family therapy: Reflecting on the necessity of collaborative healthcare research. *Families, Systems, & Health, 38,* 150–157.

Lipari v. Sears, Roebuck & Co., 836 F.2d 209 (1987).

Lisa M. v. Henry Mayo Newhall Memorial Hosp., 12 Cal.4th 291, 48 Cal.Rptr.2d 510, 907 P.2d 358 (1995).

Little, J. N. (2001). Embracing gay, lesbian, bisexual, and transgendered youth in school-based settings. *Child and Youth Care Forum, 30,* 99–110.

Lloyd, A. P. (1992). Dual relationship problems in counselor education. In B. Herlihy & G. Corey (Eds.), *Dual relationships in counseling* (pp. 59–64). Alexandria, VA: American Association for Counseling and Development.

Logan v. District of Columbia, D.C.D.C. 1978, 447 F.Supp. 1328.

Logan, C. R. (2006). Counseling lesbian clients. In C. C. Lee (Ed.), *Multicultural issues in counseling: New approaches to diversity* (3rd ed., pp. 291–301). Alexandria, VA: American Counseling Association.

Lonner, W. J., & Ibrahim, F. A. (1996). Appraisal and assessment in cross-cultural counseling. In P. B. Pedersen, J. G. Draguns, W. J. Lonner, & J. E. Trimble (Eds.), *Counseling across cultures* (4th ed., pp. 293–322). Thousand Oaks, CA: Sage.

Louisell, D. W., & Sinclair, K., Jr. (1971). The Supreme Court of California, 1969–70–Forward: Reflections on the law of privileged communications—The psychotherapist–patient privilege in perspective. *California Law Review, 59,* 30–55.

Louisiana Licensed Mental Health Counselor Act, La. Rev. Stat. Ann. §37. (West, 1999).

Lowman, R. L. (2006). Case 58: Confronting unethical behavior. In R. L. Lowman (Ed.), *The ethical practice of psychology in organizations* (2nd ed., pp. 241–244). Washington, DC: American Psychological Association.

Ludes, F. J., & Gilbert, H. J. (1998). Fiduciary. *Corpus Juris Secundum, 36A,* 381–389.

Luepker, E. T. (2012). *Record keeping in psychotherapy and counseling* (2nd ed.). New York: Routledge.

Lum, D. (2007). *Culturally competent practice: A framework for understanding diverse groups and justice issues.* Belmont, CA: Thomson Brooks/Cole.

Lunceford, B. (2011). The new pornographers: Legal and ethical considerations of sexting. In B. E. Drushel & K. German (Eds.), *The ethics of emerging media: Information, social norms, and new media* (pp. 99–118). New York: Continuum International.

Lynch, G. (2002). *Pastoral care and counselling.* London: Sage.

Lynch, R. T., & Gussel, L. (1996). Disclosure and self-advocacy regarding disability-related needs: Strategies to maximize integration in postsecondary education. *Journal of Counseling & Development, 74,* 352–358.

Lyons, M. L. (2015). If you will excuse me. In B. Herlihy & G. Corey, *ACA ethical standards casebook* (7th ed., pp. 226–229). Alexandria, VA: American Counseling Association.

Macbeth, J. E., Wheeler, A. M., Sither, J. W., & Onek, J. N. (1994). *Legal and risk management issues in the practice of psychiatry.* Washington, DC: Psychiatrists Purchasing Group.

MacCluskie, K. C. (2001). Responsible documentation. In E. R. Welfel & R. E. Ingersoll (Eds.), *The mental health desk reference* (pp. 459–465). New York: Wiley.

Machuca, R. (2015). Boundary issues in counseling Latino clients. In B. Herlihy & G. Corey, *Boundary issues in counseling* (3rd ed., pp. 100–103). Alexandria, VA: American Counseling Association.

MacNair, R. R. (1992). Ethical dilemmas of child abuse reporting: Implications for mental health counselors. *Journal of Mental Health Counseling, 14,* 127–136.

Madden, R. G. (1998). *Legal issues in social work, counseling, and mental health.* Thousand Oaks, CA: Sage.

Magaldi-Dopman, D. (2014). An "afterthought": Counseling trainees' multicultural competence within the spiritual/religious domain. *Journal of Multicultural Counseling and Development, 42,* 194–204.

Magnuson, S., Norem, K., & Wilcoxon, A. (2000). Clinical supervision of prelicensed counselors: Recommendations for consideration and practice. *Journal of Mental Health Counseling, 22,* 176–188.

Maloney, D. M. (1984). *Protection of human research subjects.* New York: Plenum.

Malott, K. M. (2010). Multicultural counselor training in a single course: Review of research. *Journal of Multicultural Counseling and Development, 38,* 51–63.

Manderscheid, R., & Barrett, S. (Eds.). (1991). *Mental health in the United States, 1987* (National Institute of Mental Health, DHHS Publication No. ADM-87–1518). Washington, DC: U.S. Government Printing Office.

Manfrini, A. (2006). Boundary issues in counseling couples and families. In B. Herlihy & G. Corey (Eds.), *Boundary issues in counseling: Multiple roles and responsibilities* (2nd ed., pp. 152–158). Alexandria, VA: American Counseling Association.

Manhal-Baugus, M. (2001). E-therapy: Practical, ethical, and legal issues. *CyberPsychology & Behavior, 4,* 551–563.

Manis, A. A. (2012). A review of the literature on promoting cultural competence and social justice agency among students and counselor trainees: Piecing the evidence together to advance pedagogy and research. *The Professional Counselor, 2,* 48–57.

Manis, A. A., & Bodenhorn, N. (2006). Preparation for counseling adults with terminal illness: Personal and professional parallels. *Counseling & Values, 50,* 197–207.

Manno v. McIntosh, 519 NW2d 815 (Iowa App. 1994).

Maramba, G. G., & Nagayama Hall, G. C. (2002). Meta-analyses of ethnic match as a predictor of dropout, utilization, and level of functioning. *Cultural Diversity & Ethnic Minority Psychology, 8,* 290–297.

Marczyk, G. R., & Wertheimer, E. (2001). The bitter pill of empiricism: Health maintenance organizations, informed consent and the reasonable psychotherapist standard of care. *Villanova Law Review, 46.* Retrieved from http://works.bepress.com/ellen_wertheimer/4

Margolin, G. (1982). Ethical and legal considerations in marital and family therapy. *American Psychologist, 37,* 788–801.

Margolin, G., Chien, D., & Duman, S. E. (2005). Ethical issues in couple and family research. *Journal of Family Psychology, 19,* 157–167.

Martz, E., & Kaplan, D. (2014, October). New responsibilities when making referrals. *Counseling Today, 57*(4), 24–25.

Mascari, J. B., & Webber, J. M. (2006). Salting the slippery slope: What licensing violations tell us about preventing dangerous ethical situations. In G. R. Walz, J. Bleuer, & R. K. Yep (Eds.), *VISTAS: Compelling perspectives on counseling, 2006* (pp. 165–168). Alexandria, VA: American Counseling Association.

Mascari, J. B., & Webber, J. (2013). CACREP accreditation: A solution to license portability and counselor identity problems. *Journal of Counseling & Development, 91,* 15–25. doi: 10.1002/j.1556-6676.2013.00066.x

Maslow, A. (1968). *Toward a psychology of being* (Rev. ed.). New York: Van Nostrand Reinhold.

Masur, P. K., Reinecke, L., Ziegele, M., & Quiring, O. (2014). The interplay of intrinsic need satisfaction and Facebook specific motives in explaining addictive behavior on Facebook. *Computers in Human Behavior, 39,* 376–386. doi:10.1016/j.chb.2014.05.047

Matarazzo, J. D. (1986). Computerized clinical psychological test interpretations: Unvalidated plus all mean and no sigma. *American Psychologist, 41,* 14–24.

Mathews, L. L., & Gerrity, D. A. (2002). Therapists' use of boundaries in sexual abuse groups: An exploratory study. *Journal for Specialists in Group Work, 27,* 78–91.

Mattie T. v. Johnson, D.C. Miss. 74 F.R.D. 498 (1976).

Matusek, J. A., & O'Dougherty, A. (2010). Ethical dilemmas in treating clients with eating disorders: A review and application of an integrative ethical decision-making model. *European Eating Disorders Review, 18,* 434-452.

Mayfield, A. C. (1996). *Receptivity of counselors to insurance fraud in mental health.* Unpublished doctoral dissertation, University of New Orleans, Louisiana.

McAdams, C. R., & Foster, V. A. (2000). Client suicides: Its frequency and impact on counselors. *Journal of Mental Health Counseling, 22,* 107–121.

McAdams, C. R., & Foster, V. A. (2007). A guide to just and fair remediation of counseling students with professional performance deficiencies. *Counselor Education & Supervision, 47,* 2–13.

McAdams, C. R., Foster, V. A., & Ward, T. T. (2007). Remediation and dismissal policies in counselor education: Lessons learned from a challenge in federal court. *Counselor Education & Supervision, 46,* 212–229.

McAdams, C. R., & Wyatt, K. L. (2010). The regulation of technology-assisted distance counseling and supervision in the United States: An analysis of current extent, trends, and implications. *Counselor Education & Supervision, 49,* 179–192.

McAuliffe, G. J., & Eriksen, K. P. (1999). Toward a constructivist and developmental identity for the counseling profession: The context-phase-stage-style model. *Journal of Counseling & Development, 77,* 267–280.

McCarthy, C. J., & Mejía, O. L. (2001). Using groups to promote preventive coping: A case example with college students from migrant farm-working families. *The Journal for Specialists in Group Work, 26,* 267–275.

McCarthy, P., Sugden, S., Koker, M., Lamendola, F., Maurer, S., & Renninger, S. (1995). A practical guide to informed consent in clinical supervision. *Counselor Education and Supervision, 35,* 130–138.

McCaughan, A. M., & Hill, N. R. (2014). The gatekeeping imperative in counselor education admission protocols: The criticality of personal qualities. *International Journal for the Advancement of Counselling, 36,* 445–453. doi: 10.1007/s10444-014-9223-2

McClarren, G. M. (1987). The psychiatric duty to warn: Walking a tightrope of uncertainty. *University of Cincinnati Law Review, 56,* 269–293.

McConnell, W. A., & Kerbs, J. J. (1993). Providing feedback in research with human subjects. *Professional Psychology: Research and Practice, 24,* 266–270.

McCormac, M. E. (2014). Preventing and responding to bullying: An elementary school's 4-year journey. *Professional School Counseling, 18,* 1–14.

McCreary, J. R. (2011). Tell me no secrets: Sharing, discipline, and the clash of ecclesiastical abstention and psychotherapeutic confidentiality. *Quinnipiac Law Review, 29,* 77–122.

McDonald v. Hogness, 598 P.2d 707 (Wash. 1979).

McEachern, A. G., Aluede, O., & Kenny, M. C. (2008). Emotional abuse in the classroom: Implications and interventions for counselors. *Journal of Counseling & Development, 86,* 3–10.

McFarland, W. P., & Dupuis, M. (2001). The legal duty to protect gay and lesbian students from violence in school. *Professional School Counseling, 4,* 171–179.

McGlothlin, J. M., Rainey, S., & Kindsvatter, A. (2005). Suicidal clients and supervisees: A model for considering supervisor roles. *Counselor Education and Supervision, 45,* 135–146.

McGuckin, C., Perren, S., Corcoran, L., Cowie, H., Dehue, F., Sevcikova, A., & Vollink, T. (2013). Coping with cyberbullying: How can we prevent cyberbulling and how victims can cope with it. In P. K. Smith & G. Steffgen (Eds), *Cyberbullying through the new media: Findings from an international network* (pp. 121–135). East Sussex, England: Psychology Press.

McGuire, J. M., Toal, P., & Blau, B. (1985). The adult client's conception of confidentiality in the therapeutic relationship. *Professional Psychology: Research and Practice, 16,* 375–384.

McIntosh, P. (1998). White privilege, color, and crime: A personal account. In C. R. Mann & M. S. Zatz (Eds.), *Images of color, images of crime* (pp. 207–216). Los Angeles: Roxbury.

McKinney, B. L. (2011). *Therapists' perceptions of walk and talk therapy: A grounded study.* Unpublished dissertation, University of New Orleans.

Meany-Walen, K. K., Carnes-Holt, K., Minton, C. A. B., Purswell, K., & Pronchenko-Jain, Y. (2013). An exploration of counselors' professional leadership development. *Journal of Counseling & Development, 91,* 206-215. doi: 10.1002/j.1556-6676.2013.00087.x

Meara, N. M., Schmidt, L. D., & Day, J. D. (1996). Principles and virtues: A foundation for ethical decisions, policies, and character. *Counseling Psychologist, 24,* 4–77.

MedicineNet. (2008). *Definition of psychiatrist.* Retrieved from http://www.medterms.com/script/main/art.asp?articlekey=5107

Megargee, E. (1979). *Classifying criminal offenders: A new system based on the MMPI.* Beverly Hills, CA: Sage.

Mehr, K. E., Ladany, N., & Caskie, G. I. L. (2014, March 24). Factors influencing trainee willingness to disclose in supervision. *Training and Education in Professional Psychology,* [No pagination specified].

Mellin, E. A., Hunt, B., & Nichols, L. M. (2011). Counselor professional identity: Findings and implications for counseling and interprofessional collaboration. *Journal of Counseling & Development, 89,* 140–147.

Melonas, J. M. (2011). Patients at risk for suicide: Risk management and patient safety considerations to protect the patient and the physician. *Innovations in Clinical Neuroscience, 8,* 45–49.

Meloy, J. R. (1987). Unrequited love and the wish to kill: Diagnosis and treatment of borderline erotomania. *Bulletin of the Menniger Clinic, 53,* 477–492.

Melton, G. B. (1991). Ethical judgments amid uncertainty: Dilemmas in the AIDS epidemic. *Counseling Psychology, 19,* 561–565.

Meneese, W. B., & Yutrzenka, B. A. (1990). Correlates of suicidal ideation among rural adolescents. *Suicide and Life-Threatening Behavior, 20,* 206–212.

Merlone, L. (2005). Record keeping and the school counselor. *Professional School Counseling, 8,* 272–276.

Merluzzi, T. V., & Brischetto, C. S. (1983). Breach of confidentiality and perceived trustworthiness of counselors. *Journal of Counseling Psychology, 30,* 245–251.

Merry, S. N., & Stasiak, K. (2012). The effectiveness of SPARX, a computerised self help intervention for adolescents seeking help for depression: Randomised controlled non-inferiority trial. *British Medical Journal, 344* (e2598). doi:10.1136/bmj.e2598

Merta, R. J., Wolfgang, L., & McNeil, K. (1993). Five models for using the experiential group in the preparation of group counselors. *Journal for Specialists in Group Work, 18,* 143–150.

Messina, J. J. (1999). What's next for the profession of mental health counseling? *Journal of Mental Health Counseling, 21,* 285–294.

Miller, D. J., & Hersen, M. (1992). *Research fraud in the behavioral and biomedical sciences.* New York: Wiley.

Miller, D. J., & Thelan, M. H. (1986). Knowledge and beliefs about confidentiality in psychotherapy. *Professional Psychology: Research and Practice, 17,* 15–19.

Miller, G. M., & Larrabee, M. J. (1995). Sexual intimacy in counselor education and supervision: A national survey. *Counselor Education and Supervision, 34,* 332–343.

Miller, G. M., & Wooten, H. R., Jr. (1995). Sports counseling: A new counseling specialty area. *Journal of Counseling & Development, 74,* 172–173.

Miller, L. D., Short, C., Garland, E. J., & Clark, S. (2010). The ABCs of CBT (Cognitive Behavior Therapy): Evidence-based approaches to child anxiety in public school settings. *Journal of Counseling & Development, 88,* 432–439.

Miller, L. G., McGlothlin, J. M., & West, J. D. (2013). Taking the

fear out of suicide assessment and intervention: A pedagogical and humanistic practice. *The Journal of Humanistic Counseling, 52,* 106–121. doi: 10.1002/j.2161-1939.2013.00036.x

Millner, V. S., & Hanks, R. B. (2002). Induced abortion: An ethical conundrum for counselors. *Journal of Counseling & Development, 80,* 57–63.

Millner, V. S., & Kiser, J. D. (2002). Sexual information and Internet resources. *The Family Journal, 10,* 234–239.

Milsome, A. S. (2002). Students with disabilities: School counselor involvement and preparation. *Professional School Counseling, 5,* 331–338.

Mitchell, C. W., Disque, J. G., & Robertson, P. (2002). When parents want to know: Responding to parental demands for confidential information. *Professional School Counseling, 6,* 156–161.

Mitchell, C. W., & Rogers, R. E. (2003). Rape, statutory rape, and child abuse: Legal distinctions and counselor duties. *Professional School Counseling, 6,* 332–338.

Mitchell, K. J., Finkelhor, D., Jones, L. M., & Wolak, J. (2012). Prevalence and characteristics of youth sexting: A national study. *Pediatrics, 129,* 13–20. doi: 10.1542/peds.2011-1730

Mitchell, R. W. (2007). *Documentation in counseling records: An overview of ethical, legal, and clinical issues* (3rd ed.). Alexandria, VA: American Counseling Association.

Mnookin, R. H., & Weisberg, D. K. (1995). *Child, family and state: Problems and materials on children and the law.* Boston: Little, Brown.

Moberly, M. D. (2007). Protecting confidential communications: Employees and work counseling. *Arizona Attorney, 44,* 10–11.

Moleski, S. M., & Kiselica, M. S. (2005). Dual relationships: A continuum ranging from the destructive to the therapeutic. *Journal of Counseling & Development, 83,* 3–11.

Morgan, E. (1943). Suggested remedy for obstructions to expert testimony by rules of evidence. *University of Chicago Law Review, 10,* 285–298.

Moore, E. M. (1997). *The relationship between clinical graduate students' experiences with their educators and their views on therapist-client dual role relationships.* Unpublished dissertation, University of Windsor.

Moore, M. T., & Griffin, B. W. (2007). Identification of factors that influence authorship name placement and decisions to collaborate in peer-reviewed, education-related publications. *Studies in Educational Evaluation, 32,* 125–135.

Morris, C. A. W., & Minton C. A. B. (2012). Crisis in the curriculum? New counselors' crisis preparation, experiences, and self-efficacy. *Counselor Education and Supervision, 51,* 256–269. doi: 10.1002/j.1556-6978.2012.00019.x

Morris, W. O. (1984). *Revocation of professional licenses by governmental agencies.* Charlottesville, VA: Michie.

Moss, J. M., Gibson, D. M., & Dollarhide, C. T. (2014). Professional identity development: A grounded theory of transformational tasks of counselors. *Journal of Counseling & Development, 92,* 3–12. doi: 10.1002/j.1556-6676.2014.00124.x

Moyer, M., & Sullivan, J. (2008). Student risk-taking behaviors: When do school counselors break confidentiality? *Professional School Counseling, 11,* 236–245.

Moyer, M., Sullivan, J., & Growcock, J. (2012). When is it ethical to inform administrators about student risk-taking behaviors? Perceptions of school counselors. *Professional School Counseling, 15,* 98–109.

Muehleman, T., Pickens, B. K., & Robinson, F. (1985). Informing clients about the limits to confidentiality, risks, and their rights: Is self-disclosure inhibited? *Professional Psychology: Research and Practice, 16,* 385–397.

Muench, F. (2010, April 8). Technology and mental health: Using technology to improve our lives. *Psychology Today.* Retrieved from http://www.psychologytoday.com

Mulvey, E., & Lidz, C. (1995). Conditional prediction: A model for research on dangerousness to others in a new era. *International Journal of Law and Psychiatry, 18,* 129–143.

Muratori, M. C. (2001). Examining supervisor impairment from the counselor trainee's perspective. *Counselor Education and Supervision, 41,* 41–56.

Murphy, E. J., Speidel, R. E., & Ayres, I. (1997). *Contract law* (5th ed.). Westbury, NY: The Foundation Press.

Murray, C. E. (2009). Diffusion of innovation theory: A bridge for the research-practice gap in counseling. *Journal of Counseling & Development, 87,* 108–116.

Myer, R. A. (2001). *Assessment for crisis intervention: A triage assessment model.* Belmont, CA: Brooks/Cole.

Myers, J. E. (1995). Specialties in counseling: Rich heritage or force for fragmentation? *Journal of Counseling & Development, 74,* 115–116.

Myers, J. E. (2007). Combating ageism: Advocacy for older persons.

In C. C. Lee (Ed.), *Counseling for social justice* (2nd ed., pp. 51–74). Alexandria, VA: American Counseling Association.

Myers, J. E., Mobley, A. K., & Booth, C. S. (2003). Wellness of counseling students: Practicing what we preach. *Counselor Education and Supervision, 42,* 264–274.

Myers, J. E., & Sweeney, T. J. (2001). Specialties in counseling. In D. C. Locke, J. E. Myers, & E. L. Herr (Eds.), *The handbook of counseling* (pp. 43–54). Thousand Oaks, CA: Sage.

Myers, J. E., & Sweeney, T. J. (2004). Advocacy for the counseling profession: Results of a national survey. *Journal of Counseling & Development, 82,* 466–472.

Myers, J. E., Sweeney, T. J., & Witmer, J. M. (2000). The wheel of wellness counseling for wellness: A holistic model for treatment planning. *Journal of Counseling & Development, 78,* 251–266.

Myers, J. E., & Truluck, M. (1998). Health beliefs, religious values, and the counseling process: A comparison of counselor and other mental health professionals. *Counseling and Values, 42,* 106–123.

NAADAC: The Association for Addiction Professionals. (2011). *Code of Ethics.* Standard 3: Dual Relationships. Retrieved from http://www.naadac.org

NAADAC: The Association for Addiction Professionals. (2014). Retrieved from http://www.naadac.org

Nadal, K. L., Griffin, K. E., Wong, Y., Hamit, S., & Rasmus, M. (2014). The impact of racial microaggressions on mental health: Counseling implications for clients of color. *Journal of Counseling & Development, 92,* 57–66. doi: 10.1002/j.1556-6676.2014.00130.x

Nagayama-Hall, G. C. (2001). Psychotherapy research with ethnic minorities: Empirical, ethical, and conceptual issues. *Journal of Consulting and Clinical Psychology, 69,* 502–510. doi: 10.1037/0022-006X.69.3.502

Nagle v. Hooks, 295 Md. 133, 460 A.2d 49 (1983).

Napoli, D. S. (1981). *Architects of adjustment: The history of the psychological profession in the United States.* Port Washington, NY: Kennikat Press.

National Alliance on Mental Illness. (2014). *Technology is used to access mental health care and information.* Retrieved from http://www.nami.org

National Association of Social Workers. (1997). *Social work speaks: NASW policy statements* (4th ed., pp. 156–163). Washington, DC: Author.

National Board for Certified Counselors. (2014). Retrieved from http://www.nbcc.org

National Career Development Association. (2014). *NCDA Guidelines for the Use of the Internet for Provision of Career Information and Planning Services.* Retrieved from http://ncda.org/aws/NCDA/pt/sp/guidelines_internet

National Center on Elder Abuse. (2014). *Statistics/data.* Retrieved from http://www.ncea.aoa.gov/Library/Data

National Coalition on Health Care. (2008). *Health insurance costs.* Retrieved from http://www.nchc.org/facts/cost.shtml

National Conference of State Legislatures. (2015). *Defining marriage: Defense of marriage acts and same sex marriage laws.* Washington, DC: Author. Retrieved from http://www.ncsl.org

National Fair Access Coalition on Testing. (2014). Retrieved from fairaccess.org

National Research Act of 1974 Regulations, 45 Code of Federal Regulations 46.

Navin, S., Beamish, P., & Johanson, G. (1995). Ethical practices of field-based mental health counselor supervisors. *Journal of Mental Health Counseling, 17,* 243–253.

NBCC International. (2014). Retrieved from http://www.nbccinternational.org

Neighbors, H. W., Ford, B. C., Trierweiler, S. J., & Stillman, P. (2002). African American mental health disparities: Prevalence, utilization, diagnosis, and treatment. In J. Berry, D. Baldwin, & P. Marshall (Eds.), *Eliminating disparities in the treatment of African Americans with mental health and substance abuse disorders.* Rockville, MD: Substance Abuse & Mental Health Services Administration.

Neighbors, H. W., Trierweiler, S. J., Ford, B. C., & Muroff, J. A. (2003). Racial differences in DSM diagnosis using semi-structured instruments: The importance of clinical judgment in the diagnosis of African Americans. *Journal of Health and Social Behavior, 43,* 237–256.

Nelson, K. W., Oliver, M., Reeve, J., & McNichols, C. (2010). *Gatekeeping and supervisory intervention: Complex ethical processes.* Retrieved from http://www.counselingoutfitters.com/vistas/vistas10/Article_42.pdf

Nelson, M. L., Gizara, S., Hope, A. C., Phelps, R., Steward, R., & Weitzman, L. (2006). A feminist multicultural perspective on supervision. *Journal of Multicultural Counseling and Development, 34,* 116–128.

Neufeld, P. J. (2002). School violence—Family responsibility. *The Family Journal, 10,* 207–209.

Neukrug, E., Milliken, T., & Walden, S. (2001). Ethical complaints made against credentialed counselors: An updated survey of state licensing boards. *Counselor Education and Supervision, 41,* 57–70.

Neukrug, E. S., Healy, M., & Herlihy, B. (1992). Ethical practices of licensed professional counselors: An updated survey of state licensing boards. *Counselor Education and Supervision, 32,* 130–141.

Neukrug, E. S., & Milliken, T. (2011). Counselors' perceptions of ethical behaviors. *Journal of Counseling & Development, 89,* 206–216.

New York State Task Force on Life and the Law. (1994). *When death is sought: Assisted suicide and euthanasia in the medical context.* Albany, NY: Author.

Newlin, C. M., Adolph, J. L., & Kreber, L. A. (2004). Factors that influence fee setting by male and female psychologists. *Professional Psychology: Research and Practice, 35,* 548–552.

Newman, J. L. (1993). Ethical issues in consultation. *Journal of Counseling & Development, 72,* 148–156.

Newsome, S., Waldo, M., & Gruszka, C. (2012). Mindfulness group work: Preventing stress and increasing self-compassion among helping professionals in training. *Journal for Specialists in Group Work, 37,* 297–311.

Ngui, E. M., Khasakhals, L., Ndetei, D., & Roberts, L.W. (2010). Mental disorders, health inequalities and ethics: A global perspective. *International Review of Psychiatry, 22,* 235–244.

Nichols, M. P., & Schwartz, R. C. (2004). *Family therapy: Concepts and methods* (6th ed.). Boston: Allyn & Bacon.

Nixon, J. A. (1993). Gender considerations in the case of "The Jealous Husband": Strategic therapy in review. *The Family Journal, 1,* 161–163.

Nock, M. K., & Marzuk, P. M. (1999). Murder-suicide. In D. G. Jacobs (Ed.), *Guide to suicide assessment and intervention* (pp. 188–209). San Francisco: Jossey-Bass.

Nugent, F. (1981). *Professional counseling: An overview.* Pacific Grove, CA: Brooks/Cole.

O'Dwyer, K. (2012). Camus's challenge: The question of suicide. *Journal of Humanistic Psychology, 52,* 165–177. doi: 10.1177/0022167811402999

O'Mahony, K. (2011). *The 10 biggest mistakes physicians make after a licensing board complaint has been filed against them.* Atlanta, GA: Allen, McCain & O'Mahony. Retrieved from http://www.amolawfirm.com

Office of Research Integrity. (2011). *Guidelines for avoiding plagiarism, self-plagiarism, and other questionable writing practices.* Washington, DC: U.S. Department of Health and Human Services. Retrieved from http://www.ori.hhs.gov/education

Ojeda, L., Flores, L. Y., Meza, R. R., & Morales, A. (2011). Culturally competent qualitative research with Latino immigrants. *Hispanic Journal of Behavioral Sciences, 33,* 184–203.

Orton, G. L. (1997). *Strategies for counseling with children and their parents.* Pacific Grove, CA: Brooks/Cole.

Ossana, S. M., Helms, J. E., & Leonard, M. M. (1992). Do "womanist" identity attitudes influence college women's self-esteem and perceptions of environmental bias? *Journal of Counseling & Development, 70,* 402–408.

Overton, S. L., & Medina, S. L. (2008). The stigma of mental illness. *Journal of Counseling & Development, 86,* 143–151.

Owen, D. W., Jr., & Weikel, W. J. (1999). Computer utilization by school counselors. *Professional School Counseling, 2,* 179–182.

Owens, P. C., & Kulic, K. R. (2001). What's needed now: Using groups for prevention. *The Journal for Specialists in Group Work, 26,* 205–210.

Pabian, Y. L., Welfel, E., & Beebe, R. S. (2009). Psychologists' knowledge of their states' laws pertaining to Tarasoff-type situations. *Professional Psychology: Research and Practice, 40,* 8–14. doi: 10.1037/a0014784

Pack-Brown, S. P., Thomas, T. L., & Seymour, J. M. (2008). Infusing professional ethics into counselor education programs: A multicultural/social justice perspective. *Journal of Counseling & Development, 86,* 296–302.

Packman, W. L., & Harris, E. A. (1998). Legal issues and risk management in suicidal patients. In B. Bongar, A. I. Berman, R. W. Maris, M. M. Silverman, E. A. Harris, & W. L. Packman (Eds.), *Risk management with suicidal patients* (pp. 150–186). New York: Guilford Press.

Page, R. C., & Bailey, J. B. (1995). Addictions counseling certification: An emerging counseling specialty. *Journal of Counseling & Development, 74,* 167–171.

Paisley, P. O. (1997). Personalizing our history: Profiles of theorists, researchers, practitioners, and issues. *Journal of Counseling & Development, 76,* 4–5.

Paisley, P. O., & Borders, L. D. (1995). School counseling: An evolving specialty. *Journal of Counseling & Development, 74,* 150–153.

Palmo, A. J. (1999). The MHC child reaches maturity: Does the child seem short for its age? *Journal of Mental Health Counseling, 21,* 215–228.

Palusci, V. J., Hicks, R. A., & Vandervort, F. E. (2001). "You are hereby commanded to appear": Pediatrician subpoena and court appearance in child maltreatment. *Pediatrics, 107,* 1427–1430.

Paone, T. R., & Malott, K. M. (2008). Using interpreters in mental health counseling. A literature review and recommendations. *Journal of Multicultural Counseling and Development, 36,* 130–141.

Parham, T. A., & Caldwell, L. D. (2015). Boundaries in the context of a collective community: An African-centered perspective. In B. Herlihy & G. Corey, *Boundary issues in counseling* (3rd ed., pp. 96–100). Alexandria, VA: American Counseling Association.

Parigi, P., & Henson, W., II. (2014). Social isolation in America. *Annual Review of Sociology, 40,* 153–171. doi: 10.1146/annurev-soc-071312-145646

Parker, L. K., Chang, C. Y., Corthell, K. K., Walsh, M. E., Brack, G., & Grubbs, N. K. (2014). A grounded theory of counseling students who report problematic peers. *Counselor Education & Supervision, 53,* 111–125.

Paterson, R. J. (2011). *Private practice made simple: Everything you need to know to set up and manage a successful mental health practice.* Oakland, CA: New Harbinger Publications.

Patry, W. F. (1986). *Latman's The copyright law* (6th ed.). Washington, DC: The Bureau of National Affairs.

Patsiopoulos, A. T., & Buchanan, M. J. (2011). The practice of self-compassion in counseling: A narrative inquiry. *Professional Psychology: Research and Practice, 42,* 301–307. doi: 10.1037/a0024482

Patureau-Hatchett, M. (2008). *Counselors' perceptions of training, theoretical orientation, cultural and gender bias, and use of the Diagnostic and Statistical Manual of Mental Disorders-IV-Text Revision.* Unpublished doctoral dissertation, University of New Orleans.

Paulson, B. L., & Worth, M. (2002). Counseling for suicide: Client perspectives. *Journal of Counseling & Development, 80,* 86–93.

Pavkov, T. W., Lewis, D. A., & Lyons, J. S. (1989). Psychiatric diagnosis and racial bias: An empirical investigation. *Professional Psychology: Research and Practice, 20,* 364–368.

Pease-Carter, C., & Barrio Minton, C. (2012). Counseling programs' informed consent processes: A survey of student preferences. *Counselor Education & Supervision, 51,* 308–319.

Peck v. Counseling Service of Addison County, Inc., 146 Vt. 61, 499 A.2d 422 (1985).

Pedersen, P. B. (1991). Multiculturalism as a generic approach to counseling. *Journal of Counseling & Development, 70,* 6–12.

Pedersen, P. B., Draguns, J. G., Lonner, W. J., & Trimble, J. E. (2002). *Counseling across cultures* (5th ed.). Thousand Oaks, CA: Sage.

People v. Cohen, 98 Misc.2d 874, 414 N.Y.S.2d 642 (1979).

People v. Lobaito, 133 Mich. App. 547, 351 N.W.2d 233 (App. 1984).

People v. Taylor, 618 P.2d 1127 (Colo. 1980).

Perez v. City of Chicago, 2004 U.S. Dist. LEXIS 7415, April 28, 2004.

Perosa, L. M., & Perosa, S. L. (2010). Assessing competencies in couples and family therapy/counseling: A call to the profession. *Journal of Marital and Family Therapy, 36,* 126–143.

Perr, I. N. (1985). Suicide litigation and risk management: A review of 32 cases. *The Bulletin of the American Academy of Psychiatry and the Law, 13,* 209–219.

Perritt, H. H., Jr. (2013). *Employee dismissal law and practice* (5th ed. & Supp. 2007–2012). New York: Aspen Publishers.

Perry, J. C., Satiani, A., Henze, K. T., Mascher, J., & Helms, J. E. (2008). Why is there *still* no study of cultural equivalence in standardized cognitive ability tests? *Journal of Multicultural Counseling and Development, 36,* 155–167.

Perry, S. (1989). Warning third parties at risk of AIDS: American Psychiatric Association's policy is a barrier to treatment. *Hospital and Community Psychiatry, 40,* 158–161.

Petersen v. State, 100 Wash. 2d 421, 671 P.2d 230 (1983) (en banc).

Peterson, C. (1996). Common problem areas and their causes resulting in disciplinary action. In L. J. Bass, S. T. DeMers, J. R. Ogloff, C. Peterson, J. L. Pettifor, R. P. Reaves, et al. (Eds.), *Professional conduct and discipline in psychology* (pp. 71–89). Washington, DC: American Psychological Association.

Peterson, D. B., Hautamaki, J. B., & Walton, J. L. (2007). Ethics and technology. In R. R. Cottone & V. M. Tarvydas (Eds.), *Counseling ethics and decision making* (pp. 184–211). Upper Saddle River, NJ: Pearson Merrill Prentice Hall.

Petrashek v. Petrashek, 232 Neb. 212, 440 N.W.2d 220 (1989).

Phillips, B. N. (1982). Regulation and control in psychology. *American Psychologist, 37,* 919–926.

Phillips-Green, M. J. (2002). Sibling incest. *The Family Journal, 10,* 195–202.

Phillis, N. (2011). When sixteen ain't so sweet: Rethinking the regulation of adolescent sexuality. *Michigan Journal of Gender & Law, 17,* 271–312. Retrieved from http://www.lexisnexis.com

Piazza, N. J., & Baruth, N. E. (1990). Client record guidelines. *Journal of Counseling & Development, 68,* 313–316.

Pierce, K. A., & Baldwin, C. (1990). Participation versus privacy in the training of group counselors. *Journal for Specialists in Group Work, 15,* 149–158.

Pilkington, N. W., & D'Augelli, A. R. (1995). Victimization of lesbian, gay, and bisexual youth in community settings. *Journal of Community Psychology, 23,* 34–56.

Pine, A. M., & Aronson, E. (1988). *Career burnout: Causes and cures.* New York: The Free Press.

Plaintiff v. Rector and Board of Visitors of The College of William and Mary, No. 03-2119 (4th Cir. February 8, 2005).

Pope, K. S. (1986). Research and laws regarding therapist-patient sexual involvement: Implications for therapists. *American Journal of Psychotherapy, 40,* 564–571.

Pope, K. S. (1988). How clients are harmed by sexual contact with mental health professionals: The syndrome and its prevalence. *Journal of Counseling & Development, 67,* 222–226.

Pope, K. S., & Bouhoutsos, J. C. (1986). *Sexual intimacy between therapists and patients.* New York: Praeger Press.

Pope, K. S., Butcher, J. N., & Sheelen, J. (1993). *The MMPI, MMPI-2, and MMPI-A in court: A practical guide for expert witnesses and attorneys.* Washington, DC: American Psychological Association.

Pope, K. S., & Keith-Spiegel, P. (2008). A practical approach to boundaries in psychotherapy: Making decisions, bypassing blunders, and mending fences. *Journal of Clinical Psychology: In Session, 64,* 638–652.

Pope, K. S., Keith-Spiegel, P., & Tabachnick, B. G. (1986). Sexual attraction to clients: The human therapist and the (sometimes) inhuman training system. *American Psychologist, 41,* 147–158.

Pope, K. S., Levinson, H., & Schover, L. R. (1979). Sexual intimacy in psychology training: Results and implications of a national survey. *American Psychologist, 34,* 682–689.

Pope, K. S., Sonne, J. L., & Holroyd, J. (1993). *Sexual feelings in psychotherapy: Explorations for therapists and therapists-in-training.* Washington, DC: American Psychological Association.

Pope, K. S., Tabachnick, B. G., & Keith-Spiegel, P. (1987a). Ethics of practice: The beliefs and behaviors of psychologists as therapists. *American Psychologist, 42,* 993–1006.

Pope, K. S., Tabachnick, B. G., & Keith-Spiegel, P. (1987b). Good and poor practices in psychotherapy: National survey of beliefs of psychologists. *Professional Psychology: Research and Practice, 19,* 547–552.

Pope, K. S., & Vasquez, M. J. T. (2005). *How to survive and thrive as a therapist: Information, ideas, and resources for psychologists in practice.* Washington, DC: American Psychological Association. doi: 10.1037/11088-005

Pope, K. S., & Vasquez, M. J. T. (2010). *Ethics in psychotherapy and counseling: A practical guide* (4th ed.). San Francisco: Jossey-Bass.

Pope, K. S., & Vetter, V. A. (1991). Prior counselor-patient sexual involvement among patients seen by psychologists. *Psychocounseling, 28,* 429–438.

Priester, P. E., Jones, J. E., Jackson-Bailey, C. M., Jana-Masri, A., Jordan, E. X., & Metz, A. J. (2008). An analysis of content and instructional strategies in multicultural counseling courses. *Journal of Multicultural Counseling and Development, 36,* 29–39.

Prober, M. (2005). Please don't tell my parents: The validity of school policies mandating parental notification of a student's pregnancy. *Brooklyn Law Review, 71,* 557–580.

Prochaska, J. O., DiClemente, C. C., & Norcross, J. C. (1992). In search of how people change. *American Psychologist, 47,* 1102–1114.

Prochaska, J. O., & Norcross, J. (1983). Psychotherapists' perspectives on treating themselves and their clients for psychic distress. *Professional Psychology: Research and Practice, 14,* 642–655.

Prosek, E. A., Holm, J. M., & Daly, C. M. (2013). Benefits of required counseling for counseling students. *Counselor Education & Supervision, 52,* 242–254.

Prosser, W. L. (1971). *The law of torts.* St. Paul, MN: West.

Pruett, M. K., & DiFonzo, J. H. (2014). AFCC Think Tank Final Report: Closing the gap: Research, policy, practice, and shared parenting. *Family Court Review, 52,* 152.

Przybylski, A. K., Murayama, K., DeHaan, C. R., & Gladwell, V. (2013). Motivational, emotional, and behavioral correlates of fear of missing out. *Computers in Human Behavior, 29,* 1841–1848. doi: 10.1016/j.chb.2013.02.014

Quinn, M. J., & Tomita, S. K. (1997). *Elder abuse and neglect: Causes, diagnosis, and intervention strategies* (2nd ed.). New York: Springer.

Rapp, C. A., & Goscha, R. J. (2012). *The strengths model: A recovery-oriented approach to mental health services* (3rd ed.). New York: Oxford University Press.

Rappleyea, D. L., Harris, S. M., White, M., & Simon, K. (2009). Termination: Legal and ethical considerations for marriage and family therapists. *American Journal of Family Therapy, 37,* 12–27. doi: 10.1080/01926180801960617

Randall, V. R. (1994). Impact of managed care organizations on ethnic Americans and underserved populations. *Journal of Health Care for the Poor and Underserved, 5,* 224–236.

Ratts, M. J. (2011). Multiculturalism and social justice: Two sides of the same coin. *Journal of Counseling & Development, 89,* 24–37.

Ratts, M. J., Anthony, L., & Santos, K. N. T. (2012). The dimensions of social justice model: Transforming traditional group work into a socially just framework. *Journal for Specialists in Group Work, 35,* 160–168.

Rave, E. J., & Larsen, C. C. (1995). *Ethical decision making in therapy: Feminist perspectives.* New York: Guilford Press.

Ray, D. C., Hull, D. M., Thacker, A. J., Pace, L. S., Swan, K. L., Carlson, S. E., & Sullivan, J. M. (2011). Research in counseling: A 10-year review to inform practice. *Journal of Counseling & Development, 89,* 349–359.

Reese, R. J., Conoley, C. W., & Brossart, D. F. (2006). The attractiveness of telephone counseling: An empirical investigation of client perceptions. *Journal of Counseling & Development, 84,* 54–60.

Reeve, D. (2000). Oppression within the counseling room. *Disability and Society, 15,* 669–682.

Reeves, A. (2011, September/October). Therapy and Skype. *Family Therapy Magazine,* 48–49.

Regents of the University of Michigan v. Ewing, 474 U.S. 214 (1985).

Reid, W. H. (2010). When lawyers call clinicians. *Journal of Psychiatric Practice, 16,* 253–257.

Reiner, S. M., Dobmeier, R. A., & Hernandez, T. J. (2013). Perceived impact of professional counselor identity: An exploratory study. *Journal of Counseling & Development, 91,* 174–183. doi: 10.1002/j.1556-6676. 2013.00084.x

Remley, T. P., Jr. (1993). Consultation contracts. *Journal of Counseling & Development, 72,* 157–158.

Remley, T. P., Jr. (1995). A proposed alternative to the licensing of specialties in counseling. *Journal of Counseling & Development, 74,* 126–129.

Remley, T. P., Jr., Bacchini, E., & Krieg, P. (2010). Counseling in Italy. *Journal of Counseling & Development, 88,* 28–32.

Remley, T. P., Jr., Benshoff, J. M., & Mowbray, C. A. (1987). A proposed model for peer supervision. *Counselor Education and Supervision, 27,* 53–60.

Remley, T. P., Jr., & Fry, L. J. (1993). Reporting suspected child abuse: Conflicting roles for the counselor. *The School Counselor, 40,* 253–259.

Remley, T. P., Jr., Herlihy, B., & Herlihy, S. (1997). The U.S.

Supreme Court decision in *Jaffee v. Redmond:* Implications for counselors. *Journal of Counseling & Development, 75,* 213–218.

Remley, T. P., Jr., Hulse-Killacky, D., Ashton, L., Keene, K., Kippers, S., Lazzari, S., et al. (1998, October). *Advanced students supervising other students.* Paper presented at Louisiana Counseling Association conference, Lafayette, LA; and Southern Association for Counselor Education and Supervision conference, Montgomery, AL.

Renshaw, D. C. (2001). Bullies. *The Family Journal, 9,* 341–342.

Reppucci, N. D., Weithorn, L. A., Mulvey, E. P., & Monahan, J. (1984). *Children, mental health, and the law.* Beverly Hills, CA: Sage.

Rice, P. R. (1993). *Attorney-client privilege in the United States.* Rochester, NY: Lawyers Cooperative Publishing.

Richards, D., & Vigano, N. (2013). Online counseling: A narrative and critical review of the literature. *Journal of Clinical Psychology, 69,* 994–1011. doi: 10.1002/jclp.21974

Ridley, C. R. (1989). *Overcoming unintentional racism in counseling and therapy.* Thousand Oaks, CA: Sage.

Ridley, C. R. (1995). *Overcoming unintentional racism in counseling and therapy: A practitioner's guide to intentional interventions.* Thousand Oaks, CA: Sage.

Ridley, C. R., & Lingle, D. W. (1996). Cultural empathy in multicultural counseling: A multidimensional process model. In P. B. Pedersen, J. C. Draguns, W. J. Lonner, & J. E. Trimble (Eds.), *Counseling across cultures* (4th ed., pp. 21–46). Thousand Oaks, CA: Sage.

Rios v. Read, D.C.N.Y. 73 F.R.D. 589 (1977).

Ritchie, M. H., & Huss, S. N. (2000). Recruitment and screening of minors for group counseling. *Journal for Specialists in Group Work, 25,* 146–156.

Rivera, D. P., Forquer, E. E., & Rangel, R. (2010). Microaggressions and the life experience of Latina/o Americans. In D. W. Sue (Ed.), *Microaggressions and marginality: Manifestation, dynamics, and impact* (pp. 59–84). New York: Wiley.

Roach, L. F., & Young, M. E. (2007). Do counselor education programs promote wellness in their students? *Counselor Education and Supervision, 47,* 29–45.

Roberts v. Superior Court, 9 Cal.3d 330, 107 Cal. Rptr. 309, 508 P.2d 309 (1973).

Roberts, A. R., Monferrari, I., & Yeager, K. R. (2008). Avoiding malpractice lawsuits by following risk assessment and suicide prevention guidelines. *Brief Treatment and Crisis Intervention, 8,* 5–14.

Roberts, W. B., & Morotti, A. A. (2000). The bully as victim: Understanding bully behaviors to increase the effectiveness of interventions in the bully-victim dyad. *Professional School Counseling, 4,* 148–155.

Roberts-Henry, M. (1995). Criminalization of therapist sexual misconduct in Colorado. In J. C. Gonsiorek (Ed.), *Breach of trust: Sexual exploitation by health care professionals and clergy* (pp. 347–388). Thousand Oaks, CA: Sage.

Robertson, D. W., Powers, W., Jr., Anderson, D. A., & Wellborn, O. G. (2011). *Cases and materials on torts* (4th ed.). St. Paul, MN: West.

Robinson, E., Amburgey, R., Swank, E., & Faulker, C. (2004). Test cheating in a rural college: Studying the

importance of individual and situational factors. *College Student Journal, 38,* 380–395.

Robinson, T. L., & Watt, S. K. (2001). "Where no one goes begging": Converging gender, sexuality, and religious diversity in counseling. In D. C. Locke, J. E. Myers, & E. L. Herr (Eds.), *Handbook of multicultural counseling* (pp. 589–599). Thousand Oaks, CA: Sage.

Robinson-Wood, T. L. (2009). *The convergence of race, ethnicity, and gender: Multiple identities in counseling* (3rd ed.). Upper Saddle River, NJ: Pearson.

Rochlen, A. B., Beretvas, N. S., & Zack, J. S. (2004). The online and face-to-face counseling attitudes scales: A validation study. *Measurement and Evaluation in Counseling and Development, 36,* 95–111.

Rock, M., Carlson, T. S., & McGeorge, C. R. (2010). Does affirmative training matter? Assessing CFT students' beliefs about sexual orientation and their level of affirmative training. *Journal of Marital & Family Therapy, 36,* 171–184.

Rogers, J. R. (2001). Suicide risk assessment. In E. R. Welfel & R. E. Ingersoll (Eds.), *The mental health desk reference* (pp. 259–264). New York: Wiley.

Rogers, J. R., Lewis, M. M., & Subich, L. M. (2002). Validity of the Suicide Assessment Checklist in an emergency crisis center. *Journal of Counseling & Development, 80,* 493–502.

Roig, M. (2009). *Avoiding plagiarism, self-plagiarism, and other questionable writing practices: A guide to ethical writing.* Retrieved from http://facpub.stjohns.edu/~roigm/plagiarism

Rosenbach, W. E. (1993). Mentoring: Empowering followers to become leaders. In W. E. Rosenbach & R. L. Taylor (Eds.), *Contemporary issues in leadership* (3rd ed., pp. 141–151). Boulder, CO: Westview Press.

Rosenhan, D. L. (1973). On being sane in insane places. *Science, 179,* 250–258.

Rothstein, L. F. (1997). Disability discrimination in higher education: A review of the 1995 judicial decision. *Journal of College and University Law, 23,* 475–487.

Rottenberg, S. (Ed.). (1980). *Occupational licensure and regulation.* Washington, DC: American Enterprise Institute for Public Policy Research.

Rowell, J. A. C., & Green, M. A. (2003). *Understanding health insurance: A guide to professional billing.* Clifton Park, NY: Thompson Delmar Learning.

Roy, E. D. (2008). The end of custody in Florida: Finally parents are just parents. *The Florida Bar Journal, 82,* 49. Retrieved from http://www.lexisnexis.com

Rudolph, J. (1990). Counselors' attitudes toward homosexuality: Selective review of the literature. *Journal of Counseling & Development, 65,* 165–168.

Rudow, H. (2013). *Resolution of EMU case confirms ACA Code of Ethics, counseling profession's stance against client discrimination.* Retrieved from http://ct.counseling.org/2013/01/resolution-of-emu-case-confirms-aca-code-of-ethics-counseling-professions-stance-against-client-discrimination/

Rummell, C. M., & Joyce, N. R. (2010). "So wat do u want to wrk on 2day?": The ethical implications of online counseling. *Ethics & Behavior, 20,* 482–496.

Rupert, P. A., & Baird, K. A. (2004). Managed care and the independent practice of psychology. *Professional Psychology: Research and Practice, 35,* 185–193.

Rust, J. P., Raskin, J. D., & Hill, M. S. (2013). Problems of professional competence among counselor trainees: Programmatic issues and guidelines. *Counselor Education & Supervision, 52,* 30–42.

Safran, J. D., & Kriss, A. (2014). Psychoanalytic psychotherapies. In D. Wedding & R. J. Corsini (Eds.), *Current psychotherapies* (10th ed., pp. 19–54). Belmont, CA: Brooks/Cole, Cengage Learning.

Salgo v. Leland Stanford Jr. Univ. Bd. of Trustees, 317 P.2d 170 (Cal. Ct. App. 1957).

Salisbury, W. A., & Kinnier, R. T. (1996). Posttermination friendship between counselors and clients. *Journal of Counseling & Development, 74,* 495–500.

Salo, M. (2015). *Counseling minor clients.* In B. Herlihy & G. Corey (Eds.), *ACA ethical standards casebook* (7th ed., pp. 205–207). Alexandria, VA: American Counseling Association.

Sampson, J. P., Jr. (1996). A computer-aided violation of confidentiality. In B. Herlihy & G. Corey (Eds.), *ACA ethical standards casebook* (5th ed., pp. 213–215). Alexandria, VA: American Counseling Association.

Sampson, J. P., Jr. (2000). Using the Internet to enhance testing in counseling. *Journal of Counseling & Development, 78,* 348–356.

Sampson, J. P., Jr., & Bloom, J. W. (2001). The potential for success and failure of computer applications in counseling and guidance. In D. C. Locke, J. E. Myers, & E. L. Herr (Eds.), *The handbook of counseling* (pp. 613–627). Thousand Oaks, CA: Sage.

Sampson, J. P., Jr., Kolodinsky, R. W., & Greeno, B. P. (1997). Counseling on the information highway: Future possibilities and potential problems. *Journal of Counseling & Development, 75,* 203–212.

Sandhu, D. S. (2000). Special issue: School violence and counselors. *Professional School Counseling, 4,* iv–v.

Sapia, J. L. (2001). Using groups for the prevention of eating disorders among college women. *The Journal for Specialists in Group Work, 26,* 256–266.

Sapyta, J., Goldston, D. B., Erkanli, A., Daniel, S. S., Heilbron, N., Mayfield, A., & Treadway, S. L. (2012). Evaluating the predictive validity of suicidal intent and medical lethality in youth. *Journal of Consulting and Clinical Psychology, 80,* 222–231. doi: 10.1037/a0026870

Saunders, J. L., Barros-Bailey, M., Rudman, R., Dew, D. W., & Garcia, J. (2007). Ethical complaints and violations in rehabilitation counseling: An analysis of Commission on Rehabilitation Counselor Certification data. *Rehabilitation Counseling Bulletin, 51,* 7–13.

Savage, T. A., Harley, D. A., & Nowak, T. M. (2005). Applying social empowerment strategies as tools for self-advocacy in counseling lesbian and gay male clients. *Journal of Counseling & Development, 83,* 131–137.

Scarborough, J. L., Bernard, J. M., & Morse, R. E. (2006). Boundary considerations between doctoral students and master's students. *Counseling and Values, 51,* 53–65.

Schaffer, S. J. (1997). Don't be aloof about record-keeping; it may be your best liability coverage. *The National Psychologist, 6,* 21.

Schank, J. A., & Skovholt, T. M. (2006). *Ethical practice in small communities: Challenges and rewards for psychologists.* Washington, DC: American Psychological Association.

Schmid, D., Applebaum, P., Roth, L. H., & Lidz, C. (1983). Confidentiality in psychiatry. A study of the patient's view. *Hospital and Community, Psychiatry, 34,* 353–356.

Schoener, G. R. (1989). Self-help and consumer groups. In G. R. Schoener, J. H. Milgrom, J. C. Gonsiorek, E. T. Luepker, & R. M. Conroe (Eds.), *Psychotherapists' sexual involvement with clients: Intervention and prevention* (pp. 375–399). Minneapolis, MN: Walk-In Counseling Center.

Schoener, G. R., & Gonsiorek, J. (1988). Assessment and development of rehabilitation plans for counselors who have sexually exploited their clients. *Journal of Counseling & Development, 67,* 227–232.

Schofield, M. J. (2013). Counseling in Australia: Past, present, and future. *Journal of Counseling & Development, 91,* 234–239. doi: 10.1002/j.1556-6676.2013.00090.x

Schultze, N. G. (2006). Success factors in Internet-based psychological counseling. *Cyberpsychology & Behavior, 9,* 623–626.

Schutz, B. M. (1990). *Legal liability in psychotherapy.* San Francisco: Jossey-Bass.

Schwab, R., & Neukrug, E. (1994). A survey of counselor educators' ethical concerns. *Counseling and Values, 39,* 42–45.

Schwartz, R. C. (2000). Suicidality in schizophrenia: Implications for the counseling profession. *Journal of Counseling & Development, 78,* 496–499.

Schwartz, R. C., Lent, J., & Geihsler, J. (2011). Gender and diagnosis of mental disorders: Implications for mental health counseling.

Journal of Mental Health Counseling, 33, 347–358.

Schwartz, V. E., Kelly, K., & Partlett, D. F. (2010). *Cases and materials on torts* (12th ed.). Westbury, NY: Foundation Press.

Schweiger, W. K., Henderson, D. A., McCaskill, K., Clawson, T. W., & Collins, D. R. (2011). *Counselor preparation: Programs, faculty, trends* (13th ed.). New York: Routledge.

Schwiebert, V. L., Myers, J. E., & Dice, C. (2000). Ethical guidelines for counselors working with older adults. *Journal of Counseling & Development, 78,* 123–129.

Sciarra, D. T. (1999). *Multiculturalism in counseling.* Itasca, IL: F. E. Peacock.

Scott, W. R. (1969). Professional employees in a bureaucratic structure: Social work. In A. Etzioni (Ed.), *The semi-professions and their organization* (pp. 102–156). New York: The Free Press.

Sekaran, U. (1986). *Dual career families.* San Francisco: Jossey-Bass.

Seligman, L. (1999). Twenty years of diagnosis and the DSM. *Journal of Mental Health Counseling, 21,* 229–239.

Senyonyi, R. M., & Ochieng, L. A. (2012). The development of professional counseling in Uganda: Current status and future trends. *Journal of Counseling & Development, 90,* 500–504. doi: 10.1002/j.1556-6676.2012.00062.x

Sexton, T. L. (2001). Evidence-based counseling intervention programs: Practicing "best practices." In D. C. Locke, J. E. Myers, & E. L. Herr (Eds.), *The handbook of counseling* (pp. 499–512). Thousand Oaks, CA: Sage.

Shaw, H. E., & Shaw, S. F. (2006). Critical ethical issues in online

counseling: Assessing current practices with an ethical intent checklist. *Journal of Counseling & Development, 84,* 41–53.

Shin, R. Q. (2008). Advocating for social justice in academia through recruitment, retention, admissions, and professional survival. *Journal of Multicultural Counseling and Development, 36,* 180–191.

Shuman, D. W., & Weiner, M. F. (1987). *The psychotherapist-patient privilege: A critical examination.* Springfield, IL: Charles C Thomas.

Simon, R. I. (1987). *Clinical psychiatry and the law.* Washington, DC: American Psychiatric Press.

Simon, R. I. (1989). Sexual exploitation of patients: How it begins before it happens. *Psychiatric Annals, 19,* 104–112.

Simon, R. I. (1991). Psychological injury caused by boundary violations: Precursors to therapist-patient sex. *Psychiatry Annals, 19,* 104–112.

Simon, R. I. (1998). Boundary violations in psychotherapy. In L. E. Lifson & R. I. Simon (Eds.), *The mental health practitioner and the law* (pp. 195–215). Cambridge, MA: Harvard University Press.

Simpson, L. R., & Glowiak, M. V. (2012). Supervision, coaching, and consultation. In D. Capuzzi & M. D. Stauffer (Eds.), *Career counseling: Foundations, perspectives, and applications* (2nd ed., pp. 279–312). New York: Routledge.

Sims v. State, 251 Ga. 877, 311 S.E.2d 161 (1984).

Singley, S. J. (1998). Failure to report suspected child abuse: Civil liability of mandated reporters. *Journal of Juvenile Law, 19,* 236. Retrieved from http://seg802.ocs.lsu.edu:2077/universe/document?_m=8868c24f3aca250

391ddeb692e4f286a&_docnum=12&wchp=dGLbVzz-zSkVb&_md5=875a5ad9f921317af340d225e56a7b93

Skovholt, T. M. (2001). *The resilient practitioner: Burnout prevention and self-care strategies for counselors, therapists, teachers, and health professionals.* Boston: Allyn & Bacon.

Skovholt, T. M. (2012). *Becoming a therapist: On the path to mastery.* Hoboken, NJ: Wiley.

Slaby, A. E. (1999). Outpatient management of suicidal patients. In B. Bongar, A. L. Berman, R. W. Maris, M. M. Silverman, E. A. Harris, & W. L. Packman (Eds.), *Risk management with suicidal patients* (pp. 34–64). New York: Guilford Press.

Sleek, P. (1996, April). Ensuring accuracy in clinical decisions. *APA Monitor, 26,* 30.

Slovenko, R. (1960). Psychiatry and a second look at the medical privilege. *Wayne Law Review, 6,* 174–203.

Slovenko, R. (1966). *Psychotherapy, confidentiality, and privileged communication.* Springfield, IL: Charles C Thomas.

Slovenko, R., & Usdin, G. (1961). The psychiatrist and privileged communication. *Archives of General Psychiatry, 4,* 431–444.

Slovic, P., & Monahan, J. (1995). Probability, danger, and coercion: A study of risk perception and decision making in mental health law. *Law and Human Behavior, 19,* 49–73.

Smaby, M. H., Maddux, C. D., Richmond, A. S., Lepkowski, W. J., & Packman, J. (2005). Academic admissions requirements as predictors of counseling knowledge, personal development, and counseling skills. *Counselor Education and Supervision, 43,* 43–57.

Small Business Administration. (2014). *Thinking about starting a business?* Retrieved from http://www.sba.gov

Smart, D. W., & Smart, J. F. (1997). *DSM-IV* and culturally sensitive diagnosis: Some observations for counselors. *Journal of Counseling & Development, 75,* 392–398.

Smart, J. F., & Smart, D. W. (2006). Models of disability: Implications for the counseling profession. *Journal of Counseling & Development, 84,* 29–40.

Smith, D., & Fitzpatrick, M. (1995). Patient-therapist boundary issues: An integrative review of theory and research. *Professional Psychology: Research and Practice, 26,* 499–506.

Smith, D. C., & Sandhu, D. S. (2004). Toward a positive perspective on violence prevention in schools: Building connections. *Journal of Counseling & Development, 82,* 287–293.

Smith, H. B. (2001). Counseling: Professional identity for counselors. In D. C. Locke, J. E. Myers, & E. L. Herr (Eds.), *The handbook of counseling* (pp. 569–579). Thousand Oaks, CA: Sage.

Smith, H. B., & Robinson, G. P. (1995). Mental health counseling: Past, present, and future. *Journal of Counseling & Development, 75,* 158–162.

Smith, J. A., & Smith, A. H. (2001). Dual relationships and professional integrity: An ethical dilemma case of a family counselor as clergy. *The Family Journal, 9,* 438–443.

Smith, J. M., & Mallen, R. E. (1989). *Preventing legal malpractice.* St. Paul, MN: West.

Smith, K. A. (2010). *Correlates of perceived multicultural competence: Experience and ethnic identity.* Unpublished

master's thesis, California State University Sacramento.

Smith, L., Foley, P. F., & Chaney, M. P. (2008). Addressing classism, ableism, and heterosexism in counselor education. *Journal of Counseling & Development, 86,* 303–309.

Smith, R. L., Carlson, J., Stevens-Smith, P., & Dennison, M. (1995). Marriage and family counseling. *Journal of Counseling & Development, 74,* 154–157.

Smith, R. L., & Valarezo, M. A. (2013). The foundation of counseling in the Republic of Ecuador. *Journal of Counseling & Development, 91,* 120–124. doi: 10.1002/j.1556-6676.2013.00080.x

Smith, S. (2006). Confronting the unethical vocational counselor in forensic practice. *Journal of Vocational Rehabilitation, 25,* 133–136.

Snider, P. D. (1985). The duty to warn: A potential issue of litigation for the counseling supervisor. *Counselor Education and Supervision, 25,* 66–73.

Snider, P. D. (1987). Client records: Inexpensive liability protection for mental health counselors. *Journal of Mental Health Counseling, 9,* 134–141.

Snyder, D. K., & Doss, B. D. (2005). Treating infidelity: Clinical and ethical directions. *Journal of Clinical Psychology: In Session, 61,* 1453–1465.

Sommer, C. A. (2008). Vicarious traumatization, trauma-sensitive supervision, and counselor preparation. *Counselor Education & Supervision, 48,* 61–71.

Sommers-Flanagan, R., Sommers-Flanagan, J., & Lynch, K. L. (2001). Counseling interventions with suicidal clients. In E. R. Welfel & R. E. Ingersoll (Eds.),

The mental health desk reference (pp. 264–270). New York: Wiley.

Sonne, J. L. (1994). Multiple relationships: Does the new ethics code answer the right questions? *Professional Psychology: Research and Practice, 25,* 336–443.

Sonne, J. L. (2005). Dual relationships, multiple relationships, and boundary decisions. *The Independent Practitioner, 25,* 1–14.

Spargo, A. L., Orr, J., & Chang, C. (2010). Group counseling pedagogy: A comparison of counselor training groups and clinical growth groups. Retrieved from http://www.counselingoutfitters .com/vistas/vistas10/Article_ 55.pdf

Speight, S. L. (2012). An exploration of boundaries and solidarity in counseling relationships. *The Counseling Psychologist, 40,* 133–157.

Sperry, L. (2007). *The ethical and professional practice of counseling and psychotherapy.* Boston: Pearson.

Squyres, E. (1986). An alternative view of the spouse of the therapist. *Journal of Contemporary Psychology, 16,* 97–106.

St. Germaine, J. (1993). Dual relationships: What's wrong with them? *American Counselor, 2,* 25–30.

Stadler, H., Willing, K., Eberhage, M., & Ward, W. (1988). Impairment: Implications for the counseling profession. *Journal of Counseling & Development, 66,* 258–260.

Stadler, H. A. (2001). Impairment in the mental health professions. In E. R. Welfel & R. E. Ingersoll (Eds.), *The mental health desk reference* (pp. 413–418). New York: Wiley.

Stanard, R. P. (2000). Assessment and treatment of adolescent

depression and suicidality. *Journal of Mental Health Counseling, 22,* 204–217.

State of Louisiana v. Atterberry. 664 So.2d 1216, La. App. 1 Cir., 1995.

State v. Andring, 342 N.W.2d 128 (Minn. 1984).

State v. Brown, 376 N.W.2d 451, review denied (Minn. App. 1985).

State v. Hungerford, 84 Wisc.2d 236, 267 N.W.2d 258 (1978).

State v. Kupchun, 117 N.H. 417, 373 A.2d 1325 (1977).

State v. Magnuson, 682 P.2d 1365, 210 Mont. 401 (Mont. 1984).

Steele, D. (2012). *The million dollar private practice: Using your expertise to build a business that makes a difference.* Hoboken, NJ: John Wiley.

Steele, J. M., Bischof, G. H., & Craig, S. E. (2014). Political ideology and perceptions of social justice advocacy among members of the American Counseling Association. *International Journal for the Advancement of Counseling, 36,* 450–467.

Steen, R. L., Engels, D., & Thweatt, W. T. (2006). Ethical aspects of spirituality in counseling. *Counseling and Values, 50,* 108–118.

Stern, E. B., & Havlicek, L. (1986). Academic misconduct: Results of faculty and undergraduate student surveys. *Journal of Allied Health, 15,* 129–142.

Stern, R. C., & DiFonzo, J. H. (2007). Terminal ambiguity: Law, ethics and policy in the assisted dying debate. *The Boston University Public Interest Law Journal, 17,* 99–135.

Stetson University College of Law. (2014). *Statutory updates.* Gulfport, FL: Author. Retrieved from http://www.stetson.edu/law /academics/elder/ecpp/statutory-updates.php

Stiegel, L., & Klem, E. (2006). *Information about laws related to*

elder abuse. Washington, DC: American Bar Association Commission on Law and Aging. Retrieved from http://www .americanbar.org

Stokes, L. S., & Remley, T. P., Jr. (2001). Counselors as expert witnesses. In E. R. Welfel & R. E. Ingersoll (Eds.), *The mental health desk reference* (pp. 404–410). New York: Wiley.

Stoltenberg, C. D., McNeill, B., & Delworth, U. (1998). *IDM supervision: An Integrated Developmental Model for supervising counselors and therapists.* San Francisco: Jossey-Bass.

Stone, C. (2002). Negligence in academic advising and abortion counseling: Courts rulings and implications. *Professional School Counseling, 6,* 28–35.

Stone, C. B., & Hanson, C. (2002). Selection of school counselor candidates: Future directions at two universities. *Counselor Education and Supervision, 41,* 175–192.

Stone, L. A. (1985). National Board for Certified Counselors: History, relationships, and projections. *Journal of Counseling & Development, 63,* 605–606.

Storm, C. L., Todd, T. C., Sprenkle, D. H., & Morgan, M. M. (2001). Gaps between MFT supervision assumptions and common practice: Suggested best practices. *Journal of Marital and Family Therapy, 27,* 227–239.

Stout, C. E., & Grand, L. C. (2006). *Getting started in private practice: The complete guide to building your mental health practice.* Hoboken, NJ: John Wiley.

Strasburger, L. H. (1998). Suggestions for expert witnesses. In L. E. Lifson & R. I. Simon (Eds.), *The mental health practitioner and the law* (pp. 281–298). Cambridge, MA: Harvard University Press.

Straus, M. A. (1999). The controversy over domestic violence by women: A methodological, theoretical, and sociology of science analysis. In X. B. Arriaga & S. Oskamp (Eds.), *Violence in intimate relationships* (pp. 17–44). Thousand Oaks, CA: Sage.

Straus, M. A., & Gelles, R. J. (1992). *Physical violence in American families.* New Brunswick, NJ: Transaction.

Sudak, H., Ford, A., & Rushforth, N. (1984). Adolescent suicide: An overview. *American Journal of Psychotherapy, 38,* 350–369.

Sue, D. W. (1996). Ethical issues in multicultural counseling. In B. Herlihy & G. Corey (Eds.), *ACA ethical standards casebook* (5th ed., pp. 193–197). Alexandria, VA: American Counseling Association.

Sue, D. W., Bucceri, J., Lin, A. I., Nadal, K. L., & Torino, G. C. (2007). Racial microaggression and the Asian American experience. *Cultural Diversity and Ethnic Minority Psychology, 13,* 72–81. doi: 10.1037/1948-1985.S.1.88

Sue, D. W., Capodilupo, C. M., & Holder, A. M. B. (2008). Racial microaggressions in the life experience of Black Americans. *Professional Psychology: Research and Practice, 39,* 329–336. doi: 10.1037/0735-7028.39.3.329

Sue, D. W., & Sue, D. (2013). *Counseling the culturally diverse: Theory and practice* (6th ed.). New York: Wiley.

Sue, S., Fujino, D., Takeuchi, D., Hu, L.-T., & Zane, N. (1991). Community mental health services for ethnic minority groups: A test of the cultural responsiveness hypothesis. *Journal of Consulting and Clinical Psychology, 59,* 533–540.

Sullivan, T., Martin, W. L., & Handelsman, M. M. (1993). Practical benefits of an informed consent procedure: An empirical investigation. *Professional Psychology: Research and Practice, 24,* 160–163.

Sumerel, M. B., & Borders, L. D. (1996). Addressing personal issues in supervision: Impact of counselors' experience level on various aspects of the supervisory relationship. *Counselor Education and Supervision, 35,* 268–285.

Suzuki, L. A., & Ponterotto, J. G. (Eds.). (2007). *Handbook of multicultural assessment: Clinical, psychological, and educational applications* (3rd ed.). San Francisco: Jossey-Bass.

Swank, J. M., & Smith-Adcock, S. (2014). Gatekeeping during admissions: A survey of counselor education programs. *Counselor Education & Supervision, 53,* 47–61. doi: 10.1002/j.1556-6987.2014.00048.x

Sweeney, T. (1995). Accreditation, credentialing, professionalization: The role of specialties. *Journal of Counseling & Development, 74,* 117–125.

Sweeney, T. J. (2001). Counseling: Historical origins and philosophical roots. In D. C. Locke, J. E. Myers, & E. L. Herr (Eds.), *The handbook of counseling* (pp. 3–26). Thousand Oaks, CA: Sage.

Swenson, L. C. (1997). *Psychology and the law for the helping professions* (2nd ed.). Pacific Grove, CA: Brooks/Cole.

Sydow, N. (2006). A "shrink"-ing privilege: United States v. Romano and the "course of diagnosis" requirement of the psychotherapist-patient privilege. *Harvard Civil Rights–Civil Liberties Law Review, 41,* 265–270.

Szymanski, E. M., & Parker, R. M. (2001). Epistemological and

methodological issues in counseling. In D. C. Locke, J. E. Myers, & E. L. Herr (Eds.), *Handbook of counseling* (pp. 455–466). Thousand Oaks, CA: Sage.

Tanigoshi, H., Kontos, A. P., & Remley, T. P., Jr. (2008). The effectiveness of individual wellness counseling on the wellness of law enforcement officers. *Journal of Counseling & Development, 86,* 64–75.

Tarasoff v. Regents of University of California, 529 P.2d 553, 118 Cal. Rptr. 129 (1974), vacated, 17 Cal. 3d 425, 551 P.2d 334, 131 Cal. Rptr. 14 (1976).

Tarka v. Franklin, C.A.5 (Tex.) 891 F.2d 102, certiori denied 110 S.Ct. 1809, 494 U.S. 1080, 108 (1989).

Tarvydas, V. M. (1998). Ethical decision-making processes. In R. R. Cottone & V. M. Tarvydas (Eds.), *Ethical and professional issues in counseling* (pp. 144–154). Upper Saddle River, NJ: Prentice Hall.

Tatara, T. (1996). *Elder abuse: Questions and answers.* Washington, DC: National Center on Elder Abuse.

Taube, D. O., & Elwork, A. (1990). Researching the effects of confidentiality law on patients' self-disclosures. *Professional Psychology: Research and Practice, 21,* 72–75.

Taylor, K. (1995). *The ethics of caring.* Santa Cruz, CA: Hanford Mead.

Tebes, J. K., Matlin, S. L., Migdole, S. J., Farkas, M. S., Money, R. W., Shulman, L., & Hoge, M. A. (2011). *Providing competency training to clinical supervisors through an interactional supervision approach.* Retrieved from http://rsw.sagepub.com

Thapar v. Zezulka, 994 S.W.2d 635 (Tex. 1999).

The Reporters Committee for Freedom of the Press. (2008). *How to avoid copyright infringement.* Arlington, VA: Author.

The Writing Place. (2005). *Avoiding plagiarism.* Evanston, IL: Northwestern University. Retrieved from http://www.writing.northwestern.edu/avoiding_plagiarism.html

Thomas, R., & Henning, S. (2012). Counseling in Switzerland: Past, present, and future. *Journal of Counseling & Development, 90,* 505–509. doi: 10.1002/j.1556-6676.2012.00063.x

Thomas, R. V., & Pender, D. A. (2008). Association for Specialists in Group Work: Best Practice Guidelines 2007 Revisions. *The Journal for Specialists in Group Work, 33,* 111–117.

Thompson, A. (2008, August). Counselors' right to privacy: Potential boundary crossings through membership in online communities. *Counseling Today,* 44–45.

Thompson, T. L. (1999). Managed care: Views, practices, and burnout of psychologists. *Dissertation Abstracts International: Section B, The Sciences and Engineering, 60,* 1318. (UMI No. 91–14).

Thoreson, R., Nathan, P., Skorina, J., & Kilberg, R. (1983). The alcoholic psychologist: Issues, problems, and implications for the profession. *Professional Psychology: Research and Practice, 14,* 670–684.

Thoreson, R. W., Morrow, K. A., Frazier, P. A., & Kerstner, P. L. (1990, March). *Needs and concerns of women in AACD: Preliminary results.* Paper presented at the annual convention of the American Association for Counseling and Development, Cincinnati, OH.

Thoreson, R. W., Shaughnessy, P., & Frazier, P. A. (1995). Sexual contact during and after professional relationships: Practices and attitudes of female counselors. *Journal of Counseling & Development, 74,* 84–88.

Thoreson, R. W., Shaughnessy, P., Heppner, P. P., & Cook, S. W. (1993). Sexual contact during and after the professional relationship: Attitudes and practices of male counselors. *Journal of Counseling & Development, 71,* 429–434.

Tigertext. (2014). *Secure texting for physicians.* Santa Monica, CA: Author. Retrieved from http://www.tigertext.com

Ting, S. A., Sullivan, A. F., Boudreaux, E. D., Miller, I., & Camargo, C. (2012). Trends in US emergency department visits for attempted suicide and self-inflicted injury, 1993–2008. *General Hospital Psychiatry, 34,* 557–565. doi: 10.1016/j.genhosppsych.2012.03.020

Title I of the Americans with Disabilities Act of 1990, 42 U.S.C. §1211 et seq.

Title VII of the Civil Rights Act of 1964, 42 U.S.C. §2000f et seq.

Tomm, K. (1993, January/February). The ethics of dual relationships. *The California Therapist,* 7–19.

Toporek, R. L., Ortega-Villalobos, L., & Pope-Davis, D. B. (2004). Critical incidents in multicultural supervision: Exploring supervisees' and supervisors' experiences. *Journal of Multicultural Counseling and Development, 32,* 66–83.

Toren, N. (1969). Semi-professionalism and social work: A theoretical perspective. In A. Etzioni (Ed.), *The semi-professions and their organization* (pp. 12–63). New York: The Free Press.

Tracey, T. J. (1991). Counseling research as an applied science. In C. E. Watkins, Jr. & L. J. Schneider (Eds.), *Research in counseling* (pp. 3–31). Hillsdale, NJ: Erlbaum.

Trepal, H., Haberstroh, S., Duffey, T., & Evans, M. (2007). Considerations and strategies for teaching online counseling skills: Establishing relationships in cyberspace. *Counselor Education and Supervision, 46,* 266–279.

Tromski-Klingshirn, D. M., & Davis, T. E. (2007). Supervisees' perceptions of their clinical supervision: A study of the dual role of clinical and administrative supervisor. *Counselor Education and Supervision, 46,* 294–304.

Truax v. Raich, 239 U.S. 33, 36 S.Ct. 7, 60 L.Ed. 131 (1915).

Trudeau, L. S., Russell, D. W., de la Mora, A., & Schmitz, M. F. (2001). Comparisons of marriage and family therapists, psychologists, psychiatrists, and social workers on job-related measures and reactions to managed care in Iowa. *Journal of Marital and Family Therapy, 27,* 501–507.

Truffo, C. (2007). *Be a wealthy therapist: Finally, you can make a living making a difference.* Saint Peters, MO: MP Presss.

Truneckova, D., Viney, L. L., Maitland, H., & Seaborn, B. (2010). Personal construct peer consultation: Caring for the psychotherapists. *The Clinical Supervisor, 29,* 128–148.

Truscott, D., & Evans, J. (2001). Responding to dangerous clients. In E. R. Welfel & R. E. Ingersoll (Eds.), *The mental health desk reference* (pp. 271–276). New York: Wiley.

Truscott, D., Evans, J., & Mansell, S. (1995). Outpatient psychotherapy with dangerous clients: A model for clinical decision making. *Professional Psychology: Research and Practice, 26,* 484–490.

Tubbs, P., & Pomerantz, A. M. (2001). Ethical behavior of

psychologists: Changes since 1987. *Journal of Clinical Psychology, 57,* 395–399.

Tyler, J. M., & Tyler, C. (1994). Ethics in supervision: Managing supervisee rights and supervisor responsibilities. *Directions in Mental Health Counseling, 4,* 4–25.

Tylitzki v. Triple X Service, Inc., 126 Ill. App.2d 144, 261 N.E.2d 533 (1970).

University of Essex. (2013, April 29). Do you fear you are missing out? *ScienceDaily.* Retrieved from www.sciencedaily.com

United States v. Miami University, 294 F.3d 797 (6th Cir. 2002).

Urofsky, R. I. (2013). The Council for Accreditation of Counseling and Related Educational Programs: Promoting quality in counselor education. *Journal of Counseling & Development, 91,* 6–14. doi: 10.1002/j.1556-6676.2013.00065.x

U.S. Census Bureau. (2009). *Household computers 2009.* Retrieved from http://www.census.gov/hhes/computer

U.S. Census Bureau. (2014). *Computers and Internet use in the United States: 2013.* Retrieved from http://www.census.gov/content/dam/Census/library/publications/2014/acs/acs-28.pdf

U.S. Department of Education. (1998). *Early Warning, Timely Response: A Guide to Safe Schools.* Retrieved from http://cecp.air.org/guide/guide.pdf

U.S. Department of Education. (2014). *Family Education Rights and Privacy Act (FERPA).* Retrieved from http://www2.ed.gov/policy/gen/guid/fpco/ferpa/index.html

U.S. Department of Health and Human Services. (n.d.). *Health Information Privacy Complaints Received by Calendar Year.*

Retrieved from http://www.hhs.gov/ocr/privacy/hipaa/enforcement/data/complaintsyear.html

U.S. Department of Health and Human Services. (2014a). *Health Information Privacy.* Retrieved from http://www.hhs.gov/ocr/privacy

U.S. Department of Health and Human Services. (2014b). *HIPAA enforcement.* Retrieved from http://www.hhs.gov/ocr/privacy/hipaa/enforcement/index.html

Usher, C. H., & Borders, L. D. (1993). Practicing counselors' preferences for supervisory style and supervisory emphasis. *Counselor Education and Supervision, 33,* 66–79.

Utsey, S. O., Ponterotto, J. G., & Porter, J. S. (2008). Prejudice and racism, year 2008—still going strong: Research on reducing prejudice with recommended methodological advances. *Journal of Counseling & Development, 86,* 339–347.

Vaccaro, N., & Lambie, G. W. (2007). Computer-based counselor-in-training supervision: Ethical and practical implications for counselor educators and supervisors. *Counselor Education & Supervision, 47,* 46–57.

VandeCreek, L., Miars, R. D., & Herzog, C. E. (1987). Client anticipations and preferences for confidentiality of records. *Journal of Counseling Psychology, 34,* 62–67.

Vasquez, L. A. (1996). A systemic multicultural curriculum model: The pedagogical process. In D. B. Pope-Davis & H. L. K. Coleman (Eds.), *Multicultural counseling competencies: Assessment, education, training, and supervision* (pp. 159–179). Thousand Oaks, CA: Sage.

Vasquez, M. J. T. (1988). Counselor-client sexual contact: Implications

for ethics training. *Journal of Counseling & Development, 67,* 238–241.

Vasquez, M. J. T. (1991). Sexual intimacies with clients after termination: Should a prohibition be explicit? *Ethics and Behavior, 1,* 45–61.

Vasquez, M. J. T., Bingham, R. P., & Barnett, J. E. (2008). Psychotherapy termination: Clinical and ethical responsibilities. *Journal of Clinical Psychology: In Session, 64,* 653–665.

Veach, L. J. (2015). Boundary issues in addictions and substance abuse counseling. In B. Herlihy & G. Corey, *Boundary issues in counseling* (3rd ed., pp. 237–241). Alexandria, VA: American Counseling Association.

Vidmar, N. (1995). *Medical malpractice and the American jury: Confronting the myths about jury incompetence, deep pockets, and outrageous damage awards.* Ann Arbor: University of Michigan Press.

Vilardaga, R., Luoma, J. B., Hayes, S. C., Pistorello, J., Levin, M. E., Hildebrandt, M. J., Kohlenberg, B., Roget, F., & Bond, F. (2011). Burnout among the addiction counseling workforce: The differential roles of mindfulness and values-based processes and worksite factors. *Journal of Substance Abuse Treatment, 40,* 323–335.

Walden v. Centers for Disease Control and Prevention. No. 1:08-cv-02278-JEC (U.S. District Court for the Northern District of Georgia, March 18, 2010).

Walfish, S., & Barnett, J. E. (2009). *Financial success in mental health practice: Essential tools and strategies for practitioners.* Washington, DC: American Psychological Association.

Walsh, W. B., & Betz, N. E. (1995). *Tests and assessment* (3rd ed.).

Upper Saddle River, NJ: Prentice Hall.

Ward v. Wilbanks. (2010). U.S. Dist. LEXIS 127038 (E.D. Mich., July 26, 2010). Retrieved from http://www.lexisnexis.com

Ward v. Wilbanks. (2012). 667 F.3d 727; 2012 U.S. App. LEXIS 1479; 2012 FED App. 0024P (6th Cir.). Retrieved from http://www.lexisnexis.com

Ware, J. N., & Dillman Taylor, D. (2014). Concerns about confidentiality: The application of ethical decision-making within group play therapy. *International Journal of Play Therapy, 23,* 173–186. doi: 10.1037/a0036667

Warnke, M. A. (2001). In E. R. Welfel & R. E. Ingersoll (Eds.), *The mental health desk reference* (pp. 379–383). New York: Wiley.

Warren, J., & Douglas, K. I. (2012). Falling from grace: Understanding an ethical sanctioning experience. *Counseling and Values, 57,* 131–146. doi: 10.1002/j.2161-007X.2012.00013.x

Warren, J., Morgan, M. M., Morris, L. B., & Morris, T. M. (2010). Breathing words slowly: Creative writing and counselor self-care—the writing workout. *Journal of Creativity in Mental Health, 5,* 109–124. doi: 10.1080/15401383.2010.485074

Watson, J. C., & Sheperis, C. J. (2010). *Counselors and the right to test: Working toward professional parity (ACAPCD-31).* Alexandria, VA: American Counseling Association.

Watson, Z. E., Herlihy, B. R., & Pierce, L. A. (2006). Forging the link between multicultural competence and ethical practice: A historical perspective. *Counseling & Values, 50,* 99–108.

Watts, R. E. (2015). Research and publication. In B. Herlihy & G. Corey, *ACA ethical standards casebook* (7th ed., pp. 273–275). Alexandria, VA: American Counseling Association.

Webb v. Quincy City Lines, Inc., 73 Ill. App.2d 405, 219 N.E.2d 165 (1966).

Wehrly, B. (1991). Preparing multicultural counselors. *Counseling and Human Development, 24*(3), 1–24.

Weil, R. I. (1983). Are professional corporations dead? *The North Carolina State Bar Quarterly, 30,* 8–9.

Weinrach, S. G. (1989). Guidelines for clients of private practitioners: Committing the structure to print. *Journal of Counseling & Development, 67,* 299–300.

Weinrach, S. G., Lustig, D., Chan, F., & Thomas, K. R. (1998). Publication patterns of *The Personnel and Guidance Journal/Journal of Counseling & Development:* 1978–1993. *Journal of Counseling & Development, 76,* 427–435.

Weinrach, S. G., & Thomas, K. R. (1996). The counseling profession's commitment to diversity-sensitive counseling: A critical reassessment. *Journal of Counseling & Development, 74,* 472–477.

Weinrach, S. G., Thomas, K. R., & Chan, F. (2001). The professional identity of contributors to the *Journal of Counseling & Development:* Does it matter? *Journal of Counseling & Development, 79,* 166–170.

Welfare, L. E., & Sackett, C. R. (2011). The authorship determination process in student-faculty collaborative research. *Journal of Counseling & Development, 89,* 479–487.

Welfel, E. R. (2013). *Ethics in counseling and psychotherapy: Standards, research, and emerging issues* (5th ed.). Pacific Grove, CA: Brooks/Cole.

Welfel, E. R., Danzinger, P. R., & Santoro, S. (2000). Mandated reporting of abuse/maltreatment of older adults: A primer for counselors. *Journal of Counseling & Development, 78,* 284–293.

Welfel, E. R., & Heinlen, K. T. (2001). The responsible use of technology in mental health practice. In E. R. Welfel & R. E. Ingersoll (Eds.), *The mental health desk reference* (pp. 484–490). New York: Wiley.

Wendorf, D. J., & Wendorf, R. J. (1992). A systemic view of family therapy ethics. In R. L. Smith & P. Stevens-Smith (Eds.), *Family counseling and therapy* (pp. 304–320). Ann Arbor, MI: ERIC/CAPS.

Werth, J. L., Jr. (Ed.). (2013). *Counseling clients near the end of life: A practical guide for mental health professionals.* New York: Springer.

Werth, J. L., & Crow, L. (2009). End-of-life care: An overview for professional counselors. *Journal of Counseling & Development, 87,* 194–202. doi: 10.1002/j:1556

Werth, J. L., & Gordon, J. R. (2002). Amicus curiae brief for the United States Supreme Court on mental health issues associated with "physician-assisted suicide." *Journal of Counseling & Development, 80,* 160–163.

Westbook v. Penley, 231 S.W.3d 389, 392 (Tex. 2007).

Wester, K. L. (2007). Teaching research integrity in the field of counseling. *Counselor Education and Supervision, 46,* 199–211.

Wester, K. L. (2011). Publishing ethical research: A step-by-step overview. *Journal of Counseling & Development, 89,* 301–307.

Westgate, C. E. (1996). Spiritual wellness and depression. *Journal of Counseling & Development, 75,* 26–36.

Wheeler, A. M., & Bertram, B. (2012). *The counselor and the law* (6th ed.). Alexandria, VA: American Counseling Association.

Whisenhunt, J. L., & Kress, V. E. (2013). The use of visual arts activities in counseling clients who engage in nonsuicidal self-injury. *Journal of Creativity in Mental Health, 8,* 120–135.

Whiston, S. C., Tai, W. L., Rahardja, D., & Eder, K. (2011). School counseling outcome: A meta-analytic examination of interventions. *Journal of Counseling & Development, 89,* 37–55.

White, J. (2013). Research finds link between social media and the "fear of missing out." *Washington Post.* Retrieved from http://www.washingtonpost.com

White, M. G. (2014). *What types of social networks exist?* Retrieved from http://socialnetworking.lovetoknow.com

Whitman, J. S., Glosoff, H. L., Kocet, M. M., & Tarvydas, V. (2006). Exploring ethical issues related to conversion or reparative therapy. Retrieved from http://ct.counseling.org/2006/05/exploring-ethical-issues-related-to-conversion-or-reparative-therapy/

Whitman, M. A., & Wagers, T. P. (2005). Assessing relationship betrayals. *Journal of Clinical Psychology: In Session, 61,* 1383–1391.

Wichansky v. Wichansky, 126 N.J. Super. 156, 313 A.2d 222 (1973).

Wickline v. State of California, 192 Cal.App.3d 1630 (1986); 239 Cal. Rptr. 810 (Ct. App. 1986).

Wiger, D. E. (1999). *The clinical documentation sourcebook* (2nd ed.). New York: Wiley.

Wigmore, J. H. (1961). *Evidence in trials at common law* (Vol. 8, McNaughton Rev.). Boston: Little, Brown.

Wilcoxon, A., & Fennel, D. (1983). Engaging non-attending spouse in marital therapy through the use of therapist-initiated written communication. *Journal of Marital and Family Therapy, 9,* 199–203.

Wilcoxon, S. A., & Magnuson, S. (1999). Considerations for school counselors serving noncustodial parents: Premises and suggestions. *Professional School Counseling, 2,* 275–279.

Wilcoxon, S. A., Magnuson, S., & Norem, K. (2008). Institutional values of managed mental health care: Efficiency or oppression? *Journal of Multicultural Counseling and Development, 36,* 143–154.

Wilcoxon, S. A., Remley, T. P., Jr., & Gladding, S. T. (2013). *Ethical, legal, and professional issues in the practice of marriage and family therapy* (updated 5th ed.). Upper Saddle River, NJ: Pearson.

Wilkinson, W. K., & McNeil, K. (1996). *Research for the helping professions.* Pacific Grove, CA: Brooks/Cole.

Williams, C. B. (2001). Ethics complaints: Procedures for filing and responding. In E. R. Welfel & R. E. Ingersoll (Eds.), *The mental health desk reference* (pp. 441–447). New York: Wiley.

Williams, K. M., Craig, N., & Paulhus, D. L. (2010). Identifying and profiling scholastic cheaters: Their personality, cognitive ability, and motivation. *Journal of Experimental Psychology: Applied, 16,* 293–307. doi: 10:1037/a0020773

Wilson, F. R., Jencius, M., & Duncan, D. (1997). Introduction to the Internet: Opportunities and dilemmas. *Counseling and Human Development, 29*(6), 1–16.

Wilson, F. R., & Owens, P. C. (2001). Group-based prevention programs for at-risk adolescents and adults.

The Journal for Specialists in Group Work, 26, 246–255.

Wilson v. Blue Cross, 271 Cal.Rptr. 876 (Ct. App. 1990).

Wineburgh, M. (1998). Ethics, managed care and outpatient psychotherapy. *Clinical Social Work Journal, 26,* 433–443.

Winston, M. E. (1991). AIDS, confidentiality, and the right to know. In T. A. Mappes & J. S. Zembaty (Eds.), *Biomedical ethics* (3rd ed., pp. 173–180). New York: McGraw-Hill.

Witmer, J. M., & Young, M. E. (1996). Preventing counselor impairment: A wellness approach. *Journal of Humanistic Education and Development, 34,* 141–155.

Wohlberg, J. W. (1999). Treatment subsequent to abuse by a mental health professional: The victim's perspective of what works and what doesn't. *Journal of Sex Education & Counseling, 24,* 252–261.

Wolfe, S. E., Marcum, C. D., Higgins, G. E., & Ricketts, M. L. (2014). Routine cell phone activity and exposure to sext messages. *Crime & Delinquency.* doi: 10.1177/0011128714541192

Wong, L. C. J., Wong, P. T., & Ishiyama, F. I. (2013). What helps and what hinders in cross-cultural clinical supervision: A critical incident study. *The Counseling Psychologist, 41,* 66–85.

Woody, R. H. (1988a). *Fifty ways to avoid malpractice.* Sarasota, FL: Professional Resource Exchange.

Woody, R. H. (1988b). *Protecting your mental health practice: How to minimize legal and financial risk.* San Francisco: Jossey-Bass.

Woody, R. H. (2011). The financial conundrum for mental health practitioners. *American Journal of Family Therapy, 39,* 1–10. doi: 10.1080/01926187.2010.530170

Woody, R. H. (2013). *Legal self-defense for mental health practitioners.* New York: Springer.

Worell, J., & Remer, P. (2003). *Feminist perspectives in therapy: Empowering diverse women.* New York: Wiley.

Wortham, J. (2011, April 9). Feel like a wallflower? Maybe it's your Facebook wall." *New York Times.* Retrieved from http://www.nytimes.com

Wrenn, G. (1962). *The counselor in a changing world.* Washington, DC: American Personnel and Guidance Association.

Wyatt, T., & Daniels, M. H. (2000). Noncompetition agreements and the counseling profession: An unrecognized reality for private practitioners. *Journal of Counseling & Development, 78,* 14–20.

Wylie, M. S. (1995, May/June). The power of *DSM-IV*: Diagnosing for dollars. *Networker,* 22–32.

Yakunina, E. S., Weigold, I. K., & McCarthy, A. S. (2011). Group counseling with international students: Practical, ethical, and cultural considerations. *Journal of College Student Psychotherapy, 25,* 67–78. doi: 10.1080/87568225.2011.532672

Yalom, I. D. (2005). *The theory and practice of group psychotherapy* (5th ed.). New York: Basic Books.

Yamamoto, J., & Chang, C. (1987, August). *Empathy for the family and individual in the racial context.* Paper presented at the Interactive Forum on Transference and Empathy in Psychotherapy with Asian Americans, Boston, MA.

Yaron v. Yaron, 83 Misc.2d 276, 372 N.Y.S.2d 518 (Sup. 1975).

Yeh, C. J. (2001). An exploratory study of school counselors' experiences with and perceptions of Asian-American students. *Professional School Counseling, 4,* 349–356.

Young, J., Cashwell, C., & Shcherbakova, J. (2000). The moderating relationship of spirituality on negative life events and psychological adjustment. *Counseling and Values, 45,* 49–57.

Younggren, J. N. (2002). Ethical decision-making and dual relationships. Retrieved from http://kspope.com/dual/younggren.php

Yuen, M., Leung, A., & Chan, R. T. H. (2014). Professional counseling in Hong Kong. *Journal of Counseling & Development, 92,* 99–103. doi: 10.1002/j.1556-6676.2014.00135.x

Zalaquett, C. P., Fuerth, K. M., Stein, C., Ivey, A. E., & Ivey, M. B. (2008). Reframing the *DSM-IV-TR* from a multicultural/social justice perspective. *Journal of Counseling & Development, 86,* 364–371.

Ziskin, J. (1995). *Coping with psychiatric and psychological testimony* (Vols. I–III, 5th ed.). Los Angeles, CA: Law and Psychology Press.

Ziv, S. (2014, November 12). Technology's latest quest: Tracking mental health. *Newsweek.* Retrieved from http://www.newsweek.com

Zur, O. (2007). *Boundaries in psychotherapy: Ethical and clinical explorations.* Washington, DC: American Psychological Association.

Zur, O. (2011a). *Therapist burnout: Fact, causes and prevention.* Retrieved from http://www.zurinstitute.com/therapeutic_ethics

Zur, O. (2011b). *When the board comes knocking: How to respond to a licensing board investigation and protect your license, professional career, and livelihood.* Sonoma, CA: Zur Institute. Retrieved from http://www.zurinstitute.com/index.html

Zur, O., & Nordmarken, N. (2010). *DSM: Diagnosing for money and power: Summary of the critique of the DSM.* Retrieved from http://www.zurinstitute.com/dsmcritique.html

AUTHOR INDEX

SUBJECT INDEX